ARBITRATION COSTS

Arbitration Costs

MYTHS AND REALITIES IN INVESTMENT TREATY ARBITRATION

Susan D. Franck

OXFORD
UNIVERSITY PRESS

OXFORD
UNIVERSITY PRESS

Oxford University Press is a department of the University of Oxford. It furthers the University's objective of excellence in research, scholarship, and education by publishing worldwide. Oxford is a registered trademark of Oxford University Press in the UK and certain other countries.

Published in the United States of America by Oxford University Press
198 Madison Avenue, New York, NY 10016, United States of America.

Library of Congress Cataloging-in-Publication Data

Names: Franck, Susan D., author.
Title: Arbitration costs : myths and realities in investment treaty arbitration / Susan D. Franck.
Description: New York : Oxford University Press, 2019. | Includes bibliographical references and index.
Identifiers: LCCN 2018052696 | ISBN 9780190054434 ((hardback) : alk. paper)
Subjects: LCSH: Investments, Foreign—Law and legislation. | Investments, Foreign (International law) | International commercial arbitration. | International commercial arbitration—Economic aspects. | Commercial treaties.
Classification: LCC K3830 .F73 2019 | DDC 346/.092—dc23
LC record available at https://lccn.loc.gov/2018052696

9 8 7 6 5 4 3 2 1

Printed by Sheridan Books, Inc., United States of America

Note to Readers
This publication is designed to provide accurate and authoritative information in regard to the subject matter covered. It is based upon sources believed to be accurate and reliable and is intended to be current as of the time it was written. It is sold with the understanding that the publisher is not engaged in rendering legal, accounting, or other professional services. If legal advice or other expert assistance is required, the services of a competent professional person should be sought. Also, to confirm that the information has not been affected or changed by recent developments, traditional legal research techniques should be used, including checking primary sources where appropriate.

(Based on the Declaration of Principles jointly adopted by a Committee of the American Bar Association and a Committee of Publishers and Associations.)

To my husband Kevin, the physicist and engineer who encouraged me to focus on the data, remember the importance of scientific evolution of knowledge, and who lives the values of collaboration, methodological integrity, and human kindness.

Contents

Preface

HUMANS ARE HUMAN. Humans make errors. Humans create law. Law, and debate about law, inevitably has embedded error. This book is an effort to understand the humanity and psychology underpinning conversations about international investment law and dispute settlement, with a focus on using data to debias and reframe conversations about the future of investment treaty dispute settlement. The hope is to offer data-driven base rates and statistical information to ensure that debates are more likely to be driven by balanced (rather than skewed or inaccurate) information. Recognizing the powerful, potentially pernicious, and prevalent influence of cognitive illusions, I have worked to remain conscious of their potential limitations throughout the research and writing of this book to avoid committing the errors that I sought to explore and redress with data. Yet recognizing the possibility of bias blind spots, to model the humility and care that I wish to see from other stakeholders, I apologize in advance for any inadvertent imbalance, omissions, and failures that derive from the challenges of analyzing limited and timebound data (and focusing on sources primarily in English), while acknowledging that space constraints meant much analysis was left "on the cutting room floor." I also encourage stakeholders to consider their own human limitations in how they perceive the data and context offered in this book, ask *why* they might have a particularly positive or negative reaction, and then explore how moving beyond initial perceptions may help constructively evolve international investment law. The quest of making scientific insights into international law is one of gradual evolution, and my hope is that this book is a single step on a larger journey.

Acknowledgments

THIS BOOK WOULD not have been possible without the support and effort of many people, as it truly took a village. There was exemplary support by dedicated librarians (Stephanie Miller and Caroline Osborne), methodological assistance from the University of Nebraska (the Bureau of Sociological Research, Calvin P. Garbin, and Lindsey E. Wiley), student assistance with diligent coding (Jason Ratigan, Gene Hamilton, Brandon Hasbrouck, and Melanie Neely), helpful editing (Lorena Guzman-Diaz, Rachael Kurzweil, and Emily Tichenor), and outstanding research support (Alexandra Klein, Kellen Lavin, Denis Metin, and Anaeli Sandoval). The design of the cover art would not have been possible without Ann-Marie Schelvis and David Lipp. I am also indebted to the multitude of individuals who were willing to review draft chapters to improve the ultimate work product including: Christina Beharry, Colin Brown, Huiping Chen, Jeffrey Commission, Diane Desierto, Joshua A.T. Fairfield, James Freda, Mariana Hernandez Crespo Gonstead, John Gotanda, Anna Joubin-Bret, M. Imad Khan, Meg Kinnear, Irina Manta, Andrea Kupfer Schneider, Victoria Shannon Sahani, Maya Steinitz, and Nancy Welsh. I thank my colleagues at the American University, Washington College of Law's Business Faculty Workshop for thoughtful comments of draft chapters and Dean Camille Nelson for her support of this project. I am also grateful to Oxford University Press editors, particularly Catherine Rogers and Blake Ratcliffe, who showed me the light at the end of the tunnel and for the diligent editorial support of Balamurugan Rajendran, Meera Seth, and Brooke Smith.

Abbreviations

ADR	Appropriate Dispute Resolution
BIT	Bilateral Investment Treaty
CETA	Comprehensive Economic and Trade Agreement between Canada and the European Union
CPTPPP	Comprehensive and Progressive Agreement for Trans-Pacific Partnership
CPI	Consumer Price Index
CAFTA-DR	Dominican Republic-Central American Free Trade Agreement
DSD	Dispute Systems Design
ECT	Energy Charter Treaty
FDI	Foreign Direct Investment
HKIAC	Hong Kong International Arbitration Centre
HSD	Tukey's Honestly Significant Difference
HDI	Human Development Index
IBA	International Bar Association
ICSID	International Centre for Settlement of Investment Disputes
ICC	International Chamber of Commerce
ICA	International Commercial Arbitration
ICJ	International Court of Justice
ITA	Investment Treaty Arbitration
ISDS	Investor-State Dispute Settlement
LDC	Least Development Country
LCIA	London Court of International Arbitration
LSD	Least Significant Difference
NYC	New York Convention

NAFTA	North American Free Trade Agreement
NDPs	Non-Disputing Parties
NGOs	Non-Governmental Organizations
NHST	Null Hypothesis Significance Testing
OS	One-Shot players
OECD	Organisation for Economic Co-operation and Development
PLC	Parties' Legal Costs
PCA	Permanent Court of Arbitration
RP	Repeat Player
SIAC	Singapore International Arbitration
SCC	Stockholm Chamber of Commerce
TPF	Third-Party Funding
TPP	Trans-Pacific Partnership
TCE	Tribunal Costs and administrative Expenses
UNCITRAL	United Nations Commission on International Trade Law
UNCTAD	United Nations Conference on Trade and Development
UNDP	United Nations Development Programme
USMCA	United States-Mexico-Canada Agreement

1 Introduction to Investment Treaty Arbitration (ITA) and Framing the Debate

GLOBAL ECONOMIC ACTIVITY and international economic law are lynchpins of the international political economy. Conflicts that derive from commercial activity, finance, trade, and investment are at the heart of the current and future faces of globalization, and the derivative disputes offer insights into the net value of the international economic activity and whether stakeholders are satisfied with the underlying legal regimes. The evolution of international investment law has become an area of mounting interest and increased political, economic, and legal scrutiny. Within the last several years, the backlash against globalization and the resurgence of state sovereignty and isolationism have risen off the back of critiques of international trade and investment agreements.[1] In an effort to provide an evidence-based approach to international lawmaking that minimizes the impact of errors from cognitive illusions[2] and maximizes strategic policy choices, this book explores international investment law with a focus on treaty-based dispute settlement.

The landscape of international investment and dispute resolution has shifted radically during the last half century. Despite the 2008 global economic crisis and the growing discontent with globalization, international investment is rising and between 2012 and 2017, the global total of FDI (foreign direct investment) stock ranged from roughly US$23–31 trillion.[3] Meanwhile, the

---

[1] *See generally* José E. Alvarez, *The Return of the State*, 20 MINN. J. INT'L L. 223 (2011); Robert J. Samuelson, *The (Largely False) Globalization Narrative*, WASH. POST (Aug. 7, 2016), http://wapo.st/2b7lWG1 (last visited Aug. 8, 2018).

[2] *See* Chapter 2.

[3] U.N. Conference on Trade and Dev. [UNCTAD], *World Investment Report 2018: Investment and New Industrial Policies*, 188, UNCTAD/WIR/2018 (June 6, 2018) [hereinafter UNCTAD, *WIR* 2018]; UNCTAD, *World Investment Report 2016: Investor Nationality: Policy Challenges*, 200, UNCTAD/WIR/2016 (June

Arbitration Costs. Susan D. Franck.

number of investment treaties, which enumerate substantive international law rights and contain ex ante consent to dispute settlement, which permit investors to require states to arbitrate treaty violations, continues to expand. We have moved from a world without a single investment treaty containing enforceable dispute resolution rights to a global economy with more than 3,000 investment treaties.[4] Based upon United Nations Conference on Trade and Development (UNCTAD) estimates, the convergence of these factors means that roughly US$15.6 trillion in international investment is protected by at least one investment treaty and theoretically subject to treaty-based arbitration.[5]

With trillions of dollars in investment protected by thousands of treaties, imperfect human beings acting in an imperfect world create conflict. Conflict is inevitable as commercial interests diverge, political and economic circumstances change, and interpersonal friction emerges. When conflicts crystalize, they generate formal disputes[6] where investors exercise their international law rights. The number of formal disputes under investment treaties has grown since the first award in 1990. Around 2012, UNCTAD estimated the historical number of "known" disputes to be around 450;[7] some institutions suggest figures of formal disputes were closer to 700 by 2016,[8] yet verifying these assertions to prevent inadvertent double-counting, improper attribution, or accidental confusion is challenging.

21, 2016) [hereinafter UNCTAD, *WIR 2016*]; Susan D. Franck & Lindsey E. Wylie, *Predicting Outcomes in Investment Treaty Arbitration*, 65 DUKE L.J. 459, 461–62 (2016); Susan D. Franck, *Conflating Politics and Development?, Examining Investment Treaty Arbitration Outcomes*, 55 VA. J. INT'L L. 13, 15 (2013); UNCTAD, *World Investment Report 2013: Global Value Chains: Investment and Trade for Development*, xv, 217, UNCTAD/WIR/2013 (June 26, 2013) [hereinafter UNCTAD, *WIR 2013*]; UNCTAD, *World Investment Report 2012: Towards a New Generation of Investment Policies*, 84–86, UNCTAD/WIR/2012 (May 7, 2012) [hereinafter UNCTAD, *WIR 2012*]; UNCTAD, *World Investment Report 2011: Non-equity Modes of International Production and Development*, xii, 191, UNCTAD/WIR2011 (July 26, 2011) [hereinafter UNCTAD, *WIR 2011*].

[4] *See* UNCTAD, *WIR 2018, supra* note 3, at 88 ("In 2017, 18 new [investment treaties] were concluded, bringing the total to 3,322 treaties by year-end."); UNCTAD, *WIR 2013, supra* note 3, at x, xix–xx; UNCTAD, *WIR 2012 supra* note 3, at 84–86.

[5] *See infra* notes 24, 27; Charles N. Brower & Sadie Blanchard, *What's in a Meme? The Truth About Investor-State Arbitration: Why It Need Not, and Must Not, Be Repossessed by States*, 52 COLUM. J. TRANSNAT'L L. 689, 696–97 (2014) (stating TPP and TTIP could "govern the investment relations of 65% of the world economy"); Michael Froman, *Remarks by Ambassador Michael Froman at the Council on Foreign Relations the Strategic Logic of Trade*, 20 L. & BUS. REV. AM. 373 (2014); Mark Weaver, *The Proposed Transatlantic Trade and Investment Partnership (TTIP): ISDS Provisions, Reconciliation, and Future Trade Implications*, 29 EMORY INT'L L. REV. 225, 226 (2014).

[6] Abe Felstiner et al., *The Emergence and Transformation of Disputes: Naming, Blaming, Claiming*, 15 L. & SOC'Y REV. 630 (1981).

[7] UNCTAD, *WIR 2013, supra* note 3, at 110–11; UNCTAD, *WIR 2012, supra* note 3, at 84–86. Unfortunately, it is not always possible to identify how cases are "known" to verify them for scientific replicability. The availability of the online UNCTAD Policy Hub is, however, improving transparency. *See, e.g.*, UNCTAD, *Investment Policy Hub*, http://investmentpolicyhub.unctad.org (last visited Aug. 8, 2018).

[8] UNCTAD, *WIR, supra* note 3, at 70, 104. UNCTAD estimates jumped to roughly 855 in 2017. UNCTAD, *WIR 2018, supra* note 3, at 92. By the end of 2017, ICISD (the International Centre for the Settlement of Investment Disputes) had historically registered 650 disputes, which includes treaty-based *and* non-treaty-based disputes. ICSID Secetariat, *The ICSID Caseload—Statistics*, Issue 2018-1, https://bit.ly/2HS5k2y (last visited Aug. 8, 2018); *see also* ICSID Secretariat, *The ICSID Caseload—Statistics*, Issue 2016-2 (June 2016), https://bit.ly/2tFVaia (last visited Aug. 8, 2018) (identifying, in 2016, ICSID's registered cases were around 570).

As rights granted to investors under investment treaties last roughly 10 years, for at least the next decade, ITA will be a fact of economic life. Conflicts related to international investments will continue to percolate, and some may evolve into full-fledged arbitrations. Some disputes may address policy issues, and some disputes may claim compensation high enough to affect a state's fiscal position.[9] There has, unfortunately, been minimal attention paid to investment that has *not* generated formal treaty disputes. In contrast, there is an increasingly vocal public debate about the utility of investment treaties and ITA,[10] with anecdotal observations that even taxi drivers are actively debating ITA (or the so-called ISDS)[11] to pass time with passengers.[12]

Combined, these factors set the scene for a perfect storm. There are increases in scope of arbitration risk (in the form of number of covered investments), increases in formalized investor disputes, a rise of nationalistic sentiment, and clear expressions of dissatisfaction with the current paradigm for managing international investment conflict. Meanwhile, states vote with their feet. Some states strategically exit the international investment law regime,[13] whereas others enter the system or "stay the course," exhibiting path-dependent reliance on existing dispute resolution paradigms. With increased political, economic, and legal scrutiny on international investment and dispute resolution, ITA became part of debates about sensitive multi-lateral treaties.[14] Stakeholders express concerns that ITA is unpredictable and

---

[9] Organisation for Economic Co-operation and Development, Investor-State Dispute Settlement, Public Consultation: 16 May–9 July 2012 5 (2012), http://bit.ly/1dOxFTc (last visited Aug. 8, 2018).

[10] The "growing" ITA backlash, and whether there has been a meaningful shift in rhetoric, could be empirically studied. In the interim, it is noteworthy that mainstream English-speaking media, such as the *New York Times, Wall Street Journal, Washington Post, Economist, Financial Times, Guardian*, and BBC, have run multiple articles on ITA.

[11] Commentators sometimes use "ISDS," or Investor-State Dispute Settlement, in a doctrinally inaccurate way. Some ISDS cases involve commercial disputes created under national law, rather than rights provided granted through international investment treaties. The broad brush of ISDS inaccurately sweeps nontreaty disputes into the controversy, when concerns involve treaty standards and their application. ITA is a more accurate and the preferable term.

[12] Stephen M. Schwebel, *Outlook for the Continued Vitality, or Lack Thereof, of Investor-State Arbitration, in* 9 Contemporary Issues in International Arbitration 1, 2 (Art W. Rovine ed., 2016); Susan D. Franck, *Crafting Appropriate Dispute Settlement: The Politics of International Investment Disputes, in id.* at 134, 141.

[13] *See* UNCTAD, *WIR 2018, supra* note 3, at 88 (noting 2017 "marks the lowest number of [investment treaties] concluded since 1983, and for the first time, effective treaty terminations exceeded the number of new treaty conclusions").

[14] ITA became an area of focus during renegotiations of North American Free Trade Agreement (NAFTA), which led to the United States-Mexico-Canada Agreement (USMCA). Robert Landicho & Andrea Cohen, *What's in a Name Change? For Investment Claims Under the New USMCA Instead of NAFTA, (Nearly) Everything*, Kluwer Arb. Blog (Oct. 5, 2018), https://bit.ly/2ScWPVw (last visited Dec. 19, 2018). The Transpacific Partnership (TPP) and Transatlantic Trade and Investment Partnership (TTIP) also debated the inclusion and scope of ITA; Leon E. Trakman, *Investment Dispute Resolution Under the Proposed Transpacific Partnership Agreement: Prelude to a Slippery Slope?*, 5 Geo. Mason J. Int'l Comm. L. 1 (2013); Daniel J. Ikenson, *A Compromise to Advance the Trade Agenda: Purge Negotiations of Investor-State Dispute Settlement*, 57 Free Trade Bulletin (Mar. 4, 2014), http://bit.ly/OX7LWs (last visited Aug. 7, 2018); Jos Dings & Pieter de Pous, *As It Stands, the TTIP Could Threaten Democracy*, Fin. Times (Feb. 18, 2014), https://on.ft.com/2OjMpRT (last visited Aug. 7, 2018); George Monbiot, *This Transatlantic Trade Deal Is a Full-Frontal Assault on Democracy*, The Guardian (Nov. 4, 2013), https://bit.ly/2aYToxk (last visited Aug. 7, 2018); Kyriaki Karadelis, *Germany Shuns Arbitration in EU-US Treaty*, Global Arb. Rev. (Mar. 19, 2014), http://bit.ly/1nyNsox (last visited Aug. 7, 2018).

illegitimate.[15] As a result, there has been a re-examination of how investment treaty disputes should be resolved.[16] Some have proposed alternative or supplementary methods of managing investment treaty conflict,[17] whereas others advocate for wholesale elimination of investor-state arbitration[18] or creating a separate public international law court to resolve disputes.[19]

In the midst of debates about retaining, increasing, rejecting, or transforming investment law, there has been a dearth of empirical research carefully and quantitatively analyzing ITA.[20] Given the peculiar, novel, sensitive, and empirically under-explored nature of international

---

[15] Susan D. Franck, *The Legitimacy Crisis in Investment Treaty Arbitration: Privatizing Public International Law Through Inconsistent Decisions*, 73 FORDHAM L. REV. 1521 (2005); *compare* Pia Eberhardt & Ceclia Olivet, *Profiting from Injustice: How Law Firms, Arbitrators and Financiers Are Fueling an Investment Arbitration Boom*, CORP. EUROPE OBSERVATORY & TRANSNAT'L INST. (Nov. 2012), http://bit.ly/1e30kHT (last visited Aug. 7, 2018) *with* Charles N. Brower & Sadie Blanchard, *From "Dealing in Virtue" to "Profiting from Injustice": The Case Against "Re-statification" of Investment Dispute Settlement*, 55 HARV. INT'L L.J. (Jan. 2014); *but see* Sebastian Perry, *Supporters of Investment Arbitration Launch EU Think Tank*, GLOBAL ARB. REV. (July 7, 2014), http://bit.ly/1pFbRyy (last visited Aug. 7, 2018).

[16] MICHAEL WAIBEL ET AL., THE BACKLASH AGAINST INVESTMENT ARBITRATION: PERCEPTIONS AND REALITY (2010); Stavros Brekoulakis, *Systemic Bias and the Institution of International Arbitration: A New Approach to Arbitral Decision-Making*, 5 J. INT'L DISP. SETTLE. 1 (2013); Asha Kaushal, *Revising History: How the Past Matters for the Present Backlash Against the Foreign Investment Regime*, 50 HARV. INT'L L.J. 491 (2009); Sebastian Perry, *Public Consultation Opens on EU-US Treaty*, GLOBAL ARB. REV. (Mar. 28, 2014), http://bit.ly/2aUa9Oo (last visited Aug. 7, 2018).

[17] Susan D. Franck, *Integrating Investment Treaty Conflict and Dispute Systems Design*, 92 MINN. L. REV. 161 (2007); Susan D. Franck, *Using Investor-State Mediation Rules to Promote Conflict Management: An Introductory Guide*, 29 ICSID REV. 66 (2014); Nancy Welsh & Andrea K. Schneider, *The Thoughtful Integration of Mediation into Bilateral Investment Treaty Arbitration*, 18 HARV. NEG. L. REV. 71 (2013).

[18] *See* Section IV; *supra* note 8.

[19] European Commission, *Commission Welcomes Adoption of Negotiating Directives for a Multilateral Investment Court*, EUR. COMM'N (Mar. 20, 2018), https://bit.ly/2Mv2dkl (last visited Aug. 7, 2018); Fernanda Nicola & Daniele Gallo, *The External Dimension of EU Investment Law: Jurisdictional Clashes and Transformative Adjudication*, 39 FORDHAM. INT'L L.J. 1081 (2016); Horia Ciurtin, *Across the Strait: The Case for a Special EU-Taiwan Trade and Investment Partnership*, EFILABLOG (May 3, 2016), http://bit.ly/2bhy4T4 (last visited Aug. 7, 2018).

[20] Some research analyzes jurisdiction. Kathleen McArthur & Pablo A. Ormachea, *International Investor-State Arbitration: An Empirical Analysis of ICSID Decisions on Jurisdiction*, 28 REV. LIT. 559 (2009); Gus Van Harten, *Arbitrator Behavior in Asymmetrical Adjudication: An Empirical Study of Investment Treaty Arbitration*, 40 OSGOODE HALL L.J. 211 (2012); Ole K. Fauchald et al., *The Legal Reasoning of ICSID Tribunals—An Empirical Analysis*, 19 EUR. J. INT'L L. 301 (2008). Other research focused on holistic outcomes. Susan D. Franck, *Empirically Evaluating Claims About Investment Treaty Arbitration*, 86 N.C. L. REV. 1 (2007) [hereinafter Franck, *Empirically Evaluating*]; Susan D. Franck, *Development and Outcomes in Investment Treaty Arbitration*, 50 HARV. INT'L L.J. 435 (2009); Susan D. Franck, *The ICSID Effect? Considering Potential Variations in Arbitration Awards*, 51 VA. J. INT'L L. 825 (2011); Daphna Kapeliuk, *The Repeat Appointment Factor: Exploring Decision Patterns of Elite Investment Arbitrators*, 96 CORNELL L. REV. 47 (2010); Daphna Kapeliuk, *Collegial Games: Analyzing the Effect of Panel Comparison on Outcome in Investment Arbitration*, 31 REV. LIT. 267 (2012). During the multi-year process of drafting this book, ITA empirical research expanded, often focusing on outcomes or assessing arbitrators. *See, e.g.*, Scott Miller & Gregory N. Hicks, *Investor-State Dispute Settlement: A Reality Check*, CENTER FOR STRATEGIC & INTERNATIONAL STUDIES 10–11 (Jan. 2015), https://bit.ly/2VcjMdr (last visited Dec. 25, 2018); Daniel Behn, *Legitimacy, Evolution, and Growth in Investment Treaty Arbitration: Empirically Evaluating the State-of-the-Art*, 46 GEO. J. INT'L L. 363 (2015);

investment law, this book considers the functionality of investment treaty dispute resolution as regards the fiscal costs to provide evidence-based insights stakeholders can use to make normative choices. The objective is to enable stakeholders to engage in a lively and informed normative policy debate about the future of international investment dispute resolution. The book tests conventional wisdom about ITA, with a focus on costs, to evaluate its normative future. Yet the intention is deeper; by using a data-driven approach, the book aims to aid debates about ITA by providing perspectives from cognitive psychology. The book offers building blocks to move beyond what we *think* that we might know about international investment law and costs to reality-test assessments using scientific methods to ensure that assumptions—and derivative normative choices—are informed both by information and context.

This chapter grounds the discussion within legal doctrine and policy. Chapter 2 explores how cognitive illusions may inadvertently affect assessments of investment law and how social science, with appropriate ex ante methodology, can be used as an opportunity to reality check and de-bias both our cognition and our conversations. The heart of the book explores the functional reality of ITA in context and ITA's fiscal costs. Overall, the data reflected ITA is neither wholly positive nor wholly negative, suggesting singular narratives are likely misleading. Failing to recognize the complicated nature of ITA generates normative reforms that likely will fail to address actual challenges and run a risk of creating more harm than good. It would be unfortunate if angst, populism, and the economic malaise of a world order in transition lead to international economic law reforms violating the credo made famous by physicians, namely: "first, do no harm."[21] Rather, the general and cost-specific data reflect that ITA is a complicated, multivariate phenomenon with both positive and negative attributes. Chapter 9 synthesizes the data and points the way forward, using costs as a platform for thinking systematically about investment treaty dispute resolution and how to bring international investment law into alignment with anti-bullying and rule-of-law norms to prevent abuse by investors, states, counsel, arbitrators, and other stakeholders while also promoting access to justice, equality of treatment, and efficiency.

To begin the journey, this chapter first provides an overview of international investment, with a historic context and a matrix for understanding dispute resolution options. It then provides ITA's doctrinal foundation to explore the debate about ITA. The final section addresses the relative value of options to make grounded, evidence-based normative choices for investment treaty dispute resolution.

Franck & Wylie, *supra* note 3; Joost Pauwelyn, *The Rule of Law Without the Rule of Lawyers? Why Investment Arbitrators Are from Mars, Trade Adjudicators from Venus*, 109 AM. J. INT'L L. 761 (2015); Sergio Puig, *Social Capital in the Arbitration Market*, 25 EUR. J. INT'L L. 387 (2014); Thomas Schultz & Cederic Dupont, *Investment Arbitration: Promoting the Rule of Law or Over-empowering Investors? A Quantitative Empirical Study*, 25 EUR. J. INT'L L. 1147; Alec Stone Sweet et al., *Arbitral Lawmaking and State Power: Empirical Analysis of Investor–State Arbitration*, 8 J. INT'L DISP. SETTLEMENT 579 (2017). Standards for identifying quality research are discussed elsewhere. Susan D. Franck, *The Promise and Peril of Empiricism and International Investment Law Disputes*, *in* CAMBRIDGE COMPENDIUM OF INTERNATIONAL COMMERCIAL AND INVESTMENT ARBITRATION (Andrea Bjorklund et al., eds., forthcoming 2019).

[21] Franck, *supra* note 12, at 143.

I. Context of Foreign Investment

Countries continue to promote foreign investment in order to support local economic growth and development. Despite the global economic crisis, total international investment is generally on an upward trajectory. In 2010, the United Nations estimated that global FDI stock was in the order of US$19–20 trillion;[22] and despite some fluctuations,[23] by 2017, the volume of global FDI stock rose to US$31 trillion.[24] Simultaneously, although the volume of investment treaties may be slowing, the number of investment treaties containing ex ante agreements permitting investors to arbitrate disputes with states to redress violations of a treaty's substantive rights continues to expand.[25] Sources suggest there are roughly 2,000–2,500 treaties in force.[26] The convergence of these factors suggests: treaties cover 68% of foreign investment, and US$15.6 trillion in FDI stock is protected by an ex ante agreement to resolve treaty-based conflicts through arbitration.[27]

Historically, the developed world dominated capital exports. More recently, yearly investment flows have ebbed and flowed but are no longer unidirectional.[28] Developed countries

---

[22] *See* UNCTAD, *WIR 2012, supra* note 3, at 169, 173 (identifying 2011 levels of worldwide inbound FDI stock at US$20 trillion and outbound FDI stock of $21 trillion).

[23] *See* UNCTAD, *WIR 2016, supra* note 3, at 200 (identifying 2015 levels of worldwide inbound FDI stock at US$25 trillion and global outbound FDI stock at US$25 trillion); *see also* UNCTAD, *WIR 2013, supra* note 3, at 217 (identifying levels of global FDI stock around US$23 trillion); UNCTAD, *WIR 2011, supra* note 3, at 191.

[24] *See* UNCTAD, *WIR 2018, supra* note 3, at 188 (identifying levels of global inward FDI stock at US$31.5 trillion and outbound global FDI stock at US$30.8 trillion). There are, of course, year-to-year variations in specific amounts of annual investment inflows and outflows. UNCTAD's *World Investment Reports* document this over time, particularly in annex table 1 of their annual reporting.

[25] *See* UNCTAD, *WIR 2018, supra* note 3, at 88 (observing that roughly 18 new treaties brought the investment treaties universe to 3,322 treaties).

[26] *Compare* U.N. Comm'n on Int'l Trade Law, *Report of Working Group II (Arbitration and Conciliation) on the work of its 53d Sess., Oct. 4–8, 2010*, at 20, U.N. Doc. A/CN.9/712, (Oct. 20, 2010), https://bit.ly/2QRXoaA (last visited Dec. 25, 2018) (referring to "more than 2,500 investment treaties in force") *with* Catherine M. Amirfar & Elyse M. Dreyer, *Thirteen Years of NAFTAs Chapter 11*, 20 N.Y. INT'L L. REV. 39, 39 (2007) (indicating over 2,000 investment treaties were in effect); ORGANISATION FOR ECONOMIC COOPERATION & DEVELOPMENT, INTERNATIONAL INVESTMENT PERSPECTIVES: 2006, at 144 (2006) (suggesting only 1700 investment treaties were in force); *but see* S.I. Strong, *Truth in a Post-truth Society: How Sticky Defaults, Status Quo Bias, and the Sovereign Prerogative Influence the Perceived Legitimacy of International Arbitration*, 2018 U. ILL. L. REV. 533, 534 (2018) *citing* ORGANISATION FOR ECONOMIC COOPERATION & DEVELOPMENT [OECD], DISPUTE SETTLEMENT PROVISIONS IN INTERNATIONAL INVESTMENT AGREEMENTS: A LARGE SAMPLE SURVEY 5 (2012), https://bit.ly/2kqP78Q (last visited Aug. 7, 2018) (stating "approximately 93% of the 3,000–5,000 investment treaties now in effect" contain arbitration provisions and citing to a 2012 OECD report without noting the report only referred to "93% of the treaties [surveyed] contain language on ISDS").

[27] UNCTAD, *WIR 2011, supra* note 3, at 102–03; *see also* UNCTAD, *WIR 2016, supra* note 3, at 104 (discussing investment treaties "and multiple dispute-settlement mechanisms, which nevertheless offers protection to only two-thirds of global FDI stock").

[28] Markus Wagner, *Regulatory Space in International Trade Law and International Investment Law*, 36 U. PA. J. INT'L L. 1, 24 (2015).

continue to have the largest overall capital flows, but annual inflows to and capital outflows from developed countries have dropped somewhat.[29] In contrast, capital inflows to developing states have been somewhat stable, but capital *outflows* from developing states have grown.[30] Historically, rates of capital outflows from developing states and transitioning economies was proportionately low when compared to their developed world counterparts, with annual investment outflows regularly around 10% and never more than a quarter of worldwide outbound investment until 2009.[31] But starting around 2010, developing and transitioning economies together began accounting for roughly 30% of worldwide outbound investment.[32] With existing dominance in outbound investment from China and Hong Kong[33] and the Belt and Road Initiative,[34] the influence of developing and transitioning economies will likely expand.[35] In combination, the modern reality of investment flows is not about the fall of the West, but rather reflects "the rise of the rest."[36]

---

[29] UNCTAD, *Global Investment Trend Monitor, Issue No. 28*, 1-2, UNCTAD/DIAE/IA/2018/1 (Jan. 22, 2018). Annual investment inflows to developed economies were US$858,263 million, US$1,141,251, and US$712,383 in 2012, 2015, and 2017 respectively. These figures were from total worldwide investment inflows of US$1,574,712 million (or 54.5%), US$1,921,306 million (or 59.4%), and US$1,429,807 million (or 49.8%) for the same years. UNCTAD, *WIR 2018, supra* note 3, at 184.

[30] UNCTAD, *WIR 2018, supra* note 3, at xi. When considering annual flows—rather than total global investment stock—investment inflows into developing economies were US$651,500 million in 2012 (or 41.4% of all inbound investment), US$744,032 in 2015 (or 38.7% of all inbound investment) and US$670,658 in 2017 (or 46.9% of all inbound investment). In contrast, development outflows during those same time periods from developing economies were US$362,661 (or 26.3% of all worldwide outbound investment), US$406,237 (or 25% of worldwide outbound investment), and US$380,775 million (or 26.6% of worldwide outbound investment). Investment inflows for transition economies were US$64,948 million in 2012, US$36,022 in 2015, and US$46,767 in 2017; investment outflows were US$33,193, US$32,085, and US$39,989 million respectively. *Id.* at 184–87.

[31] UNCTAD, *WIR 2012, supra* note 3, at 4, figure 1.4; *see also id.* at 169–72 (providing details of FDI inflows and outflows on an annual basis for developed, developing, and transitional economies); *id.* at 173–76 (comparing global FDI stock in UNCTAD-defined developed, developing, and transitional economies during 1990, 2000, and 2011).

[32] UNCTAD, *WIR 2012, supra* note 3, at 169–72 (reflecting developed states only had 68% of investment outflows in 2010, leaving developing and transitioning economies with 32%; and identifying developed states had 73% of investment outflows in 2011, leaving 27% from developing and transitional economies); *see also* UNCTAD, *WIR 2018, supra* note 3, at 5, figure 1.5 (reflecting that, with the exception of 2014 when developing and transitional economies accounted for roughly 40% of all outbound investment, between 2009 and 2018 developing and transitioning economies typically accounted for roughly 30% of outbound investment); UNCTAD, *WIR 2018, supra* note 3, at 184–87 (reflecting that developed states had 70.6% of outbound investment in 2017, leaving 29.4% of annual outbound investment from developing and transitional economies).

[33] *See* UNCTAD, *WIR 2016, supra* note 3, at 6 (reflecting that China is the third largest source of outbound investment and Hong Kong is ninth); UNCTAD, *WIR 2018, supra* note 3, at 6 (identifying China as the third-largest source of outbound investment and Hong Kong as the fifth-largest source).

[34] State Council of the People's Republic of China, *The Belt and Road Initiative*, ENGLISH.GOV.CH, https://bit.ly/2eurSrW (last visited Aug. 7, 2018); *see also* Jac Depczky, *Will China's Belt and Road Initiative Outdo the Marshall Plan?*, THE ECONOMIST (Mar. 8, 2018), https://econ.st/2O9gm72 (last visited Aug. 7, 2018).

[35] UNCTAD, *WIR 2018, supra* note 3, at 4–6, 14–15.

[36] FAREED ZAKARIA, THE POST-AMERICAN WORLD (2008); *see also* Gordon H. Haonson, *The Rise of Middle Kingdoms: Emerging Economies in Global Trade*, 25 J. ECON. PERSP. 41 (2012); Christoph Lakner & Branko Milanovic, *Global Income Distribution: From the Fall of the Berlin Wall to the Great Recession*, WORLD BANK POL'Y RESEARCH WORKING PAPER 6719 (Dec. 2013), https://bit.ly/2onMjOb (last visited Aug. 7, 2018).

A full explanation for these investment shifts is beyond the scope of this book, but explanations are likely multivariate. One theory is that investors engage in rent-seeking to lower costs while expanding profits. In global competition for capital, investment occurs where states generate incentives and regulatory schemes to maximize their return on natural resources, which may involve nonrenewable resources in the air or in the ground, human capital with unique expertise or low costs, or other local infrastructure that facilitates commercial activity.[37] Another explanation could derive from globalization byproducts and increased openness where, as relationships and ideas flourish, new markets expand and established markets expand in new directions.[38] A final theory might reflect that investment levels reflect the predictability provided by property rights, regulatory stability, and good governance.[39] Or, perhaps, elements of each theory work in tandem, depending upon the circumstances and personalities involved.

Irrespective of how investment decisions occur,[40] there are challenges when anticipated benefits of investment deviate from reality. Expectations about investment can vary depending upon stakeholder type, including what kind of actor makes the investment, how states attempt to procure the benefits of inbound investment and balance domestic political considerations, or what civil society concerns are implicated by investment and regulatory activity. It is unrealistic to presume that, in all circumstances, all stakeholders will view investment effects similarly. A simplistic framework evaluating outcomes using three broad stakeholder groups, which fails to account for intra-group variation, demonstrates complete positive alignment occurs in only one of eight permutations.[41] *See* Table 1.1.

---

[37] Tamir Agmon & Avi Messica, *Financial Foreign Direct Investment: The Role of Private Equity Investments in the Globalization of Firms from Emerging Markets*, 49 MGMT. INT'L 5 (2009); M. Blomström & A. Kokko, *Multinational Corporations and Spillovers*, 12 J. ECON. SURVEYS 247 (1998); H. Gorg & D. Greenway, *Much Ado About Nothing? Do Domestic Firms Really Benefit from Foreign Direct Investment?*, 19 WORLD BANK RESEARCH OBSERVER 171 (2004); Kelly Liu et al., *Regional Determinants of Foreign Direct Investment in Manufacturing Industry*, 4 INT'L J. ECON. & FIN. 178 (2012); Argiro Moudatsou & Dimitrios Kyrkillis, *FDI and Economic Growth: Causality for the EU and ASEAN*, 26 J. ECON. INTEGRATION 544 (2011); Mariana Papanastassiou, *Foreign Direct Investment and Small Countries*, 49 MGMT. INT'L 5 (2009).

[38] WERNER BAER & WILLIAM R. MILES, FOREIGN DIRECT INVESTMENT IN LATIN AMERICAN: ITS CHANGING NATURE AT THE TURN OF THE CENTURY (2001); Glen Biglaiser & Karl DeRouen, *Economic Reforms and Inflows of Foreign Direct Investment in Latin America*, 41 LATIN AM. RESEARCH REV. 51 (2007); Kishor Sharma & Yapa Bandara, *Trends, Patterns and Determinants of Foreign Direct Investment*, 44 J. ECONOMICS 661 (2010).

[39] NATHAN M. JENSEN, NATION-STATES AND THE MULTINATIONAL CORPORATIONS: A POLITICAL ECONOMY OF FOREIGN DIRECT INVESTMENT (2006); Glen Biglaiser & Joseph L. Staats, *Do Political Institutions Affect Foreign Direct Investment? A Survey of U.S. Corporations in Latin America*, 63 POL. RESEARCH Q. 508 (2010); Tim Buthe & Helen V. Miner, *The Politics of Foreign Direct Investment into Developing Countries: Increasing FDI Through International Trade Agreements?*, 52 AM. J. POL. SCI. 741 (2008); Quan Li, *Democracy, Autocracy, and Tax Incentives to Foreign Investors: A Cross-national Analysis*, 68 J. POL. 62 (2006).

[40] Susan D. Franck, *Foreign Direct Investment, Investment Treaty Arbitration and the Rule of Law*, 19 MCGEORGE GLOBAL BUS. & DEV. L.J. 337, 338–40 (2007); *see also* Jason W. Yackee, *Do Bilateral Investment Treaties Promote Foreign Investment: Hints from Alternative Evidence*, 51 VA. J. INT'L L. 397 (2010).

[41] Susan D. Franck, *Managing Expectations: Beyond Formal Adjudication*, *in* PROSPECTS IN INTERNATIONAL INVESTMENT LAW AND POLICY: WORLD TRADE FORUM 371, 376–78 (Roberto Echandi & Pierre Suave, eds., 2013) [hereinafter PIILP].

TABLE 1.1

Matrix of Stakeholder Perspectives in Theoretical Alignment in Investment Outcomes.

Investor	State	Civil Society
Positive Effect	Positive Effect	Positive Effect
Positive Effect	Positive Effect	Neutral or Negative Effect
Positive Effect	Neutral or Negative Effect	Neutral or Negative Effect
Neutral or Negative Effect	Neutral or Negative Effect	Neutral or Negative Effect
Neutral or Negative Effect	Neutral or Negative Effect	Positive Effect
Neutral or Negative Effect	Positive Effect	Positive Effect
Neutral or Negative Effect	Positive Effect	Neutral or Negative Effect
Positive Effect	Neutral or Negative Effect	Positive Effect

Given the realistic likelihood of systemic dissatisfaction with investment outcomes, the availability of cost-effective enforcement mechanisms is central to regulating conflict.[42] Historical approaches to dispute settlement included "primitive remedies such as hostage taking, ransom demands and reprisals in ancient times,"[43] but modern approaches instead focus on promoting rule-of-law values and judicialization.[44] Rather than uncertainty deriving from using power politics or violence to resolve disputes, judicialized procedures create opportunities for rule-driven, neutral, predictable dispute settlement. Generally, reliability aids parties in establishing reasonable baselines for addressing unforeseen contingencies that otherwise would disrupt expectations.[45] It is not, however, empirically certain that arbitration provisions in treaties impact decisions to invest,[46] which necessitates a deeper exploration of the history of investment dispute resolution.

[42] Antonio R. Parra, *Settlement of Investment Disputes: The Experience of ICSID in Transition Countries and Elsewhere*, *in* EUROPEAN BANK OF RECONSTRUCTION AND DEVELOPMENT, LAW IN TRANSITION: CONTRACT ENFORCEMENT 39 (2001); Frances Delacey, *Enforcing Contracts in Developing Countries*, *in id.* at 18–22, 24.

[43] Delacey, *supra* note 42, at 16.

[44] PATRICK BOLTON & MATHIAS DEWATRIPONT, CONTRACT (2005); Anne van Aaken, *International Investment Law Between Commitment and Flexibility: A Contract Theory Analysis*, 12 J. INT'L ECON. L. 507 (2009).

[45] ROBERT E. SCOTT & PAUL B. STEPHEN, THE LIMITS OF LEVIATHAN: CONTRACT THEORY AND THE ENFORCEMENT OF INTERNATIONAL LAW (2006); Robert E. Scott, *The Law and Economics of Incomplete Contracts*, 2 ANN. REV. LAW & SOC. SCI. 279 (2006).

[46] *Compare* Todd Allee & Clint Peinhardt, *Delegating Differences: Bilateral Investment Treaties and Bargaining over Dispute Resolution Provisions*, 54 INT'L STUD. QUART. 1 (2010) *with* Yackee, *supra* note 40; *see also* Jonathan Bonnitcha, *Assessing the Impacts of Investment Treaties: Overview of the Evidence*, INTERNATIONAL INSTITUTE FOR SUSTAINABLE DEVELOPMENT, IISD REPORT 3–4 (2017), https://bit.ly/2ynM39u (last visited Aug. 7, 2018).

II. History of Investment Dispute Resolution

ITA is a hybrid sui generis creature that owes its doctrinal and policy basis to both public and private international law.[47] For private law, it involves the rights of private individuals, their commercial activities, and vindicating rights using adjudicative forums and fiscal awards of damages. From a public law perspective, ITA involves the law of state responsibility, state regulatory conduct, and states' capacity to craft international law instruments that voluntarily set boundaries on their own regulatory capacity in a bid to incentivize private commercial activity.[48]

ITA is a relatively new international law phenomenon but fits within a larger historical framework. For centuries, people made their way to other countries searching for economic opportunities. Sometimes this involved trade in goods or services; other times, there were more developed commercial enterprises with deeper commitments. Whenever people are involved in commercial activity, there is inevitably friction that can transform into investment-related conflict and possibly escalate into crystalized disputes. Historical options for addressing conflict included: ignoring investment conflict and accepting it as a cost of doing business (and pricing commercial risks accordingly), obtaining political risk insurance coverage and passing the cost of conflict onto a secondary market, soliciting the investor's home state to privately engage in diplomacy on investors' behalves, engaging in "gunboat diplomacy," or making formal declarations of war to protect the underlying economic interests. Over time, formal adjudicative rule-of-law options developed, including espousal of investors' disputes in a public international venue or state-to-state adjudication.[49]

One might conceptualize these conflict management options as quadrants with two dimensions. The first dimension involves informal versus formal options, and the second dimension involves adjudicative or non-adjudicative mechanisms. As dispute resolution options are not a pure binary continuum, managing conflict requires broader options including: (1) informal non-adjudicative options, such as those related to private negotiation and mediation; (2) informal adjudicative options, such as expert determination or assessments by ombuds; (3) formal non-adjudicative options, including diplomacy, gunboat diplomacy, and declarations of war; and (4) formal adjudicative options, including national courts or other international courts and tribunals.[50] *See* Table 1.2. Methods are not per se "right" or "wrong"; rather optimal choices require contextual evaluation of how well processes meet stakeholder needs.

---

47 Franck & Wylie, *supra* note 3; Anthea Roberts, *Clash of Paradigms: Actors and Analogies Shaping the Investment Treaty System*, 107 Am. J. Int'l L. 45 (2013).

48 Jose E. Alvarez, The Public International Law Regime Governing International Investment (2011); Roberts, *supra* note 47.

49 Anthea Roberts, *State-to-State Investment Treaty Arbitration: A Hybrid Theory of Interdependent Rights and Shared Interpretive Authority*, 55 Harv. Int'l L.J. 1 (2014).

50 Franck, *in* PIILP, *supra* note 41, at 380–86.

TABLE 1.2

Matrix of Theoretical Dispute Resolution Options for Managing International Investment Law Conflict.

	Rulemaking or Non-Adjudicative	Adjudicative
Formal	***Formal Rulemaking:*** Diplomacy, Declarations of War, Treaty Drafting, Free Trade Commission Statements, Negotiated Rulemaking	***Formal Adjudication:*** International Courts and Tribunals, International Arbitration, National Courts
Informal	***Informal Rulemaking:*** Negotiation, Mediation, Dispute Prevention Policies, etc.	***Informal Adjudication:*** Early Neutral Evaluation, Expert Determination, Ombuds

Other areas of international law—particularly international economic law in areas such as international trade—have likewise become more judicialized.[51] Following a strong current in a related discipline, international investment law developed towards valuing formalized adjudication.

History also explains this evolution. In the past, foreign investors were caught between a rock and a hard place when trying to obtain redress for state activity arguably harming their investment. Investors had a limited range of non-adjudicative, direct options. Investors were dependent upon: internal capacity to absorb losses, ability to negotiate directly with host states, or political capital and willingness of their home state to use diplomacy to secure favorable outcomes. Without a clear, independent, reliable, and predictable adjudicative baseline, the non-adjudicative options meant commercial risk and uncertainty. While investors could manage risks with their local counterparties, they had limited capacity to manage risks involving host state regulation, particularly when local expertise in limited or sovereign immunity prevented redress. This could make investment either untenable or lead investors to pass the cost of uncertainty on to the market through increased costs.[52]

The historical lack of adjudicative options was a function of two overlapping issues, namely the substantive law and procedural forum. Substantively, there debates about the meaning of public international law on expropriation and compensation, meaning core

[51] Robert E. Hudec, *The Judicialization of GATT Dispute Settlement, in* In Whose Interest? Due Process and Transparency in International Grade (Michael Hart & Debra Steger, eds. 1992); *see also* John H. Jackson, The World Trading System: Law and Policy of International Economic Relations (2d ed. 1997).

[52] *See, e.g.*, Witold J. Henisz & Bennet A. Zelner, *The Hidden Risks in Emerging Markets*, Harv. Bus. Rev. 4 (Apr. 2010), https://bit.ly/1JVW63k (last visited Aug. 7, 2018) (discussing a case where "high-priced lawyers constructed an ironclad set of guarantees that allowed [investors] to pass the costs of policy and other risks on to Georgian consumers").

property rights were hotly contested and not subject to universal agreement.[53] Given the uncertainty, states sometimes enumerated substantive rights in treaties of Friendship, Navigation, and Commerce to offer clarity.[54] Yet those were functionally "ghostly" rights, creating rights without a forum to secure a remedy.[55] Some international tribunals provided a forum for adjudicating investment-related rights. While there have been others,[56] mixed Claims Commissions have redressed commercial harm related to the bombing of the *Lusitania*, claims related to damages for disputes involving U.S. and Mexican nationals (the American-Mexican Claims Commission), and disputes related to the Iranian revolution and hostage crisis (the Iran-U.S. Claims Tribunal).[57] Yet, such tribunals were ad hoc byproducts of political negotiations brokered by states. Because choice-of-law and choice-of-forum were historically conflated, non-adjudicative options were the only viable direct method for investors to vindicate damages incurred from international law violations.

Rights could be adjudicated indirectly, however, but in a manner making investors wholly dependent upon states. The International Court of Justice (ICJ) provides adjudication for investment-related international law rights, but only when states make the political decision to espouse their investors' claims. The byproduct of states' decisions about whether and under what conditions to transform an investment dispute to a public inter-state dispute involves high political stakes and heightening tension in international relations. As such, initiating litigation was not done lightly or frequently.[58] Yet, even should the ICJ identify a breach of international investment rights, the indirect nature of the remedy and enforcement is suboptimal for investors. First, the ICJ does not typically award monetary damages. Since its inception, the ICJ has awarded monetary damages in only two cases, including *Diallo*.[59] The only other case was *Corfu Chanel*,[60] decided nearly seventy years

[53] ANDREW NEWCOMBE ET AL., LAW AND PRACTICE OF INTERNATIONAL INVESTMENT TREATIES: STANDARDS OF TREATMENT (2009); Andrew Guzman, *Why LDCs Sign Treaties That Hurt Them: Explaining the Popularity of Bilateral Investment Treaties*, 38 VA. J. INT'L L. 639, 641(1998). *See also* L. Yves Fortier & Stephen L. Drymer, *Indirect Expropriation in the Law of International Investment: I Know It When I See It, or Caveat Investor*, 13 ASIA PAC. L. REV. 79, 81 (2005); Matthew C. Porterfield, *State Practice and the (Purported) Obligation Under Customary International Law to Provide Compensation for Regulatory Expropriations*, 37 N.C. J. INT'L L. & COM. REG. 159, 171–72 (2011).

[54] H.P. Connell, *United States Protection of Private Foreign Investment Through Treaties of Friendship, Commerce and Navigation*, 9 ARCHIV DES VÖLKERRECHTS 256 (1961).

[55] *See* Western Maid v. Thompson, 257 U.S. 419, 433 (1922) (Holmes, J.) ("[l]egal obligations that exist but cannot be enforced are ghosts that are seen in the law but that are elusive to the grasp"); Karl N. Llewellyn, *Some Realism About Realism—Responding to Dean Pound*, 44 HARV. L. REV. 1222, 1244 (1931) (noting law's fundamental value quality is not just the right but "what can be done: not only 'no remedy, no right' but 'precisely as much right as remedy'").

[56] This might include claims from the Jay Treaty and the Alabama Claims Commission. JOHN COLLIER & VAUGHN LOWE, THE SETTLEMENT OF DISPUTES IN INTERNATIONAL LAW 31–44 (1999).

[57] Maurizio Brunetti, *The* Lex Mercatoria *in Practice: The Experience of the Iran-United States Claims Tribunal*, 18 ARB. INT'L 355 (2002); Abraham H. Feller, *The Mexican Claims Commission*, 19 IOWA L. REV. 225, 225–29 (1934); Joseph C. Fehr, *American and German War Claims Settled*, 18 ABA 896, 897 (1932).

[58] Franck, *supra* note 15, at 1536–37.

[59] *In re* Diallo (Guinea v. Congo), Compensation owed by the Democratic Republic of the Congo to the Republic of Guinea, 51 I.L.M. 737 (June 19, 2012).

[60] Corfu Channel Damages Case (U.K. v. Alb.), 1949 I.C.J. 244 (Dec. 15).

ago, and full compliance only occurred after fifty-seven years. Second, compliance with ICJ decisions can be challenging. Should states fail to comply voluntarily with an adverse judgment, the dispute returns to the political arena, and the United Nations Security Council must secure enforcement.[61] Third, even if a favorable ICJ award becomes liquid, the winning state—not the investor—is the official recipient of damages, and the state need not disgorge the proceeds.

The indirect access to adjudication generated a legal vacuum in international law that largely meant that the default position required foreign investors to invoke national law (presumably the national law of the host states) in a national forum.[62] If an investor was fortunate enough to have a separate agreement with a state, its organ, or instrumentality, an investor could select a forum—such as international commercial arbitration or an appropriate national court—to have jurisdiction over the investment dispute governed by national law. Yet, not all foreign investors were so lucky. Not all investors can seek relief in national courts for allegedly problematic state conduct. Investors might not be in direct privity with a state-party, or national law might not permit foreign investors to challenge state regulatory activity.[63] Even if states did permit investors to sue states for state conduct in a national court, concerns may nevertheless remain. Irrespective of whether they are real or imagined, investors may have lingering concerns about the integrity and independence of the local adjudicative process.[64] Mixed empirical results suggest that this concern may be warranted, as foreign litigants have been sufficiently concerned about anti-foreigner bias that only the most meritorious claims were brought to national courts,[65] and some research on U.S. domestic courts suggests courts may favor in-state litigants.[66] Even if an investor pursued national court litigation, there is still no viable, broad international enforcement regime for foreign court judgments.[67] This means that, even if an investor secured a favorable judgment against the state in the state's own courts, there would still be challenges—including more time and cost—in procuring enforcement of a national judgment, let alone securing voluntary compliance by recalcitrant states. These factors create incentives for states to ensure

---

[61] U.N. Charter art. 94, para. 2.

[62] The nature of investors' international legal rights is uncertain, as is seen from questions about what constitutes a legal expropriation under international law. NEWCOMBE ET AL., *supra* note 53, at 12–41; Fortier, *supra* note 53, at 81–84; Porterfield, *supra* note 53, at 171.

[63] Julian Arato, *Corporations as Lawmakers*, 56 HARV. INT'L L.J. 229, 256–58, 288–89 (2015).

[64] Maya Steinitz & Paul Gowder, *Transnational Litigation as a Prisoner's Dilemma*, 594 N.C. L. REV. 751, 751, 753 (2016); *see also* William S. Dodge & Scott Dodson, *Personal Jurisdiction and Aliens*, 116 MICH. L. REV. 1205, 1125 (2018) (exploring literature on perceived "local bias" and "judicial hellholes").

[65] Given case selection effects where foreigners only pursued their strongest cases, research demonstrates that foreign plaintiffs did not necessarily lose in greater proportion to their domestic litigants. Kevin M. Clermont & Theodore Eisenberg, *Xenophilia or Xenophobia in U.S. Courts? Before and After 9/11*, 4 J. EMPIRICAL L. STUD. 441 (2007); Kevin M. Clermont & Theodore Eisenberg, *Xenophilia in American Courts*, 109 HARV. L. REV. 1120 (1996).

[66] Jeffrey J. Rachlinski et al., *Can Judges Make Reliable Numeric Decisions? Distorted Damages and Skewed Sentences*, 90 IND. L.J. 695 (2015); Kimberly A. More, *Xenophobia in American Courts*, 97 NW. U. L. REV. 1497 (2003).

[67] The Convention has limited scope and application. Hague Convention on Choice of Court Agreements, June 30, 2005, 44 I.L.M. 1294, http://bit.ly/18x6Gbv (last visited Aug. 7, 2018).

some viable venue to seek clarification of whether state conduct generated liability and to ensure those decisions, whether adverse to states or favorable, were respected.

Against this backdrop, states and investors began using investment treaties to permit arbitration. ITA was an evolutionary step providing investors with direct rights and a meaningful forum for rule-of-law adjudication. It avoided states having to make difficult, time-consuming, and politically challenging decisions of whether to espouse an investor's claim; it granted investors the choice to decide whether, given costs and benefits, pursuing a claim was appropriate; and it offered a tried and tested process, namely international arbitration, with a historical pedigree of adjudicative neutrality. The existence of two preexisting treaties, namely the New York Convention and ICSID Convention, offered clear but tailored grounds for challenging awards that permitted ITA to have some degree of review while benefitting from established and streamlined enforcement regimes. In theory, ITA offered a more balanced playing field and fostered adjudication that minimized commercial risk and maximized rule-of-law. Whether ITA has secured those theoretical benefits is, however, a subject of debate.[68]

III. Doctrinal Foundation of ITA

Understanding the current policy debates and options normative reform requires appreciating ITA's doctrinal framework. ITA has three doctrinal foundations, namely: investment treaties that supply the basis of the arbitration agreement and identify the applicable law, institutional rules applicable to the arbitration procedure, and enforcement conventions. While others have thoughtfully explored substantive treaty law,[69] this section offers an overview to aid subsequent empirical inquiry.

Doctrinally, ITA derives from investment treaties. Germany and Pakistan signed the first investment treaty in 1959. By 1990, 300 investment treaties were concluded, and there was only one ITA dispute. With over 3,000 investment treaties and approximately 700 formal disputes initiated over three decades, investment treaties and ITA remain a relatively modern phenomenon in international law. The net objective of the treaties was to entice inbound foreign investment and to protect a state's own investors abroad, while minimizing the risk of state liability when foreign investors receive unilateral international economic rights. Treaties typically involve a pair or group of countries signing a treaty, like the Dominican Republic-Central American Free Trade Agreement (CAFTA-DR), where states exchange promises to protect others' investments. Treaties grant reciprocal investment rights—both procedural and substantive—to the foreign investors of the signatory countries. In some, but not all, instances, states secure the intended benefit of investment treaties, namely increased foreign investment.[70]

---

[68] Franck & Wylie, *supra* note 3, at 472.

[69] Doak Bishop et al., Foreign Investment Disputes (2005); Rudolf Dolzer & Christoph Schreuer, Principles of International Investment Law (2012); Campbell McLachlan et al., International Investment Arbitration: Substantive Principles (2008); Newcombe et al., *supra* note 53.

[70] Jennifer L. Tobin & Susan Rose-Ackerman, *When BITs Have Some Bite: The Political-Economic Environment for Bilateral Investment Treaties*, 6 Rev. Int'l Org. 1 (2011); *see also* Franck, *in* PIILP, *supra* note 41 (reviewing literature).

Procedurally, treaties offer dispute resolution rights, including the right to arbitrate treaty disputes. After complying with prerequisites, like notification of disputes and amicable settlement efforts, treaties permit investors to directly bring a dispute against a state to a tribunal in which both parties can appoint adjudicators. This serves as an alternative to political negotiations, soliciting an investor's home state to espouse a claim before a public international law tribunal, avoiding the domestic courts of a state that may have to render a decision against a coequal branch of government, or simply absorbing the loss. ITA also has the virtue of preventing blanket claims of immunity from suit—whether by virtue of sovereign immunity or political question doctrines—that might otherwise prevent investors from bringing claims in national courts.[71] Despite hoping to provide a neutral, legitimate forum for states to resolve disputes without allegations of bias, ITA has fallen prey to claims that it is politicized and biased—particularly against developing states.[72]

Substantively, investment treaties involve state promises that foreign investors will receive basic protections, including freedom from unlawful expropriation without proper compensation, freedom from discrimination, and guarantees of fair and equitable treatment (FET). These rights are analogous to using international law to provide an economic bill of rights for foreign investors.[73] Some disputes arising under treaties involve public law elements, such as questions about Zimbabwe's expropriation of land that displaced some white farmers or imposing environmental regulations disparately impacting foreign companies.[74] Other disputes have a more commercial flavor, such as a state's revocation of a banking license or breach of contract.[75] Certain disputes, although not necessarily representative, have become iconic symbols in ITA. For example, groups of investors sued Argentina for its 2001 currency crisis that led to the devaluation of the Argentine peso and decreased the value of investments, particularly those denominated in U.S. dollars;[76] and Philip Morris sued—and lost to—Australia and Uruguay for plain-packaging cigarette regulations that allegedly expropriated intellectual property.[77]

---

[71] Stephen E. Blythe, *The Advantages of Investor-State Arbitration as a Dispute Resolution Mechanism in International Law*, 47 INT'L LAW. 273, 274–79 (2013).

[72] Leon Trakman, *The ICSID Under Siege*, 45 CORNELL INT'L L.J. 603 (2012).

[73] David Schneidermann, *Investment Rules and the New Constitutionalism*, 25 LAW & SOC. INQUIRY 757, 767 (2000); Susan D. Franck, *The Nature and Enforcement of Investor Rights Under Investment Treaties: Do Investment Treaties Have a Bright Future?*, 12 U.C. DAVIS J. INT'L L. & POL'Y 47, 48 (2005).

[74] Jason Webb Yackee, *Pacta Sunt Servanda and State Promises to Foreign Investors Before Bilateral Investment Treaties: Myth and Reality*, 32 FORDHAM INT'L L.J. 1550, 1554–57 (2009); *see also* Julie A. Maupin, *Differentiating Among International Investment Disputes*, THE FOUNDATIONS OF INTERNATIONAL INVESTMENT LAW: BRIDGING THEORY INTO PRACTICE (2014), http://bit.ly/Xpaqwp (last visited Aug. 7, 2018).

[75] Ross P. Buckley & Paul Blyshak, *Guarding the Open Door: Non-party Participation Before the International Centre for Settlement of Investment Disputes*, 22 BANK. & FIN. L. REV. 353, 366 (2007); Michael Waibel, *Opening Pandora's Box: Sovereign Bonds in International Arbitration*, 101 AM. J. INT'L L. 711, 712–13 (2007).

[76] JOSE E. ALVAREZ, THE PUBLIC INTERNATIONAL LAW REGIME GOVERNING INTERNATIONAL INVESTMENT (2011).

[77] Philip Morris Asia Ltd. v. Commonwealth of Austl., UNCITRAL, PCA Case No. 2012-12, Award on Jurisdiction and Admissibility (Dec. 17, 2015), http://bit.ly/1R4XEqe (last visited Aug. 7, 2018); Philip Morris Brand Sàrl et al. v. Oriental Republic of Uru., Decision on Jurisdiction, ICSID ARB/10/7 (July 8, 2016), http://bit.ly/29G1ewI (last visited Aug. 7, 2018).

If a foreign investor believes a host state violated its substantive treaty rights, treaties permit direct redress against the state through treaty-based dispute resolution. This is the genesis of ITA, as treaties permit investors to resolve their disputes directly and finally through arbitration. A cause of action under an investment treaty generally involves a foreign investor asserting that host state conduct violated the treaty and damaged the investment. If the dispute is not otherwise resolved through negotiation or mediation, the investor requires the state to arbitrate. While treaties vary, investors can generally elect to arbitrate before: an ad hoc tribunal organized under the United Nations Commission on International Trade Law (UNCITRAL) Arbitration Rules; the Stockholm Chamber of Commerce (SCC), a tribunal organized through the World Bank's International Centre for Settlement of Investment Dispute (ICSID); or another designated venue.[78] The rules offer the procedural backbone for ITA. While there are variations, the rules typically operate as an individualized civil procedure code—subject to party modification—and offer baselines for filing pleadings, selecting and challenging arbitrators, contesting jurisdiction, gathering and assessing evidence, and writing awards.[79]

After parties select their arbitrators, either an arbitral institution or the two co-arbitrators appoint the tribunal chair.[80] Arbitrators make undertakings of independence and impartiality; panels resolve investment disputes[81] in accordance with the applicable law,[82] which generally includes the substantive provisions of the investment treaty and other relevant principles of law.[83]

Parties must, in turn, marshal their facts and legal arguments to address four core aspects: namely, jurisdiction, merits, quantum, and costs. The investor must first establish that it meets the three jurisdictional thresholds, namely, that there is: (1) a qualifying investor, (2) a qualifying investment that is (3) brought under an enforceable treaty within a proper time frame. If those prerequisites are not established, the case terminates, and the state is not liable. Otherwise, the dispute continues. The merits phase involves an assessment of whether the respondent breached the treaty's substantive obligations and specific protections promised. If there is no substantive breach, the case terminates without state

---

[78] Some treaties permit investors to arbitrate at the International Chamber of Commerce (ICC). Jason W. Yackee, *Bilateral Investment Treaties, Credible Commitment and the Rule of (International) Law*, 42 LAW & SOC'Y REV. 805 (2008); *see also* UNCTAD, IIA ISSUES NOTE, No. 1 (Apr. 2012), https://bit.ly/WETAcp (last visited Aug. 7, 2018) (identifying seven known ICC cases).

[79] Chiarra Giorgetti, *Who Decides in International Investment Arbitration*, 35 U. PENN. J. INT'L L. 431 (2013).

[80] GARY B. BORN, INTERNATIONAL COMMERCIAL ARBITRATION 1696 (2009); Franck, *supra* note 15, at 1543–44.

[81] RUDOLF DOLZER & MARGRETE STEVENS, BILATERAL INVESTMENT TREATIES 124 (1995); Franck, *supra* note 20, at 77.

[82] Toby Landau, *Composition and Establishment of the Tribunal*, 9 AM. REV. INT'L ARB. 45, 52–53 (1998); Andreas F. Lowenfeld, *The Party-Appointed Arbitrator in International Controversies: Some Reflections*, 30 TEX. INT'L L.J. 59, 65 (1995); Claudia T. Salomon, *Selecting an International Arbitrator: Five Factors to Consider*, 17 MEALEY'S INT'L ARB. REP. No. 10, 2, 3 (2002).

[83] Yas Banifatemi, *Mapping the Future of Investment Treaty Arbitration as a System of Law*, 103 AM. SOC'Y INT'L L. PROC. 323 (2009); Andrea K. Bjorklund, *Mandatory Rules of Law and Investment Arbitration*, 18 AM. REV. INT'L ARB. 175 (2007).

liability; otherwise, the dispute continues. At the quantum phase, the parties establish the value of the treaty breach. Cost awards and assessments can be made at any point during the dispute. Although tribunals can issue several decisions, ultimately, the tribunal must render a final award.[84]

The final doctrinal foundation relates to recognition and enforcement of awards. The two primary treaties permitting enforcement are the ICSID Convention and New York Convention.[85] Despite differences in methodology, both treaties generally provide narrow bases for challenging awards and permitting final awards to be enforceable worldwide.[86]

Although beyond the scope of this book, there is evidence that states voluntarily comply with awards, often after reviewing awards within ICSID or through national courts. Mexico paid the full amount of the *Metalclad* arbitration award after exhausting opportunities to overturn the award through national courts.[87] When compared with *Corfu Chanel* and the need to wait nearly six decades to obtain compliance with a monetary damage award, the prevalence of compliance and payment of awards is noteworthy.[88] Yet, full and immediate compliance is not necessarily uniform and can re-politicize disputes. Argentina contested adverse decisions resulting from its 2001 currency crisis through the normal challenge procedures.[89] After several years of unpaid awards, the United States suspended preferential Argentine tariffs under the Generalized System of Preferences program.[90] Argentina settled several cases in 2013,[91] and in an effort to secure more international lending, Argentina agreed to pay a variety of other claims.[92] Like other public international law adjudication, some states inevitably can fail to participate in ITA or fail to abide by the arbitration awards. Nevertheless, despite non-enforcement risks, states can and do participate in ITA and comply with adverse awards.

---

[84] *See, e.g.*, Lucy Reed et al., Guide to ICSID Arbitration (2d ed. 2010); Andrew Newcombe & Lluis Paradell, Law and Practice of Investment Treaties: Standards of Treatment (2009).

[85] Convention on the Recognition and Enforcement of Foreign Arbitral Awards, June 10, 1958, 21 U.S.T. 2518 [hereinafter New York Convention]; Convention on the Settlement of Investment Disputes between States and Nationals of Other States (Mar. 18, 1965), 17 U.S.T. 1270, 575 U.N.T.S. 159 [hereinafter ICSID Convention]; *see also* Inter-American Convention on International Commercial Arbitration of 1975, Pub. L. No. 101-369, 104 Stat. 448 (1990).

[86] Susan D. Franck, *Integrating Investment Treaty Conflict and Dispute Systems Design*, 92 Minn. L. Rev. 161, 193–94 (2007). There is doctrinal variation. ICSID Convention arbitrations issue one final "award"; earlier decisions are not enforceable "awards." *See* ICSID Convention art. 37(2)(b); *but see* Franck, *supra* note 15, at 1547–57 (comparing ICSID and New York Convention enforcement).

[87] Bureau National Affairs, *Mexico Pays $16 Million to Metalclad, Ending First NAFTA Chapter 11 Dispute* (Oct. 2001); ICSID, *Survey for ICSID Member States on Compliance with ICSID Awards*, ICSID.WorldBank.org (Nov. 6, 2017), https://bit.ly/2NggiGn (last visited Aug. 17, 2018); *BG Group PLC v. Republic of Arg.*, 134 S. Ct. 1198 (2014) (contesting ITA enforcement).

[88] OECD, *Government Perspectives on Investor-State Dispute Settlement: A Progress Report* 11–12 (Dec. 14, 2012), http://bit.ly/19H3Elf (last visited Aug. 7, 2018).

[89] Edward Baldwin et al., *Limits to Enforcement of ICSID Awards*, 23 J. Int'l Arb. 1 (2006).

[90] Doug Palmer, *Obama Says to Suspend Trade Benefits for Argentina*, Reuters (Mar. 26, 2012).

[91] Juliana Castilla, *Argentina Agrees $217 Million Arbitration Deal with Energy Companies*, Reuters (May 14, 2015), http://reut.rs/1OqRLtd (last visited Aug. 7, 2018).

[92] Palmer, *supra* note 90; *see also* Ezequiel Vetulli & Emmanuel E. Kaufman, *Is Argentina Looking for Reconciliation with ISDS?*, Kluwer Arb. Blog (Oct. 13, 2016), https://bit.ly/2BwD7Nr (last visited Dec. 20, 2018).

IV. ITA "Success" and "Backlash"

Tensions about the value of investment treaties have existed since their inception. The strength of the competing voices ebbs and flows over time and "[t]he debate is set to intensify."[93] The challenge is, as ITA has moved from the margin to the center of debates about globalization, that the pace of debate has become frenetic with major evolutions occurring quickly and ITA-related protests organized with remarkable efficiency.

During the early phase of the international investment system, many gave ITA "overwhelming praise" for its "unmitigated" success.[94] Supportive commentary came from international law luminaries such as Judge Stephen Schwebel, who praised the benefits of ITA for both capital-importing and exporting states.[95] Extolling these virtues by investment-law triumphalists may have been a byproduct of a time when there was growth in foreign investment flows: more treaties, but a small number of treaty disputes. In other words, the benefits seemed tangible and the risks appeared minimal. Yet human cognition may have affected how stakeholders, at that time, perceived those experiences. For example, primacy—which involves an undue focus upon first impressions[96]—contributes to ensuring that the initial cases leave a lasting impression, forming the basis for conscious or subconscious comparisons,[97] and the representativeness heuristic may mean, should those initial cases be easily to recollect, that one might presume that easily recalled cases are representative of the larger population. Early adjudication under the North American Free Trade Agreement (NAFTA) could have been viewed more favorably when contrasted with then-contemporaneous or prominent ICJ litigation. The United States, for instance, was unable to establish a claim for expropriation on behalf of investors in *ELSI*.[98] Unlike the nearly six decades required to secure compliance in *Corfu Chanel*, ITA cases—like *Metalclad*, where U.S. investors received a prompt payment after Mexico unsuccessfully challenged the award in a Canadian court—were comparatively attractive. Some commentators continue to praise ITA, suggesting that "States and investors both stand to benefit from international arbitration."[99]

Despite the initial wave of satisfaction, matters have shifted. Concerns come from various quarters, including international organizations, nongovernmental organizations (NGOs), academics, and states. UNCTAD has discussed "perceived shortcomings" of the system,

---

93 Paul M. Blyschak, *State Consent, Investor Interests and the Future of Investment Arbitration: Reanalyzing the Jurisdiction of Investor-State Tribunals in Hard Cases*, 9 ASPER REV. INT'L BUS. 99, 99 (2009).

94 David P. Riesenberg, *Fee Shifting in Investor-State Arbitration: Doctrine and Policy Justifying Application of the English Rule*, 60 DUKE L.J. 977, 985 (2011) (discussing the satisfaction and praise for the existing ITA system and citing Jeswald Salacuse, Stephen Schwebel, Thomas Waelde, Ian Laird, and Joel Beauvais).

95 Stephen M. Schwebel, *The Overwhelming Merits of Bilateral Investment Treaties*, 32 SUFFOLK TRANSNAT'L L. REV. 263 (2009).

96 *See* Chapter 2.

97 Flashbulb memories involve highlighted, detailed, and emotionally vivid memories seem fresh, precise, and easy to recollect. They can, however, be decidedly inaccurate. Should experience with ITA generate a flashbulb memory, this could theoretically facilitate inaccurate impressions and perceptions. *See* CHRISTOPHER CHABRIS & DANIEL SIMONS, THE INVISIBLE GORILLA: AND OTHER WAYS OUR INTUITIONS DECEIVE US 68–78 (2010) (discussing flashbulb memories).

98 Elettronica Sicula S.p.A. (ELSI) (U.S. v. Italy), 1989 I.C.J. 15 (July 20).

99 Joshua B. Simmons, *Valuation in Investor-State Arbitration: Toward a More Exact Science*, 30 BERKELEY J. INT'L L. 196, 202 (2012); *see also* Brower & Blanchard, *supra* note 5; Brower & Blanchard, *supra* note 15.

particularly opportunities about "reigning in the growing number of [ITA] cases, fostering the legitimacy and increasing the transparency of the [ITA] proceedings, dealing with inconsistent readings of key provisions investment treaties and poor treaty interpretation, improving the impartiality and quality of arbitrators, reducing the lengthy and costs of proceedings, assisting developing countries in handling [ITA] cases, and addressing overall concerns about the functioning of the system."[100] Others suggest ITA involves considerable time and costs, and that cases "run, on average, several years and entail large costs for both claimants and respondent States,"[101] which presumably has a disparate impact on developing states with fewer fiscal resources. Meanwhile, reports with emotionally evocative and tantalizing headlines suggest ITA amounts to "Profiting from Injustice" since "agreeing to arbitration [means] states have accepted to be sued by the devil in hell."[102] Others suggest ITA is a "legal monster," using vivid and emotive symbols.[103] While focusing argumentation on potentially unrepresentative examples and emotional impulses may offer effective marketing, particularly in the Twitter age,[104] it also facilitates intuitive assessments and generalizations tapping into suboptimal aspects of cognitive illusions.

Some states have voted with their feet.[105] Russia withdrew from the Energy Charter Treaty after an investor established jurisdiction over disputes related to the dissolution of Yukos Oil, which resulted in an adverse award against Russia in excess of US$50 billion.[106] Bolivia and Ecuador withdrew from the ICSID Convention.[107] The president of Ecuador rejected ICSID, claiming ICSID "signifies colonialism, slavery with respect to transnationals, with respect to Washington, with respect to the World Bank."[108] In 2012, Ecuador's Minister of Foreign Affairs, Trade and Integration called an ICSID award "unjust, illegal, illegitimate and absurd."[109]

---

[100] UNCTAD, *WIR 2012, supra* note 3, at 86–88; *see also* UNCTAD, *WIR 2013, supra* note 3, at 110–17.

[101] Kyla Tienharra, *Third-Party Participation in Investment-Environment Disputes: Recent Developments*, 16 Rev. Eur. Cmty. & Int'l Envtl. L. 230 (2007).

[102] Eberhardt & Olivet, *supra* note 15.

[103] Mahnaz Malik, *The Legal Monster That Lets Companies Sue Countries*, The Guardian, Nov. 4, 2011; Eberhardt & Olivet, *supra* note 15; Transnational Law Institute, *Discover the Dark Side of Investment* (June 27, 2012), http://bit.ly/1mBGYYs (last visited Aug. 7, 2018); Global Europe, *A Response to the Critic of "Profiting from Injustice"* (Jan. 4, 2013), http://bit.ly/1p8mhVT (last visited Aug. 7, 2018); *see also* Corporate Europe, *The Zombie ISDS: Rebranded as ICS, Rights for Corporations to Sue States Refuse to Die* (Feb. 17, 2016), http://bit.ly/1PVOJIx (last visited Aug. 7, 2018); Jonathan Green, *ISDS: The Devil in the Trade Deal,* Australian Radio National (Sept. 14, 2014), http://ab.co/1rYKBAV (last visited Aug. 7, 2018).

[104] *See, e.g.*, Tom Nichols, The Death of Expertise: The Campaign Against Established Knowledge and Why It Matters (2018).

[105] Michael Waibel et al, *The Backlash Against Investment Arbitration: Perceptions and Reality, in* The Backlash Against Investment Arbitration: Perceptions and Reality (Michael Waibel et al., eds., 2010).

[106] Megan Davies et al., *Court Orders Russia to Pay $50 Billion for Seizing Yukos Assets*, Reuters (July 28, 2014), http://reut.rs/1mUISnn (last visited Aug. 7, 2018). A Dutch court, however, set aside the award, ruling the tribunal lacked jurisdiction. Stanley Reed, *Dutch Court Overturns $50 Billion Ruling Against Russia in Yukos Case*, N.Y. Times (Apr. 20, 2016), https://nyti.ms/2TodPhK (last visited Dec. 20, 2018).

[107] *See generally* Susan D. Franck, *The ICSID Effect?: Considering Potential Variations in Arbitration Awards*, 51 Va. J. Int'l L. 825, 828–29 (2011).

[108] Trakman, *supra* note 72, at 604 (citing *ICSID in Crisis: Straight-Jacket or Investment Protection?*, Bretton Woods Project (July 10, 2009)).

[109] Republica del Ecuador, Ministerio de Relaciones Exteriores Comercio e Integracion, *Ecaudor Will Require Invalidity of Fault of the International Center for Settlement of Investment Disputes (ICSID) in Favor of Western. Minister: Ricardo Patiño* (Oct. 10, 2012), http://bit.ly/1bO24Ts [Spanish language presentation at http://bit.ly/W2zZOu] (last visited Aug. 7, 2018).

Other states have encouraged the "reemergence of the 'toothless' investment treaty,"[110] which, much like older treaties of Friendship Navigation and Commerce, provides substantive rights but no forum resolving disputes.[111] India materially altered its investment treaty program.[112] South Africa has generally stopped signing new investment treaties, letting older ones expire.[113] The Czech Republic attempted to cancel its investment treaties with the United States,[114] and other countries, such as Ecuador and Venezuela, gave notice to terminate their treaties.[115] Indonesia has reviewed its investment treaty program.[116] The German judiciary has led the charge to reject international courts and tribunals, stating investment

---

[110] Riesenberg, *supra* note 94, at 980, 987; *see also* Trakman, *supra* note 72.

[111] *See* UNCTAD, *WIR 2012, supra* note 3, at 139–40 (suggesting ITA's display of "serious shortcomings" warrants the use of ADR, tribunals considering investor behavior and "limiting resort to ISDS and increasing the role of domestic judicial systems, providing for the possibility of counterclaims by States, or even refraining from offering [ITA]").

[112] Won Kidane, *China and India's Different Investment Treaty Dispute Resolution Experiences and Implications for Africa*, 49 Loyola U. Chi. L. Rev. 405 (2018); *see also* Kavaljit Singh, *ISDS Is Unsuited to Meet Today's Global Challenges*, Fin. Times (May 7, 2017), https://on.ft.com/2MfrBKA (last visited Aug. 7, 2018) ("Within a span of four years (2013–16), India has radically restructured its BIT policy and practice to protect itself from costly investor to state arbitration. Not only did India terminated [*sic*] 57 of its existing BITs, it also recently negotiated a new BIT with Brazil which does not contain ISDS and other controversial provisions.").

[113] *See, e.g.*, Brower & Blanchard, *supra* note 5, at 693; Anna T. Katselas, *Exit, Voice, and Loyalty in Investment Treaty Arbitration*, 93 Neb. L. Rev. 313, 344–45 (2014); Jennifer Reed, *South Africa Revolutionizing Foreign Investment Protection System*, 6 Y.B. on Arb. & Med. 295 (2014); Republic of South Africa, *Statement on the Cabinet Meeting of 20 July 2010* (July 20, 2010), https://bit.ly/2vJNCdn (last visited Aug. 7, 2018); Dr. Rob Davies, *Minister of Trade and Industry, Speech Delivered at UNCTAD Investment Policy Framework for Sustainable Development* (July 26, 2012), https://bit.ly/2npm8WV (last visited Aug. 7, 2018); Agreement Between the Government of the Republic of South African and the Republic of Zimbabwe for the Promotion and Reciprocal Protection of Investments (Nov. 27, 2009), https://bit.ly/2LYTnPw (last visited Aug. 7, 2018); *see also* Republic of South Africa, *Statement on Cabinet Meeting of 24 March 2010* (Mar. 25, 2010), https://bit.ly/2MraIfZ (last visited Aug. 7, 2018); Webber Wentzel, *South Africa Declines to Renew Bilateral Investment Treaties with European Union Member States*, Mondaq (Oct. 5, 2012), http://bit.ly/15AwcQt (last visited Aug. 7, 2018). The exception to this was that South Africa signed investment treaties where it was the dominant capital exporter. *See* Erin O'Hara O'Connor & Susan D. Franck, *Foreign Investments and the Market for Law*, 2014 U. Ill. L. Rev. 1617, 1644–45 (2014) (collecting sources); *see also* Nyasha N. Katsenga, *Revisiting Zimbabwe's First Generation BITs: A Case for Balancing* (LLM Thesis submitted Sept. 7, 2017), https://bit.ly/2OQRFx7 (last visited Aug. 7, 2018).

[114] Martin Shabu, *Czechs Face Uphill Battle to Cancel US Investment Treaty*, ISDS.Bilaterals.org (Apr. 7, 2011), https://bit.ly/2KzB79R (last visited Aug. 7, 2018).

[115] Mercedes Alvaro, *Ecuador Plans to Audit Bilateral Investment Treaties*, JustInvestemt.Org (Mar. 11, 2013), https://bit.ly/2Mv7JD6 (last visited Aug. 7, 2018); Luke E. Peterson, *Venezuela Surprises the Netherlands with Termination Notice for BIT* (May 16, 2008), http://bit.ly/18aYUFt (last visited Aug. 7, 2018); U.S. Department of State, *2011 Investment Climate Statement—Ecuador* (Mar. 2011), http://1.usa.gov/19ME5OA (last visited Aug. 7, 2018) (describing July 2009 action by Ecuador to withdraw from ICSID and September 2009 request to terminate 13 treaties). Latin American states have suggested that—as an alternative to ICSID—a regional Latin American body should be created to settle investment-related disputes. Third World Network, *Latin American States Form Alliance to Tackle Investment Treaties* (Apr. 30, 2013), https://bit.ly/2M864Ho (last visited Aug. 7, 2018).

[116] *See* Luke Nottage, *Do Many of Australia's Bilateral Treaties Really Not Provide Full Advance Consent to Investor-State Arbitration?*, Sydney Law School Legal Studies Research Paper No. 14/39, 1–2 (Apr. 2014), http://bit.ly/1pm2MNm (last visited Aug. 7, 2018) (discussing Indonesia's potential termination and review of the Indonesian investment treaty program).

law violations must be addressed exclusively by "the proven system of national and European legal protection."[117] Australia, by contrast, has a complicated relationship with investment treaties.[118] Australia's love-hate relationship with ISDS is not unique. In the United States—despite revising the U.S. model BIT in 2012[119] and including ITA in the Transpacific Partnership (TPP)[120]—local officials have opposed ITA in treaties.[121] The Trump administration has withdrawn from TPP but also suggested it may reconsider that decision,[122] and in 2018, the administration negotiated NAFTA revisions eliminating U.S.-Canada ITA after three years and curtailing U.S.-Mexico ITA.[123]

---

[117] Deutscher Ricterbund, *Opinion on the Establishment of an Investment Tribunal in TTIP—The Proposal from the European Commission on 16.09.2015 and 11.12.2015* (Feb. 2016), http://bit.ly/2bsIS3L (last visited Aug. 7, 2018); *see also* BBC, *German Judges Oppose New Investor Courts*, British Broad. Co. (Feb. 5, 2016), http://bbc.in/2bz72Hc (last visited Aug. 7, 2018); Caroline Simson, *German Judges Slam TTIP Investment Arbitration Model*, Law360 (Feb. 4, 2016), http://bit.ly/2b6eooU (last visited Aug. 7, 2018).

[118] Australia historically embraced the substantive international law norms and ITA, yet its approach has fluctuated. While under threat of suit in the Philip Morris case, Australia issued a policy statement rejecting ITA, concluding it would "discontinue" the practice. Australian Gov't, Dep't of Foreign Affairs & Trade, *Gillard Government Trade Policy Statement: Trading Our Way to More Jobs and Prosperity* 14 (Apr. 2011), https://bit.ly/TEghet (last visited Jan. 18, 2019). As Jurgen Kurz explained, where parties to investment treaties are "transition state[s] (with an underdeveloped judicial system), it may not be desirable for Australia to forego investor-state arbitration because of purely defensive reasons" as "Australian investors abroad (especially in the resources sector) would be significantly exposed to regulatory risk as they would be limited to poorly equipped domestic court mechanisms and, even more importantly, could not 'bargain in the shadow of an investment treaty' when dealing with host governments." Jurgen Kurtz, *The Australia Trade Policy Statement on Investor-State Dispute Settlement*, 15 ASIL Insights (Aug. 2, 2011), https://bit.ly/2MpFN3C (last visited Aug. 7, 2018); *see also* Jurgen Kurtz, *Australia's Rejection of Investor-State Arbitration: Causation, Omission and Implication*, 27 ICSID Rev. 65 (2012). Yet when concluding TPP in October 2015—two months before its victory against Philip Morris—Australia agreed to ITA but prohibited arbitration for tobacco disputes. Office of the U.S. Trade Representative, *Summary of the Trans-Pacific Partnership Agreement* (Oct. 4, 2015), http://bit.ly/1QUf3UC (last visited Aug 7, 2018); Thomas J. Bollyky, *TPP Exception Proves the New Rule in Trade*, Council on For. Rel. (Feb. 4, 2016), http://on.cfr.org/1LFYHfl (last visited Aug. 7, 2018).

[119] U.S. Department of State, *Model Bilateral Investment Treaty* (Apr. 20, 2012), https://bit.ly/2KCi2DP (last visited Aug. 7, 2018).

[120] *See, e.g.*, Todd Tucker, *The TPP Has a Provision Many Will Love to Hate: ISDS. What Is It, and Why Does It Matter?*, Wash. Post (Oct. 6, 2015), http://wapo.st/1LQjGuD (last visited Aug. 7, 2018); *compare* Ted Bromund et al., *Straight Talk on the ISDS Provisions in the Trans-Pacific Partnership*, Heritage Foundation: Issue Brief 4564 on Economic Freedom (May 17, 2016), http://bit.ly/2b9ofY2 (last visited Aug. 7, 2018), *with* Joesph Stiglitz, *Beware of TPP's Investor-State Dispute Settlement Provision*, Roosevelt Institute (Mar. 28, 2016), http://bit.ly/23it1GQ (last visited Aug. 7, 2018).

[121] *See* "An Open Letter from Lawyers to the Negotiators of the Trans-Pacific Partnership Urging the Rejection of Investor-State Settlement" (May 8, 2012), http://bit.ly/1kVPvWT (last visited Aug. 7, 2018).

[122] Alana Abramson, *White House Explains Trump's Reversal on TPP*, Fortune (Apr. 12, 2018), https://for.tn/2M1yJxk (last visited Aug. 7, 2018). While this book was being revised, the White House announced a new approach to ITA for NAFTA, which narrows substantive rights subject to arbitration for most investors while privileging extractive industries. Jacob M. Schlesinger, *U.S., Mexico Agree to Weaken Rights to Dispute Trade Practices*, Wall St. J., (Aug. 27, 2018), https://on.wsj.com/2PjM5D2 (last visited Aug. 30, 2018).

[123] United States-Mexico-Canada Agreement (Oct. 1, 2018), art. 14.2(4), Annexes 14-C-14-E, https://bit.ly/2O5Pbi1 (last visited October 3, 2018); *see also supra* note 14.

Yet not all states believe that investment treaties and ITA are suboptimal. China broadened its treaties to permit arbitration tribunals to assess both merits and damages for treaty claims.[124] Canada, who has had its investors bring claims and been a respondent, made changes to its model treaty in 2003 to reflect its experience in NAFTA arbitration, retaining ITA.[125] The 2012 trilateral investment treaty among China, Japan and Korea retained ITA as a means of dispute settlement. Australia included ITA in a treaty negotiated with South Korea[126] and permitted it in the TPP. Meanwhile, states continue to renegotiate investment treaties, and the European Union (EU) has taken a firm stand on excluding ITA, especially after the European Court of Justice (ECJ) held that arbitral clauses in intra-European investment treaties are incompatible with EU law.[127] The EU hopes to provide a substitute form of adjudication through a multilateral investment court.[128]

Ultimately, the debate about ITA is a live issue with critical ramifications. Should stakeholders wish to debate using quality evidence, rather than manufactured rhetoric, it is useful to have a balanced understanding. This requires data, gathered using sound ex ante research protocols, to inform discussions about appropriate dispute resolution.

V. Moving beyond Debate to Grounded Reform

Choices about how best to pursue investment treaty dispute resolution should be made based upon evidence. While it may feel as if policy debates have been spinning out of control and changing daily, it is necessary to keep perspective. Should we give into an emotive, instinctual, and non-rational approach to decisions about major international economic law debates, we are likely to suffer the consequences for decades and spawn more problems than we solve. The better course of conduct is to carefully, methodically, and consciously recognize the constructive and negative aspects of options, moving beyond pure ideological preferences, to consider what strategies provide the highest chance of solving core problems.

The costs and benefits of normative options for reforming the ITA system—or engaging in business as usual—vary based upon the reform proposed. Given the variance, no single

---

124 Norah Gallagher & Wenhua Shan, Chinese Investment Treaties: Policies and Practice (2009). In the Canadian-EU Trade Agreement (CETA), during the scrubbing process to revise minor terms, Canada changed its approach to dispute settlement in favor of a standing court (rather than arbitration). August Reinisch, *Will the EU's Proposal Concerning an Investment Court System for CETA and TTIP Lead to Enforceable Awards?—The Limits of Modifying the ICSID Convention and the Nature of Investment Arbitration*, 19 J. Int'l Econ. L. 761 (2016).

125 Foreign Affairs & Int'l Trade Canada, *Canada's Foreign Investment Promotion and Protection Agreements (FIPAs)*, https://bit.ly/2puQiZ5 (last visited Aug. 7, 2018).

126 Australian Gov't, Minister for Trade and Inv., *Press Release: Australia Concludes FTA Negotiations with the Republic of Korea* (Dec. 5, 2013), http://bit.ly/1noVdED (last visited Aug. 7, 2018); Australian Gov't, Dep't of Foreign Affairs and Trade, Korea-Australia Free Trade Agreement, arts. 11.15–11.28, https://bit.ly/2KAGSE3 (last visited Aug. 7, 2018) (providing the text of the Korean-Australia investment agreement recently negotiated that provides for ITA).

127 Case C-284/16, Slovak Republic v. Achmea BV, 2018 (Mar. 6, 2018), https://bit.ly/2NZ5CI3 (last visited Aug. 7, 2018).

128 *See supra* note 19 and accompanying text; *see also* Reinisch, *supra* note 24 (discussing CETA).

critique (or normative reform) is likely to be the "silver bullet" that generates a unitary solution that works for all stakeholders across all circumstances. In choosing appropriate processes, the goal should be to strive for investment law dispute resolution that has procedural integrity with quality processes likely to generate substantively appropriate results. Evidence-based insights from quality research can elucidate this process by providing information on the reality of dispute resolution to inform strategic adjustments to treaties, rules, and party agreements.

In both medicine and business, there has been a growth in efforts to subject conventional wisdom to empirical testing to generate data-driven problem-solving. False myths and factual misconceptions in those areas can lead to erroneous treatment or support costly business practices.[129] Evidence-based approaches test fundamental assumptions; so, when critical resources are involved, whether a human life or capital is on the line, problem-solving generates solutions that are more likely to provide intended benefits. The underlying assumption is, rather than risking reliance on "dangerous half-truths and total nonsense," even the most innocuous assumptions are subjected to empirical scrutiny.[130]

Law stands to benefit from an evidence-based approach. As Richard Posner explained, "[w]e need evidence-based law."[131] International investment likewise needs evidence, not emotive rhetoric. It is possible that assertions about ITA and dispute resolution may be correct and accurate as to an individual experience; but there is also a risk of reality distortions or a failure to appreciate a larger context, making normative choices inapposite. We must therefore explore legal phenomenon in international investment law scientifically, without resort to anecdote, idiosyncrasy, bias, or preconception, and with the overall objective of moving past unexamined path dependence and toward systemized verification of knowledge.[132] Given the risk of error in creating international law, implications for sovereign responsibility, and meaningful fiscal exposure, such an approach is prudent and necessary.

Appreciation of evidence-based strategies is not unknown in international law.[133] Yet, such reforms can be difficult to implement, and the proverbial jury is still out as to whether evidence-based scholarship can "create better law—law informed by reality."[134] Evidence-based problem-solving has been particularly successful, like in medicine and business, when there are clear and measurable goals. Law, by contrast, involves multiple and sometimes

---

[129] Jeffrey J. Rachlinski, *Evidence-Based Law*, 96 CORNELL L. REV. 901 (2011).

[130] JEFFREY PFEFFER & ROBERT I. SUTTON, HARD FACTS, DANGEROUS HALF-TRUTHS AND TOTAL NONSENSE: PROFITING FROM EVIDENCE-BASED MANAGEMENT (2006); *see also* IAN AYRES, SUPERCRUNCHERS: WHY THINKING-BY-NUMBERS IS THE NEW WAY TO BE SMART (2007); David L. Sackett et al., *Evidence-Based Medicine: What It Is and What It Isn't*, 312 BRIT. MED. J. 71 (1996).

[131] Richard A. Posner, *Judicial Opinions and Appellate Advocacy in Federal Courts—One Judge's Opinion*, 51 DUQ. L. REV. 3, 16 (2013).

[132] Bernard Trujillo, *Patterns in a Complex System*, 53 UCLA L. REV. 356, 363 (2005).

[133] DEBORA ISSER, CUSTOMARY JUSTICE AND THE RULE OF LAW IN WAR-TORN SOCIETIES (2011); Jim Chen, *Soft Law and the Global Financial System*, 25 EMORY INT'L L. REV. 1561, 1566 (2011); Kevin E. Davis, *Legal Universalism: Persistent Objections*, 60 U. TORONTO L.J. 537, 548 (2010); William Onzivu, *Globalism, Regionalism or Both: Health Policy and Regional Economic Integration in Developing* Countries, 15 MINN. J. INT'L L. 111, 129–38 (2006).

[134] Rachlinski, *supra* note 129, at 910–11; Bryan Lammon, *Rules, Standards and Experimentation in Appellate Jurisdiction*, 74 OHIO ST. L.J. 423, 460–61 (2013).

conflicting objectives, and lacks a single, unifying organizational principle such as patient health or wealth maximization. Yet, empirical assessments of legal phenomena can aid stakeholders in ruling out some narratives by testing them; but ruling *out* error is not the same as ruling *in* viable normative choices. Human inference and error likewise generate impediments to evidence-based law. Anecdotes—with easily understandable narratives that inspire trust—have a particular power and can be sticky, particularly as "[s]tatistics are invariably more pallid than anecdotes."[135] Additionally the timbre of anecdotes may resonate with more deeply held political, cultural, or social beliefs making them hard to dislodge, and when data contradicts core beliefs or disrupts conventional wisdom, people may react strongly when perceiving an implicit threat to their sense of identity.[136] Although politics and psychology may generate challenges, as "politics seems often dominated by extremists," we can hope that "a vast middle of the polity may be open to listening to the consensus of the research."[137]

These challenges may be poignant in international investment law where a new form of intellectual tribalism is appearing upon the horizon.[138] One might hope that a careful and rational approach may appeal to a broader constituency—particularly lawyers trained in the value of logic and evidence—and other stakeholders may use empirical insights to consider evidence-based ways of engaging with international investment law. Although empirical study may not always provide clear answers and may conflict with preexisting beliefs, taking a data-driven approach facilitates debates and normative solutions that derive from better information.

---

[135] Rachlinski, *supra* note 129, at 919–20; *see also* MALCOLM GLADWELL, THE TIPPING POINT (2000).

[136] Dan M. Kahan, *The Cognitively Illiberal State*, 60 STAN. L. REV. 115, 120–42 (2007).

[137] Rachlinski, *supra* note 129, at 923.

[138] *See* AMY CHUA, POLITICAL TRIBES: GROUP INSTINCT AND THE FATE OF NATIONS 2–13, 204 (2018) (discussing political tribalism and ideological divides); Stephen Pinker, *Steven Pinker on Intellectual Tribalism: Conversations with Tyler* (Nov. 4, 2016), https://bit.ly/2KzpejS (last visited Aug. 7, 2018) (discussing intellectual tribalism); *see also* JONATHAN HAIDT, THE RIGHTEOUS MIND: WHY GOOD PEOPLE ARE DIVIDED BY POLITICS AND RELIGION 156–67, 161–63 (2012) (identifying how impulses toward tribalism can become maladaptive in an era of globalization); David Brooks, *The Retreat to Tribalism*, Opinion, N.Y. TIMES (Jan. 1, 2018), https://nyti.ms/2CuMrUJ (last visited Aug. 7, 2018).

2 Cognitive Psychology and Empirical Insights for ITA

COGNITIVE PSYCHOLOGY AND empiricism provide unique insights for international investment law and evidence-based normative reform. Using quality scientific research[1] to generate evidence that reduces the risk of cognitive illusions[2] adversely influencing debates about ITA, can help correct unconscious, instinctive, or non-adaptive error. Although evidence-based methods have challenges,[3] international investment law can and should draw on interdisciplinary synergies and has done so in some disciplines.[4] Yet psychology is a relatively untapped social science discipline, although it has deeply embedded affinities with law. Psychological influences affect information gathering, analysis, and decision-making. There is no evidence that international investment law is immune from these influences, and clear data to the contrary.[5] Yet, psychology been remarkably under-scrutinized. To begin bridging

[1] *See, e.g.*, Susan D. Franck, *The Promise and Peril of Empiricism and International Investment Law Disputes*, *in* CAMBRIDGE COMPENDIUM OF INTERNATIONAL COMMERCIAL AND INVESTMENT ARBITRATION (Andrea Bjorklund et al., eds., forthcoming 2019).

[2] The term "cognitive illusions" is shorthand for what cognitive psychologists and behavioral economists often call "biases and heuristics," reflecting intuitive, simple, and quick cognitive assessments. Susan D. Franck et al., *Inside the Arbitrator's Mind*, 66 EMORY L.J. 1117, 1120 n.10 (2017). Given the legally specific meaning of "bias" involving arbitrator challenges and the use of undefined terms such as "bias" in discussions about ITA, this book prefers the term "cognitive illusion" to aid focus on intuitive decision-making.

[3] *See* Franck, *supra* note 1.

[4] *See* Susan D. Franck, *Empiricism and International Law: Insights for Investment Treaty Dispute Resolution*, 48 VA. J. INT'L L. 767, 775–80. (2007) (discussing links with economics and political science).

[5] Franck et al., *supra* note 2. Since this chapter was originally drafted, others have become interested in psychology. *See* THE ROLE OF PSYCHOLOGY IN INTERNATIONAL ARBITRATION (Tony Cole ed., 2017) (compiling papers discussing psychology and international arbitration); *infra* notes 20 and 154.

Arbitration Costs. Susan D. Franck.

the divide, this chapter first explores the roots of law and psychology in international law. It next posits that cognitive illusions are implicit in information collection, processing, and decision-making to explore how cognition errors might impact international investment law. It then describes the literature on cognitive illusions and preliminarily explores how they might affect the debate about international investment law and dispute settlement. The final section explores debiasing opportunities from quality empiricism.

I. Law and Psychology Meets International Law

Integrating psychological insights into law is not a new phenomenon. "Law and Psychology" has used psychological insights to understand and improve national courts.[6] Psychological research has improved court systems' normative operations. For example, by identifying disconnects between legal rules for admitting "reliable" eyewitness testimony and generating eyewitness testimony that was actually reliable, psychologists identified reforms for how police gather and how courts use eyewitness testimony.[7]

Historically, international law expressed mild interest in psychology. In the 1920s, Roscoe Pound observed a "functional critique of international law" required "legal philosophy [to] take account of the social psychology."[8] Sir Geoffrey Butler encouraged international law to explore psychological perspectives in debates about sovereignty.[9] The true pioneer was Howard Lasswell. Lasswell, a social science legend,[10] explored the personalities, power, and politics behind behavior, particularly international political figures.[11] Lasswell used insights from then-current Freudian theories of psychology,[12] earning him the title of "the founder of political psychology."[13] His scholarship fostered collaboration with luminaries such as Myres McDougal[14] and Michael

---

[6] HUGO MUSTENBERG, ON THE WITNESS STAND (1908).

[7] ELIZABETH LOFTUS, EYEWITNESS TESTIMONY (1996); Brandon L. Garrett, *Eyewitnesses and Exclusion*, 65 VAND. L. REV. 451 (2012); Gary L. Wells et al., *Eyewitness Identification Procedures: Recommendations for Lineups and Photospreads*, 22 LAW & HUM. BEH. 603 (1998); Gary L. Wells, *Eyewitness Identification: Systematic Reforms*, 2006 WIS. L. REV. 615 (2006).

[8] ANTHONY ANGHIE, IMPERIALISM, SOVEREIGNTY AND THE MAKING OF INTERNATIONAL LAW 129 (2004) (quoting Roscoe Pound, *Philosophical Theory and International Law*, 1 BIBLIOTECA VISSERIANA DISSERTATIONUM IUS INTERNATIONALE ILLUSTRANTIUM 79, 89–90 (1923)); *see also id.* at 134 n.77 (quoting Sir Geoffrey Butler).

[9] Geoffrey Butler, *Sovereignty and the League of Nations*, 1 BRIT. Y.B. INT'L L. 35, 42 (1920).

[10] *See* W. Michael Reisman et al., *The New Haven School: A Brief Introduction*, 32 YALE J. INT'L L. 575, 575 n.3 (2007); HAROLD D. LASSWELL, HAROLD D. LASSWELL ON POLITICAL PSYCHOLOGY (1977); POLITICS, PERSONALITY AND SOCIAL SCIENCE IN the TWENTIETH CENTURY: ESSAYS IN HONOR OF HAROLD D. LASSWELL (Arnold A. Rogow ed., 1969).

[11] HAROLD D. LASSWELL, PSYCHOPATHOLOGY AND POLITICS (1930).

[12] Harold D. Lasswell, *The Impact of Crowd Psychology and International Law*, 9 WM. & MARY L. REV. 664 (1968); Harold D. Lasswell, *The Interconnections of Political Power, Psychotherapy and World Community*, 1 POL. COMM. & PERSUASION 107 (1981).

[13] RODNEY MUTH ET AL., HAROLD D. LASSWELL: AN ANNOTATED BIBLIOGRAPHY 11 (1990).

[14] Harold D. Lasswell & Myres S. McDougal, *Legal Education and Public Policy: Professional: Professional Training in the Public Interest*, 52 YALE L.J. 203 (1943); Myres S. McDougal et al., *The Intellectual Function of the World Public Order*, *in* INTERNATIONAL LAW ESSAYS: A SUPPLEMENT TO INTERNATIONAL LAW

Reisman,[15] which ultimately infused the "New Haven School"[16] of international legal theory. Others have gently cultivated interdisciplinary seeds.[17] Richard Steinberg and Jonathan Zasloff explore the reflexive relationship among psychology, cognition, and international law.[18] Others, such as Soia Mentschikof, Christopher Drahozal, and Mark Drumbl, used psychological insights to explore decision-making of international adjudicators.[19] More recently, key international economic law and key scholars have begun exploring law and psychology.[20]

---

in Contemporary Perspective (Myres S. McDougal & W. Michael Reisman eds., 1981); W. Michael Reisman, *Myres S. McDougal: Architect of a Jurisprudence for a Free Society* 66 Miss. L.J. 15 (1996).

15 W. Michael Reisman, *In Memoriam: Harold D. Lasswell*, 4 Yale Studies in World Public Order 154 (1978); Harold D. Lasswell et al., *The World Constitutive Process of Authoritative Design*, 19 J. Legal Ed. 253 (1967); Myres S. McDougal et al., *Theories About International Law: Prologue to Configurative Jurisprudence*, 8 Va. J. Int'l L. 188 (1968); Myres S. McDougal et al., *The Intelligence Function and World Public Order*, 46 Temple L. Quart. 365 (1973); Myres S. McDougal & W. Michael Reisman, *Harold D. Lasswell*, 73 Am. J. Int'l L. 55 (1979); W. Michael Reisman, *Sanctions and International Law*, 4 Intercultural Hum. Rts. L. Rev. 9 (2009); W. Michael Reisman, *Development and Nation-Building: A Framework for Policy-Oriented Inquiry*, 60 Me. L. Rev 309 (2008).

16 Reisman et al., *supra* note 10. *See also* Harold D. Lasswell & Myres S. McDougal, Jurisprudence for a Free Society: Studies in Law, Science and Policy (1992); W. Michael Reisman, *The View from the New Haven School of International Law*, 86 Am. Soc. Int'l L. Proc. 118 (1992).

17 Jerome Frank, Law and the Modern Mind (1930); Raynard West, International Law and Psychology: Two Studies (1974); Thomas M. Franck, *Some Psychological Factors in International Third-Party Decision-Making*, 19 Stan. L. Rev. 1217 (1967); *see also* Douglas M. Johnston, The Historical Foundations of World Order: The Tower and the Arena 116, 272, 257 (2008) (discussing various historic and international law scholars who have valued insights from psychology); Theodore Schroeder, *The Psychologic Study of Judicial Opinions*, 6 Calif. L. Rev. 89, 89 (1918).

18 Richard H. Steinberg & Jonathan Zasloff, *Power and International Law*, 100 Am. J. Int'l L. 64, 85 (2006).

19 *See, e.g.*, Mark A. Drumbl, Atrocity, Punishment and International Law 29–35 (2007); Soia Mentschikoff & Ernest A. Haggard, *Decision Making and Decision Consensus in Commercial Arbitration*, *in* Law, Justice and the Individual in Society: Psychological and Legal Issues Law Journal 295 (June L. Tapp & Felice J. Levine eds., 1977); Christopher Drahozal, *A Behavioral Analysis of Private Judging*, 67 Law & Contemp. Probs. 105 (2004); Giacomo R. Elgueta, *Understanding Discovery in International Commercial Arbitration Through Behavior Law and Economics: A Journey Inside the Minds of Parties and Arbitrators*, 16 Harv. Negot. L. Rev. 165 (2011); Christopher A. Whytock, *Domestic Courts and Global Governance: The Politics of Private International Law* (2007) (unpublished Ph.D. dissertation, Duke University), http://bit.ly/194TdvM (last visited Aug. 7, 2018); *see also* Brian D. Lepard, *Is the United States Obligated to Drive on the Right? A Multidisciplinary Inquiry into the Normative Authority of Contemporary International Law Using the Arm's Length Standard as a Case Study*, 10 Duke J. Comp. & Int'l L. 43 (1999); Bradford S. Simon, *Intellectual Property and Traditional Knowledge: A Psychological Approach to Conflicting Claims of Creativity in International Law*, 20 Berkeley Tech. L.J. 1613 (2005).

20 Scholars like Tomer Brode, van Aaken, and the author have been slowly developing the intersection of law and psychology since around 2012. Tomer Broude, *Behavioral International Law*, 163 Penn. L. Rev. 1099 (2015); Franck et al., *supra* note 2; Anne van Aaken, *Behavioral Law and Economics*, 55 Harv. Int'l L. J. 421 (2014). Others have begun exploring potential psychological insights. *See* Tae Jung Park, *Behavioral Economics in International Investment Law: Bounded Rationality and the Choice of the Reservation List Modality*, 5 Penn. St. J.L. & Int'l Aff. 398 (2017); S.I. Strong, *Truth in a Post-truth Society: How Sticky Defaults, Status Quo Bias, and the Sovereign Prerogative Influence the Perceived Legitimacy of International Arbitration* 2018 Ill. L. Rev. 533 (2018); *see also supra* note 5; *infra* note 154.

Despite the preliminary interest,[21] little literature has actively integrated psychology into international law.[22] Multiple elements contribute to the disconnect. Psychologists use experiments to explore social phenomenon; lawyers may be unfamiliar with these methods, and it may not be possible to design experiments where scientists randomly assign states to experimental conditions (thereby proscribing state sovereignty).[23] Psychologists interested in legal decision-making have historically focused on national legal frameworks. Yet, both psychologists and international lawyers could benefit from deeper conversations, as the growing body of international courts and tribunals means there are new frameworks, individuals, groups, and bodies to understand. Likewise, psychologists can explore human behavior, legal frameworks, and legal decision-making in contexts transcending national boundaries.

Psychology is a broad discipline including developmental, industrial, social, and cognitive psychology. This book focuses on one possible fruitful area, namely cognitive psychology insights for international investment law. Given its relatively recent development, it is understandable that international law historically did not address cognition.[24] Yet, as Professors Robbennolt and Sternlight explain, cognitive psychology has much to teach lawyers,[25] as it offers a prism for evaluating, understanding, and perhaps even improving decision-making of systemic actors. With investment law and dispute resolution created and shaped by humans,[26] cognitive processes inevitably affect how information is gathered, processed, and

---

[21] *See* Gabcikovo-Nagymoros Project (Hung. v. Slovk.), 1997 I.C.J. 7, 96–97 (Sept. 25) (Weeramantry J.) ("[E]specially at the frontiers of the discipline of international law, it needs to be multi-disciplinary, drawing from other disciplines such as history, sociology, anthropology, and psychology such wisdom as may be relevant for its purpose.").

[22] Roda Mushkat, *International Legal Compliance as a Rational Act*, 20 TRANSNAT'L L. & CONTEMP. PROBLS. 633, 648–49 (2012). In July 2013, a Westlaw search for titles containing the words "international law" and psychology generated only a single document. Louraine C. Arkfeld, *Ethics for the Problem-Solving Court Judge: The New ABA Model Code*, 28 JUST. SYS. J. 317, 317 n.1 (2007). That article did not involve international law; rather, it related to a law and psychology conference involving international participants. In June 2016, a search using root expanders ([TI(internation! /s psycholog!)] generated eighteen documents; and only eight of those touched international or comparative law topics in any way, often involving psychological trauma from international child abduction. A June 2016 search looking for articles discussing international law and bounded rationality [(international /2 law) /s "bounded rationality"] generated six documents; a search for behavioral economics [(international /2 law) /s "behavioral economics"] generated twenty-two documents. Both searches included the articles by Broude and van Aaken. *See also* Park, *supra* note 20 (using behavioral economics to explain negotiating outcomes for a proposed multilateral free trade agreement among ASEAN countries).

[23] Randomly assigning subjects into experimental conditions, a favorite tool of psychologists, may not be suitable for examining state behavior in negotiating real international law instruments. The small number of agreements and high stakes create ethical or methodological challenges. *See* Appendix I. Because of methodological variations and the needs of different areas, not all aspects of international law will necessarily benefit from psychology.

[24] REID HASTIE & ROBYN M. DAWES, RATIONAL CHOICE IN AN UNCERTAIN WORLD 3 (2d ed. 2010); Barbara A. Spellman & Simone Schnall, *Embodied Rationality*, 35 QUEEN'S L.J. 117 (2009).

[25] JENNIFER K. ROBBENNOLT & JEAN R. STERNLIGHT, PSYCHOLOGY FOR LAWYERS (2012).

[26] This book focuses primarily on individual cognition. Group and social psychology may also offer interesting insights for international law, as research identifies groups and panels involved in decision-making sometimes balance out or exacerbate psychological deficiencies. DENNIS DEVINE, JURY DECISION MAKING: THE STATE OF THE SCIENCE (2012); Broude, *supra* note 20, at 1143–56; Daniel Gigone & Reid Hastie, *Proper Analysis of the Accuracy of Group Judgments*, 121 PSYCH. BULL. 149 (1997); Pauline T. Kim, *Deliberation and Strategy on the United States Courts of Appeals: An Empirical Exploration of Panel Effects*, 157 U. PA.

used to: negotiate and sign treaties; make decisions about investing in states; sublimate or escalate conflict into formalized disputes; channel and manage disputes; abide by, challenge, or ignore adjudicative outcomes; and think critically about relative cost and value of managing investment conflicts.

One core area of cognitive psychology involves biases and heuristics,[27] what this book calls "cognitive illusions." In 1969, Daniel Kahneman and Amos Tversky's original research explored the cognitive errors of mathematicians and psychologists, who were well-versed in statistics but nevertheless used intuition to make inaccurate predications.[28] Since those initial insights,[29] scholars have explored cognitive illusions in other areas, generating new literatures such as behavioral economics[30] focusing on what decision-makers *actually* do, as opposed to theories about what we *hope* people *should* do.[31]

There is value in exploring how psychological phenomenon, such as cognitive illusions, could influence international investment law, particularly for costs. A data-driven approach could improve our understanding about cost implications and provide insights about optimal system design. This chapter focuses on cognitive illusions with the most immediate relevance to international investment law and dispute settlement, serving as an

L. Rev. 1319, 1329–31 (2009); David Schkade et al., *What Happened on Deliberation Day?*, 95 Cal. L. Rev. 915 (2007); Cass R. Sunstein, *Deliberative Trouble? Why Groups Go to Extremes*, 110 Yale L.J. 71 (2000); van Aaken, *supra* note 20, at 443–49; Adrian Vermeule, *Many-Minds Arguments in Legal Theory*, 1 J. Leg. Analysis 1, 26–35 (2009).

[27] Gideon Keren & Karh H. Tiegen, *Yet Another Look at the Heuristics and Biases Approach*, *in* Blackwell Handbook of Judgment and Decision Making 89, 91–100 (Derek J. Koehler & Nigel Harvey eds., 2004) [hereinafter Handbook of Judgment]. There is a debate within cognitive psychology about how to use biases and heuristics. Kahneman and Tversky view cognitive illusions as mechanisms that prevent decisions that maximize expected value and conventional rational choice through miscomputation probabilities and misevaluation of information. In this paradigm, cognitive illusions generate deviations in judgment whereby people draw illogical or irrational inferences. Others view heuristics as "fast and frugal" shortcuts, irrespective of whether there is a "bias" or error. Gerd Gigerenzer, *Heuristics*, *in* Heuristics and the Law 18 (Gerd Gigerenzer & Christoph Engel eds., 2006); Marie G. Haselton et al., *The Evolution of Cognitive Bias*, *in* Handbook of Evolutionary Psychology 724 (David M. Buss ed., 2005); Mark Kelman, The Heuristics Debate (2011); Daniel G. Goldstein & Gerd Gigerenzer, *Models of Ecological Rationality*, 109 Psychol. Rev. 75 (2002).

[28] Daniel Kahneman & Amos Tversky, *Subjective Probability: A Judgment of Representativeness*, 3 Cog. Psychol. 430 (1972); *see also* Daniel Kahneman & Shane Frederick, *Representativeness Revisited: Attribute Substitution in Intuitive Judgment*, *in* Heuristics and Biases: The Psychology of Intuitive Judgment 49 (Daniel Kahneman et al., eds., 2002).

[29] Daniel Kahneman, Thinking, Fast and Slow (2011) [hereinafter Fast and Slow]; Judgment Under Uncertainty: Heuristics and Biases (Daniel Kahneman et al., eds., 1982) [hereinafter Judgment Under Uncertainty].

[30] John M. Dowling & Yap Chin-Fang, Modern Developments in Behavioral Economics (2007); Behavioral Law and Economics (Cass R. Sunstein ed., 2000); Handbook of Contemporary Behavioral Economics: Foundations and Developments (Morris Altman ed., 2006).

[31] Behavioral Law & Economics (Cass R. Sunstein ed., 2000); Christine Jolls et al., *A Behavioral Approach to Law and Economics*, 50 Stan. L. Rev. 1471 (1998); Russell B. Korobkin & Thomas S. Ulen, *Law and Behavioral Science: Removing the Rationality Assumption from Law and Economics*, 88 Calif. L. Rev. 1051 (2000); Jeffrey J. Rachlinski, *The Psychological Foundations of Behavioral Law and Economics*, 2011 U. Ill. L. Rev. 1675, 1679–81 (2011); Cass R. Sunstein, *Behavioral Analysis of* Law, 64 U. Chi. L. Rev. 1175 (1997).

invitation for others to explore synergies between cognitive psychology and international law. Although cognitive psychology may not integrate with all aspects of international law, enivitably, there is a larger intellectual iceberg to explore.[32]

II. Cognition and Investment Law: To Err Is Human

Data collection, information processing, and decision-making involve the cognition of individuals and also the collective cognition of groups. Part of the human condition means that individuals (and groups of individuals) implicitly use intuition.[33] Kahneman and Tversky discovered how, despite our best intentions, human decision-making is not as rational as we would like to believe.[34] Psychology has focused on understanding how cognition generates decisions, and observes that cognition is a function of two independent systems, called "System 1" and "System 2."[35] Under this "dual system" processing approach, System 1 conducts automatic operations that are typically quick, emotional, and instinctive, which happen below conscious awareness. System 1 "operates automatically and quickly with little or no effort and no sense of voluntary control."[36] In contrast, System 2 involves slow, rational, and logical reasoning. As Kahneman explains, it "allocates attention to the effortful mental activities that demand it, including complex computations. The operations of System 2 are often associated with the subjective experience of agency, choice and concentration."[37] Cognitive illusions generally derive from System 1's quick, instinctual reactions, but they can also derive from System 2's "lazy" thinking deriving from overstimulation, lack of attention to detail, and need for cognitive ease.[38]

Stakeholders in international investment law could be rational actors generating optimal decisions after carefully considering relative costs and benefits.[39] Yet, it is also

---

[32] Like any system of knowledge, cognitive psychology applied to law has limitations. Gregory Mitchell, *Why Law and Economics' Perfect Rationality Should Not Be Traded for Behavioral Law and Economics' Equal Incompetence*, 91 Geo. L.J. 67, 87 (2002); Joshua D. Wright & Douglas H. Ginsburg, *Behavioral Law and Economics: Its Origins, Fatal Flaws, and Implications for Liberty*, 106 Nw. U. L. Rev. 1033 (2012). Cognitive psychology itself has been critiqued. Some observe that cognitive illusions can generate correct answers. Others in naturalistic decision-making argue, in complex natural situations, experts use instinct to generate correct choices in conditions of uncertainty and time pressures. Susan T. Fiske & Shelly E. Taylor, Social Cognition: From Brains to Culture (2d ed. 2013); Daniel Kahneman & Gary Klein, *Conditions for Intuitive Expertise: A Failure to Disagree*, 64 Am. Psych. 515 (2009); Daniel Kahneman & Amos Tversky, *On the Reality of Cognitive Illusions*, 103 Psych. Rev. 582 (1996).

[33] Note 26, *supra*, identifies literature exploring how errors can reflect individual or group decision-making.

[34] Scott O. Lilienfeld et al., *Giving Debiasing Away: Can Psychological Research on Correcting Cognitive Errors Promote Human Welfare?*, 4 Persp. Psychol. Sci. 390 (2009).

[35] Fiske & Taylor, *supra* note 32.

[36] Kahneman, Fast and Slow, *supra* note 29; *see also* Richard H. Thaler & Cass R. Sunstein, Nudge: Improving Decisions About Health, Wealth and Happiness 19–22 (2009) (describing the two systems as: (1) "Automatic" or Human; and (2) "Reflective" and "Econs").

[37] Kahneman, Fast and Slow, *supra* note 29.

[38] *Id.* at 39–49; On Amir & Orly Lobel, *Stumble, Predict and Nudge: How Behavioral Economics Informs Law and Policy*, 108 Colum. L. Rev. 2098 (2008); Spellman & Schall, *supra* note 24.

[39] Gary S. Becker, The Economic Approach to Human Behavior (1976); Jack L. Goldsmith & Eric A. Posner, The Limits of International Law (2005); Andrew T. Guzman, How

possible that stakeholders behave in ways failing to comply with the rational actor model,[40] just like other humans. If true, international investment law stakeholders are not unique. A large body of scholarship demonstrates that cognitive illusions influence choices of many elite professionals.[41] Decades of psychological research demonstrate that humans preselect (whether intentionally or inadvertently) information during the collection process, leading to misrepresentations. When processing information, individuals also fill in gaps, impose patterns, change perceptions, and selectively interpret information. When making decisions, cognitive illusions influence perceived choices and ultimate assessments.[42] Expert decision-making—by political scientists, physicians, accountants, judges, and lawyers—is not immune to cognitive illusions.[43] In some circumstances, cognitive shortcuts are useful and adaptive, but in others, they generate error. Cognitive illusions sometimes affect how humans process information, partially because, as we navigate the social world while being inundated with unending information with finite time and capacity for attention, we require mental "shortcuts" to function given limited cognitive resources.[44]

International Law Works: A Rational Choice Theory (2008); Amartya Sen, *Rational Behaviour*, *in* New Palgrave Dictionary of Economics (Steven N. Durlauf & Laurence E. Blume eds., 2d ed. 2008); *see also* David Zaring, *Finding Legal Principle in Global Financial Regulation*, 52 Va. J. Int'l L. 685, 688 (2012).

[40] Paul Schiff Berman, Global Legal Pluralism: A Jurisprudence Beyond Borders (2012); George W. Downs & David M. Rocke, Optimal Imperfection? Domestic Uncertainty and Institutions in International Relations (1995); Anne Van Aaken, *Towards Behavioral International Law and Economics*, 2008 Ill. L. Rev. 47 (2008).

[41] Russell Korobkin, *The Problems with Heuristics for Law*, *in* Heuristics and the Law 45, 47 (Gerd Gigerenzer & Christoph Engel eds., 2006).

[42] Dan Ariely, Predictably Irrational (2008); Kahneman & Tversky, Judgment under Uncertainty, *supra* note 29; Scott Plous, The Psychology of Judgment and Decision Making (1993); Hans Rosling, Factfulness: Ten Reasons Why We're Wrong About the World—and Why Things Are Better Than You Think (2018); Jane Risen & Thomas Gilovitch, *Informal Logical Fallacies*, *in* Critical Thinking in Psychology 110 (Robert J. Sternberg et al., eds., 2007); Robbennolt & Sternlight, *supra* note 25, at 7; Ronald Chen & Jon Hanson, *Categorically Biased: The Influence of Knowledge Structures on Law and Legal Theory*, 77 S. Cal. L. Rev. 1103 (2004); Justin Kruger & David Dunning, *Unskilled and Unaware of It: How Difficulties in Recognizing One's Own Incompetence Lead to Inflated Self-Assessments*, 77 J. Personality & Soc. Psychol. 1121 (1999); Donald C. Langevoort, *Behavioral Theories of Judgment and Decision Making in Legal Scholarship: A Literature Review*, 51 Vand. L. Rev. 1499 (1998).

[43] Robyn M. Dawes, Everyday Irrationality: How Pseudo-Scientists, Lunatics, and the Rest of Us Fail to Think Rationally (2001); Heuristics and Biases: The Psychology of Intuitive Judgment (Thomas Gilovich et al., eds., 2002) [hereinafter Heuristics and Biases]; Philip E. Tetlock, Expert Political Judgment: How Good Is It? How Can We Know? (2005); Philip E. Tetlock & Dan Gardner, Superforecasting: The Art and Science of Prediction (2016); Hal R. Arkes et al., *Hindsight Bias Among Physicians Weighing the Likelihood of Diagnoses*, 66 J. Applied Psychol. 252 (1981); Stephen K. Asare, *The Auditor's Going-Concern Decision: Interaction of Task Variables and the Sequential Processing of Evidence*, 67 Acct. Rev. 379 (1992); Chris Guthrie et al., *Inside the Judicial Mind*, 86 Cornell L. Rev. 777 (2001); Elizabeth F. Loftus & Willem A. Wagenaar, *Lawyers' Predictions of Success*, 28 Jurimetrics J. 437 (1988).

[44] Fiske & Taylor, *supra* note 32.

Simons and Chabris's research revealed how unknown errors and faulty perception inadvertently creep into cognition. When people were instructed to watch a video of two basketball teams and asked to count the number of passes for only the team wearing white T-shirts, 50% of the people failed to notice a woman wearing a gorilla suit walking among the players, even though the gorilla was visible for seven seconds and beat her chest in the center of the screen.[45] The lesson was simple: people did not always notice what was literally in front of them. These findings were not confined to the laboratory. Simons and Levin explored cognitive blindness—and indeed our blindness to our own blindness—in real-world environments. In one study, an experimenter asked a stranger for directions while outside. During the conversation, people carrying a door between the experimenter and the stranger interrupted the dialogue. While obscured from the stranger's view, the experimenter was replaced with a completely different individual. Half of the time, the subject was completely unaware that the original experimenter had been replaced with an entirely different person.[46] Once again, studies confirmed that people might not have the capacity to perceive information in their immediate environment when they are distracted or otherwise focused. Even when asked, subjects believed that while *others* might be affected by the cognitive deficit, they did not believe that they *personally* could fall prey to the faulty perception.

For international investment law and dispute resolution, cognitive psychology raises two questions: what are we missing, particularly when it comes to the cost-benefit calculus of pursuing dispute settlement, and how can we avoid complications from undesired errors? Stakeholders in investment law are likely not immune from the promise and peril of normal human cognition. Adaptive cognitive illusions could theoretically generate value; yet they could also lead to inefficiencies in reasoning and facilitate suboptimal choices with stakeholders ignoring, underweighting, or overweighting information. While investment treaty dispute resolution may not involve proverbial gorillas, we cannot exclude the possibility that cognitive illusions could impact treaty negotiations, influence dispute resolution counseling with clients, affect lawyer advocacy, impact clients making choices about how to resolve disputes, animate stakeholder choices about normative reforms, and affect tribunals rendering decisions involving substantive outcomes and costs.[47] Given what is at stake, it is vital for decision-making in international investment law to avoid inferences from "stylized facts" or "truthiness"[48] deriving from the undue influence of System 1 cognition; instead, there is value in ensuring mental shortcuts are adaptive rather than generating error, and focus on using System 2 cognition to explore evidence carefully. As Hans Rosling argues in *Factfulness*, which Bill Gates endorsed as "[o]ne of the most important books [he's] ever read,"[49] the objective should be to use data to put reality in perspective and not be overly

---

[45] Christopher Chabris & Daniel Simons, The Invisible Gorilla (2010).

[46] Daniel J. Simons & Daniel T. Levin, *Failure to Detect Changes to People During a Real-World Interaction*, 5 Psychonomic Bull. & Rev. 644 (1998).

[47] Franck et al., *supra* note 2.

[48] Farhad Manjoo, True Enough: Learning to Live in a Post-Fact Society 198 (2008); Keith E. Stanovich, How to Think Straight About Psychology 13 (9th ed. 2010).

[49] *See, e.g.*, Rosling, *supra* note 42; Sarah Begley, *Bill Gates Says This Book Is "One of the Most Important" He's Ever Read*, Time (Apr. 3, 2018), https://bit.ly/2ARoPYn (last visited Aug. 8, 2018).

optimistic, pessimistic, or dramatic. The following sections explore basic cognitive illusions and debiasing opportunities to reflect Rosling's insights.

III. Identifying Errors: A Review of Cognitive Illusions

The literature on cognitive illusions is large and growing.[50] While inevitably a limited snapshot, the section offers an overview for international lawyers by focusing on three groups of cognitive illusions.[51] First, it explores cognitive illusions related to the accessibility of information, including, availability, representativeness, as well as primacy and recency effects. Second, it considers cognitive illusions involving the provision and presentation of information, including, negativity, framing, loss aversion, and anchoring. Third, it addresses cognitive illusions related to the self, including confirmation bias, self-serving biases (such as egocentrism and illusory superiority), and bias blind spots. Each subsection defines the cognitive illusion, describes classic and more recent research, and identifies the potential application to international investment law.

A. Cognitive Illusions Related to Accessibility of Information

Some cognitive illusions relate to the availability of information and how people create inferences, make predictions, and generate decisions using intuitive processes. This group of cognitive illusions typically involves availability, representativeness, primacy, and recency.

1. Availability

The **availability heuristic** occurs when we inform judgments about an event's likelihood by identifying the ease with which we retrieve relevant associations from long-term memory.[52] To the extent that memories are more easily recalled and therefore "available," we judge events to occur more frequently and be more typical. In other words, the likelihood of an event is judged by the ease through which we can recall a number of cases.

Unfortunately, the availability of a memory can be influenced by factors unrelated to actual frequency of occurrence, such as primacy or recency, an event's vividness, and exposure. These factors can cause overestimation of highly public events and underestimation of less public events. A classic example involves a plane crash discussed on the news, which causes someone to believe plane crashes are typical. The vivid event—complete with graphic pictures and emotional stories—becomes lodged in memory, making the story easy to recall, thereby suggesting the easily recalled event is common.[53] In contrast, statistical summaries of information about plane crashes may not be recalled, even though more accurate.

---

[50] *See* Joachim I. Krueger & David C. Funder, *Towards a Balanced Social Psychology*, 27 Behav. & Brain Sci. 313, 317 (2004) (providing a table of cognition errors).

[51] *See generally id.*; Anuj K. Shah & Daniel M. Oppenheimer, *Heuristics Made Easy: An Effort-Reduction Framework*, 134 Psych. Bull. 207 (2008).

[52] Kahneman & Tversky, *supra* note 28.

[53] Robbennolt & Sternlight, *supra* note 25, at 72–73; *see also* Rosling, *supra* note 42, at 61, 107, 231.

In Kahneman and Tversky's classic study on availability,[54] participants were asked whether it was more likely for the letter K to be the first or third letter in the English language. Because participants could more readily think of words that began with K than words with "K" as the third letter, participants indicated that words beginning with "K" were more frequent. Yet, an extensive word count conducted by other researchers indicated that the letter "K" occurs more frequently in the third rather than first position.[55] The same results occurred when participants were asked about the letters "L," "N," "R," and "V," which suggested there was nothing special about the letter chosen. Rather, results—and the mistaken belief that words beginning with a letter were more frequent—were tied to the ease with which individuals could recall words beginning with a letter. By contrast, the difficulty in recalling words with a letter in the third position was mentally translated into the mistaken belief that those words occurred less frequently.[56]

Availability illusions may impact the ongoing debate about the net value of international investment law. In ITA, one might easily recall the details of a single investment dispute those with vivid, extreme, or unusual details—for example an outsized damages award or a dramatic cost-shifting decision. When evaluating the risk and frequency of investment treaty disputes, one might focus on the easily recalled case and presume that the entire universe of cases and risk mirrors the one case that is easily recalled. Availability could work in the opposite manner. Where disputes involve less vivid facts, the information may not be easily recalled and the prevalence of those disputes may be deemed as less frequent. Similarly, where information about investment treaty conflict does not enter the public domain (such as settlements or other resolutions occurring through conflict management) or when modest cost awards do not make the mainstream press or social media, those phenomena might be perceived as less frequent and atypical, when in fact they could be quite standard. In combination, these two risks lay the foundation net effect whereby stakeholders perceive rare conflicts as more typical, even though they are not. Should stakeholders—whether counsel, clients, arbitrators, or policymakers—base decisions on mistaken impressions, there will likely be a downstream cost.

2. Representativeness and the Base Rate Fallacy

The **representative heuristic** involves the tendency to base estimates of risk on events that are presumably representative of the greater whole when, in fact, they are not. The unrepresentative anecdotes then create misperceptions about chance events, affect decision-making, and generate insensitivity to quantitative information.[57]

---

[54] Amos Tversky & Daniel Kahneman, *Availability: A Heuristic for Judging Frequency and Probability*, 5 Cog. Psychol. 207 (1973).

[55] Mark E. Mayzner & Mary E. Tresselt, *Tables of Single-Letter and Diagram Frequency Counts for Various Word-Length and Letter-Position Combinations*, 1 Psychol. Monograph Supplement 13 (1965).

[56] Norbert Schwarz et al., *Ease of Retrieval as Information: Another Look at the Availability Heuristic*, 61 J. Person. & Soci. Psych. 195 (1991).

[57] Robbennolt & Sternlight, *supra* note 25, at 73–74.

Kahneman and Tversky's original 1969 experiment demonstrated how representativeness even affects mathematical experts. Their research revealed, when experts attempted to classify events, they used instinct to evaluate informational accuracy and neglected other key sources of information, such as the actual base rate or frequency of events. In other words, even when statisticians considered: "Is it likely that X is Y?" they did not actually answer the question. Rather, they generated answers to a different question—namely "Does X *seem* like Y?" The representativeness heuristic reflects an unconscious and instinctive inference that like goes with like. As applied in another context, representativeness can mean that the "*perception* of a stranger as menacing is inseparable from a *prediction* of future harm."[58] A modern example that has made "representativeness" famous comes from *Moneyball*, where Billy Beane—the manager of the Oakland Athletics baseball team—picked a team of baseball players using their statistical success. Others, probably influenced by representativeness, overlooked players' potential capacity because they did not "look right" or appear to have characteristics people thought of when they imagined "stars." By focusing on statistical rates of quality, not interpretive assumptions, Beane created a team that was more successful than others.[59]

In ITA, representativeness could impact decisions. Recent research demonstrated—similar to how representativeness affected national court judges—that representativeness affected international arbitrators' assessments of probabilities in a mock commercial dispute.[60] This suggests ITA arbitrators, like other elite adjudicators, could be affected similarly. When considering whether it is likely that investors will win disputes and generate financial damages for states or when estimating potential costs (rather than focusing on base rates about actual likelihoods, the base rates about costs, and baseline data about costs shifts), stakeholders might consider whether it *seems* like investors will win and how much they may win. Representativeness may prevent stakeholders from distinguishing between perceived risks and actual fiscal exposure. Like the error-prone baseball scouts in *Moneyball*, when considering which lawyers to hire or which arbitrators to appoint, stakeholders may inadvertently focus on an existing pedigree, "look", or a relationship, rather than more carefully examining underlying credentials, approaches to core issues (including case management, disclosure, or settlement),[61] future capacity, or relative historic statistical success. While representativeness has the potential to be adaptive, in other instances, it may overestimate value or underestimate quality.

Representativeness affects cognition in other ways. Rather than making individual assessments by comparison to existing data, social narratives that fit within an existing social script can feel

---

58 Kahneman & Frederick, *supra* note 28, at 49–50.

59 Michael Lewis, Moneyball: The Art of Winning an Unfair Game (2003); Nate Silver, The Signal and the Noise: Why So Many Predictions Fail—But Some Don't (2012).

60 Franck et al., *supra* note 2.

61 Ema Vidak-Gojkovic et al., *Puppies or Kittens? How to Better Match Arbitrators to Party Expectations*, 2016 Australian Y.B. on Int'l Arbitration 61, 64–65 (2016); Klaus Peter Berger & J. Ole Jensen, *The Arbitrator's Mandate to Facilitate Settlement*, 40 Ford. Int'l L.J. 887, 917 (2017).

compelling; but this can mean that stakeholders ignore logical fallacies.[62] Representativeness can create misperceptions and misinterpretation of arguably random events.[63]

In ITA, there is a risk that stakeholders may ignore logical fallacies and the peculiar risk of each dispute or otherwise misinterpret random events. When combined with availability, representativeness might facilitate intuitive processing where stories of extreme cases may be easily recalled and may be deemed to be representative, when in fact they are not. For example, past commentary suggests some cases are "emblematic," and a paper from around 2012 suggested that a damage award of US$350 million[64] was standard;[65] yet, at the time, data reflected that measures of central tendency indicated typical awards ranged from approximately US$18 to US$45 million.[66] Prior to the 2012 *Occidental v. Ecuador* award[67] and the 2014 *Yukos* award, which was vacated,[68] the largest ITA award for roughly ten years was approximately US$270 million in 2003 award in *CME v. Czech Republic*. Focusing on unusual examples, as if they were representative, generates a possibility that both debate and

---

[62] The "Linda Problem" is a classic example of a problem related to representativeness and the conjunction fallacy. Participants receive a short description about "Linda": namely that "Linda is a 31 year-old, single, outspoken, and very bright. She majored in philosophy. As a student, she was deeply concerned with issues of discrimination and social justice and she also participated in anti-nuclear demonstrations." After that, participants were given several statements that classified Linda and asked to rank the probability that Linda belonged to the group. Statements included singular categories such as "Linda is a bank teller" *or* "Linda is active in the feminist movement," or conjunctive categories, such as "Linda is a bank teller *and* active in the feminist movement." Given the description, the majority of participants stated that it is more likely that Linda was *both* a bank teller *and* a feminist, even though it is statistically more probable for Linda to belong to only one of those categories, rather than members of both categories simultaneously. Because Linda's characteristics conform to stereotyped ideas of social categories that we believe are representative, it is common to over-rely on how similar "Linda" might fit to a stereotype and ignore the logic of the probabilities. KAHNEMAN, FAST AND SLOW, *supra* note 29, at 146–65.

[63] For example, after observing a roulette wheel, you observe a number of spins in a row have all come up red and predict that "black" is to come back up next; yet, on any individual spin of the wheel, the odds of coming up with black or red remain unchanged and are not influenced by previous spins. The tendency to mis-predict and misinterpret is known as the gambler's fallacy; this is related to "hot-hand fallacy" that one who has experienced success in the past has a greater chance of further success in an additional attempt. ROBBENNOLT & STERNLIGHT, *supra* note 25, at 74–75; Amos Tversky & Daniel Kahneman, *Judgment Under Uncertainty: Heuristics and Biases*, 185 SCI. 1124 (1974); Thomas Gilovitch et al., *The Hot Hand in Basketball: On the Misperception of Random Sequences*, 17 COGNITIVE PSYCHOL. 295 (1985); *but see* Mark Raab et al., *The Hot Hand Exists in Volleyball and Is Used for Allocation Decisions*, 18 J. EXPERIMENTAL PSYCHOL. APPLIED 81 (2012).

[64] *See* Pia Eberhardt & Ceclia Olivet, *Profiting from Injustice: How Law Firms, Arbitrators and Financiers Are Fueling an Investment Arbitration Boom*, CORP. EUROPE OBSERVATORY & TRANSNAT'L INST. 13-14 (Nov. 2012), http://bit.ly/1e30kHT (last visited Aug. 7, 2018).

[65] *See also* UNCTAD, *Reform of Investor-State Dispute Settlement: In Search of a Roadmap*, IIA ISSUES NOTE: No 2., 3 (May 28, 2013), http://bit.ly/19heJeA (last visited Aug. 7, 2018).

[66] *See* Chapter 5; Susan D. Franck & Lindsey E. Wylie, *Predicting Outcomes in Investment Treaty Arbitration*, 65 DUKE L.J. 459, 494–95 (2016).

[67] Occidental Petroleum Corp. v. Republic of Ecuador, ICSID Case No. ARB/06/11, Award (Oct. 5, 2012), https://bit.ly/2wuOe5e (last visited Aug. 7, 2018).

[68] Yukos Universal v. Russian Fed'n, PCA Case No. AA227, Final Award (July 18, 2014), http://bit.ly/Z08v21 (last visited Aug. 7, 2018); Stanley Reed, *Dutch Court Overturns $50 Billion Ruling Against Russia in Yukos Case*, N.Y. TIMES (Apr. 20, 2016), http://nyti.ms/28WmM89 (last visited Aug. 7, 2018).

normative choices are tailored toward systemic outliers, rather than representative disputes.[69] The beauty of data means that it is possible to identify core parameters, to assess the data's limitations, and to acknowledge the possibility that new data may arise in the future, thereby changing what is representative. In this way, the entirety of an experience—whether it be both the forest and the trees or, as Chapter 9 explains, different component parts of an elephant—can be appreciated.

Representativeness is linked to the **base rate fallacy**, which occurs when people either ignore or discount probabilistic evidence and other relevant statistical information.[70] Instead of considering the actual frequency of activities when making assessments, we inject error by instead relying on what instinctively feels correct.

In a classic experiment demonstrating the failure to consider base rates, researchers asked Harvard Medical School students and staff to estimate the risk of a patient contracting a disease. Subjects were asked: "If a test to detect a disease whose prevalence is 1/1000 has a false positive rate of 5%, what is the chance that a person found to have a positive test actually has the disease, assuming you know nothing about the person's symptoms or signs?" Given the underlying base rate of disease, the mathematically correct response was 2%. The logic is: assuming 1,000 people were tested and only one of those actually has the disease, the test will be positive in another 50 or so cases (5%); and the chance that a person with a positive result actually has the disease is about 1/50 or 2%. Less than 20% of subjects properly identified the correct answer. Rather, most subjects failed to calculate the probabilities and responded 95%, presumably reasoning that if the false-positive rate is 5%, the test will be correct 95% of the time.[71]

In ITA, parties and their lawyers may neglect base rates when estimating the likelihood of winning a dispute, amounts awarded, and potential costs of pursuing the dispute. Some may be skilled at assessing probabilistic outcomes whereas others may not. Every dispute may *feel* unique to the parties involved, and lawyers might believe it is good advocacy to treat every case as distinct. Yet, there is ultimately a range of outcomes and costs,[72] which could be normally distributed. Appreciating both base rates and the risk of cognitive illusions inadvertently misdirecting decision-making enhances the value of counsel's advice, parties' choices,

---

[69] This same point requires acknowledging that new data—as part of ITA's evolving population—may change over time. This may mean, at different moments, different cases may be emblematic of a "median dispute."

[70] Maya Bar-Hillel, *The Base-Rate Fallacy in Probability Judgments*, 44 ACTA PSYCHOLOGICA 211, 211–12 (1980); Daniel Kahneman & Amos Tversky, *Evidential Impact of Base Rates*, *in* JUDGMENT UNDER UNCERTAINTY, *supra* note 29, at 153; Alex Stein, *Are People Probabilistically Challenged?*, 111 MICH. L. REV. 855 (2013); *but see* Jonathan J. Koehler, *The Base Rate Fallacy Reconsidered: Descriptive, Methodological and Normative Challenges*, 19 BEHAV. & BRAIN SCI. 1 (1996). Base rate neglect is related to extension neglect, where "unless attention is specifically directed to it, the size of the set has little or no influence on its valuation." Daniel Kahneman, *Evaluation by Moments, Past and Future*, *in* CHOICES, VALUES AND FRAMES 707–08 (Daniel Kahneman & Amos Tversky eds., 2000).

[71] Ward Casscells et al., *Interpretation by Physicians of Clinical Laboratory Results*, 299 NEW ENGLAND J. MED. 999 (1978); Amos Tversky & Daniel Kahneman, *Evidential Impact of Base Rates*, JUDGMENT UNDER UNCERTAINTY, *supra* note 29, at 153–55; *but see* Leda Cosmides & John Tooby, *Are Humans Good Intuitive Statisticians After All? Rethinking Some Conclusions from the Literature on Judgment Under Uncertainty*, 58 COGNITION 1 (1996) (varying conditions to make the question clearer and finding the change improved accuracy).

[72] IAN AYRES, SUPERCRUNCHERS: HOW ANYTHING CAN BE PREDICTED 192–99 (2008).

and arbitrators' determinations. If nothing else, base rates manage stakeholder expectations by generating information to be considered when negotiating treaties, revising arbitration rules, and pursuing dispute settlement.

While base rate information should be considered, it need not be the exclusive basis for decisions. Qualitative data can also be constructive to offer context.[73] As Nate Silver wrote in *Signal and the Noise* about Billy Beane's success, both quantitative and qualitative information was necessary as, "If we in Oakland happen to be right on a gut-feel decision one time, my guess is it would be random' . . . The key to making a good forecast . . . is not in limiting yourself to quantitative information. Rather it's having a good process for weighing the information appropriately. This is the essence of [*Moneyball*]: collect as much information as possible, but then be as rigorous and disciplined as possible when analyzing it."[74] Statistical information and base rates aid careful decision-making and help to avoid errors from instinctive reasoning. As Ian Ayers likewise explained, "Increasingly, decision makers will switch back and forth between their intuitions and data-based decision making. Their intuitions will guide them to ask new questions of the data that a non-intuitive number crunchers would miss. And databases will increasingly allow decision makers to test their intuitions."[75] More than a hundred years ago, Justice Holmes likewise urged that, for the future, "the rational study of the law" requires lawyers to be "the man [or person] of statistics and the master of economics."[76] ITA likewise offers an opportunity to use data to evaluate dispute settlement, with a careful focus on costs.

3. Primacy and Recency

Both primacy and recency effects involve the ease of accessing information. A **primacy effect** occurs when information is presented early, captures attention, and influences the processing of subsequent information. A **recency effect** occurs when information presented at a later stage is more easily recalled.[77] In combination, the effects mean information gathered at the earliest or latest stages have disproportionate influence on memory and decision-making.[78]

Psychologists studying primacy and recency traditionally studied word recollection. For example, subjects were presented with a series of words they were told to remember; and

---

[73] *See* ROSLING, *supra* note 42, at 130 (identifying the value of providing quantitative numbers and context).

[74] SILVER, *supra* note 59, at 100.

[75] AYRES, *supra* note 72.

[76] Oliver Wendell Holmes, Jr., *The Path of the Law*, 10 HARV. L. REV. 457, 469 (1897).

[77] *See, e.g.*, ROBBENNOLT & STERNLIGHT, *supra* note 25, at 123; Daniel T. Gilbert & Jane E.J. Ebert, *Decisions and Revisions: The Affective Forecasting of Changeable Outcomes*, 82 J. PERSONALITY & SOC. PSYCHOL. 503 (2002); Dirk D. Steiner & Jeffrey S. Rain, *Immediate and Delayed Primacy and Recency Effects in Performance Evaluation*, 74 J. APPLIED PSYCHOL. 136 (1989).

[78] Delbert A. Brodie & Bennet B. Murdock, Jr., *Effects of Presentation Time on Nominal and Functional Serial Position Curves in Free Recall*, 16 J. VERBAL LEARNING & VERBAL BEHAV. 185 (1977); Robert L. Greene, *Sources of Recency Effects in Free Recall*, 99 PSYCHOL. BULL. 221 (1986); Martin F. Kaplan, *Stimulus Inconsistency and Response Dispositions in Forming Judgments of Other Persons*, 25 J. PERSONALITY & SOC. PSYCHOL. 58 (1973); Robert E. Lana, *Three Theoretical Interpretations of Order Effects in Persuasive Communications*, 61 PSYCHOL. BULL. 314 (1964); Bennet B. Murdock, Jr., *The Serial Position Effect of Free Recall*, 64 J. EXPERIMENTAL PSYCHOL. 482 (1962).

after a delay, they are asked to recall as many of the items as possible. The impact of primacy and recency depended upon other aspects, such as the number of items tested and time delay between giving information and the point of recollection.[79] Many subjects focused on aspects coming at the outset of their experience, namely when their memories were fresh and subjects could mentally rehearse the experience in an effort to store memories.[80] Where, however, there were long delays between the end of the task and information recall, the recency effect dominated memory recollection, and biased information accurately recalled, with the last aspects more typically recalled.[81]

Primacy and recency also affect quality assessments. For example, primacy and recency affect students' assessment of professor quality. Steiner and Rain asked students to view four videotaped lectures, with all students watching three average lectures and one lecture that involved an experimental manipulation. The researchers randomly assigned students to: (1) watch either "poor" quality (i.e. acting nervous, monotone voice, and no facial expressions) or "good" quality lectures; and (2) whether the "good" or "poor" lecture was first or last in the series. The position of the lectures affected students evaluations of professor quality. Students watching all four lectures in a single day and seeing the good lecture last (recency), evaluated the professor's quality as reliably higher; and when other students watched the lectures over four consequctive days, they ranked professor quality as reliably lower after watching the poor lecture last (recency). Primacy also played a role. For students seeing either the good or bad lecture first, subsequent evaluations tended to conform to earlier assesments.[82]

Primacy and recency effects could impact ITA. While counsel may already be unconsciously exploiting these effects during advocacy, they may wish to do so with greater precision to add value. For example, counsel could schedule regular-reassessments of a case, to consider initial impressions, as a dispute evolves. Similarly, they may wish to use memory cues in crafting closing arguments, and they should also be alert to the possibility that opposing counsel may attempt to exploit these effects to distort arbitrators' perceptions and assessments. Arbitrators may wish to both be aware of these effects and consciously reconsider their first and last impressions. By providing a strategic check to address the effects of primacy and recency, arbitrators could ensure that "sandwiched" evidence is not inadvertently

---

79 Arthur M. Glenberg et al., *A Two-Process Account of Long-Term Serial Position Effects*, 6 J. Experimental Psychol.: Hum. Learning & Memory 355 (1980); Norman Miller & Donald T. Campbell, *Recency and Primacy in Persuasion as a Function of the Timing of Speeches and Measurements*, 59 J. Abnormal & Soc. Psychol. 1 (1959); Dewey Rundus, *An Analysis of Rehearsal Processes in Free Recall*, 89 J. Experimental Psychol. 63 (1971).

80 The foremost explanation for primacy is rehearsal; unconsciously repeating the list (as new items appear) results in more repetition of earlier items and may facilitate easy recall. Brodie & Murdock, *supra* note 78; Murdock, *supra* note 78.

81 One of the main explanations for recency is that, during recall, earlier items are suppressed and replaced with later items. Murdock, *supra* note 78; *see also* Simon Farrell & Stephan Lewandowsky, *Response Suppression Contributes to Recency in Serial Recall*, 40 Memory Cognition 1070 (2012).

82 Dirk D. Steiner & Jeffrey S. Rain, *Immediate and Delayed Primacy and Recency Effects in Performance Evaluation*, 74 J. Applied Psychol. 136 (1989); *see also* Shelly J.C. Turcotte & Les Leventhal, *Gain-Loss versus Reinforcement-Affect Ordering of Student Rating of Teaching: Effect of Rating Instructors*, 76 J. Ed. Psychol. 782 (1984).

ignored and that "bookends" of arguments at the start or end of a case do not receive undue attention.

Primacy and recency might influence investment law stakeholders. For example, those pleased with a single result may view ITA more favorably, even though the data suggest that investors won at statistically lower rates than states and investors' relative success was well below 40%.[83] Similarly, poor initial impressions deriving from large claims and the threat of massive liability may cause stakeholders to view ITA unfavorably, even though ultimate results are relatively favorable. For example, in *Philip Morris v. Australia*, there was a serious damage claim and a challenge the regulation of cigarette packaging, which sparked a public outcry. Although Australia won, there has been minimal focus upon the outcome and continued focus on the evils of the threat of a lawsuit.[84] Irrespective of whether one lauds or loathes the system, the risk remains that the cognitive illusions influence policy debates.

B. COGNITIVE ILLUSIONS RELATED TO INFORMATION PROVIDED

A second group of cognitive illusions, which relate to the information people receive, also affect decision-making. These cognitive illusions include the negativity bias, framing effects, loss aversion, and anchoring.

1. Negativity Bias

Psychological research consistently demonstrates that negative information is weighted more heavily and more strongly influences judgments than positive information.[85] This **negativity bias** or negativity dominance means that, all things being equal, negative events are viewed more negatively than corresponding positive events, with negative effects exhibiting a

---

[83] *See* Chapter 5; *see also* Franck & Wylie, *supra* note 46, at 489–90, 495.

[84] Nikos Lavranos, *The Deafening Silence of the Anti-ISDS Groups After the* Philip Morris *Decision*, KLUWER ARB. BLOG (Feb. 24. 2016), http://bit.ly/28WpJ8R (last visited Aug. 7, 2018); *see also* Deborah R. Hensler & Damira Khatam, *Re-investing Arbitration; How Expanding the Scope of Arbitration Is Re-shaping Its Form and Blurring the Line Between Private and Public Adjudication*, 18 NEV. L.J. 381, 414–15 (2018) (discussing the evolution of plain-packaging adjudication, without focusing on arbitration results).

[85] *See, e.g.*, David E. Kanouse & L. Reid Hanson, *Negativity in Evaluations*, *in* ATTRIBUTION: PERCEIVING THE CAUSES OF BEHAVIOR 47 (Edward E. Jones et al., eds., 1972); John J. Skowronski & Donal E. Carlston, *Negativity and Extremity Biases in Impression Formation: A Review of Explanations*, 105 PSYCHOL. BULL. 131 (1989); *see also* ROSLING, *supra* note 42, at.47–74. One counterpoint to this is the optimism bias, which causes people to believe that they are less at risk of experiencing negative events as compared to others. Technically, optimism bias can impact perception of likelihood both for positive events (such as winning the lottery, winning a case, or being awarded a large amount in an ITA) or negative events (such as being less likely to have a drinking problem, being sued, or being subject to a large award in ITA). Yet, much research suggests that the bias exhibits a stronger effect on negative events. The optimism bias in ITA may be worthy of further consideration in whether both parties overestimate the likelihood of their success, underestimate exposure to potential costs, or states may underestimate the risk of being subject to an ITA dispute. *See, e.g.*, TALI SHAROT, THE OPTIMISM BIAS: A TOUR OF THE IRRATIONALLY POSITIVE BRAIN (2012); Susana O. Gouveia & Valerie Clarke, *Optimistic Bias for Negative and Positive Events*, 101 HEALTH EDUC. 228 (2001); James A. Sheppard et al., *Exploring the Causes of Comparative Optimism*, 42 PSYCHOLOGICA BELGICA 65 (2002).

stronger effect on cognition than positive ones.[86] Baumeister's classic paper, "Bad Is Stronger than Good," explained:

> The power of bad events over good ones is found in everyday events, major life events [], close relationship outcomes, social network patterns, interpersonal interactions, and learning processes. Bad emotions, bad parents, and bad feedback have more impact than good ones, and bad information is processed more thoroughly than good. . . . Bad impressions and bad stereotypes are quicker to form and more resistant to disconfirmation than good ones.[87]

To offer another classic (yet emotive) example, the presence of a single cockroach in a bowl of otherwise ripe and luscious cherries will wreck the cherries' appeal, as the negativity associated with the cockroach becomes the center of focus. In contrast, the image of adding cherries to a bowl of cockroaches exerts minimal influence over the initial impression.[88]

Negativity bias expresses itself in multiple ways. First, the negativity illusion exerts an outsized effect on how people form impressions, particularly in quality assessments.[89] In ITA, the negativity illusion may mean stakeholders form an impression of a new international law area and potentially focus unduly on negative information (and ignore counterpoints of potentially positive information). Rather than focusing on the value generated by investment, identifying the scope of investments that do not generate disputes, or identifying cases where cost decisions operated in a party's favor, stakeholders become focused upon the negative information related to formal dispute settlement. When people focus, negative information commands more attention than positive information, and negative events elicit more rapid and prominent responses than non-negative events.[90] Second, the negativity illusion may facilitate an undue focus upon the fiscal consequences of adverse cost assessments. Unless this

---

[86] Paul Rozin & Carol Nemeroff, *Sympathetic Magical Thinking: The Contagion and Similarity "Heuristics," in* HEURISTICS AND BIASES, *supra* note 43, at 201, 207–08. The negativity bias is manifested by: negative potency where negative entities are viewed more strongly than equivalent positive entities, steeper negative gradients where the negativity of negative events grows more rapidly than comparable positive events, negativity dominance where combinations of negative and positive experiences yield evaluations that are more negative than the sum of individual experience, and negative differentiation where negative experiences are more varied and yield complex responses. Paul Rozin & Edward B. Royzman, *Negativity Bias, Negativity Dominance and Contagion*, 5 PERSONALITY & SOC. PSYCHOL. REV. 296 (2001).

[87] Ro Roy F. Baumeister, *Bad Is Stronger than Good*, 4 REV. GEN. PSYCHOL. 323, 323 (2001).

[88] KAHNEMAN, FAST AND SLOW, *supra* note 29, at 301–03; *see also* Rozin & Royzman, *supra* note 86, at 296 (discussing the contagion effect of cockroaches and quoting a Russian adage that a "spoonful of tar can spoil a barrel of honey, but a spoonful of honey does nothing for a barrel of tar.").

[89] Edward E. Jones & Daniel McGillis, *Correspondent Inferences and the Attribution Cube: A Comparative Reappraisal, in* 1 NEW DIRECTIONS IN ATTRIBUTION RESEARCH 389 (John H. Harvey et al., eds., 1976); Norman H. Anderson, *Averaging Versus Adding as a Stimulus-Combination Rule in Impression Formation*, 70 J. EXPERIMENTAL PSYCHOL. 394 (1965); Skowronski & Carlston, *supra* note 85.

[90] Rozin & Royzman, *supra* note 86; *see also* Louis Carretié, *Emotion, Attention and the "Negativity Bias", Studied Through Event-Related Potentials*, 41 INT'L J. PSYCHOPHYSIOLOGY 75, 83–84 (2001); Christine H. Hansen & Ranald D. Hansen, *Finding a Face in the Crowd: An Anger Superiority Effect*, 54 J. PERSONALITY & SOC. PSYCHOL. 917 (1988); Jacob E. Steiner, *Innate, Discriminative Human Facial Expressions to Taste and Smell Stimulation*, 237 ANN. N.Y. ACAD. SCI. 229 (1974).

impression is supported by data, the focus risks improperly influencing impressions about the efficacy of ITA. Third, negativity illusions partially explain why some stakeholders instinctively focus on negative and extreme cases. It is possible that negative and extreme (and recent) cases receive undue focus even though they are non-representative. To prevent the negativity bias from unduly dominating discussions, stakeholders should have opportunities to round out their attention and debias perception, and ensure that their perceptions are both grounded in data and have a proper context for assessment.

2. Framing

Framing occurs when equivalent descriptions of a choice generate systematically different decisions. Put simply, when given choices that have identical effects, people reliably make different decisions depending upon how the choices are presented. Three types of framing issues involve: risk-related choices, attributive framing, and goal framing.[91]

For risk-related choices, framing choices as a potential gain or potential loss influences willingness to take risks.[92] Even where choices are economically equivalent, people behave differently depending on whether options are framed positively or negatively. In theory, rational choice means decisions should *not* fluctuate depending upon framing; yet, in practice, they do.[93] In the classic "Asian Disease Problem,"[94] Kahneman and Tversky asked participants to imagine the outbreak of a disease that would kill 600 people. Participants chose between two options:

(1) Program A: "If Program A is adopted, 200 people will be saved."
(2) Program B: "If Program B is adopted, there is a 1/3 probability that 600 people will be saved and a 2/3 probability that no people will be saved."

When the options were framed to focus on the number of lives saved (i.e., a positive frame), participants were more likely to be *risk averse* and selected the certain option (72% selected Program A) instead of the gamble (28% selected Program B). In other words, when outcomes were framed in terms of lives saved (i.e., a potential gain), decision-makers preferred the certain positive outcome over an outcome framed as a probabilistic gamble.

---

[91] Eyal Gamliel & Eyal Peer, *Positive Versus Negative Framing Affects Justice Judgments*, 19 SOC. JUST. RES. 307 (2006); Irwin P. Levin et al., *All Frames Are Not Created Equal: A Typology and Critical Analysis of Framing Effects*, 76 ORGANIZATIONAL BEH. HUM. 149 (1998). Attributive framing involves an object's attribute being described either positively or negatively. Risky choice framing involves presenting two options in a forced choice, one of which is certain and the other of which is a gamble. Goal framing relates to assessing the advantages of participation versus disadvantages of nonparticipation. Levin et al., *supra*.

[92] Daniel Kahneman & Amos Tversky, *Choices, Values and Frames*, 39 AM. PSYCHOL. 341 (1984); Daniel Kahneman & Amos Tversky, *The Framing of Decisions and Psychology of Choice*, 211 SCI. 453 (1981) [hereinafter *Framing*]; Daniel Kahneman & Amos Tversky, *Prospect Theory: An Analysis of Decision Under Risk*, 47 ECONOMETRICA 263 (1979) [hereinafter *Prospect Theory*]; Amos Tversky & Daniel Kahneman, *Rational Choice and the Framing of Decisions*, 59 J. BUS. 251 (1986).

[93] ROBBENNOLT & STERNLIGHT, *supra* note 25.

[94] Kahneman & Tversky, *supra* note 28.

Other participants, however, received a different framing. They were asked to choose between two similar options but outcomes were framed negatively, focusing on deaths. Although all options were, once again, statistically equivalent, one option was framed in terms of a certain number of lives lost, whereas the alternative was framed as a gamble about potential loss of life:

(1) Program C: "If Program C is adopted, 400 people will die."
(2) Program D: "If Program D is adopted, there is a 1/3 probability that nobody will die and a 2/3 probability that 600 people will die."

Statistically, all four options (A–D) have the exact same success likelihood (33%) and, theoretically, decision-makers should view all options as equivalent. Yet, framing revealed different preferences.

If the earlier pattern of preferring certainty over risk-seeking persisted (i.e., participants preferred a fixed number of lives saved and lost), re-framing to focus on death theoretically should have meant participants selected Program C over Program D (i.e., choosing a fixed number of lives saved and lost). That was not the case, however. Instead, when options involved a negative frame (i.e., a focus on death), risk-seeking preferences reversed. When two statistically equivalent options were framed as a loss, participants became *risk seeking* and selected the gamble (72% selected Program D) over the certain outcome (28% selected Program C). In other words, decision-makers rejected a certain outcome and accepted a risky gamble when choices had negative overtones.[95]

Attribute framing involves describing an object's attributes as either positive or negative. Even with equivalent conditions, focusing on either positive or negative attributes of objects or events affects people's evaluations. Classic research asked consumers to evaluate the quality of ground beef. Consumers who were given a positive frame, and told that the beef was 75% lean, viewed the beef more favorably than consumers who had a negative frame and were told the beef was 25% fat.[96]

When framing goals, stakeholders consider the advantages of participating in an activity (a positive/gain frame) rather than the lost opportunity of not participating (a negative/loss frame). Studies generally find that people are more likely to participate in activities when the disadvantages of not engaging (rather than the advantages of engaging) are emphasized. Other researchers gave women information that either stressed the positive consequences of conducting breast self-examinations (i.e., a gain frame) or the negative consequences of not conducting breast self-examinations (i.e., a loss frame). The study found, four months after exposure to framing, women exposed to the "negative" frame were more likely than those

---

[95] KAHNEMAN, FAST AND SLOW, *supra* note 29, at 366–67; Kahneman & Tversky, *Prospect Theory*, *supra* note 92. Similar effects have been observed in university professors and physicians. Kahneman & Tversky, *Framing*, *supra* note 92; Kahneman & Tversky, *supra* note 28; *see also* Simon Gachter et al., *Are Experimental Economists Prone to Framing Effects? A Natural Field Experiment*, 70 J. ECON. BEH. & ORG. 443 (2009) (finding Ph.D. economics students were more susceptible to framing effects than economics faculty members).

[96] Irwin P. Levin & Gary J. Gaeth, *How Consumers Are Affected by the Framing of Attribute Information Before and After Consuming the Product*, 15 J. CONSUMER RES. 374 (1988).

receiving a "positive" frame to have both a constructive approach to breast self-examinations and actually have conducted a self-examination.[97]

Given the reliable influence of framing on assessments and conduct in other areas, framing could affect ITA in multiple ways. First, framing has the potential to affect risk assessments and decision-making. Like the "Asian Disease Problem," framing could directly affect assessments of the utility of dispute settlement and the choice for how best to resolve disputes. Dispute settlement generates an inherent frame where investors choose between accepting settlements or gambling that adjudication will produce larger gains. By contrast, respondents either must pay a settlement or gamble to reduce liability. To claimants, ITA creates a gain frame, whereas respondents are always in a loss condition. Other research on framing reveals that framing affects litigation choices both in the laboratory and in the real world.[98] Given that ITA's doctrinal framework naturally creates frames, it is likely that framing affects how parties evaluate claims, perceive risks and adjudication costs, and consider the value of potential settlement.

Moreover, experimental evidence confirmed that framing has affected the decision-making of both international arbitrators and national judges. Multiple hypotheticals identified that, when international arbitrators resolved international commercial disputes, framing exhibited a small—but statistically reliable—effect.[99] Judges, at least those in the United States, responded similarly to framing effects—even on the identical hypothetical given to arbitrators,[100] suggesting the framing, rather than adjudicator type, influences legal decision-making. It stands to reason that ITA arbitrators, many of whom have been commercial arbitrators or judges, may likewise be affected by framing. If framing affects elite international adjudicators and judges, it is possible that framing impacts other stakeholders, including policymakers, parties, counsel, and third-party funders making assessments about the potential net value and cost of dispute resolution.

Attribute framing may impact stakeholder perceptions, whereby negative frames generate more antipathy and assessments of the quality of ITA. Relatedly, goal framing may influence public discourse about ITA. Much discussion of ITA focuses on its disadvantages risks to states; but focusing on advantages of retained sovereignty or the value of demonstrating adherence to rule-of-law, could offer alternative frames to prevent imbalanced impressions. Debates using negative frames, in particular, inevitably tap into cognitive illusions and exert

---

[97] Beth E. Meyerowitz & Shelly Chaiken, *The Effect of Message Framing on Breast Self-Examination Attitudes, Intentions and Behavior*, 52 J. PERSONALITY & SOC. PSYCHOL. 400 (1987).

[98] Chris Guthrie, *Framing Frivolous Litigation: A Psychological Theory*, 67 U. CHI. L. REV. 163 (2000); Guthrie et al., *supra* note 43; Russell Korobkin & Chris Guthrie, *Psychological Barriers to Litigation Settlement: An Experimental Approach*, 93 MICH. L. REV. 107 (1994); Jeffrey J. Rachlinski, *Gains, Loses, and the Psychology of Litigation*, 70 CALIF. L. REV. 113 (1996).

[99] Franck et al., *supra* note 2, at 1155–60.

[100] Unpublished research by Professor Rachlinski, testing the same hypothetical on U.S. judges, identified that framing affected judges' decisions about contract rescission. Email on file with author from Jeffrey J. Rachlinski (Feb. 15, 2017), 12:11pm; *see also* Franck et al., *supra* note 2, at 1158–59; Guthrie et al., *supra* note 43, at 794–98; Chris Guthrie et al., *Heuristics and Biases in Specialized Judges: The Case of Bankruptcy Judges*, 86 B.U. L. REV. 1227, 1237–40 (2006) [hereinafter *Specialized Judges*]; Chris Guthrie et al., *The "Hidden Judiciary": An Empirical Examination of Executive Branch Justice*, 58 DUKE L.J. 1477, 1506–09 [hereinafter *Hidden Judiciary*] (exploring framing affects in administrative law judges).

a powerful effect. When considering the future of ITA and rebalancing international investment law, the dialogue may itself require rebalancing or debiasing to address implicit frames.

3. Loss Aversion

Research demonstrates that people are more concerned with avoiding losses than acquiring gains of a similar magnitude.[101] Put bluntly: we hate to lose more than we love to win. This tendency is called **loss aversion**. A classic problem illustrates the effect. "Imagine you are offered a gamble on the toss of a coin. If the coin shows tails, you lose $100. If the coin shows heads, you win $150. Is this gamble attractive? Would you accept it?" As Kahneman explained, when making a choice, people balance the psychological benefit of getting US$150 against the psychological cost of losing US$100. Even where the expected value of the gamble is positive, because one stands to gain more than one loses, the risk may be more distasteful; and the fear of losing can be more intense than the hope of winning. Affective responses to losses may also be a function of the size of the stakes; when the stakes rise, loss aversion increases. As Kahneman explains, "All bets are off, of course, if the possible loss is potentially ruinous, or if your lifestyle is threatened."[102]

Loss aversion extends beyond the laboratory to other economic behaviors.[103] In one study, researchers sent letters to credit card holders who had not used their card for several months. The letter contained a message either: (1) focusing on the benefits of using the card, or (2) focusing on the benefits they would lose if they did not use the card. Results showed that, those in the "loss" condition were twice as likely to begin using the card when they were reminded of the risk of loss.[104] While most research focuses on a person's own loss aversion, loss aversion affects choices related to the health, wealth, and welfare of others.[105]

Loss aversion might manifest itself in different ways in ITA. First, investors faced with a fiscal loss related to investment-related conflict may focus on the loss or potential loss (rather than gains), and this could affect an investor's dispute resolution strategy, including decisions about pursuing settlement or ITA. Second, states may likewise become fixated with potential losses, whether viewed as a potential limitation on discretion or the risk of

---

[101] Kahneman & Tversky, *Prospect Theory*, *supra* note 92; Robyn S. Wilson et al., *My Loss Is Your Loss . . . Sometimes: Loss Aversion and the Effect of Motivational Biases*, 4 RISK ANALYSIS 929 (2008); *see also* KAHNEMAN, FAST AND SLOW, *supra* note 29, at 283–86; Dilip Soman, *Framing, Loss Aversion, and Mental Accounting*, *in* HANDBOOK OF JUDGMENT, *supra* note 27, at 379; A. Peter McGraw et al., *Comparing Gains and Losses*, 21 PSYCHOL. SCI. 1438 (2010).

[102] KAHNEMAN, FAST AND SLOW, *supra* note 29, at 283–84; *see also* Soman, *supra* note 101, at 387.

[103] Colin Cramerer, *Prospect Theory in the Wild: Evidence from the Field*, *in* CHOICES, VALUES, AND FRAMES (Daniel Kahneman & Amos Tversky eds., 2000); Stefano DellaVigna, *Psychology and Economics: Evidence from the Field*, 47 J. ECON. LITERATURE 315, 324–36 (2009).

[104] Yoav Ganzach & Nili Karashi, *Message Framing and Buying Behavior: A Field Experiment*, 32 J. BUS. RES. 11 (1995).

[105] Avital Moshinsky & Maya Bar-Hillel, *Loss Aversion and the Status Quo Label Bias*, 28 SOC. COGNITION 191 (2010); Ilana Ritov & Jonathan Baron, *Reluctance to Vaccinate: Omission Bias and Ambiguity*, 3 J. BEH. DECISION MAKING 263 (1990); Wilson et al., *supra* note 101; Eyal Zamir & Ilana Ritov, *Loss Aversion, Omission Bias, and the Burden of Proof in Civil Litigation*, 41 J. LEG. STUD. 165, 169 (2012).

losing fiscal resources to defend state action. Third, literature on the ITA backlash suggests that the stakes are large and substantial. To the extent that data support the claim, ITA may be the quintessential example of how loss aversion generates extreme dislike. For investors, amounts claimed may involve "potentially ruinous" or "bet the company" risk. For states, amounts claimed may be sufficiently large to involve ruinous liability, amount to a "bet the country" dispute, or otherwise threaten state identity. Combining a negative frame and loss aversion may mean risk of loss is perceived as more poignant. Although potential risk may not result in an *actual* loss, the cognitive focus on *possible* loss may leave a more deep, lasting, and memorable impression than positive ultimate outcomes. In either event, the effect may impact normative policy choices related to international investment law and dispute resolution.

The combined effect of framing and loss aversion likely affects ITA. Depending upon the degree of risk and how an option is framed, parties behave differently.[106] ITA—given the rights states bestow on investors—naturally frames outcomes as gains or loses. If there is a low probability of gain, claimants will view disputes as potential gains and are theoretically more likely to pursue dispute resolution rather settle. If there is only a 10% chance of winning, claimants may prefer to take the chance of winning a large amount rather than settling for a certain smaller amount. In contrast, when claimants face a high probability gain, they become risk-avoiding, pursue settlement, and seek to avoid losing a potential gain. When faced with potential losses, respondents behave differently. When there is a low probability loss, respondents are more likely to pursue settlement; presumably the nuisance of settling a small and certain loss outweighs the risk of an uncertain larger loss. Should the probabilities be larger, however, respondents become more likely to engage in risk-seeking behavior and pursue adjudication; presumably, the value in avoiding a potentially larger loss motivates respondents to avoid smaller, but certain, settlements.[107] Using Kahneman and Tversky's conceptions of prospect theory, framing, and loss aversion, Table 2.1 provides a matrix of dispute resolution strategies in ITA given probable outcomes and whether outcomes are framed as gains or losses.

This matrix has tangible implications for ITA. As treaty rights primarily impose *only* state liability, framing effects are both fixed and asymmetric. As perpetual respondents,[108] states inevitably view ITA from the loss frame. This means if states perceive a low probability of loss, they may be inclined to settle. But should states perceive a medium or high probability

---

[106] This is known as prospect theory, where people make decisions based upon potential value of losses or gains, rather than outcomes, and framing reliably influences decisions. Amos Tversky & Daniel Kahneman, *Prospect Theory: An Analysis of Decision Under Risk*, 47 ECONOMETRICA 263 (1979).

[107] Amos Tversky & Daniel Kahneman, *Advances in Prospect Theory: Cumulative Representation of Uncertainty*, 5 J. RISK & UNCERTAINTY 297 (1992); *see also* Guthrie, *supra* note 98; Jeffrey J. Rachlinski, *Gains, Loses, and the Psychology of Litigation*, 70 CALIF. L. REV. 113 (1996); John M.A. Dippa, *How Prospect Theory Can Improve Legal Counseling*, 24 U. ARK. LITTLE ROCK L. REV. 81, 90–91 (2001).

[108] In theory, states could initiate G2G (government to government) dispute settlement. As opportunity costs of bringing a private investment dispute into the international relations sphere are high, states rarely relied upon the G2G dispute settlement. Some states have begun drafting treaty language that imposes affirmative obligations upon foreign investors. Jesse Coleman et al., *International Investment Agreements, 2015–16: A Review of Trends and New Approaches*, 2017 Y.B. INT'L INV. L. 42, 90–95 (2017).

TABLE 2.1

Matrix of Dispute Resolution Tactics as a Function of Outcome Probability and Framing.

	Low Probability (10% risk)	Medium to High Probability (50% or greater risk)
Gain (Claimant / Investor)	Arbitrate: Investor Preference for Risk-Seeking Behavior • Low Probability Gain • Claimant prefers to take a risk on a potential gain and overweights possibility of winning the case • *Example: For choice between 10% chance of winning US$500 and a certain gain of US$50, 78% preferred to risk an uncertain US$500 gain*	Settle: Investor Preference for Risk-Averse Option • Medium to High Probability Gain • When choosing between two potential gains, claimant underweights probability of winning and seeks to avoid losing a potential gain • *Example: For choice between 50%+ chance of a US$500 win and a 100% chance of a US$250 gain, 88% preferred certain US$250 gain*
Loss (Respondent / State)	Settle: State Preference for Risk-Averse Option • Low Probability Loss • Respondent prefers a small and certain loss because overweights the probability of possible loss • *Example: For choice between 10% chance of US$500 loss or 100% chance of US$50 loss, 80% preferred certain US$50 loss*	Arbitrate: State Preference for Risk-Seeking Behavior • Medium to High Probability Loss • When choosing between two potential losses, respondent underweights probability of loss and seeks to avoid greater loss • *Example: For choice between 50%+ chance of a US$500 loss and a certain US$250 loss, 87% preferred to risk an uncertain US$500 loss*

of a loss, even though the ultimate outcomes could generate greater state liability, states will nevertheless engage in risk-seeking behavior and pursue ITA to avoid a certain loss. The major challenge of applying Kahneman and Tversky's theory is that they presume that outcomes and probabilities are certain, which is not necessarily the case in ITA. Although some outcome data is available,[109] an information vacuum persists, meaning gaps on data about

[109] *See* Chapter 5; Franck & Wylie, *supra* note 46; Daniel Behn, *Legitimacy, Evolution, and Growth in Investment Treaty Arbitration: Empirically Evaluating the State-of-the-Art*, 46 GEO. J. INT'L L. 363 (2015).

outcome probabilities makes it difficult to reliably estimate the value of dispute resolution, and fear of risk and negativity illusions may create inaccurate risk assessments, facilitating suboptimal decisions. This may partially explain why states fail to pursue settlement options as, when states must choose between two potential losses, they could undervalue the probability of an investor win and overweight the value of avoiding a larger loss.

4. Anchoring

Anchoring is a form of intuitive decision-making involving numerical estimates. When people make estimates, they tend to rely upon an initial value that is readily available, with that number becoming an "anchor" for subsequent numerical estimations, even when the initial figure is irrelevant or an intentional distractor.[110] While people can adjust away from initial anchors with deliberation, they often fail to adjust sufficiently. Thus, both reasonable anchors and completely irrelevant anchors have an outsized impact on final estimates.

In the classic "wheel of fortune experiment," Kahenman and Tversky had subjects spin a wheel of fortune to generate a random number.[111] After the wheel generated a random number, subjects estimated the percentage of African states in the United Nations. The different numerical starting points—even though fundamentally random—yielded different estimations, with responses biased toward the wheel's initial value. Even paying people to guess did not necessarily improve accuracy or reduce anchoring.[112]

Irrelevant anchors can affect legal judgments.[113] Scholars have demonstrated that anchoring affects the reasoning of U.S. judges and claim valuations.[114] The research showed how anchors trigger intuitive, automatic processing that judges were unable to override, even when anchors had no relation to the magnitude of the claim or judges knew they must ignore the anchor. Other research has revealed how anchoring impacted the criminal sentences of German judges; where anchors were low, sentences were lower, and where anchors were high, sentences were higher.[115]

Anchoring can affect international arbitrators. Like the judges, experimental research demonstrated that both relevant and irrelevant anchors affected arbitrators resolving ITA disputes.[116] One experiment with a relevant anchor involved expert reports assessing the value of expropriated beachfront property. In both conditions, the respondent state conceded that the value of the land was at US$1 million; but in the low anchor condition, the state assessed

---

[110] ROBBENNOLT & STERNLIGHT, *supra* note 25; Thomas Mussweiler & Fritz Stack, *Heuristic Strategies for Estimation Under Uncertainty: The Enigmatic Case of Anchoring, in* FOUNDATIONS OF SOCIAL COGNITION 79 (Galen V. Bodenhausen & Alan Lambert eds., 2003); Nicholas Epley, *A Tale of Tuned Decks? Anchoring as Accessibility and Anchoring as Adjustment, in* HANDBOOK OF JUDGMENT, *supra* note 27, at 240.

[111] Daniel Kahneman & Amos Tversky, *Judgment Under Uncertainty: Heuristics and Biases*, 185 SCI. 1124 (1974).

[112] JUDGMENT UNDER UNCERTAINTY, *supra* note 29.

[113] ROBBENNOLT & STERNLIGHT, *supra* note 25.

[114] Chris Guthrie et al., *Blinking on the Bench: How Judges Decide Cases*, 93 CORNELL L. REV. 1 (2007); Guthrie et al., *Specialized Judges, supra* note 100; Guthrie et al., *supra* note 43; Guthrie et al., *Hidden Judiciary, supra* note 100.

[115] Brite Englich & Thomas Mussweiler, *Sentencing Under Uncertainty: Anchoring Effects in the Courtroom*, 31 J. APPLIED SOC. PSYCHOL. 1535 (2001).

[116] Franck et al., *supra* note 2, at 1144–53.

the value at US$10 million, but in the high anchor condition, the valuation was US$50 million. In an example of how cognitive illusions can be adaptive, the relevant anchor reliably affected tribunal damage assessments. Although arbitrators sometimes awarded *less* than even the state asserted was due, investors' expert reports always constrained arbitrators' damages awards.[117] For ITA costs, it will be vital to ensure that costs documentation is driven by real and relevant anchors to ensure cost assessments, like the expert submissions in the experiment, are influenced by relevant anchors.

More troublingly, another experiment demonstrated that utterly irrelevant anchors affected damage assessments. In a hypothetical involving an ITA dispute about an investment in a law firm, arbitrators were instructed to presume there was jurisdiction, a violation of a treaty's "fair and equitable treatment" standard, and a viable claim for damage including moral damages. They were then told about post-deliberation dinnertime conversation that involved a conversation about an irrelevant and inapplicable U.S. federal court case involving U.S. domestic tort law. The only words that varied in the experiment was what arbitrators were told about the amount of the damage award in the U.S. tort litigation, including: nothing (control condition), US$1 million (low anchor), US$50 million (medium anchor), and US$300 million (high anchor). All arbitrators were then asked how much they would award. The results demonstrated that the irrelevant anchors influenced arbitrator assessments, the mean award in the medium anchor condition being roughly US$5.5 million and US$16.3 million in the high anchor condition.[118] While the results involved damage—and not cost—assessments, it stands to reason that ITA cost assessments risk manipulation from anchoring. As later chapters describe, arbitration costs are nontrivial, involving material proportions of amounts awarded. The potential unintentional, yet pernicious, effect of anchoring on ITA costs should be monitored to ensure costs are based upon legal, rather than intuitive, assessment principles.

The results also suggested that international arbitrators are not superhuman, much like other experts. This opens up the possibility that arbitrators are not the only ITA stakeholders affected by anchoring. Anchoring could also affect parties. Investors might become unduly focused on an original claim and generate a default baseline of what their case is worth, even in the face of subsequent contradictory evidence. When combined with loss aversion, deviation from an initial claim may feel like an unwarranted loss for investors. States, by contrast, may become anchored on initial damage claims. Even if actual liability is nonexistent or considerably lower than claimed, an initial arbitration request may anchor states' perceptions of ITA. Where state agents must explain the claim on multiple occasions to other officials, primacy and anchoring effects could make it difficult to dislodge the perception of ITA's actual risk and could affect choices about how to manage the disputes and inform policy choices about the state's future approach to international investment law.

Anchors could also influence counsel's willingness to recommend and to engage in negotiation or other forms of ADR. If lawyers become focused on initial damage claims or calculations of success (or loss), this focus may interact with framing and loss aversion to decrease the incentive

[117] *Id.* at 1145, 1147.

[118] *Id.* at 1148–52.

to adjust the dispute resolution strategy and may lead to the continuation of ITA.[119] The willingness to adapt and disrupt anchors, however, may permit counsel to reconsider their frame of reference and pursue more advantageous forms of dispute settlement. Finally, initial liability assessments might anchor stakeholders' assessment of international investment law and ITA. By focusing on initial or extreme claims, which may be inflated compared to later assessments,[120] their perceptions—while based upon preliminary information—may be anchored to an inaccurate, un-contextualized claim, and it may be difficult to disrupt the impression even when faced with contradictory information. This may partially explain why commentators, parties, and policymakers may focus on large and potentially unrepresentative amounts.

C. COGNITIVE ILLUSIONS RELATED TO SELF

Having explored illusions related to information accessibility and assessments of social phenomena, it is now useful to explore how cognitive illusions impact one's self. This section examines three cognitive illusions affecting how people collect information and derivative decision-making.

1. Confirmation Bias

Confirmation bias involves the tendency to seek out, evaluate, and remember information in a way confirming preexisting beliefs. Rather than systematically gathering all information, confirmation bias facilitates the disregard of conflicting information and supports increased confidence in original beliefs.[121] Confirmation bias can generate conscious strategic cherry-picking of information; it can also engender unconscious or instinctual selectivity in the acquisition and use of information.[122] Confirmation bias involves selective perception where preexisting expectations affect perception, leading to a focus on information corresponding to expected outcomes and downgrading data that conflict with initial expectations.[123]

Experimental research confirms people seek out information supporting favored hypotheses and interpret information in ways favorable to those hypotheses. Conversely, people do not necessarily seek out (and sometimes avoid) information that is counter-indicative of their beliefs or supportive of alternative hypotheses. To demonstrate confirmation bias in an

---

[119] While analysis of third-party funding is beyond the scope of this book, cognitive illusions could influence funding decisions. Existing research shows that anchoring influences insurance professionals, although there is some evidence that the degree of influence is lower than for other types of experts. Chris Guthrie & Jeffrey J. Rachlinski, *Insurers, Illusions of Judgment and Litigation*, 49 VAND. L. REV. 2017 (2006).

[120] In theory, amounts claimed could either increase or decrease in value over the lifetime of the dispute.

[121] Craig R.M. McKenzie, *Hypothesis Testing and Evaluation, in* HANDBOOK OF JUDGMENT, *supra* note 27, at 200; Raymond S. Nickerson, *Confirmation Bias: A Ubiquitous Phenomenon in Many Guises*. 2 REV. GEN. PSCYHOL. 175 (1998).

[122] Technologically sophisticated search engines using algorithms designed to weed out information presumably people do not wish to see can unwittingly generate confirmation bias. ELI PARISER, THE FILTER BUBBLE: WHAT THE INTERNET IS HIDING FROM YOU (2012); MANJOO, *supra* note 48.

[123] Lyle A. Brenner et al., *On the Evaluation of One-Sided Evidence*, 9 J. BEHAV. DECISION MAKING 59 (1996); Dan Simon, *A Third View of the Black Box: Cognitive Coherence in Legal Decision Making*, 71 U. CHI. L. REV. 511 (2004); Mary Snyder & William B. Swann, Jr., *Hypothesis-Testing Processes in Social Interaction*, 36 J. PERSONALITY & SOC. PSYCHOL. 1202 (1978).

uncontroversial setting, Wason created a simple test to determine whether people are willing to consider alternatives that differ from their initial beliefs. Subjects received the number sequence "2-4-6" and were then asked to guess what numerical pattern the experimenter was attempting to demonstrate with the number sequence. Most participants believed the scientists were only testing numbers that were increasing by rates of two, and subjects then only guessed about the pattern using pairs of numbers, such as "10-12-14," that would confirm the original hypothesis. In reality, experimenters simply offered numbers that sequentially increased in magnitude, but subjects did not explore any patterns that would assess the more general hypothesis—instead only testing numerical patterns that confirmed their ideas. As they were unwilling to test theories disconfirming their initial assessment, few subjects ever discovered the correct rule.[124] Confirmation bias influences evidence evaluation in other settings. Experiments demonstrate that when people receive new information inconsistent with their original beliefs, they are skeptical of the new information, downplay the evidence, and overweight information confirming the original belief. Even with ambiguous information, individuals interpret evidence to favor an original hypothesis.[125]

Confirmation can affect legal reasoning and adjudication.[126] Although jurors are asked to remain open-minded until deliberation, research demonstrates they favor a verdict early during trial, and their final decision is usually the same as the initial assessment. Pennington and Hastie found mock jurors were more likely to remember evidence supporting their verdict and discounted contradictory evidence.[127]

Confirmation bias may likewise affect ITA. First, lawyers—whose job it is to search out confirmatory information that supports their client's case—must guard against becoming overly polarized and unable to identify the weaknesses in their evidence, experts, and case law.[128] Arbitrators must also strive to dislodge ideological beliefs—as opposed to reasoned legal positions—that either discount evidence or legal logic that contradicts initial impressions. While following preliminary impressions may be adaptive where instincts reflect adherence to clear legal principles, in areas of legal ambiguity, the value is more questionable. ITA does contain, however, procedural mechanisms to root out actual bias or partiality, including removal for bias and partiality. Yet, arbitrators (or institutions) could consider implementing supplementary procedures to guard against experiencing confirmation bias unwittingly.

---

[124] Peter C. Wason, *On the Failure to Eliminate Hypotheses in a Conceptual Task*, 12 Q.J. Experimental Psychol. 129 (1960).

[125] Jonathan J. Koehler, *The Influence of Prior Beliefs on Scientific Judgments of Evidence Quality*, 56 Organizational Beh. & Human Decision Processes 28 (1993); McKenzie, *supra* note 121; Nickerson, *supra* note 121.

[126] Patricia G. Devine & Thomas M. Ostrom, *Cognitive Mediation of Inconsistency Discounting*, 59 J. Personality & Soc. Psychol. 5 (1985); Nickerson, *supra* note 121; *see also* Richard A. Posner, How Judges Think 110–11 (2008); Marsha S. Berzon, *Dissent, "Dissentials," and Decision-Making*, 100 Calif. L. Rev. 1479, 1483 (2012).

[127] Nancy Pennington & Reid Hastie, *The Story Model for Juror Decision* Making, *in* Inside the Juror: The Psychology of Juror Decision Making 192 (Reid Hastie ed., 1993); Stephen J. Choi & G. Mitu Gulati, *Bias in Judicial Citations. A Window into the Behavior of Judges?*, 37 J. Leg. Stud. 87 (2008); Robert G. Lawson, *Order of Presentation as a Factor in Jury Persuasion*, 56 Kent. L.J. 523 (1968).

[128] Robbennolt & Sternlight, *supra* note 25, at 14–16, 223–28.

Second, stakeholders may also have preexisting beliefs about the value or underlying utility (or lack thereof) of ITA. Fixed policy preferences may mean stakeholders gather information that confirms preexisting beliefs and generates cognitive ease, whereas disruptive evidence may be disregarded or marginalized. Irrespective of whether one is a "true believer" or an "avid critic" of ITA, confirmation bias likely contributes to polarized debates. Policymakers, as much as ITA participants, must recognize the value in slower, more deliberative, and balanced discussion so as to prevent suboptimal decisions.

2. Self-Serving Biases

Self-serving biases impact judgment by protecting and enhancing one's self-esteem. One type of self-serving cognition is the **egocentrism bias**, in which people have unrealistically positive views of themselves and their abilities. One form of this egocentrism relates to an overconfidence bias[129] of **illusory superiority** where one evaluates one's skills as better than they objectively are.[130] The classic research driving showed, when asked to assess whether they are better than average drivers, 75% of people studied typically asserted that they are better than average drivers. Statistically, this cannot be true; but people nevertheless presume that it is correct, with more than a majority believing they are above average.[131]

---

[129] A related cognitive illusion involves overconfidence, which can manifest itself in two ways. First, subjective confidence in one's own judgment could be reliably greater than objective accuracy. Second, confidence can cause other individuals to interpret those signals (possibly wrongly) as accurate signals of the individual's abilities, knowledge, and accuracy. In other words, people who are incompetent may be perceived as competent purely due to adopting an air of confidence. CHABRIS & SIMONS, *supra* note 45, at 85–92, 110–15. In ITA, this might mean that parties (or counsel) are overconfident in the merits of claims, defenses, or lines of argument given the law and facts. Overconfident mis-predictions can generate unnecessary disputes, lead parties to pass up settlement opportunities, or facilitate other poor decisions. ROBBENNOLT & STERNLIGHT, *supra* note 25, at 69. It may also mean tribunals evaluate confident witnesses as more reliable (even when wrong) or witnesses showing a lack of confidence as less credible (even when they are accurate). In a study to evaluate the information provided about a dispute's effect on the predictions of the dispute's outcome, one group received only plaintiff's arguments, a second group received only defendant's arguments, and a third group received both sets. Those receiving unilateral information typically failed to account for incomplete information and made less accurate predictions than those receiving both sets of information; oddly, subjects incorrectly predicting outcomes were more confident in their error-prone predictions. Brenner, *supra* note 123.

[130] ROBBENNOLT & STERNLIGHT, *supra* note 25, at 70–71; Jonathon D. Brown, *Understanding the Better than Average Effect: Motives (Still) Matter*, 38 PERSONALITY & SOC. PSYCHOL. BULL. 209 (2012); David Dunning et al., *Flawed Self-Assessment: Implications for Health, Education, and the Workplace*, 5 PSYCHOL. SCI. PUB. INST. 69 (2004); Vera Hoorens, *Self-Favoring Biases, Self-Presentation, and the Self-Other Asymmetry in Social Comparison*, 63 J. PERSONALITY 4 (1995). People often judge themselves to be above average on a variety of scales. *See* Mark D. Alicke, *Global Self-Evaluation as Determined by the Desirability and Controllability of Trait Adjectives*, 49 J. PERSONALITY & SOC. PSYCHOL. 1621 (1985) (more competent than others); Hoorens, *supra* (less likely to be a victim of crime); Laurie Larwood & William Whittaker, *Managerial Myopia: Self-Serving Biases in Organizational Planning*, 62 J. APPLIED PSYCHOL 194 (1977) (more successful than others); Neil D. Weinstein, *Unrealistic Optimism About Susceptibility to Health Problems*, 5 J. BEH. MED. 441 (1982) (fewer health problems than others).

[131] Ola Svenson, *Are We All Less Risky and More Skillful than Our Fellow Drivers?*, 47 ACTA PSYCHOLOGICA 143 (1981).

While egocentrism can be adaptive,[132] it also facilities dispute resolution inefficiency. Egocentrism can cause lawyers—and clients—to overestimate counseling skills, negotiation skills, the quality of advocacy, and the capacity to accurately assess the relative merits of cases, which undermine settlement efforts.[133] Similarly, people generally believe that they are more objective, fairer, and more ethical than others.[134] In one experiment, over 85% of U.S. magistrate judges believed their reversal rate on appeal was lower than average. A similar experiment on administrative law judges revealed that 83% believed they were above average in evaluating witness credibility, 87% believed they were above average in facilitating settlement, and 97% believed they were above average in avoiding prejudice.[135] Lawyers with considerable experience exhibited similar failings.[136]

Illusory superiority likely effects ITA. Research revealed that international arbitrators—like their brethren in national courts—were affected by egocentrism.[137] They were, as a group, overconfident in their own assessment of witness credibility and ability to render impartial decisions. Similarly, 92% of arbitrators believed they were above average in procedural efficiency—even though that is statistically impossible. Like the administrative law judges who nearly universally believed that they were all above average, arbitrators should consider the realistic possibility that they may, in fact, be prone to cognitive illusions, and should work to safeguard against improper influence when making decisions involving high-value disputes about sovereign conduct with material cost implications.

Arbitrators, as one set of human stakeholders, are likely not alone. Illusory superiority likely affects others in ITA. For parties, it may affect counsel and may require an adjustment of counsel's assessment of witness credibility, the quality of their case, and their likely degree of success. Lawyers advising clients might consider the possibility that they may be less persuasive, less effective, and less influential than they internally believe; and they should take steps to avoid potential illusory superiority and overconfidence limiting their clients' dispute resolution options. Even law professors writing books could be skewed by this cognitive illusion. The better course, rather than ignoring the risk, is to acknowledge the potential effect and work to combat the potential effect. For example, the risk of skewed assessments means dispute resolution procedures

---

[132] Jason K. Lopez & Matthew J. Fuxjager, *Self-Deception's Adaptive Value: Effects of Positive Thinking and the Winner Effect*, 21 CONSCIOUSNESS & COGNITION 315 (2012).

[133] Linda Babcock & Greg Pogarsky, *Damage Caps and Settlement: A Behavioral Approach*, 28 J. LEG. STUD. 341 (1999); Linda Babcock & George Loewenstein, *Explaining Bargaining Impasse: The Role of Self-Serving Biases*, 11 J. ECON. PERSPECTIVES 109 (1997); Linda Babcock et al., *Forming Beliefs About Adjudicated Outcomes: Perceptions of Risk and Reservation Values*, 15 INT'L REV. L. & ECON. 289 (1995); Guthrie et al., *supra* note 43; Roderick M. Kramer et al., *Self-Enhancement Biases and Negotiator Judgment: Effects of Self-Esteem and Mood*, 56 ORGANIZATIONAL BEH. & HUMAN DECISION PROCESSES 110 (1993).

[134] Nicholas Epley & David Dunning, *Feeling "Holier Than Thou": Are Self-Serving Assessments Produced by Errors in Self- or Social Prediction?*, 79 J. PERSONALITY & SOC. PSYCHOL. 861 (2000); Wim B.G Liebrand et al., *Why We Are Fairer than Others*, 21 J. EXPERIMENTAL SOC. PSYCHOL. 480 (1985).

[135] Guthrie et al., *Hidden Judiciary*, *supra* note 100, at 1518–20; Guthrie et al., *supra* note 43, at 811–20; *see also* Theodore Eisenberg, *Differing Perceptions of Attorney Fees in Bankruptcy Cases*, 72 WASH. U. L.Q. 979, 982–87 (1994).

[136] Jane Goodman-Delahunty et al., *Insightful or Wishful: Lawyers' Ability to Predict Case Outcomes*, 16 PSCYCHOL. PUB. POL'Y & L. 133 (2010).

[137] Franck et al., *supra* note 2, at 1166–68.

in investment law should be crafted with an acknowledgment that a degree of hubris may have been injected into assessments of the value of a claim or dispute, the skills of lawyers, witnesses, and adjudicators. The idea is to use rule-of-law mechanisms (for example, an appeal facility or mediation protocol) to provide structural opportunities for corrective mechanisms.

3. Bias Blind Spot

A final cognitive bias is the failure to compensate for one's own cognitive biases. Much like a visual blind spot, a **bias blind spot** exists where one is unaware of the limitations of one's own cognitive biases. Put simply, we are blind to our own blindness.[138] While it may be perfectly fine to acknowledge that *others* are subject to cognitive illusions (and knowing that illusions could theoretically affect our own cognition), we can nevertheless believe (and can act as if) we are immune from the effects of cognition errors. This "blindness blindness" can manifest itself in various ways. In vision studies, people can be blissfully unaware that cognitive biases influence their judgments. Research suggests that people regularly are unable to identify key changes occurring within their field of vision, whether it involves the introduction of a gorilla or even the substitution of human beings during a conversation.[139] The lack of awareness about the limitations of cognitive illusions is acute where people are unable to reconcile the belief that they perceive information accurately when faced with the reality of their inaccurate perception.[140]

Pronin, Lin, and Ross conducted seminal research on the bias blind spot.[141] They identified that, although participants can be aware of the existence and impact of biases in others, those same participants failed to recognize how those same illusions affected their own judgment.[142] Others have identified how individuals are more inclined to believe that cognitive illusions affect their cognition *in the abstract* rather than in a specific instance.[143] Although people might admit succumbing to illusions in the past, they may nevertheless fail

---

[138] David Dunning, Self-Insight: Roadblocks and Detours on the Path to Knowing Thyself (2005); Robbennolt & Sternlight, *supra* note 25, at 4; Emily Pronin, *The Introspection Illusion*, 41 Advances Experimental Soc. Psychol. 1 (2009); *see also* Thomas Gilovich et al., *Shallow Thoughts About the Self: The Automatic Components of Self-Assessment*, *in* The Self in Social Judgment 67 (Mark D. Alicke et al., eds., 2005).

[139] *See* Simons & Levin, *supra* note 46; Daniel T. Levin & Bonnie Angelone, *Visual Metacognition Questionnaire: A Measure of Intuitions About Vision*, 121 Am. J. Psychol. 451 (2008).

[140] Ronald A. Rensink, *Change Detection*, 53 Ann. Rev. of Psychol. 245 (2002).

[141] Emily Pronin et al., *Objectivity in the Eye of the Beholder: Divergent Perceptions in Self Versus Others*, 111 Psychol. Rev. 781 (2004).

[142] Scholars suggest various reasons for the inability to detect one's own cognition biases. Some suggest it derives from illusory superiority and overconfidence bias. John R. Chambers & Paul D. Windschitl, *Biases in Social Comparative Judgments: The Role of Nonmotivated Factors in Above-Average and Comparative Optimism Effects*, 130 Psychol. Bull. 813 (2004). Others suggest it derives from naïve realism, whereby individuals believe their version of reality is the most accurate and others' views are uniformed or biased. Lee Ross & Andrew Ward, *Psychological Barriers to Dispute Resolution*, 27 Advances Experimental Soc. Psychol. 255 (1995).

[143] Joyce Ehrlinger et al., *Peering into the Bias Blind Spot: People's Assessments of Bias in Themselves and Others*, 31 Personality & Soc. Psychol. Bull. 680 (2005).

to recognize how illusions affect their current behavior.[144] Bias blind spots ultimately mean that cognition slants toward doubting others' cognitive skills while presuming one's own cognition is immune from error.

The implications for ITA are critical. With information being gathered, impressions being formed, decisions being made, outcomes being decided, or choices being made about costs and cost allocation, the bias blind spot creates various risks. First, stakeholders may be unaware of how cognitive illusions influence the discourse about international investment law in general and how it may affect the dispute resolution process. Second, when stakeholders are unaware of how the blind spot may directly apply to them, it is not possible to take corrective measures. To the extent there is already a demonstrated relationship where cognitive illusions, including anchoring and framing, causally affect arbitrators' decisions, tribunals and other stakeholders should have their eyes wide open about how cognitive illusions could disrupt dispute resolution. Arbitrators, in particular, make material decisions on outcomes and costs, and they should be open to a conversation about structural correctives. Counsel, parties, and policymakers should avoid narratives suggesting that they are resistant to cognitive illusions. Instead, we should all be aware that we are at risk of cognitive illusions affecting information collection and processing, argumentation, and decision-making. This applies irrespective of whether one is an international arbitrator, a government official making policy decisions, or a law professor writing scholarship. To err is human, but creating a fantasy of superhuman capacity when the data tells us otherwise is both misguided and silly. The better course is to seek opportunities for debiasing to minimize the pernicious effects of cognitive illusions, potentially harness their useful aspects, and enhance international investment law and the rule-of-law.

D. SYNTHESIS

When considering the strategic use of ITA, the implications of costs, or normative reforms, there is a legitimate possibility that cognitive illusions skew our assessments and conversations. Focusing upon recent, negative, and extreme cases (whether the decisions adversely affect states or investors) and relying on potentially unrepresentative cases to serve as a prototypical example could lead to suboptimal reforms. It could, for example, lead to the creation of systemic responses that address outliers, rather than the totality or more representative examples. Alternatively, reform might be tailored to solve a problem that does not exist, and thereby generate new problems. Reforms might solve a nonexistent problem while leaving meaningful problems unresolved. These suboptimal responses, potentially driven by intuitive reasoning, could sacrifice long-term quality and sustainability in search of short-term solutions that generate cognitive ease.

Ultimately, whether and how cognitive illusions affect ITA generally is an empirical question. This will require experiments to ascertain their potential existence and relative influence. There is value in recognizing that cognitive illusions may unwittingly

[144] Emily Pronin & Matthew Kugler, *Valuing Thoughts, Ignoring Behavior: The Introspection Illusion as a Source of Bias Blind* Spot, 43 J. EXPERIMENTAL SOC. PSYCHOL. 565 (2007); *see also* Ehrlinger et al., *supra* note 143 (exploring how personal views may be identified as a source of enlightenment, but others' views as a source of bias).

affect our understanding of ITA. By slowing down decision-making to reassess underlying assumptions, stakeholders can identify whether original impressions are substantiated or whether cognitive illusions influence the impression. The objective should be to ensure that policy discussions and dispute settlement decisions are made with the best information so as to increase the likelihood of optimal choices.

IV. Debiasing

Having identified experimental evidence demonstrating that cognitive illusions affect international arbitrators and raising the realistic possibility that they pervade investment law, it is vital to explore how to minimize negative aspects of cognitive illusions, to draw upon the potential positive elements, and to enhance decision-making. "Debiasing" involves the prevention, elimination, or mitigation of cognitive illusions.[145] Debiasing can be complex, however. Some debiasing techniques mitigate—but do not eliminate—negative externalities of cognitive illusions. This section explores debiasing techniques, including the provision of reliable statistical information. It examines how, in other contexts, scholars targeted debiasing mechanisms to improve legal choices. It then considers theoretical mechanisms for debiasing. Finally, it explores the value and challenges of applying debiasing techniques to ITA.

A. DEBIASING INSIGHTS FROM DOMESTIC LAW

Appreciating how cognitive illusions might operate, domestic legal scholars have explored how to reinforce positive elements of intuitive processing while minimizing risk.[146] Both substantive law and legal procedures can be a constructive tool for decreasing bounded rationality and generating more optimal results.[147] Debiasing recommendations run the gamut of substance and procedure and possibly offer insights to investment law.

Substantively, in consumer protection, scholars recommend debiasing for decision-making about mortgages, loans, credit cards, and other purchases; these scholars recommend requiring lenders to provide consumers with real examples of harm or additional affirmative disclosures prior to the financial acquisition.[148] Employment scholars advocate that reform

---

[145] *See* Pat Croskerry, *The Importance of Cognitive Errors in Diagnosis and Strategies to Minimize Them*, 78 ACAD. MED. 775, 776, 779 (2003) ("there are, indeed, cognitive pills for cognitive ills"); *see also* Elizabeth J. Reese, *Techniques for Mitigating Cognitive Biases in Fingerprint Identification*, 59 UCLA L. REV. 1252 (2012).

[146] Despite the scope of research on cognitive illusions, there is less research on debiasing. *See* Lilienfeld et al., *supra* note 34, at 391. One study identified nearly 2,000 papers on cognitive illusions but fewer than 200 papers on debiasing. *Id.*; *see also* Reese, *supra* note 145, at 1268.

[147] THALER & SUNSTEIN, *supra* note 37; Oren Bar-Gill & Chaim Fershtman, *Law and Preferences*, 20 J.L. ECON. & ORG., 331 (2004); Christine Jolls & Cass R. Sunstein, *Debiasing Through Law*, 35 J. LEG. STUD. 199 (2006).

[148] Colin Camerer et al., *Regulation for Conservatives: Behavioral Economics and the Case for "Asymmetric Paternalism,"* 151 U. PA. L. REV. 1211 (2003); Andrea Freeman, *Payback: A Structural Analysis of the Credit Card Problem*, 55 ARIZ. L. REV. 141, 156 (2013); Ron Harris & Asher Meir, *Non-Recourse Mortgages—A Fresh Start*, 21 AM. BANKR. L. REV. 11, 140–41 (2013); Ronald J. Mann, *"Contracting" for Credit*, 104 MICH. L. REV. 899 (2006); Scott R. Peppet, *Freedom of Contract in an Augmented Reality: The Case of Consumer Contracts*, 59 UCLA L. REV. 676 (2012).

of the jury process to debias cognition and improve deliberation quality.[149] Constitutional scholars have explored how structural changes—including institutional reforms such as creating specialized tribunals—may improve decision-making.[150] These strategies may prove useful for investment treaty dispute resolution, as informing and structuring adjudicative authority within bounded rules seems sensible to identify the potential risk of cognitive illusions and provide remedies designed to constrain risks from intuitive and unintentional error.

Other scholars focus on procedural safeguards to limit the effect of cognitive illusions. Procedural debiasing reforms focus on shifting the decision-making process for strategic decision-makers such as jurors or judges, counsel, and litigation funders making critical decisions.[151] Procedural debiasing could be simple, namely just informing decision-makers about the risks of cognitive illusions. This sometimes involves educating judges, or it sometimes involves requiring jury instructions to minimize the negative effects of cognitive illusions or giving jurors opportunities to make judgments with feedback. While these debiasing techniques have mixed success, one debiasing technique changing cognitive focus has been reasonably successful. For instance, subjects being required to generate their own descriptions of possible outcomes or reasons for probability assessments, rather than be subject to the influence of other stimuli, has reduced the effect of cognitive illusions.[152] The objective is to require people to forgo quick thinking and unlearn an instinctive reaction to create a more rational and balanced conclusion.

Along a similar vein, there is evidence that decision-makers processing in a language other than their mother tongue either reduce or eliminate the manipulative effects of cognitive illusions. Although this procedural technique may not translate well into domestic legal systems where a single language is spoken, there may be applications and opportunities for investment treaty dispute settlement where many people are multilingual.[153]

---

[149] Avani M. Sood & John M. Darley, *The Plasticity of Harm in the Service of Criminalization Goals*, 100 CALIF. L. REV. 1313, 1357–58 (2012).

[150] Dan M. Kahan, *The Supreme Court, 2010 Term--Foreword: Neutral Principles, Motivated Cognition, and Some Problems for Constitutional Law*, 125 HARV. L. REV. 1 (2011); Paul M. Secunda, *Cognitive Illiberalism and Institutional Debiasing Strategies*, 49 S.D. L. REV. 373 (2012); Paul M. Secunda, *Cultural Cognition at Work*, 38 FLA. ST. U. L. REV. 107 (2010); Cass R. Sunstein, *Trimming*, 122 HARV. L. REV. 1049 (2009).

[151] Guthrie et al., *Specialized Judges*, *supra* note 100; Guthrie et al., *Hidden Judiciary, supra* note 100; Guthrie et al., *supra* note 43; Guthrie & Rachlinski, *supra* note 119; Reid Hastie & W. Kip Viscusi, *What Juries Can't Do Well: The Jury's Performance as Risk Manager*, 40 ARIZ. L. REV. 901 (1998); Kim A. Kamin & Jeffrey J. Rachlinski, *Ex Post ≠ Ex Ante: Determining Liability in Hindsight*, 19 L. & HUM. BEH. 89 (1995); Kramer et al., *supra* note 133; Guthrie & Korobkin, *supra* note 98; Jeffrey J. Rachlinski et al., *Can Judges Make Reliable Numeric Judgments? Distorted Damages and Skewed Sentences*, 90 IND. L.J. 695 (2015); Jeffrey J. Rachlinski, *A Positive Psychological Theory of Judging in Hindsight*, 65 U. CHI. L. REV. 571 (1998).

[152] These studies were often about hindsight bias. John C. Anderson et al., *Evaluation of Auditor Decisions: Hind-Sight Bias Effects and the Expectation Gap*, 14 J. ECON. PSYCHOL. 711, 722 (1993); Hal R. Arkes et al., *Eliminating the Hindsight Bias*, 73 J. APPLIED PSYCHOL. 305, 306–07 (1988); Martin F. Davies, *Field-Dependence and Hindsight Bias: Output Interference in the Generation of Reasons*, 27 J. RES. PERSONALITY 222, 278–80 (1993); Martin F. Davies, *Reduction of Hindsight Bias by Restoration of Foresight Perspective: Effectiveness of Foresight-Encoding and Hindsight-Retrieval Strategies*, 40 ORGANIZATIONAL BEH. & HUM. DECISION PROCESSES 50, 53 (1987); Wolfgang Hell et al., *Hindsight Bias: An Interaction of Automatic and Motivational Factors?*, 16 MEMORY & COGNITION 533, 535 (1988); Paul Slovic & Baruch Fischhoff, *On the Psychology of Experimental Surprise*, 3 J. EXPERIMENTAL PSYCHOL. 544 (1977).

[153] *See* Franck et al., *supra* note 2, at 1174.

B. FISCHHOFF'S DEBIASING FRAMEWORK

Minimal scholarship has explored debiasing in international law.[154] Given the gamut of domestic debiasing techniques, when considering the potential application to ITA or international law, it is helpful to return to first principles on debiasing. Baruch Fischhoff, a pioneer in debiasing, created the core classification for debiasing techniques.[155] Fischhoff targeted three categories of problems from cognitive illusions, namely: faulty tasks, faulty decision-makers, or a mismatch between tasks and decision-makers.[156] Although appropriate debiasing will require adaption to the type of decision-maker and cognitive illusion,[157] this section offers preliminary ideas about application to ITA to promote debiasing, reduce risk, and increase accuracy in investment law dispute settlement. Given debates about ITA and the fiscal implications of outcomes and costs, there is value in exploring how to minimize the negative consequences of cognitive illusions.

1. Faulty Tasks

For "faulty tasks," Fischhoff argues that some tests of cognitive decision-making involve "unfair" or "misunderstood" tasks generating spurious results. Fischhoff's primary concern is that methods for identifying cognitive illusions are complex and may lead researchers to misidentify the presence of illusions. He likewise recognizes that decision-making tasks might involve overlooked distinctions or semantic disagreement, meaning the precise task simply requires clarification to facilitate debiasing.[158]

Fischhoff recommends that debiasing occur through procedural reforms, particularly methodologies that streamline and clarify decision-making.[159] First, he encourages people to engage with the subject matter and objectives of decision-making. Second, he recommends that decision-makers request clarification of instructions, definitions, and mandates to reduce error.[160] Third, Fischhoff recommends generating procedures that nudge decision-makers to

---

[154] *But see* Anne van Aaken, *Das deliberativ Element juristischer Verfahren als Instrument zur Überwindung nachteiliger Verhaltensanomalien—Ein Plädoyer für die Einbeziehung diskursiver Elemente in die Verhaltensökonomik des Rechts*, *in* RECHT UND VERHALEN: BETRÄGE ZU BEHAVIORAL LAW (C Christoph Engel et al., eds., 2007). After this chapter was initially drafted, commentators began discussing scholarship on psychology and investment dispute settlement more actively. *See, e.g., supra* notes 5 and 20 and accompanying text; Cornel Marian & Sean P. Wright, THE ROLES OF PSYCHOLOGY IN INTERNATIONAL ARBITRATION 231–64 (Tony Cole ed., 2017); Jose Maria Figaredo, *Cognitive Biases: What Are They, Do They Affect Arbitrators, And if So, Can That Influence Be Avoided?*, 40 UNDER 40: INTERNATIONAL ARBITRATION (Carlos González-Bueno ed., 2018).

[155] Other scholars have explored debiasing. *See, e.g.*, SERENA SANDRI, REFLEXIVITY IN ECONOMICS 110–18 (2009); Pat Croskerry et al., *Cognitive Debiasing 2: Impediments to and Strategies for Change*, 22 BMJ QUAL. & SAF. (2013); Richard P. Larrick, *Debiasing, in* HANDBOOK OF JUDGMENT AND DECISION MAKING, *supra* note 27, at 318, 321–31 (focusing on motivational, cognitive, and technological strategies); Katherine L. Milkman et al., *How Can Decision Making Be Improved?*, 4 PERSPECTIVES PSYCHOL. SCI. 379 (2009).

[156] Baruch Fischhoff, *Debiasing, in* JUDGMENT UNDER UNCERTAINTY, *supra* note 29, at 422–40.

[157] Amir & Lobel, *supra* note 38, at 2117.

[158] Fischhoff, *supra* note 156, at 422–47.

[159] *Id.* at 425–26.

[160] This might also involve presenting questions in a more readily understood manner. Frequencies, for example, appear to be easier to understand than probabilistic data. Gerd Gigerenzer, *How to Make Cognitive Illusions Disappear: Beyond "Heuristics and Biases,"* 2 EUR. REV. SOC. PSYCHOL. 83 (1991); *but see* Steven A. Sloman et al., *Frequency Illusions and Other Fallacies*, 91 ORGANIZATIONAL BEH. & HUM. DECISION PROCESSES 296 (2003).

provide more clear and structured mandates. Fourth, he encourages streamlining tasks by asking fewer questions and permitting decision-makers to focus.[161] Finally, Fischhoff argues that, by reassessing assumptions under their decisions, decision-makers can ensure they do not misunderstand their mandate.

Addressing "faulty tasks" could prove useful for debiasing international investment law. Intriguing options include requesting clarification of definitions, restructuring tasks, and testing assumptions. As investment treaties contain a variety of broad standards and definitions vary among treaties, policy debates could be enhanced by ensuring all stakeholders share common definitions of contested areas. At a bare minimum, it should be made clear what the precise issues and disaffections are, rather than using nebulous terms—including "policy space," "development," or "mediation"—that could mean different things to different stakeholders in different contexts. There has been interest, for example, in UNCITRAL Working Group III in creating shared definitions to decrease confusion and increase cohesive discussions.[162] While generating a working definition could become contentious, an agreed baseline for discussion informs debate.[163]

Restructuring tasks could also create value for investment dispute settlement. States, for example, might choose to narrow the scope of discretion in arbitral decision-making or provide precise parameters for how arbitrators must exercise their mandate and discretion. Particularly for ITA costs where there is, by and large, large pockets of unfettered discretion, this shift could aid arbitrators and reorient their cognition to enhance decision-making. Other procedures—such as checklists for parties considering whether and how to arbitrate claims, or structured formats for arbitrators generating awards, particularly factors for making cost assessments—offer opportunities to mitigate risk from cognitive illusions.[164] Nevertheless attempting to debias "faulty tasks" in isolation has limits. ITA is complex, and it is unlikely that some problems can be avoided.[165] Creating additional incentives to reorient decision-making may have marginal impact. Deeper engagement could have diminishing marginal returns or promote further polarization, which may ironically exacerbate preexisting biases, meaning a degree of caution is required.

2. Faulty Decision-Makers

Error is not just a function of how questions are asked and how decisions are structured. Fischhoff also identifies that some error derives from "faulty decision-makers." Arguing that debiasing can occur by improving the reasoning of those making decisions, he nevertheless

---

[161] Fischhoff, *supra* note 156, at 424–25.

[162] *See* CIDS, *Academic Forum on ISDS*, https://bit.ly/2ScWKBj (last visited Dec. 22, 2018).

[163] Focusing on common definitions for international arbitrators may have less value, as arbitrators must apply the applicable law. Nevertheless, ITA arbitrators might proactively ask questions during dispute settlement to test this assumption.

[164] Atul Gawande, The Checklist Manifesto: How to Get Things Right (2009); Lucy Reed, *Arbitral Decision-Making: Art, Science or Sport?*, 30 J. Int'l Arb. 85 (2013).

[165] States might use this strategy to limit the scope of rights in IIAs to eliminate the risk of cognition error impacting decision-makers. The decision to remove the rights could also be influenced by cognitive illusions.

identified groups of "perfectible" and "incorrigible" decision-makers who make reliable errors.[166] Each type of decision-maker requires unique debiasing interventions.

For "perfectible" individuals, debiasing involves educational opportunities. At the mild end of the spectrum, debiasing involves nudges or subtle warnings about the possibility of error from cognitive illusions generally. A more direct strategy involves warning people about the risks of specific cognitive illusions, describing how the illusion operates, and identifying the impact on decision-making. The strongest intervention requires providing direct feedback and personalized explanations of how cognitive illusions affect individual choices, and then providing training to redress errors.[167] The objective of debiasing for the "perfectible" individuals is to offer corrective opportunities to decrease error and enhance the quality of decisions.

Yet, some decision-makers either cannot be educated or are unsuitable for training. Fischhoff reasons these "incorrigible" individuals' judgments cannot be improved even with information, training, and feedback. When faced with this unfortunate situation, he recommends three debiasing techniques. First, he suggests replacing "incorrigible" individuals with those who possess superior cognition or adaptability. Second, he recommends recalibrating the range of potential decisions to reflect that cognitive illusions are influencing the decision matrix. Proper recalibration, however, requires notice of the direction and degree of cognition illusions. Fischhoff's final debiasing technique involves accepting that decisions from these individuals are inherently imprecise. In such a situation, he recommends planning for inevitable error.[168]

Debiasing "faulty decision-makers" also holds promise for investment law. On the theory that policymakers, counsel, arbitrators, and other stakeholders are "perfectible," becoming aware of the cognition literature could, in itself, provide a subtle debiasing mechanism. In theory, when stakeholders can describe cognitive illusions, consider how cognitive illusions may inadvertently affect decisions, and alert themselves of the potential negative effects, they are in a better position to adjust conduct to minimize the risk of error. For those requiring greater intervention, individual assessment and training could decrease negative effects. Unfortunately, there are no cognitive retraining problems currently available in international investment law.

Should investment law stakeholders be deemed "incorrigible," other debiasing strategies would be warranted. Replacement of individuals could be effective. If the Pareto Principle applies and 20% of investment law stakeholders generate 80% of problems,[169] theoretically, strategically replacing the small subset of suboptimal decision-makers with more "perfectible" individuals could minimize error. Arbitrators and other transnational adjudicators might be a group of "incorrigible" decision-makers. Where parties control the appointment process, it would be relatively straightforward to debias effort to eliminate party appointment. Yet as not all parties have the same incentive to avoid appointing incorrigible

[166] Fischhoff, *supra* note 156, at 424–25.

[167] *Id.*

[168] *Id.* at 425–27.

[169] Joseph M. Juran, *The Quality Control Process*, *in* JURAN'S QUALITY HANDBOOK 5.1, 5.20–5.24 (Joseph M. Juran & A. Blanton Godfrey eds., 5th ed. 1999); Ian Ayres, *Regulating Opt-Out: An Economic Theory of Altering Rules*, 121 YALE L.J. 2032, 2050–51 (2012).

arbitrators, there may be value in reforms that reconsider the prominence of party-appointed arbitrators. Relatedly, where institutions direct appointment, within the broader matrix of factors, they might also consider arbitrators' potential susceptibility to cognitive illusions.

Other stakeholders may fall within Fischhoff's "incorrigible" classification, but the implementation of debiasing techniques may prove more challenging. Voters, for example, may elect political officials precisely because they are "incorrigible"; removing elected representatives is antithetical to democratic principles. While counsel could benefit from training and education on cognitive illusions, replacement may be unnecessary. Competition within the marketplace for legal services may weed out individuals overly susceptible to cognitive illusions; but this also requires clients choosing counsel to be aware of cognitive error and to prioritize it in their selection process. Parties to ITA also might be "incorrigible." Investors, for example, may not respond to debiasing, and removing investors may prove problematic in two respects. First, eliminating investors from investment would undermine the purpose of treaties. Second, as the data reflected most investors are not repeat players, attempting to replace investors in ITA (or their individual representatives) has limited value. By contrast, states are repeat players in the negotiation of ITAs and the defense of ITA disputes. States, however, cannot be removed from either treaty negotiating or arbitration defense as their exercise of sovereignty create the very rights at issue; but, presuming the desirability of rationality, there may be value in substituting government officials who are less influenced by cognitive illusions.

3. Mismatched Tasks and Decision-Makers

Fischhoff has a third category of debiasing, focusing on a mismatch between decision-maker and task type that generates decision-making errors. In this context, debiasing requires both providing education and restructuring decision-making tasks.[170] The first element involves using education to decrease the negative externalities of cognitive illusions,[171] using knowledge and repeated experiences to reduce error.[172] While Fischhoff primarily focuses on training to understand probabilistic and computational assessments, he posits experts in other areas can similarly train themselves to decrease the risk of error.[173]

For restructuring, Fischhoff cautions, "the most charitable, and psychological, viewpoint is to point no fingers and blame neither the judge nor the task."[174] These debiasing techniques assume decision-makers have the requisite skills to avoid cognitive illusions but just are not engaging properly. The objective is to construct mechanisms to bridge the gap. Restructuring requires re-engineering decision-making mechanics to make tasks and decision-makers more compatible. For example, tasks might require decision-makers to search for discrepant evidence, rather than collecting details that corroborate a preferred answer. Likewise restructuring may require decision-makers to identify their assumptions expressly (rather than letting them remain "in the head"), to deconstruct a problem into familiar and discrete components, or to use an alternative framework to the problem.[175] These debiasing

---

[170] *Id.* at 427, 430, 438.

[171] Fischhoff, *supra* note 156, at 427.

[172] Kahneman & Klein, *supra* note 32.

[173] Fischhoff, *supra* note 156, at 430.

[174] *Id.* at 427.

[175] *Id.* at 425–27.

techniques re-channel historically path-dependent, and error-prone, cognition by requiring decisions to be conducted in atypical ways.[176] Professor Korobkin similarly recommends reframing problems to imagine how a "disagreeable" adjudicator might resolve disputes and generate new insights.[177] Kahneman advocates taking an "outside view," requiring decision-makers to base assessments and forecasts upon past experiences, probability distributions, and comparisons to existing statistical baselines.[178] The core objective is to impose external information or perspectives to override intuitive decisions, reduce error, and prevent inadvertent use of *post-hoc* justifications for prior intuitive conclusions.

In theory, recalibrating investment law rules or making choices about dispute settlement could prove fruitful. Little, however, is known about how cognitive illusions affect all stakeholders in international investment law. The limited amount that is known, however, demonstrates that cognitive illusions affected the legal decisions of individual arbitrators, rather than how arbitrators interacted in real cases.[179] Attempting recalibration, but without a more systemic understanding of how the cognitive illusions operate and the size of the effects, has an undeniable risk. With better information, a viable option may be adjusting legal rules to remove discretion from poor decision-makers.[180] In any event, stakeholders would be wise to plan for some inevitable error by different stakeholders on core issues including treaty negotiation, dispute outcomes, and cost assessments. Signatories to treaties, parties to disputes, and counsel providing advice should anticipate a degree of imprecision, strategize about how best to prepare for uncertainty, and reduce risk where possible. Should arbitrators or other adjudicators prove "incorrigible," parties may wish to avoid arbitration and craft their own settlements through processes such as mediation. Although a shift from adjudication may only shift the influence of cognitive illusions from arbitrators to parties and counsel, this may be desirable given norms of party control, autonomy, and cost savings.

Addressing mismatches between decisions and decision-makers may prove constructive. Restructuring decision-making, for example, could require decision-makers to use an "outside perspective,"[181] test parties' frames using tribunal-appointed experts with different perspectives,[182] or consider how "disagreeable"[183] arbitrators or policymakers make decisions; this could restructure preliminary conclusions to more fully test the value of choices. Similarly, lawyers counseling

---

[176] *See, e.g.*, Adam S. Zimmerman, *Funding Irrationality*, 59 DUKE L.J. 1105 (2010); *see also* Strong, *supra* note 5, at 552–65 (discussing the challenges of the status quo bias in international arbitration).

[177] Russell Korobkin, *Psychological Impediments to Mediation Success: Theory and Practice*, 21 OHIO ST. J. ON DISP. RESOL. 281, 296 (2006).

[178] Daniel Kahneman & Dan Lovallo, T*imid Choices and Bold Forecasts: A Cognitive Perspective on Risk Taking*, 39 MGMT. SCI. 17, 24–27 (1993); Daniel Kahneman & Amos Tversky, *Intuitive Prediction: Biases and Corrective Procedures*, *in* JUDGMENT UNDER UNCERTAINTY, *supra* note 29, at 414; KAHNEMAN, FAST AND SLOW, *supra* note 29.

[179] There may be distinctions between how cognitive illusions affect individuals and groups. *Supra* note 26.

[180] Hindsight bias might be redressed by adjusting rules, including "[r]aising the standard of persuasion, by requiring 'clear and convincing evidence' for findings that the bias is likely to affect, may undo its impact on judgment." Rachlinski, *supra* note 151, at 606–07.

[181] ROBBENNOLT & STERNLIGHT, *supra* note 25, at 78, 80–82; *see also supra note* 178.

[182] KAHNEMAN, FAST AND SLOW, *supra* note 29.

[183] Korobkin, *supra* note 177.

clients could require and structure counseling to require clients to reassess their claims.[184] Creating and normalizing such an infrastructure, however, may be challenging.

Given various limitations, education may prove the most useful debiasing tools. The most powerful way to debias decisions is "perhaps most straightforwardly, when there are data available that speak to the judgment, they can be obtained and used."[185] For ITA, basic information about dispute resolution and costs will enable stakeholders to make more informed decisions.[186] Despite theoretical interest in exploring how cognitive illusions affect international investment law,[187] there is minimal data to educate, inform, and debias decision-making. This underpins the value of using psychology, debiasing techniques, and education to aid decisions about the future of international investment law and dispute settlement.[188]

C. THE PROMISE AND PERIL OF EMPIRICISM

Experimental data demonstrated that cognitive illusions influenced assessments of international arbitrators. It is likely that cognitive illusions affect other stakeholders, meaning it is vital to consider how to use debiasing tools effectively. For Fischhoff, information about cognitive illusions and education about decision-making tasks are vital tools. Yet education requires more. It requires quality data to inform the conversation. The challenge, however, is how to create, identify, and use quality empirical work for debiasing.[189]

Data, derived from scientifically sound processes, provides an opportunity to debias and inform international investment law. While it may not be possible (or desirable) to wholly eliminate cognitive illusions from international investment law and generate "fully rational" decisions, it is constructive to consider how to benefit from instinct, reduce the negative

---

[184] Linda Babcock et al., *Creating Convergence: Debiasing Biased Litigants*, 22 LAW & SOC. INQUIRY 913 (1997) (discussing debiasing occurred where parties were required to evaluate the weaknesses of their own cases); Gregory Mitchell, *Libertarian Paternalism Is an Oxymoron*, 99 NW. U. L. REV. 1245, 1256 n.40 (2005) ("Asking . . . subjects to consider alternative or opposing arguments . . . has been found to ameliorate the adverse effects of several biases."); Jeffrey J. Rachlinski, *The Uncertain Psychological Case for Paternalism*, 97 NW. U. L. REV. 1165, 1207–11 (2003) (describing methods to reduce bias through "alternative representational structure[s]").

[185] ROBBENNOLT & STERNLIGHT, *supra* note 25, at 78, 80–82.

[186] Jolls et al., *supra* note 31.

[187] Broude, *supra* note 20; Drahozal, *supra* note 19; Elgueta, *supra* note 19; Reed, *supra* note 164; van Aaken, *supra* note 20.

[188] Domestically, legal scholars do not agree psychological insights are worth exploring. Some argue empirical insights are inherently limited, or "behavioral" insights are neither better nor worse than other forms of knowledge. *See, e.g.*, Jonathan Klick & Gregory Mitchell, *Government Regulation of Irrationality: Moral and Cognitive Hazards*, 90 MINN. L. REV. 1620 (2006); Mark Klock, *Contrasting the Art of Economic Science with Pseudo-economic Nonsense*, 37 PEPP. L. REV. 153 (2010); *see also* Richard A. Posner, *Rational Choice, Behavioral Economics, and the Law*, 50 STAN. L. REV. 1551, 1559–75 (1998) (critiquing behavioral theories as "confus[ing] explanation and prediction," lacking "theoretical ambition," and failing to provide a useful and applicable model).

[189] *See* Franck, *supra* note 1 (identifying criteria of quality research, including concerns about populations of interest and sampling, relevancy, multiple forms of validity, reliability, replicability, transparency, and identification of limitations).

externalities, or avoid the powerful pull of intuitive decision-making.[190] While some instincts can be adaptive, when complexity is involved, intuition has a high risk of error or inefficiency.[191] One need only think of debates about "alternative facts" and intuitive assessments articulated on Twitter that demonstrate that intuitive assessments and assertions are problematic. At the core, empirical data can inform a more accurate understanding of international investment law and offer a prophylactic to the negative effects of cognitive illusions.

The modern rhetoric of ITA has become polarized, focusing upon low nuance false dichotomies—whether the "pro-ISDS" versus "anti-ISDS"[192] divide or the "pro state" or "pro investor" debate—and using emotionally evocative characterizations.[193] Rather than appreciating the inevitable complexities of transnational dispute settlement and derivative empirical research, it has become easy to rush to judgment with one's "favorite" piece of research that justifies one's policy preferences.[194] Policymakers should be careful in how they rely on data and how they use data to influence the debate and normative choices, lest the system that we create, in a "hot" cognitive state,[195] be suboptimal and unsustainable for the longer term. Rather, there should be an honest appreciation both for quality data and for the research limitations. Failure to do otherwise creates a risk of implementing normative solutions that overpromise and underperform, possibly leading to disaffection with a purported "cure" that is potentially worse than the original "disease."

This book is premised upon empiricism offering a constructive lens for assessment and debiasing dialogues about international investment law and offering baselines for issues impacting costs. While no empirical research is perfect—just as no form of knowledge is perfect—provided it is methodologically sound ex ante and its limitations are identified, empiricism is preferable to no research at all or the substitution of chance, personal opinion, instinct, political power, or unrepresentative but emotionally "sticky" examples.

Empirical perspectives have valuable aspects. First, they permit the holistic analysis of data, rather than arguably unrepresentative examples that fit neatly into perceived reality and generate cognitive ease. While experiences are hypotheses to be tested, it is preferable to understand whether examples are outliers or typical when making major fiscal choices involving

---

[190] *See* Henry J. Watt, The Sensory Basis and Structure of Knowledge 168 (1925) (noting intuition involves reactions that are "carried forwards by some inborn machinery not the result of learning—in a direction not anticipated or foreseen and without any knowledge of the end of its action.").

[191] *See* Stanovich, *supra* note 48 ("We all have implicit models of behavior that govern our interactions and our thoughts about ourselves and other people. . . . we carry around a ragbag of general principles, homilies and clichés about human behavior that we draw on when we feel we need an explanation. The problem with this commonsense knowledge about behavior is that much of it contradicts itself and is, therefore, unfalsifiable"); *id.* at 29 (discussing "truthiness").

[192] The Kluwer Arbitration Blog has a subdivision of articles called "Anti-ISDS Propaganda". *See* http://arbitrationblog.kluwerarbitration.com/category/anti-isds-propaganda/ (last visited Aug. 7, 2018); Gus Van Harten has a category on his website called "Spin by ISDS promoters." *See* https://gusvanharten.wordpress.com/category/spin-by-isds-promoters/ (last visited Aug. 7, 2018).

[193] *See* Chapter 1.

[194] Chiara Giorgetti, *Is the Truth in the Eyes of the Beholder? The Perils and Benefits of Empirical Research in International Investment Arbitration*, 12 Santa Clara J. Int'l L. 268, 268 (2013).

[195] Shiri Krebs, *The Legalization of Truth in International Fact-Finding*, 18 Chi. J. Int'l L. 83 (2017).

sovereignty. Second, data offers a baseline for testing assumptions. Third, empiricism uses a research loop that first seeks to describe the world, then looks for reliable relationships, before exploring causal links. This systematic approach prevents causal assertions from being generated without verification and aids differentiation between correlation and cause. Fourth, results are subject to verification by others asking the same (or similar) questions using the same (or similar) methodologies. As no single piece of research is perfect, definitive, or irrefutable for all time, empiricism necessitates replication. While there is an inherent inability to make definitive conclusions, this reflects that statistics are probabilistic and social phenomenon can change.[196] Finally, empiricism offers an opportunity to connect choices and data. A healthy appreciation of the value and limitations of research increases the likelihood that choices will achieve desired objectives, or at a minimum, provide an opportunity for managing expectations.

Despite its value, empirical analysis of ITA is not a silver bullet.[197] Stakeholders—whether policymakers, institutions, clients, counsel, or arbitrators—may never read the research or may ignore it. Some may misrepresent or misunderstand the research, while others may prioritize research that accords with their objectives. As reflected by the evisceration of expertise when making international law choices, such as the Brexit vote,[198] even if experts are correct, there is no guarantee the expertise will be properly used, acknowledged, or respected.

Even when experts make predictions, experts who are ideologically bound, or unable to appreciate the nuance of data, may find themselves making predictions that are *less* accurate than random chance. Philip Tetlock's classic research exploring expert political judgments sampled nearly 300 experts from different contexts across the political spectrums and asked for predictions about the future. In twenty years, those predictions were tested against reality. On the whole, the expert judgments were only slightly more accurate than chance alone, and their expert predictions were worse than guesses generated by computer algorithms.[199]

Yet, not all experts were similarly bad. Experts who were amenable to receiving new information and thinking beyond ideological constraints (whom Tetlock called "foxes") were reliably better at making predictions. In contrast, experts who tended to follow reductionist narratives, simple explanations, or ideological party lines (whom Tetlock called "hedgehogs") were comparatively worse at making accurate predictions. The irony is: the hedgehogs who speak forcefully and predict with confidence—even when they are wrong—tend to get the spotlight, garner the attention of new and old media, and are rewarded for outspoken opinions.[200] This means that incorrect knowledge can be transmitted as

---

[196] Franck, *supra* note 1.

[197] Franck, *supra* note 4, at 790.

[198] Griff Witte, *9 out of 10 Experts Agree: Britain Doesn't Trust the Experts on Brexit*, WASH. POST (June 21, 2016), http://wapo.st/28LP3kg (last visited Aug. 7, 2018); *see also* Michael Deacon, *EU Referendum: Who Needs Experts When We've Got Michael Gove?*, THE TELEGRAPH (June 6, 2016), http://bit.ly/28SHYcr (last visited Aug. 7, 2018) (quoting Michael Gove that "'I think people in this country have had enough of experts' and stating "In short: experts schmexperts. What do they know? Follow your heart! Trust your instincts! Believe in Britain!").

[199] Some experts, however, were better than others; those experts who were not wedded to a universal ideology exhibited better judgment. TETLOCK, *supra* note 43.

[200] *See, e.g.*, TETLOCK, *supra* note 43; TETLOCK & GARDNER, *supra* note 43; *see also* ROSLING, *supra* note 42; at 66–68 (discussing how a focus on dramatic extremes by activists and the media prevents a full appreciation of the breath of data).

legitimate information.[201] Put another way, human nature, even with the best of intentions, requires that we be cautious with empirical research. A healthy skepticism and careful inquiry prevents maladaptive, hedgehog-like tendencies seeking to fit research into a grand universal narrative, and generating a risk of being intuitive, ideological, or wrong.[202] The better course is to be careful, skeptical, and reduce error for matters that are of practical, political, and policy importance.

Like any other scientific endeavor, when data evolves, policy and debate about that data should evolve as well. The job of good consumers of empirical work—and not just the producers—is to scrutinize the work, differentiate between quality work and other material, understand limitations and risk of error, and appreciate the relative value of evidence-based normative choices. While we can never eliminate all error from knowledge acquisition, empiricism makes it possible to increase confidence in results through replication over time. This book is therefore only a starting point for testing assumptions, analyzing conventional wisdom, and preventing cognitive illusions from improperly influencing the development of international investment law dispute resolution and ITA costs.

---

[201] Earl Babbie, The Basics of Social Research 7–8 (4th ed. 2008); Chabris & Simons, *supra* note 45, at 95–115.

[202] Gary Saul Morson & Morton Schapiro, Cents and Sensibility: What Economics Can Learn from the Humanities 391 (2017) ("Foxy approaches are far less sexy, but they are more likely to be right."); *see also* Robert A. Burton, On Being Certain: Believing You Are Right Even When You Are Not 8–13, 223–24 (2009) (identifying how cognitive processes facilitate and encourage people to "tolerate the unpleasantness of uncertainty").

3 Introduction to the Data and Basic Demographics

UNDERSTANDING EMPIRICAL ANALYSIS may not come naturally to international law scholars, practitioners, arbitrators, and stakeholders. Yet data is fundamental to disrupting cognitive illusions. This chapter therefore has an unenviable task: namely it must orient readers to the data to aid understanding of the potential value (and risks) of derivative inferences. To aid information accessibility and ensure requisite scientific integrity and rigor, Appendices (including online materials) offer core methodological information.[1] As that material underlies information within this book, readers are presumed to be familiar with those extensive and transparently described methodological choices, which set the stage for the data and analyses.

This chapter has two objectives to contextualize data and cost-related variables at the heart of this book. Initially, it demarcates among data from complete cases, individual awards, and separate opinions. It does so largely because costs—within a single case—could be assessed in multiple awards. Separate opinions are discussed, as subsequent chapters explore their cost implications. Second, the chapter focuses on core descriptive aspects, both to identify what have been paradigmatic characteristics of ITA disputes and to set the stage for mapping ITA costs. It focuses on party identity—including investors (one of the most under-explored

[1] Readers are particularly encouraged to review Appendix I. Appendix I offers detailed information about awards analyzed, methodology, coding and transformation protocols, and underlying statistical analyses. Whenever readers have questions as to why descriptive or inferential tests were used, Appendix I offers the general background to social science protocols and the selection of appropriate tests. Whenever readers wish to understand in more detail how a variable was coded or how concepts were operationalized, Appendix IV (online) contains the Codebook, which provides detailed explanations of coding protocols and choices related to the variables analyzed in this book or otherwise contained in the dataset (online Appendix V).

actors of ITA) and state identity—before moving to other stakeholders, including non-disputing parties (NDPs) and counsel. It then offers core information about industries and institutions administering ITA cases.

I. Cases, Final Awards, and Separate Opinions

As the research was designed to focus upon costs and cost-shifting, awards were the core unit of analysis. Although a dispute's life cycle can involve post-award review, court enforcement, award negotiation, and compliance, data on these topics are more sporadic and subject to case selection bias. This research therefore focused on first-instance decision-making. Yet, a dispute could generate decisions through several dispositive awards, meaning data on individual disputes was inevitably nested. The next section explores alternative analytical frames, namely: cases (disputes spawning multiple awards), final awards (cases finally resolving ITA claims), and separate opinions.

A. CASES

A "case" was defined as a dispute submitted to arbitration that spawned at least one award, whether the decision was final or not. Filed cases that did not spawn a public award (i.e., the tribunal was never empaneled, the case terminated, public activity involved only a preliminary order, or awards remained private) were not coded. In total, the research analyzed 202 different cases, generating 272 different awards from awards made public by 2012.

Like previous research, the majority of cases (73.8%; $n = 149$) resulted in a single award. The remaining cases (26.2%; $n = 53$) generated multiple awards, most of which ($n = 48$) generated two awards. For the remaining cases with multiple awards, only four cases spawned three awards, and a solitary early NAFTA case spawned four separate awards on jurisdiction, merits, damages, and costs).

B. FINAL AWARDS

Some research on ITA has focused purely on ITA's jurisdictional awards,[2] whereas others focus exclusively on final awards.[3] A more balanced approach requires appreciation of both frames, namely understanding the entire body and which issues tribunals addressed in final outcomes. The next section identifies the awards finally resolving a treaty-based claim and explores when they became final to enable identification of when tribunals assessed costs.

More than 75% of all cases ($n = 159$) resulted in an award finally resolving treaty claims, nearly a 300% expansion compared to earlier costs research. For final awards, disputes became final during different phases. Final awards did not collapse neatly into categories where disputes were final after purely resolving either "jurisdiction" or the "merits." Rather, final awards addressed a range of substantive issues. *See* Figure 3.1.

---

[2] Kathleen S. McArthur & Pablo A. Ormachea, *International Investor-State Arbitration: An Empirical Analysis of ICSID Decisions on Jurisdiction*, 28 Rev. Lit. 559 (2009); Gus Van Harten, *Arbitrator Behaviour in Asymmetrical Adjudication: An Empirical Study of Investment Treaty Arbitration*, 50 Osgoode Hall L.J. 211 (2012).

[3] Daphna Kapeliuk, *The Repeat Appointment Factor: Exploring Decision Patterns of Elite Investment Arbitrators*, 96 Cornell L. Rev. 47 (2010).

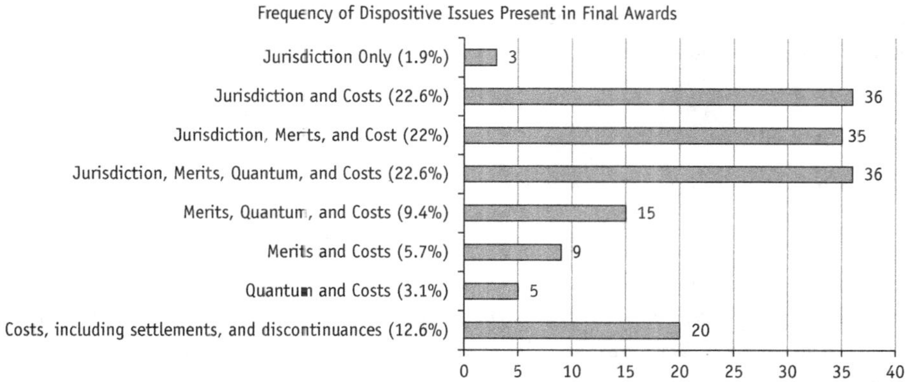

FIGURE 3.1 Bar Chart—Frequency of Dispositive Issues Present in Awards Finally Resolving ITA Cases ($n = 159$).

Three awards finally adjudicated treaty claims after addressing only jurisdiction but then proceeded under a different jurisdictional basis, such as in *CSOB v. Slovak Republic*, without addressing ITA costs.[4] Thirty-six cases were final after awards addressing jurisdiction and costs; thirty-five cases were final after addressing jurisdiction, merits, and costs; thirty-six cases were final after addressing the full range of jurisdiction, merits, damages, and costs; nine cases were final after assessing the merits and costs; fifteen cases were final after addressing merits, damages, and costs; five cases were final after assessing damages and costs; and twenty cases were final in awards addressing costs. Of those last twenty cases, six involved disputes where there had been an earlier substantive decision to resolve the case in either party's favor, eight embodied parties' settlement agreements, three were discontinuances for nonpayment, and three were discontinuances in softwood lumber disputes for withdrawn claims.[5]

The data suggest tribunals exhibited certain patterns when resolving disputes. First, tribunals tended to resolve cases in a single award, often at jurisdiction. Second, tribunals were willing to bifurcate proceedings to separately address issues of jurisdiction and merits and/or damages. Although this trend was more visually prevalent in earlier cases, tribunals throughout the dataset bifurcated, and it was not possible to identify any meaningful difference across time.[6] Third, there was a small but disfavored micro-trend whereby tribunals

---

[4] Československá Obchodní Banka, a.s. v. Slovak Republic, ICSID Case No. ARB/97/4, Decision of the Tribunal on Objections to Jurisdiction (May 24,1999), 14 ICSID REV.-FOREIGN INV. L.J. 251 (1999).

[5] Two of these cases, *Canfor v. United States* and *Terminal Forest v. United States*, involved the investors' withdrawal of claims upon implementation of the Canada-U.S. Softwood Lumber Agreement. In contrast, *Tembec v. United States*, involved a withdrawal on the eve of jurisdictional hearings and protracted submissions involving costs. *See* John Crook, *NAFTA Panel Awards Costs to United States in Termination of Softwood Lumber Claim*, 101 AM. J. INT'L L. 897 (2007).

[6] When looking for a reliable mean difference between bifurcated and non-bifurcated final cases, it was not possible to detect a reliable difference in the year filed ($t\,(157) = -0.075; p = .94; r = .01; n = 159$) or year award rendered ($t\,(157) = 0.302; p = .76; r = .02; n = 159$). Similarly, when looking for a reliable median difference related to bifurcation, it was not possible to detect a meaningful pattern for year filed ($U = 2496.5; p = .22$) or year of the award ($U = 2722.5; p = .68$). In theory, these analyses were underpowered, but as effect sizes were

separated damages from the remainder of the dispute.[7] Ultimately, tribunals' dominant approach was to either generate a single award or have a single bifurcation.

C. SEPARATE OPINIONS

Arbitrators' separate opinions, particularly dissents, are an area of debate.[8] Alan Redfern argued that dissents are dangerous and "the time has perhaps come to enquire whether the present leniency towards dissenting opinions, however offensive they may be, has gone too far."[9] There is concern that the availability of a dissent (or some separate opinion) may be used by party-appointed arbitrators who feel pressured to express support for an appointing party.[10] The use of separate opinions, however, is nuanced. Separate opinions can have elements both of agreement and disagreement in reasoning, issues, and/or outcomes. Placing separate opinions in a broader context is therefore constructive.

Some research analyzed ITA dissents but not necessarily with a precise ex ante definition of a dissent or other times without a holistic assessment of potential separate opinions. Professor Kapeliuk thoughtfully studied tribunal voting patterns and dissents in ITA. She delineated critical variables, including repeat arbitrators and newcomers, but failed to define how she measured the presence of a dissent.[11] In contrast, van den Berg's empirical research recognizes distinctions between dissents and concurrences, but without defining other separate opinions, defined a "dissent" as a separate opinion involving a "disagreement on the dispositive outcome of the majority holding," and explained a disagreement on reasoning was not a "dissent." Van den Berg provided a useful annex revealing his assessments of which opinions were "dissents." While the view of an esteemed arbitrator provides a useful baseline for operationalizing "dissent," it did not ex ante identify which elements conclusively define a dissent or dissent subcategories. A reverse engineering of coding choices suggests that a "dispositive" issue could relate to: any sub-element of jurisdiction, whether *ratione personae, materiae,* or *temporis*; any substantive claim under a treaty, whether expropriation, discrimination, MFN, FPS, FET, umbrella clause claims or similar; any head of damage or damage calculations; any decision on costs, whether the parties' legal costs, the tribunal costs, or cost-shifting assessments; or any element of an interest assessment, whether pre-award interest,

---

close to zero, the issue may not be statistical power. In an abundance of caution, over 700 final awards would be required to definitively exclude the possibility of a meaningful change in tribunals' approach to bifurcation over time. For questions about statistical tests used and coding protocols, readers are reminded to review Appendices I and IV. *See supra* note 1.

[7] Although there was a facial increase in awards only addressing costs, this was a function of the awards reflecting parties' settlements and discontinuances. In G1 research, only four cases involved pure cost assessments.

[8] Albert Jan van den Berg, *Dissenting Opinions by Party-Appointed Arbitrators in Investment Arbitration, in* LOOKING TO THE FUTURE: ESSAYS ON INTERNATIONAL LAW IN HONOR OF W. MICHAEL REISMAN 822, 837–43 (Mahnoush Arsanjani et al., eds., 2011); Domenico Di Pietro, *The Controversial Role of Dissenting Opinions in International Arbitral Awards*, TRANSNATIONAL NOTES (Oct. 24, 2011), https://bit.ly/2GEhnFn (last visited Dec. 23, 2018).

[9] Alan Redfern, *Dangerous Dissents*, 71 ARBITRATION 200, 207–08, 210 (2005).

[10] Kapeliuk, *supra* note 3, at 309.

[11] *Id.* at 300–02.

post-award interest, or interest on costs. Such an ex ante definition would be doctrinally sound, more useful than no definition, and preferable to an impressionistic gestalt.

To be more inclusive of opinion type and not limit exploration of opinions to specific appointment types, this research defined a "Separate Opinions" as any arbitrator's opinion that was separate from the dispositive decision. One variable coded a "separate opinion" irrespective of substantive content. A second variable identified the option using the arbitrator's own description, including: no description, dissent, concurring, or dissenting and concurring. A third variable classified the type of a second opinion (if any) using a second arbitrator. While these variables create clear categories, the measurement relies upon arbitrators' characterization. Future research may consider recoding this data to use theoretically sound categories, perhaps using van den Berg's re-engineered definitions or consider assessing the degree of disagreement.

The overwhelming majority of awards (80.1%; $n = 218$) did *not* contain a separate opinion. Roughly 20% of awards (19.9%; $n = 54$) contained at least one separate opinion. When compared to rates of separate opinions rendered by other international law tribunals or U.S. courts, separate opinions in ITA were not comparatively large.

Other international courts and tribunals have had higher rates of separate opinions. Chilton and Tingley's classic research on separate opinions—in concurrences or dissents—in international adjudicative bodies provides useful comparisons. Their research revealed the European Court of Justice never delivered a unanimous opinion. The ICJ had separate opinions in 95% of contentious cases. The European Court of Human Rights rendered separate opinions in 53% of cases. The Iran-U.S. Claims Tribunal had separate opinions in 23% of cases. The WTO was the only international tribunal with lower rates, namely separate opinions in 5% of cases.[12] Put another way, separate opinions in ITA were somewhat more prevalent than in trade disputes but more like other investment disputes involving states. The rate of separate opinions was also not dissimilar to U.S. courts. Rates of separate opinions in ITA were lower than the 70% of separate opinions issued by the U.S. Supreme Court, and the dissent rate at the U.S. Supreme Court has been around 62%.[13] U.S. appellate courts, by contrast, had slightly lower levels of separate opinions, with roughly 16% of cases containing separate opinions and a dissent rate of less than 8%.[14] In other words, ITA rates of separate opinions are not necessarily dissimilar from other forms of adjudication.

With 20% of cases containing a separate opinion, the question remains about the content of those opinions. Most separate opinions were labeled as dissents (59.2%; $n = 32$); But another major group refused to label the separate opinion or classify its content (29.6%; $n = 16$). For the remaining opinions, three arbitrators labeled their opinion as a "dissent and concurrence" (5.6%), and three were pure concurrences (5.6%). An fraction of awards had

[12] Adam Chilton & Dustin Tingley, *The Doctrinal Paradox and International Law*, 34 U. Pa. J. Int'l L. 67, 99–103 (2012). Although they claimed 7% of ICSID cases contain separate opinions, Chilton and Tingley neither identified their coding methodology nor evaluated non-ICSID ITA cases. *Id.* at 100-01.

[13] Lee Epstein, William M. Landes & Richard A. Posner, *Why (and When) Judges Dissent: A Theoretical and Empirical Analysis*, 3 J. Legal Analysis 101, 102 n.4, 106 n.9 (2011).

[14] *Id.* at 99–109.

two separate opinions (1.8%; $n = 5$). Of that group, one opinion was labeled as a dissent, two were concurrences, one was dissenting and concurring, and the remaining opinion in *American Manufacturing v. Zaire* was unclassified.[15] In other words, the dominant use of separate opinions was to express substantive disagreement with colleagues, and the minority trend involved concurrences with alternative reasoning.

U.S. empirical scholars have explored judicial "dissent aversion." Their empirical models identified self-interested behavior where: judges dissent less when dockets are heavy, dissents were linked with judicial ideology, and dissents increased collegiality costs by increasing decision-making length and making adjudicative work more difficult.[16] It could be constructive to consider whether arbitrators exhibited meaningfully different patterns than judges, particularly given normative debates about using adjudication to resolve investment disputes. Likewise, it may be useful to explore whether arbitrators focused on substantive legal issues or matters involving discretion (such as costs) when making separate opinions.

II. Party Demographics: Investors

When this research was initiated, there was minimal reliable information about which investors initiated ITA.[17] Yet investors are the actors initiating ITA.[18] Unfortunately, ICSID does not provide information on investor nationality or distinguishing characteristics, such

---

[15] American Mfg. & Trading, Inc. v. Republic of Zaire, ICSID Case No. ARB/93/1, Statement of Individual Opinion and Declaration (Feb. 10, 1997), 36 I.L.M. 1534 (1997).

[16] Nuno Garoupa & Tom Ginsburg, *Building Reputation in Constitutional Courts: Political and Judicial Audiences*, 28 ARIZ. J. INT'L & COMP. L. 539 (2011); Dennis Te-chung Tang, *Dafaguanjieshi Butongyijian de Shizhengyanjiu* [An Empirical Study of Separate Opinions in the Council of Grand Justices of Taiwan], *in* QUANLIFENLI XINLUN: JUANER. WEIXIANSHENCHA YU DONGTAIPINGHENG [Separation of Powers Revisited: Volume II. Constitutional Review and Dynamic Balance] 427–89 (3d ed. 2005). There is a rich domestic literature discussing the value of dissenting opinions. Antonin Scalia, *Remarks on Dissenting Opinions*, *in* L'OPINIONE DISSENZIENTE 411 (Adele Anzon ed., 1995); William J. Brennan, *In Defense of Dissents*, 37 HASTINGS L.J. 427 (1986); Ruth Bader Ginsburg, *Remarks on Writing Separately*, 65 WASH. L. REV. 133 (1990); Ruth Bader Ginsburg, *The Role of Dissenting Opinions*, 95 MINN. L. REV. 1 (2010).

[17] *See, e.g.*, Susan D. Franck, *The Promise and Peril of Empiricism and International Investment Law Disputes*, *in* CAMBRIDGE COMPENDIUM OF INTERNATIONAL COMMERCIAL AND INVESTMENT ARBITRATION (Andrea Bjorklund et al., eds., forthcoming 2019)] (discussing how some recent research has attempted to measure investor identity, with varying levels of success); *compare* Daniel Behn, *Legitimacy, Evolution, and Growth in Investment Treaty Arbitration: Empirically Evaluating the State-of-the-Art*, 46 GEO. J. INT'L L. 363, 383–88 (2015); Scott Miller & Gregory N. Hicks, *Investor-State Dispute Settlement: A Reality Check*, CENTER FOR STRATEGIC & INTERNATIONAL STUDIES 10–11 (Jan. 2015), https://bit.ly/2VcjMdr (last visited Dec. 25, 2018).

[18] Although states can theoretically initiate arbitration against another state under an investment treaty, there is limited evidence that this occurs, arguably reflecting an "unusual" choice according to some commentators. Luke Eric Peterson, *Ecuador Initiates Unusual State-to-State Arbitration Against United States in Bid to Clarify Scope of Investment Treaty Arbitration*, INV. ARBITRATION REPORTER (July 4, 2011), https://bit.ly/2vqvYw3 (last visited Aug. 7, 2018); *see also* KENNETH J. VANDEVELDE, BILATERAL INVESTMENT TREATIES: HISTORY POLICY, AND INTERPRETATION 499 (2010).

as firm size or type.[19] UNCTAD publishes some information on investor nationality.[20] Meanwhile, without explaining their unit of analysis or methodology, others have stated that, "[t]he proportion of cases filed against G8 countries is 1.4 per cent, all of which have been filed by US investors. . . . Twenty per cent of ICSID cases are brought by companies that rank within the top 500 globally, seven of these companies have revenues that exceed the GDP of the country they are bringing a case against."[21] These omissions necessitate a careful examination of investors and claimed nationality. The confusion about investor identity reminds one of Paul Newman's oft-repeated question in *Butch Cassidy and the Sundance Kid* about their relentless pursuers, namely: "Who are those guys?"

There is, unfortunately, no preexisting established scale to classify investor identity. Recognizing that any single measure is limited and that best practice requires assessment of multiple measures when analyzing an untested phenomenon, this research explored investor identity using multiple measures. First, it examined the total number of investors bringing claims, irrespective of whether they were foreign or locally incorporated. Second, it identified investors' nationality and development status of investors' claimed origin.[22] Given the dominance of investors from High Income states, the research further analyzes investor background exploring whether cases involved: humans, corporations, or a combination thereof; privately held or publicly listed entities; or involved at least one commercial entity classified as a leading multinational enterprise according to the *Financial Times 500*.

A. NUMBER OF INVESTORS

There is minimal research on number of investors bringing ITA claims. Previous research suggested the average number of investors in a case was 1.3, usually not more than five investors in a single case.[23] Although the average number of investors was relatively stable,[24] the data reflected a small subset of mass claims.

For the 202 cases analyzed, there were 180,893 named claimants, including the investors from *Abaclat v. Argentina*.[25] The median number of investors in a case was one. The average

---

[19] International Centre for Settlement of Investment Disputes [ICSID] Secretariat, *The ICSID Caseload–Statistics, Issue 2012-1*, 3–4 (Feb. 7, 2012), https://bit.ly/2ttZlMS (last visited Aug. 7, 2018). ICSID released some clustered information involving the European Union. ICSID Secretariat, *The ICSID Caseload–Statistics (Special Focus—European Union)*, 11 (Mar. 1, 2014), https://bit.ly/2vt4qWC (last visited Aug. 7, 2018).

[20] UNCTAD's Issues Notes did not analyze investor nationality but provided Annexes sometimes reporting an investor's home country. *See* UNCTAD, IIA Issues Note: Latest Developments in Investor-State Dispute Settlement No. 1 Annex (Apr. 2012) [hereinafter UNCTAD, 2012 Issues Note].

[21] *The International Center for the Settlement of Investment Disputes (ICSID)*, Bretton Woods Project (July 10, 2009), http://bit.ly/1Az6fNA (last visited Aug. 7, 2018).

[22] The research used a case's first award to assess named claimants and to avoid omitting claimants who were potentially dismissed.

[23] Susan D. Franck, *Empirically Evaluating Claims About Investment Treaty Arbitration*, 86 N.C. L. Rev. 1, 36 (2007).

[24] *See infra* note 30.

[25] Locally incorporated companies not listed as formal claimants were not analyzed. Codebook protocols meant the figure includes the total number of investors identified in awards, such as *Abaclat*. Abaclat v. Argentine Republic, ICSID Case No. ARB/07/5, Decision on Jurisdiction and Admissibility, 10 (Aug. 4, 2011), https://bit.ly/2C1a489 (last visited Aug. 7, 2018).

number of investors in a case was 896, largely because the broad standard deviation[26] from a few cases with a large number of investors, such as *Abaclat*, skewed the mean.

Most typically, cases had one ($n = 140$), two ($n = 33$), three ($n = 14$), or a maximum of four ($n = 4$) investors, which accounted for 94.6% of the caseload. Fewer than 5% of cases had over five claimants. At the other end of the spectrum, some cases had a large number of investors. Six cases had over ten investors, namely *Abaclat* (180,285 investors), *Alasdair Ross Anderson v. Costa Rica* (137 investors), *Canadian Cattlemen for Fair Trade v. United States* (one named investor comprising 109 individuals), *Bayview v. Mexico* (forty-six investors), *Funnekotter v. Zimbabwe* (thirteen investors), and *Foresti v. South Africa* (eleven investors).[27] Two other cases, *Mobil v. Venezuela* and *Renta 4 v. Russian Federation*, had either six or seven investors.[28] The phenomenon of a large number of investors within a single proceeding was unusual, but not irrelevant. Filing mass claims was not a recent evolution. Every case with ten or more investors was filed between 2002 and 2006. Nevertheless, the jurisdictional flexibility granted from *Abaclat* provides a potential path for expanding this micro-trend.

B. INVESTOR NATIONALITY

There is minimal research on investor nationality. Earlier research identified that of 175 states signing investment treaties, investors came from twenty-three different countries, predominantly from developed states.[29] This analysis expands upon those findings by: providing general information on investors' claimed nationality, exploring investors' development status, and offering a context for the data.[30]

Overall, there were investors from twenty-three different countries, and investors overwhelmingly hailed from developed economies. Like earlier research, the largest number of investors came from the United States, explaining why treaties involving the United States were the most frequently arbitrated. The next largest group of investors were from North America and Western Europe, particularly Canada, the Netherlands, Italy, the United Kingdom, Germany, Spain, France, Belgium, Sweden, and Greece. Russian investors were also relatively prevalent. Investors from other regions, such as Latin America and Asia, occurred in smaller proportions.[31]

---

[26] *SD* = 12,684.

[27] *Abaclat, supra* note 25; Alasdair Ross Anderson v. Republic of Costa Rica, ICSID Case No. ARB(AF)/07/3, Award (May 19, 2010), https://bit.ly/2sBCZYS (last visited Dec. 27, 2018); Canadian Cattlemen for Fair Trade v. United States, UNCITRAL, Award on Jurisdiction (Jan. 28, 2008), https://bit.ly/2R1f7rH (last visited Dec. 27, 2018); Bayview Irrigation Dist. v. United Mexican States, ICSID Case No. ARB(AF)/05/1, Award (Jun. 19, 2007), 19 World Trade & Arb. Materials 1 (2007); Bernardus Funnekotter v. Republic of Zimbabwe, ICSID Case No. ARB/05/6, Award (Apr. 22, 2009), 21 World Trade & Arb. Materials 1019 (2009); Foresti v. Republic of S. Afr., ICSID Case No. ARB(AF)07/01, Award (Aug. 4, 2010), https://bit.ly/2EWJOMi (last visited Dec. 27, 2018).

[28] Mobil Corp. v. Bolivarian Republic of Venez., ICSID Case No. ARB/07/27, Decision on Jurisdiction (June 10, 2010), 22 World Trade & Arb. Materials 999 (2010); Renta 4 v. Russian Fed'n, SCC No. 24/2007, Award on Preliminary Objections (Mar. 20, 2009), https://bit.ly/2wEhE1h (last visited Dec. 27, 2018).

[29] Franck, *supra* note 23, at 27, 29.

[30] As most cases had fewer than five investors, the research focused upon the first five named investors. When focusing on the first five named investors, the research coded 318 investors in the 202 cases, generating a mean number of 1.4 investors and a median number of one investor per case. Appendix III.

[31] *See* Appendix III.

The dominance of investors from economically developed states becomes starker when framed against other established metrics, namely: whether the investor was from an OECD (Organisation for Economic Co-operation and Development) state, how the World Bank classified the investor's home state, and how the U.N. Development Programme (UNDP) Human Development Index scored the state of investors' claimed nationality. Using OECD status, 88.4% (n = 281) of all investors were from OECD states. Only 11.6% (n = 37) of investors were from non-OECD states. A limited number of cases involved investors from both OECD and non-OECD states.[32] World Bank classifications revealed investors typically came from developed states, with the overwhelming majority of investors coming from High Income states (90.57%; n = 288). There were a minimal number from either Upper-Middle (8.17%; n = 26) and Lower-Middle (1.26%; n = 4) Income states. There were no investors from Low Income states in the dataset.[33] *See* Figure 3.2. The World Bank measurement revealed a minimal number of cases where developing world investors were local partners of investors from High Income states.[34]

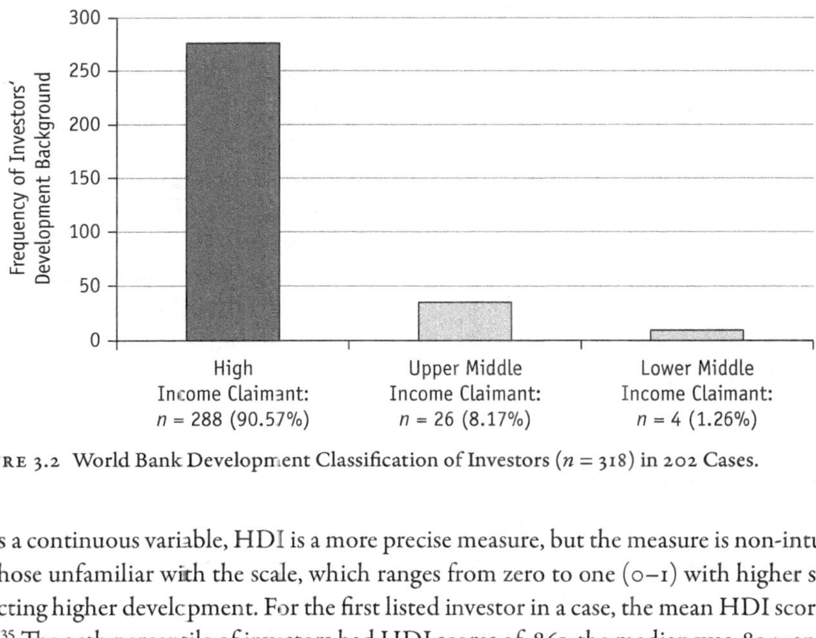

FIGURE 3.2 World Bank Development Classification of Investors (n = 318) in 202 Cases.

As a continuous variable, HDI is a more precise measure, but the measure is non-intuitive for those unfamiliar with the scale, which ranges from zero to one (0–1) with higher scores reflecting higher development. For the first listed investor in a case, the mean HDI score was .872.[35] The 25th percentile of investors had HDI scores of .861, the median was .894, and the

[32] The relevant cases were *EP America v. Argentina* (one U.S. investor and three Argentine claimants), *AIG v. Kazakhstan* (one U.S. investor and one Kazak investor), and *Millicom v. Senegal* (one investor from the Netherlands and one from Senegal).

[33] *Millicom v. Senegal* and *Goetz v. Burundi* were the only cases where investors were nationals of states classified by the U.N. as a Least Developed Country (LDC).

[34] The only additional case was *Gemplus v. Mexico*, with two French investors and one local Mexican investor (i.e., Mexico was an OECD, Upper-Middle income state).

[35] n = 202; SD = .050. The mean HDI for the first investor was similar to the second (M = .848; SD = .135; n = 51), third (M = .881; SD = .057; n = 29), fourth (M = .887; SD = .034; n = 15), and fifth (M = .801; SD = .268; n = 11) listed investors.

75th percentile was .904. To contextualize that result, even at the 25th percentile of claims brought by investors from the least developed states, UNDP reports reflect that those scores mean that investors came from countries with "very high human development," sometimes within the top twenty-eight most developed countries in the world.[36]

C. INVESTOR TYPOLOGIES

There is minimal data about the nature and size of the investors in ITA, which makes it a source of speculation. Historically, the OECD conducted research on investor identity in ninety-five cases. They determined that roughly one-third of cases contained no information on investors. They nevertheless made three findings based upon their data. First, they identified that, "[f]ar from supporting the view that smaller claimants are excluded" from ITA, 22% of claimants were either individuals or small corporations with limited foreign operations. Second, medium and large multinational enterprises were involved with roughly half the cases. Third, extremely large multinational corporations accounted for less than 10% of the cases.[37] While difficult to assess the utility of derivative inferences,[38] it provides a baseline for exploring investor identity.

As a preliminary matter—given the lack of established scales tied to historically tried and tested variables—this research is inevitably exploratory, and other researchers presuming to analyze investor identity must acknowledge that core limitation of the lack of ex ante tried and tested definitions. This research makes the choice, rather than operating in an information vacuum, to rely on publicly available data to generate three variables to offer proxies for investor identity. The first subsection analyzes named investors using a blunt three-category variable for investor identity. It then evaluates whether the named corporate entities were private entities or related to a publicly traded corporation. Third, it explored whether claimants were from large—presumably powerful—multinational corporations, by identifying whether at least one claimant (or a parent) was listed as a *Financial Times* 500 entity.

1. Investors: Corporations, People, or Both?

Claimants were first analyzed to assess whether, claiming investors were: individuals, corporations, or a combination thereof. The vast majority of investors bringing ITA claims were corporate entities. In contrast, 11.4% of cases[39] involved claims brought solely by private individuals. A combination of at least one human and a corporate entity initiated 7.4%[40] of

[36] U.N. Dev. Programme, Human Development Report 2013, The Rise of the South: Human Progress in a Diverse World, 144 (2013), http://bit.ly/1jtTjS6 (last visited Aug. 7, 2018).

[37] Org. for Econ. Co-operation & Dev., Government Perspectives on Investor-State Dispute Settlement: A Progress Report (Dec. 14, 2012), http://bit.ly/19H3Elf (last visited Aug. 7, 2018) [hereinafter OECD, *Progress Report*].

[38] The OECD failed to define "very small," "small," "medium," or "large" investors and multinational enterprises. They did, however, explain "extremely large multinationals" derived from UNCTAD's top list of 100 multinational enterprises. *Id.* at 7.

[39] $n = 23$.

[40] $n = 15$.

cases, meaning people were involved in some way in roughly 19% of the caseload. This was similar to the OECD's finding that around 20% of the cases involved individuals or smaller claimants. The vast majority of cases[41] involved claimants that were exclusively corporate entities. This is initial evidence that corporate investors, potentially larger and with more resources than individuals, dominated ITA. Yet cases involving individuals were a notable subcomponent.

2. Investors: Privately Owned or Publicly Traded?

Another way to explore investor identity is whether a publicly traded corporation was involved. Given the administrative complexity and scrutiny of public listings, smaller businesses may prefer to remain privately held, whereas larger businesses may be willing to incur the costs associated with public listing. Assessing the involvement of a publicly listed corporation is an imperfect, but intriguing, proxy for investor size and relative economic strength.[42] Data from Bloomberg, government listings, and other websites identified whether any of the first five investors were: publicly traded or otherwise listed on any worldwide stock exchange, privately held, or people.[43] To assess whether ITA is used to " 'protect from regulation the assets of multinational firms,' "[44] the hypothesis was that publicly listed firms would dominate ITA cases.

Like the missing data in the OECD's analysis, there was no data on investor identity in roughly 15% of cases.[45] Visual assessment of cases without data suggested the entities were likely privately held, possibly small-to-medium sized businesses, which had a narrow commercial focus. Unlike cases involving corporations such as IBM, UPS, or Chevron, the cases with missing data involved disputes such as: *Bogdanov v. Moldova, Bayview v. Mexico, Europe Cement v. Turkey, Fedax v. Venezuela, HICEE v. Slovakia, Tokeles v. Ukraine,* and *Wena Hotels v. Egypt*. This suggests that privately held, arguably smaller, investors were potentially under-represented in this initial analysis.

The data cast doubt on assertions that large publicly traded entities dominated the investors bringing claims. For the 172 cases with data, only 29.7% (n = 51) contained at least one publicly traded investor. Cases where the named investors were publicly listed at the time of the award included *Waste Management v. Mexico, Siemens v. Argentina, AES v. Argentina, Mytilineos Holdings v. Serbia, OKO v. Estonia, Occidental v. Ecuador, Glamis*

41 81.2%; n = 164.

42 Other ways to capture investor size were considered, including annual revenues to determine investor size and capitalization, as more than 75% of cases lacked investor revenue data.

43 For this definition, cases where investors were in bankruptcy or had administrators in bankruptcy, were classified as privately held. The only two cases where investors fell within this category were *Enron v. Argentina* and *Inmaris v. Ukraine*. *Walter Bau v. Thailand*, which involved an investor in bankruptcy, was classified through the original entity rather than the administrator.

44 Pratap Chatterjee, *Global Ambulance Chasers: Lawyers Profit from Suing States for Multinationals*, CorpWatch Blog (Dec. 17, 2012), http://bit.ly/296qddV (last accessed Aug. 7, 2018) (quoting Gus van Harten).

45 This figure made up 14.9% of the 202 cases (n = 30). Those cases were similar to others as they spanned a similar time frame, had roughly equivalent distributions of party nationality, and finished in similar amounts of time.

Gold v. United States, Mobil v. Venezuela, and *GEA v. Ukraine*.[46] The results provided an initial piece of evidence suggesting larger corporate investors were a critical subgroup—but not the core—in ITA.

Rather, 70% (n = 121) of cases involved private investors, human beings, or a combination thereof. Of this subgroup, most cases involved investors that were privately owned (50.6%; n = 87); but a small fraction (6.4%; n = 11) involved claimants that were people and private companies; and the remainder (11.4%; n = 23) were cases initiated exclusively by people. *See* Figure 3.3. The finding that approximately 43% of investors were privately held was vaguely akin to the OECD assessment that "medium and large" enterprises accounted for "about half" of cases.

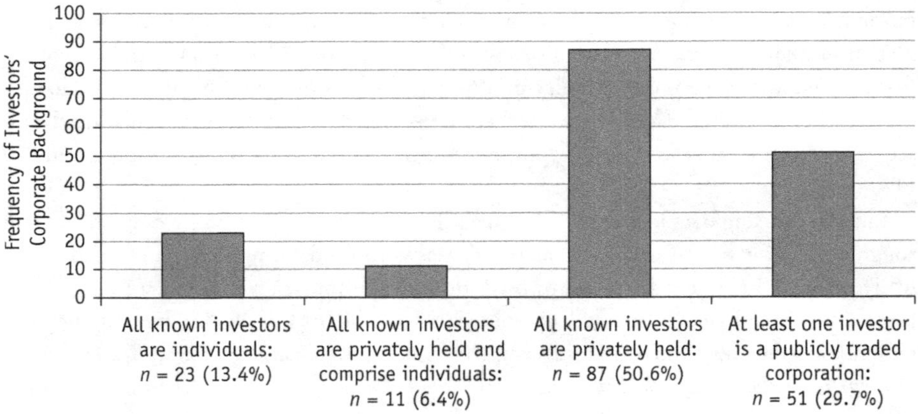

FIGURE 3.3 Frequency of Named Investors' Corporate Identity in Cases (n = 172).

Some private companies could be "large" or "medium" corporations. Although arguably atypical, Cargill and Vattenfall were large (but privately held) corporations. Private entities could run the gamut from large, medium, or small investors. Some private investors either functioned similarly to publicly listed corporations and others were indirectly related to publicly listed companies.[47]

Given the dominance of private investors, it is useful to reconsider the classification using a lens considering a broader corporate chain (and ignoring people), focusing on whether investors, a direct parent, or an entity in the corporate chain was publicly listed. Approximately half of the cases contained at least one investor linked to a publicly listed

---

[46] In *Enron v. Argentina*, the claimant was not classified as a publicly listed corporation, as it was de-registered by 2002. Although Enron acquired Azurix in 2001, data on public or private ownership was unavailable for *Azurix v. Argentina*.

[47] The investor in *Cargill v. Mexico* was a large privately held multinational. *IBM v. Ecuador* involved a private subsidiary of a publicly held corporation. *Occidental v. Ecuador* involved the private subsidiary of a publicly held corporation. *Saluka v. Czech Republic* involved an investor owned by a public traded holding company. *Murphy Exploration v. Ecuador* involved an investor owned by a publicly traded company. *See* Appendix V.

company. Generally, publicly listed corporations were the named claimants. It was less frequent for publicly listed entities to be involved via a direct or an indirect parent. Privately held companies, where no party in the investors' corporate chain was publicly listed, remained the dominant category. Even omitting cases where data on corporate ownership was unavailable and public ownership was unlikely, private investors accounted for nearly half of cases involving corporations.[48] *See* Table 3.1.

TABLE 3.1

Frequency Breakdown of Cases for Types of Corporate Investor(s) involved (n = 149), Excluding those Cases Involving Only Individuals (n = 23) or Where Investor Data was Unavailable (n = 30).

Type of Named Investor(s) in Case	Number of Cases	Relative Percentage of Cases with Corporate Investors
One or more corporate investor(s) was publicly listed[49]	51	34.23%
Corporate investor(s) were private, but at least one direct corporate parent was publicly listed[50]	27	18.12%
Corporate investor(s) were private, but at least one parent in corporate chain was publicly listed	3	2.01%
Corporate investor was private, with no direct or indirect publicly listed corporate parent[51]	68	45.64%

While public listing is an imperfect proxy for investor size and power,[52] there was evidence of some influence of publicly listed entities for roughly half the cases. Conversely, non-large investors participated heavily in ITA. One example, *Champion Trading*

[48] Using a blunter metric of investor type that did not consider the larger corporate chain, there were: twenty-three cases brought by people, eleven cases brought by a combination of people and corporate entities, eighty-seven cases where investors were privately held entities, fifty-one cases where at least one investor was a publicly listed corporation; and thirty cases that did not have publicly available information on the corporate investor, which likely means that they were privately owned.

[49] Fifteen cases involved claims from mixed groups of corporations and people. This included *Loewen v. United States*, where one investor was a person and another was publicly listed when the case was filed.

[50] This included one case, *Paushok v. Mongolia*, where one investor was a person and another investor was a private corporation that was a subsidiary of a publicly traded company. *See* Appendix V.

[51] For the remaining thirteen cases involving claims brought by a consortium of people and corporations, ten cases involved individuals and privately owned corporations (without indication of public ownership). Corporate identity of investors in *Bogdanov v. Moldova, Bayview v. Mexico*, and *Abaclat v. Argentina* was unavailable. *See* Appendix V.

[52] Efforts were made to identify investors' corporate revenue as another proxy. As that data was woefully incomplete with material omissions, it was included in the dataset but not scientifically appropriate for analysis.

v. Egypt, was a case brought by family members who owned 75% of an investment, and two corporate entities, which were wholly owned by family members, owned the remainder of the investment.[53] This pattern suggests that smaller corporations use or, at the bare minimum, have access ITA. Missing data creates a possibility that cases involving smaller corporations were under-represented and generates the possibility that privately held corporations—presumably small or medium-sized enterprises—may be more prevalent claimants.

3. Investors: *Financial Times* Global 500 Corporations?

Conversations about investor identity can involve generalized discussions about "multinationals" without specific definitions. Technically, "multinational" simply means relating to "more than two nationalities,"[54] suggesting every foreign investor operating abroad is, by definition, a multinational.

Yet, connotations about multinationals are emotionally evocative, potentially triggering intuitive assessments, cognitive illusions, and caricatures. Referring to multinationals as "large and powerful," with budgets exceeding those of small countries and exploiting developing nations,[55] characterizes ITA claimants as monolithic, large, powerful, and potentially overprivileged. Professor Sornarajah focuses on companies such as Enron and Parmalat.[56] Other commentators concentrate on "large multinational corporations" using ITA[57] or assert that "multinational corporations have wielded [treaties'] investor rights like a weapon,"[58] concluding the system is "tilted . . . in favour of large multinational corporations."[59] Other perspectives are more nuanced. The Bretton Woods Project posited that approximately 20% of ICSID cases involve companies ranked within the top 500 globally, while failing to explain the methodology or excise non-ITA disputes from analysis. Some have reproduced Bretton Woods' claim that 20% of ITA cases come from the "Global 500," thereby concluding this is

---

[53] Champion Trading Co. v. Arab Republic of Egypt, ICSID Case No. ARB/02/9, Decision on Jurisdiction, 18 (Oct. 21, 2003), https://bit.ly/2Lb7Siy (last visited Dec. 27, 2018).

[54] *Multinational Definition*, MIRIAM WEBSTER DICTIONARY, http://bit.ly/iknrpb (last visited Aug. 7, 2018).

[55] *See Multinational Definition*, CAMBRIDGE DICTIONARY ONLINE, http://bit.ly/16TiRO9 (last visited Aug. 7, 2018); *Multinational Corporation Definition*, Investopedia, http://bit.ly/174rpmo (last visited Aug. 11, 2014).

[56] M. Sornarajah, *Power and Justice: Third World Resistance in International Law*, 10 SINGAPORE Y.B. INT'L L. 19 (2006).

[57] Glenn Kelley, *Multilateral Investment Treaties: A Balanced Approach to Multinational Corporations*, 39 COLUM. J. TRANSNAT'L L. 483, 484, 508–09 (2001); *see also* Simon Lester, *Liberalization or Litigation: A Time to Rethink the International Investment*, POLICY ANALYSIS, CATO INST. NO. 730 (July 8, 2003), http://bit.ly/1aza9rt (last visited Aug. 7, 2018).

[58] *NAFTA's Broken Promises 1994–2013: Outcomes of the North American Free Trade Agreement*, PUBLIC CITIZEN (Mar. 15, 2013), http://bit.ly/tvKuIU (last visited Aug. 7, 2018).

[59] Pia Eberhardt & Cecilia Olivet, *Profiting from Injustice: How Law Firms, Arbitrators and Financiers Are Fueling an Investment Arbitration Boom*, CORP. EUROPE OBSERVATORY & TRANSNAT'L INST., 70 (Nov. 2012), https://bit.ly/2Mb20nJ (last visited Aug. 7, 2018). Rights granted in treaties flow only to foreign investors (rather than states), albeit investors from both signatory states. A doctrinal critique about rights flowing only in the direction to private entities (rather than private entities owning a duty to a state under international law) is different from the characterizations of claimants accessing transitional justice systems.

"unprecedented power."[60] The Bretton Woods narrative contrasts with OECD's analysis that only 8% of claimants were in UNCTAD's list of top 100 multinational investors.[61]

Given the conventional wisdom, the research hypothesis was that larger (presumably powerful), multinational companies dominated ITA claimants. A variable evaluated whether the *Financial Times* designated any of the five listed investors (or an immediate parent) was an elite "Global 500" company (the FT500).[62] Despite the hypothesis, cases with at least one investor, or an immediate parent from an FT500 company, did *not* dominate the ITA caseload, accounting for less than 12% of the cases (11.9%; $n = 24$). Rather, 88% of cases ($n = 177$)[63] did *not* have any investors—or an immediate corporate parent—ranked on the FT500. *See* Figure 3.4.

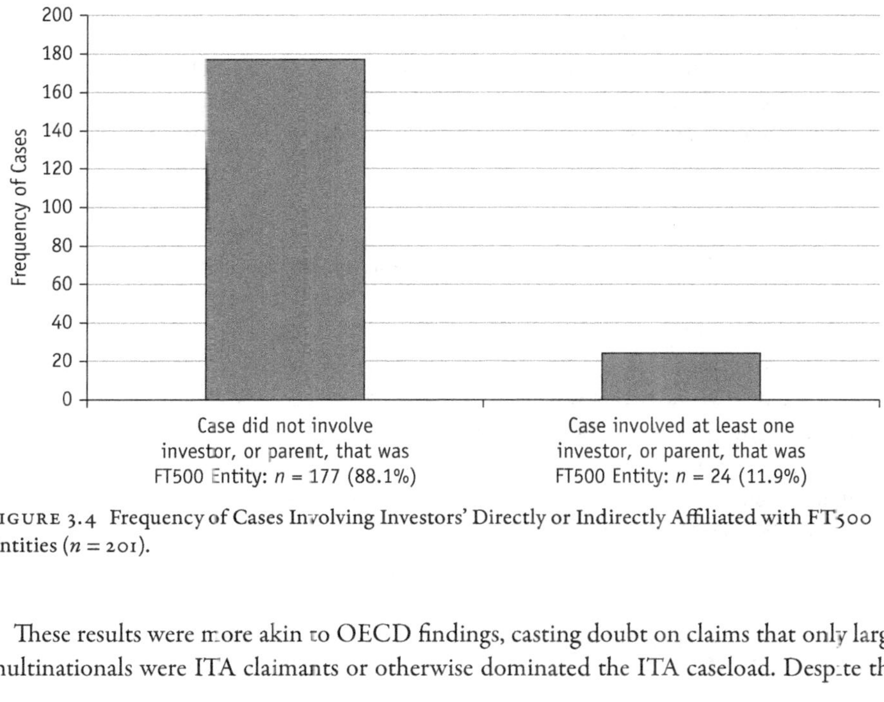

FIGURE 3.4 Frequency of Cases Involving Investors' Directly or Indirectly Affiliated with FT500 Entities ($n = 201$).

These results were more akin to OECD findings, casting doubt on claims that only large multinationals were ITA claimants or otherwise dominated the ITA caseload. Despite the

[60] *Obscure World Bank Court Grants Too Much Power to Corporations*, FOOD AND WATER WATCH (Apr. 30, 2007), http://bit.ly/16JoBcf (last visited Aug. 11, 2014).

[61] OECD, *Progress Report*, *supra* note 37, at 7.

[62] Previous scholarship analyzed FT500 entities, finding that the presence of an FT500-related entity was reliably linked with a "winning" outcome for investors, but it was not possible to identify that these same investors experienced higher (or lower) levels of amounts awarded or relative success. Susan D. Franck & Lindsey Wylie, *Predicting Outcomes in Investment Treaty Arbitration*, 65 DUKE L.J. 459, 508–09, 516–17 (2015). Coding for FT500 was made using 2012 rankings. Future researchers may wish to analyze classifications at the time of the award, time of filing, or time of investment. The operationalization may have affected two cases, *Enron v. Argentina* and *Azurix v. Argentina*. Although the cases were filed late in 2001, Enron was a global leader before its 2001 demise.

[63] *Abaclat*, *supra* note 25, was not coded given the extensive number of corporations involved (180,000–); the unavailability of Annex C, which listed the corporate investors; and the focus on the first five investors.

conventional wisdom, the "median claimant" in ITA was not an elite, powerful multinational. While cognitive illusions—including availability and representativeness—may facilitate the easy retrieval of household names on the FT500, it is improper to conclude those were typical claimants. Although large corporations did use ITA, most cases did not involve large multinationals. Moreover, claims initiated by major multinationals existed at roughly the equivalent levels to claims initiated by individuals.

Overall, the data revealed variance in investors using ITA. At one end of the spectrum, there was a relatively small—but critical—set of cases brought by people, and at the other end, a small but powerful group of FT500 corporations used ITA. The majority of claims tended to be a group of corporations, roughly half of which were purely private entities. Although caution is warranted given missing data and proxy variables, several themes emerged. First, the conception that large multinationals dominate ITA was unsupported. Second, there was evidence that people and private (presumably smaller) corporate entities were critical ITA participants. Third, large multinationals and publicly listed (presumably larger) corporate entities played a role in ITA but were not necessarily dominant. While larger commercial entities pursued ITA, they constituted neither the exclusive actors nor the majority.

D. SYNTHESIS AND CONTEXT

The data both confirmed and disproved narratives about investors bringing ITA claims. It confirmed both that the "median investor" bringing a claim was from a developed state and the rarity of investors from developing states bringing claims. Second, it cast doubt upon claims that investors initiating ITA were elite multinationals. Rather, the median claimant was a privately held entity that might—but also might not—be related to a publicly listed corporate entity. The data bolstered findings of the Center for Strategic and International Studies that posited (for U.S. investors only) two-thirds of claims involved individuals or "small and medium-sized enterprises."[64] While somewhat rare for cases to be brought by FT500 entities, cases initiated by people were also a roughly equivalent proportion.

Where data did not confirm certain claims about ITA, discussions about investor identity require adjustment. Given the power of intuitive cognition—and the ease of recalling names consumers may see regularly (such as Chevron, IBM, Philip Morris, or Siemens)—the dialogue about ITA is likely infected by cognitive illusions of availability and representativeness. The power of the ease of name recall and a presumption that capacity to recall investors' names may lead to quick (and incorrect) assessments that the names easily recalled were dominant players in the overall caseload, and that cases were representative of the broader whole, when in fact they were atypical. Rather, typical players were the privately owned entities—that most normal people have likely not heard of—who may not have the same incentives for due diligence in initiating adjudication as publicly held entities, who are responsible to shareholders (and the media) and must file disclosures with national regulators, or individuals, who may be more careful in deciding to pursue serious international law claims.

---

[64] Scott Miller & Gregory N. Hicks, *Investor-State Dispute Settlement: A Reality* Check, CENTER FOR STRATEGIC INTERNATIONAL STUDIES 10 (Jan. 2015). When defining SMEs, CSIS used the U.S. Small Business Administration's classification of businesses with fewer than 500 employees.

The data, however, revealed the dominance of developed world investors. This raises a question about disparity of those initiating ITA and requires context to understand the stark lack of developing world investors. OECD countries historically had active investment treaty programs and high investment flows. UNCTAD has explored how the developed world has been largely responsible for FDI flows, with developed economies historically nearly 90% of outbound investment and developing and transitioning economies responsible for roughly 11% of outbound investment flows.[65] Given the time-lag between making an investment and a dispute crystallizing after a conflict erupts,[66] with roughly 10% of historical investment deriving from the developing world, it is roughly proportionate for the developing world to initiate 10% of ITA disputes. Yet, UNCTAD's data reflects that investment flows are shifting, and as annual outbound investment from the developing world and transition economies is headed for the 30% range (with current total worldwide investment stock from developing and transitional economics now around 25%),[67] it would be unsurprising for the proportion of ITA disputes from those economies to also increase. Potentially emblematic claims include cases such as *Ping An v. Belgium*.[68] With China's Belt and Road initiative, the identified baseline of the nationality of investors bringing claims may likewise evolve. While the prevalence of developed country investors is notable, relative investment flows for the period studied provide a baseline for recontextualizing concerns of ITA being overused by the developed world and potentially underutilized by the developing world.[69]

Other aspects may contribute to under-representation of developing world claimants. The value of investments may not justify expending fiscal resources. Developing world investors may lack the financial or legal resources to pursue claims. Roberto Echandi argued that for small and

[65] In 1990, the developed world contributed 93% of global outbound investment stock (US$1,946,833 million out of US$2,092,92 million); but by 2011, developed economies contributed only 80.6% (US$17,055,964 million out of the total of global investment outbound stock of US$21,168,489 million), whereas developing and transitional economics contributed nearly 20%. U.N. Conference on Trade and Dev. [UNCTAD], *World Investment Report 2012: Towards a New Generation of Investment Policies*, 173–76, UNCTAD/WIR/2012 (July 5, 2012), https://bit.ly/2ECaDSZ (last visited Aug. 7, 2018); *see also id.* at 4, figure 1.4 (showing increases of annual outbound investment flows to developing and transitional economies).

[66] In international commercial arbitration, data from the LCIA's Director General suggested it is rare (usually less than 10% of the cases) for arbitrations to be commenced within a year of contract formation. Rather, for the eleven-year period from 2000–2011, the bulk of the disputes were filed three to five years after contract formation. *See Director General Reports 2000–2011*, LONDON COURT INT'L ARB., https://bit.ly/2APMLoD (last visited Aug. 7, 2018).

[67] UNCTAD reported, in 2017, that developed economies accounted for roughly 76% (US$23,498,002 million) of the total global FDI outbound stock (US$30,839,927). Developing and transitional economies were responsible for the remainder. UNCTAD, *World Investment Report 2018: Investment and New Industrial Policies*, 188–91, UNCTAD/WIR/2018 (June 6, 2018) [hereinafter UNCTAD, *WIR 2018*].

[68] Simon Rabinovitch & James Fontanella-Khan, *Ping An in Arbitration Claim over Fortis*, FIN. TIMES, Sept. 24, 2012. Ping An Insurance is listed as one of the top companies in the FT's Global 500 2012 ranking. *Global 500 2012 Ranking*, FIN. TIMES, 4 (Mar. 30, 2012), http://bit.ly/1fmRDms (last visited Aug. 7, 2018). Belgium won, with a dismissal on jurisdiction, and there was no shift of any costs. Ping An Life Ins. Co. v. Belg., ICSID Case No. ARB/12/29, Award, 58-59 (Apr. 30, 2015), https://bit.ly/2oruHkg (last visited Aug. 7, 2018).

[69] Paul M. Blyschak, *State Consent, Investor Interests and the Future of Investment Arbitration: Reanalyzing the Jurisdiction of Investor-State Tribunals in Hard Cases*, 9 ASPER REV. INT'L BUS. & TRADE L. 99, 118 (2009).

medium sized enterprises (SMEs), "investments . . . which may represent only several million US Dollars but [ITA] may be *de facto* unavailable if the costs of bringing a proceeding exceed the value of the investment" underpins the concern that ITA can disempower developing world investors.[70] Cultural or business relationship constraints may impact pursuit of ITA. Some legal cultures or business relationships may value other forms of conflict management. For example, Chinese investment abroad has grown, and Chinese culture has historically valued non-adjudicative dispute settlement.[71] Accounting for culture and history may prove useful prior to drawing firm conclusions about the lack of representation by developing country investors. Nevertheless, the dominance of developed world investors must be acknowledged given implications for systemic functionality and perceived legitimacy.

III. Party Demographics: Respondent States

Unlike investors, there is more information on respondent state identity. As states are the authors of treaties and subjects of disputes, the focus is prudent. Earlier research identified only thirty-seven states subjected to ITA, and the average respondent was sued twice.[72] As the caseload expanded, more states have become involved. Focusing on "known" claims rather than awards, UNCTAD historically reported the development status of states sued, and that data was contemporaneous with the dataset in this book.[73] In 2012, UNCTAD explained their data revealed that "over the past years at least 89 governments have responded to one or more investment treaty arbitration: 55 developing countries, 18 developed countries and 16 countries with economies in transition."[74] Meanwhile, around 2012, ICSID recorded the geographical affiliation of respondents for its cases rather than development status. At that time, ICSID observed the greatest majority of state respondents hailed from South America (30%), quickly followed by Eastern Europe and Central Asia (23%), sub-Saharan

---

[70] Roberto Echandi, *Towards a New Approach to Address Investor-State Conflict: Developing a Conceptual Framework for Dispute Prevention*, World Trade Inst. Working Paper No. 2011/46 (Aug. 2011), https://bit.ly/2vqU3me (last visited Aug. 7, 2018).

[71] Huiping Chen, *China's Innovative ISDS Mechanisms and Their Implications*, 112 AJIL UNBOUND 207, 208–09 (Aug. 27, 2018), https://bit.ly/2C5y5uY (last visited Aug. 30, 2018); Wang Guiguo & HE Xiaoli, *Mediation and International Investment: A Chinese Perspective*, 65 ME. L. REV. 215, 221–33 (2012); Tiffany M. Lin, *Chinese Attitudes Toward Third-Party Dispute Resolution in International Law*, 48 N.Y.U. J. INT'L L. & POL. 581, 585–88 (2016).

[72] Franck, *supra* note 23, at 31.

[73] More recent UNCTAD publications tend to identify only the number of countries sued in a particular year (rather than providing specific holistic information or historical context), some of the most frequently sued states, and the total number of states sued. *See, e.g.*, UNCTAD, *WIR 2018*, *supra* note 67, at 92.

[74] UNCTAD, 2012 ISSUES NOTE, *supra* note 20, at 2; *see also* UNCTAD, *World Investment Report 2016: Investor Nationality: Policy Challenges*, 105, UNCTAD/WIR/2016 (June 21, 2016) (identifying that six new countries "faced their first (known) ISDS claims"); *see also* UNCTAD, *WIR 2018*, *supra* note 67, at 92 (identifying four new countries experiencing their first claim). Unfortunately, more recent UNCTAD publications tend to identify only the number of countries sued in a particular year (rather than providing specific information or historical context) and identify some of the most frequently sued states. *See, e.g.*, UNCTAD, *WIR 2018*, *supra* note 67, at 92.

Africa (16%), Middle East and North Africa (10%), South East Asia and the Pacific (8%), and Central America and Caribbean (7%). A small fraction of respondents then were from North America (5%) and Western Europe (1%).[75] ICSID's 2018 data suggests that, while there were a few less cases against South American states and a few more cases against Western European states, not much otherwise changed.[76]

These studies, despite different time periods and different units of analysis, provide a useful backdrop. The next section offers a reflection on those baselines by using the dataset to explore information about respondents, identifying elements regarding states' development background using preexisting scales, and contextualizing the information.

A. NUMBER AND NATIONALITY OF STATES

The time-bound data revealed fifty-seven states were ITA respondents. The U.S. Department of State recognizes the existence of 195 different states, and UNCTAD has identified 175 states with at least one investment treaty in force,[77] meaning roughly one-third of countries that were theoretical respondents were subjected to ITA. Put another way, when the dataset closed, and recognizing evolution since then,[78] roughly two-thirds of states had *not* been sued.[79]

Like ICSID's findings, respondents ran the gamut in geographic distribution. Appendix III provides a breakdown of the cases against every state in the dataset. It reflects that states from South America, Central America, and North America were frequent respondents.[80] Eastern Europe, Central Asia, and African respondents are also frequent. Cases against Western European states were rare at that time. It also plots the data against the number of cases brought by the state's nationals and the number of cases where nationals served as arbitrators.

Argentina was the most frequent respondent in the dataset, with Mexico a close runner-up. The remaining "Top 5" respondents in the pre-2012 dataset were: Ecuador, Ukraine,

---

[75] ICSID Secretariat, *The ICSID Caseload-Statistics, Issue 2012-1*, 11 (2012), https://bit.ly/2ttZlMS (last visited Aug. 7, 2018); *see also* ICSID Secretariat, *ICSID Caseload-Statistics, Issue 2013-1*, 11 (2013), https://bit.ly/2MhZ4nl (last visited Aug. 7, 2018) (offering similar statistics); ICSID Secretariat, *The ICSID Caseload–Statistics, Issue 2014-2*, 11 (July 30, 2014), https://bit.ly/2vsevDl (last visited Aug. 7, 2018) (same).

[76] ICSID Secretariat, *The ICSID Caseload-Statistics, Issue 2018-1*, 11 (2018), https://bit.ly/2HS5k2y (last visited Aug. 7, 2018) (observing that 26% of respondents were from Eastern Europe and Central Asia, 23% from South America, 15% from sub-Saharan Africa, 11% from the Middle East and North Africa, 8% from South East Asia and the Pacific, 8% from Western Europe (8%), 6% from Central America and the Caribbean, and 4% from North America.

[77] UNCTAD, *The Entry into Force of Bilateral Investment Treaties (BITs)*, 2, U.N. Doc. UNCTAD/WEB/ITE/IIA/2006/9 (Jan. 10, 2006), http://bit.ly/18eoQNu (last visited Aug. 7, 2018).

[78] For example, UNCTAD's most recent data suggests that 113 countries have now been subject to one or more claims. UNCTAD, *WIR 2018, supra* note 67, at 92. This means that there has arguably been a historical transition from 66% of states *not* being sued to 75% of states being sued at least once.

[79] This figure has evolved. Since the dataset closed, two cases were brought against China, one that settled and one that China won; and there were ten claims filed against India. Won Kidane, *China and India's Different Investment Treaty Dispute Resolution Experiences and Implications for Africa*, 49 LOYOLA U. CHI. L. REV. 405, 425, 438 (2018).

[80] Of the 202 cases in the dataset, 38% ($n = 77$) involved cases against Latin American states, with twenty-eight of the cases involving disputes with Argentina.

Egypt, and the United States. Other states subjected to seven cases were Canada, Russia, and the Czech Republic. Romania experienced six cases. Other states, namely Turkey, Slovakia, and Venezuela, had five cases each. Like findings from earlier research, many states only experienced one dispute; and the "median state" experienced two claims. There was, however, a noteworthy shift. Earlier research identified that the average number of claims against a state was 2.2, whereas the average number of claims in the current dataset was 3.2. The facial increase suggests the risk of being a repeat respondent should not be ignored.

B. RESPONDENT DEVELOPMENT STATUS

Considering respondents' development status contextualizes the variance of state experience. The research used the award date to consider: whether the respondent was an OECD state, how the World Bank classified the state's development status, how the UNDP ranked the state's HDI level, and whether the U.N. classified states as a Least Developed Country (LDC).

Unlike investors, respondents were *not* concentrated in developed states. Rather, respondents came from various backgrounds. Using an OECD classification, nearly three-quarters of respondents were *not* OECD members (74.3%; n = 150). There were multiple claims against Canada, the Czech Republic, Hungary, Mexico, Turkey, and the United States; and there was a solitary case against Germany.

World Bank classifications provide a more nuanced four-category classification. The World Bank measure demonstrated two things. First, there were respondents in all four development categories. Second, claims were not distributed equally across all categories. Middle-income states were the most typical respondents. Close to half (47.5%;) of respondents were Upper-Middle Income states; the second core contingency (30.7%) were Lower-Middle Income states. There were smaller proportions of High Income respondents (13.9%); Low Income states (7.9%) experienced the smallest proportion of claims. *See* Figure 3.5. Overall, proportions were similar to earlier research, with shifts of only 1–4%. The only noteworthy facial change was a 4.1% decrease in cases against High Income respondents.

Finally, using the UNDP's 0-1 index, the average HDI score was .720.[81] Ecuador, in *Perenco v. Ecuador* (2011), was the average (.720) respondent. The United States had the highest HDI score (.907) in *Canadian Cattlemen for Fair Trade v. United States* (2008). Burundi, in *Goetz* (1999), was the least developed state (.246). The median respondent had an HDI score of .734, including states such as: Venezuela in *Nova Scotia Power* (2010), *Mobil* (2010) and *CEMEX* (2010); Albania in *Pantechniki* (2009); and Mexico in *Gami Investments* (2004). Table 3.2 provides a quartile breakdown of HDI scores.

Using a UNDP report as a baseline,[82] with the exception of Romania, all states in the top quartile had "very high human development." For the second quartile, the UNDP classified the remaining states "high human development." Argentina, Slovakia, Chile, and Latvia transitioned

---

[81] n = 200; SD = .114. HDI data was missing for Macedonia in *EVN v. Macedonia* and Azerbaijan in *Azpetrol v. Azerbaijan*.

[82] Human Development Report 2011, *Sustainability and Equity: A Better Future for All*, U.N. DEVEL. PROG. 127 (Nov. 2, 2011), http://bit.ly/WlZnTw (last visited Aug. 7, 2018).

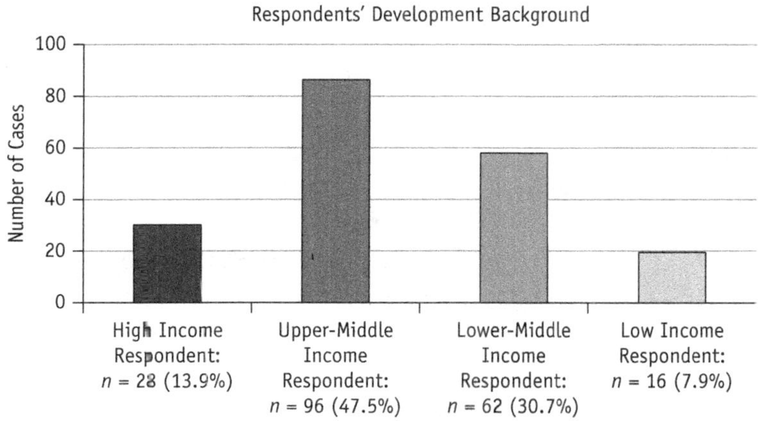

FIGURE 3.5 World Bank Development Classification of Respondents in Cases (n = 202).

to "very high" development. In the third quartile, Lebanon, Russia, Mexico, Venezuela, Ukraine, Kazakhstan, Georgia, Peru, Ecuador, Malaysia, and Turkey had "high human development" but Jordan and the Dominican Republic were "medium human development." In the bottom quartile, Macedonia and Azerbaijan had "high human development," but El Salvador, Algeria, Mongolia, Paraguay, Bolivia, Egypt, Moldova, Sri Lanka, Uzbekistan, Philippines, South Africa, Tajikistan, Kyrgyzstan, Guatemala, Morocco, and Ghana had "medium human development". For states in the bottom quartile, the UNDP classified Pakistan, Myanmar, Bangladesh, Senegal, Tanzania, Yemen, Zimbabwe, and the Congo as "low human development." Like other classifications, HDI scores suggest that respondents had various development levels, but that the majority of states exhibited lower levels of development, particularly when compared to the development levels of states from which investors originated. The bulk of respondents were states that exhibited either "high" or "medium" human development using HDI.

Finally, only 3% of respondents analyzed were LDCs. This was a slight drop (less than 1%) from earlier research. LDC respondents were Bangladesh, Burundi, Democratic Republic of the Congo, Myanmar, Senegal, and Tanzania, or 12.5% of the forty-eight designated LDC states.[83] All LDCs except Bhutan, Kiribati, Samoa, and Tuvalu had at least one treaty, and usually multiple treaties,[84] meaning most LDCs theoretically subject to ITA had not been sued. While the most vulnerable economies were subjected to treaty disputes, they were a fraction of the caseload.

---

[83] LDCs were coded based upon the date of the award. *See* Codebook, Appendix IV; *see also UN List of Least Developed Countries*, UNCTAD, http://bit.ly/163Ue4H (last visited Aug. 11, 2014).

[84] According to the UNCTAD database available in 2012–2014 (and compared to 2018's Investment Policy Hub), Afghanistan had one (currently three), Angola had three (currently five), Bangladesh had twenty (currently twenty-four), Benin had twelve (currently eight), Burkina Faso had twelve (currently fourteen), Burundi had six, Cambodia had fifteen (currently thirteen), Central African Republic had five (currently two), Chad had five (currently three), Comros had five (currently two), Congo had nine (currently eight), Dijbouti had three (currently four), Equatorial Guinea had four, Eritrea had two (currently one), Ethiopia had twenty (currently twenty-one), Gambia had three (currently five), Guinea had eleven (currently six), Guinea-Bissau

TABLE 3.2

HDI Quartile Breakdown of Respondents Subject to ITA (n = 201) and Year (where HDI Ranking Changed Over Time).

HDI Quartiles from ITA Cases	HDI Range	States (years identified when states were were present in multiple quartiles)
Top Quartile	.907–.775	United States; Canada; Germany; Spain; Estonia, Slovakia (2010, 2011); Lithuania; Czech Republic; Hungary; United Arab Emirates; Poland; Chile (2007, 2008); Argentina (2007; 2008; 2010; 2011); Romania (2008–2011)
Second Quartile	.773–.734	Argentina (1998, 2000, 2003-2006); Slovakia (1999); Chile (2002, 2004); Romania (2005); Bulgaria; Mexico (2004, 2006–2010); Panama, Latvia (2003); Serbia; Russia (2007, 2009); Malaysia, Grenada, Costa Rica (2010); Trinidad & Tobago; Venezuela (2010); Albania (2009)
Third Quartile	.733–.677	Lebanon; Russia (1998; 2006); Latvia (2000); Mexico (1999, 2000, 2002, 2003); Venezuela (2008); Ukraine (2003, 2004, 2010, 2011); Kazakhstan; Georgia; Peru; Ecuador (2003, 2004, 2006–2011); Malaysia; Turkey (2007, 2009–2011); Jordan (2009, 2010); Dominican Republic
Bottom Quartile	.674–.246	El Salvador; Algeria; Thailand; Ukraine (2000); Jordan (2004); Turkey (2004); Albania (1996); Mongolia; Venezuela (1998); Paraguay; Bolivia; Egypt; Moldova; Sri Lanka; Uzbekistan; Philippines; South Africa; Tajikistan; Kyrgyzstan; Guatemala; Pakistan; Myanmar; Morocco; Ghana; Bangladesh; Senegal; Tanzania; Yemen; Zimbabwe; Congo; Macedonia; Azerbaijan

had one, Haiti had four (currently three), Laos had fourteen (currently twenty-one), Lesotho had two (currently three), Liberia had three, Madagascar had seven (currently eight), Malawi had one (currently three), Mali had five (currently eight), Mauritania had eight (currently nine), Mozambique had six (currently twenty), Myanmar had two (currently six), Nepal had six (currently four), Niger had three (currently two), Rwanda had three (currently four), Sao Tome and Principe had one (currently two are signed and none in force), Senegal had eleven (currently seventeen), Timor-Leste had two (currently one), Togo had three (currently two), Uganda had twelve (currently six), United Republic of Tanzania had twelve (currently eleven), Vanuatu had one (currently two signed but none in force), Yemen had twenty (currently twenty-three), and Zambia had six. *Investment Instruments Online: Bilateral Investment Treaties*, UNCTAD (formerly http://iiadbcases.unctad.org); *Investment Policy Hub: International Investment Agreements Navigator*, UNCTAD, https://bit.ly/2toiT50 (last visited June 23, 2018).

A broad spectrum of states were sued. Irrespective of how "development" was defined, all measures indicated that: both developing and developed states experienced claims, states from the developing world experienced the majority of claims, and the poorest states were unlikely to be involved in ITA.

Although many respondents were developing states, their prevalence as respondents was not proportionate to worldwide levels of inbound investment. UNCTAD previously reported, in 2000, that nearly 76% of global inbound investment stock occurred in the developed world, leaving developing and transitional economies with the remaining 24% of global inbound investment stock.[85] Around the contemporaneous closure of the dataset, the total global inbound stock for those economies rose to roughly 36%.[86] Given the time required from when investment is made to the time a dispute crystalizes, a core question lingers, namely: Why is the proportion of the world with a quarter of global investment inflows nevertheless the object of half of ITA disputes? While beyond the scope of this book, there have been analyses suggesting that corruption, democracy, and rule-of-law indicators may be the more influential drivers, and debates about ITA potentially conflate variance attributable to development and other variables.[87] Yet it remains an open question worthy of ongoing dialogue and assessment.

Other research[88] has laid groundwork to suggest that there is an exceedingly complex web of relationships involving states' development, corruption, and democracy levels. It is possible that respondent development status, while important, need not be the sole critical aspect upon which to focus. States are not monolithic actors. Different government conduct gives rise to different ITA risks. Caddell and Jensen, for example, observed differences for democratic governments, which find themselves with an ITA risk due to irregular behavior by subnational units. They also observed that different forms of government conduct—particularly executive branch actions—were predominantly responsible for ITA risk, as

---

[85] *See* UNCTAD, *WIR 2012*, *supra* note 65, at 173–76 (reflecting that 2000 total FDI inward stock was US$7,340,022 million, with developed economies accounting for US$5,653,715 million (75.9%), with the remaining 24.1% attributable to developing or transitioning economies).

[86] *See id.* at 173–76 (reflecting total FDI inward stock in 2011 was US$20,438,199 million and developed economies accounted for US$13,055,903 million (63.9%), leaving the remainder of 36.1% to developing or transitioning economies). UNCTAD data indicates, in 2017, the share of global investment stock was roughly similar, with 64.5% for developed economies, and 35.5% for developing and transitional economies. *See* UNCTAD, *WIR 2018*, *supra* note 67, at 188–91 (identifying total worldwide inbound investment stock at US$31,524,356 million and attributing US$30,331,171 million to developed economies).

[87] *See* Susan D. Franck, *Conflating Politics and Development? Examining Investment Treaty Arbitration Outcomes*, 55 VA. J. INT'L L. 13 (2014) (noting potential conflation of risks while identifying that only World Bank development classifications was reliably linked with raw wins and amounts awarded but not relative investor success); Franck & Wylie, *supra* note 62, at 506–09, 514, 517 (2015) (running regression analyses and observing respondents' World Bank development status sometimes predicted outcomes, namely amounts awarded, but not raw outcomes or relative success).

[88] Julian Donaubauer & Peter Nunnenkamp, *International Arbitration of Investment Disputes: Are Poor and Badly Governed Respondent States More Likely to Lose?*, 25 APPLIED ECON. LETTERS 1 (2017); Daniel Behn, Tarald Laudal Berge & Malcolm Langford, *Poor States or Poor Governance? Explaining Outcomes in Investment Treaty Arbitration*, 38 N.W. J. INT'L L. & BUS. 333 (2018).

opposed to legislative or judicial conduct.[89] Williams's detailed classification of government conduct similarly identified that 85% of ITA disputes derived from executive branch or a related administrative entity activity; legislative conduct only generated 11% of disputes.[90] Together, these research strands suggest that while politics and development are linked to ITA disputes, over-reliance on blunt, grand narratives about "development" risk oversimplification, under-specification, or inaccuracy. Rather than focusing on monolithic, possibly emotive, narratives about state constraints on undefined "regulatory space"[91] or "check[s] on executive branch misbehavior,"[92] the better course is to begin a thoughtful dialogue about demographics and variables contributing to investment conflict and ITA costs.

C. Reciprocity and Context

States are both subjects and objects of investment law. Theoretically, states' investors have an opportunity to sue and states risk being sued. The question remains whether states—particularly developing ones—have disproportionate exposure to ITA. There have been concerns that investment treaties are bilateral in theory but unilateral in effect.[93]

Earlier research demonstrated only roughly 20% of states were both the subject (through an investor) and object (as a respondent) of ITA.[94] The updated analyses largely replicated the finding of imbalance, finding 20.7% of states were both subjects and objects of ITA. When excluding local investors with the same nationality of the respondent, the picture shifted slightly. The refined perspective demonstrated that only 16.1% ($n = 14$) of states were simultaneously subjects and objects of ITA. The vast majority of states experienced ITA unilaterally, either purely as a respondent or having their investors bringing claims. *See* Appendix III. When it comes to dispute resolution, the data continued to suggest ITA is reciprocal primarily in theory.

While states' net benefits (from protecting their investors abroad) and risks (from their own fiscal exposure) of granting investors substantive rights and access to dispute resolution was not proportionate, this does not inevitably lead to a conclusion of fundamental imbalance. Investment treaties are complex instruments supporting multiple goals. Derivative benefits might also include increased domestic investment, improved knowledge transfer and capacity building, and the development of good governance practices. As the initial data suggested that risks and benefits of ITA were not equally distributed, on a case-by-case basis, states may wish to assess both the net value of ITA and treaties. But to do so requires data

---

[89] Jeremy Caddel & Nathan M. Jensen, *Which Host Country Government Actors Are Most Involved in Disputes with Foreign Investments?*, Columbia FDI Perspectives (Apr. 29, 2014), http://bit.ly/1nVYAPe (last visited Aug. 7, 2018).

[90] Zoe P. Williams, *Risky Business or Risky Politics: What Explains Investor-State Disputes?*, IISD Investment Treaty News (Aug. 12, 2014), http://bit.ly/299De6y (last visited Aug. 7, 2018).

[91] *See* Tomer Broude et al., *Who Cares About Regulatory Space in BITs? A Comparative International* Approach, *in* Comparative International Law (Anthea Roberts et al., eds., 2018) (observing the debates and lack of systemic measurement of "regulatory space").

[92] Cadell & Jensen, *supra* note 89.

[93] William S. Dodge, *Investor-State Dispute Settlement Between Developed Countries: Reflections on the Australia-United States Free Trade Agreement*, 39 Vand. J. Transnat'l L. 1, 3 (2006).

[94] Franck, *supra* note 23.

rather than intuition. Rather than focusing only on losses or gains, to avoid the pernicious effect of cognitive illusions such as framing, consideration of the whole is essential. Chapter 2's discussion of the "Asian disease" problem demonstrates how positive and negative frames influence strategic decisions, even when outcomes are quantitatively identical. Framing could similarly affect decisions about treaty negotiations and ITA. The better course is to acknowledge the framing risk and minimize risk by introducing better data, as credible information can ameliorate or eliminate framing's improper influence[95] so as to more effectively allow assessment of the costs of ITA and the net benefit of investment treaties.

Data provides that better perspective by identifying typical or median respondents for understanding the regular operation of ITA. Cases such as *Philip Morris v. Australia* and *Vattenfall v. Germany*, against developed states, are atypical. Meanwhile, some have focused on "emblematic" cases[96] in a tactical way. While lawyers might select "emblematic" cases as a calculated exercise or well-intentioned belief, the choice nevertheless risks stimulating negative strains from cognitive illusions such as: availability, namely focusing on recent or emotionally charged memories and presuming the examples are dominant and representative; base rate neglect, namely ignoring statistical background information to predict future events; negativity, causing people to pay more attention and give more weight to negative experiences; recency, weighting recent cases more heavily than earlier events even if they are unrepresentative; and confirmation bias, where people gather, rely upon, and use information in a manner that confirms preexisting beliefs. Data offers a prophylactic to correct misperception about standard ITA cases or, at a minimum, identify median characteristics to craft normative preferences around typical (rather than extreme) situations. The objective should be to avoid inadvertent manipulation by cognitive illusions when making material policy decisions in international investment law.

IV. Participation of Non-Disputing Parties

While investors and states primarily control ITA, they are not the only potential participants. ITA involves adjudicating treaty rights by assessing state conduct to determine whether state liability, which derivatively impacts others. While "others" could be other treaty counterparties, citizens and other groups experience spillover effects where ITA influences policy activities when disputes involve sensitive regulatory activity or investment sectors.[97] Third parties can therefore serve as fundamental actors within ITA.[98]

International commercial arbitration (ICA) was historically confidential. With that initial model, core ITA doctrinal sources, such as the ICSID Convention and 1976 UNCITRAL

[95] James N. Druckman, *Using Credible Advice to Overcome Framing Effects*, 17 J.L. Econ. & Org. 62 (2001).

[96] Eberhardt & Olivet, *supra* note 59, at 13.

[97] Regulatory activity might involve regulation of health, safety, labor law, human rights, and indigenous peoples; sensitive sectors might involve oil, gas, mining, water, or waste disposal. The former was not coded, as there was no preexisting, reliable, and valid measure to categorize government activity, but it did code the primary industrial sector involved.

[98] Katia F. Gomez, *Rethinking the Role of Amicus Curiae in International Investment Arbitration: How to Draw the Line Favorably for the Public Interest*, 35 Ford. Int'l L.J. 510, 523 (2012).

Rules, either required confidentiality of proceedings or were silent on the status of third parties. Given the value of transparency when adjudicating state liability, the United States and Canada pioneered innovations opening ITA to Non-Disputing Parties (NDPs) in NAFTA, the NAFTA Free Trade Commission Statement, and model investment treaties.[99] The United States improved NDP access in its 2004 and 2012 model BITs. The 2012 U.S. Model BIT provides for open hearings, the publication of awards, the availability of case materials, and amicus curiae briefs.[100] ICSID also made strides, despite ICSID Convention confidentiality restrictions, and revised rules to permit NDP participation. ICSID's current Rule 37(2) allows NDP written submissions after tribunals consider: the extent to which the submission would be within the scope of the dispute at issue, if the submission would be useful, and if the NDP has a significant interest in the proceeding.[101] Existing ICSID Rules also permit NDPs to view hearings when parties agree. The Mauritius Convention[102] and revised UNCITRAL Rules for ITA[103] likewise reflect modern norms of open access.

Normative preference, rather than empirical evidence, drove reform.[104] Yet data aids assessment of normative choices. As Professor Trakman explained, "there is no suitable macro data which satisfactorily identifies when third parties are involved in investment arbitration proceedings. What is needed, at the outset, is: comprehensive information on the nature of petitions by third parties to participate in ICSID proceedings" and that, in turn assists "in allaying concerns about biases in arbitration proceedings against developing countries and public interests being represented in those countries."[105] While Chapter 8 identifies evidence that diverges with claims NDP participation "increases arbitration costs and generates delays,"[106] this section provides background on NDP identity, type, and scope of participation.

A. PRESENCE AND IDENTITY OF NDPS

NDPs represent multiple types of international law stakeholders. More traditionally, NDPs can be states or international organizations. NDPs can also represent private entities, whether

---

[99] 2012 United States Model Bilateral Investment Treaty, art. 20(3)(b)(iv) (2012), http://1.usa.gov/UgIyXP (last visited Aug. 7, 2018); [hereinafter 2012 U.S. Model BIT]; Canada Model Bilateral Investment Treaty, Agreement Between Canada and for the Promotion and Protection of Investment, arts. 38(1), 38(3), 39 (2004), https://bit.ly/2M6hLoB (last visited Aug. 7, 2018).

[100] *See* 2012 U.S. Model BIT, *supra* note 99, art. 28(3) ("The Tribunal shall have the authority to accept and consider amicus curiae submissions from a person or entity that is not a disputing party.").

[101] ICSID Rules of Procedure for Arbitration Proceedings, Rule 37(b), (Apr. 10, 2006), https://bit.ly/2sjVvVg (last visited Aug. 7, 2018); *see also* Chapter 9 (discussing ICSID's proposed NDP-related reforms).

[102] U.N. Comm'n Int'l Trade Law [UNCITRAL], United Nations Convention on Transparency in Treaty-based Investor-State Arbitration, Mauritius Convention (Dec. 10, 2014), A/RES/69/116, http://bit.ly/1N2UemB (last visited Aug. 7, 2018); *see also* James D. Fry & Odysseas G. Repousis, *Towards a New World for Investor-State Arbitration Through Transparency*, 48 N.Y.U. J. INT'L L. & POL. 795 (2016).

[103] UNCITRAL, *UNCITRAL Rules on Transparency in Treaty-Based Investor-State Arbitration* (Apr. 1, 2014), https://bit.ly/2nlgDZg (last visited Aug. 7, 2018).

[104] Susan D. Franck, *The Nature and Enforcement of Investor Rights Under Investment Treaties: Do Investment Treaties Have a Bright Future?*, 12 U.C. DAVIS J. INT'L L. & POLICY 57, 89–92 (2005).

[105] Leon Trakman, *The ICSID Under Siege*, 45 CORNELL INT'L L.J. 603 (2012).

[106] Gomez, *supra* note 98, at 552–53.

citizens or nongovernmental organizations (NGOs) representing civil society. Existing literature emphasizes the importance of civil society in ITA and identifies NGOs as key actors;[107] but the same literature focuses less on state NDPs.[108] To explore a broad range of NDP participation in ITA, the research explored actual or attempted NDP participation by states, international organizations, NGOs, for-profit corporate entities, or individuals acting in a private capacity.

The data revealed that roughly 17% of cases[109] involved some form of actual or attempted NDP participation. This suggests, for the historical snapshot analyzed, that NDP activity was the exception rather than the rule.

NDPs were typically successful in obtaining some type of ITA participation rights. The dataset contained only two cases where NDPs were not granted the right to participate.[110] First, in *Suez v. Argentina*, despite the tribunal's rejecting participation during the jurisdictional phase, the tribunal invited further participation in later phases, but the NDPs failed to pursue the invitation.[111] Second, in *Aguas del Tunari v. Bolivia,* the tribunal refused NDP participation during jurisdiction; but it expressed a willingness to entertain amicus submissions on the merits.[112] In several cases, NDPs were invited to participate immediately;

---

[107] *Id.*; Amokura Kawharu, *Participation of Non-governmental Organizations in Investment Arbitration as Amici Curiae, in* THE BACKLASH AGAINST: INVESTMENT ARBITRATION: PERCEPTIONS AND REALITY 275, 279–80 (Michael Waibel et al., eds., 2010); Trakman, *supra* note 105; Valentina Vadi, *When Cultures Collide: Foreign Direct Investment, Natural Resources and Indigenous Heritage in International Investment Law*, 42 COLUM. HUM. RTS. L. REV. 797, 837–928 (2011).

[108] Anthea Roberts and Federico Ortino thoughtfully explored states' ITA submissions. Federico Ortino, *The Impact of Amicus Curiae Briefs in the Settlement of Trade and Investment Disputes: An Analysis of the Shrimp/Turtle and Methanex Decisions, in* ECONOMIC LAW AS AN ECONOMIC GOOD 301, 304–05, 310–11 (K. M. Meessen ed., 2009); Anthea Roberts, *Power and Persuasion in Investment Treaty Arbitration: The Dual Role of States*, 104 AM. J. INT'L L. 179, 194 (2010).

[109] 16.8%; $n = 34$.

[110] Although it was not in the dataset as the case did not involve a public award before January 2012, the *Apotex* tribuna denied NDP participation. The Study Center for Sustainable Finance, described as a for-profit nongovernmental organization that is the "research and development arm of the Business Neatness Magnanimity," sought to become an NDP. The tribunal rejected the application, at least for jurisdiction, given the failure to identify any significant interest or a public interest. Apotex Inc. v. United States, UNCITRAL Procedural Order No. 2 on the Participation of a Non-Disputing Party (Oct. 11, 2011), http://1.usa.gov/16JprG1 (last visited Aug. 7, 2018). Although the for-profit nature of the NGO was unusual, the result was standard in that it denied participation only for jurisdictional purposes.

[111] Suez v. Argentine Republic, ICSID Case No. ARB/03/19, Decision on Liability (July 30, 2010), https://bit.ly/2Huk8Js (last visited Dec. 27, 2018). There is some evidence that, despite a tribunal's specific invitation for NDP participation, NDPs have not followed through on the opportunity. In *Commerce Group v. El Slavador*, although the tribunal issued standards for accepting amicus submissions and two states made NDP submissions, there was no evidence of NGO participation. Commerce Group Corp. v. El Salvador, ICSID Case No. ARB/09/17, Award (Mar. 14, 2011), https://bit.ly/2QX2EoH (last visited Dec. 27, 2018). In *Foresti v. South Africa, supra* note 27, there was no indication that NDPs, who requested the right to submit an amicus brief and receive documents, participated in this manner; but this may be a by-product of the settlement, which made the next phase unnecessary.

[112] *See* Aguas del Tunari v. Republic of Bol., ICSID Case No. ARB/02/3, Decision on Jurisdiction (Oct. 21, 2005), 20 ICSID REV.-FOR. INV. L.J. 450, 574–76 (2005), https://bit.ly/2IkUbHG (last visited Aug. 7, 2018) (referring to the January 29, 2003 Letter from the Tribunal to Earthjustice).In cases that were not in the dataset given their procedural posture, tribunals denied NGOs requests to act as amici and submit a brief. *See* Apotex v. United

or in some instances, where tribunals did not permit NDPs (particularly NGOs) to participate at the jurisdiction phase, those tribunals accepted NDP activity later, particularly for merit-related issues. Put simply: persistence paid off for NDPs in *Methanex v. United States, S.D. Myers v. Canada*, and *UPS v. Canada,* even in consolidated proceedings such as *Suez and Vivendi v. Argentina* and *AWG v. Argentina*.

When NDPs participated, they often acted in concert with other NDPs. There were solitary NDPs in only four cases. All other cases[113] involved two or more NDPs.[114] When states acted as NDPs, they tended to do so in pairs; likewise, NGOs tended to work together and pool resources.

Given the literature focusing on NGO participation, intuitively one would believe they were the most prevalent NDP type. Yet, data revealed that *states* were the most prevalent, appearing in nearly 80% of cases where any NDP was present.[115] Those states tended to be the United States, Canada, and Mexico; but other sovereigns included the Netherlands, the Quechan Indian Nation, Costa Rica, the Dominican Republic, Nicaragua, and El Salvador. Given the dominance of NAFTA states and NAFTA rules permitting state participation, choice architecture of investment treaties likely facilitated state NDP participation.

NGOs were the second most prevalent NDP type, appearing in close to 30% of cases where any NDP was present.[116] NGOs generally had a specific focus, whether issues related to the environment (such as the Center for International Environmental Law, Sierra Club, and Friends of the Earth), development (such as International Institute for Sustainable Development), or labor (such as Canadian Union of Postal Workers or United Steelworkers). There were also a small group of cases involving international organizations or private individuals. In the cases analyzed, the European Commission acted as an NDP twice (6.3%).[117] In one case, a private individual participated as an NDP (3.1%).[118] No cases contained a business or for-profit entity appearing as an NDP.

Cognitive illusions could partially explain the arguable underemphasis on state participation and over-focus on NGOs. Discussion about NDP activity could, for example, make those discussions more readily available. As policy debates involve discussions about the role and activity of NGOs, those examples may be most recent and easiest to retrieve from memory. As such, the availability and representativeness illusions could make the scope of

---

States, *supra* note 110; Von Penzold v. Republic of Zim., ICSID Case Nos. ARB/10/15 & ARB/10/25, Procedural Order No. 2 (June 26, 2012), http://bit.ly/1dPzxLm (last visited Jan. 18, 2019) (denying NGO participation where the NGO failed to establish its independence and, as neither the investor nor respondent had yet raised issues upon which the NGOs wished to make submissions, the matter was beyond the scope of the dispute); Chevron Corp. & Texaco Petroleum Co. v. Republic of Ecuador, PCA Case No. 2009-23, Letter of April 26, 2011 (Apr. 26, 2011), http://bit.ly/1ePZJZl (last visited Aug. 7, 2018) (denying participation in the jurisdictional phase).

[113] 87.5%; $n = 28$.

[114] The median was two NDPs per case. $M = 2.69$; $SD = 1.469$; $n = 32$.

[115] 84.3%; $n = 27$.

[116] 28.1%; $n = 9$.

[117] AES Summit Generation Ltd. v. Republic of Hung., ICSID Case No. ARB/07/22, Award (Sept. 23, 2010), https://bit.ly/2Cwz6cs (last visited Dec. 27, 2018); Eureko B.V. v. Slovak Republic, UNCITRAL, PCA Case No. 2008-13, Award on Jurisdiction, Arbitrability and Suspension (Oct. 26, 2010), 23 World Trade & Arb. Materials 171 (2011).

[118] This was Phil Fontaine in *Grand River v. United States*. There were two cases of attempted intervention by people in *Aguas del Tunari v. Bolivia* and *Suez v. Argentina*.

NGO activity "feel" more prevalent than a statistical base rate would suggest. With state NDP activity a lesser focus of debate, the availability heuristic could facilitate a conclusion that state participation was smaller. Reorienting perceptions of NDP participation with data could aid policy debates. First, the data identifies the weight of state NDP activity in ITA. Second, given normative concerns about lost sovereignty, the evidence of proactive state intervention requires reorientation of discussions. Third, as treaties typically have provisions permitting state NDP activity, states may also wish to consider providing similar provisions facilitating NGO participation.

B. CHARACTERISTICS OF CASES WITH NDPS

NDP activity is, in part, an effort to address concerns related to public policy concerns and the spillover effects of investment and government regulation. To explore cases at that intersection, this subsection explores industries involved, doctrinal basis of participation, and temporal evolution of NDP participation.

One might hypothesize that NDP participation would be concentrated in environmental disputes, particularly disputes involving energy, mining, waste management, and water. The data, however, revealed only partial support for that theory. NDP activity was broadly dispersed across twelve different industrial sectors, including waste management, water, chemical and mining, energy, entertainment, industrial supplies, food and beverage, industrial supplies, transportation, real estate, insurance, postal services, and consumer goods. NDPs were present in environmental disputes. Yet the overall pattern was for NDP participation across cases affecting a variety of industries.

There was, however, a narrow doctrinal commonality for cases with NDPs. With one exception, *Eureko v. Slovak Republic*, NDP activity occurred only in ICSID cases and/or when the case involved a multilateral treaty. The result may derive the doctrinal flexibility of ICSID Rule 37, NAFTA, or CAFTA-DR.

In contrast to theories that NDP participation is a new phenomenon, the data revealed that NDP participation has been present since ITA's inception. The fifth known award ever rendered, *Ethyl v. Canada*,[119] involved an NDP submission from Mexico. As early as 2002, NGOs sought access in cases such as *Methanex* and *UPS*. Between 2003 and 2009, roughly two awards each year involved NDP participation. Although there was a spike in NDP participation for awards rendered in 2010, this may reflect the overall caseload increase. Focusing on the year of filing revealed that roughly two cases per year involved NDP participation—without a spike in participation in a single year. Together, this suggests that NDP participation has been a regular feature of ITA. The potential benefit from NDP participation, without necessarily increasing time or costs, suggests that there should be minimal hesitation in including NDPs—whether those contributions be from states or other stakeholders—capable of adding critical perspectives to aid quality decision-making and support rule-of-law.

---

[119] Ethyl Corp. v. Gov't of Can., UNCITRAL, Award on Jurisdiction (Jun. 24, 1998), 16 J. INT'L ARB. 149 (1998).

C. TYPE OF NDP ACTIVITY

The role of NDPs has varied depending on tribunals involved and rights in dispute.[120] Theoretically, NDP activity in ITA could involve a broad range of participation. At the narrow range, activity involves basic participation, such as attending a hearing. Activity could be more involved, including gaining access to case materials, filing written submissions, making oral presentations, or even cross-examining witnesses. This research evaluated all NDPs within an award and type of NDP activity.[121] First, it identified whether NDPs acted as "observers" and attended hearings with tribunal permission. Second, it explored whether NDPs served as "*amicus curiae*" with the capacity to submit written briefs and respond to tribunal requests for information. Third, it classified whether NDPs acted as a formal "intervener" capable of requesting production of documents, submitting briefs, and attending hearings. A final classification identified whether the award involved hearings generally open to the public, rather than a specific NDP activity.

Most cases involved active NDP participation. Nearly 62% of cases with NDPs involved NDPs acting as an intervener.[122] This activity, however, was the exclusive province of states, and NGOs did not achieve this degree of involvement. Notably, there was a statistically reliable pattern,[123] with a large effect size and practical significance, between the existence of a multilateral investment treaty—such as NAFTA[124] and CAFTA-DR (Dominican Republic Central American Free Trade Agreement)—and an NDP's intervention through submissions or requests for documents. It was atypical for NDPs to act as interveners without a multilateral treaty, underscoring the value of granting a clear doctrinal framework for NDP access. Or, to paraphrase the movie *Field of Dreams*, "If you build it, they will come."[125]

For cases with NDPs, the second most typical form of NDP participation involved actual or attempted provision of an amicus submission.[126] Various entities served as amici. In two cases, states—the Netherlands and the Quechan Indian Nation—acted as NDPs.[127] In two other cases, an international organization—the European Commission—submitted an amicus brief. In an unusual case, an individual—namely Phil Fontaine, the National Chief of the Assembly of First Nations—submitted a letter functioning as an amicus submission. NGOs, however, most typically made amicus submissions. NGOs with multiple

---

[120] *See generally* CIVIL SOCIETY, INTERNATIONAL COURTS AND COMPLIANCE BODIES (Tullio Treves et al., eds. 2005); Arthur Watts, *Enhancing Effectiveness of Procedures in International Dispute Settlement*, 5 MAX PLANCK Y.B. U.N. L. 21 (2001).

[121] Each award was coded to amalgamate all NDP activity within the award; but each NDP identity was coded separately. *See* Codebook, Appendix IV.

[122] 61.8%; $n = 21$.

[123] A chi-square test explored presence of a multi-lateral and bilateral treaty with whether an NDP intervenor present. The pattern was that multilateral treaties were more likely to have intervenors than bilateral treaties (χ^2 (1) = 9.000; $p = .003$; $r = .55$; $n = 30$).

[124] NAFTA Articles 1128 and 1129 permit NAFTA states to make submissions to tribunals on questions of interpretation as well as request evidence or written arguments.

[125] *See* FIELD OF DREAMS (1989) (using the phrase "If you build it, he will come" as a major plot point).

[126] $n = 11$; 32.4%.

[127] In the only case of its kind, a subdivision of a state entity acted as an NDP. In *Bayview v. Mexico*, the State of Texas, acting through the Attorney General and Department of Agriculture, submitted letters to the tribunal, and the United States also made an Article 1128 submission.

interventions included the Center for International Environmental Law, International Institute for Sustainable Development, and Friends of the Earth. The remaining NGOs represented various interests related to human rights and development, labor unions, academic centers (such as the Centre for Applied Legal Studies), and one commercially focused NGO, the U.S. Chamber of Commerce. One noteworthy aspect was NGO success in obtaining amicus status and obtaining leave to make submissions; although typically granted leave to submit briefs, they were not otherwise granted access to documents or to hearings, or permitted to make oral submissions. The broadest scope of NGO participation in the analyzed cases was in *Foresti v. South Africa*, where the tribunal mandated an innovative methodology for parties to share documents with amici.[128] While NGO participation evolves with transparency norms in flux and moving toward greater public access, NDP activity is still far from full participation.

The least typical NDP activity analyzed was also least invasive and also, arguably, the hardest to measure reliably. For cases involving some form of NDP participation, less than a quarter involved pure observation or attendance at hearings.[129] A handful of cases studied involved public hearings, and sometimes webcasts, accessible to the general public.[130] Given the difficulty in identifying who attended public hearings, whether a high school class touring the World Bank or individuals streaming on a computer, it is possible that an even larger proportion of the public acted as "observers." ICSID's 2018 analysis reflects public in-person access and internet streaming,[131] opening the possibility of innumerable members of the public having access to proceedings. This raises a risk that the true scope of public participation in ITA is both difficult to measure and broader than information available in awards.

Overall, data supported claims of various NDP activity. Although states had the broadest range of participation, NGOs were actively involved in amicus activity. NGO participation may become both broader or less invasive through public or electronically streamed hearings. Although NDP activity has evolved since 2012, this information provides a useful baseline for comparing future NDP activity.

V. The Arbitration Ear and Repeat Players

Lawyers—and their relative value—generates well-trodden debates harking back to Shakespeare's sentiment that: "[t]he first thing we do, let's kill all the lawyers."[132] As ITA has diffused, perennial debates about lawyers became grafted onto ITA. Whether characterized as wise counselors, functional tools, angels or devils, the commentary on lawyers runs the gamut from sharp to observational; and it has become arguably fashionable to pillory the

[128] *Foresti v. South Africa*, ICSID Case No. ARB(AF)07/01, Letter Regarding Non-Disputing Parties (Oct. 5, 2009), https://bit.ly/2W5aFvM (last visited Jan. 18, 2019).

[129] 23.5%; $n = 8$.

[130] 21.9%; $n = 7$. When analyzing all 202 cases, this was only 3.5%. ICSID webcast the hearing of *Commerce Group v. El Salvador*; the webcast was available online at https://bit.ly/2lAC73c (last visited Aug. 7, 2018). For cases with public hearings, only *Commerce Group* and *Pac Rim Cayman v. El Salvador* had states acting as observers.

[131] ICSID Secretariat, Proposals for Amendment of the ICSID Rules—Working Paper, Vol. 3, 936–40, 959–61 (Aug. 2, 2018), https://bit.ly/2whvXdh (last visited Aug. 17, 2018).

[132] William Shakespeare, The Second Part of King Henry the Sixth act 4, sc. 2, 71–78 (1623).

international bar. Yet there has been minimal empirical research systematically considering the role of counsel.[133]

Some commentators have used somewhat evocative language, calling ITA lawyers "the new international 'ambulance chasers'"[134] who are "profiting from injustice" or otherwise engaging in "legalized profiteering." They suggest, without empirical quantification, that "the evidence suggests that the lawyers not only have a strong interest in the current international investment regime, but actually perpetuate and exacerbate its profound injustice. At great personal financial gain, arbitration lawyers have actively pursued cases, exploited loopholes and created an explosion in the number and costs of dispute settlement cases."[135] Placing the blame for ITA's negative externalities at the feet of counsel, they assert lawyers "seek out every opportunity to sue countries" and "aggressively promote investment arbitration" to generate "bonanza profits."[136]

Others offer more balanced observations, suggesting such claims may be "'somewhat misleading.'"[137] Professor Yackee expressed concern about counsel's role in creating and interpreting international investment law.[138] Others raise concerns about "issue conflicts," and the profound ethical dilemma of "double hatting" to prevent lawyers serving simultaneously as both counsel and arbitrator on cases involving related issues.[139] When it comes to international investment law, lawyers are rarely lauded as instruments of social justice. Professor Rogers, perhaps, comes the closest when indicating that some states' internal lawyers have "built up impressive expertise" in ITA or have "retained prestigious international law firms, often at deeply discounted rates."[140] Dezalay and Garth suggested that law firms can serve as tools to spread the values of liberal democracies, including recognition of individual civil rights.[141]

---

[133] The exception to this was scholarship previously produced using this dataset. Franck & Wylie, *supra* note 62. The closest analogy involves literature on the role of counsel in national court litigation. *See* Francisco González De Cossío, *National Report for Mexico*, at 44 *in* International Handbook on International Commercial Arbitration (Jan Paulsson ed., 2011) (discussing Mexico's defense team in investment-related domestic litigation).

[134] Eberhardt & Olivet, *supra* note 59, 8, 19; *see also id.* at 24, 48, 50; Pratap Chatterjee, *Global Ambulance Chasers: Lawyers Profit from Suing States for Multinationals*, CorpWatch Blog (Dec. 17, 2012), https://bit.ly/2KACrcd (last visited Aug. 7, 2018); Julio Godoy, *The Evils of Bilateral Investment Treaties*, Arab News (Dec. 13, 2012), https://bit.ly/2OPhiyk (last visited Aug. 7, 2018); Cecelia Olivet & Pia Eberhardt, *Profiting from Injustice: Challenging the Investment Arbitration Industry*, Open Democracy Net (Feb. 9, 2013), https://bit.ly/2nfJfTw (last visited Aug. 7, 2018).

[135] Nick Buxton, *Legalised Profiteering?* Corporate Europe Observatory, 3–7 (Nov. 2011), https://bit.ly/2KCo5s1 (last visited Aug. 7, 2018).

[136] Eberhardt & Olivet, *supra* note 59, at 7–9.

[137] Peter O'Neil, *Lawyers, Companies Set to Profit from Huge Growth in Global Arbitration Against Canadian Government*, Van. Sun. (Dec. 3, 2012), https://bit.ly/2lzgSib (quoting Marc Lalonde) (last visited Aug. 7, 2018).

[138] Jason Yackee, *Controlling the International Investment Law Agency*, 53 Harv. Int'l L.J. 391, 405, 411 (2012).

[139] Marc Viet, *Investment Treaty Arbitration: Session on Issue Conflicts*, 15 No. 1 IBA ARB. News 22 (2010).

[140] Catherine Rogers, *The Arrival of the "Have-Nots" in International Arbitration*, 8 Nev. L.J. 341, 358 (2007).

[141] Bryant Garth & Yves M. Dezalay, *Corporate Law Firms, NGOs, and Issues of Legitimacy for a Global Legal Order*, 80 Fordham L. Rev. 6, 2309, 2312 (2012).

Much like the undiscovered country of investor identity and the question from *Butch Cassidy*, there is an open issue: Who are the lawyers involved, and what is their level of expertise? Seminal scholarship by Marc Galanter suggests that it is not the availability of lawyers that matters but a lawyer's status and power that marks strategic advantage. For this reason, Galanter set up the classic distinction between counsel who are "one-shotters" or "one shot" (OS) players, who are newcomers to a system, or those who have extensive experience as "repeat players" (RPs). He then argued that RPs have critical advantages in dispute resolution.[142]

Applying Galanter's typology in international arbitration,[143] previous research explored RP lawyers and ITA outcomes. The results demonstrated a reliable relationship between counsel and outcomes, but the link was subtle, working in slightly different ways for investors and states across different outcome variables. For investors, the presence of experienced counsel was linked to winning a case and amounts awarded (but not relative investor success). Meanwhile, for states, the presence of experienced counsel was linked to decreased relative success for investors (but not with winning a case or amounts awarded).[144]

The question remains whether those outcomes are worth the cost. Chapter 8 explores counsel expertise and ITA costs, with this section setting the stage. It first explores basic counsel demographics and how parties used counsel. It then identifies who has represented investors and states in the past as well as the marketplace for legal representation. Third, it explores RP counsel and "lawyering up" in response to expertise on the opposite side.

A. BASIC DEMOGRAPHICS ON REPRESENTATION

In ITA, parties could theoretically represent themselves *pro se*, use internal counsel, secure external counsel as its exclusive representative, or use a hybrid approach. Commentary in the popular press focuses on the private bar and law firms.[145] In her classic article, Professor Rogers posited that "foreign investors typically hire[] one of the major international law firms, which have practice groups that specialize" in ITA but that "many developing countries have their own government attorneys defend them in investment arbitrations."[146] While Rogers references an early ITA case against Argentina and one non-ITA case against the Seychelles to support her paradigm,[147] the question remains whether it reflects the market for ITA legal services.

[142] Marc Galanter, *Why the "Haves" Come Out Ahead: Speculations on the Limits of Legal Change*, 9 LAW & SOC'Y REV. 95 (1974).

[143] Rogers, *supra* note 140, at 343; Carrie Menkel-Meadow, *Do the "Haves" Come Out Ahead in Alternative Judicial Systems?: Repeat Players in ADR*, 15 OHIO ST. J. DISP. RESOL. 19 (1999).

[144] Franck & Wylie, *supra* note 62, at 460, 508–09, 514, 517, 522–23.

[145] *See, e.g.*, Michael D. Goldhaber, *High Stakes*, AMERICAN LAWYER: FOCUS EUROPE, Summer 2011, at 19, 20; David Samuels, *Guide to "Approved" Specialist International Arbitration Firms*, GLOBAL ARB. REV. (Feb. 11, 2013); Global Arbitration Review, *GAR 100: 9th Edition*, GLOBAL ARB. REV. (Jan. 1. 2016).

[146] Rogers, *supra* note 140, at 257.

[147] *Id.* (citing Eric Gottwald, *Leveling the Playing Field: Is It Time for a Legal Assistance Center for Developing Nations in Investment Treaty Arbitration?*, 22 AM. U. INT'L L. REV. 237, 252–56 (2007)). The author supervised Mr. Gottwald's student article and organized his interviews with government officials.

The data explored counsel of record to test theories about legal representation. Although lawyers can, and did, change over the course of a dispute, the dataset coded up to seven different legal entities representing either the investor or respondent for every public award.[148] While this may undercount lawyers involved earlier or withdrawing from representation, the objective was to create a replicable coding protocol that other researchers could verify.[149]

Assessing the distinct entities involved (not typically people)[150] revealed that investors and states had similar, but slightly different, representation patterns. Investors tended to primarily secure representation from external sources. By contrast, states used external counsel but to a lesser degree, having greater involvement with internal counsel.

In roughly 90% of cases studied, investors had at least one external law firm involved.[151] In approximately 15% of cases, investors themselves were identified as advisors of record.[152] In a fraction of cases, by the end of the award if not earlier, the investor was *pro se* (3.5%).[153] The size of claimants' legal teams, on average, involved two separate legal entities.[154] While nearly half (42.6%; $n = 86$) the investors had a single legal representative, another cluster (38.1%; $n = 77$) used two sets of legal representatives.[155]

---

148 *See* Codebook, Appendix IV. To promote reliability, coding primarily addressed counsel of record on the first page of the award; where information was not available, award text and the last phase of representation was evaluated. Representation involved not mere attendance but some indication of legal advocacy. Future research should consider additional coding to develop the metric of legal representation. In the interim, this research provides an initial baseline.

149 Over the period studied, some legal entities changed names or merged. After consulting corporate histories and lawyers in cases, specific coding assessments were individually detailed in the Codebook. For example, cases originally from either Hale & Door or Wilmer Cutler & Pickering were all coded as "Wilmer Hale."

150 Coders originally attempted to identify the number of people within legal entities, but given the information provided by tribunals and variance, the codes varied widely and failed to precisely capture the variable of interest. In the author's experience, there have been cases where lawyers—whether external or internal—are used strategically but their participation need not be credited in submitted briefs or reflected in awards. Such "shadow" counsel may be worthy of future exploration.

151 90.1%; $n = 182$. For the 202 cases, information about claimant's counsel was unavailable in 13 cases. The data, when filtered for final awards, reflected similar representation patterns.

152 $n = 30$. This may be a function of how tribunals identified counsel of record in the case as, in several awards, tribunals indicated the parties' internal representative attended hearings but there was no evidence indicating they were formal counsel or actively involved in formal advocacy. It is possible that such activity may have occurred but it was not reflected in the award.

153 The seven cases were *Tokios Tokeles v. Ukraine, Quadrant v. Costa Rica, Gruslin v. Malaysia, Europe Cement v. Turkey, Cemetownia v. Turkey, Howard v. Canada*, and *Lemire v. Ukraine* [I]. As coding protocols focused on representation at the time of the award, there were three cases where lawyers had withdrawn from representation but were involved in earlier phases of the representation, namely: Mannheimer Swartling in *Cementownia "Nowa Huta"* and *Europe Cement*, and Appleton Associates in *Quadrant*. In the remaining four cases, there was no indication investors used external counsel.

154 $M = 1.73$; $SD = .818$.

155 The number of entities ranged from a minimum of one to five. Only two cases, *Yaung Chi Oo v. Myanmar* and *Mhilay v. Sri Lanka*, had five legal entities (including in-house counsel). A smattering of investors had teams of three ($n = 20$; 9.9%) or four ($n = 4$; 2%) legal entities.

States' legal teams were somewhat similar. Like investors, states tended to have two or more firms involved in the defense,[156] with states typically using one[157] or two[158] legal entities for defense. Unlike investors, in nearly a quarter of cases (n = 43; 21.3%) states secured representation from *three* different legal entities. States also nearly always sent some representatives to participate in ITA. In only three cases (1.5% of cases analyzed), states refused to participate in ITA. But in each of those three cases—*Mohammad Ammar al-Bahloul v. Tajikistan, Iurii Bogdanov v. Moldova*, and *Goetz v. Burundi*—tribunals repeatedly encouraged state participation without success. Even in *Goetz*, where Burundi failed to send representatives to hearings or submit memorials, the state contacted ICSID at key stages requesting time to settle the dispute.[159]

Legal representation of states exhibited a few other variations. Primarily, states were more likely to proceed *pro se* (24.8%; n = 50) and without external counsel.[160] But like investors, even where internal state counsel was involved, respondents used some external representation in nearly 70% of cases.[161] This created four main patterns of how states utilized counsel in ITA. The first pattern involved exclusive or nearly exclusive internal representation by states. The United States, for example, never relied on external legal counsel.[162] Argentina rarely (11% of its cases) retained external legal counsel, in high-stakes cases such as *Compañiá de Aguas del Aconquija & Vivendi Universal* and *Abaclat*;[163] Argentina often collaborated with internal entities for defense.[164]

A second pattern involved states exhibiting moderate collaboration with external legal expertise. Canada did so in roughly 30% of its caseload, twice by hiring Donald McRae and Garvey, Shubert & Barer. Mexico was similarly active in retaining counsel in 40% of its caseload. In six cases, it retained at least one of the following entities: Thomas & Partners, Pillsbury Winthrop Shaw Pittman, or counsel from Matrix Chambers.

The third pattern was use of internal counsel, but primarily in collaboration with external counsel. Ecuador, for example, typically worked in collaboration (75% of its caseload)[165] with a team of lawyers from a large multinational law firm.[166] Egypt similarly tended to partner

---

156 $M = 2.02$; $SD = 1.147$.

157 38.1%; n = 77.

158 24.8%; n = 50.

159 *Goetz et al. v. Republic of Burundi*, ICSID ARB/95/3, 458 ICSID Rev.-F.I.L.J. 457 (2009).

160 For respondents, information about counsel was missing from 11 of the 202 cases.

161 68.3%; n = 138.

162 In only one case, *Loewen*, the U.S. Department of Justice was involved with representation. Spain was the only other state analyzed exclusively relying on in-house counsel, but it was only sued once in the period analyzed.

163 The entities in the three cases were: Pérez Alati, Grondona, Benites, Arntsen & Martínez de Hoz, Arnold & Porter, Matrix Chambers and Bruce Heyman; and Cleary Gottlieb Steen & Hamilton.

164 These included the Embassy of Argentina in Washington, DC, and the Argentine Ministry of the Economy.

165 Information about legal counsel was missing in one case. Once, Ecuador used internal lawyers from various departments to represent itself; and in another case, Ecuador exclusively used Weil Gotshal & Manges. In the remaining nine cases, representation was a collaboration between Ecuador and the private sector.

166 In one case, the information about Ecuador's counsel is unknown; another case has Weil Gotshal & Manges as the sole representative. For the other ten cases, in addition to internal government assistance and the activity of the Procuradoria General del Estado, the law firms involved were Foley Hoag; Winston & Strawn; Dechert, Latham & Watkins; Squire Sanders; Weil Gotshal; Arnold & Porter; Cabezas y Wray Abogados; Fabara & Compañía Abogados; and Bustamante y Bustamante.

with private law firms (75% of its caseload), many of which had a local partner,[167] and in one case, *Champion Trading*, relied exclusively upon the services of Bredin Prat. The final, but minor, trend involved states *exclusively* using external counsel. These were typically states with one ITA dispute, namely: Azerbaijan, Macedonia, Thailand, Lebanon, United Arab Emirates, Serbia, Kyrgyzstan, and Bangladesh. The only exceptions, where a state with multiple ITA disputes only used external counsel, were Turkey[168] and Russia.[169]

Ultimately, data suggested a degree of balance in ITA legal representation, at least for the sheer number of legal entities involved in party representation. This, however, did not evaluate quality of legal services, impact of RPs, or representation cost. It also indicates that, for both investors and respondents, only a fraction avoided using counsel, and most parties secured legal representation. Although they used internal and external counsel in slightly different proportions, both investors and states relied heavily on the private bar to adjudicate ITA disputes.

B. THE MARKETPLACE FOR COUNSEL

Having identified parties use of counsel and the contributions of in-house and external lawyers, the question remains: Who exactly are the entities, and what is their experience? The dataset synthesized information focusing *only* on counsel identified in awards through a painstaking process that merged compiled lists of legal representatives, including in-house and external counsel for all parties, and cross-checked to prevent double-counting for cases with multiple awards. The compiled data revealed several things.

First, there were 420 different legal entities representing parties in ITA disputes.[170] This rebuts the suggestion that ITA is a completely closed shop, and begins to suggest opportunities for market participants to enter the fray and expand the scope of legal services. It also begins to cast doubt on statements that there is "a concentrated market that is difficult for newcomers to enter."[171]

Second, although each legal entity represented a client in an average of two cases, the median number of cases was one. Roughly 75% of the known legal entities involved in ITA

[167] The Egyptian government's external lawyers were Freshfields Bruckhaus Deringer; Bredin Prat; Kosheri Rashed & Riad; Abdel Raouf Law Firm; Baker & McKenzie's local Egyptian branch, Hafez, Andreas Reiner & Partners; Thomas H. Webster; and Dr. Aktham El Kholy.

[168] Turkey tended to use groups of lawyers for cases. Freshfields Bruckhaus Deringer often worked in collaboration with Cosar Avukatlik Burosu; Sidley Austin worked in collaboration with Stephen Schwebel and Paksoy & Company. In one case, Turkey consolidated its work with Derains & Gharavi.

[169] In each case, Russia consolidated its defense into a single law firm. The law firms in each case were Granrut Avocats, Baker Botts, and Cleary Gottlieb Steen & Hamilton.

[170] Given variation tribunals' procedures for identifying counsel, legal entities were the unit of analysis. Legal entities were external law firms, barristers' chambers, business units, and government departments. Individuals, such as Stephen Schwebel, were only coded as distinct legal entities when s/he had no other formal affiliation. Counsel were primarily identified using the award cover page or descriptions as to who appeared in hearings. This creates a risk the coding did not fully reflect lawyers who were silently assisting or ghost-writing. *See* Codebook, Appendix IV. As law firms have incentives to serve as counsel of record, control proceedings, and participate in hearings, this risk could be small.

[171] Eberhardt & Olivet, *supra* note 59, at 22.

were one-shot-players who arbitrated a single case and had no further demonstrated participation in ITA. By contrast, 25% of legal representatives were RPs serving in multiple cases. Recognizing that the caseload and scope of representation has evolved, Appendix III identifies the "Top 21" legal entities derived from the dataset, with breakdowns in the numbers of representation of investors and/or states. State agencies, including the Argentine Procuración del Tesoro de la Nación, Secretaria de Economia de Ecuador, the U.S. Department of State, the Canadian Department of Foreign Affairs, Egyptian State Lawsuits Authority, and the Mexican government (primarily through the Secretaria de Economia) made the list of the most elite state RPs. Intriguingly, private sector firms did not necessarily represent one party type. Of RPs, 30% exclusively represented investors and 41% exclusively represented states, but 29% of legal representatives were "side switchers," representing both investors and states over time.

Having identified RPs, we note there are intriguing implications for the growth in the transnational marketplace for legal services and the growth of legal capacity worldwide. There were, for example, a cluster of entities with moderate levels of experience (2–5 cases); and their expertise has arguably grown since the dataset closed. These slightly smaller players reflect a robust, possibly growing, competition for legal services; presumably, a strong market for services permits the dissemination of knowledge, prevents monopolization, and encourages price competition that benefits the parties by way of lower prices. There was also an interesting micro-trend whereby historically smaller players either grew or developed in a local capacity in countries perhaps not historically known for their arbitration practice. For example, Pérez Alati, Grondona, Benites, Arntsen & Martínez de Hoz (an Argentine firm), defended Argentina in one case and later worked with King & Spalding representing investors in five other cases. Likewise, Griskenko & Partners was involved in five cases representing Ukraine, usually in tandem with the state and another local firm. Another firm experiencing growth was Bonelli Erede Pappalardo Studio Legale, which partnered with Sidley Austin and Judge Schwebel in one case, *Impreglio v. Pakistan*, but then had solo representation in *Van de Nul v. Egypt*, thereby having RP expertise in six cases exclusively representing investors. In other words, elements of the market for ITA legal services grew organically, and being part of a smaller or non-Western firm did not prohibit counsel from being retained.[172] Rather, representation choices may be about requisite expertise, competence, price competitiveness, and unique factors of the dispute.

C. IDENTIFYING REPEAT PLAYERS AND "LAWYERING UP"

When it comes to counsel, no one has previously defined RPs in ITA. Empirically, this means that it is appropriate to draw on methodological choices from related research. This research therefore used Galanter's framework for evaluating the effect of being an "arbitration insider," namely by first making a binary distinction between "one-shot" (OS) firms and RPs. Yet, Galanter also argued expertise can be more "a continuum rather than a dichotomous

[172] While many prevalent firms were larger firms from North America and western Europe, the organic growth of firms provides some evidence to rebut the assertion that "Non-Western law firms from the countries most sued by investors scarcely get a look in." *Id.* at 22.

pair,"[173] which warrants a second measure to weight experience using continuous variable to reflect relative participation in ITA. These two approaches were called a "binary" approach and a "weighted" approach.

First, for the 420 legal entities involved, a binary variable identified whether the firm had either one or more than one appointment as counsel—irrespective of whether the firm represented investors, respondents, or both. Then, for every case, another variable calculated the total number of RPs involved to identify the expertise of the total legal team for both investors and states. Second, another variable evaluated the relative weight and experience of counsel. To avoid skewing given the outsized influence of a minority of RPs,[174] the variable used five categories on a scale of 0 (one-shot player) to 4 (most experienced) to identify a firm's weighted experience, using categorical breakpoints based upon the data's own distribution.[175] After coding firms' experience, such as the binary measure, the final weighted variable calculated the total relative expertise of all counsel on each party's legal team.

Using the binary approach, counsel's experience for investors and states were roughly equivalent. The average number of RPs was just under one on the investors' prosecution team and just over one on the states' defense team.[176] Tests using the binary measure failed to identify, as a whole, meaningful difference in the relative experience of investors' and states' legal teams.[177]

Yet that was not the end of the story. The weighted measure suggested a degree of nuance. When investors secured experienced arbitration counsel, so too did states; but states' counsel tended to have even more experience under their belts. Specifically, RP counsel on states' defense teams tended to have been active in roughly twice as many cases as RPs on investors'

---

[173] Galanter, *supra* note 142, at 97–98.

[174] For example, cases involving RPs Freshfields or Argentine Procuración had nearly 200% more experience than other legal entities.

[175] Firms with a single appointment were ranked as "0" to reflect that they were OS. The distribution indicated that at the 90th percentile, the average number of cases involved were 3.9. For that reason, RPs with two-four appointments were ranked as "1." The next clear break occurred at the 95th percentile, where the average number of cases was 6.95 and there was a meaningful clump of firms with five to six cases; for that reason, RPs with five to six cases were ranked as "2." The next clear break came for the group of twelve law firms that were on the bottom portion of the "Top 21" list (those law firms that were ranked in the top ten to fourteen entities); and RPs with seven to nine cases were ranked as "3." Finally, the remaining top nine RPs, namely those with eleven or more cases, were classified as "4." Each of the 420 legal entities were then transformed to a ranked score using the 0–4 categorical approach. *See* Codebook, Appendix IV.

[176] Using the Binary approach, investors had an average of .95 RPs in a case (n = 189; SD = .742); and respondents had 1.31 RPs (n = 188; SD = .932).

[177] A chi-square test compared cases involving exclusively OS counsel on both investors' and states' legal teams (n = 9), OS counsel on investors' legal teams but RPs on states' legal teams (n = 39), RPs on investors' legal teams and OS counsel on states' legal teams, (n = 19), and RPs representing both parties (n = 119). The test failed to reveal a reliable pattern between the presence (or absence) of at least one RP on either party's legal team (χ^2 (1) = −0.406; p = .48; r = .06; n = 186). Similarly, a bivariate correlation explored links between the number of RPs on investors' legal teams and the number of RPs on states' legal teams, but failed to identify a meaningful linear relationship (r (186) = .08; p = .27). Given the small effect sizes, the power of the analysis is approximately .30, creating a 70% risk of a Type II error. As the lack of a result does not prove the lack of a relationship, future analyses could reveal different results.

legal teams.[178] Some variance may reflect that states, as the ultimate repeat players in the arbitration process, had internal legal teams with more experience; and some of the variance may have occurred in how states staffed their defense teams (often *pro se* defense like the United States and Argentina but often with strategic co-counsel like Canada and Mexico).

The difference was not just superficial. There was a reliable relationship between the relative weight of experience of the parties' legal teams. The significant—but relatively small—effect reflected that, as the weighted expertise of investors' teams increased, so too did the weighted expertise of states' defense team.[179] Likewise, the lower the relative expertise of investors' counsel, the lower the relative expertise of respondents' counsel. The tests offer initial evidence supporting a theory that states tended to "lawyer up" with expert counsel in ITA when there were RPs on investors' legal teams. It is an intriguing possibility, as retaining expert counsel may be a signal of a case's relative merits or the seriousness of parties' intentions to vigorously pursue ITA by selecting counsel with experience in procedure, substantive law, and culture of ITA. It is critical to remember that the tests explored linkages between variables—not a causal chain—making it improper to conclude that one party retaining more sophisticated counsel causes retention of similarly experienced counsel by the counter-party. While investors presumably initiate ITA with the aid of counsel (thereby theoretically starting a battle for relative counsel expertise), counsel for both investors' and states' legal teams can also (and sometimes did) change over the case's lifecycle.[180] Moreover, counsel choice can be influenced by factors beyond opposing counsel's expertise, for reasons including costs, recommendations of constituents or third-party funders, or state procurement laws on bidding for external legal services. Leaping too far with the correlation, therefore, is improper and a likely by-product of intuitive reasoning searching for cognitive ease. Nevertheless, future research could replicate these initial analyses to explore "lawyering up" in ITA. Those questions should include: what are the implications for the capacity building of new entrants into the legal marketplace; what role will the ratcheting up of lawyer expertise have upon the cost that both parties pay for legal representation; and what does this mean for equality of arms and access to justice both for smaller investors and less developed countries?

VI. Industry and Institutions

Case-related variables aid identification of paradigmatic ITA disputes. This requires an appreciation of the industries involved in ITA to have a sense of historical risk. Likewise, doctrinal distinctions in ITA are critical, as the legal framework implicates potential reform. This section explores the industries affected as well as the institutions and applicable rules.

---

[178] For investors' counsel, the average weighted score was 2.23 (n = 189; SD = 2.038), reflecting that claimants' counsel had been involved in approximately five to six ITA cases. In slight contrast, respondents' teams had a mean weighted score of 3.31 (n = 188; SD = 2.341), suggesting that state counsel teams had been involved with roughly ten to fourteen cases.

[179] A bivariate correlation identified a significant positive relationship between the weighted experience of investors' and states' legal teams (r (186) = .15; p = .04). A linear regression likewise identified a meaningful relationship (F (1, 184) = 4.254; p = .04; r = .15; n = 186).

[180] *See supra* notes 148–153, 165–169 (discussing coding and counsel); *see also* Codebook, Appendix IV.

The data revealed that, despite various sectors involved, energy-related disputes had the largest (and arguably outsized footprint) in ITA. Doctrinally, ICSID remained the dominant player administrating cases.

A. INDUSTRIES AFFECTED

Little research has focused on the investment sectors producing ITA disputes. Historically, UNCTAD used an undefined coding method to estimate that "less than half the cases (39%) involved the services sector, including electricity distribution, telecommunications, debt instruments, water services and waste management";[181] they further estimated 24% of cases involved "mining and oil and gas exploration."[182] Although UNCTAD typically offers an annual update,[183] they continue to find many cases involve electricity, oil, and gas.[184]

ICSID offers some data on the underlying industrial sectors generating disputes. For the time period similar to data analyzed in this book, ICSID reported their disputes covered a variety of sectors, reflecting eleven primary types of investments. The most common sectors were oil, gas, and mining (25%); and there was a large subcomponent of disputes (13%) involving electric power and other energy cases. Other industries with more than 5% of ICSID's docket involved transportation (11%), "other industry" (11%), finance (7%), construction (7%), water (6%), and information and communication (6%).[185] The difficulty with drawing inferences from ICSID statistics, however, is threefold. First, its coding methodology and definitions are somewhat vague. Second, it does not include non-ICSID ITA cases. Third, their docket does not distinguish between ITA and non-ITA disputes arising under national law.

One problem in understanding industry information is the lack of a standard measurement system for coding investment sectors. This means, first, that researchers may be using the same words but referring to different industries; second, researchers may use different words to refer to the same industry; and third, the blunt measure of a single industry may mask the complex nature of the commercial activity in the investment. Recognizing the inevitable challenges of using valid, reliable, and precise definitions,[186] this research used coding

---

[181] UNCTAD, *Latest Developments in Investor-State Dispute Settlement*, IIA Monitor No. 1, 2–3, U.N. Doc. UNCTAD/WEB/ITE/IIA/2008/3 (2008).

[182] *Id.*

[183] *See* UNCTAD, *Investor State Dispute Settlement: Review of Developments in 2015*, IIA Issues Note No. 2, 5, UNCTAD/WEB/DIAE/PCB/2016/4 (June 8, 2016), https://bit.ly/2tDuFrF (last visited Aug. 7, 2018) (noting 76% of cases filed in 2015 related to the services sector, with twenty-three cases supplying electricity and gas, seven cases in construction, seven cases in financial and insurance services, and seven cases in transportation and storage.)

[184] UNCTAD, *WIR 2018*, *supra* note 67, at 93 (describing cases filed in 2017, including eleven cases relating to financial and insurance services; nine cases relating to construction; seven cases relating to electricity, gas, steam, and air; six cases relating to information and communication; and four cases relating to transportation and storage).

[185] ICSID Secretariat, *The ICSID Caseload–Statistics, Issue 2012-1*, ICSID 3–4 (Feb. 7, 2012), https://bit.ly/2ttZlMS (last visited Aug. 7, 2018).

[186] *See* Franck, *supra* note 17.

methodology from previous research, with nineteen different industries in ITA that focused upon the primary industrial sector in dispute.[187] While the largest subgroup of disputes occurred in the energy sector, there were other relatively large subgroups in sectors related to financial investments, food and beverage, industrial supplies, real estate, transportation, waste management, and water. The lingering question is whether earlier research remained representative.

The ITA caseload analyzed covered a broad range of investment activity. The bulk of claims remained in the energy sector, accounting for nearly 30% of cases.[188] Other extractive industries, including chemical and mining (7.4%), were also contentious. Other common sectors generating disputes involved food and beverage investments (9.4%), transportation (9.4%), real estate (5.9%), telecommunications (5.4%), and industrial supplies (5.4%). *See* Figure 3.6.

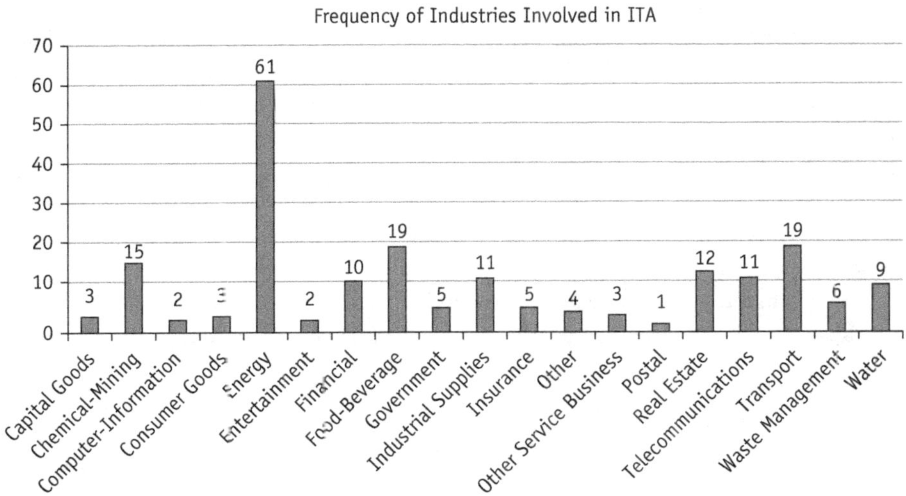

FIGURE 3.6 Frequency of Industries Involved in ITA. Mean Cases per Industry = 9.64 (*SD* = 7.726; *n* = 201).[189]

Compared to earlier research, some industries experienced relative growth. Industries with the greatest proportions of ITA growth (listed highest to lowest) were energy, food-beverage, transportation, chemical-mining, capital goods, and telecommunications. Other investment sectors experienced no new disputes, including: computer and information services, postal, and waste management.

---

[187] Franck, *supra* note 23, at 42 n.180; *see also* Codebook, Appendix IV.

[188] 30.2%; *n* = 61. Energy disputes were defined as involving: electricity generation, transmission, and distribution; natural gas exploration, transmission, or distribution; oil exploration, transmission or distribution; or dam construction and/or hydroelectric projects. *See* Codebook, Appendix IV.

[189] Industry data from *Austrian Airlines v. Slovak Republic* was unavailable given redactions. One might hypothesize that the dispute involved transportation.

Commentators rightly focus on energy sector disputes,[190] as energy cases remained the single largest category and experienced the largest proportionate increase. Yet, ITA conflict encompasses more than just energy disputes, and it is critical to prevent cognitive illusions from creating an intuitively appealing perception that overemphasizes energy disputes and underemphasizes other sectors. Recent and prominent energy disputes, whether deriving from nationalizations in Latin America or Yukos oil, may facilitate the easy recollection of energy disputes. Similarly, oil disputes initiated by companies who are household names, such as Chevron or Enron, may be easy to recall. Availability and recency could contribute to overestimating that energy disputes are representative[191] and wrongly presume most ITA cases involve energy-related disputes. Failing to appreciate base rate information that energy disputes comprised 30% of disputes could create errors about industries benefitting from ITA or creating ITA risk. While energy disputes were a fundamental subset, energy cases were not the only risky sector. This has three implications.

First, as they comprise a core of ITA disputes, there is value in considering the variance attributable to energy disputes. Second, other industries with relatively large proportions of cases, including transportation and food and beverage, may have received insufficient attention as prototypical ITA disputes. Third, as the majority of the cases did *not* derive from the energy sector, ITA reform need not be designed exclusively for energy disputes. Rather, reform should be structured to nimbly address disputes across multiple sectors. As ITA could evolve, other areas (such as investments in services) may become more prevalent, and it is critical to have a system of resolving disputes that can handle a variety of cases, rather than one paradigm of disputes or creating a dispute system for cases that are, fundamentally, outliers. Put simply, the tail should not "wag the dog," and stakeholders should focus on systematic concerns. If, however, energy disputes are meaningfully different than other disputes, there may be value in designing specific dispute resolution systems to address the issues unique to the energy sector.[192]

B. INSTITUTIONS AND RULES

An impressionistic literature review might suggest ITA disputes are resolved exclusively at ICSID. Some commentators conflate doctrinal regimes underlying ITA and ICSID cases, and the two are sometimes used in a synonymous manner.[193] The critique of ITA as "ISDS" (i.e., investor-state dispute settlement) is doctrinally wrongheaded, ignoring that ITA involves adjudication of international law.[194] Some have tapped this vein to critique ICSID.[195] Rather than focusing on substantive treaty rights, states critique the outcome of

---

[190] Kabir Duggal, *The Energy Sector, Investment Arbitration, and the ECT: Carving Out a Special Regime*, *in* INVESTMENT TREATY ARBITRATION AND INTERNATIONAL LAW 3, 5–14 (Ian A. Laird et al., eds., 2014).

[191] DANIEL KAHNEMAN ET AL., JUDGMENT UNDER UNCERTAINTY: HEURISTICS AND BIASES (Daniel Kahneman et al., eds., 1982).

[192] *See* Chapter 9.

[193] *See, e.g.*, Katia F. Gomez, *Latin American and ICSID: David Versus Goliath*, 17 L. & BUS. REV. AM. 194 (2011); Trakman, *supra* note 105; Stephan W. Schill, *System-Building in Investment Treaty Arbitration and Lawmaking*, 12 GERMAN L.J. 1083, 1084 (2011).

[194] "Investor-State Dispute Settlement" need not involve treaty claims; instead it can involve claims under domestic commercial law or domestic investment law, meaning the governing law is the host state's internal law.

[195] Sergey Ripinsky, *Venezuela's Withdrawal from ICSID: What It Does and Does Not Achieve*, INVESTMENT TREATY NEWS (Apr. 13, 2012), http://bit.ly/HD7L8e (last visited Aug. 7, 2018).

dispute resolution. Chavez justified Venezuela's ICSID withdrawal by claiming, "ICSID has ruled 232 times in favor of transnational interests in the 234 cases heard throughout its history."[196] He did not critique the expropriation rights within the treaty. Nor did he discuss the treaty's failure to constrain arbitral discretion in interpreting treaty rights. Rather, systemic blame was laid at ICSID's feet without appreciation of the subtleties of international law or the role of unique facts.

Conflating ICSID and ITA is legally incorrect and scientifically improper. First, as a matter of law, while ICSID's caseload contains cases arising under treaties, ICSID's jurisdiction extends to domestic commercial and domestic investment law. It is improper to make inferences about ICSID cases without first excluding ICSID's non-ITA cases. Second, focusing exclusively on ICSID ignores ITA cases originating from different doctrinal regimes and generates unrepresentative information. Both errors have consequences. Critical explanatory variables, for example, may be misattributed. Policy determinations based on improper assumptions or misattributions are unlikely to achieve their goals or can generate negative externalities; meanwhile, fruitful policy opportunities may remain unexplored. To create normative reform tailored to address actual problems, it is vital to compare "apples to apples."

While matters have somewhat improved, there has been less focus on holistically analyzing ITA, irrespective of the forum. UNCTAD has worked hard to offer a framework. In its 2012 *Issues Note*, one arguable interpretation of the data was that cases at ICSID accounted for roughly 64% of disputes, UNCITRAL accounted for roughly 29%, SCC accounted for 5%, and other known institutions (namely the ICC, LCIA (London Court of International Arbitration), and CRCICA (Cairo Regional Centre for International Commercial Arbitration)) carried 2% of the caseload.[197] Together, these figures suggest that—for the time period contemporaneous[198] to the dataset this book analyzes—roughly 71% of ITA cases were institutional and the remainder were non-institutional. This was similar to earlier research identifying that approximately 79% of ITA cases involved institutional arbitration.[199]

---

[196] *Spain's Valle Verde Brings Arbitration Cases Against Venezuela to 25*, Lat. Am. Herald Trib. (July 26, 2012), http://bit.ly/18evC8S (last visited Aug. 7, 2018); *but see* Chapter 5 (providing data contradicting the claim).

[197] UNCTAD's Note referred to "known treaty-based cases reached 450 in 2011," but later referred to 279 ICSID cases, 126 UNCITRAL cases, twenty-one SCC cases, seven ICC cases, one CRCICA case, and one LCIA case, totaling only 435 cases. UNCTAD, *2012 Issues Note, supra* note 17, at 1–2. Although the Note also identifies (without enumerating) that for "the remaining cases, the applicable arbitration rules/venues are unknown," it is not certain if the unknown cases were counted elsewhere or are novel. The calculations therefore used 435 as the denominator.

[198] The situation was not dissimilar in UNCTAD's 2017 data. Focusing on "known" cases, UNCTAD explained "[s]ixty-one percent of all known [ISDS] cases have been filed under the ICSID Convention or the ICSID Additional Facility Rules. The UNCITRAL Arbitration Rules were the second most used procedural basis, followed by the Arbitration Rules of the SCC Arbitration Institute." UNCTAD, *Special Update on Investor-State Dispute Settlement: Facts and Figures*, IIA Issues Note No. 3, 1, 5, UNCTAD/DIA/PCB/2017/7 (Nov. 2017), https://bit.ly/2lWvfQO (last visited Aug. 7, 2018). A more specific breakdown of 2017 data suggests roughly 68% of ITA cases were institutional, and the remaining 32% were some ad hoc arbitration. *Id.* at 5.

[199] Franck, *supra* note 23, at 39–40.

It is critical to demarcate between institutions and rules, as institutions can apply different rules, and ad hoc arbitrations can apply different institutional rules, such as *Yaung Chi Oo Trading v. Myanmar*, which used ICSID-Additional Facility Rules.[200] This research distinguishes between institutional versus ad hoc arbitration and separately analyzes applicable rules.

Consistent with UNCTAD's findings, most ITA cases occurred at institutions, with built-in administrative support for arbitration. Like the baseline from earlier research, 78.7% of cases analyzed were arbitrated before institutions, namely ICSID and the SCC. ICSID retained the primary caseload (73.3%; $n = 148$). The SCC (5.4%; $n = 11$) had a core of ITA disputes but remained comparatively smaller. *See* Figure 3.7. At the time, despite coding for the possibility, there were no publicly available ITA awards from the ICC. UNCTAD's data suggested that the ICC (and other institutions including the LCIA, HKIAC (Hong Kong International Arbitration Centre) among others) plays a minimal or, at the least, smaller role in ITA cases than the SCC. As ICSID provides limited public information on registered cases, but not all venues have the same transparency obligations, case selection effects may under-represent non-ICSID cases and over represent ICSID cases. Yet UNCTAD's data on "known" cases reasonably aligns with this research.

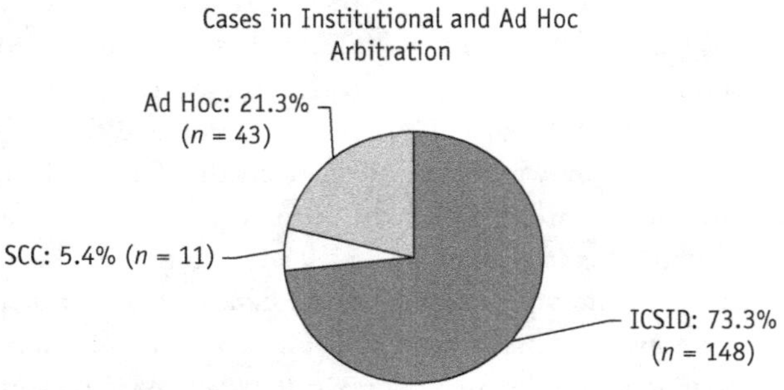

FIGURE 3.7 Frequency and Percentage of Cases in Institutional and *ad hoc* Arbitration ($n = 202$).

The remainder of cases analyzed (21.3%) involved ad hoc arbitration.[201] UNCTAD's reported proportions of ad hoc arbitrations (29%)[202] were roughly similar to the 21% observed

[200] Yaung Chi Oo Trading Ltd. v. Myanmar, ASEAN I.D. Case No. ARB/01/1, Award (Mar. 31, 2003), 42 I.L.M. 540 (2003); Franck, *supra* note 23, at 39–40.

[201] Cases were coded as ad hoc where institutions provided some administrative assistance, whether ICSID, the LCIA, or the PCA. Administrative assistance of an institution did not doctrinally transform ad hoc arbitration into an institutional one as the case was: not conducted according to the institution's arbitration rules, and there is no reference to the institution's administrative body to resolve questions of procedure. *Occidental v. Ecuador* was an ad hoc arbitration conducted pursuant to the UNCITRAL Rules, with the LCIA managing financial matters and assisting with hearing rooms, but it was not administered under the LCIA Rules.

[202] Comparing the 29% with data in the 2017 Issues Note, *supra* note 198, suggesting 32% of cases were ad hoc and/or UNCITRAL cases, the facial distinction need not be statistically meaningful. As minor fluctuations can be due to chance alone, UNCTAD data does not readily lend itself to direct statistical comparison, particularly as measurement differences could account for small variances. Alternatively, there may be a verifiable

here. The replication and convergence of results from different methodologies suggests that, as a population parameter, at least 70–79% of the ITA caseload involved institutional arbitration and the remainder was ad hoc arbitration. Nevertheless, possible selection effects—where private awards that were not analyzed could involve ad hoc cases—may have skewed the data and under-represented the number of ad hoc ITA cases.

Exploring whether cases were institutional or ad hoc is only one aspect of applicable law. Arbitration rules also provide applicable doctrine, with four core paradigms. The largest group of cases occurred at ICSID under ICSID Convention Rules (61.9%; $n = 125$). The next largest tranche in the pre-2012 caseload occurred in ad hoc arbitration under UNCITRAL Rules (19.8%; $n = 40$). A third group of cases were rendered at ICSID pursuit to Additional Facility Rules (11.9%; $n = 24$). A fourth trend was for the SCC to administer ITA under SCC Rules (5.4%; $n = 11$).

The data demonstrated a strong reliance on ICSID and the ICSID Convention. Other forums, particularly ad hoc UNCITRAL arbitration, had a substantial footprint. The data did not reveal an abandonment of ICSID, or a strong decrease in ICSID's use as a legal framework. Although the caseload increased approximately 250% from earlier research, the ICSID-Additional Facility and SCC caseload doubled, but experienced a slight proportionate decrease.[203] By contrast, rates of the ICSID Convention and ad hoc UNCITRAL cases both slightly increased in proportion.[204] This suggests that there was not a per se "flight" from ICSID,[205] and such claims could be overstated and potentially influenced by cognitive illusions of recency or availability.[206] Rather, there may be a phenomenon whereby other forums, particularly UNCITRAL, are growing in proportion compared to their historical levels, which may make their prevalence appear greater. Put simply, there may not be a decline of ICSID, but rather a "rise of the rest."[207]

Other elements warrant attention when assessing institutions and rules. Issues related to cost, time, and outcome are chief among concerns affecting strategic choices.[208] Chapter 8 explores potential links to arbitration costs, as a function of arbitration institutions. The common thread, however, was that arbitral forums were *not* reliably associated with differences in critical cost variables and the timing of the proceedings. When considering

---

phenomenon of a move toward ad hoc arbitration, but that is not proven in a statistically reliable manner. Future research may test the historical baseline.

[203] In 2006, there were five SCC cases (now eleven) and twelve ICSID-AF cases (now twenty-four). The number of ad hoc cases under non-UNCITRAL rules remained constant.

[204] Earlier research identified forty-nine ICSID Convention cases (now 125) and fourteen UNCITRAL ad hoc cases (now forty).

[205] *See, e.g.*, Katia Fach Gómez, *Latin America and ICSID: David v. Goliath?*, 17 L. & Bus. Rev. Am. 195, 227 (2011) (discussing efforts to avoid ICSID arbitration); *but see* Ruth MacKenzie et al., The Manual on International Courts and Tribunals 150 (2d ed. 2010) (suggesting ICSID's transparency reform "has not led to any flight from ICSID").

[206] *See* Chapter 2.

[207] Fareed Zakaria, The Post-American World (2008). It is possible that the use of institutions—such as the ICC, HKIAC, SIAC (Singapore International Arbitration), LCIA, ICDR (International Center for Dispute Resolution), and others—has changed.

[208] Anthony Sinclair et al., *ICSID Arbitration: How Long Does It Take?*, 4 Global Arb. Rev. J. 18 (2009).

ITA as a whole, having a case at ICSID or outside ICSID was likewise not reliably associated with outcomes, including whether an investor won or lost a case, amounts awarded, or relative investor success.[209] So perhaps one need not be unduly surprised by the results involving arbitration costs.

---

[209] *See, e.g.*, Franck & Wylie, *supra* note 62, at 511, 515 (trying, but failing, to identify reliable relationships in a regression model between ICSID cases and outcomes using this dataset); *see also* Susan D. Franck, *The ICSID Effect?*, 51 VA. J. INT'L L. 825 (2011) (failing to identify links between ICSID and outcomes using more limited data).

4 ITA Expansion, Time, and Costs

I. The Growth of ITA

ITA was a material change in international investment dispute resolution.[1] It gave investors the right to sue host states directly for government conduct that arguably violated treaties and damaged investors. Without a direct right to access dispute settlement, there were no formal disputes. This does not mean investment conflict was nonexistent. Historical information suggests investment disputes existed in medieval times.[2] Between 1960 and 1974, the United Nations identified 875 acts of expropriation in sixty-two countries.[3] Only when political and economic interests were sufficiently serious did rare cases make their way to international courts[4] or state-created ad hoc Claims

[1] *See* Chapter 1.

[2] Tillmann R. Braun, *Globalization: The Driving Force in International Investment Law*, *in* The Backlash against Investment Arbitration 491 (Michael Waibel et al., eds., 2010).

[3] Jeswald W. Salacuse & Nicolas P. Sullivan, *Do BITs Really Work? An Evaluation of Bilateral Investment Treaties and Their Grand Bargain*, 35 Harv. Int'l L.J. 67, 75–76 n.54 (2005); U.N. Secretary-General, *Permanent Sovereignty over Natural Resources: Rep. of the Secretary-General*, U.N. Doc. A/9716 (1974); *see also* Don L. Piper, *New Direction in the Protection of American-Owned Property Abroad*, 4 Int'l Trade L.J. 315, 320 (1979).

[4] *See, e.g.*, Case Concerning Amadou Sadio Diallo (Guinea v. Dem. Rep. Congo), I.C.J., Preliminary Objections (May 24, 2007); Elettronica S.p.A. (ELSI) (U.S. v. It.), 1989 I.C.J. 15 (July 20); Barcelona Traction, Light, and Power Co., Ltd. (Belg. v. Spain), 1970 I.C.J. 3 (July 20); Anglo-Iranian Oil Co. (U.K. v. Iran), 1952 I.C.J. 93 (July 22).

Arbitration Costs. Susan D. Franck.

Commissions.[5] Otherwise, investors absorbed the loss directly, negotiated alternative solutions with the state, attempted to recover under political risk insurance, or sought recovery in the state's domestic courts—where states could benefit from defenses such as sovereign immunity. There is little historical data on investment conflict to offer a baseline for how investors or states fared under these alternative dispute resolution methods. Particularly when there was no direct contractual relationship, historical conflict management processes functionally insulated states from having domestic conduct evaluated under international law. Deviation from a pre-existing baseline of zero means that launching *any* case generates an undeniable increase. For states involved in the rare dispute prior to the creation of ITA, recency and availability of information about ITA facilitates cognitive illusions whereby stakeholders likely perceive the recent disputes to be both prevalent and typical.

Understanding ITA demographics helps in assessing the growth of ITA and provides a baseline. UNCTAD historically referred to a "litigation explosion,"[6] although recent reports describe an increasing caseload.[7] Focusing on "known cases," UNCTAD reported in 2012 that there were 450 known cases, but less than half those cases were concluded.[8] UNCTAD's data suggested that, starting in 1987, there were fewer than ten cases per year. After 1999, the caseload shifted, and the smallest number of new disputes UNCTAD reported was in 2002 (approximately twenty-seven), with a maximum of forty-six new cases in 2012.[9] As time marched on, UNCTAD's data reflects that the number of cases filed has continued to increase in a somewhat facially higher proportion.[10] Although ICSID does not differentiate between ITA and other disputes, ICSID's data is similar. Between 1987 and 1996, ICSID registered fewer than three cases a year; from 1997 to 2001, there were roughly 10–14 cases per year. Matters changed in 2002, after the Argentine currency crisis, when nineteen cases were filed. From then until 2011, ICSID registered approximately twenty-five to thirty-five cases per year;[11] by 2013–2017, ICSID registered around forty to fifty cases each year.[12]

---

[5] Andrea Bjorklund, *Contract Without Privity: Sovereign Offer and Investor Acceptance*, 2 Chi. J. Int'l L. 183, 185 (2001); Stephan W. Schill, *System-Building in Investment Treaty Arbitration and Lawmaking*, 12 German L.J. 1083, 1089 n.25 (2011).

[6] U.N. Conference on Trade & Dev. [UNCTAD], Investor-State Disputes Arising from Investment Treaties: A Review 4–6, U.N. Doc. UNCTAD/ITE/IIT/2005/4 (2005); *see also* Gus Van Harten, Investment Treaty Arbitration and Public Law (2008).

[7] UNCTAD, IIA Issues Note, No. 2, 1 (2018).

[8] UNCTAD, IIA Issues Note, No. 1, 3 (2012).

[9] *But see* UNCTAD, *World Investment Report 2013: Global Value Chains: Investment and Trade for Development*, 110, UNCTAD/WIR/2013 (June 26, 2013) (reporting fifty-eight new claims initiated in 2012). In 2013, UNCTAD reported fifty-six new ITA disputes. UNCTAD, *World Investment Report 2014: Investing in the SDGs: An Action Plan*, 124, UNCTAD/WIR/2014 (June 24, 2014).

[10] UNCTAD, *World Investment Report 2018: Investment and New Industrial Policies*, 91, UNCTAD/WIR/2018 (June 6, 2018) ("In 2017, at least 65 new treaty-based ISDS cases were initiated, bringing the total number of known cases to 855."); UNCTAD, *World Investment Report 2016: Investor Nationality: Policy Challenges*, 107–08, UNCTAD/WIR/2016 (June 21, 2016) ("In 2015, investors initiated 70 known ISDS cases pursuant to IIAs, which is the highest number of cases ever filed in a single year").

[11] International Centre for Settlement of Investment Disputes [ICSID] Secretariat, *The ICSID Caseload–Statistics, Issue 2012-1*, 8 (Feb. 7, 2012), https://bit.ly/2ttZlMS (last visited Aug. 7, 2018).

[12] ICSID's Annual Reports reflect cases registered within its fiscal year (July–June). *See* ICSID, 2017 Annual Report 30 (2017), https://bit.ly/2xZhZOc (last visited Sept. 28, 2018) (reflecting forty-nine registered cases

This book uses data from public awards, which can be used to assess whether different research protocols revealed similar patterns. Analysis from the dataset supported the hypothesis, like UNCTAD and ICSID data, that the ITA caseload increased over time and exhibited a general upward trajectory. Before 2000, there were a minimal number of awards. This means, to the extent that empirical analyses of ITA purport to focus on pre-1990 cases, they are likely improperly incorporating non-ITA cases, thereby improperly skewing analyses and decreasing the value of these studies. It is worthwhile recalling that, during this period, the entire ITA caseload could almost be counted on two hands. *See* Figure 4.1. When considering awards rendered after 2000, tribunals rendered roughly twenty-two awards each year.[13] This suggests two primary phases in the historical development of ITA, namely, an initial experimentation period and a secondary expansion.

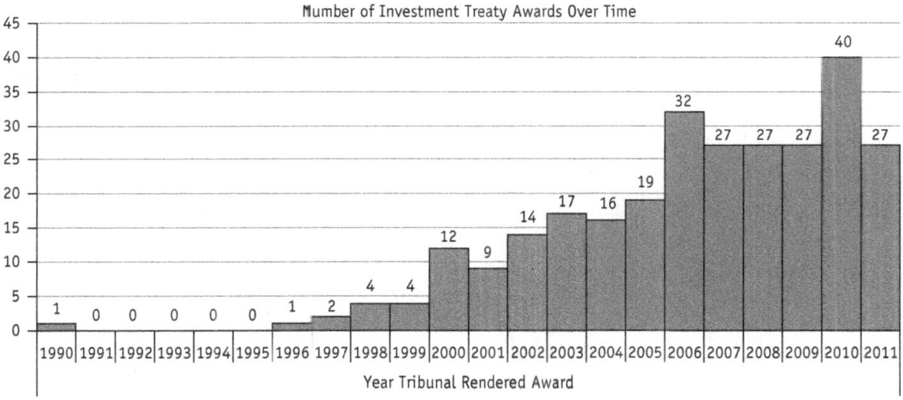

FIGURE 4.1 Histogram of Publicly Available ITA Awards Until January 1, 2012, indicating Frequency of Awards Rendered Each Year ($M = 2006$; $SD = 3.644$; $n = 272$).

Comparing the number of awards in 2012 to volumes twenty-five years ago, the data demonstrates a marked increase. Yet the interpretive question about the purported "explosion" is a function of perspective. Three paradigms offer potential frames for the data.

Under one paradigm, the term "explosion" is warranted, given a strict and non-contextual assessment of the caseload's exponential growth. Comparing the number of awards in 1990, when there was one single award, to the roughly thirty awards per year in 2011 suggests a 3,000% growth. Even comparing the average four awards per year in 1999 to the 2011 number suggests a greater than 600% increase in awards rendered per year. While this narrative is technically accurate, the sharp and compelling story about the expansion of the ITA caseload is somewhat loaded. Using a "zero to explosion" frame is the equivalent of making final

in FY2017); ICSID, 2016 ANNUAL REPORT 30 (2016), https://bit.ly/2N7NPh7 (last visited Sept. 28, 2018) (reflecting forty-five cases registered in FY2016); ICSID, 2015 ANNUAL REPORT 5 (2015), https://bit.ly/2QikYJo (last visited Sept. 28, 2018) (reflecting fifty-two cases registered in FY2015); ICSID, 2014 ANNUAL REPORT 21 (2014), https://bit.ly/2R5GBgS (last visited Sept. 28, 2018) (reflecting forty cases registered in FY2014); ICSID, 2013 ANNUAL REPORT 21 (2013), https://bit.ly/2NM74C6 (last visited Sept. 28, 2018) (reflecting forty-three cases registered in FY2013).

[13] $M = 22.25$; $SD = 9.18$; $n = 267$.

judgments about a child's evolution by focusing on the growth between birth and the first several years of life. Likewise, this strict constructionist approach fails to address alternative baselines and comparative contexts.

A second interpretive framework recognizes the increase but places information in context. Contextual frames contrast data against other baselines, including other international law adjudication, the scope of foreign investment, or investment treaties in force. For instance, other forms of public international law adjudication initially had small numbers but grew over time. The ICJ's caseload steadily increased; and by 2018, there were only 146 contentious disputes referred to the Court, averaging roughly of two cases a year.[14] The Inter-American Commission on Human Rights renders roughly one award per year. International economic law adjudication has a somewhat different pattern. GATT (and then WTO) disputes initially ranged in the single digits, but now roughly experience 30–35 new cases per year.[15] Given the private, economic nature of adjudicated rights, ITA has much doctrinally in common with its international economic law cousin. The context suggests the ITA increase was not usual; rather, like other international economic law adjudication, case numbers started smaller and then developed to around 30–40 disputes per year, with some dispersion and incremental increases in units of tens (rather than hundreds or thousands).

Levels of international investment also suggest ITA disputes were relatively low or reasonably expected. Despite the billions of dollars in investment and thousands of treaties, there was a relatively small amount of conflict leading to ITA.[16] As investors generally cannot initiate ITA without a treaty, it is worth recalling that the number of treaties quintupled during the 1990s[17] when there were few arbitration awards.[18] While focusing on investments and treaties generating ITA under-emphasizes cases where investments and treaties did not generate disputes, investors have used treaties' dispute resolution provisions. Having been given new rights, investors tested the limits. Philip Morris, for example, tested its rights—and lost—about arguable international law expropriation of intellectual property deriving from plain-packaging regulations.[19] If nothing else, data reflects that states must appreciate

---

[14] *List of Contentious Cases referred to the Court since 1946 by date of introduction*, INT'L COURT OF JUSTICE, https://bit.ly/2NZiuPc (last visited July 17, 2018); *see also Cases*, INT'L COURT OF JUSTICE, https://bit.ly/2GJLB51 (last visited July 31, 2018) (indicating that "Between 22 May 1947 and 1 January 2018, 170 cases were entered in the General List" of the ICJ docket).

[15] Robert E. Hudec, The *New WTO Dispute Settlement Procedure: An Overview of the First Three Years*, 8 MINN. J. GLOBAL TRADE 1, 15–16 (1999); Eric A. Posner & John C. Yoo, *Judicial Independence and International Tribunals*, 93 CAL. L. REV. 1, 36–37, 42–43, 46 (2005); *see also* Gary Born, *A New Generation of International Adjudication*, 61 DUKE L.J. 775, 843, 853–54 (2012). These figures also do not address state-to-state dispute resolution involving bilateral or multilateral trade agreements.

[16] W. Michael Reisman, *International Investment Arbitration and ADR: Married but Best Living Apart*, 24 ICSID REV. 185 (2009).

[17] UNCTAD, BILATERAL INVESTMENT TREATIES IN THE MID-1990S, 10, UN Doc. UNCTAD/ITE/IIT/7 (1998).

[18] Given investment levels and lack of claims, states may not have fully appreciated the realistic probability of adjudication, which may account for suggestions that states were surprised by ITA. *See* Susan D. Franck, *Empirically Evaluating Claims About Investment Treaty Arbitration*, 86 N.C. L. REV. 1, 47 (2007) and sources cited therein.

[19] Philip Morris Asia Ltd. v. Gov't of Austl., UNCITRAL, PCA Case No. 2012-12, Award on Jurisdiction and Admissibility (Dec. 17, 2015), http://bit.ly/1R4XEqe (last visited Aug. 7, 2018); Philip Morris Brand Sàrl

that signing a treaty with dispute resolution rights creates real—not theoretical—risk. Government officials should think critically about the value of investment areas most likely to lead to conflict, and types of dispute resolution likely to generate net value or minimize net loss.

A third paradigm draws upon sociology, suggesting the ITA increase exhibits a pattern that mimics normal innovation diffusion. Everett Rogers's 1962 classic *Diffusion of Innovations* examined over 500 different innovations to identify how, why, and at what rate new ideas and technologies spread.[20] Rogers observed that innovations diffuse over time, as clusters of people adapt to new ideas. His primary contribution was to identify five clusters of actors, their respective proportions, and their role in diffusing innovation. The first group, "Innovators," are a small subset, usually 2.5% of a population, who are willing to experiment with novel approaches. "Early Adopters" are the next group most willing to try innovations. Accounting for approximately 13.5%, Early Adopters take risks after some preliminary indication of how the innovation is used or how the innovation might apply. Rogers observed that the opinions and experiences of Early Adopters heavily influence the scope and rate of adoption by future groups. The third group most willing to adopt innovations is the "Early Majority." Comprising roughly 34%, this group tends to adopt innovations in varying degrees over time. For the remainder of the population, innovation spreads more slowly if at all. The "Late Majority" accounts for roughly 34% of the population, whereas "Laggards" (16%) adapt most reluctantly to innovations. *See* Figure 4.2. As innovation spreads, the market becomes saturated and use of the innovation stabilizes or decreases. In Rogers's framework, for innovation to take hold, there are five steps, namely: (1) knowledge about an innovation, (2) initial adoption, and (3) enough stakeholders to weigh up the relative advantages and disadvantages; only then can the innovation move to (4) continued deployment, and (5) confirmation within social institutions. Having become saturated with use of the innovation, however, Rogers suggests market participants may move onto another innovations.

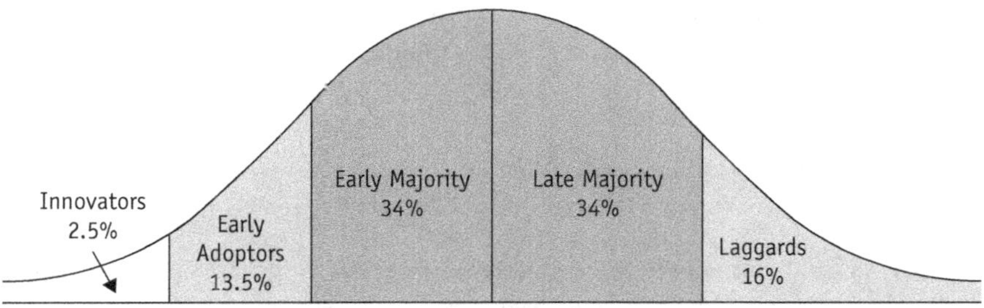

FIGURE 4.2 Everett Rogers' Adoption Curve Demonstrating the Diffusion Rate of New Ideas.

ITA was an innovation in international law. ITA's evolution roughly tracks Rogers's theory about clusters of actors diffusing ideas over time. ITA, like the initial groups in Rogers' Adoption Curve, has experienced three phases since its inception. Prior to the creation of ITA,

v. Republic of Uru., Decision on Jurisdiction, ICSID ARB/10/7 (July 8, 2016), http://bit.ly/29G1ewI (last visited Aug. 7, 2018).

[20] EVERETT M. ROGERS, DIFFUSION OF INNOVATIONS (1st ed. 1962).

there was no innovation to diffuse. Once investment treaties offered a new dispute resolution right, evolution occurred in three core phases. Phase I (experimentation) occurred in the 1990s, from 1990 to 1999. During that time, there were always fewer than five awards rendered per year, and several years of inactivity.[21] Phase II (early adoption) likely occurred during the early part of the 2000s, during which there were an increasing number of awards, but still never more than 15–20 awards per year.[22] Phase III (early majority), which is occurring now, involves some degree of stability. Although ITA may be a relatively new international law evolution, the process of diffusing the innovation has not been unusual. The rise in the case law is also not dissimilar from some growth patterns identified at the European Court of Human Rights (ECtHR)[23] or the innovation in using international investment rights as a basis for claims in a new forum.[24]

Rogers's sociological frame has implications for ITA, suggesting the current moment in ITA's evolution is critical. First, there is knowledge dissemination of the innovation, having moved beyond claims that ITA involves "rights you never knew you had,"[25] and although the scope of public information is expanding, the information diffusion has challenges to facilitate balanced evidence consumption, lest cognitive illusions skew information flows. Second, stakeholders must be sufficiently interested in the innovation to seek out information to evaluate the innovation and consider the utility of its adoption. Various stakeholders, including investors, states, counsel, non-disputing parties like NGOs, and third-party funders, have been participating in ITA, suggesting that the second step of diffusion is well underway. The third step requires weighing advantages and disadvantages of the innovation to decide about its net value. This, in theory, requires states and other stakeholders to gather balanced data to ensure the benefits and costs are weighed properly to aid balanced assessment to decide whether the ITA innovation should continue to disseminate, be curtailed, or eliminated. The final phases of Rogers' theory—implementation and confirmation—are the crux of the current ITA debate. Using his framework, the marketplace for ITA's innovation could become saturated, stabilize, and even drop, over time. Superimposing Rogers's curve on ITA awards provides a visual cue about the application of Rogers's diffusion theory to ITA. *See* Figure 4.3. Time, however, will tell whether the caseload will continue to climb, if an equilibrium point will be reached, or if there will be a drop-off.

---

[21] For final awards, there was one in 1990, one in 1996, two in 1998, and three in 1999.

[22] For final awards, there were seven in 2000, three in 2001, eight in 2002, eleven in 2003, six in 2004, and eight in 2005.

[23] *See* European Court of Human Rights, Analysis of Statistics 2016, 7 (Jan. 2017), https://bit.ly/2MG6Uvv (last visited Aug. 30, 2018) (demonstrating a similar curve in number of yearly applications allocated to a judicial formation at the ECtHR).

[24] *See* Karen J. Alter, The New Terrain of International Law: Courts, Politics, Rights 104–07 (2014) (offering graphic data on the dispersion and shifts in international courts); Balen Olmos Giupponi, *Disentangling Human Rights and Investors' Rights in International Adjudication: The Legacy of the* Yukos *Cases*, 24 Willamette J. Int'l L. & Disp. Resol. 127 (2017) (discussing how the ECtHR has become used by foreign investors increasingly in cases such as *Yukos* and *Uzan v. Turkey* to adjudicate property and investment claims); *see also* José E. Alvarez, *The Human Right of Property*, 72 U. Miami L. Rev. 580 (2018) (exploring ECtHR property rights litigation and other international courts and tribunals to explore implications for foreign investment).

[25] Jason W. Yackee, *Do Bilateral Investment Treaties Promote Foreign Direct Investment? Some Hints from Alternative Evidence*, 51 Va. J. Int'l L. 397, 426 (2011).

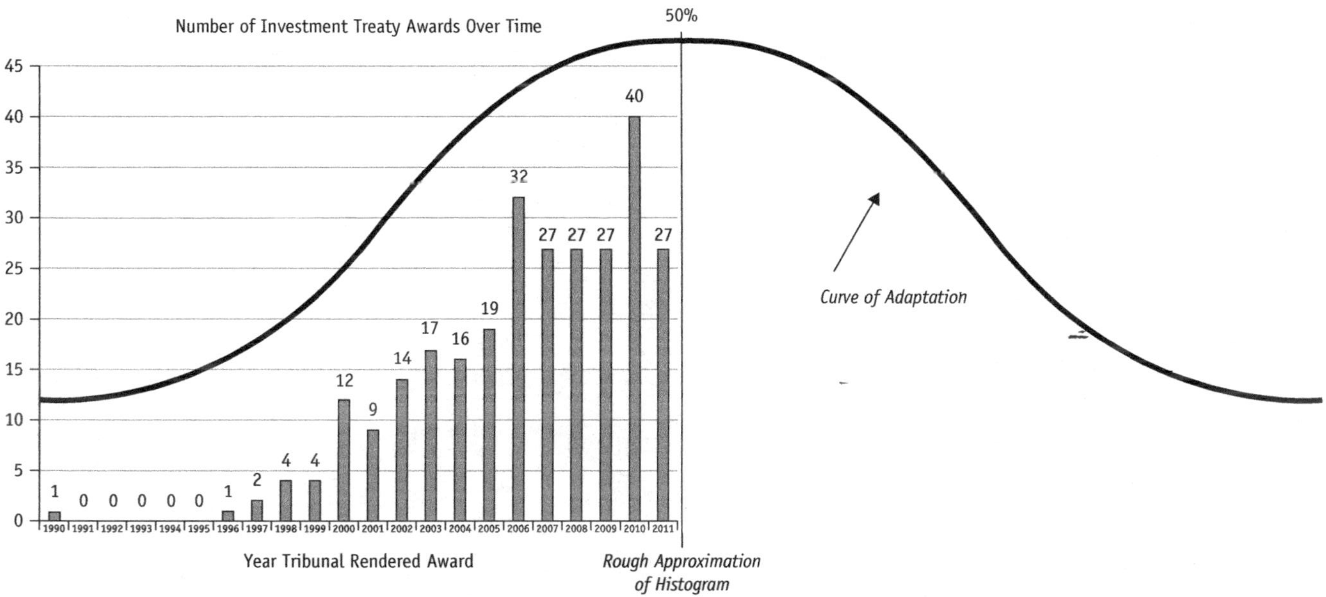

FIGURE 4.3 Approximation of Figure 4.1's Histogram of Awards Superimposed with Rogers' Adoption Curve.

Irrespective of which paradigm is used for framing, there was an increase in cases. Until substantive treaty rights are eliminated or governments become perfect actors, the risk of some investment-treaty conflict will remain. The more important element is: Which narrative should be used to frame the debate about ITA increases?

While the strict constructionist paradigm has accuracy, it has emotional salience that risks intuitive assessments and error. Rather than viewing data in isolation and injecting risk of manipulation from attention-grabbing headlines, the better course is to contextualize data by cross-referencing alternative frameworks. While one could reasonably disagree about the proper framework, any context that bears doctrinal and policy similarities to ITA is worth exploring. One would hope that stakeholders analyzing ITA would prefer to focus on context rather than sensationalism. This makes comparing ITA's evolution to other international courts and tribunals—particularly tribunals exploring similar legal phenomenon—the most reasonable comparators. Ultimately, while there are undoubtedly more cases than pure public international disputes, the increase in ITA levels does not appear to be unusual by comparison to the diffusion of innovations generally, or international economic law in particular.

II. Elements of Time

Time is not simply about ITA's temporal evolution. Time affects individual cases. As Benjamin Franklin wrote in his *Advice to a Young Tradesman*, "time is money."[26] In ITA, time to arbitrate disputes has cost implications. This section explores the length of ITA cases and how time affects efficiency. Arbitration has historically been lauded as a quick form of dispute resolution, yet this platitude need not apply to international arbitration. Some posit that international arbitration can be fast and cheap, concluding it is therefore a preferable dispute resolution method.[27] Others skeptically suggest cases take years to resolve.[28] As Sinclair and Macrory cleverly put it, "[i]f Tolstoy had been an international arbitration lawyer, he might have said that 'efficient proceedings are all alike; every inefficient proceeding is inefficient in its own way.'"[29] To test these alterative theories, this section explores different elements of time related to ITA.

There is minimal research analyzing time in ITA. UNCTAD has not published data reflecting average length of cases or other variables contributing to dispute resolution times. In August 2018, ICSID published data suggesting that average case length was around three

[26] Benjamin Franklin, Advice to a Young Tradesman (1748), *reprinted in* The Oxford Dictionary of Quotations 218 (3d ed. 1979).

[27] Russell J. Cortazzo, Jr., *Development and Trends of the Lex Maritime from International Arbitration Jurisprudence*, 43 J. Mar. L. & Com. 255, 277 (2012); Joerg Risse, *Drastic Proposals for Saving Time and Costs in Arbitral Proceedings*, 29 J. Int'l Arb. 453 (2013).

[28] Paula Hodges, *Drive for Efficiency and the Risks of Procedural Neutrality—Another Tale of the Hare and the Tortoise?*, 2 Disp. Resol. Int'l 183 (Oct. 2012); Thomas J. Stipanowich & J. Ryan Lamare, *Living with ADR: Evolving Perceptions and Use of Mediation and Conflict Management in Fortune 1,000 Corporations*, 19 Harv. Negot. L. Rev. 1 (2013) (suggesting decreases in arbitration occurred with increased time and costs that made arbitration equivalent to litigation).

[29] Anthony Sinclair & Sarah Macrory, *ICSID Arbitration: How Long Does It Take?*, 4 Global Arb. Rev. J. (2009), https://bit.ly/2APfDWI (last visited Aug. 7, 2018).

years and seven months.[30] In slight contrast, the Chartered Institute of Arbitrators' survey on commercial arbitration suggests that the average arbitration was between seventeen and twenty months.[31]

Practitioners offer preliminary observations about ITA lengths. Hodgson's study of ICSID and non-ICSID awards through 2012, covering the period analyzed in this book and offering helpful methodological detail, identified the average time to resolve an ITA dispute as 3.8 years.[32] Similarly, Sinclair and Macrory analyzed ICSID's caseload from inception to July 2009, identifying an average case length of 3.6 years. They suggested that, as cases from July 2003 to July 2009 were resolved in 3.2 years, ICSID arbitration was getting faster. The conclusion, however, focused on descriptive numbers without identifying variance, testing for reliable statistical differences, or identifying that changes could reflect chance alone. Focusing on ICSID limits the value of inferences, as it excludes non-ICSID ITA cases[33] and includes ICSID cases arising under commercial contracts and national investment law.[34] Yet, it offers a baseline for consideration.

This remainder of this section explores the average length of an ITA case, whether time to resolve ITA disputes became shorter, and time between a hearing and an award. Finally, it analyzes whether other variables, including bifurcation or separate opinions, were meaningfully associated with increased case length.

A. CASE LENGTH

Starting with the signing of the formal Request for Arbitration,[35] the research explored the number of months between the Request[36] and the award finalizing the treaty claim.[37] The

---

[30] *See* ICSID SECRETARIAT, PROPOSALS FOR AMENDMENT OF THE ICSID RULES—WORKING PAPER, VOL. 3, 977–79 (Aug. 2, 2018), https://bit.ly/2whvXdh (last visited Aug. 17, 2018) (analyzing sixty-three cases from 2015–2017 including both ITA and non-ITA disputes to indicate the average length was 1,336 days).

[31] CHARTERED INST. OF ARBS., CIARB COSTS OF INTERNATIONAL ARBITRATION SURVEY 2011 (2011).

[32] Matthew Hodgson, *Counting the Costs of Investment Treaty Arbitration*, GLOBAL ARB. REV. (Mar. 24, 2014), http://bit.ly/29UwfPi (last visited Aug. 7, 2018). The December 2017 update suggested the average ITA case length was four years. Matthew Hodgson & Alastair Campbell, *Investment Treaty Arbitration: Cost, Duration and Size of Claims all Show a Steady Increase* (Dec. 14, 2017), https://bit.ly/2NEnWqA (last visited Aug. 7, 2018). The study failed to test whether the "steady increase" was statistically reliable or rule out risk that superficial shifts could reflect chance alone.

[33] Several cases that would have qualified as part of Sinclair & Macrory's fastest and slowest cases, such as *UPS v. Canada*, were not included as they were not ICSID registered cases.

[34] Sinclair & Macrory referred to two ICSID cases including *Cable TV v. St. Kitts and Nevis* and *CDC v. Seychelles*, neither of which arose under investment treaties, and both of which were listed as the two fastest ICSID cases. Likewise, one of the longest cases, *World Duty Free v. Kenya*, did not involve a claim under an investment treaty.

[35] The Codebook, Appendix IV, provided protocols to ensure the date coded was the date investors signed the official Request for Arbitration, rather than date of dispute notice or date the Request was submitted, received, or registered.

[36] Several cases did not contain the date the request was signed—but usually provided the date ICSID received the request; a proxy variable "CaseLength_Detail," tracked receipt date. *See* Codebook, Appendix IV. Analyses were typically unable to identify meaningful differences in results between the two variables. To minimize lost data, this book primarily reports the proxy variable. Of the 159 final cases, 131 cases had complete information about case length; using the proxy variable, 156 cases contained full information, including twenty-five cases using the date of receipt (instead of signing date). Three cases contained no information about request date.

[37] As Chapter 3 explained, data focused on first-instance tribunals, not annulment, vacatur, or enforcement.

data tended to reflect practitioners' assessments. On average, the time from when an investor filed a request for ITA until when a tribunal rendered a final decision was roughly forty-three months or 3.5 years,[38] similar to ICSID's recently released figure.[39] Median case length was similar, at roughly forty months.[40] The slowest cases analyzed ranged from case lengths of 73–128 months,[41] whereas the fastest cases ranged from 9–16 months.[42]

Other international tribunals have not necessarily been faster. In 1944, Manley Hudson observed that delay was typical in mixed commissions, perhaps due to the challenges from adjudicators of different nationalities, languages, and legal systems working together.[43] Professor Bederman similarly advised that "the average duration of the approximately thirty claims tribunals for which we have accurate operational records was slightly under 5 years"; but he acknowledged that many tribunals completed their mandate in less than two years.[44] Wholly public international law tribunals also encounter lengthy adjudication times. The case length of international tribunals was not dissimilar from those of international courts. Professor Slomanson wrote, "[s]ince the 1980s, the average length of a judicial proceeding at the ICJ, from filing to disposition has grown from two-and-one-half to four years."[45]

With these alternative international baselines, ITA is not unusual in the time required to complete adjudication. Delay in adjudication can come from many vectors. For example, arbitrators are not employed full-time to resolve disputes, and they could be distracted by other professional obligations or have schedules inhibiting greater efficiencies. Yet, if arbitrator schedules are driving delay, procedural mechanisms should prohibit overly busy arbitrators from taking cases, create fiscal incentives for expeditious resolution, or fiscally penalize delay.[46] Delay is not, however, the sole province of arbitrators. Parties and counsel can contribute to delay. Some parties, for example, could strategically benefit from delays and slower procedure; and parties may also jointly resist arbitrators' suggestions to implement strict timetables or move toward expedited timelines. Meanwhile, parties juggle multiple internal responsibilities, and their lawyers—who have competing client demands—may require large blocks of time to gather evidence, secure translations, and

---

[38] *Supra* note 30.

[39] $M = 42.87$; $SD = 18.80$; $n = 155$.

[40] For pure case length, excluding cases where only the date of the receipt of the request for arbitration was available, the average number of months to complete a case was 41.65 months ($n = 131$; $SD = .18.12$) and the median was 38.43 months.

[41] *See* Dataset, Appendix V (identifying *Victor Pey Casado v. Chile* (128 months), *Bayindir v. Pakistan* (90 months); *UPS v. Canada* (86 months), *Grand River v. United States* (83 months), and *Alasdair Ross Anderson v. Costa Rica* (73 months)).

[42] *See* Dataset, Appendix V (*Yury Bogdanov v. Moldova* (9 months), *Iurii Bogdanov v. Moldova* (10 months); *Grynberg v. Grenada* (11 months), *Tembec v. United States* (13 months), and *Nagel v. Czech Republic* (16 months)).

[43] Manley O. Hudson, International Tribunals: Past and Future 6, 96 (1944).

[44] David J. Bederman, *The Glorious Past and Uncertain Future of International Claims Tribunals*, *in* International Courts for the Twenty-First Century 161, 167 (Mark W. Janis ed. 1992).

[45] William R. Slomanson, Fundamental Perspectives in International Law 395 (6th ed. 2010). Karen Alter's transformative book on international courts and tribunals, *supra* note 24, was unfortunately unable to focus on time or cost of adjudication.

[46] *See* Chapter 9.

present arguments. Perhaps more important, even if ITA experiences roughly equivalent time periods to complete transnational adjudication, even if one might wish for faster dispute resolution, increased speed can have tangible consequences. If tribunals proceed too expeditiously, parties may have concerns about the capacity of the record to be developed properly, core legal arguments to be briefed fully, and the unique merits of each case to be thoroughly considered. To the extent that parties lack faith in procedural integrity, there can be negative externalities, including award noncompliance or distrust of the process.[47] Perhaps more important, as treaty rights, state liability, and public international law are at stake, the time required to resolve the disputes may be worth the care, focus, precision, and attention.

B. INCREASING SPEED OR DELAY?

There are competing narratives as to whether the time to resolve ITA cases has increased, decreased, or possibly remained stable. Sinclair and Macrory suggested ICSID claims were becoming increasingly faster when comparing the 2003–2009 to pre-2003 cases. Their research, however, failed to provide standard deviations or tests assessing whether facial differences were statistically meaningful. Other research, which failed to distinguish among ITA and other arbitration types, argues increasing delays make international arbitration unpalatable.[48] To test both ideas, the hypothesis was that over time, there would be a decrease in the months required to resolve ITA disputes.

A simple, initial test revealed that there *was* a statistical reliable relationship between the year a tribunal rendered an award and months required to complete the dispute.[49] The direction, however, was opposite to Sinclair and Macrory's assertion, namely: *newer* cases took longer to complete, and older cases took fewer months to complete.

Other tests explored the unexpected results, analyzing whether different periods of time experienced meaningfully different case lengths. One analysis explored case length for clusters of years, namely: data for cases finishing before June 1, 2006 (Generation 1 or G1); data for cases rendered between June 1, 2006 and June 1, 2009 (Generation 2 or G2); and data for cases rendered between June 1, 2009 and January 2012 (Generation 3 or G3). Although clusters were originally a marker for when data was coded, the benefit was that the three groups were of roughly similar size and covered similar clusters of time.[50] The results confirmed there were reliable differences in

[47] *See* Tom R. Tyler, *Governing amid Diversity: The Effect of Fair Decisionmaking Procedures on the Legitimacy of Government*, 28 LAW & SOC'Y REV. 309, 827 (1994) ("the use of fair decisionmaking procedures does enhance the legitimacy of national governmental authorities"); Susan D. Franck, *Integrating Investment Treaty Conflict and Dispute Systems Design*, 92 MINN. L. REV. 161, 215–16 (2007) (discussing procedural justice in ITA).

[48] Stipanowich & Lamare, *supra* note 28; Berwin, Leighton & Paisner, *International Arbitration: Research Based Report on Perceived Delay in the Arbitration Process* (July 2012), http://bit.ly/1azIRRL (last visited Aug. 7, 2018).

[49] A bivariate correlation found a reliable and positive linear relationship between case length and the year the tribunal rendered the final ITA award ($r(156) = .24; p < .01$). *See also* Appendix I (discussing statistical tests and data selection).

[50] This variable was not perfect, as, in rare cases, an older award became public later.

the average[51] and median[52] number of months to complete ITA. The effect was, however, complex. The means suggested more recent cases took longer to complete—but the most recent set of cases were *not* the most time-consuming. *See* Table 4.1. Put simply, time was not a constant, and case length ebbed and flowed.

TABLE 4.1

Mean Time between Filing Request for Arbitration and Final ITA Award ($n = 156$).

Award Generation	*Mean Number of Months to Completion*	*Standard Deviation*	*Total Cases*
Generation 1 (until June 1, 2006)	34.77	11.59	51
Generation 2 (June 1, 2006–June 1, 2009)	50.93	19.22	47
Generation 3 (June 1, 2009–January 1, 2012)	43.48	20.78	58
Total	42.88	18.80	156

HSD follow-up tests confirmed the oldest group of cases was reliably faster than the more recent ones. Namely, when using conservative tests to compare the newer groups of cases, cases rendered prior to 2006 took the least time to resolve. Recency of completion, however, was not always reliably associated with longer case length. There was a facial pattern whereby the most recent cases (post-2009) were resolved somewhat more quickly when compared to cases finalized during 2006–2009. The difference was not meaningful, however, when examined using conservative follow-up tests.[53]

These findings provide food for thought. First, they disrupt Sinclair and Macrory's claim that more recent ITA cases reliably proceeded more quickly.[54] The facial result—whereby the latest set of cases were resolved more quickly than the middle group—likely explains the intuitive assessment. Given the potential perniciousness of cognitive illusions, statistical analysis offers value by testing intuitions about speed with base rates to assess whether patterns or meaningful or reflect chance alone. Second, parties in the earliest cases were likely systemic innovators; over time, case management likely became more complex, more lawyers became involved, disputes became more nuanced, and there was more legal analysis and case law to explore. These elements could increase the length of time required to resolve disputes, meaning first innovators experienced faster and more

[51] An ANOVA found reliable mean differences in case length ($F(2, 153) = 10.152; p < .001; r = .34; n = 156$) across the different temporal groups of data.

[52] A Kruskall-Wallis test found reliable group differences in median case length ($\chi^2 (2) = 19.32; p < .001; r = .33; n = 156$).

[53] A more sensitive LSD follow-up with higher error rates, however, found another statistically meaningful difference, whereby G3 cases were completed more quickly that G2 cases.

[54] Although ICSID introduced Rule 41(5) in 2006 to permit early termination, the rule was implicated in roughly 2% of cases in the dataset. *See* Chapter 5(II)(B); *infra* note 101.

efficient proceedings compared to their modern counterparts. Third, further analysis should explore fluctuations over time, as it is possible that the data—and the reality of case lengths—continues to evolve. Given increasing complexity, the advent of international economic crises, and incentives to create economies of scale within case administration, case lengths could continue to fluctuate. Definitive conclusions about ITA's efficiency, and whether disputes are being resolved more quickly or slowly, requires ongoing reassessment. The more important point is the vital role data plays in informing choices. Without data to debias dialogue, cognitive illusions may easily facilitate believing that one's own recent experiences (which spring readily to mind) are representative, thereby confirming one's initial impression. Even with the best of intentions, clients making strategic choices about dispute resolution may end up being influenced by gestalt or error from intuition rather than statistical baserates.

C. INSTITUTIONS AND TIME

One critical aspect implicit in previous commentary about case length was the focus upon a singular institution, namely ICSID. Even though earlier analyses confirmed that ICSID was the primary institution where ITA cases occur, there are other potential forums. Treaties frequently offer the option of arbitrating at other venues, including the SCC, the ICC, and ad hoc arbitration proceeding under UNCITRAL Rules.[55] Undue focus on ICSID cases also holds the possibility of incorporating non-treaty-based cases, which are not proper for making inferences about ITA.

Given the forum flexibility in many treaties and potential competition for cases, there is value in identifying whether temporal variations exist. ICSID arbitration has unique doctrinal obligations, including a registration requirement and extra jurisdictional hurdles. Theoretically, these additional features could increase the time of ICSID cases, making them comparatively longer. Yet doctrinally, arbitration rules at ICSID, SCC, and UNCITRAL ad hoc arbitration are relatively similar, suggesting the time to resolve disputes need not be meaningfully different. Even for ad hoc arbitration, where lack of administrative oversight could generate delay, parties can manage risk by obtaining supervisory services of entities such as the Permanent Court of Arbitration or other institutions. This section explores those competing theories—whether ITA forums take longer or are roughly equivalent. In this way, investors making a forum selection and states' dispute resolution options can take data into account. Put bluntly, multiple stakeholders may wish to understand how ICSID and other non-ICSID arbitrations vary on time, both to have information for making practical and tactical choices and to consider implications for jurisdictional competition.

Two sets of analyses approached the question of time. One set analyzed time differences between institutional arbitration generally and ad hoc arbitration (whether under UNCITRAL rules or otherwise). A second set of tests analyzed specific institutional differences, exploring how case length varied at ICSID, the SCC, or other arbitration venues.

---

[55] Todd Allee & Clint Peinhardt, *Delegating Differences: Bilateral Treaties and Bargaining over Dispute Resolution Options*, 54 INT'L STUD. Q. 54 (2010); Alison Christians, *How Nations Share*, 87 IND. L.J. 1407, 1425 (2012).

The first set of tests failed to identify a difference in time to resolve cases in institutional or ad hoc arbitration.[56] The average institutional case finished in 43 months,[57] whereas the average ad hoc arbitration took 41.5 months.[58] Despite a 1.5 month gap, the facially intriguing distinction was not statistically meaningful and could reflect chance alone. This provides initial evidence, but cannot conclusively prove, that case length did not vary among institutional and ad hoc arbitrations.[59]

The second set of tests, however, identified a meaningful difference in case length for different arbitration venues.[60] Table 4.2 summarizes average case length. The overall significant results did not mean that all arbitral fora were different. Conservative follow-up tests were unable to distinguish between ad hoc cases and ICSID cases. Yet, SCC cases were reliably shorter—by roughly 18–21 months—than both ad hoc and ICSID cases.

TABLE 4.2

Mean Time between Filing Request for Arbitration and Final Award Adjudicating ITA Disputes ($n = 156$).

Arbitral Institution	*Mean Number of Months to Completion*	*Standard Deviation*	*Total Cases*
ICSID	44.81	18.44	114
SCC	23.56	14.97	9
Ad Hoc	41.48	18.29	33
Total	42.88	18.80	156

Reliably shorter times at the SCC do not necessarily mean that the SCC arbitration processes caused faster dispute resolution. Focusing on the set of SCC cases creating the effect[61] provides vital context. Roughly 78% ($n = 7$) of SCC cases analyzed had unusual

[56] A t-test explored mean differences in case length for cases occurring either through ad hoc or institutional arbitration ($t\,(154) = 0.481$; $p = .63$; $r = .04$; $n = 156$).

[57] $M = 43.25$; $SD = 18.99$; $n = 123$.

[58] $M = 41.48$; $SD = 18.29$; $n = 33$.

[59] Although underpowered, the size of the latent effect of ad hoc arbitration on time was less statistically small. More than 700 final awards would be needed to reliably detect any potential effect. Because the variable distinguishing between ad hoc and institutional cases coded on the basis of legal doctrine (rather than administrative case management), a different operationalization could reveal different results. As it was, cases occurring on an ad hoc doctirinal basis nevertheless received assistance from institutions including: (1) ICSID in cases including *UPS v. Canada, BG Group v. Argentina, Merrill & Ring v. Canada*, and *National Grid v. Argentina*, (2) the LCIA, in cases such as *Occidental v. Ecudor, Encana v. Ecaudor*, and *Société Générale v. Dominican Republic*, and (3) the PCA, in cases like *Chevron v. Ecuador, HICEE v. Slovak Republic*, and *Nova Scotia Power v. Venezuela*. Other cases including, *Lauder v. Czech Republic, Link Trading v. Moldova, Mytilineos Holdings v. Serbia, Canadian Cattlemen for Fair Trade v. United States*, and *Pope & Talbott v. Canada* had no administrative oversight.

[60] An ANOVA analyzed mean differences in time across a multi-category variable of arbitration forum ($F\,(2, 153) = 5.783$; $p = .004$; $r = .27$; $n = 156$).

[61] Although the SCC caseload was small, there was sufficient power to identify meaningfully faster resolution.

characteristics aiding faster resolution. First, two cases, *Petrobart v. Kyrgyz Republic*[62] and *Iurii Bogdanov v. Moldova*[63] involved documents-only cases where tribunals rendered decisions without a hearing. ICSID and an ad hoc case each had one documents-only case,[64] and the documents-only cases were a small proportion of the relative caseloads; in contrast, the SCC had a larger proportion of documents-only cases. This suggests the lack of hearings, rather than the arbitral institution, could contribute to the faster resolution. Second, in another SCC case, *Mohammad Ammar Al-Bahloul v. Tajikistan*,[65] despite numerous attempts made by the tribunal to secure state participation, Tajikistan failed to appear and never mounted a defense.[66] Although Tajikistan prevailed, its failure to defend or interact with opposing counsel likely streamlined the proceedings and generated faster resolution. Third, another case, *Amto v. Ukraine*, involved the tribunal canceling the final hearing pursuant to the parties' agreement, eliminating final briefs, and circulating a draft award, which suggests procedural techniques have the potential to streamline time.[67] Finally, three SCC cases involved lower than average amounts claimed. In raw amounts unadjusted for inflation, *Yury Bogdanov v. Moldova* involved a claim that was the equivalent of US$41,620,[68] *Nykomb Synergetics v. Latvia* involved a claim equivalent to US$13.2 million,[69] and *Berschader v. Russia* involved a claim for US$13.3 million.[70] As SCC fees are partially determined by amount in controversy, comparatively small claims may reflect narrower processes that necessitated less time and attention by parties and arbitrators. Only one case roughly reflected the average time to complete an SCC case,[71] and the remaining case, *RosInvestCo v. Russia*,[72] was substantially longer than average, taking approximately 59 months (nearly five years) to finish. Inferences about the significant results must be tempered by the knowledge that SCC cases analyzed exhibited unusual characteristics and the SCC caseload may have evolved over time. The reliable relationship with shorter dispute resolution may reflect case attributes or procedural peculiarities of SCC cases, rather than the SCC causing a shorter time to completion.

---

[62] Petrobart Ltd. v. The Kyrg. Republic, SCC Case No. 126/2003, Arbitral Award (Mar. 9, 2005), https://bit.ly/2vMrfnJ (last visited Aug. 7, 2018).

[63] Iurii Bogdanov v. Republic of Mold., SCC Arb., Award (Sept. 22, 2005), https://bit.ly/2vAc5Ds (last visited Aug. 7, 2018). *Iurii Bogdanov* was also resolved before a sole arbitrator. *Id.* at 1.

[64] At ICSID, the case was *Rail World v. Estonia*, and *Link-Trading v. Moldova* was the ad hoc arbitration that proceeded on a documents-only basis.

[65] Mohammad Ammar Al-Bahloul v. Republic of Taj., SCC Case No. V (064/2008), Final Award (June 8, 2010), https://bit.ly/2AOuS1Z (last visited Aug. 7, 2018).

[66] *Id.* at 1 (noting that Tajikistan did not appear before the tribunal, despite receiving all notices).

[67] Ltd. Liability Co. AMTO v. Ukraine, SCC Case No. 080/2005, Final Award, §§ 11–13 (Mar. 26, 2008), https://bit.ly/2mpNawy (last visited Aug. 7, 2018).

[68] *Yury Bodanov v. Moldova* was also unusual in that it involved a Sole Arbitrator. *See* Yury Bogdanov v. Republic of Mold., SCC Arb. No. V (114/2009), Award, ¶¶ 35–36 (Mar. 30, 2010), https://bit.ly/2mqlurE (last visited Aug. 7, 2018). Only four other cases in the dataset exhibited this phenomenon.

[69] Nykomb Synergetics Tech. Holding AB v. Republic of Lat., SCC, Arbitral Award, 4 (Dec. 16, 2003), https://bit.ly/2tu5d7F (last visited Aug. 7, 2018).

[70] Vladimir Berschader & Moise Berschander v. Russian Fed'n, SCC Case No. 080/2004, Award, ¶ 12 (Apr. 21, 2006), https://bit.ly/2Lp76xb (last visited Aug. 7, 2017).

[71] William Nagel v. Czech Republic, SCC Case No. 049/2002, Award (Sept. 9, 2003), https://bit.ly/2JvwYTC (last visited Aug. 7, 2018).

[72] RosInvestCo UK Ltd. v. Russian Fed'n, SCC Case No. V079/2005, Final Award (Sept. 12, 2010), https://bit.ly/2gCH6BC (last visited Aug. 7, 2018).

D. DELIBERATIVE DELAY AND SEPARATE OPINIONS

Deliberation amongst arbitrators and writing awards can be a complex exercise. After a hearing, tribunals can require parties to submit post-hearing briefs or make cost submissions. Time is required to meet, discuss, draft materials, negotiate award language to identify common grounds, revise draft awards, and, in some cases, render separate opinions where unanimity is absent. This subsection focuses on time in two ways, namely first exploring the temporal gap between the last hearing and the rendering of an award (an arguable proxy for arbitrator efficiency) and then exploring linkages between case length and the presence of a separate opinion.

Both of these aspects are critical when exploring the relative efficiency of the arbitrators, who are at the heart of resolving ITA disputes. While unusual developments can occur, the critical element is that parties are not necessarily responsible for delay in the post-hearing phase. Rather this analysis puts the focus squarely upon arbitrators and whether they have lived up to their obligations to resolve cases with requisite care and the implications for time, which affect parties' satisfaction with the process ex post and willingness to create arbitration provisions ex ante. Cost implications of separate opinions are discussed in Chapter 8.

1. Temporal Gaps between Hearings and Rendering Awards

Parties and counsel care about deliberation length and the time to render an award. A Queen Mary and White & Case study identified that a "common criticism of arbitration is that tribunals take too long to render awards," observing that 30% of practitioners and in-house counsel believed tribunals take too long to render awards. Other analysis, which did not distinguish between ICA and ITA cases, indicated that for three-member tribunals, 37% of participants believed tribunals should render awards within three months; and 41% believed tribunals should render awards within three to six months. In other words, 78% of those surveyed believed awards should be rendered within a *maximum* of six months.[73] Sinclair and Macrory observed that arbitrators are sensitive to perceived delay and some have been "known to publish in their CVs data about the time it took from the hearing on the merits until the award was rendered." Their research revealed that, after a hearing, ICSID tribunals took, on average, 14 months to render an award.[74] While acknowledging its focus on non-ITA disputes, the LCIA's internal data from 2013 to 2016 suggests the average gap between the last hearing and rendering the award was three months.[75]

To explore the gap between party expectation and arbitral reality, a variable calculated the number of months between the last hearing date and the award.[76] For all awards, on average,

---

[73] Paul Friedland & Stavros Brekoulakis, *Introduction to* 2012 International Arbitration Survey: Current and Preferred Practices in the Arbitral Process, (White & Case 2012), https://bit.ly/2KZvRRI (last visited Aug. 7, 2018); Berwin, Leighton & Paisner, *supra* note 48.

[74] Sinclair & Macrory, *supra* note 29.

[75] LCIA, Facts and Figures—Costs and Duration: 2013–2016, 8–9 (Oct. 3, 2017), https://bit.ly/2uKjJKd (last visited Aug. 7, 2018); The LCIA computed this period on the basis of the time after the parties completed their submissions, which was different from the time used in this research (i.e., last hearing date).

[76] While theoretically useful to measure from the date of the parties' last submissions, tribunals' failure to report that information made it methodologically untenable. It is preferable to measure from the expressly articulated

after the last date of the hearing, parties waited ten months[77] for an award. Only twenty-four awards—less than 10% of awards studied—were rendered less than three months after the last hearing, and seventeen of those were non-final awards, typically addressing jurisdiction.

Things were not much better after excluding non-final awards. When waiting for a final decision, there was an average year-long gap between the final hearing and ultimate award;[78] and the median wait, of ten months, was not markedly better. For final awards, 25% of cases were rendered within six months; and another 25% were resolved within fifteen months. For those final awards the five fastest tribunals rendered awards within one to three months,[79] whereas the five slowest tribunals rendered awards from twenty-nine to fifty-three months after the last hearing.[80]

These results are instructive for several reasons. First, the average waiting period for ITA awards was facially *lower* than Sinclair and Macrory estimated. Given the standard deviation, the gap of roughly two months suggests rough equivalence to different waiting periods. The discrepancy may also reflect different units of analysis and time periods studied.[81]

Second, there is an expectation gap between what parties arguably want and what adjudicators provide in reality. If parties and counsel believe tribunals should render awards within six months, the fissure between arbitrator performance and expectation is material, suggesting an opportunity for either managing arbitrator coduct and/or stakeholder assumptions. Yet, as the Queen Mary study did not distinguish between ITA and other arbitration types, parties in ITA could have different expectations from those operating in the commercial realm. With states and sensitive issues of international law, stakeholders may anticipate arbitrators will take longer than six months. Nevertheless, typical ITA tribunals

common reference date (i.e., last hearing day) to ensure proper comparisons, rather than injecting unnecessary error. Should tribunals regularly provide information on date of final brief submission, this research could provide one historical baseline and a more nuanced, rich, and comparative analysis would become possible. In any event, initial deliberations and preliminary drafting of introductory information of basic facts established by on the record could and should begin prior to receiving parties' submissions. For example, at the close of the last hearing, the tribunal chair could both assign writing obligations involving the record that are not in dispute and a strict timetable for draft awards, deliberations, and final awards.

77 $M = 10.39$; $SD = 7.65$; $n = 265$. The median was 8.6 months.

78 $M = 11.93$; $SD = 7.68$; $n = 154$.

79 *See* Dataset, Appendix V (identifying *Yury Bogdanova v. Moldova* (2010) (1 month), *Grynberg v. Grenada* (2010) (2 months), *Nagel v. Czech Republic* (2003) (2 months), *Swembalt v. Latvia* (2000) (3 months), and *Pantechniki v. Albania* (2009) (3 months). For non-final awards, the fastest tribunals were: *Lanco v. Argentina* (1998) (.03 months); *Tembec v. United States* (2006) (.03 months); and *Trans-Global Petroleum v. Jordan* (2008) (.67 months). *Id.*

80 *See id.* (identifying *El Paso v. Argentina* (2011) (53 months), *Sempra v. Argentina* (2007) (32 months), *S & T Oil v. Romania* (2010) (31 months), *LG&E Energy v. Argentina* (2007) (30 months), and *Chevron v. Ecuador* (2011) (29 months). For non-final awards, the slowest tribunals were *Suez v. Argentina*, (2010) (38.5 months), *Total v. Argentina* (2010) (35.8 months), and *AWG v. Argentina* (2007) (33.17 months). *Id.*

81 An ANOVA analyzing generational effect and gap between hearing and final award revealed a statistically significant relationship (F (2, 151) = 4.031; $p = .02$; $r = .23$; $n = 154$). The superficial time to render awards increased over time: 9.47 months in G1 data; 12.76 months in G2 data; and 13.39 months in G3 data. Not all temporal changes were reliable, as HSD follow-ups indicated that the only meaningful difference was between G1 (oldest awards) and G3 (newest awards), with tribunals rendering awards more quickly in earlier cases and more slowly in the newest cases.

taking *over* six months (and twice the time for final awards) risks mismanaged expectations, disappointment, and user dissatisfaction. This raises questions, including how to use incentives and doctrinal safeguards to increase efficiency without sacrificing quality. It also raises concerns as to whether aspects, such as bifurcation or separate opinions, influence delays. ITA stakeholders should readjust their expectations of tribunal expediency given the data and consider the normative reforms discussed in Chapter 9.

2. Separate Opinions and Time

Another element that may raise concerns about the functionality of ITA involves how time intersects with the presence of separate opinions. There has been some debate about the relevant value of separate opinions. On the one hand, they can be potentially valuable in developing doctrine, promoting discourse, and enhancing legitimacy.[82] Yet, others suggest separate opinions detract from the value of ITA. Van den Berg, for example, expressed skepticism about the normative value of separate opinions.[83] Others have echoed concerns about the net effect of separate opinions.[84] Yet, despite a focus on value, there has been little systemic consideration about how separate opinions affect time (and presumably costs) of ITA. Such analysis could offer nuance to debates about the relative value of separate opinions and provide an opportunity to assess whether separate opinions are tied to meaningful differences with a practical implication.

Sinclair and Macrory came the closest to exploring links between separate opinions and arbitration functionality. Their analysis, which focused on ICSID awards, stated, "[a]s logic would suggest, awards are longer forthcoming where there is a dissenting opinion to contend with."[85] Their findings indicated, for cases without a separate opinion, parties waited for approximately 1.2 years for an award; but for cases *with* a separate opinion, parties waited 1.3 years—or forty-seven days longer.[86] Their unit of analysis focused only on ICSID awards, analyzing "cases where the tribunal has proceeded to the merits"[87] and excluding other awards. They did not test whether the descriptive differences were statistically meaningful.

In contrast to the theory of separate opinions making cases longer, data failed to demonstrate case length was reliably longer when a separate opinion was present.[88] Rather, when

---

[82] Pedro J. Martinez-Fraga & Harout Jack Samra, *A Defense of Dissents in Investment Arbitration*, 43 U. MIAMI INTER-AM. L. REV. 445, 450 (2012); *see also* Chapter 3(I)(C).

[83] Albert Jan van den Berg, *Dissenting Opinions by Party-Appointed Arbitrators in Investment Arbitration*, *in* LOOKING TO THE FUTURE: ESSAYS ON INTERNATIONAL LAW IN HONOR OF W. MICHAEL REISMAN 822, 837–43 (Mahnoush Arsanjani et al., eds. 2011).

[84] Daphna Kapeliuk, *The Repeat Appointment Factor: Exploring Decision Patterns of Elite Investment Arbitrators*, 96 CORNELL L. REV. 47 (2010); *see also* Domenico Di Pietro, *The Controversial Role of Dissenting Opinions in International Arbitral Awards*, TRANSNAT'L NOTES (Oct. 24, 2011), http://bit.ly/1AdxBpk (last visited Aug. 7, 2018).

[85] Sinclair & Macrory, *supra* note 29, at 3.

[86] Sinclar and Macrory suggested, on average, ICSID tribunals took "425 days, or just under 14 months" to render awards, which computes to 1.16 years; and the average time for cases with a separate opinion was 472 days, which computes into 1.29 years. *Id.* It is not clear whether the authors' figure of 425 days included cases with and without separate opinions or otherwise separately analyzed time for cases without separate opinions.

[87] *Id.*

[88] A t-test analyzing mean differences in case length for final cases with (or without) a separate opinion failed to identify a meaningful pattern (t (154) = 1.327; p = .19; r = .11; n = 156). Given the null effect and possibility of

tribunals rendered final awards, the cases with (or without) separate opinions exhibited roughly similar total case lengths and deliberation periods. For cases with separate opinions, the average time from the request for arbitration to the final award was forty-seven months,[89] whereas unified tribunals took on average forty-two months.[90] Although final cases facially took five months longer, the large standard deviation in case length meant that the facial difference could be due to chance alone. Put simply, the intuitively appealing data did not withstand statistical scrutiny.

Likewise, tests failed to identify a reliably different average deliberation period (i.e., time between the last hearing and the final award) for cases with and without separate opinions.[91] On average, tribunals rendering final awards with a separate opinion took thirteen months;[92] but tribunals rendering final awards without separate opinions took 11.5 months.[93] There was also evidence, when tribunals rendered final awards, cases with separate opinions did not generate meaningful delay—a one-to-two month difference is of minimal practical significance given overall case length. The lack of a reliable difference in time for deliberations undercuts arguments that separate opinions create temporal inefficiency.[94]

The time data on separate opinions offer a glimpse behind the curtains of arbitral decision-making. In other adjudicative contexts, scholars identify "peer effects" or "panel effects" in group decision-making. National judges engage in bargaining or logrolling, whistle-blowing, or avoiding dissent.[95] When judges deliberate and negotiate like "horse-swapping legislators," more time is required for a homogeneous decision, as people need time to engage in rounds of information-exchange and deliberation. Empirical evidence suggests such negotiation has occurred at the U.S. Supreme Court.[96] Other research has identified that adjudicators experience "dissent aversion" where, in an effort to avoid contentious deliberations, courts are

---

a statistically small latent effect, the analysis was arguably underpowered, requiring over 700 awards to reliably eliminate the possibility of a relationship.

[89] $M = 46.72$; $SD = 15.57$; $n = 33$.

[90] $M = 41.85$; $SD = 19.50$; $n = 123$.

[91] $t\,(152) = 1.241$; $p = .22$; $r = .10$; $n = 154$. A Mann-Whitney test was unable to detect a reliable median difference in tribunals' deliberation periods in final cases with (and without) a separate opinion ($U = 1637.5$; $p = .11$; $n = 154$). The potentially small latent effect ($r = .10$) could arguably result from insufficient power.

[92] $M = 13.39$; $SD = 7.08$; $n = 33$.

[93] $M = 11.53$; $SD = 7.82$; $n = 121$.

[94] The one counter-point involved the subset of non-final awards. Unlike final awards, non-final awards involving separate opinions were reliably longer both in terms of mean ($t\,(110) = 4.535$; $p < .001$; $r = .39$; $n = 112$) and median ($U = 554.0$; $p = .01$; $n = 112$) deliberation length. For non-final awards where there was no separate opinion, there was an average delay of seven months, whereas for those non-final awards with a separate opinion, the deliberative delay was twice as long—namely fourteen months. The discrepancy merits ongoing evaluation.

[95] Sean Farhang & Gregory Warro, *Institutional Dynamics on the U.S. Court of Appeals: Minority Representation under Panel Decision Making*, 20 J. LAW. ECON. & ORG. 299 (2004); Frank B. Cross & Emerson H. Tiller, *Judicial Partisanship and Obedience to Legal Doctrine, Whistleblowing on the Federal Courts of Appeal*, 107 YALE L.J. 2155 (1998); Lee Epstein et al. *Why (and When) Judges Dissent: A Theoretical and Empirical Analysis*, 3 J. LEGAL ANALYSIS 101 (2011).

[96] Pamela C. Corley, *Bargaining and Accommodation on the United States Supreme Court*, 90 JUDICATURE 157 (2007).

neither slower nor faster rendering decisions.[97] Not all lengthy time periods, however, reflect collaborative decision-making and could instead reflect internal complexity.[98] When judges render separate opinions to serve as a "whistle-blower," there is no need for negotiation; decision-making is streamlined, and awards can be rendered quickly.

The results could also not prove that separate opinions were linked to faster dispute settlement. Where ITA tribunals "agreed to disagree," rendering different opinions did not streamline decision-making by writing opinions independently and efficiently, suggesting arbitrators did not typically use separate opinions to engage in "whistle-blowing," There are counter-examples, including the dissent in *CME v. Czech Republic* leading a Stockholm court to question arbitrators about their deliberations.[99] A single outlier, however, does not reflect a pattern. Avoiding cognitive illusions by testing intuition against data suggests tribunals rendering separate opinions were not necessarily reliably faster. Rather—like judges—the results provide preliminary evidence that time periods with separate opinions may derive from peer-effects of dissent aversion.[100] This suggests arbitrators did not rubber-stamp outcomes but engaged with their colleagues and worked to create clear, unified decisions. Yet other factors, including busy schedules or competing obligations, could contribute to delay. Likewise, the lack of significant results may reflect the ad hoc nature of ITA and different tribunals taking various approaches to an assortment of disputes.

E. THE IMPACT OF BIFURCATION

ITA tribunals often have discretion to bifurcate cases into phases resolving distinct legal issues. In practice, tribunals have tended to: separate jurisdiction as a preliminary question, or separate jurisdiction and merits from damages.[101] Although bifurcation historically has been justified as saving time and costs, there is a general debate within international arbitration about the value of bifurcation. John Gotanda suggests there is "no consensus" as to whether bifurcation is generally appropriate, and this uncertainty increases costs and delays.[102] Having a data-driven baseline can inform the debate and reality-test concerns.

---

[97] Thomas J. Miles, *The Law's Delay: A Test of the Mechanisms of Judicial Peer Effects*, 4 J. LEGAL ANALYSIS 301, 304 (2012).

[98] *See* DEBORAH J. BARROW & THOMAS G. WALKER, A COURT DIVIDED: THE FIFTH CIRCUIT COURT OF APPEALS AND THE POLITICS OF JUDICIAL REFORM (1998); Tracey E. George & Chris Guthrie, *The Threes: Re-imagining Supreme Court Decisionmaking*, 61 VAND. L. REV. 1825 (2008).

[99] CME Czech Republic B.V. v. Czech Republic, UNCITRAL, Challenge to Arbitration Award (May 15, 2003), 42 I.L.M. 915 (2003).

[100] Miles, *supra* note 97, at 305. Professor Miles's suggested appellate judges were more influenced by whistle-blowing incentives and less influenced by bargaining. Professor Miles, however, controlled for "ideological" makeup of tribunals and individual judges. As arbitrators come from various countries with different legal traditions, economic realities, and varying concepts of political ideology, creating such a variable for ITA is dubious.

[101] *See* Chapter 5(II)(B) (noting, although they were coded in the dataset, Rule 41(5) decisions were not analyzed as they involved only 2% of cases); *supra* note 54.

[102] John Y. Gotanda, *An Efficient Method for Determining Jurisdiction in International Arbitrations*, 40 COLUM. J. TRANSNAT'L L. 11 (2001).

While exploring variations in case length for bifurcated and non-bifurcated cases,[103] analyses revealed a statistically reliable difference in mean case length for cases that were (and were not) bifurcated.[104] Namely, bifurcated cases took a reliably *longer* number of months to complete than their non-bifurcated counterparts. The mean time to complete a bifurcated (or trifurcated) case was fifty-three months, or approximately 4.5 years. In contrast, disputes resolved in a single award were completed, on average, in thirty-seven months (i.e., three years).[105] *See* Figure 4.4.[106] Recognizing the limited historical framework and inclusion of non-ITA disputes, ICSID's review of sixty-three internal cases from 2015 to 2017, which included many non-ITA disputes, likewise found "significant discrepancies" for bifurcated and non-bifurcated cases on temporal efficiency, suggesting "that bifurcation is not the best option for all cases" where parties are trying to decrease case length.[107]

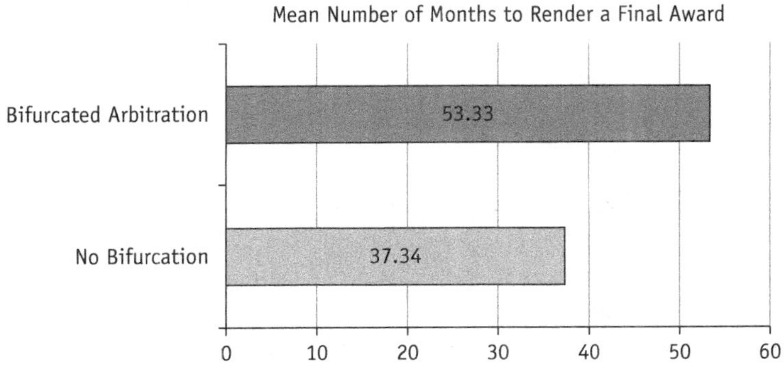

FIGURE 4.4 Mean Number of Months between Filing Request for Arbitration and Final Award Adjudicating ITA Disputes for Bifurcated ($n = 54$) and Non-bifurcated ($n = 102$) Cases.

Theoretically, bifurcation streamlines disputes and increases efficiency. The increased case length suggests bifurcation efficiency objectives were not being met in all cases, with an average 1.5 year gap.

Particularly complex or financially large cases could potentially explain both a decision to bifurcate as well as increased time. In theory, complexity or large fiscal risk may warrant extra time for parties to develop their arguments, for experts to prepare damage reports, or

[103] Bifurcation was a binary variable for whether the dispute was resolved by a single award, or if the tribunal bifurcated (or in a small number of cases trifurcated) the process. *See* Codebook, Appendix IV. Given the temporal nature of the dataset, ICSID Rule 45(1) decisions played a minimal role, involving roughly 2% of cases studied. *See supra* note 54.

[104] A t-test identified reliable mean difference in case length and the binary bifurcation variable ($t\,(154) = -5.512$; $p < .001$; $r = .41$; $n = 156$). *See* Appendix I (discussing choices about statistical tests).

[105] $n = 102$; $SD = 15.37$.

[106] For deliberation length, twelve months was the mean time between last hearing and final award ($n = 154$; $SD = 7.68$). For bifurcated cases, the mean deliberation period was thirteen months ($n = 54$; $SD = 8.37$), whereas the mean deliberation period for cases resolved in a single award was eleven months. It was not possible to identify a meaningful link between mean deliberation period and bifurcation ($t\,(152) = -1.609$; $p = .11$; $r = .13$).

[107] ICSID, WORKING PAPER, *supra* note 30, at Sch. 9, 976–80.

for tribunals to carefully analyze materials. Yet, even controlling for amounts claimed, there was a strong and reliable relationship whereby bifurcated cases took reliably more months to resolve.[108] Some other theory is therefore required to explain the variation.

The results may, however, reflect that complicated cases necessitate bifurcation because they are simply more difficult, require more time, and could have been even longer without bifurcation. Bifurcation is not an experiment where cases are randomly assigned to bifurcation or unified proceedings; instead, bifurcation involves a party request and the arbitrators' assessment that bifurcation is appropriate, presumably offering theoretical ex ante net efficiency (rather than actual ex post efficiency). When considering the deliberative delay and that an average tribunal took ten to twelve months to render an award after a hearing, the delay may be partially explained by the need to write multiple awards. Put simply, multiplying the deliberative delay to write multiple awards stands to increase the overall time to render a final award. Even in the absence of this data, but having considered their own analyses, ICSID has properly advocated a cautionary tale for inadvertently increasing case length by requesting bifurcation.[109]

III. Time and Costs

Thus far, the book has lightly touched elements of ITA costs. This section tackles costs in a way that should facilitate cognitive ease. The objective is to start with a relatively easy concept and introduce core ideas to enable readers to take a deeper dive in later chapters. Benjamin Franklin's sage advice suggested that increased time causes increased costs. Yet cognitive illusions can wreak havoc with common sense, making it vital to assess whether the conventional wisdom is, indeed, wise. This section therefore explores links between time and costs. It first offers a costs nomenclature before exploring whether Benjamin Franklin's advice is applicable to ITA.

A. DEFINING ITA COSTS

In theory, costs related to investment treaty disputes could take various forms. Social costs, for example, may relate to social unrest or other social considerations related to sensitive policy issues. Political costs likewise may involve the value of subjecting the state to any liability, voluntarily curtailing historical realms of state sovereignty, the possibility of raising domestic taxes to pay for adverse awards, or difficulties in procuring international aid. Economic costs could include reputational costs that may impact the credit rating of sovereign debt or decisions to invest in the state, opportunity costs of sinking resources into ITA, and transactional costs of paying lawyers, arbitrators, experts, and institutions for their expenses.[110]

---

[108] A partial correlation, controlling for amounts claimed using logged data, continued to identify a reliable relationship between case length and bifurcation (r (97) = .43; p < .001). *See* Appendix I (discussing inflation-adjustments, transformations, and statistical tests used); Chapter 3 (providing a methodological overview of the data analyzed).

[109] *See* Chapter 9 (commenting on ICSID proposals and making recommendations for normative reform).

[110] Susan D. Franck, *Rationalizing Costs in Investment Treaty Arbitration*, 88 WASH U. L. REV. 769, 782–83 (2011).

A full explanation of "true costs" likely includes non-fiscal elements, yet finding valid, reliable, clear, and scientifically sound ex ante ways to measure those costs is inevitably challenging. In an effort to use clear, reliable, quantifiable terms with practical relevance, this book focuses on quantifiable, fiscal costs directly associated with ITA. Two critical types of costs are readily quantifiable and required to finally adjudicate ITA claims, namely, parties' own legal costs, including their lawyer fees and related internal expenses (**PLC**), and tribunal and institutional administrative expenses for conducting the arbitration (**TCE**).

PLC consists of costs for each party's internal and external legal counsel, counsel's administrative costs (factual and research, data and document processing, expert witnesses, transnational, etc.), and other costs connected with party advocacy to resolve the dispute.[111] PLC are the normal costs of retaining lawyers when pursing formal dispute resolution. Unlike court litigation, arbitration is an ad hoc, nonpublicly funded process requiring payment of fees and expenses of arbitrators, administrative charges of any arbitral institution, costs associated with renting facilities, and fees for transcription services, interpreters, and other related expenditures. As those are necessary services, and no state entity or transnational body currently picks up the tab, those costs are inevitable. TCE consists of administrative charges, arbitrators' fees and expenses (hotel, typists, etc.), costs for those experts retained by the tribunal, costs for tribunal secretaries, and other costs arbitrators incur.[112]

The two sets of costs can involve distinct doctrinal rules.[113] The research demarcated between PLC and TCE to reflect both the doctrinal distinction and the reality that the costs involve different orders of magnitude, potentially triggering different normative concerns. Understanding the distinction between cost types aids stakeholder assessments.[114] If "the worst thing a client

[111] John Gotanda, *Awarding Costs and Attorneys' Fees in International Commercial Arbitration*, 21 MICH. J. INT'L L. 1, 9–10 (1999); J. Gillis Wetter & Charl Priem, *Costs and Their Allocation in International Commercial Arbitrations*, 2 AM. REV. INT'L ARB. 249, 253–54 (1991); *see also* Codebook, Appendix IV (defining PLC as "costs incurred by either a Claimant in bringing a claim or a Respondent in defending a claim. PLC might include, for example, (1) attorney fees, (2) expert and consultant fees, (3) travel expenses, and (4) administrative expenses.").

[112] Micha Bühler, *Awarding Costs in International Commercial Arbitration: An Overview*, 22 ASA BULL. 249, 249 (2004); *see* MAURO RUBINO-SAMMARTANO, INTERNATIONAL ARBITRATION LAW & PRACTICE 812–14 (2d ed. 2001); *see also* FOUCHARD GAILLARD GOLDMAN ON INTERNATIONAL COMMERCIAL ARBITRATION 684–85 (Emmanuel Gaillard & John Savage eds., 1999); *see also* Codebook, Appendix IV (defining TCE as "refers to the costs incurred by the tribunal and the arbitral institution (if any) in adjudicating the claims and arguments made by the parties. TCE might include, for example, (1) tribunal's fees, (2) the tribunal's travel expenses, (3) the costs of experts consulted by the tribunal, (4) the costs of hearing rooms and transcripts, and (5) the administrative expenses of the institution").

[113] U.N. Comm'n on Int'l Trade Law [UNCITRAL], Arbitration Rules, G.A. Res. 31/98, art. 40(1)–(2), U.N. Doc. A/31/17; GAOR, 31st Sess., Supp. No. 17 (Dec. 15, 1976), http://bit.ly/Paq3vX [hereinafter 1976 UNCITRAL Arbitration Rules] (last visited Aug. 7, 2018) (providing that procedural costs are "borne by the unsuccessful party," but for legal costs, the tribunal is "free to determine which party shall bear such costs or may apportion such costs between the parties if it determines that apportionment is reasonable").

[114] Cost elements may be critical for assessments of third-party funding. *See generally* LISA BENCH NIEUWVELD & VICTORIA SHANNON, THIRD-PARTY FUNDING IN INTERNATIONAL ARBITRATION (2012); Maya Steinitz, *Whose Claim Is This Anyway? Third-Party Litigation Funding*, 95 MINN. L. REV. 1268 (2011); *see also* Stavros L. Brekoulakis, *International Arbitration Scholarship and the Concept of Arbitration Law*, 36 FORD. INT'L L.J. 745, 767 (2013) ("the current arbitration zeitgeist is the use of third-party funding in international arbitration"). While a critical area, it is beyond the scope of this book but worthy of future consideration as it has profound implications for international litigation and adjudication generally.

can ever be is surprised,"[115] then precision in cost assessments aids management of expectations, encourages realistic views about results, and minimizes outcries about unfair surprise.

B. THE RELIABLE RELATIONSHIP BETWEEN TIME AND COST

Time and costs are of concern in international arbitration generally.[116] Institutions can have detailed guidelines about controlling time and costs.[117] The Chartered Institute of Arbitrators explored time and costs in international commercial arbitration, suggesting "[w]hile length [of arbitration] may affect some of the common costs, it does not appear to have been a material factor."[118] ITA stakeholders have likewise exhibited concerns about time and costs,[119] becoming a focus of attention at UNCITRAL Working Group III.[120] Yet, there is a dearth of empirical evidence exploring these aspects. To test the assumption that time is money in ITA, tests explored links between case length and fundamental arbitration costs, namely claimants' legal costs, respondents' legal costs, and the total cost of the tribunal and other institutional support. All analyses revealed a strong, reliable, and positive relationship between case length and the different ITA costs. In other words, the more months required to render a final award, the higher all forms of arbitration costs; conversely, the faster a tribunal rendered a final award, the lower the costs.

First, for claimants' PLC, data revealed a strong, positive correlation between investors' legal costs and case length, using logged data.[121] Figure 4.5 offers a visual summary using raw inflation-adjusted data, which includes statistical outliers, to aid comprehension. The results reflect that longer time periods to finalize cases were correlated with increased costs for investors' counsel; decreased time to complete cases was associated with decreased lawyer costs.

Second, there was a meaningful link between case length and respondents' PLC.[122] Like claimants, longer times to resolve disputes were associated with higher legal costs, and cases resolved more quickly had lower legal costs for states. Combining all parties' lawyer fees

---

[115] *See* Susan D. Franck, *Considering Recalibration of International Investment Agreements: Empirical Insights*, *in* THE EVOLVING INTERNATIONAL INVESTMENT REGIME: EXPECTATIONS, REALITIES, OPTIONS (José E. Alvarez et al., eds., 2011) (referring to observations by Sherry Williams).

[116] *See* Queen Mary University of London, 2015 INTERNATIONAL ARBITRATION SURVEY: IMPROVEMENTS AND INNOVATIONS IN INTERNATIONAL ARBITRATION 2 (2015), https://bit.ly/2uu7txv (last visited Aug. 7, 2018) (noting that practitioners surveyed indicated that costs are arbitration's worst feature).

[117] *See, e.g.*, ICC ARB. COMM'N., REPORT ON TECHNIQUES FOR CONTROLLING TIME AND COSTS IN ARBITRATION (2012), http://bit.ly/11ie7lb (last visited Aug. 7, 2018).

[118] Chartered Institute, *supra* note 31, at 12.

[119] Leon Trakman, *The ICSID Under Siege*, 45 CORNELL INT'L L.J. 603, 617 (2012) Jeswald W. Salacuse, *Is There a Better Way? Alternative Methods of Treaty-Based, Investor-State Dispute Resolution*, 31 FORDHAM INT'L L.J. 138, 147 (2007).

[120] *See generally* UNCITRAL, *Report of Working Group III (Investor-State Dispute Settlement Reform) on the work of its thirty-fourth session (Vienna, 27 November–1 December 2017)*, at 6–11, UN Doc. A/CN.9/930 (Dec. 19, 2017), https://bit.ly/2LbD5Sc (last visited Aug. 7, 2018); *see also* UNCITRAL, Possible Reform of Investor-State Dispute Settlement (ISDS)—Cost and Duration, Note by the Secretariat, A/CN.9/WG.III/WP.153 (Aug. 31, 2018), https://bit.ly/2CzklXp (last visited Dec. 25, 2018).

[121] $r(50) = .60$; $p < .001$. Legal costs and time are continuous variables, making correlations appropriate tests, and logged costs data exhibited the lowest skewing. See Appendix I for a discussion of methodology.

[122] $r(56) = .35$; $p = .01$.

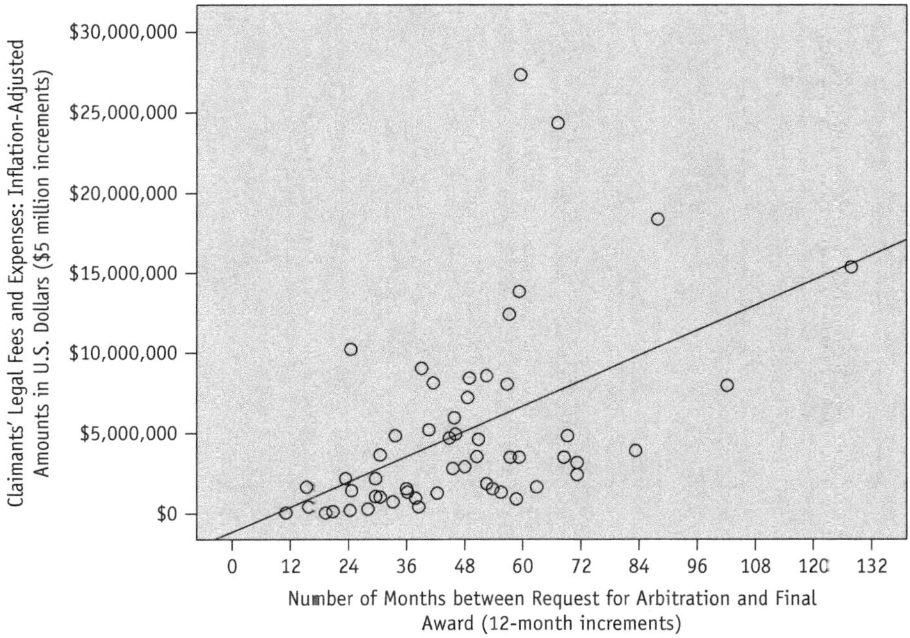

FIGURE 4.5 Scatterplot of Case Length in Final Awards and Claimants' Legal Fees, including Line of Best Fit ($n = 50$).

similarly revealed a strong and reliable relationship between case length and parties' legal fees.[123]

The final cost variable was tribunal expenses and institutional costs. Like parties' legal fees, time meant money for arbitrators. There was a strong, positive, and robust correlation between case length and TCE using logged data.[124] Longer time periods to resolve the case were correlated with increased tribunal and administrative costs; decreased time was associated with decreased costs. Figure 4.6 visually summarizes the results using raw inflation-adjusted data (including statistical outliers) to facilitate an appreciation of the relationship.

The data revealed Franklin's conventional wisdom applied to ITA: for lawyers' and tribunals' costs, time was indeed money. While correlation is not causation, statistical models reliably demonstrated links between increased time and increased costs. Comparatively, the strength of the relationship between time and cost was weakest for respondents' legal expenses, albeit still strong. For claimants' fees, large r-values suggest that approximately 50–60% of costs could be linked with case length. For tribunal expenses, high r-values suggest that 58–63% of variance could be traced to time.

Some caution is required, however. Roughly 30–40% of final cases analyzed had fiscal data on claimant, respondent, and tribunal costs. This means that, tribunals more typically tended to omit key cost data from their written awards. It is troubling that pertinent information was omitted, particularly when costs submissions are available and

[123] $r(47) = .53; p < .001$.

[124] $r(58) = .63; p < .001$.

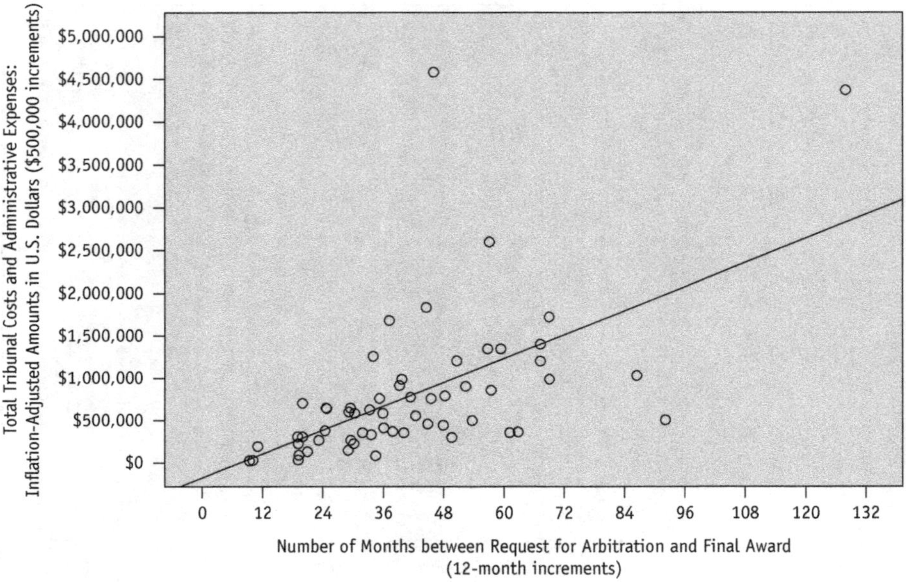

FIGURE 4.6 **Scatterplot of Case Length in Final Awards and Total Tribunal Costs and Administrative Expenses, including Line of Best Fit ($n = 58$).**

this impacts normative reform proposed in Chapter 9, as ITA would be better served by providing full cost data in disputes involving state liability and treaty interpretation. While the gap raises concerns about inferential strength, extensive analysis[125] nevertheless failed to identify—on other core variables related to the investor identity,[126] respondent

[125] To examine whether missing data impacted key dependent variables, data with and without missing values were compared for each dependent variable. A dummy variable was coded to indicate whether there was missing data for each dependent variable (0 = missing data and 1 = available data). The following analyses were estimated using one-way ANOVAs (for continuous variables) and chi-square (for categorical variables) with the coded variable as the independent variable, and key predictor variables as the dependent variables. For claimant's legal costs, most variables were not significantly different for missing ($n = 110$) and available ($n = 49$) data. For respondents' legal costs, variables of interest were not significantly different for missing ($n = 104$) and available ($n = 55$) cases. Lastly, most variables of interest were not significantly different for missing ($n = 104$) and available ($n = 54$) cases on tribunal costs and expenses.

[126] When exploring potential differences between cases with and without costs data, claimant and respondent legal costs exhibited similar results as regards core variations in investor identity, both as regards development status and commercial background. For claimants' legal costs, it was not possible to distinguish between cases missing and containing costs data for investors from OECD or non-OECD states (χ^2 (1) = 0.91; p = .34), investors' World Bank development classification (χ^2 (2) = 1.70; p = .43), or HDI classifications from an investors' home state (F (1, 157) = 0.04; p = .83). Likewise, tests were unable to find a reliable difference in investors' commercial background when testing for the presence of people, corporations, or a combination thereof (χ^2 (2) = 1.36; p = .51), the presence of a publicly listed corporation (χ^2 (1) = 0.10; p = .75), or FT500-related investors (χ^2 (1) = 0.17; p = .83). For respondents' legal costs, tests were unable to reliably distinguish between cases with and without costs data where investors were from OECD or non-OECD states (χ^2 (1) = 1.10; p = .30), on the World Bank development classifications from an investors' home state (χ^2 (2) = 2.56; p = .28), or using

identity,[127] arbitrator background,[128] aspects of the underlying disputes,[129] and applicable

an investors' home state HDI score (F (1, 157) = 0.57; p = .45). It was also not possible to distinguish between cases missing or containing data on respondents' legal costs as a function of investors' commercial identity when comparing cases where investors were people, corporations, or a combination thereof (χ^2 (2) = 2.52; p = .28), where investors were a publicly listed corporation (χ^2 (1) = 0.22; p = .64), or there was an FT500-related investor (χ^2 (1) = 0.01; p = .93). For tribunal costs, it was also not possible to distinguish between cases with and without costs data by virtue of whether investors were from OECD or non-OECD states (χ^2 (1) = 0.46; p = .50;), World Bank development classifications of investors' home states (χ^2 (2) = 1.09; p = .58), and HDI background of investors' home states (F (1, 157) = 2.00; p = .16). It was also not possible to differentiate between cases containing or missing tribunal expenses as a function of investors' commercial identity when exploring whether investors were people, corporations, or a combination thereof (χ^2 (2) = 0.83; p = .66) or where investors' were a publicly listed corporation (χ^2 (1) = 0.02; p = .90). There was a slight difference for FT500-related investor (χ^2 (1) = 3.92; p < .048), whereby FT500-related entities were more likely to be missing data on tribunal expenses only, but this may be a function of the small number of cases involving FT500-related entities.

127 Claimant legal costs, respondent legal costs, and tribunal costs tests were unable to find meaningful variance in core aspects of respondent identity when comparing cases with and without data. For claimants' legal costs, it was not possible to identify meaningful difference between cases with and without costs data as a function of respondent's OECD membership (χ^2 (1) = 0.11; p = .74), respondents' World Bank development classification (χ^2 (3) = 5.57; p = .14), respondents' HDI score (F (1, 155) = 0.60; p = .44), respondents' ranking on the Perceived Corruption Index (F (1, 151) = 0.61; p = .44), and respondents' Polity IV scores (F (1, 156) = 0.71; p = .40). For respondents' legal costs, tests were likewise unable to identify any meaningful differences for cases with and without cost data when exploring respondents' OECD membership (χ^2 (1) = 0.55; p = .46), World Bank development classification (χ^2 (3) = 2.83; p = .42), HDI score (F (1, 155) = 1.36; p = .25), Perceived Corruption Index score (F (1, 151) = 0.01; p = .93), and Polity IV score (F (1, 156) = 1.37; p = .24). For tribunal expenses, it was not possible to identify a meaningful difference between cases with and without costs data as a function of respondent identity, irrespective of respondents'OECD membership (χ^2 (1) = 2.89; p = .09), World Bank development classification (χ^2 (3) = 1.83; p = .61), HDI score (F (1, 155) = 1.86; p = .18), Perceived Corruption Index score (F (1,151) = 1.10; p = .30), and Polity IV score (F (1, 156) = .12; p = .73).

128 It was generally not possible to identify meaningful tribunal-related differences with cases missing or containing cost data. For claimant's legal costs, it was not possible to identify meaningful differences in either tribunal gender composition (i.e. having at least one woman on a tribunal) (χ^2 (1) = 0.04; p = .84), or the tribunal's combined World Bank classification (i.e. the combined value of the development status of each arbitrator's home state) (χ^2 (7) = 8.30; p = .31). Data on tribunal development classification suggested that tribunals with all arbitrators derived exclusively from OECD states (χ^2 (3) = 10.52; p < .05) and tribunals with a higher combined HDI score (F (1, 155) = 3.979; p = .048) were slightly more likely to provide data on claimant's legal costs (and tribunals with lower development status backgrounds were more likely to omit data on claimants' legal costs). For respondents' legal costs, it was not possible to identify the availability of costs data as a function of tribunal gender (χ^2 (1) = 0.01; p = .92) and World Bank combined classifications (χ^2 (7) = 12.424; p = .09). Like the earlier finding for investors, for respondents' legal costs, tests suggested that the composite score of tribuanls development background was that where tribunals had fewer arbitrators from OECD states OECD (χ^2 (3) = 10.53; p < .05) or lower composite HDI scores (F (1, 155) = 4.81; p < .05), the cases missing data on respondents' costs were slightly more likely to be promulgated by tribunals with arbitrators from less developed countries; yet the failure to replicate with the World Bank measure requires caution. For tribunal expenses, it was never possible to identify a meaningful difference in tribunals providing or omitting costs data as a function of tribunal gender composition (χ^2 (1) = 0.01; p = .99), tribunals' combined development status under the OECD (χ^2 (3) = 4.84; p = .18), World Bank (χ^2 (7) = 12.896; p = .08), or HDI (F (1, 155) = 0.83; p = .36) classifications.

129 Tests failed to distinguish between cases missing or containing cost data for the industry in dispute and procedural aspects of the dispute. For claimants' legal costs, it was not possible to distinguish between cases based upon the industry involved (χ^2 (19) = 18.550; p = .49), presence of an energy dispute (r (159) = .033; p = .68), presence of

law[130]—that cases *omitting* cost data were meaningfully different from cases *with* cost data. To the extent the cases omitting data were not otherwise atypical, a reasonable possibility (but not a definitive conclusion), is that the cases containing full costs data were necessarily unusual on costs. The one exception was that, for only *party* legal fees, older cases tended to have *less* data and recent cases tended to have more complete cost data.[131] Inferences must therefore be made with caution, as there is a risk that missing data could skew results and undermine inferences about the oldest arbitration cases.

Yet the objective is to offer this historic data with a view considering of the ongoing value of this baseline. This snapshot of costs should, at a minimum, encourage tribunals to provide greater data and incentivize institutions to develop practices codifying the inclusion of critical fiscal information that—in multiple instances—may be representing 20–30% of amounts awarded. Given what is at stake in a contentious area of international law, transparency on critical fiscal elements will promote a more informed debate and generate better analysis in the future.

---

a non-disputing party (NDP) ($r\,(159) = -.037; p = .64$), bifurcation ($\chi^2\,(1) = 0.13; p = .72$), or existence of a separate opinion ($\chi^2\,(1) = 2.12; p = .15$). For respondents' legal costs, it was not possible to distinguish between cases with or without costs for the industry involved ($\chi^2\,(19) = 20.896; p = .34$), energy disputes ($r\,(159) = .014; p = .86$), participation of an NDP ($r\,(159) = -.036; p = .66$), bifurcation ($\chi^2\,(1) = 0.56, p = .45$), or a separate opinion ($\chi^2\,(1) = 2.34; p = .13$). For tribunal expenses, it was not possible to distinguish between cases with or without data for the industry involved ($\chi^2\,(19) = 24.578; p = .16$), energy disputes ($r\,(159) = .121; p = .13$), NDP participation ($r\,(159) = -.06; p = .45$), bifurcation ($\chi^2\,(1) = 0.06, p = .80$), or a separate opinion ($\chi^2\,(1) = 0.30; p = .58$).

130 For claimants' legal costs, it was not possible to identify meaningful differences between cases with complete and missing data that derived from a multilateral or bilateral treaty ($\chi^2\,(1) = 0.02; p = .89$), but the type of multilateral treaty was significant ($\chi^2\,(4) = 9.79; p < .05$) as, proportionally, ECT cases had more costs data than the early NAFTA cases. Similarly, for respondents' legal costs, it was not possible to distinguish between those cases with complete or missing data on the basis of whether the dispute derived from a multilateral or bilateral treaty ($\chi^2\,(1) = 0.54; p = .46$); but testing type of multilateral treaty did identify a significant difference, as ECT cases had more costs data available than early NAFTA cases ($\chi^2\,(4) = 9.51; p = <.05$). For tribunal costs, it was not possible to identify a meaningful difference between cases with and without costs as a function of a specific treaty ($\chi^2\,(4) = 9.13; p = .06$). In a small twist, when comparing cases deriving from bilateral or multilateral treaties, tribunal costs were more likely to be omitted in cases from bilateral investment treaties and more likely to be present in cases under multilateral treaties ($\chi^2\,(1) = 3.88; p =.049$). The only other variation was that tribunal costs were more likely to be missing data in institutional arbitration as compared to ad hoc arbitration ($\chi^2\,(2) = 36.42; p < .001$); and institutional rules indicated ICSID-Convention and ICSID-AF cases had more missing cost data compared to cases proceeding under SCC or UNCITRAL Rules ($\chi^2\,(4) = 39.11; p < .001$). Seventy-four ICSID-Convention cases, nineteen ICSID-AF cases, two SCC cases, and eleven UNCITRAL omitted data on tribunal costs; only nineteen ICSID-Convention cases, three ICSID-Additional Facility, eight SCC and twenty-two UNCITRAL cases contained data on tribunal costs. The missing costs data from ICSID-related cases may derive from the current gap within the existing rules explaining costs application, suggesting that revising ICSID Rules to require transparent costs information is an area decidedly ripe for reform. *See* Chapter 9.

131 For claimants' legal costs, cases containing or missing costs data reliably differed in the year the award was rendered ($F\,(1, 157) = 25.62; p < .001$). Cases without data were rendered earlier ($M = 2005; SD = 3.96$) than cases with data ($M = 2009, SD = 2.34$). For respondents' legal costs, cases with and without data were likewise meaningfully different ($F\,(1, 157) = 30.47; p < .001$). Cases without data were rendered in an earlier year ($M = 2005; SD = 3.98$) than cases with data ($M = 2009; SD = 2.32$). The year an award was rendered failed to predict whether a dispute contained or was missing tribunal cost data ($F\,(1, 157) = 1.967; p = .16$); likewise, it was not possible to detect a reliable difference in case length based upon the presence or absence of tribunal cost data ($F\,(1, 154) = 0.041; p = .84$).

5 Claims and Outcomes in ITA

I. Introduction

ITA is no longer a theoretical risk. It is now a practical reality. ITA risks involve a potential loss for investors, when investment losses are not covered by international law, and a risk for states that they will incur liability. These risks, in turn, can influence perceived relative cost and the net benefit of pursuing or defending investment disputes. Data offers a key debiasing tool to prevent cognitive illusions from skewing debates about the reality of realized risk.

Literature suggests considerable disagreement over who wins and who loses in ITA. This derives from multiple challenges. The core challenge involves definitions, namely what it means to "win." Subjective definitions create confusion about what is being analyzed, inject variance, and impede measurement. Some investors receive financial compensation, but nevertheless view the outcome as a "loss."[1] Others suggest, even if a state is not liable, the mere existence of the claim is a "loss."[2] Where the mere risk of an adverse outcome is itself "losing," commentators focus on the "threat of massive damage awards"[3] without framing potential

[1] *See* Jack J. Coe, Jr., *Toward a Complementary Use of Conciliation in Investor-State Disputes—A Preliminary Sketch*, 12 U.C. Davis J. Int'l L. & Pol'y 7, 8 (2005) (referring to remarks by Grant Kesler, CEO of Metalclad who successfully recovered over US$16 million from Mexico).

[2] Nathalie Bernasconi-Osterwalder, *Who Wins and Who Loses in Investment Arbitration? Are Investors and Host States on a Level Playing Field?*, 6 J. World Inv. & Trade 69, 69 (2005).

[3] Sarah Anderson & Sara Grusky, *Challenging Corporate Investor Rule: How the World Bank's Investment Court, Free Trade Agreements, and Bilateral Investment Treaties have Unleashed a New Era of Corporate Power and What to Do About It*, Food & Water Watch, 4 (Apr. 2007), https://bit.ly/2RovggO (last visited Jan. 18, 2019).

Arbitration Costs. Susan D. Franck.

loss against actual results. More sophisticated permutations suggest investors are primarily successful and have a high chance of success, and therefore "host States cannot be winners in investment arbitration."[4] The net result is: measuring a "win" or "loss" is emotionally evocative and likely sparks intuitive responses. Still others might classify a settlement as a "loss"—even where parties agree a mutually acceptable outcome—because not everyone received everything they wanted.[5] Yet if all parties could obtain precisely what they wanted, there would be no conflict. A dispute inevitably leaves one or both parties dissatisfied on some vector. Given emotive reactions, relying on subjective and non-generalizable perceptions makes reliable comparison infeasible. The validity and reliability of fiscal measures recorded in cases—although imperfect—are preferable to intuitive, subjective, and non-generalizable assessments.[6]

Second, disagreements about the meaning of ITA outcomes occur when commentators use methodology failing to comport with social science standards. Without explaining the unit of analysis or methodology—and without acknowledging distinctions between ITA and other arbitrations at ICSID—one group historically stated:

> Seventy per cent of ICSID cases have favored the investor. The legal fees and arbitration costs are borne by the losing party. The implications for developing countries are substantial, in respect to the technical capacity to handle investment reputation to the country.[7]

Similarly, work claiming to demonstrate a "pro-investor" bias in ITA[8] through tribunals making "expansive" decisions: failed to control for whether treaty language was itself expansive (i.e., making a broad interpretation appropriate) or narrow (i.e., making a broad interpretation inappropriate);[9] focused exclusively on issues in jurisdiction awards, thereby

---

[4] Anderson & Grusky, *supra* note 3, at ix; Bernasconi-Osterwalder, *supra* note 2, at 69.

[5] Pia Eberhardt & Cecilia Olivet, *Profiting from Injustice: How Law Firms, Arbitrators and Financiers Are Fueling an Investment Arbitration Boom*, CORP. EUR. OBSERVATORY & TRANSNAT'L INST., 9, 13, 22, 30, 58 (Nov. 2012), http://bit.ly/1e30kHT (last visited Aug. 7, 2018); *see also* Douglas Thomson, *"A Negotiated Surrender": Counsel in Belize Cases Criticises Settlement*, GLOBAL ARB. REV. (Aug. 2, 2016), http://bit.ly/2aCRH7n (last visited Aug. 7, 2018).

[6] Susan D. Franck, *The Promise and Peril of Empiricism and International Investment Law Disputes*, *in* CAMBRIDGE COMPENDIUM OF INTERNATIONAL COMMERCIAL AND INVESTMENT ARBITRATION (Andrea Bjorklund et al., eds., forthcoming 2019); Susan D. Franck & Lindsey E. Wylie, *Predicting Outcomes in Investment Treaty Arbitration*, 65 DUKE L.J. 459, 484–85 (2015).

[7] *ICSID-International Centre for Settlement of Investment Disputes (ICSID)*, BRETTON WOODS PROJ. (July 10, 2009), https://bit.ly/1Az6fNA (last visited Aug. 7, 2018).

[8] *See generally* Gus Van Harten, *Arbitrator Behavior in Asymmetrical Adjudication: An Empirical Study of Investment Treaty Arbitration*, 50 OSGOODE HALL L.J. 211 (2012) (claiming to find "statistically significant" evidence that arbitrators favor claimants).

[9] *See id.* at 240 (listing the controls for a hypothesis that predicted an expansive approach as "claimant's state of nationality; the specific issue among the coded issues; the treaty or treaty type; the total appointments per arbitrator; and the total issue resolutions per case").

overweighting cases with multiple jurisdictional issues and failing to address final outcomes;[10] and failed to define the meaning of "expansive" while simultaneously excluding cases from analysis where "the treaty was clear and express," meaning core awards involving arbitrators' adjudicative authority were omitted.[11]

Third, interpreting outcomes is challenging where commentators select examples fitting preexisting conceptions but without acknowledging contrary examples. Some suggest, for example, that ITA generally results in multimillion-dollar awards or other "emblematic" cases that are at the extreme end of the spectrum.[12] Reflecting backlash and "pro-investor" bias concerns, even though Bolivia has won ITA disputes, Bolivian president Evo Morales previously said, "'[g]overnments from Latin America and I think all over the world never win cases. The transnationals always win.'"[13] Although "[e]mpirical studies suggest that the [claim that Latin American governments never win] is unfounded, but the overall perception has, nonetheless, been difficult to shed."[14]

A final challenge involves the lack of a preexisting, reliable baseline for legal correctness. Doctrinal variations in treaty text, lack of de jure precedent, inability to access case records, inconsistency in application of core legal principles, and absence of an appellate body makes it difficult to make reliable ex ante assessments about legally "correct" results.[15] Professor Rogers observed, "it is impossible to control for the most essential variable," namely, "the 'correct' legal outcome in a particular case."[16] Rather than abandoning efforts to offer empirical insights altogether, the difficulty must be acknowledged; nevertheless, as it uses a common scale to evaluate cases and partially controls for relative merit, relative investor success is the best metric currently available.[17]

Without clear definitions and a baseline from which to evaluate parties' success and failure, discussions of "bias" remain undefined, malleable, emotive, and affiliated with potentially unrepresentative experiences. The risk of improper influence from cognitive illusions means

---

[10] Van Harten "focused on legal issues arising from decisions at or after the jurisdictional stage." *Id.* at 231. Van Harten thoughtfully notes his methodology failed to "address situations where a known case has not led to a publicly available award." *Id.*

[11] *Id.* at 226–27, 230.

[12] *See* Franck, *supra* note 6 (identifying both positive and problematic methodological aspects of the asymmetric adjudication study).

[13] Leslie Mazoch, *Chavez Takes Cool View Toward OAS, Says Latin America Better Off Without World Bank*, HUFFINGTON POST (Apr. 30, 2007, 11:09 AM), http://tinyurl.com/knnl8xp (last visited Aug. 11, 2014); *see also* Peter K. Yu, *The Investment-Related Aspects of Intellectual Property Rights*, 66 AM. U. L. REV. 829, 853 (2017) (discussing the same article and quotation).

[14] David P. Reisenberg, *Fee Shifting in Investor-State Arbitration: Doctrine and Policy Justifying Application of the English Rule*, 60 DUKE L.J. 977, 988 (2011) (footnotes omitted).

[15] When thinking about how to define legal correctness ex ante, one might recall the quip by U.S. Supreme Court Justice Robert Jackson, also a prosecutor in the Nuremburg Trials, who remarked the U.S. Supreme Court was "not final because we are infallible, but we are infallible only because we are final." Maximillian Koessler, *Robert H. Jackson: Lawyer's Judge*, 62 COLUM. L. REV. 395, 396–97 (1962).

[16] Catherine A. Rogers, *The Politics of International Investment Arbitration*, 12 SANTA CLARA J. INT'L L. 223, 234 (2013).

[17] *See id.* at 235 (arguing "relative strength of a particular party's case" serves as a control for correct outcomes); *see also* Franck & Wylie, *supra* note 6, at 486.

it is necessary to test beliefs against verifiable measures, which is an award's final *dispositif* in ITA. Dialogues about whether a party obtaining a favorable outcome has "won" or whether "losing in a curious way is winning"[18] provide constructive information about subjective experience; but the *dispositif* provides an objective measure of compensable breaches and derivative damages.

This chapter uses objective measures to assess outcomes related to fiscal elements as these generate direct, verifiable figures, which, in combination with costs, permit parties to undertake evidence-based cost-benefit assessment of ITA's net value. First, it explores ultimate outcome by identifying whether tribunals awarded investors damages, whether respondents did not experience damages, or whether parties settled or otherwise discontinued the case. Second, it identifies the amount awarded, including awards reflecting settlements or discontinuances. Third, it describes investors' relative success, comparing amounts claimed and awarded.

II. Winning and Losing

ITA outcomes fall roughly into three categories: win, lose, or draw. This framework manifests in two different ways, namely the ultimate outcome when a tribunal renders a final award and during distinct phases where arbitrators resolve determinative matters. The first subsection analyzes ultimate outcomes using a blunt three-category classification.[19] The second subsection offers a more granular view, analyzing critical junctures of a case's lifecycle, namely: jurisdiction, merits, quantum, and costs.[20]

A. Overall Outcomes

In earlier research, investors won 38.5% of cases, respondents won 57.7%, and the remaining awards memorialized settlements.[21] First-generation (G1) research failed to identify a reliable difference in cases won by investors or states. Professor Alvarez wrote that these "numbers pour cold water on unexamined assertions by many critics of the [ITA] regime."[22] But as time marches on, the initial snapshot requires reconsideration. Given the 300% increase in cases in this dataset, tests reconsidered whether parameters changed.

[18] Richard Bach, The Bridge Across Forever 91 (1984).

[19] An investor "win" involved awarding an investor any amount over US$0 or equivalent remedy. A state win involved a respondent successfully avoiding any damage award (i.e., US$0 liability). *See* Codebook, Appendix IV. Settlements, whether memorialized in an award, separately settled, or otherwise discontinued, were grouped together.

[20] Chapter 3 identified the dataset does not address post-award review, enforcement, award negotiation, and compliance, as data is sporadic and subject to enhanced case selection bias.

[21] Susan D. Franck, *Empirically Evaluating Claims About Investment Treaty Arbitration*, 86 N.C. L. Rev. 1, 49–50 (2007).

[22] Jose E. Alvarez, The Public International Law Regime Governing International Investment 391 (2011).

For the 159 final awards analyzed, tribunals awarded investors damages or an equivalent remedy[23] in roughly 36% of cases. Respondents won, paying no damages, in nearly 55% of cases; and around 9% of cases involved settlement or discontinuance.[24] *See* Figure 5.1.

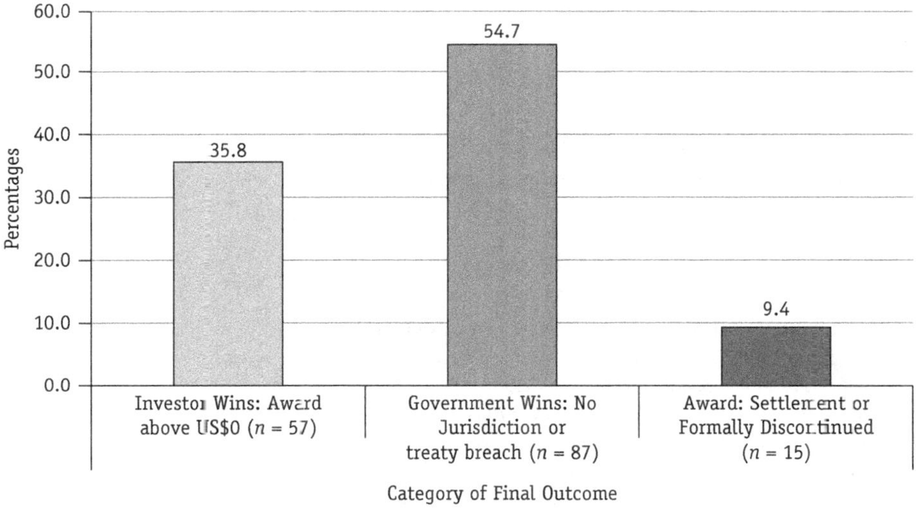

FIGURE 5.1 Percentage of Ultimate Winners, Losers and Settlements in ITA (n = 159) Categorizing Outcome by: Cases where Tribunals Awarded Damages (or an Equivalent Remedy), Cases where the Award was in a State's Favor, and Awards reflecting a Final Settlement Agreement or Discontinuance.

The categorical breakdown was roughly equivalent to earlier research. Over time, both governments and investors were successful in ITA, although states won in slightly larger proportions. This replication suggests that the initial research was robust, providing preliminary evidence that the proportionate outcomes are a population parameter,[25] and also roughly reflect contemporaneous data from UNCTAD.[26] Nevertheless, given temporal evolution, and because others have used different analyses of outcomes,[27] that benchmark

[23] *ATA Construction v. Jordan* was the only case awarding specific performance in lieu of damages; this was coded as an investor win, as specific performance was substituted for damage. *See* ATA Constr., Indus. & Trading Co. v. Jordan, ICSID Case No. ARB/08/2, Award 66–68 (May 18, 2010), 22 WORLD TRADE & ARB. MATERIALS 945, 994–95 (2010).

[24] This group included eight cases with awards embodying settlement agreements, three discontinuances where investors abandoned their claims, three discontinuances where respondents paid damages to settle, and one discontinuance where the respondent paid nothing to settle.

[25] Franck & Wylie, *supra* note 6, at 491.

[26] UNCTAD historically analyzed investor-state treaty-based cases, identifying that investors won less and states won more often. U.N. Conference on Trade and Dev. [UNCTAD], *Latest Developments in Investor–State Dispute Settlement*, IIA ISSUES NOTE, No. 1 (Apr. 2012), https://bit.ly/WETAcp (last visited Aug. 7, 2018) ("Out of these, approximately 40% were decided in favour of the State and approximately30% in favour of the investor. Approximately 30% of the cases were settled.").

[27] UNCTAD's more recent reports focus on "ISDS tribunals," meaning investor-state contract cases governed by national laws (rather than treaties) may be inadvertently included, and thus inferences should be made

should continue to be evaluated. Failure to do so, or focusing only on specific years, risks cognitive illusions (such as recency, negativity, confirmation bias among others) inadvertently skewing understanding.

1. Comparing Investor and State Wins

Although states facially won more, earlier research failed to identify a reliable difference in outcomes. The newer data, however, revealed a statistically meaningful pattern whereby states won reliably more often than investors.[28] For roughly every two claims an investor won, states won three cases (2:3); and the size of the effect was statistically small-to-medium.[29] The results provide a piece of evidence suggesting generalized claims that overall ITA outcomes exhibited a "pro-investor" bias[30] require more precision. Rather, results suggest a potential

---

cautiously. Likewise, ICSID's mandate has been to resolve investor-state claims arising under treaties, commercial disputes under national law, and disputes under national investment law, meaning one must appreciate the inferential limitations and potential for error in drawing conclusions. *See* UNCTAD, *World Investment Report 2018: Investment and New Industrial Policies*, 94–95, UNCTAD/WIR/2018 (June 6, 2018) [hereinafter UNCTAD, *WIR* 2018] ("About one-third of all concluded cases were decided in favour of the State (claims were dismissed either on jurisdictional grounds or on the merits), and about one-quarter were decided in favour of the investor, with monetary compensation awarded"); UNCTAD, *World Investment Report 2016: Investor Nationality: Policy Challenges*, 107-08, UNCTAD/WIR/2016 (June 21, 2016) [hereinafter UNCTAD, *WIR* 2016] ("About one third of all concluded cases were decided in favour of the State (claims dismissed either on jurisdictional grounds or on the merits) and about one quarter were decided in favour of the investor, with monetary compensation awarded."); *see also* International Centre for Settlement of Investment Disputes [ICSID] Secretariat, *The ICSID Caseload–Statistics, Issue 2018-1*,14–15 (2018), https://bit.ly/2HS5k2y (last visited Aug. 7, 2018) [hereinafter ICSID, *2018 Statistics*] (providing data for ISDS cases generally that, excluding settlements, investors won in part or in full in 48% of cases and that states were wholly responsible on jurisdiction or merits in 52% of cases); ICSID Secretariat, *The ICSID Caseload–Statistics, Issue 2016-1*, 14 (2016), https://bit.ly/2N4Mt7o (last visited Aug. 7, 2018) [hereinafter ICSID, *2016 Statistics*] (providing data for ISDS cases generally that, excluding settlements, investors won in part or in full in 46% of cases and states were wholly responsible on jurisdictional or merits grounds in 54% of cases). *But see* Matthew Hodgson & Alastair Campbell, *Investment Treaty Arbitration: Cost, Duration and Size of Claims All Show a Steady Increase* (Dec. 14, 2017), https://bit.ly/2NEnWqA (last visited Aug. 7, 2018) (suggesting 59% of ITA disputes involve state wins, as compared to 56% of state wins in a 2012 study, but failing to conduct statistical tests to identify whether the shift was attributable to statistical chance).

[28] Excluding settlements and discontinuances, chi-square analyses comparing expected and obtained frequencies demonstrated a meaningful statistical pattern (χ^2 (1) = 6.25; $p < .05$; $r = .21$; $n = 144$) of investor wins and respondent wins. *See also* Franck & Wylie, *supra* note 6, at 490–91.

[29] In addition to other methodological explanations, Appendix I discusses effect sizes and Cohen's conventions.

[30] While one might hope for more sophisticated terminology than an essentializing "pro-investor" and "prostate" dichotomy, the terms are commonly used, perhaps generating cognitive ease or flattening social discourse to facilitate intellectual tribalism. *See* Julian Donanbauer, Eric Neumayer & Peter Nunnenkamp, *Winning or Losing in Investor-to-State Dispute Resolution: The Role of Arbitrator Bias and Experience*, 26 Rev. Int'l Econ. 892 (2018) (exploring "pro-investor" bias of tribunal chairs based on previous appointments and finding significant effects but not finding a similar effect for "pro state" bias from appointments); Franck, *supra* note 6 (discussing cognition, dichotomies, and intellectual tribalism); Chiara Giorgetti, *Is the Truth in the Eyes of the Beholder? The Perils and Benefits of Empirical Research in International Investment Arbitration*, 12 Santa Clara J. Int'l L. 263, 265 (2012) ("questioning whether someone or something is 'pro-investor' or 'pro-State' is already attaching a value judgment on the issue studied").

"pro-state" bias[31] in outcomes, with states reliably faring better. The historical snapshot has multiple implications.

First, claims of a "pro-investor" bias on this point have been arguably overstated. If such a bias existed, data would have revealed that investors won more than states. Instead, the results were reversed, with states winning in a reliably greater proportion. Unlike the "anti-defendant bias" in the International Trade Commission's treatment of patent cases[32] or Clermont and Eisenberg's early research suggesting foreign plaintiffs experienced higher win rates in U.S. courts than U.S. plaintiffs,[33] ITA did not exhibit an "anti-respondent" bias. Rather, the overall pattern favored state respondents. Although some ICSID data suggested that, for half a year, investors won more often,[34] a single year does not make a reliable pattern and may be a statistical aberration, but it may also reflect a population parameter in flux.

In an era of rising nationalism and antiglobalization, it is possible that more states engage in more problematic conduct, giving rise to claims for breaches of states' international law obligations.[35] It is also possible that tribunals are shifting in their approach to analyzing disputes. Likewise, investors (and potentially their counsel) could be becoming more selective in bringing claims and only bringing the most meritorious disputes. Like Clermont and Eisenberg's research on U.S. litigation, it is possible that in a tumultuous period of low trust and high risk for foreigners, foreigners may be cautious in initiating adjudication, with only the most serious claims being pursued. No matter the cause, the possibility of changing circumstances does not disrupt the finding that data demonstrated that, on the whole, states won reliably more for the period studied.

Second, for states considering whether to exclude or include arbitration in treaties, ITA outcomes did not disfavor them as a group ex post. This is perhaps unsurprising. Eisenberg and Farber identified that claimants in U.S. litigation generally win at lower rates when suing

---

[31] *See* Chapter 1; *see also* George Kahale III, *Kahale Calls for Overhaul of BIT System*, GLOBAL ARB. REV. (Apr. 11, 2014), https://bit.ly/2vNox1j (last visited Aug. 7, 2018) (arguing ITA exhibits "systematic bias against states").

[32] *See* Colleen V. Chien, *Patently Protectionist? An Empirical Analysis of Patent Cases at the International Trade Commission*, 50 WM. & MARY L. REV. 63, 63–64 (2008); Robert W. Hahn & Hal J. Singer, *Assessing Bias in Patent Infringement Cases: A Review of International Trade Commission Decisions*, 21 HARV. J.L. & TECH. 457, 462 (2008); *but see* MARK A. LEMLEY, *The Fractioning of Patent Law*, *in* INTELLECTUAL PROPERTY AND THE COMMON LAW 504, 506 n.14 (Shyamkrishna Balganesh ed., 2013).

[33] Kevin M. Clermont & Theodore Eisenberg, *Xenophilia in American Courts*, 109 HARV. L. REV. 1120, 1127–30 (1996) [hereinafter Clermont & Eisenberg, *Xenophilia*] (noting foreign plaintiffs won 67–83% of cases in U.S. courts between 1986 and 1994); *but see* Kevin M. Clermont & Theodore Eisenberg, *Xenophilia or Xenophobia in U.S. Courts? Before and After 9/11*, 4 J. EMP. LEG. STUD. 441, 456–59 (2007) [hereinafter Clermont & Eisenberg, *After 9/11*] (noting that as globalization prospered, fears of foreign courts diminished, and cases other than the most meritorious entered litigation, "more standard win rates are now reasserting themselves").

[34] ICSID Secretariat, *The ICSID Caseload–Statistics, Issue 2016-2*, 13 (2016), https://bit.ly/2tFVaia (last visited Aug. 7, 2018); Ali Khan, *ICSID Stats Show Winning Streak for Investors*, GLOBAL ARB. REV. (Aug. 4, 2016), https://bit.ly/2mpnzUw (last visited Aug. 7, 2018).

[35] A macroeconomic analysis of commodity prices—such as oil, gas, electricity, and telecommunications—might reveal that when investments became more valuable, this perhaps incentivized state nationalization of valuable assets and investors bringing claims given disruption to anticipated revenue. Testing these theories is beyond the scope of this book.

states,[36] suggesting states have a natural advantage when creating and participating in dispute resolution. As states "hold the pen" when drafting both substantive treaty rights and offering procedural remedies, states' capacity to draft "pro-state" terms to nudge pro-state outcomes should be expected. Meanwhile, for investors, although they may wish to assess whether to bring a specific claim, as a group, investors sometimes won.[37]

Third, results suggest that the Priest-Klein litigation model, predicting claimants generally win 50% of the cases irrespective of applicable legal standards,[38] may not apply to ITA. The Priest-Klein model was normed on U.S. courts using certain assumptions—namely, application of U.S. law, clear and available precedent, and "close" cases going to trial. By contrast, most treaties do not permit cases to go to national courts, ITA precedent is not always available,[39] and application of legal principles is not necessarily clear.

While the 50/50 baseline may be inapplicable to ITA,[40] it is an open question as to what should be the appropriate baseline for ITA outcomes. One might argue that a situation where either investors or states won 100% of cases would likely be problematic. This means, rather than looking for a system favoring extreme outcomes (namely exclusively pro-state, exclusively pro-investor, or a pure toss-up), the truth is likely somewhere in the middle. As Hans Rosling explained, rather than focusing on extremes, stakeholders should appreciate that reality occurs within a range of reasonable possibilities.[41]

ITA has similarities to adjudication where there were outcomes favoring respondents. Respondents were most successful in U.S. litigation research when claims tended to involve large amounts, there were gaps in informational access, or settlement costs were larger than litigation costs.[42] Given the large amounts at stake, high costs, and information asymmetries, ITA has structural similarities to adjudication where parties should expect respondents to have a relative advantage. A better comparison appropriate to ITA outcomes may be

---

[36] *See* Theodore Eisenberg & Henry Farber, *The Government as Litigant: Further Tests of the Case Selection Model*, 9 AM. L. & ECON. REV. 94, 96, (2003); Theodore Eisenberg, *Litigation Models and Trial Outcomes in Civil Rights and Prisoner Cases*, 77 GEO. L.J. 1567, 1569 (1989); Stewart J. Schwab & Theodore Eisenberg, *Explaining Constitutional Tort Litigation: The Influence of the Attorney Fees Statute and the Government as Defendant*, 73 CORNELL L. REV. 719, 750–52 (1988).

[37] Franck & Wylie, *supra* note 6, at 492.

[38] George L. Priest & Benjamin Klein, *The Selection of Disputes for Litigation*, 13 J. LEGAL STUD. 1 (1984); Donald Whittman, *Dispute Resolution, Bargaining, and the Selection of Cases for Trial: A Study of the Generation of Biased and Unbiased Data*, 17 J. LEGAL STUD. 313 (1988).

[39] Raj Bhala, *The Power of the Past: Towards De Jure Stare Decisis in WTO Adjudication (Part Three of a Trilogy)*, 33 GEO. WASH. INT'L L. REV. 873, 950 (2001); Jeffery Commission, *Precedent in Investment Treaty Arbitration: A Citation Analysis of a Developing Jurisprudence*, 24 J. INT'L ARB. 129 (2007).

[40] Franck & Wylie, *supra* note 6, at 492–93.

[41] HANS ROSLING, FACTFULNESS: TEN REASONS WHY WE'RE WRONG ABOUT THE WORLD—AND WHY THINGS ARE BETTER THAN YOU THINK 19–46 (2018) (discussing "the Gap Instinct" and how most reality is found in the middle, rather than in extremes).

[42] Theodore Eisenberg, *Testing the Selection Effect: A New Theoretical Framework with Empirical Tests*, 19 J. LEGAL STUD. 337 (1990); Keith N. Hylton, *Information, Litigation and Common Law Evolution*, 9 AM. L. & ECON. REV. 33 (2006); Daniel Kessler et al., *Explaining Deviations from the Fifty-Percent Rule: A Multimodal Approach to the Selection of Cases for Litigation*, 25 J. LEGAL STUD. 233 (1996).

whistle-blower lawsuits,[43] qui tam litigation,[44] *Bivens* lawsuits against government officials for violations of citizens' constitutional rights,[45] citizen complaints against agency action,[46] civil or prisoner rights cases,[47] or medical malpractice litigation.[48] These areas have doctrinal similarities to ITA, as they involve claims by individuals, claims against a state, claims related to allegedly improper state regulatory activity, and/or claims seeking fiscal compensation.[49]

2. The Rise of Settlements and Discontinuances

Earlier research found that fewer than five cases ended in settlements. The current research identified a limited number of settlements and discontinuances but identified a facial increase in non-adjudicative resolutions. Namely, the proportion of cases (with a public award) terminating from settlements or discontinuances rose from approximately 3% to 9%.

Although not meaningful,[50] the shift toward non-adjudicative options—whether negotiation, mediation, claim abandonment, or otherwise absorbing the loss—is worthy of consideration. There has been a growing interest in alternatives to treaty conflict management. ICSID has a Panel of Conciliators who could facilitate mediation and non-adjudicative dispute resolution.[51] The International Bar Association finalized Investor-State Mediation Rules for use in treaty disputes[52] and the United Nations promulgated a convention for enforcing mediated settlements,[53] with the U.N. Secretary General making mediation a core plank of

---

[43] *See* Richard E. Moberly, *Unfulfilled Expectations: An Empirical Analysis of Why Sarbanes-Oxley Whistleblowers Rarely Win*, 49 WM. & MARY L. REV. 65 (2007); Richard E. Moberly, *Sarbanes-Oxley's Whistleblower Provisions: Ten Years Later*, 64 S.C. L. REV. 1 (2012); Nancy M. Modesitt, *Why Whistleblowers Lose. An Empirical and Qualitative Analysis of State Court Cases*, 62 KAN. L. REV. 165 (2013).

[44] *See* David Freeman Engstrom, *Harnessing the Private Attorney General: Evidence from Qui Tam Litigation*, 112 COLUM. L. REV. 1244, 1288–90, 1296, 1299, 1306, 1319–20 (2012).

[45] Alexander A. Reinert, *Measuring the Success of* Bivens *Litigation and Its Consequences for the Individual Liability Model*, 62 STAN. L. REV 809, 827–30, 839–46 (2010).

[46] *See* Michael A. Carrier & Daryl Wander, *Citizen Petitions: An Empirical Study*, 34 CARDOZO L. REV. 249, 249 (2012); *see also* William N. Eskridge, Jr. & Lauren E. Baer, *The Continuum of Deference: Supreme Court Treatment of Agency Statutory Interpretations from Chevron to Hamdan*, 96 GEO. L.J. 1084, 1099 (2008).

[47] *See* Eisenberg, *supra* note 36, at 1578–80; Franck & Wylie, *supra* note 6, at 493–94.

[48] *See* Thomas H. Cohen, *Tort Bench and Jury Trials in State Courts, 2005*, U.S. DEPT. OF JUSTICE, BUREAU OF JUSTICE STATS. BULL. 4 (2009), https://bit.ly/2NZOnrg (last visited Aug. 7, 2018); David A. Hyman & Charles Silver, *Medical Malpractice Litigation and Tort Reform: It's the Incentives, Stupid*, 59 VAND. L. REV. 1085, 1126 (2006).

[49] Franck & Wylie, *supra* note 6, at 493–94.

[50] Units of analysis were slightly different, making comparisons between proportions arguably improper. Nevertheless, current research expanded to explore discontinuances. It was not possible to identify increases (or decreases) in settlements and discontinuances ($t\,(157) = 1.792; p = .08; r = .14; n = 159$).

[51] ICSID Secretariat, *Designations to the ICSID Panel of Conciliators and of Arbitrators by the Chairman of the ICSID Administrative Council* (June 4, 2018), https://bit.ly/2wAOIqp (last visited Aug. 7, 2018).

[52] INT'L BAR ASSOC., RULES FOR INVESTOR-STATE MEDIATION (Oct. 2012), https://bit.ly/2pdbJoY (last visited Aug. 7, 2018).

[53] Christina Hioureas, *A New Legal Framework for the Enforcement of Settlement Agreements Reached Through International Mediation: UNCITRAL Concludes Negotiations on Convention and Draft Model Law*, EJIL TALK! (Mar. 26, 2018), https://bit.ly/2L1MDyM (last visited Aug. 7, 2018).

his platform.[54] Meanwhile, conference programs explore mediation opportunities for investment treaty disputes,[55] and organizations such as the International Mediation Institute position themselves to provide criteria for mediator competency.[56] ICSID has likewise begun training mediators for future disputes and proposed new mediation rules.[57]

Case selection effects limit the strength of inferences. As the dataset focused on cases with a public award, all of the cases settled or discontinued had taken the provocative step of initiating arbitration (rather than negotiating settlement prior to filing a case) and receiving an initial tribunal award. This means the data inevitably under-represents settled cases and does not address treaty conflict settled prior to an arbitration request or disputes settled after initiating arbitration but before an award.

ICSID's 2014 statistics—which combined commercial and treaty cases—suggested tribunals concluded 65% of ICSID's registered cases, whereas 35% of cases were settled or otherwise discontinued.[58] More recent data from UNCTAD and ICSID suggest that roughly 25–35% of cases settle.[59] Likewise, Waibel and Wu's ICSID analysis, which did not consider ITA generally and included ICSID's commercial cases, identified the "percentage of settled cases is also high. Almost every third case is settled."[60] Roberto Echandi explored settlements in investment treaty disputes, reflecting a core and growing group of non-adjudicative resolutions.[61]

---

[54] U.N. Sec'y Gen., *Secretary-General's Remarks to Security Council's Debate on the Maintenance of International Peace and Security: Mediation and the Peaceful Resolution of Conflicts* (Aug. 29, 2018), https://bit.ly/2olroLo (last visited Sept. 1, 2018).

[55] Am. Soc'y of Int'l Law, Advancing Mediation in International Investment Disputes, 2013 Annual Meeting (Apr. 4, 2013); Am. Bar Ass'n, Adding Mediation to the Process Choices in Global Investment Disputes, Dispute Resolution Section Annual Meeting, Int'l Comm. Workshop (Apr. 6, 2013), http://bit.ly/2axın4J (last visited Aug. 7, 2018).

[56] Int'l Mediation Inst., IMI Competency Criteria for Investor-State Mediators (May 2, 2016), https://bit.ly/2OgK8GU (last visited Aug. 7, 2018).

[57] ICSID, *Investor-State Mediator Training*, ICSID Newsletter (Feb. 2017), http://bit.ly/2pTihBi (last visited Aug. 7, 2018); *see also* Chapter 9 (discussing ICSID's mediation reform efforts in greater detail).

[58] ICSID Secretariat, *The ICSID Caseload–Statistics, Issue 2014-2*, 13 (2014), https://bit.ly/2mtSPSp (last visited Aug. 7, 2018).

[59] *See, e.g.*, UNCTAD, *WIR* 2018, *supra* note 27, at 94 (finding 25% of claims completed in 2017 were settled); UNCTAD, *WIR* 2016, *supra* note 27, at 107 (observing 26% of claims completed in 2015 were settled). As ICSID resolves ITA and non-ITA disputes, these statistics must be viewed with care to prevent unwarranted inferences. *See, e.g.*, ICSID, *2018 Statistics, supra* note 27, at 13–14, 16 (analyzing data at the end of 2017, finding that 34% of cases were settled or discontinued, and identifying that, of that 34%, 47% were discontinued at both parties' request and 15% involved an award embodying a settlement agreement and providing information on the type of discontinuance); ICSID, *2016 Statistics, supra* note 27, at 13, 15 (2016) (analyzing data at the end of 2015, finding 36% of cases overall were settled or discontinued, and further identifying that, of that 36%, 47% of those cases were discontinued at both parties' request and 15% involved an award embodying a settlement agreement).

[60] Michael Waiben & Yanhui Wu, *Are Arbitrators Political?* (draft manuscript at 24, 26), https://bit.ly/2Lvuwyf (last visited Aug. 7, 2018).

[61] Roberto Echandi & Priyanka Kher, *Can International Investor-State Disputes Be Prevented? Empirical Evidence from Settlements in ICSID Arbitration*, 29 ICSID Rev. 41 (2014).

Nevertheless, settlements and discontinuances occurred after critical junctures—including after determinations of preliminary issues permitting dismissal of cases "manifestly without legal merit,"[62] jurisdictional determinations, or merits claims. Case selection effects mean data failed to capture settlement-related variance and further study would be valuable. Yet, even the limited data suggests parties should consider the value of non-adjudicative dispute resolution processes both before and during arbitration to narrow the scope of controversy or wholly dispose of disputes. It also means, for stakeholders failing to consider non-adjudicative dispute settlement, they have likely lost an opportunity to maximize the value of dispute resolution and to minimize unnecessary loss.

B. JURISDICTION: WINNING AND LOSING

Ultimate outcomes do not reflect party success at each potentially determinative phase. Although others may wish to consider sub-issues within each phase, this section focuses on who was successful at jurisdiction, merits, and damages. For each phase, "winning" was classified as complete investor success on all dispositive issues, complete state success on all dispositive issues, or mixed success. This next section addresses what occurred at each juncture for all awards.

Jurisdiction decisions are fundamental, as they permit disputes to continue. Irrespective of ultimate outcomes, some suggest ITA is unbalanced because tribunals find they have jurisdiction to decide disputes, claiming broad jurisdictional interpretation demonstrates "pro-investor" bias.[63] Without controlling for breadth or narrowness of jurisdictional treaty language,[64] one scholar suggested empirical analyses reflected a "strong tendency in favor of an expansive approach" to core jurisdictional issues and "provide tentative cause for concern for those who expect the system to deliver a degree of evenness—between the interests of claimants and respondent states—in the resolution of jurisdictional issues."[65] Others have disagreed, instead suggesting arbitrators decide cases "according to their particular . . . jurisdictional merits. The cases show no propensity of arbitrators to rubber stamp investors' claims."[66] Evaluating those competing claims is constructive.

---

[62] ICSID, *Rules of Procedure for Arbitration Proceedings (Arbitration Rules)*, Rule 41(5) *compiled in* ICSID CONVENTION, REGULATIONS AND RULES, 119 (2006), https://bit.ly/2sjVvVg (last accessed Aug. 7, 2018) [hereinafter ICSID Arbitration Rules]; ICSID ADDITIONAL FACILITY RULES, Rule 45(6), 63 (2006), https://bit.ly/2nLUMIp (last accessed Aug. 7, 2018) [hereinafter ICSID Additional Facility Rules].

[63] Cecilia Olivet, *The Dark Side of Investment Agreements*, TRADE & INV. (Dec. 2011), https://bit.ly/2LS6qRW (last accessed Aug. 7, 2018).

[64] The published study failed to control for treaty language. *See supra* note 9.

[65] Gus Van Harten, *Pro-Investment or Pro-State Bias in Investment-Treaty Arbitration? Forthcoming Study Gives Cause for Concern*, INV. TREATY NEWS (Apr. 13, 2012), https://bit.ly/2LHjUR8 (last accessed Aug. 7, 2018) (footnote omitted); *see also* Van Harten, *supra* note 8, at 251 ("There was strong support for the anticipated tendency toward an expansive approach in the resolution of contested issues of jurisdiction and admissibility and for the expected accentuation of this tendency for claimants from France, Germany, the United Kingdom, or the United States.").

[66] William W. Park, *Arbitrator Integrity*, *in* THE BACKLASH AGAINST INVESTMENT ARBITRATION: PERCEPTIONS AND REALITY 189, 217 (Michael Waibel, ed., 2010).

From awards involving jurisdiction issues,[67] three patterns of success emerged.[68] The first, and dominant, pattern was for complete investor success on jurisdictional issues. Investors successfully established jurisdiction in 56.6% of awards, and the pattern of investor success was relatively stable for the time analyzed.[69] Irrespective of how many jurisdictional issues were argued, more than half of the time, investors were wholly successful in establishing jurisdiction. The prominence of pure investor success explains the results for the study analyzing jurisdiction on an issue-by-issue basis (rather than focusing on awards or cases).[70]

Pure investor success in jurisdiction, however, did not guarantee ultimate success. In *Pac Rim Cayman*,[71] jurisdictional success did generate an investor win on the merits. Complete jurisdictional success did not translate into compensable damages for *Gustav Hamester*[72] and *Thunderbird Gaming*.[73] Some investors wholly successful on jurisdiction also succeeded in establishing a treaty breach and some form of (usually reduced) damages, as in *Feldman*,[74] *Enron*,[75] and *Fuchs*.[76]

The second most prevalent pattern was mixed jurisdictional success. For awards with jurisdictional issues, 24.5%[77] exhibited mixed jurisdictional success in which both parties were successful on some aspect. Put another way, investors established at least one basis of jurisdiction and respondents eliminated at least one jurisdictional issue. This was similar to earlier research, finding mixed success in 31% of awards.[78]

---

[67] $n = 212$. Where the 202 cases contained jurisdictional assessments in multiple awards (i.e., both an initial jurisdictional award and supplementary jurisdictional issue determination), both awards in the same case were analyzed, resulting in a very small degree of double-counting of cases (but single-counting of awards).

[68] The dataset includes information about Rule 41(5), which was not analyzed separately as it reflected roughly 2% of cases. Others have thoughtfully analyzed those cases and others, with results that mirrored preliminary assessments deriving from the dataset, which were omitted due to space restrictions. Michele Potestà & Marija Sobat, *Frivolous Claims in International Adjudication: A Study of ICSID Rule 41(5) and of Procedures of Other Courts and Tribunals to Dismiss Claims Summarily*, 3 J. Int'l Disp. Settlement 137 (2012).

[69] $n = 120$. Earlier research found 57.5% of cases involved pure investor success in jurisdiction determinations. Franck, *supra* note 21, at 52.

[70] *See* Van Harten, *supra* note 8, at 214 (explaining the study analyzed "awards dealing with jurisdictional matters" and coding for "legal issues of jurisdiction and admissibility").

[71] Pac Rim Cayman LLC v. Republic of El Sal., ICSID Case No. ARB/09/12, Decision on Respondent's Jurisdictional Objections (June 1, 2012), https://bit.ly/2v2rpHl (last visited Aug. 7, 2018).

[72] Gustav F W Hamester GmbH v. Republic of Ghana, ICSID Case No. ARB/07/24, Award (June 18, 2010), 22 World Trade & Arb. Materials 1275 (2010).

[73] International Thunderbird Gaming Corp. v. United Mexican States, UNCITRAL, Award, 213 (Jan. 26, 2006), 18 World Trade & Arb. Materials 59 (2006).

[74] Marvin Roy Feldman Karpa v. United Mexican States, ICSID Case No. ARB(AF)/99/1, Award (Dec. 16, 2002), https://bit.ly/2NwN2XE (last visited Aug. 7, 2018).

[75] Enron Corp. & Ponderosa Assets, L.P. v. Argentine Republic, ICSID Case No. ARB/01/3, Award (May 22, 2007), https://bit.ly/2LcKVvw (last visited Aug. 7, 2018).

[76] Ron Fuchs v. Republic of Geor., ICSID Case No. ARB/07/15, Decision on Jurisdiction (July 6, 2007), https://bit.ly/2zYEAi1 (last visited Aug. 7, 2018); ICSID Case No. ARB/07/15, Award (Mar. 3, 2010), https://bit.ly/2whb8hr (last visited Aug. 7, 2018).

[77] $n = 52$.

[78] When comparing pure investor and mixed wins for earliest and later data, it was not possible to identify a pattern change that was statistically meaningful (χ^2 (1) = 1.543; $p = .21$; $r = .10$; $n = 172$).

Mixed jurisdictional success also generated mixed ultimate outcomes. The slight majority of cases with mixed jurisdictional success resulted in states' ultimate success. This group of cases is exemplified by *Champion Trading v. Egypt*,[79] there was no jurisdiction over three U.S.-Egypt dual nationals, but there was jurisdiction over an entity they controlled. Despite partial investor success at jurisdiction, Egypt prevailed on the merits.[80] Similarly, *Biwater Gauff v. Tanzania*[81] identified limited grounds for jurisdiction—and although it found substantive treaty violations—dismissed the damages claim.[82] A minority of cases involving mixed jurisdictional success generated ultimate investor success. In *Continental Casualty v. Argentina*[83] and *Iurii Bogdanov v. Moldova*,[84] investors had mixed jurisdictional success and tribunals awarded a portion of claimed damages. *ATA Construction v. Jordan*,[85] by contrast, was the only case studied where investors were partially successful on jurisdiction but wholly successful in securing requested relief.

The third, and least dominant, pattern involved states defeating all jurisdictional claims. Of the 212 awards, states defeated all jurisdictional arguments in forty awards (18.9%). Cases exemplifying pure respondent jurisdictional success were *Soufraki*,[86] *Wintershall*,[87] *Phoenix Action*,[88] *HICEE*,[89] and *Libananco*.[90] In earlier research, respondents were completely successful in 11.5% of awards. As time has gone on, respondents have apparently done better at defeating investors' jurisdictional claims.[91] Statistical tests, however, were unable to identify that the facial shift toward full respondent success on jurisdiction was statistically meaningful.[92]

---

[79] Champion Trading Co. v. Islamic Republic of Egypt, ICSID Case No. ARB/02/9, Decision on Jurisdiction (Oct. 23, 2003), https://bit.ly/2Lb7Siy (last visited Aug. 7, 2018).

[80] Champion Trading Co. v. Islamic Republic of Egypt, ICSID Case No. ARB/02/9, Award (Oct. 27, 2006), https://bit.ly/2uTyoDO (last visited Aug. 7, 2018).

[81] Biwater Gauff (Tanzania) Ltd. v. United Republic of Tanz., ICSID Case No. ARB/05/22, Award (July 24, 2008), https://bit.ly/2O6pgCQ (last visited Aug. 7, 2018).

[82] *See id.* at 239 (dismissing claims for damages).

[83] Continental Cas. Co. v. Argentine Republic, ICSID Case No. ARB/03/9, Decision on Application for Partial Annulment (Sept. 16, 2011), 24 World Trade & Arb. Materials 145 (2012).

[84] Iurii Bogdanov v. Republic of Mold., SCC, Award (Sept. 22, 2005), https://bit.ly/2Jst79P (last visited Aug 7, 2018).

[85] ATA Constr., Indus. and Trading Co. v. Hashemite Kingdom of Jordan, ICSID Case No. ARB/08/2, Award (May 18, 2010), https://bit.ly/1u1PNAP (last visited Aug. 7, 2018).

[86] Hussein Nuaman Soufraki v. United Arab Emirates, ICSID Case No. ARB/02/7, Award (July 7, 2004), 17 World Trade & Arb. Materials 129 (2005).

[87] Wintershall Aktiengesellschaft v. Argentine Republic, ICSID Case No. ARB/04/14, Award (Dec. 8, 2008), https://bit.ly/2uVnP1o (last visited Aug. 7, 2018).

[88] Phoenix Action, Ltd. v. Czech Republic, ICSID Case No. ARB/06/5, Award (Apr. 15, 2009), 21 World Trade & Arb. Materials 729 (2009).

[89] HICEE B.V. v. Slovak Republic, UNCITRAL, PCA Case No. 2009-11, Supplementary & Final Award (Oct 17, 2011), https://bit.ly/2O9d98q (last visited Aug. 7, 2018).

[90] Libananco Holdings Co. Ltd. v. Republic of Turk., ICSID Case No. ARB/06/8, Award (Sept. 2, 2011), https://bit.ly/1SppzCO (last visited Aug. 7, 2018).

[91] This may account for the study's findings, as the dataset closed earlier. *See* Van Harten, *supra* note 8, at 229 (noting the primary source was awards decided by May 10, 2010, and publicly available by June 1, 2010).

[92] Comparing respondent jurisdictional wins in G1 (pre-2006) versus G2–G3 data (2006–2012), it was not possible to identify a reliably different pattern in jurisdictional success (χ^2 (1) = 3.555; p = .06; r = .15; n = 160). As

Overall, there were various noteworthy aspects of jurisdictional determinations. First, 75% of cases resulted in either a complete denial or complete grant of jurisdiction. This suggests that tribunals made sharp jurisdictional assessments and appeared less interested in "splitting the jurisdictional baby." Second, the stability of the pure investor jurisdictional wins across the time studied was intriguing, although the baseline may be evolving. Third, it would be prudent to evaluate states' pure jurisdictional success given the facial shift towards enhanced state success. Ultimately, to avoid the pernicious influence of cognitive illusions such as framing, jurisdictional success must be contextualized with both past practice and ultimate outcomes, lest there be an over-focus on one element at the expense of the broader context.

C. MERITS: WINNING AND LOSING

Merits are the next critical phase. As 19% of cases terminated at jurisdiction, there was a smaller subset of awards analyzing merits.[93] Patterns of merits success differed from jurisdiction.

First, although mixed success was unusual for jurisdiction, mixed success was the hallmark of tribunals' merits assessments. For merits-related awards, 49.1%[94] exhibited mixed party success. In other words, for half the cases, an investor established a violation of one substantive cause of action (i.e., discrimination) but was unsuccessful on another aspect (i.e., expropriation). Mixed merits awards had two different jurisdictional patterns. First, with mixed merits success, investors were wholly successful on jurisdiction in cases such as the 2004 *Occidental* case,[95] *Alpha Projektholding*,[96] and *Total*.[97] A second cluster of investors with mixed merits success likewise experienced mixed jurisdictional success, such as *Tecmed*,[98] *PSEG Global*,[99] and *Walter Bau*.[100]

Not all awards were mixed, however. Some tribunals wholly favored the investor or the state. Unlike jurisdiction, states were more likely to be wholly successful on the merits. States successfully defeated all treaty-based merits claims in 37.5% of awards.[101] Some state successes involved cases where, although investors were wholly successful during the jurisdictional

---

results were on the cusp of significance—but with a relatively small effect size—the results bear watching. Post hoc power analyses suggest that a minimum sample of 343 final cases would be required to reliably identify any latent result.

[93] $n = 112$.

[94] $n = 55$.

[95] Occidental Expl. and Prod. Co. v. Republic of Ecuador LCIA Case No. UN3467, Final Award (July 1, 2004), https://bit.ly/1PTn6hO (last visited Aug. 7, 2018).

[96] Alpha Projektholding GMBH v. Ukr., ICSID Case No. ARB/07/16, Award (Nov. 8, 2010), https://bit.ly/2wuyGyC (last visited Aug. 7, 2018).

[97] Total S.A. v. Argentine Republic, ICSID Case No. ARB/04/01, Decision on Liability (Dec. 27, 2010), https://bit.ly/2uFlWGO (last visited Aug. 7, 2018).

[98] Técnicas Medioambientales Tecmed S.A. v. United Mexican States, ICSID Case No. ARB (AF)/00/2, Award (May 29, 2003), 43 I.L.M. 143 (2004).

[99] PSEG Global, Inc v. Republic of Turk., ICSID Case No. ARB/02/5, Decision on Jurisdiction (June 4, 2004), 44 I.L.M. 465 (2005).

[100] Walter Bau AG v. Kingdom of Tha., UNCITRAL, Award (Jul. 1, 2009), 22 World Trade & Arb. Materials 681, 782 (2010).

[101] $n = 42$.

phase, the same investors were wholly unsuccessful on the merits, including *Azinian*[102] and *Pantechniki*.[103] Other cases involved mixed state jurisdictional success but complete state success on the merits, such as *Grand River Enterprises Six Nations*[104] and *MCI*.[105]

Investors experienced complete success on the merits in a minority of cases—unlike their jurisdictional success. Investors were only completely successful on the merits in 13.4% of cases. *ADC v. Hungary*[106] and *Tza Yap Shum v. Peru*[107] exemplify this rare phenomenon.

Based on data analyzed, party success on merits was relatively stable over time with minor variations (1–2%). Earlier, investors were wholly successful on the merits in 12.2% of cases, as opposed to the 13.4% analyzed. Similarly, respondents were previously wholly successful on the merits in 39% of cases, as opposed to the 37.5% analyzed. In earlier research, 48.8% of the cases experienced mixed results as contrasted with 49.1% in the current dataset. Given the small variation, while recognizing the possibility of continued evolution, it is unlikely those slight shifts were meaningful; and those rates may offer a standard baseline.

The data about success on the merits was blunt, however. It did not analyze specific claims—including expropriation, discrimination, umbrella clause, fair and equitable treatment, or full protection and security. Future researchers may consider how to code for this, reflecting upon which causes of action were more or less successful.[108] Given the primacy of treaty text in adjudicating specific legal issues of jurisdiction and merits, issue-by-issue assessment of treaty provisions will need to control for treaty language, lest variations in treaty obligations limit derivative inferences. In the interim, generic assessments of the merits offer a starting point for future consideration.[109]

E. DAMAGES: WINNING AND LOSING

As later chapters address costs, damages are the last phase analyzed here. Tribunals rarely gave 100% of requested damages. This stands in stark contrast to pro-investor jurisdictional decisions and mixed (or low) rates of investor success on the merits.

---

102 Robert Azinian v. United Mexican States, ICSID Case No. ARB (AF)/97/2, Award (Nov. 1, 1999), 39 I.L.M. 537 (2000).

103 Pantechniki S.A. Contractors & Engineers v. Republic of Alb., ICSID Case No. ARB/07/21, Award (July 30, 2009), https://bit.ly/2b81FkL (last visited Aug. 7, 2018).

104 Grand River Enterprises Six Nations, Ltd. v. United States, UNCITRAL, Award (Jan. 1, 2011), https://bit.ly/2O2J3lV (last visited Aug. 7, 2018).

105 M.C.I. Power Group L.C. v. Republic of Ecuador, ICSID Case No. ARB/03/6, Award (July 31, 2007), https://bit.ly/2LH2EeE (last visited Aug. 7, 2018).

106 ADC Affiliate Ltd. v. Republic of Hung., ICSID Case No. ARB/03/16, Award (Oct. 2, 2006), 18 World Trade & Arb. Materials 285 (2006).

107 Tza Yap Shum v. Republic of Peru, ICSID Case No. ARB/07/6, Award (July 7, 2011), https://bit.ly/2zWATcP (last visited Aug. 7, 2018).

108 *See also* Jeremy Caddel & Nathan M. Jensen, *Which Host Country Government Actors Are Most Involved with Disputes with Foreign Investors?*, Columbia FDI Perspectives, No. 120 (Apr. 28, 2014), http://bit.ly/1nVYAPe (last visited Aug. 7, 2018) (beginning to explore type of government activity or branch of government allegedly responsible for the treaty breach). There will, however, inevitably be challenges in reliably coding for the standard with variations in treaty text and the evolvution of the meaning of the rights, which may require dynamic and retroactive interpretation of prior coding.

109 Other scholarship explored variables affecting raw outcomes. Franck & Wylie, *supra* note 6, at 505–09.

After weeding out cases at jurisdiction or merits, a small set of cases remained.[110] Of those, 91.5% granted mixed damages,[111] where neither states' nor investors' damage arguments fully succeeded. In *S.D. Myers*,[112] the investor recovered on its net income claim, but the tribunal denied lost opportunity damages.[113] The dominance of mixed success replicates earlier research identifying a high proportion of mixed damage assessments (85.7%). Testing for variation in parties' damages success failed to detect a meaningful difference, so the small variation (roughly 6%) could reflect chance alone.[114]

Cases where either investors or governments were completely successful on damages were the exception, rather than the rule. For awards analyzed, investors were only wholly successful on damage claims in two cases.[115] *Maffezini v. Spain*[116] and *Fedax v. Venezuela*[117] shared two common features: they were early cases and involved financial instruments with discrete liability. States were only wholly successful on damages in three cases. In *Lauder v. Czech Republic*,[118] *Biwater Gauff v. Tanzania*,[119] and *al-Bahloul v. Tajikistan*,[120] despite finding a state treaty breach, tribunals failed to award damages.

III. Amounts Claimed and Awarded

Dispute resolution risk involves more than a flat assessment of basic outcomes. Rather, the matrix of ITA fiscal risk is complex, likely including political costs that are not easily amenable to empirical analysis.[121] Five core risks involve: amounts claimed, damages awarded, parties' legal costs (PLC) and who is ultimately liable for PLC, tribunals' legal costs and administrative expenses (TCE) and who is ultimately liable for TCE, and interest awarded. While later chapters address costs in detail, this section focuses on claims and how to appreciate the magnitude of realized risk and place ITA costs in context.

---

110 $n = 59$.

111 $n = 54$.

112 S.D. Myers, Inc. v. Governemnt of Can., UNCITRAL, Second Partial Award (Oct. 21, 2002), https://bit.ly/2ta39jg (last visited Aug. 7, 2018).

113 *See id.* at ¶ 161.

114 When comparing mixed damage awards in G1 versus G2–G3, it was not possible to identify a meaningfully different pattern (χ^2 (1) = 0.000; $p = .99$; $r = .00$; $n = 57$).

115 *ATA Construction v. Jordan* was the only case of its kind involving a tribunal determination of breach of international law but granting equitable relief. Damages were therefore not analyzed for purposes of this subsection.

116 Emilio Agustín Maffezini v. Kingdom of Spain, ICSID Case No. ARB/97/7, Award (Nov. 13, 2000), 40 I.L.M. 1148 (2001).

117 Fedax N.V. v. Republic of Venez., ICSID Case No. ARB/96/3, Award (Mar. 9, 1998), 37 I.L.M. 1391 (1998).

118 Ronald S. Lauder v. Czech Republic, UNCITRAL, Award (Sept. 3, 2001), https://bit.ly/1Pyu4te (last visited Aug. 7, 2018).

119 Biwater Gauff v. Tanzania, *supra* note 81.

120 Mohammad Ammar al-Bahloul v. Republic of Taj., SCC Case No. V (064/2008), Award (June 8, 2010), https://bit.ly/2uDmuge (last visited Aug. 7, 2018).

121 Susan D. Franck, *Rationalizing Costs in Investment Arbitration*, 88 Wash U. L. Rev. 769, 782–84 (2011).

A. INTRODUCTION

Commentators make assertions about amounts in controversy and investor recovery. The question is whether this commentary withstands systematic inquiry, as concerns about claims may be strongly held and honestly made but fail to consider holistic data or focus on potentially unrepresentative, yet evocative, examples.

Some have suggested arbitrators "can force taxpayers to pay billions of dollars in lawsuits."[122] Similarly, others historically posited that "stakes have [] skyrocketed" and warn that "'[b]ringing a billion-dollar claim is no longer enough to stand out'" in arbitration as the stakes will rise "even further."[123] Practitioners identified that "several pending cases involve claims for billions of dollars."[124] Professor Schreuer stated, "stakes are often high. Claims for several hundred million pounds are by no means unusual."[125] A 2012 OECD discussion paper stated ITA "cases frequently involve huge claims."[126] More recent comments reflect that amounts claimed for cases filed during one single year ranged from amounts as low as US$15 million to as high as US$1.5 billion.[127]

Other concerns involve liability. Some observe threats are significant, as governments "find themselves hauled before arbitration panels and compelled to pay large amounts of compensation for enacting regulation they had considered in their sovereign domain."[128] Some commentary refers to a single extreme example as if it were representative; others refer to groups of cases, perhaps by reference to award size[129] or date rendered,[130] but without a representative baseline. Still others focus on press reports, claiming that "[w]hat it takes to distinguish yourself these days is a US$350 million award, minimum."[131] This claim is unfortunate as, even adjusted for inflation, the largest damage award (*CME v. Czech Republic*)[132]

---

[122] *NOW with Bill Moyers: Trading Democracy* (PBS television broadcast Feb. 1, 2001), http://to.pbs.org/ISEnfZ (last visited Aug. 7, 2018) (transcript); Jose E. Alvarez, *How We Teach: The Final Reel*, ASIL Newsletter (Am. Soc'y Int'l Law, Washington, DC) Oct. 11, 2007.

[123] Eberhardt & Olivet, *supra* note 5, at 14 (citing Michael D. Goldhaber, *High Stakes*, Focus Europe: An American Lawyer Supplement, Summer 2011, at 22).

[124] Joshua B. Simmons, *Valuation in Investor-State Arbitration: Toward a More Exact Science*, 30 Berkeley J. Int'l L. 195, 196 (2012).

[125] Christoph Schreuer, *Investment Arbitration: A Voyage of Discovery*, 71 Arbitration 73, 73 (2005); *see also* Jack J. Coe, Jr. *Taking Stock of NAFTA Chapter 11 in Its Tenth Year: An Interim Sketch of Selected Themes, Issues and Methods*, 36 Vand. J. Transnat'l L. 1381, 1400 (2003) (observing investors "alleged extensive damages" by referencing two cases).

[126] Org. for Econ. Co-operation and Dev. [OECD], Investor-State Dispute Settlement: Public Consultation 16 May–9 July 2012, 62 (2012), http://bit.ly/1dOxFTc (last visited Aug. 7, 2018).

[127] UNCTAD, *WIR* 2018, *supra* note 27, at 94–95.

[128] Anderson & Grusky, *supra* note 3, at 29.

[129] *See* Franck, *supra* note 21, at 56–57 (gathering sources).

[130] *See* Simmons, *supra* note 124, at 196 (stating "at least seven arbitral awards have topped one hundred million dollars in the past five years").

[131] Eberhardt & Olivet, *supra* note 5, at 14 (quoting and prominently focusing upon an article by Goldhaber, *supra* note 123); *but see infra* note 132 and accompanying text.

[132] CME Czech Republic B.V. v. Czech Republic, UNCITRAL, Award (Mar. 14, 2003), https://bit.ly/1nqyL1x (last visited Aug. 7, 2018); *see also* Dataset, Appendix V (noting the 2011-inflation adjusted amount of the original US$269,814,000 *CME* damage award was US$329,788,959.80).

rendered around the time the assertion was made was under that amount.[133] As time marches on, and there are now larger awards, there has been public focus upon outsized, potentially unrepresentative, cases.

Commentators sometimes confuse awards in *commercial* "Investor-State" cases—involving national law claims—with adjudication of international law and treaty rights. UNCTAD has sometimes conflated the two.[134] Others refer to *CSOB v. Slovak Republic*'s[135] US$824 million damage award as representative of ITA outcomes[136]—even though those damages derived from breach of a commercial obligation governed by national law (with the ITA claim failing, i.e., US$0).[137]

It is vital to test data and provide appropriate comparators. Theoretical perceptions about high claims and large awards could be accurate, yet they require assessment. Cognitive illusions can skew impressions and affect how stakeholders gather information, form conclusions, make decisions, and generally influence perceptions about risk.[138] Recency may aid the easy recollection of recent, particularly negative, events, and the cognitive illusion of availability facilitates the recall of events related to large claims or large awards. Loss aversion, in which people respond negatively to risk of loss, may compound this. Representativeness may then lead people to presume memorable experiences are attributable to the broader population, even when they are not. Meanwhile, base rate neglect means debate can ignore or minimize statistical information, and anchoring may inaccurately skew recollections of amounts claimed and awarded. A single, large, unrepresentative case—such as *CME* or *CSOB*—can fuel misperceptions. Those perceptions may prove difficult to disrupt. Confirmation bias may compound matters by encouraging people to avoid data disrupting their beliefs. The bias blind spot intensifies these potential effects and can prevent stakeholders from being aware of how cognitive illusions have skewed their perception and decision-making. In the age of

---

[133] The three largest awards in ITA's history were rendered after the dataset closed. *See* Crystallex Int'l Corp. v. Bolivarian Republic of Venez., ICSID Case No. ARB(AF)/11/2, Award (Apr. 4. 2016), https://bit.ly/2LQc5Uf (last visited Aug 7.2018); Occidental Petroleum Corp. v. Republic of Ecuador, ICSID Case No. ARB/06/11, Award (Oct. 5, 2012), https://bit.ly/2A2i3kx (last visited Aug. 7, 2018); Yukos Universal Ltd. v. Russian Fed'n, UNCITRAL PCA Case No. AA 227, Final Award (Jul. 18, 2014), https://bit.ly/Z08v21 (last visited Aug. 7, 2018). Those cases were, and remain, outliers. Tai-Heng Cheng & Lucas Bento, *ICSID's Largest Award in History: An Overview of Occidental Petroleum v. the Republic of Ecuador*, KLUWER ARB. BLOG (Dec. 19, 2012), http://bit.ly/ZP2Roi (last visited Aug. 7, 2018).

[134] *See* UNCTAD, *Investor-State Disputes Arising from Investment Treaties: A Review*, 8, U.N. Doc. UNCTAD/ITE/IIT/2005/4 (2005).

[135] Československá Obchodní Banka A.S. v. Slovak Republic, ICSID Case No. ARB/97/4, Award (Dec. 29, 2004), 13 ICSID REP. 181 (2008).

[136] Anderson & Grusky, *supra* note 3, at ix; August Reinsch, *How Bad Is Investor-State Arbitration for the Development of Host Countries?*, slide 9 (Dec. 6, 2010), https://bit.ly/2A36V6Q (last visited Aug. 7, 2018); David P. Riesenberg, *Fee Shifting in Investor-State Arbitration: Doctrine and Policy Justifying Application of the English Rule*, 60 DUKE L. J. 977, 984 (2011).

[137] Československá Obchodní Banka A.S. v. Slovak Republic, ICSID Case No. ARB/97/4, Decision of the Tribunal on Objections to Jurisdiction, ¶¶ 43, 48 (May 24, 1999), https://bit.ly/2tpFlbU (last visited Aug. 7, 2018).

[138] *See* Chapter 2.

blogs, Facebook, and Twitter becoming regularized news outlets, errors and misperceptions promulgated through social media can become exacerbated.[139]

Together, these influences arguably create the "perfect storm" of misperception about ITA. Should intuitive reasoning, rather than deliberative assessments, affect ITA, this may partially explain ITA's polarization. Stakeholders should explore debiasing opportunities to aid rational assessment of emotive perceptions. Evidence-based research provides this service. Rather than ignoring relevant base rates, data can test perceptions, improve decision-making, and aid the evaluation of normative choices. Focusing on balanced facts—rather than unrepresentative realities or skewed models reinforcing preexisting conclusions—facilitates conversations likely to generate policy options that remedy actual problems, rather than improperly tailored solutions that exacerbate existing difficulties but feel intuitively appealing. Likewise, as data changes, baselines and derivative assessments require updating, as adhering to a single historical baseline from outmoded statistical conclusions is also problematic. The broader point is to let data be our guide, so norms evolve from evidence, not intuition, power, or manipulation.

B. AMOUNTS CLAIMED

Of the 202 cases studied, 117 contained either partial or full quantification of investors' claimed damages. To avoid inflating claims and focus the most recent information, where cases contained multiple awards, analysis focused on the most recent claim calculation.[140] While missing data inevitably creates a risk of error, the preference was to focus public awards where claims were verifiable while recognizing the limitation, rather than relying on non-verifiable, non-testable assertions that were potentially influenced by cognitive illusions. Moreover, extensive analysis on the analyzed data (comparing cases in the dataset missing or containing amount claimed information)[141] failed to identify that cases without amounts claimed otherwise varied meaningfully on core variables such as investors,[142]

---

[139] *See* Tom Nichols, The Death of Expertise: The Campaign Against Established Knowledge and Why It Matters 110–15, 130–33 (2017) (describing how "bad information can stay online for years" even after deletion, and identifying the challenges related to Twitter and internet-based news and the difficulties of correcting factually incorrect information in the public sphere).

[140] Amounts were recorded in the original currency with appropriate conversion to U.S. dollar values. The Codebook contains detailed coding instructions for amounts claimed, and those protocols were strictly adhered to so as to prevent unnecessary inflation or tactical choices. *See* Codebook, Appendix IV.

[141] To examine whether missing data impacted analyses of amounts claimed, a dummy variable was coded to indicate whether cases were missing data (0 = missing data and 1 = available data). It was generally not possible to identify any meaningful differences for cases had missing data (n = 111) and claim data available (n = 91). The analyses used ANOVA (for continuous variables) and chi-square (for categorical variables) to assess the impact of the dummy variable. *See also* Appendix 1 (discussing methodological and coding choices).

[142] For variables related to investors' development status, it was not possible to identify a meaningful difference in cases with and without claimed damages as a function of investors' OECD status (χ^2 (1) = 2.24; p = .14), World Bank classification (χ^2 (2) = 1.85; p = .49), or HDI score (F (1, 200) = 1.16; p = .62). Likewise, for variables related to investors' corporate identity, it was not possible to identify a meaningful difference in cases missing or containing amounts claimed when analyzing whether named investors were: people, corporations, or a combination thereof (χ^2 (2) = 0.97; p = .62), publicly listed corporations (χ^2 (1) = 0.25; p = .62), or FT500-related investors (χ^2 (1) = 0.14; p = .71).

states,[143] arbitrators,[144] underlying disputes,[145] and applicable law.[146] As cases with and without data on amounts claimed were not generally unusual, a reasonable (but non-definitive) inference is that these cases did not differ meaningfully in amounts claimed.

For cases containing damage claims—adjusted for inflation to 2011[147] to account for claims spanning nearly twenty years—the raw average claim was roughly US$623 million[148] and the median was US$100 million.[149] Adjusting those figures to June 2018, those amounts had the same buying power as US$712 million[150] and the US$115 million,[151] respectively.

Claims varied widely.[152] Using the amount claimed converted to a common currency, the lowest amount claimed was US$41,621 in *Yury Bogdanov*.[153] Other low claims were

---

[143] For variables related to states' development status, it was typically not possible to identify a reliable difference in cases with missing or containing amounts claimed as a function of respondents' OECD (χ^2 (1) = 0.26; p = .61), World Bank (χ^2 (3) = 6.85; p = .08), or Perceived Corruption Index (F (1, 192) = 0.23; p = .63) classifications. There were, however, differences in cases with and without claims data using respondents' HDI (F (1, 198) = 5.99; p = .02) and Polity IV (F (1, 199) = 5.71; p = .02) scores. Cases with missing claim information claimed had higher HDI scores and higher Polity scores, suggesting that amounts claimed were more likely to be missing when states were more developed and more democratic. Those states were a small proportion of the caseload.

[144] For arbitrator-related variables, tests were unable to identify a reliable difference in cases containing or missing amounts claimed when considering chair gender (χ^2 (1) = 0.03; p = .86) or chair World Bank classification (χ^2 (2) = 1.36; p = .24); likewise, the Tribunal's composite OECD (χ^2 (3) = 3.513; p = .32), World Bank (χ^2 (7) = 4.269; p = .78), and HDI (F (1, 197) = 1.454; p = .23) classifications were unable to identify a meaningful relationship with the presence or absence of data on amounts claimed.

[145] For variables involving the underlying dispute, it was not possible to identify a meaningful difference between energy and non-energy disputes for cases with and without amounts claimed (χ^2 (1) = 2.85; p = .09). There was, however, a possibility that disputes in some sectors were more likely to be missing data on amounts claimed (χ^2 (19) = 32.52; p = .03), although this may also be a function of the large number of categories analyzed. The largest differences were for disputes involving: energy (thirty-nine missing, twenty-two available), real estate (two missing, ten available), financial (eight missing, two available), government services (zero missing, five available), and chemicals (ten missing, five available). It was also not possible to identify meaningful differences in cases missing or containing amounts claimed as a function of the year of the award (F (1, 200) = 0.39; p = .54), case length (F (1, 165) = 0.01; p = .94), presence of an NDP (r (202) = −.014; p = .84), bifurcation (χ^2 (1) = 1.79; p = .18), or presence of a separate opinion (χ^2 (1) = 0.32; p = .58).

[146] For claimants' legal costs, there were not meaningful differences between cases with complete and missing data use of a multilateral or bilateral treaty (r (201) = −.001; p = .98), the type of underlying treaty (χ^2 (4) = 2.43; p = .66), the use of ad hoc or institutional arbitration (χ^2 (2) = 0.514; p = .77), or applicable arbitration rules (χ^2 (4) = 0.696; p = .95).

[147] *See* Appendix I (discussing inflation-adjustments and transformations).

[148] The mean for raw data, which contained outliers, was US$622,633,418 ($SD$ = 2331828846; n = 117). The winsorized mean, which minimizes the impact of outliers, was US$186,109,214 ($SD$ = 201690605; n = 117). *See also* Appendix I (discussing skewing of original data and tranformations, including winsorization, to adjust for outliers).

[149] The raw median was US$100,426,693; the winsorized median was US$100,426,693.

[150] The adjustment of the raw mean was calculated using the U.S. Bureau of Labor Statistics (BLS) inflation calculator, which reveals that adjusted to June 2018 the mean had the same buying power as roughly US$712,444,510. *See* https://data.bls.gov/cgi-bin/cpicalc.pl. The 2018-adjusted winsorized mean was US$212,954,240.

[151] Using the BLS calculator to adjust to June 2018, the raw median became US$114,913,060. The winsorized median was the same.

[152] Franck & Wylie, *supra* note 6, at 487–89.

[153] Yury Bogdanov v. Republic of Mold., SCC Arbitration No. V (114/2009), Award, 22 (Mar. 30, 2010), https://bit.ly/1nhHYGg (last visited Aug. 7, 2018).

US$155,314 in *Maffezini*,[154] US$582,397 in *Olguin*,[155] and US$2,023,907 in *Tradex Hellas*.[156] The highest amount claimed was US$19 billion in *Saba Fakes*.[157] Other large claims were US$10.1 billion in *Libananco*,[158] US$9.4 billion in *Generation Ukraine*,[159] and US$4.65 billion in *Europe Cement*.[160]

These large claims were noteworthy. The average raw claim nearly facially doubled from earlier research, identifying a mean claim of US$343 million.[161] This raised the question as to whether claims meaningfully increased over time. The short version is, given the wide variance in claims, tests were unable to identify a reliable difference in claims over time.[162] The doubling of average claims was instead influenced by six out of the top eight claims (namely cases with raw amounts claimed over US$900 million) deriving from awards rendered after July 2009, with inflation-adjusted claims from: *Saba Fakes v. Turkey* (US$19,593,287,175), *Libananco v. Turkey* (US$10,100,090,000), *Cementownia "Nowa Huta" v. Turkey* (US$4,872,386,864), *Europe Cement v. Turkey* (US$3,983,313,913), and *Total v. Argentina* (US$1,332,446,650).[163]

To prevent the largest eight claims from exerting undue influence, a boxplot reflects claim distributions, using quartiles. Figure 5.2 demonstrates that approximately 25% of claims were US$50 million or under, another 25% ranged from between US$50–100 million, another quartile involved claims between US$100–250 million, and the upper quartile ranged from approximately US$250–500 million. Excluding the eight cases with

[154] *Maffezini v. Spain*, *supra* note 116, at 31.

[155] Eudoro Armando Olguín v. Republic of Paraguay, ICSID Case No. ARB/98/5, Award (July 6, 2001), https://bit.ly/2JLKEtZ (last visited Aug. 7, 2018).

[156] Tradex Hellas S.A. v. Republic of Alb., ICSID Case No. ARB/94/2, Award, ¶ 60 (Apr. 29, 1996), https://bit.ly/2aNhNK6 (last visited Aug. 7, 2018).

[157] Saba Fakes v. Republic of Turkey, ICSID Case No. ARB/07/20, Award, ¶ 2 (July 14, 2010), https://bit.ly/2JNIklY (last visited Aug. 7, 2018).

[158] Libananco v. Turkey, *supra* note 90, at ¶ 562(a).

[159] Generation Ukraine, Inc. v. Ukraine, ICSID Case No. ARB/00/9, Award, ¶ 1.1 (Sept. 16, 2003), https://bit.ly/2JOwzvF (last visited Aug. 7, 2018).

[160] Europe Cement Inv. & Trade S.A. v. Republic of Turk., ICSID Case No. ARB (AF)/07/2, Award (Aug. 13, 2009), https://bit.ly/2LEqzYs (last visited Aug. 7, 2018). Adjusting for inflation, *Bogdanov* was still the smallest claim and *Saba Fakes* remained the highest.

[161] Franck, *supra* note 21, at 57–59. The mean amount claimed was similar: US$370,898,027 in G2 research. Susan D. Franck, *The Public International Law Regime Governing International Investment by Jose Alvarez*, 106 Am. J. Int'l L. 890 (2012).

[162] When comparing three generations of data, tests failed to identify a meaningful link between time periods and amounts claimed using logged data (F (2, 114) = 2.664; p = .07; r = .21; n = 117). HSD follow-up tests suggested awards rendered between 2006 and 2009 tended to involve larger claims than pre-2006 awards, but those awards were not meaningfully different claims from post-2009 cases. The bivariate correlation exploring the year of arbitration request and logged amounts claimed was unable to detect a meaningful linear relationship (r (117) = .16; p = .09). As tests were on the cusp of significance and effect sizes were small-to-medium, failure to detect a meaningful difference may result from a lack of power; future tests with more data (likely over 340 cases) could detect a difference.

[163] The remaining "Top 8" claims were *Generation Ukraine v. Ukraine* (US$11,489,456,522), *Occidental v. Ecuador* (US$3,983,313,913), and *Methanex v. United States* (US$1,117,186,460); *see also* Dataset, Appendix V (providing original and inflation-adjusted coding for amounts claimed).

amounts claimed over US$900 million, there was a cluster of seven outlying claims in the US$600–700 million range.

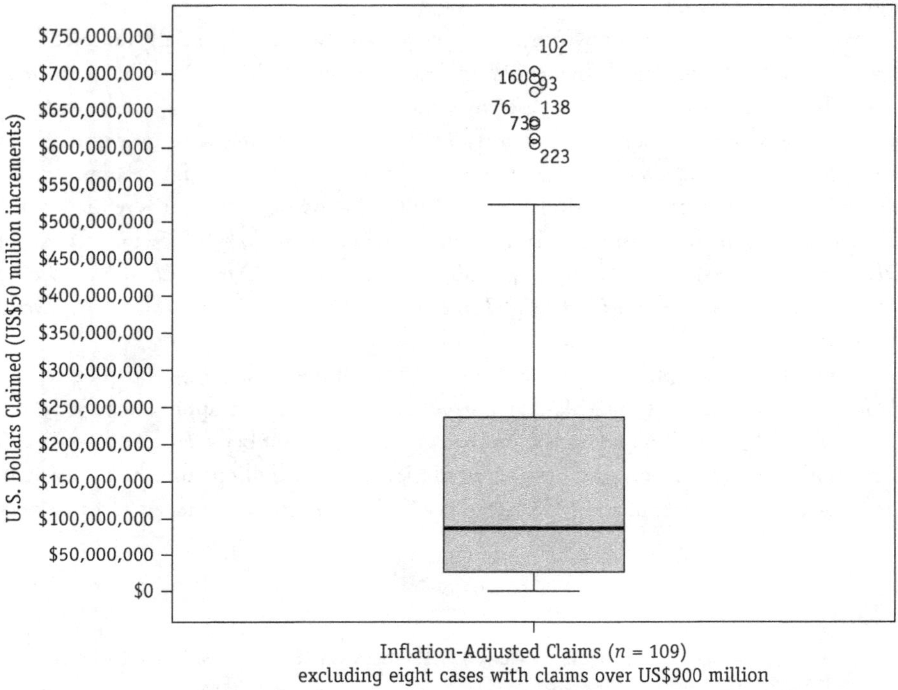

FIGURE 5.2 Boxplot Reflecting Median and Quartile Distributions of Inflation-adjusted Raw Amounts Claimed ($n = 109$).

Amounts claimed clustered toward the lower end of the distribution, rather than being evenly distributed or clumped at the top. Nevertheless, large damage claims—and more recent cases with particularly large claims—may generate concerns. Any commercial entity sued for sufficiently large claims may intuit a dispute involves a "bet the company" dispute,[164] or in the case of ITA, a "bet the state"[165] claim. For states with limited reserves or poor economic resources, it is little wonder that large claims generate serious concerns.[166] When faced with high initial claims, at least two potential cognitive illusions come in play. First, primacy may facilitate recollection of information occurring at the start of ITA, rather than ultimate

[164] Christopher R. Drahozal, *Why Arbitrate? Substantive Versus Procedural Theories of Private Judging*, 22 AM. REV. INT'L ARB. 1, 63, 177–78 (2011).

[165] Susan D. Franck, *The Legitimacy Crisis in Investment Treaty Arbitration: Privatizing Public International Law Through Inconsistent Decisions*, 73 FORDHAM. L. REV. 1521, 1605 (2005).

[166] *See* Lauge N. Skovgaard Poulsen, *Sacrificing Sovereignty by Chance: Investment Treaties, Developed Countries, and Bounded Rationality*, 15 (2011) (Ph.D. Thesis, London School of Econ. & Pol. Sci.), http://bit.ly/1fQxngI (last visited Aug. 7, 2018) ("2006 the 30 pending cases against Argentina for measures taken during its 2001 financial crisis amounted to an estimated US$17 billion in claims, which almost equaled the entire annual budget of the Argentinean government").

results or later-arising information. Second, where such large amounts are claimed, those figures may remain anchored in parties' minds. Should stakeholders recall the first pleading that hits the desk of a state official, the figure could anchor perception going forward. Even with contradictory information, a high initial claim may leave an emotive impression about ITA that is difficult to dislodge.[167] Rather than economically rational decision-making, cases may remain in ITA even when other conflict management mechanisms could resolve matters. Where claims are extreme, the small or nonexistent zone of possible agreement[168] may prevent settlement. It is noteworthy that tests revealed, when comparing average claims in energy and non-energy cases,[169] energy-related disputes had meaningfully higher average claims, suggesting specific protocols may be warranted for managing energy disputes.

Data on claims offer a counter-point to commentators' observations while revealing non-trivial fiscal resources were at risk. Given the relative rarity of billion dollar claims within the period analyzed, contemporaneous observations that it took a billion-dollar claim "to stand out" seem somewhat overstated. While more recent cases were at the larger end of the distribution, a US$250 million claim should garner attention—particularly when several billion-dollar claims were unsuccessful. Investors may wish to avoid association with cohorts with reputations for minimal success, such as the billion-dollar unsuccessful claims in *Saba Fakes v. Turkey, Libananco v. Turkey, Generation Ukraine v. Ukraine, Cementonia v. Turkey,*[170] *Europe Cement v. Turkey*, and *Methanex v. United States.*[171] States may likewise be reasonably skeptical about US$1 billion claims, and investors—to the extent they are credible—should take particular care to substantiate their claims.[172]

C. AMOUNTS AWARDED

Potential risk, however, is not realized risk. Cognitive illusions facilitate inaccurate perceptions about ITA when focusing exclusively on amounts claimed. Primacy (more easily recalling initial information)[173] facilitates easier recollection of the first demand, claim, or amount identified in the request for arbitration rather than the ultimate exposure. Like the billion-dollar claims discussed previously that were utterly unsuccessful—including the

[167] *See generally* Chapter 2.

[168] Roger Fisher & William Ury, Getting to Yes (1983); *see also infra* note 241.

[169] Tests identified reliable mean differences in claims alleged in energy and non-energy disputes using logged data (t (1, 115) = −3.041; p = .003; r = .27; n = 117). With nearly acceptable skewing, winsorized data identified a reliable mean difference (t (1, 115) = −3.612; p < .001; r = .32; n = 117), with average energy claims were US$295,274,370 ($SD$ = 228453042 n = 30), whereas average non-energy claims were US$148,466,056 ($SD$ = 17798751; n = 87) A test of median claims also revealed a reliable difference between energy and non-energy disputes (U = 700; p = .002).

[170] Cementownia "Nowa Huta" S.A. v. Republic of Turk., ICSID Case No. ARB(AF)/06/2, Award (Sept. 17, 2009), 21 World Trade & Arb. Materials 1513 (2009).

[171] Methanex Corp. v. United States, UNCITRAL, Award (Aug. 3, 2005), 44 I.L.M. 1345 (2005).

[172] Franck & Wylie, *supra* note 6, at 489.

[173] William D. Crano, *Primacy Versus Recency in Retention of Information and Opinion Change*, 101 J. Soc Psychol. 87 (1977); Peter A. Frensch, *Composition During Serial Learning: A Serial Position Effect*, 20 J Experimental Psychol. Learning Memory & Cognition 423 (1994); Norman Miller & Donald T Campbell, *Recency and Primacy in Persuasion as a Function of the Timing of Speeches and Measurements*, 59 J. Abnormal Soc. Psychol. 1 (1959); *see also* Chapter 2.

Methanex claim that was the subject of a PBS documentary—focusing upon only one aspect gives an improper perception of the whole. Meanwhile, exaggerated expectation bias could cause people to focus on perceived expectations about how they *feel* the world to be, rather than real-world evidence.[174] Outcome data is, therefore, a fundamental corrective for misperception and a validation of accurate impressions. The next section explores both amounts awarded and changes over time.

Damages relate to liability for treaty breaches, rather than interest or arbitration costs.[175] Tribunals awarded damages for a treaty-based claims in 159 cases.[176] There were 101 cases where investors were awarded nothing, whether by virtue of a tribunal award, settlement agreement, or discontinuance.[177] For the remaining fifty-eight cases, awards reflected a tribunal's damage award[178] or respondent's agreement to pay damages.

For all awards, including investor losses, the average amount awarded in the raw 2011 inflation-adjusted data was US$16.6 million,[179] or roughly US$19 million in 2018 dollars.[180] The median (and mode) awarded was zero.

For the subset of cases where investors obtained damage awards—namely one-third of the studied caseload—the raw inflation-adjusted 2011 mean award was US$46.6 million[181] (or US$52 million in 2018 dollars).[182] The raw median award was US$11 million[183] (or US$12.4 million in 2018 dollars).[184] Yet, as Has Rosling reminds us in

---

[174] Martin Hilbert, *Towards a Synthesis of Cognitive Biases: How Noisy Information Processing Can Bias Human Decision Making*, 132 PSYCHOL. BULL. 211 (2012); Willem A. Wagennar & Gideon B. Keren, *Calibration of Probability Assessments by Professional Blackjack Dealers, Statistical Experts and Lay People*, 36 ORG. BEHAV. & HUM. DECISION PROCESSES 406 (1985).

[175] Where damages were awarded—either by tribunals or in settlement agreement or discontinuance—amounts were recorded in the original currency and converted to a U.S. dollar value at the award date. *See* Codebook, Appendix IV.

[176] Not every case, let alone the same award within a case, contained both a claim and damage assessment. Of the 159 cases, only 103 contained information both about damages claimed and awarded. In fifty-six cases, there was no information available on claimed damages.

[177] This includes discontinuances and settlement agreements where awards did not reflect whether cash changed hands, including *EVN v. Macedonia, Piero Foresti v. South Africa, Howard v. Canada, Lemire v. Ukraine I, Quadrant. v. Costa Rica*, and *Vattenfall v. Germany*.

[178] This includes settlements and discontinuances that indicated a respondent's agreement to pay damages. There were only two cases like this. *See* Goetz v. Republic of Burundi [I], ICSID Case No. ARB/95/3, Award, 527 (Feb. 10, 1999), https://bit.ly/2O7Xc26f (last visited Aug. 7, 2018) (reflecting agreement to pay US$2,989,636); Impregilo S.p.A. v. Islamic Republic of Pak., ICSID Case No. ARB/03/3, Order of Discontinuance of the Proceeding (Sept. 25, 2005), https://bit.ly/2myI5Ce (last visited Aug. 7, 2018) (reflecting agreement to pay US$98,000,000).

[179] $M = 16{,}623{,}985.80$; $SD = 16623986$; $n = 159$. For winsorized data, which controlled the influence of statistical outliers, the mean was US$2,950,324 ($SD = 4766128$; $n = 159$).

[180] Using the BLS calculator revealed that the raw mean adjusted to June 2018 was US$19,021,912.40. The winsorized mean, adjusted to June 2018, was US$3,375,793.74.

[181] $M = 45{,}572{,}651$; $SD = 68283499$; $n = 58$. For winsorized data, the mean was US$42,120,095 ($SD = 57037330$; $n = 58$).

[182] Using the BLS calculator, the raw mean award for successful cases adjusted to June 2018 was US$52,146,263. The winsorized mean adjusted to June 2018 was US$48,196,701.

[183] Median = 10,866,790. The figures include settlements and discontinuances reflecting states' agreement to pay damages. *See supra* note 178.

[184] The BLS calculator indicates that the raw median award for successful cases adjusted to June 2018 was US$12,434,267.

Factfulness,[185] measures of central tendency hide variance, and reality is often found by considering overall spread of data. The remainder of this section attempts to provide context for the data.

Earlier research identified only four cases with awards over US$10 million. In contrast to that historical snapshot, more recent data suggests a different—somewhat bimodal—distribution of damages overall. Of the 159 final awards, states' capacity to avoid damages was markedly similar (64%; *n* = 101). Yet, damages for awards *under* US$10 million were only 17%, as compared to 33% in the earlier analysis. Roughly 23% (*n* = 37) of cases produced damage awards in the US$1–25 million range. A small tranche of cases (4%; *n* = 6) generated damages in the US$25–75 million range. In sharp contrast to earlier research, an increased proportion (9%; *n* = 15) produced US$75+ million awards.

Recognizing that the dataset closed before the *Crystallex, Occidental,* and *Yukos* awards,[186] the cases with the most extreme damage awards were unchanged from earlier research. Excluding cases with no damages, the smallest award was in *Iurii Bogdanov v. Moldova*, with an award of approximately US$24,603.[187] Using inflation-adjusted data, tribunals also awarded less than under US$1 million elsewhere: *Yury Bogdanov v. Moldova*,[188] *Maffezini v. Spain*,[189] *Pope & Talbot v. Canada*,[190] *Tza Yap Shum v. Peru*,[191] and *Feldman v. Mexico*.[192] At the other end of the spectrum, *CME v. Czech Republic*, where the investor secured an award of nearly US$270 million,[193] which *Forbes* reported as equivalent to the Czech Republic's "entire health care budget"[194] remained the largest award analyzed. Other top awards, which exceeded US$150 million in inflation-adjusted form, were *Siemens v. Argentina*,[195] *BG v. Argentina*,[196] *Azurix v. Argentina*,[197] and *CMS Gas Transmission v. Argentina*.[198] Out of the nine largest awards in the dataset, seven were against Argentina.[199]

---

185 *See* ROSLING, *supra* note 41.

186 *See supra* note 133 and accompanying text.

187 *Iurii Bogdanov v. Moldova, supra* note 84, at 21.

188 *Yury Bogdanov v. Moldova, supra* note 153, at 22.

189 *Maffezini v. Spain, supra* note 116, at ¶ 96.

190 Pope & Talbot, Inc. v. Government of Can., UNCITRAL, Award in Respect of Damages, ¶ 88 (May 31, 2002), https://bit.ly/2vA7scO (last visited Aug. 7, 2018).

191 *Tza Yap Shum v. Peru, supra* note 107, at 107, 120.

192 *Feldman v. Mexico, supra* note 74, at 88. With the exception of *Feldman*, adjusted for inflation to 2011, all of these awards were under US$1 million.

193 *CME v. Czech Republic, supra* note 132, at 161; *see also supra* note 132.

194 Tomas Kellner, *Call It the Ronald Lauder Tax*, FORBES (Apr. 28, 2003, 12:00 AM), https://bit.ly/2LOym9h (last visited Aug. 7, 2018).

195 Siemens A.G. v. Argentine Republic, ICSID Case No. ARB/02/8, Award, 128 (Feb. 16, 2007), 19 WORLD TRADE & ARB. MATERIALS 103, 230 (2007).

196 BG Group Plc v. Argentine Republic, UNCITRAL, Award, 138 (Dec. 24, 2007), https://bit.ly/2Obbtez (last visited Aug. 7, 2018).

197 Azurix Corp. v. Argentine Republic, ICSID Case No. ARB/01/12, Award, ¶ 442 (July 14, 2006), 18 WORLD TRADE & ARB. MATERIALS 199, 279 (2006).

198 CMS Gas Transmission Co. v. Argentine Republic, ICSID Case No. ARB/01/8, Award, 139 (May 12, 2005), https://bit.ly/2gXzgxe (last visited Aug. 7, 2018).

199 Argentina was only wholly successful on damage awards in four cases: *Compañiá de Aguas del Aconquija v. Argentina, Metalpar v. Argentina, TSA Spectrum v. Argentina*, and *Wintershall v. Argentina* (2008). In

Given the previously identified large cluster of awards at US$0, growth in cases over US$75 million, and general ITA growth, focusing on the subset of disputes where investors obtained damages is prudent. There, damages were still weighted toward lower amounts, but there was a long tail with a proverbial sting. Figures 5.3 and 5.7 demonstrate that, where investors won, amounts awarded were weighted toward the lower end of the distribution. Roughly, the bottom two damage quartiles of both were under US$25 million. The third quartile had a larger span, in the range of US$25–75million. In other words, approximately 75% of awards were under US$75 million. Figures 5.3 and 5.7 demonstrate that, for data analyzed, the minority of awards in the upper quartile spanned US$75–180 million, with only three awards over US$200 million. Although awards of US$75 million or more were atypical, they nevertheless represented a subcomponent and suggested that cases with substantial fiscal damages were no longer outliers. It remains noteworthy that the median—a measure of central tendency less susceptible to skewing—award was around US$20 million.[200]

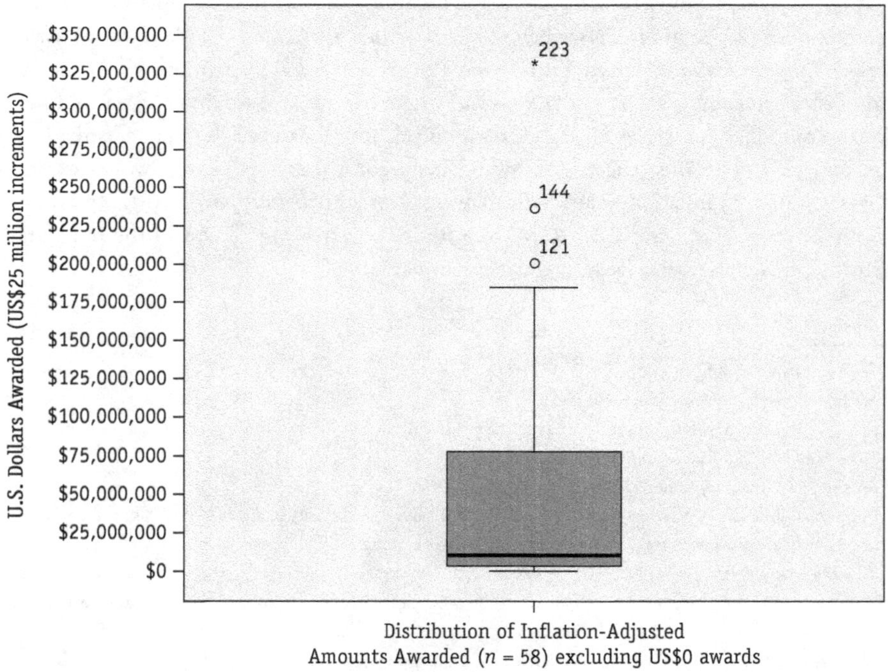

FIGURE 5.3 Boxplot Reflecting Median and Quartile Distributions of Inflation-adjusted Raw Damages Awarded or Reflected in Settlement Agreements and Discontinuances ($n = 58$). The three outliers were: *CME v. Czech Republic* (2003), *Siemens v. Argentina* (2007) and *BG v. Argentina* (2007).

Compañiá de Aguas, although the 2002 award was annulled, a tribunal reached a damage award in 2007. *See* Compañiá de Aguas del Aconquija S.A. v. Argentine Republic, ICSID Case No. ARB/97/3, Award, 264 (Aug. 20, 2007) (finding an award of US$105 million and costs against Argentina).

200 With time marching on, UNCTAD's most recent data suggests that the average amount awarded in claims in 2017 was around US$504 million, which UNCTAD acknowledges was likely skewed by three cases against the Russian Federation. UNCTAD, *WIR* 2018, *supra* note 27, at 95.

Overall, the distribution of damages was both similar and dissimilar to earlier research. The similarity was, when investors won, the damages were not necessarily large. Approximately 80% of the caseload resulted in awards of less than US$10 million, and roughly 87% of cases were under US$25 million; only 13% of the awards generated outcomes over US$25 million. Even if we focus on the subset where investors won, we see that 64% of those "wins" were under US$25 million. This demonstrates that damage awards were relatively small as a quantitative figure, but not necessarily as regards to the proportionate spending power of the state.

There were marked dissimilarities, however, from previous research. Namely, the group of cases involving large damages was facially larger. The arguable shift in damage distribution raises the question whether damage awards increased or otherwise changed over time. While it may be intuitively appealing to believe, as time goes on, that the size of awards increased, the data did not necessarily reflect that theory. Rather, while there were increases, the size of inflation-adjusted awards ebbed and flowed over time. Figure 5.4 reflects amounts awarded over time. Recalling the data's temporal limitations, the most fiscally extreme cases were rendered between 2003 and 2009.

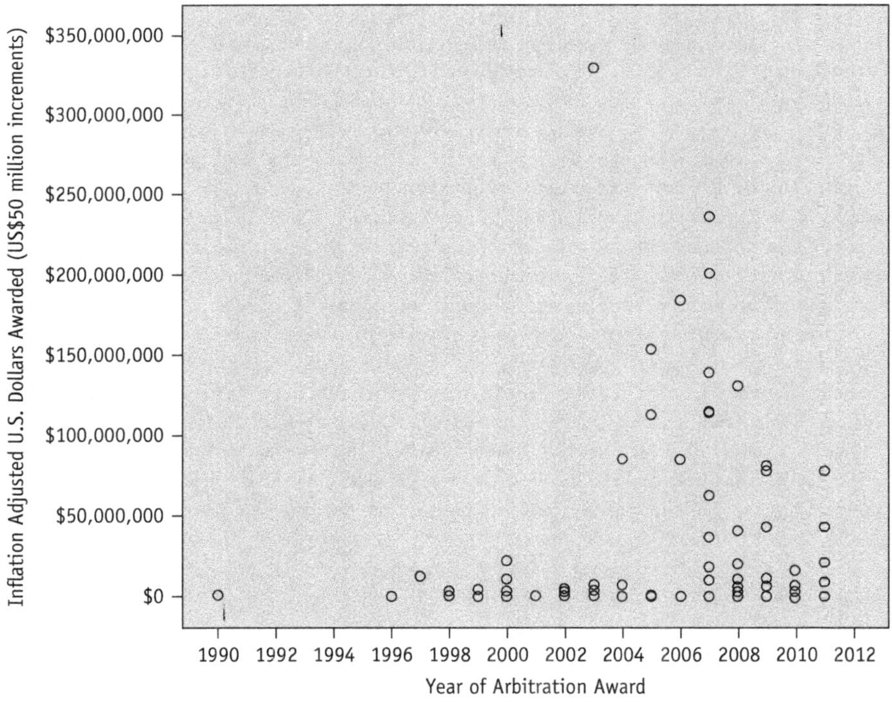

FIGURE 5.4 Scatterplot, using Inflation-adjusted Raw U.S. Dollars in US$50 Million Increments, Reflecting Amounts Awarded and Year in which the Award was Rendered ($n = 159$).

Pictorial impressions, however, require statistical analysis, lest impressions be misleading. The reality of damages was complicated and not easily reduced to a single narrative. For all awards, it was not possible to detect that amounts awarded increased over time.[201] Yet, for the subset of cases where investors won, amounts awarded *were* meaningfully different and effect sizes suggested that the practical significance was large.[202] Follow-up tests revealed that amounts awarded spiked *only* between 2006 and 2009.[203] While the "heyday" of high awards may have passed, the more recent awards of US$1.7 billion award in *Occidental*[204] and the US$50 billion award in *Yukos*[205] will influence future analyses, raising the possibility that damage awards may simply ebb and flow somewhat randomly over time. Yet, the aggregate data does not parse the variance of amounts awarded. Readers are reminded that data has evolved since earlier analysis,[206] for example, on states' development status, whereby Upper-Middle income states experienced reliably larger amounts awarded, but the effect typically dissipated after controlling democracy levels,[207] and the best predictor of amounts awarded was the experience of investors' counsel.[208]

---

[201] When examining all final cases over different time periods, it was not possible to identify a meaningful change. Tests analyzed time using the three time periods reflecting natural breakpoints containing roughly equivalent numbers of cases, namely G1 research (up to mid-2006), G2 research (mid-2006 to mid-2009), and G3 research (mid-2009 to January 2012). ANOVAs exploring potential mean differences in amounts awarded in the three periods and failed to find a meaningful difference using logged data (F (2, 156) = 0.557; p = .57; r = .08; n = 159), and HSD follow-up tests failed to reveal any latent relationship. A Kruskal-Wallis test was unable to identify a meaningful median difference in amounts awarded across the three periods (χ^2 (2) = 1.612; p = .45; r = .10; n = 159). A bivariate correlation analyzing award year and logged amounts awarded was likewise unable to detect a reliable relationship (r (159) = −.12; p = .14); and the negative relationship of the correlation suggested that the direction of any potential latent relationship was that earlier final awards exhibited higher damages whereas later awards provided lower damages. Although technically underpowered and requiring replication (with a minimum of 781 cases to detect the smallest likely effect size), the results provide initial evidence that amounts awarded did not generally increase meaningfully over time.

[202] For the subset of final cases where investors obtained damages, an ANOVA identified a reliable and statistically large mean difference in amounts awarded across different generations of data using logged data (F (2, 55) = 8.031; p = .001; r = .48; n = 58). A Kruskal-Wallis test likewise identified a meaningful median difference in amounts awarded (χ^2 (2) = 13.975; p = .001; r = .44; n = 58). A bivariate correlation likewise identified a reliable, positive linear relationship between award year and amounts awarded (r (58) = .27; p = .04); the direction of the relationship was: the newer the award, the higher the amount awarded.

[203] For logged data, conservative HSD follow-ups revealed G1 awards were reliably lower than G2 awards; and more error-prone LSD follow-ups suggested G3 awards were reliably lower than G2 awards.

[204] Nathan Gill & Mike Lee, *Occidental Awarded $1.77 Billion in Ecuador Contract Dispute*, BLOOMBERG (Oct. 6, 2012, 6:05 PM), https://bloom.bg/2KeQYKx (last visited Aug. 7, 2018); *see also* note 132 (identifying the US$1.2 billion *Crystallex* award).

[205] *Yukos*, *supra* note 133, at ¶ 1827.

[206] Franck, *supra* note 21; Susan D. Franck, *Development and Outcomes of Investment Treaty Arbitration*, 50 HARV. J. INT'L L. 446 (2009).

[207] Susan D. Franck, *Conflating Politics and Development? Examining Investment Treaty Arbitration Outcomes*, 55 VA. J. INT'L L. 13, 48, 57–59 (2014); *see also* Franck & Wylie, *supra* note 6, at 507–09 (using a two-part model of outcomes to explore multiple variables but failing to find respondents' development status was robustly associated with outcomes in all models); *id.* at 513–18 (repeatedly failing to find that respondents' World Bank development status was reliably linked to investors' relative success); *but see* Daniel Behn et al., *Poor States or Poor Governance? Explaining Outcomes in Investment Treaty Arbitration*, 38 NW. J. INT'L L. & BUS. 333 (2018) (using different data and methodologies and identifying a different result).

[208] Franck & Wylie, *supra* note 6, at 507–09.

Ignoring data on damages creates a risk of potential downstream harm. Figures, such as the reference to US$350million, constitute an irrelevant fiscal anchor that could prove difficult to correct. Some figures have moved into the broader public domain.[209] Availability[210] may facilitate conclusions that inaccurate anchors are representative and correct, even when they are not. Meanwhile, commentators can point to individual awards, discussed without context, to suggest they are representative, when the data may suggest otherwise.[211] These choices could be inadvertently influenced by cognitive illusions such as confirmation bias, which involves "unconsciously seek[ing] out information that confirms existing views and disregard[ing] conflicting information rather than attempting to systematically gather accurate information."[212] This would be unfortunate for several reasons. First, it compounds other cognitive illusions by focusing on negative information (i.e., focusing exclusively on losses), which can generate framing effects.[213] Second, it could trigger an alarmist bias where, when confronted with a range of probabilities, individuals focus on the most alarming situations identified.[214] Third, without holistic information, availability may influence stakeholders to believe inaccurate facts by virtue of their prevalence within the public domain. An availability cascade could then create a self-reinforcing process in which collective beliefs become plausible through repetition in the public discourse, even when verifiably wrong.

Put simply, "stylized facts" about ITA that are repeated enough can become the equivalent of "truth."[215] We should seek to avoid unwittingly becoming "availability entrepreneurs"[216] who generate error when searching for attention-grabbing headlines or other narratives. One critical debiasing mechanism is to first acknowledge the possibility of cognition error and avoid the bias blind spot. It is then possible to use data to correct impressions (when necessary) to assist making decision-making supported by verifiable and contextualized data, rather than intuitive perception. Cognitive illusions, such as framing and availability,

---

[209] *See* Nick Buxton, *Legalised Profiteering?* CORPORATE EUROPE OBSERVATORY, 3–7 (Nov. 2011), https://bit.ly/2KCo5sI (last visited Aug. 7, 2018; Frances Russell, *The Age of the Billion-Dollar Global Corporate Shakedown*, IPOLITICS (Jan. 5, 2013, 8:58 PM), http://bit.ly/13dod4k (last visited Aug. 7, 2018); Stuart Trew, *Profiting from Injustice: New European Report Puts Investor-State Industry Under the Microscope*, RABBLE.CA BLOGS (Nov. 28, 2012), http://bit.ly/Tlg5dZ (last visited Aug. 7, 2018).

[210] *See* Chapter 2.

[211] For example, one report rendered around when the dataset contemporaneously closed, identified a US$217 million award in *Siemens v. Argentina* as representative, but failed to appreciate that before 2012, it was the second largest public award. *See* Anderson & Grusky, *supra* note 3, at 1 (noting that Argentina has lost four cases in two years and referencing *Siemens*). After referencing a case Bolivia settled, the report failed to identify where Bolivia won a dispute. *See id.* at 18 (describing *Bechtel v. Bolivia* and noting ICSID accepted jurisdiction but providing little information about the settlement). The report otherwise lacks holistic information about the number of cases states won in ITA. *See id.* at ix (identifying key findings but ignoring state wins). The report also references the US$877 million CSOB award that arose under a commercial contract and failed to identify that the state won the treaty claim. *Id.* at ix, 10.

[212] JENNIFER K. ROBBENNOLT & JEAN R. STERNLIGHT, PSYCHOLOGY FOR LAWYERS, 15 (2012).

[213] Amos Tversky & Daniel Kahneman, *The Framing of Decisions and the Psychology of Choice*, 211 SCI. 453 (1981).

[214] Timur Kuran & Cass Sunstein, *Availability Cascades and Risk Regulation*, 41 STAN. L. REV. 683, 706 (1999); W. Kip Viscusi, *Alarmist Decisions with Divergent Risk Information*, 107 ECON. J. 1657, 1665–70 (1997).

[215] DANIEL KAHNEMAN THINKING FAST AND SLOW, 142, 144–45 (2011); Kuran & Sunstein, *supra* note 214.

[216] KAHNEMAN, *supra* note 215, at 142.

could be reduced by data[217] to realign perception with reality. Or, when data is verified, it becomes appropriate to acknowledge that data supports pre-existing assessments, while acknowledging that data may change as reality continues to unfold.

IV. Relative Success: Comparing Claims and Awards

While examining amounts awarded aids in assessing ITA outcomes, it fails to reflect variance between claimants' initial demands, the value of specific investments, and ultimate results. This section initially explores differences—for all cases—between amounts claimed and awarded. It next focuses on investors' relative success. To offer a more nuanced analysis, it then turns to the subset of cases where investors were awarded damages.

A. ALL AWARDS

Earlier research observed a decided gap between mean claims and awards. Eliminating one statistical outlier, the earlier generation of research identified a meaningful difference between mean amounts claimed (US$343m) and awarded (US$10m).[218] To reassess those findings, and given the two decades of awards involved, the replication used inflation-adjusted data. As before, there was a stark distinction between mean claims and awards.[219] When considering outcomes of all awards finally resolving treaty claims (including settlements and discontinuances resulting in liability), the average amount claimed in 2011-adjusted dollars, which included outliers, was US$622.6 million,[220] whereas the average award was US$16.6 million.[221] *See* Figure 5.5.

The US$606 million difference between the two figures is visually stark. It is nearly twice the size of the US$333 million difference identified previously. An earlier section identified a group of claims over US$900 million, which inflated mean claims. Analyzing medians was less dramatic but revealed a roughly US$100 million gap between claims and awards.[222] This was aggregate data, however. Not every case with a claim had an amount awarded, or vice versa. Comparing only those cases with both a claim *and* award replicated the aggregate data identified a mean gap of US$619 million (and a median gap of US$89 million) between amounts requested and awarded.[223]

---

[217] James N. Druckman, *Evaluating Framing Effects*, 22 J. ECON. PSYCHOL. 91 (2001); James N. Druckman, *Using Credible Advice to Overcome Framing Effects*, 17 J.L. ECON. & ORG. 62 (2001).

[218] Franck, *supra* note 21, at 59.

[219] This section includes inflation-adjusted raw data, which included statistical outliers.

[220] *See supra* notes 148–151.

[221] *See supra* notes 179–184.

[222] While the median claim was US$100 million, the median award was zero. *See supra* notes 149 and 179.

[223] For the subset with complete data, the mean claim using raw inflation-adjusted data was US$644,198,075 ($SD = 2468620879$; $n = 103$), the mean award was US$25,194,027 ($SD = 2337172721$; $n = 103$); and the median claim was US$89,268,172 with a median award of US$202,858. The winsorized mean claim was US$179,993,755 ($SD = 199681776$; $n = 103$), and the winsorized mean award was US$4,322,363 ($SD = 5275309$; $n = 103$).

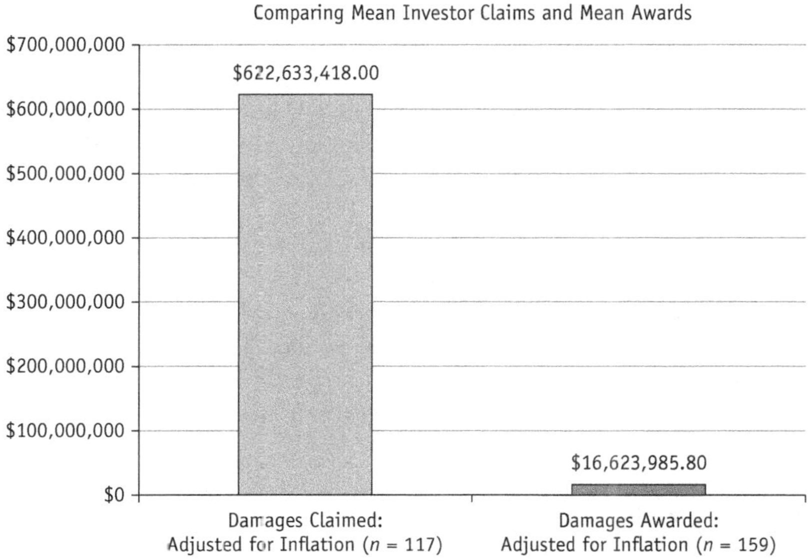

FIGURE 5.5 Bar Chart, using Inflation-adjusted Raw U.S. Dollars in US$1 Million Increments, Reflecting Investors' Mean Claims in Cases with Available Data and Mean Damage Awards in Final Awards (including Settlement Agreements and Discontinuances).

A gap between claims and awards is not necessarily surprising and could reflect a natural phenomenon found elsewhere in dispute settlement. In U.S. employment law disputes, Stewart Schwab and Michael Heise found that using natural mathematical logarithms, to help evaluate differences between plaintiff claims and defendant settlement offers, revealed a "persistent pattern." Although their outcomes initially looked more "defendant-focused," disputes were resolved in a way that split the difference between parties' positions. When logging plaintiff claims and respondent counterclaims, if there was initially a 3.0 gap between the two parties' demands, the ultimate outcome was roughly halfway between.[224] Schwab and Heise called this pattern "'splitting the logs.'" When analyzing U.S. personal injury disputes, after transforming the data using logarithms, they also found reliable gaps between amounts claimed and awarded.[225] Schwab and Heise therefore argued that dispute resolution generally involves an intuitive weighing the order of magnitude of the parties' positions, and using logs—rather than raw numbers—reflects that damage assessments can involve intuitive approaches.

ITA likewise arguably reflects some "splitting the logs." For the 103 cases with both amounts claimed and awarded, the mean logged claim was 7.9. Presuming respondents' position was for investors to receive nothing (i.e., no state liability), Schwab and Heise's approach

---

[224] Stewart J. Schwab & Michael Heise, *Splitting Logs: An Empirical Perspective on Employment Discrimination Settlements*, 96 CORNELL L. REV. 931, 936, 946–47 (2011). The author is grateful, prior to his death, that Professor Eisenberg explored her data and suggested Schwab and Heise's theory offered a constructive framework for considering the logged data to understand divergence between claims and awards.

[225] Schwab & Heise, *supra* note 224, at 946–47.

to "splitting the logs" should generate a mean logged award of 3.95. In slight contrast, the mean log award was 3.67. While ITA roughly fits within the "splitting the logs" theory, the split was not perfect. Several aspects likely explain the variation. First, ITA does not have the good-faith pleading rules of U.S. domestic litigation, which could distort claims. Second, differences in substantive law or procedural posture could contribute to variation. Given the close approximation, a "splitting the logs" theory is a thoughtful paradigm for understanding gaps between ITA claims and awards.

Examining investors' relative success on a case-by-case basis offers another useful frame, as it offers a common scale and partially controls for the merits by injecting a uniform measure, namely amounts in dispute.[226] Relative success was calculated as a function of the proportionate difference between amounts requested and awarded. The mean investor success rate for all cases—which included cases where respondents both won and lost—was 18%, and the median was 2%.[227] For every US$1 claimed, investors were awarded roughly between 2–18¢.

Quartile distributions provide context. The least successful quartile of investors experienced 0% success, namely a 100% loss. The second lowest quartile reflected relative investor success between 0–18.6%. The second highest quartile involved investors recovering 18.6–29.5%. The most successful quartile of investors obtained awards in excess of 29.5% of their claims. Put differently, 75% of investors recovered less than 30% of their request.[228]

B. SUBSET OF INVESTOR WINS

Focusing on the subset where investors obtained damages minimizes variance and offers an alternative frame for outcomes.[229] While low levels of relative investor success continued,

---

[226] *See* Rogers, *supra* note 16, at 235 (arguing "the relative strength of a particular party's case" serves as a control for correct outcomes); *supra* Section I.

[227] $M = 18.00$; Median = 1.86; $SD = 26.04$; $n = 103$.

[228] The largest single group of cases (n = 60) involved claims brought by investors with minimal recovery rates (0–10%). Out of the eleven cases with the largest gap between claims and awards, ten involved tribunals dismissing claims, such as *Saba Fakes v. Turkey, Libananco v. Turkey, Generation Ukraine v. Ukraine*, and *Methanex v. United States. TCW v. Dominican Republic* ended through a consent award. UNCITRAL, Consent Award (July 16, 2009), https://bit.ly/2NDUSPq (last visited Aug. 7, 2018); Uzma Balkss Sulaiman, *Dominican Republic Settles Triple Proceedings*, GLOBAL ARB. REV. (Sept. 21, 2009), http://bit.ly/2fzNeX (last visited Aug. 7, 2018). The next largest group of cases involved investors (n = 25) recovering between 10–35% of claimed damages. This group included *Occidental v. Ecuador* (35%), *Talsud v. Mexico* (31%), *Alpha Projektholding v. Ukraine* (30%), *Walter Bau v. Thailand* (27%), *Enron v. Argentina* (18%), *Chevron v. Ecuador* (15%), and *Tecmed v. Mexico* (11%). Investors obtained a success rate of 35% or higher in eighteen cases; investors obtained awards that reflected 36–59% of claimed damages in seven cases. Tribunals awarded eleven investors more than 60% of amounts claimed. The most successful investor was *Maffezinizi v. Spain* (second lowest amount claimed) where the investor received 100% for a financial instrument. Other cases with a 60% or greater success rate were: *Yury Bogdanov v. Moldova* was the smallest amount claimed (90%), *Ron Fuchs v. Georgia* and *Kardassopolous v. Georgia* (83%), *BG v. Argentina* (78%), *ADC v. Hungary* (76%), and *Cargill v. Mexico* (63%). Data suggests that tribunals can—and do—weed out unmeritorious and inflated claims.

[229] Figure 5.6 included cases where investors were not awarded anything because: states won, a tribunal awarded specific performance in lieu of damages, or settlements and discontinuances failed to reveal that states incurred liability. The zero values, while reflective of ITA as a whole, mask variance.

they were not as extreme after excluding investor losses. Figure 5.6 reflects the nearly US$126 million difference between mean claims (US$171.3 million)[230] and mean damages (US$45.6 million).[231] There was a similar US$73 million difference between median claims and awards.[232]

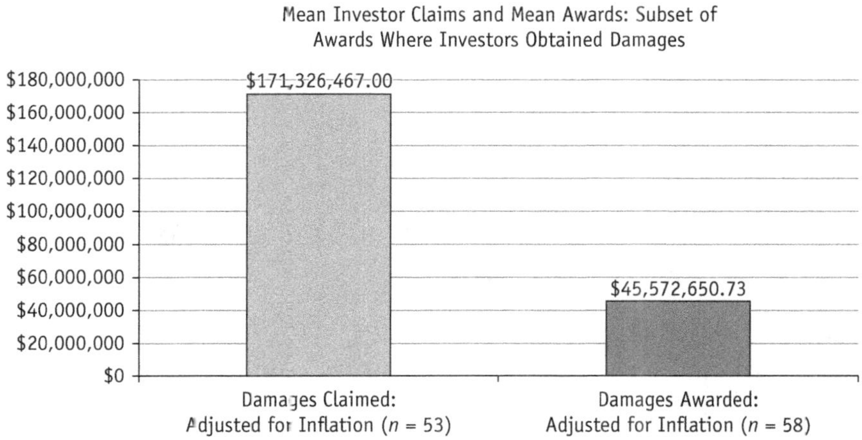

FIGURE 5.6 Bar Chart of the Subset of Investor Wins, using Inflation-adjusted Raw U.S. Dollars in US$20 Million Increments, Reflecting Investors' Mean Claims and Mean Damage Awards (including Settlement Agreements and Discontinuances).

To visualize the variation, Figure 5.7 uses a common scale for amounts claimed and damages awarded to successful investors to reflect the distribution of risk and return. The difference in investors' relative success remained for cases with complete information on amounts claimed and awarded. Excluding cases where investors lost, measures of central tendency demonstrated that investors typically recovered one-third of requested damages. Investors' mean relative success was 35% and median relative success was 28.7%. In other words, even where investors won, they obtained awards for roughly 30–35¢ for every dollar claimed.

Quartile distributions provide further context for the subset of cases where investors won. More than half of cases had relative success rates under 35%. In the lowest quartile, investors' relative success ranged from 1% to 14.7%; and the second lowest quartile exhibited success rates of 14.8–28.7%. For the second highest quartile, investors obtained awards reflecting 28.8–50.7% of their claims. Put another way, even after prevailing on the merits, 75% of investors were awarded *less than half* of their request. Only the top quartile of investors

---

230 M = 171,326,467; SD = 191861066; n = 53. For winsorized data, the mean claim was US$169,241,274 ($SD$ = 186695923; n = 53).

231 M = 45,572,651; SD = 68283499; n = 58. For winsorized data, the mean award was US$42,120,095 ($SD$ = 57037330; n = 58).

232 Using raw data, the median claim was US$87,156,098, and median award was US$10,866,791. Winsorized data had identical medians.

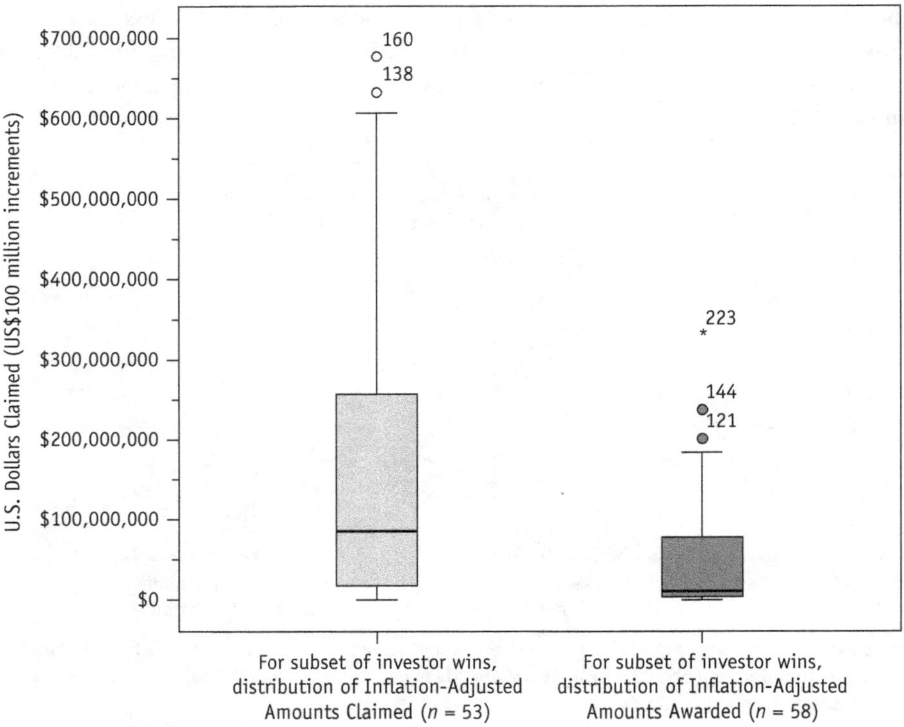

FIGURE 5.7 Side-by-Side Boxplots, for the Subset of Cases Investors Won, Reflecting Median and Quartile Distributions of Inflation-adjusted Raw Amounts Claimed ($n = 53$) and Amounts Awarded ($n = 58$). The thick black central lines represent median claims and damage awards; the shaded boxes represent the second and third quartiles; the lower black stem reflects the lowest quartile; the upper black stem reflects the upper quartile. Circles reflect outliers.

obtained awards reflecting 50.8%–100% of their claimed damages.[233] Put yet another way, only 8% of investors in all final awards obtained more than half of claimed damages.

Those cases were prominent successes and received attention. Several (but not all) of the cases—notably *BG, Cargill, CME*, and *CMS*—involved contentious set aside or annulment proceedings. The focus may facilitate easy recollection given the cognitive illusions of availability; the ease of recall may implicitly invoke representativeness to presume cases were typical when they were, in fact, extreme.[234]

[233] There were 159 final awards, and thirteen of those experienced rates greater than 59%. *See Maffezini v. Spain, Bogdanov v. Moldova, Pope & Talbot v. Canada, American Manufacturing & Trading v. Zaire, Kardassopolous v. Georgia, Fuchs v. Georgia, BG v. Argentina, ADC v. Hungary, Funnekotter v. Zimbabwe, Cargill v. Mexico, Sempra Energy v. Argentina, CME v. Czech Republic*, and *CMS Gas v. Argentina*, with 51% success. Admittedly, *Pope & Talbot* was unusual. *See supra* note 140 (discussing coding protocol). Using the Codebook protocol of coding the last award containing claimed damages, there was a high success rate given its raw US$482,622 claim for a single head of damages and US$407,646 award. Using the initial arbitration request demanding approximately US$507.6 million, the success rate would have been .08%, placing *Pope & Talbot* in the bottom quartile, rather than the top.

[234] *See* Chapter 2.

Despite conventional wisdom that tribunals "split the baby" and award 50% of claims,[235] data failed to confirm this narrative. Rather than a 50% splitting the difference, the typical case involved substantially less. Those research results roughly replicated an analysis of fifteen ITA cases of fair market value (FMV), finding tribunals awarded 20–50% of claimed damages.[236] Similar to commercial arbitration data reflecting that arbitrators do not "split the baby,"[237] experimental research has identified that, while anchoring influenced arbitrators' assessments in ITA cases, arbitrators *did not* "split the baby." Rather, damage awards were roughly tri-modal, it was the rare case that resulted in a 50% damage award, and awards tended to be respondent-favorable.[238] Even where tribunals generated investor-favorable outcomes, states successfully ratcheted down investors' relative success to decrease state liability. Recognizing these figures are blunt outcome measures that do not parse the variance influencing outcomes, readers are encouraged to recall other scholarship traced variables predicting relative success, including the reliable predictors of investor identity and respondents' counsel expertise.[239]

C. IMPLICATIONS

Irrespective of whether outcomes are viewed from the context of all awards or the subset of investor wins, there was a deviation between claims and awards. Low investor success rate was most extreme in in the general caseload; yet success rates remained low even for cases when investors won.

Given those findings, the question is whether claimants' relative success suggests ITA is worth the risk, particularly for claimants. Commentary on negotiated restructuring of Argentine bonds suggests bondholders received 25–29¢ on the dollar.[240] Where it is uncertain at the outset whether an investor will win, the baseline was that investors obtained 18¢ on the dollar on average (or 2¢ on the median), and those figures did not reflect discounts required to secure compliance—or the lost opportunity cost of pursuing arbitration rather than investing in internal development.[241]

---

[235] *See* SERGEY RIPINSKY & KEVIN WILLIAMS, DAMAGES IN INTERNATIONAL INVESTMENT LAW 122 (citing Markham Ball, *Assessing Damages in Claims by Investors Against States*, 16 ICSID REV.-FOR. INV. L.J. 408, 427–35 (2001)); *id.* at 191; Kevin T. Jacobs & Matthew G. Paulson, *The Convergence of Nationalization, Rising Commodities and "Americanization" in International Arbitration and the Need for More Rigorous Legal and Procedural Defenses*, 54 TEX. INT'L L.J. 359, 365 (2007); Richard A. Posner, *Judicial Behavior and Performance: An Economic Approach*, 32 FL. ST. L. REV. 1259, 1261 (2005); Simmons, *supra* note 124 at 200, 208–14.

[236] Simmons, *supra* note 124, at 210–13.

[237] Christopher Drahozal, *Busting Arbitration Myths*, 56 U. KAN. L. REV. 663, 665, 673–77 (2008); Stephanie E. Keer & Richard W. Naimark, *Arbitrators Do Not "Split the Baby": Empirical Evidence from International Business Arbitrations*, 18 J. INT'L ARB. 573, 574–75 (2001); Carter Greenbaum, *Putting the Baby to Rest: Dispelling a Common Arbitration Myth*, 26 AM. REV. INT'L ARB. 101, 101 (2015).

[238] Susan D. Franck et al., *Inside the Arbitrator's Mind*, 66 EMORY L.J. 1117, 1144–48 (2017).

[239] *See, e.g.*, Franck & Wylie, *supra* note 6, at 514–17.

[240] Daniel Bases, *Argentine Debt Holdouts Make Final Plea to U.S. Court for Payment*, REUTERS (Apr. 22, 2013, 5:38 AM), https://reut.rs/2njYN8K (last visited Aug. 7, 2018).

[241] In ICA, to avoid the cost of procuring compliance through enforcement proceedings, an award becomes the basis of post-award negotiation, during which successful parties take a further reduction on the amount awarded. Richard W. Naimark & Stephanie E. Keer, *Post Award Experience in International Commercial Arbitration*, *in* TOWARDS A SCIENCE OF INTERNATIONAL ARBITRATION: COLLECTED EMPIRICAL WORK 269, 272–73 (Christopher R. Drahozal & Richard W. Naimark eds., 2005).

When facing the certainty of ITA risk, investors may wish to actively consider alternatives to ITA, including restructuring an investment without arbitration[242] or using alternative dispute resolution. When considering the risk of legal fees, as discussed extensively in the next chapter, expending resources on ITA is risky. Even if an investor could guarantee success and is willing to risk future success (or failure), relative success in the future might be only marginally better than a negotiated settlement in the present. Success rates also do not reflect attorney fees, lost opportunity costs, lost goodwill, or distraction from core activities. Perhaps the scope and unpredictable risk explains the expansion in third-party funding since 2012.[243] From an investors' perspective, ITA may not be an attractive risk. It may, nevertheless, be the only or the best among a group of bad choices.

States, by contrast, should be somewhat comforted by their relative success. While states may wish to avoid negative publicity from investment claims and disruptions due to lost investment,[244] states need not seek to avoid ITA as a matter of principle. Relying on base rates, rather than intuitions facilitated by cognitive illusions, states may appreciate that the risk could be relatively smaller than sensationalist stories on Twitter or in the popular press may suggest. Moreover, states could, and should, use the uncertainty to their advantage. States might use investor success rates to generate a deeper discount when renegotiating deals, as it may splash cold water on the overly optimistic assessments of investors.

Irrespective of relative success, ITA cases proceed. The reasons are multivariate. One critical aspect may be that states, investors, and their counsel lack access to holistic data on risk factors and success rates. This means cognitive illusions could generate suboptimal decisions about whether and how to pursue dispute resolution. Philip Tetlock's work demonstrates that even expert judgment may be no better than random chance, particularly when deriving from an ideological, rather than data-driven, approach.[245] Despite one's best intent, cognitive illusions creep into decision-making. Optimism bias, for example, is pervasive and prevalent in roughly 80% of people.[246] While it has the benefit of distortions that protect self-esteem,

---

[242] Some research suggests that, where lenders and international financial institutions are involved, some of this may be happening naturally. Mark Kantor, *Negotiated Settlement of Public Infrastructure Disputes*, *in* NEW DIRECTIONS IN INTERNATIONAL ECONOMIC LAW: IN MEMORIAM THOMAS WÄLDE (Todd Weiler & Freya Baetens, eds., 2011). Where, however, investment type does not involve these stakeholders, there is government conduct at issue that is not amenable to a debt workout, or the government officials lack capacity to directly negotiate, negotiation may be impractical.

[243] Third-party funding is a complex matter beyond the scope of this book, as it impacts transational litigation and adjudication more generally. Awards rendered prior to 2012 only contained express references to third-party funding in fewer than five cases. Future research could consider the influence of third-party funders on ITA outcomes.

[244] *See, e.g.*, Todd Allee & Clint Peinhardt, *Contingent Credibility: The Impact of Investment Treaty Violations on Foreign Direct Investment*, 65 INT'L ORG. 401 (2011) (finding that treaties increase investment into states signing treaties, but only where states are not subsequently challenged at ICSID; governments suffer losses of investment when taken to ICSID, but even greater losses when they lose the dispute).

[245] PHILIP E. TETLOCK, EXPERT POLITICAL JUDGMENT: HOW GOOD IS IT? HOW CAN WE KNOW? (2005); *see also* Franck, *supra* note 6.

[246] TALI SHAROT, THE OPTIMISM BIAS: A TOUR OF THE IRRATIONALLY POSITIVE BRAIN (2012); *see also* Neil D. Weinstein & William M. Klein, *Unrealistic Optimism: Present and Future*, 15 J. SOC. & CLINICAL PSYCHOL. 1 (1996).

reduce anxiety, and create greater perceived control,[247] optimism bias could cause investors and states to believe their case or defense is stronger than appropriate, generating a false assessment in a likely positive outcome. Overconfidence bias could mean an overly optimistic assessment could create subjective confidence in a conclusion,[248] even when unwarranted. Likewise, the bias blind spot would prevent people from being unaware of their own errors and prevent identification of (and the possible correction of) one's own cognition errors. In the "invisible gorilla" scenario, people estimated whether they would have been able to spot—in the middle of an experiment on counting ball passes—a gorilla walking into their line of vision and beating its chest for nine seconds; although 90% of participants believed they would have been able to identify the gorilla, 40% of people guessed wrong. In other words, people were unable to predict accurately when cognitive illusions influenced their assessments.[249]

In ITA, investors, their lawyers, and any third-party funders may be overly optimistic about their likely relative success and may generate narratives to support this perspective, which become difficult to dislodge. Investors may believe their case is unique, better than others, and that others' poor success levels will not occur when *they* are in control rather than someone else who presumably had a worse case or is less skilled. Beyond potential overoptimism and overconfidence,[250] the planning fallacy[251] may lead investors to overestimate benefits and underestimate costs, which leads to taking on risky projects. Moreover, blind spot bias could prevent steps to correct errors from cognitive illusions. Together, this may mean investors and related stakeholders misjudge their relative skill and chance of success.

Cognitive illusions could also affect states, their counsel, and third-party funders supporting states. As states are always respondents and experience risk of loss, cognitive illusions could play a particularly prominent role. Negativity and recency biases may cause government officials to focus on recent and negative cases, making it easier to make negative inferences about cases, irrespective of the merits. Being a respondent means that disputes are fixed within a loss frame, creating challenges in positive opportunities. Anchoring, whereby states may become focused on initial claims, may make it difficult to dislodge large values or anticipate pro-state outcomes. Meanwhile, base rate neglect may cause states to underestimate their likelihood of winning or obtaining relatively favorable results.[252] The bias blind

---

[247] Cynthia T.F. Klein & Marie Helweg-Larsen, *Perceived Control and the Optimistic Bias: A Meta-analytic Review*, 17 PSYCHOL. & HEALTH 437 (2002).

[248] Gerry Pallier et al., *The Role of Individual Differences in the Accuracy of Confidence Judgments*, 129 J. GEN. PSYCHOL. 257 (2002).

[249] CHRISTOPHER CHABRIS & DANIEL SIMONS, THE INVISIBLE GORILLA 7 (2010); ROBBENNOLT & STERNLIGHT, *supra* note 212, at 8–9; Daniel T. Levin & Bonnie L. Angelone, *The Visual Metacognition Questionnaire: A Measure of Intuitions About Vision*, 121 AM. J. PSCYHOL. 451 (2008); *see also* Chapter 2.

[250] When people confidently state facts, even if incorrect, confidence becomes a proxy for accuracy. CHABRIS & SIMONS, *supra* note 249, at 112–14; Gary L. Wells et al., *The Confidence in Eyewitnesses in Their Identifications from Lineups*, 11 CURRENT DIRECTIONS PSYCHOL. SCI. 151 (2002); Steven D. Penrod & Brian L. Cutler, *Eyewitness Expert Testimony and Jury Decisionmaking*, 52 L. & CONTEMP. PROBS. 43 (1989); *see also* Chapter 2.

[251] Daniel Kahneman & Amos Tversky, *Intuitive Prediction: Biases and Corrective Procedures*, 12 TIMS: STUDIES IN MGMT. SCI. 313 (1979).

[252] Optimism bias could also cause states and their counsel to have an overly optimistic view of their defenses.

spot could also prevent state officials and their counsel from correcting errors driven by cognitive illusions.

For investors and states, data can debias decision-making and decrease the risk of inadvertent errors related to ITA.[253] Without data, lawyers and their clients will make suboptimal, and potentially incorrect, decisions. Quality lawyers may already use debiasing techniques, such as considering strong facts or arguments on the other side or imagining how a case would be resolved by a disagreeable adjudicator.[254] Yet more is necessary. Considering the "outside perspective," judging risks, and making predictions based on what is known about a similar range of cases is also fundamental. Kahneman argued that, when making decisions, more often than not "What You See Is All There Is,"[255] and a simplistic response that "every case is unique"—although a tempting response for lawyers—is insufficient.[256] Using base rates, investors, states, and other stakeholders should appreciate that, at the outset of disputes, investors face a likelihood of a relatively low success rate; even where investors are successful, they only recovered more than half of what they requested in one-quarter of the cases.

Beyond ITA-derived base rates, stakeholders should consider data from other international courts and tribunals. Other international law disputes involving individuals suggest ITA outcomes were not necessarily unusual.[257] For sheer amounts awarded, the United Nations Compensation Commission (UNCC) awarded US$44.5 billion to individuals, corporations, and states suffering damage.[258] In ITA, for the cases awarding damages, tribunals awarded approximately US$2.4 billion to investors. Although there are differences between the UNCC and ITA,[259] ITA awards were not unprecedented in international law. The Eritrean Claims Commission (ECC), like ITA tribunals, has rejected claims for moral

---

[253] ROBBENNOLT & STERNLIGHT, *supra* note 212, at 77–83.

[254] *Id.* at 78; Russell Korobkin, *Psychological Impediments to Mediation Success: Theory and Practice*, 21 OHIO ST. J. DISP. RESOL. 281, 296 (2006).

[255] KAHNEMAN, *supra* note 215, at 85–88, 154, 245–53; Daniel Kahneman & Dan Lovallo, *Timid Choices and Bold Forecasts: A Perspective on Risk Taking*, 39 MGMT. SCI. 17, 24–25 (1993).

[256] Kahneman observed: "I once asked a cousin, a distinguished lawyer, a question about a reference class 'What is the probability of a defendant winning in cases like this one?' His sharp answer that 'every case is unique' was accompanied by a look that made it clear that he found my question inappropriate and superficial." KAHNEMAN, *supra* note 215, at 249.

[257] ITA is similar to claims commissions where stakeholders experience dissatisfaction with amounts awarded. The ECC, for example, awarded approximately US$161 million to Eritrea and another US$2 million to individual Eritreans; it also awarded US$174 to Ethiopia. Eritrea stated it accepted the award "without any equivocation." Ethiopia, meanwhile, complained the award was "a very small amount given the gravity of the crime of aggression committed by Eritrea." Michael J. Matheson, *The Damage Awards of the Ethiopia-Eritrea Claims Commission*, 9 L. & PRAC. INT'L CTS. & TRIBUNALS 1, 2 (2010).

[258] *See U.N. Reparations Panel Pays Out Another $1 Billion for Iraq's Invasion of Kuwait*, U.N. NEWS CENTRE (Jan. 23, 2014), https://bit.ly/2McGvRX (last visited Aug. 7, 2018) ("The latest round of payments brings the total amount of compensation disbursed by the Commission to $44.5 billion for more than 1.5 million successful claims of individuals, corporations, Governments and international organizations, leaving some $7.8 billion remaining to be paid to the only outstanding claim.").

[259] Damages at the UNCC, for example, involved a single, albeit major, violation of international law as opposed to multiple ad hoc individual claims. In addition, the UNCC received more than 2.6 million claims, some of them very modest, from human beings, whereas ITA has a more limited number of claimants and likely larger average claims.

damages, declined to award interest, and exhibited a "skeptical attitude toward expansive claims for lost profits and revenues."[260] While there can be differences in the fiscal order of magnitude,[261] ITA nevertheless has doctrinal similarities in incentivizing states to change internal practice to prevent future harm.[262]

For relatively low levels of investor success, ITA has congruities reflecting the experience of private litigants suing states. Investors' success rates in ITA were similar to U.S. litigation where private entities sue the government.[263] Internationally, claimants at the UNCC were awarded substantially less than their claims of approximately US$352 billion. Similarly, ITA's 18% mean investor success rate was roughly equivalent to claimant success levels at the Inter-American Court of Human Rights. Dinah Shelton observed the IACHR "has never awarded the full compensation it is due under the test it has articulated."[264] One analysis of IACHR cases between 1989–2002 found typical petitioner success rate between 17–23%.[265] Although loss of human life is decidedly different than a corporate entity's fiscal loss, both ITA and human rights adjudication share a low rate of relative claimant success.

Although there are some arguable differences, ITA was not unusual when compared to other forms of international law adjudication. While the limitations of doctrines and different contexts should be considered, ITA was not necessarily markedly different from other core international courts and tribunals in terms of outcomes. Yet, the outcomes reflect that investors should neither have rose-colored glasses on when pursuing ITA nor should states be overly fearful. Rather, as there was a meaningful relationship reflecting that states won reliably more than states—at a roughly 2:3 ratio—investors must readjust their expectations about compensation and states should strategically use "power of the pen" to draft appropriate treaties and negotiate settlements on terms reflecting sovereign prerogatives. Data on ITA outcomes provides a fundamental framework—and offers the "shadow of the law"[266]—against which stakeholders can negotiate and consider their dispute resolution options.

[260] Michael J. Matheson, *Eritrea-Ethiopia Claims Commission: Damage Awards*, ASIL INSIGHTS (Sept. 4, 2009), https://bit.ly/2mEY4yw (last visited Aug. 7, 2018). The ECC is an imperfect analogy, as neither party to the dispute requested payment of attorneys' fees or costs.

[261] At the Inter-American Court of Human Rights, reparations awards between 1998–2002 ranged from roughly US$8,000 to US$65,0000, with a high award of US$153,670. Ben Saul, *Compensation for Unlawful Death in International Law: A Focus on the Inter-American Court of Human Rights*, 19 AM. U. INT'L L. REV. 523, 581–84 (2003).

[262] Jose E. Alvarez, *Are Corporations "Subjects" of International Law*, 9 SANTA CLARA J. INT'L L. 1, 20–21 (2011).

[263] *See supra* notes 44–47; Franck & Wylie, *supra* note 6, at 493–94.

[264] Saul, *supra* note 261, at 575; Dinah Shelton, *Remedies in the Inter-American System*, 92 PROC. AM. SOC. INT'L L. 202, 204 (1993).

[265] Saul, *supra* note 261, at 577–79.

[266] Robert Mnookin & Lewis Kornhauser, *Bargaining in the Shadow of the Law: The Case of Divorce*, 88 YALE L.J. 950 (1979); Robert Cooter et al., *Bargaining in the Shadow of the Law: A Testable Model of Strategic Behavior*, 11 J. LEGAL STUD. 225 (1982); *see also* OECD, *Government Perspectives on Investor-State Dispute Settlement: A Progress Report*, 6–7 (Dec. 14, 2012), http://bit.ly/19H3Elf (last visited Aug. 7, 2018).

6 Costs—Risks and Reality

COSTS OF ADJUDICATION are a subject of intense interest in dispute resolution generally and ITA in particular. There are multiple reasons for this state of affairs. First, costs affect who should bear the risk of adjudication expense and under which conditions. Second, cost allocations intersect with normative choices about legal authority, factual context, analytical reasoning, and arbitral discretion in making those choices.

ITA costs are a point of considerable interest in ongoing debates about investment treaty dispute resolution. The costs offer an object lesson in how international law provides access to justice,[1] to say nothing of providing a comparative baseline for costs in domestic litigation. Meanwhile, cost determinations affect the efficacy, vitality, and appropriateness of ITA, theoretically affecting whether investors can or should initiate claims, whether and how states should defend claims, what forms of dispute resolution are most appropriate, and whether ITA provides rule-of-law-based adjudication. With the 2015 Queen Mary and White & Case survey suggesting costs are "seen as arbitration's worst feature,"[2] ITA costs have been described as a "hot issue" or "the sting in the tail."[3] Multiple entities—such as the European

[1] *See generally* Avery W. Katz, *Indemnity of Legal Fees*, *in* 5 ENCYCLOPEDIA OF LAW AND ECONOMICS: THE ECONOMICS OF CRIME AND LITIGATION 63 (Boudewijn Bouckaert & Gerrit De Geest eds., 2000).

[2] QUEEN MARY & WHITE & CASE, 2015 INTERNATIONAL ARBITRATION SURVEY: IMPROVEMENTS AND INNOVATIONS IN INTERNATIONAL ARBITRATION 2, 5 (2015), https://bit.ly/1Xeu5sc (last visited Aug. 7, 2018).

[3] Klaus Reichert & James Hope, *Costs–The Sting in the Tail*, GLOBAL ARB. REV. (Apr. 1, 2006), https://bit.ly/2QWeWCz (last visited Dec. 27, 2018); *see also* Sébastien Manciaux, *Cirdi, Chronique des Sentences Arbitrales*, 2012 J. DROIT INT'L 263.

Union,[4] ICSID,[5] and UNCITRAL[6]— focus on costs as integral to the future of investment dispute settlement.

This chapter addresses ITA costs by initially exploring normative reasons for taking costs seriously and reviewing the doctrine underpinning cost assessments. It then tests the conventional wisdom by offering descriptive information about basic costs, and assessing claims about the "traditional" approach on cost-shifting. Having identified that "pay-your-own-way" remains dominant but investors predominantly and reliably benefit from the "loser-pays" approach, this chapter then explores percentages and dollar amounts shifted by tribunals.

I. Understanding the ITA Costs Debate

ITA costs have material repercussions for dispute resolution choices. In theory, better information about costs contributes to high-quality debates about normative choices for investment treaty dispute resolution. This section explores how costs inform adjudicative character, reflect parties' potential fiscal exposure, impact stakeholder expectations, affect strategic dispute resolution choices, and implicate ITA's systemic legitimacy.

A. Costs Inform Character of Adjudication

Cost allocation choices in dispute settlement—whether national or international—affect systemic character. Costs impact who can bring claims, who can defend them, the scope of disputes, third-parties' financial support, and potential resolution. Costs reflect how justice should be dispensed and whether justice is readily accessible (or available only to privileged elites).[7]

---

[4] *See, e.g.*, European Commission, *Council Decision Authorizing the Opening of Negotiations for a Convention Establishing a Multilateral Court for the Settlement of Investment Disputes*, COM(2017) 493 final (Sept. 13, 2017), https://bit.ly/2mcnoxp (last visited Aug. 7, 2018) (identifying, as compared to arbitration, there are various efficiencies and cost-effectiveness to be gained from creating a multilateral investment court); *see also* European Union, *Comments to the proposed amendments to the ICSID Rules submitted on behalf of the European Union and its Member States*, https://bit.ly/2Tgmc8W (last visited Dec. 24, 2018) (providing public comments to ICSID regarding its rule amendment process).

[5] *See, e.g.*, ICSID Secretariat, Proposals for Amendment of the ICSID Rules—Synopsis, Vol. 1, 4 (Aug. 2, 2018), https://bit.ly/2MhlTrv (last visited Aug. 17, 2018) [hereinafter ICSID, Synopsis]; *see also* Chapter 9; Tom Jones, *Kinnear Sheds Light on ICSID Rules Amendment*, Global Arb. Rev. (Apr. 8, 2018), https://bit.ly/2ufgjio (last visited Aug. 7, 2018).

[6] *See, e.g.*, U.N. Comm'n Int'l Trade L. [UNCITRAL], *Report of Working Group III (Investor-State Dispute Settlement Reform) on the work of its thirty-fourth session (Vienna, Nov. 27-Dec. 1, 2017)*, at 5–11, UN Doc. A/CN.9/930 (Dec. 19, 2017), https://bit.ly/2LbD5Sc (last visited Aug. 7, 2018).

[7] Richard A. Posner, Law and Legal Theory in England and America 70–83 (1996); Ronald J. Allen, *How to Think About Errors, Costs, and Their Allocation*, 64 Fla. L. Rev. 885 (2012); John J. Donohue III, Comment, *Opting for the British Rule, or if Posner and Shavell Can't Remember the Coase Theorem, Who Will?*, 104 Harv. L. Rev. 1093, 1093–94 (1991); Keith N. Hylton, *Fee Shifting and Predictability of Law*, 71 Chi.-Kent L. Rev. 427 (1995); James R. Maxeiner, *Cost and Fee Allocation in Civil Procedure*, 58 Am. J. Comp. L. 194 (2010); J. Robert S. Prichard, *A Systemic Approach to Comparative Law: The Effect of Cost, Fee, and Financing Rules on the Development of Substantive Law*, 17 J. Legal Studies 451 (1988).

The rules for compensating attorneys and addressing administrative costs involve perennial debates. Historical poles involve whether costs should be paid by the loser, on a shared basis, or in some other manner. On one end of the spectrum, in U.S. litigation, Professors Eisenberg and Miller suggest that reforming civil justice to include a "loser-pays" rule is a way to minimize the access to courts, deter frivolous claims, and induce settlement.[8] Others, however, reject this approach. Rather, they argue that the "loser-pays" rule deters small and medium-sized entities from pursuing reasonable claims or defenses and creates unfair disadvantage in disputes for risk-neutral parties.[9] Costs therefore are a defining moment for ITA, providing an opportunity to reflect norms about access to justice, equality of arms, and procedural legitimacy.

B. COSTS IMPLICATE FISCAL EXPOSURE

ITA costs are a matter of heated speculation. Theoretically, there is significant and non-trivial financial exposure. Some assertions may be based upon data, but other assertions may not be derived from systematic research and stand to be influenced by cognitive illusions.

There was, historically, various conjectures about costs. In 2010, UNCTAD suggested, "costs involved in investor-State arbitration have skyrocketed in recent years."[10] That publication cited cases where the net results meant losing states had to pay costs of roughly US$12.7 million, US$9 million, US$7.7 million, and US$10.1 million,[11] but failed to refer to other cases occurring during the same time, such as *Merrill & Ring Forestry v. Canada*, where the tribunal's costs were around US$1 million and parties split those fees evenly, absorbing internal legal fees.[12] Other unpublished research involved a limited group of states, suggesting attorneys' legal fees were non-trivial and identifying that one state's legal fees were in the order of US$2.5 million and US$1.95 million for two separate cases; another country estimated its fees were around US$1 million, and a third state had three disputes where legal fees were approximately US$1.2 million, US$1 million, and US$12 million.[13]

---

[8] Theodore Eisenberg & Geoffrey P. Miller, *The English Versus the American Rule on Attorney Fees: An Empirical Study of Public Company Contracts*, 98 CORNELL L. REV. 327, 331–33 (2013).

[9] *Id.* at 333–34; Richard Lewis, *Litigation Costs and Before-the-Event Insurance: The Key to Access to Justice?*, 74 MOD. L. REV. 272 (2011).

[10] U.N. Conference on Trade & Dev. [UNCTAD], *Investor-State Disputes: Prevention and Alternatives to Arbitration*, 16–18, UNCTAD/DIAE/IA/2009/11 (2010), http://bit.ly/18fAbQC (last visited Aug. 7, 2018) (emphasis omitted).

[11] Those cases were: Siag & Vecchi v. Arab Republic of Egypt, ICSID Case No. ARB/05/15, Award (Jun.1, 2009), 21 WORLD TRADE & ARB. MATERIALS 1171 (2009); Plama Consortium Ltd. v. Republic of Bulg., ICSID Case No. ARB/03/24, Award (Aug. 7, 2018), https://bit.ly/2LX1uMe (last visited Aug. 7, 2018); Victor Pey Casado v. Republic of Chile, ICSID Case No. ARB/98/2, Final Award (May 8, 2008), https://bit.ly/2s969gu (last visited Aug. 7, 2018); ADC Affiliate Ltd. v. Republic of Hung., ICSID Case No. ARB/03/16, Award, (Oct. 2, 2006), 18 WORLD TRADE & ARB. MATERIALS 285, 389 (2006). UNCTAD, *supra* note 10; Susan D. Franck, *Rationalizing Costs in Investment Treaty Arbitration*, 88 WASH U. L. REV. 769, 785–86 (2011).

[12] Merrill & Ring Forestry L.P. v. Government of Can., UNCITRAL, Award, 106 (Mar. 31, 2010), 22 WORLD TRADE & ARB. MATERIALS 785, 852 (2010).

[13] UNCTAD, *Iniciativa de un Centro de Asesoría Legal Sobre Derecho Internacional en Inversión y Controversias Invesionista-Estado* (May 26–27, 2009); Franck, *supra* note 11, at 786.

In slight contrast, analyzing a similar time period, the OECD suggested, on average, costs of attorneys were roughly US$3–4 million per party, resulting in a total of US$8 million for both parties lawyers as well as tribunal and administrative costs.[14] One unfortunate, yet telling, mistake is that the OECD results were later misreported by both UNCTAD and the European Commission to suggest the costs of only *one* party's legal fees were US$8 million.[15] While one might hope these were honest mistakes that can be rectified in future publications, the errors—whether influenced by cognitive illusions or otherwise—may prove difficult to dislodge from public perception, memory, and debate.[16]

Scholars also opine upon costs. Professor Trakman identified costs as a critical aspect of ICSID's legitimacy; yet he observed that length, complexity, and costs are unknown, particularly the fees of party representatives.[17] Professor Gantz called the "costs of arbitration [] significant,"[18] and Professor Sands stated ITA costs are "sometimes jaw dropping in terms of time and scale."[19] Professor Peters argued ITA can take "four years to conclude and cost millions of U.S. dollars" and explained costs "are often significant and sometimes wind up

[14] *See* David Gaukrodger & Kathryn Gordon, *Investor-State Dispute Settlement: A Scoping Paper for the Investment Policy Community*, OECD Working Papers on International Investment 2012/03, 19 (2013), https://bit.ly/2m9hGe2 (last visited Aug. 7, 2018) ("For FOI Roundtable 15, the OECD has surveyed publicly-available information about ISDS costs. This survey shows that legal and arbitration costs for the parties in recent ISDS cases have averaged over USD 8 million with costs exceeding USD 30 million in some cases"); *see also* Org. for Econ. Co-operation & Dev. [OECD], *Government Perspectives on Investor-State Dispute Settlement: A Progress Report*, 8 (Dec. 14, 2012) http://bit.ly/19H3Elf (last visited Aug. 7, 2018) ("Although information about costs is limited, it appears that legal and arbitration costs for the parties in recent ISDS cases have averaged over USD 8 million.").

[15] *See* UNCTAD, *IIA Issues Note: Reform of Investor-State Dispute Settlement: In Search of a Roadmap*, IIA Issues Note: No. 2 (June 2013), at 4, https://bit.ly/1pStIU6 (last visited Aug. 7, 2018) (stating legal fees and tribunal expenses, on average "exceeded [US]$8 million per party per case"). While citing to the correct page of the OECD study (page 19), UNCTAD misstated OECD's assessment, which referred to US$8 million overall (not on a per party basis). *See supra* note 14. The European Commission restated the same error, referring to the US$8 million figure from OECD without appreciating it constituted *both* parties' total costs (not just one party's lawyers) as well as tribunal and administrative expenses. European Commission, *Investor-to-State Dispute Settlement (ISDS)—Some Facts and Figures*, 9 (Mar. 12, 2015), https://bit.ly/18GkSEw (last visited Aug. 7, 2018) ("Research by the OECD indicates that the average legal and arbitration costs for a claimant are around $8 million.") (footnote omitted but citing page 19 of the OECD study); *see also* Jeffery Commission & Rahim Moloo, Procedural Issues in International Investment Arbitration 186–87 (2018) (identifying the error of UNCTAD and the EC); *but see* European Parliament, Directorate-General for External Policies, *Study: In Pursuit of an International Investment Court: Recently Negotiated Investment Chapters in EU Comprehensive FTA in Comparative Perspective* 20 (July 4, 2017), https://bit.ly/2v2WWZx (last visited Aug. 7, 2018) (identifying costs of an average ICSID dispute is "around USD 11.5 million").

[16] *See* Tom Nichols, The Death of Expertise: The Campaign Against Established Knowledge and Why It Matters 110–15 (2017) (describing general problems of internet misinformation and how "bad information can stay online for years" even after deletion).

[17] Leon E. Trakman, *The ICSID Under Siege*, 45 Cornell Int'l L.J. 603 (2012).

[18] David A. Gantz, *Investor-State Arbitration Under ICSID, The ICSID Additional Facility and the UNCTAD Arbitral Rules*, U.S.–Vietnam Trade Council Seminar Series, 23 (2004), http://bit.ly/18DwoMO (last visited Aug. 7, 2018).

[19] Franck, *supra* note 11, at 811–12 (quoting Philippe Sands).

exceeding actual amounts gained."[20] Similarly, Professor Gotanda observed, "disputes can also run into millions of dollars," and then cited one case, which was the most extreme case analyzed, where each side's legal fees were in excess of US$20 million.[21] In contrast analyses from pre-2007 data identified that a tribunal's average cost was roughly US$600,000, the average *shift* of counsel's legal fees (unadjusted for inflation) was also around US$600,000, and the average combined arbitration costs represented (at a minimum) 10% of the average award.[22]

Other commentators claimed, "[o]n average, respondents incur annual legal costs ranging from one to two million dollars for a single dispute," or otherwise refer to figures that each party pays US$14 million or a total of US$20 million in legal fees.[23] Those figures may reflect unusual personal experience, involve potential outliers, fail to demarcate between investor-state disputes based upon national law (rather than a treaty), or conflate costs by failing to demarcate between lawyer and tribunal costs.[24] Still others observed lawyers' costs are "often

---

[20] Don Peters, *Can We Talk? Overcoming Barriers to Mediating Private Transborder Commercial Disputes in the Americas*, 41 VAND. J. TRANSNAT'L L. 1251, 1260, 1285 (2008); Luke Eric Peterson & Nick Gallus, *International Investment Treaty Protection of Not-for-Profit Organizations*, 10 INT'L J. NOT-FOR-PROFIT L. 47, 72 (2007).

[21] John Y. Gotanda, *Consistently Inconsistent: The Need for Predictability in Awarding Costs and Fees in Investment Treaty Arbitration*, 28 ICSID REV. 420, 420 (2013). Gotanda cites to *Libananco v. Turkey*, where respondent fees were US$35 million and investor fees were US$24 million. Libananco Holdings Co. v. Republic of Turk., ICSID Case No. ARB/06/8, Award, 182–183 (Sept. 2, 2011), https://bit.ly/1SppzCO (last visited Aug. 7, 2018). As discussed later, *Libananco* is an outlier.

[22] Susan D. Franck, *Empirically Evaluating Claims About Investment Treaty Arbitration*, 86 N.C. L. REV. 1, 68–70 (2007); Franck, *supra* note 11, at 777–78, 811–16; *but see* Susan D. Franck, *The Legitimacy Crisis in Investment Treaty Arbitration: Privatizing Public International Law Through Inconsistent Decisions*, 73 FORDHAM L. REV. 1521, 1592 n.353 (2005) (using non-systematic interviews with leading practitioners to note "a case can cost 'a minimum of $1 million to develop' and . . . [yearly costs, including experts and tribunal fees] can be in the order GBP 700,000 [approximately US$1,280,000] per year but that costs could go as high as GBP 2,250,000 [approximately US$4,117,000] per year.").

[23] David P. Riesenberg, *Fee Shifting in Investor-State Arbitration: Doctrine and Policy Justifying Application of the English Rule*, 60 DUKE L.J. 977, 990, 1011 (2011); *see also* UNCTAD, *Issues Related to International Arrangements: Investor-State Disputes and Policy Implications*, ¶ 14, TD/B/COM.2/62 (Jan. 14, 2005), https://bit.ly/2QT7NTL (last visited Dec. 27, 2018) ("cursory review of cost decisions in recent awards suggests that the average legal costs incurred by Governments are $1 to $2 million, including lawyers' fees; the costs for the tribunal about $400,000 or more; and the costs for the claimant about the same as for the defendant."); David Smith, *Shifting Sands: Cost-and-Fee Allocation in International Investment Arbitration*, 51 VA. J. INT'L L. 749, 749–50 (2011) ("[i]n complex cases reaching full merits proceedings, combined party costs frequently reach into the millions of dollars, and sometimes even into the tens of millions."); Noah D. Rubins, *The Allocation of Costs and Attorney's Fees in Investor-State Arbitration*, 18 ICSID REV.-FOREIGN INV. L.J. 109, 124 (2003) (stating costs are "no small matter" and suggesting costs range from US$1–21 million).

[24] The US$14 million fee for each set of lawyers in the 2004 *CSOB v. Slovak Republic* award involved a national law contract claim, with the treaty-based claim dismissed in respondent's favor five years earlier. *See* Československá Obchodní Banka v. Slovak Republic, ICISD Case No. ARB/97/4, Decision on Objections to Jurisdiction (May 24, 1999), https://bit.ly/2NMbsgY (last visited Aug. 7, 2018). Similarly, *PSEG v. Turkey* refers to a total of US$21 million in costs but does not differentiate between attorney's fees and tribunal costs. PSEG Global, Inc. v. Republic of Turk., ICSID Case No. ARB/02/5, Award, 90 (Jan. 19, 2007), 19 WORLD TRADE & ARB. MATERIALS 107, 198 (2007).

substantial."[25] While offered prior to the expansion of third-party funding, the historical context is worthy of reflection.

More recently, practitioners have engaged in a more data-driven identification of costs. One study, covering a time period roughly contemporaneous to that analyzed in this book, identified costs of roughly US$4–5 million per party,[26] and the results were roughly similar using newer data from 2013–2017.[27] Likewise, research on the cost of investor counsel, state counsel, and tribunals—but only focusing on ICSID arbitration (which contains non-ITA cases) between 2011–2017—suggested average costs were roughly US$6 million, US$5 million, and US$1 million, respectively.[28]

Civil society has waded into the costs debate. One NGO likened ITA costs to "Legalised Profiteering," suggesting "like the infamous 'ambulance chasers', many lawyers are motivated to seek as many ways as possible to increase the number of investor-to-state disputes," which led to the provocative conclusion that those with "economic interests in arbitration should not be allowed to teach arbitration law."[29] *Profiting from Injustice* described lawyers as "legal vultures" and concluded, without holistic data, that "the consequent legal bill for countries defending cases can be staggering."[30] Press commentary has focused on the "up to $50 million"

---

[25] Joshua B. Simmons, *Valuation in Investor-State Arbitration: Towards a More Exact Science*, 30 BERKELEY. J. INT'L L. 196, 198 n.13 (2012); *see generally* Franck, *supra* note 11, at 775, 785–86.

[26] *See* Matthew Hodgson, *Counting the Costs of Investment Treaty Arbitration*, GLOBAL ARB. REV. (Mar. 24, 2014), https://bit.ly/29UwfPi (last visited Aug. 7, 2018) (identifying, for 176 cases with costs information analyzed through December 2012, the average cost for claimant counsel was US$4.4 million and respondent counsel was US$4.6 million).

[27] For the ninety-six awards analyzed arising between January 2013 and May 2017, practitioners identified average counsel cost for investors was US$7.4 million and US$5.2 million for respondents. When considering pre-2013 and post-2012 data as a whole, the mean cost was US$6 million for investors and US$5.2 for states. Matthew Hodgson & Alastair Campbell, *Investment Treaty Arbitration: Cost, Duration and Size of Claims All Show Steady Increase*, ALLENOVERY.COM, (Dec.14, 2017), https://bit.ly/2NEnWqA (last visited Aug. 7, 2018); Matthew Hodgson & Alastair Campbell, *Damages and Costs in Investment Treaty Arbitration Revisited*, GLOBAL ARB. REV. (Dec. 14, 2017), https://bit.ly/2NOTjPA (last visited Aug. 7, 2018); *see also* Matthew Hodgson & Alastair Campbell, *The Allocation of Costs in Investment Treaty Arbitraton*, *in* CONTEMPORARY AND EMERGING ISSUES ON THE LAW OF DAMAGES AND VALUATION IN INTERNATIONAL INVESTMENT ARBITRATION 398 (Christina L. Beharry ed. 2018). The study failed to report standard deviations or conduct statistical analysis indicating whether temporal shifts were statistically meaningful; the methodology also did not indicate an adjustment for inflation. Matthew Hodgson & Alastair Campbell, *Study of Costs Awards in Investment Treaty Arbitrations up to End of May 2017: Note on Methodology*, ALLENOVERY.COM, https://bit.ly/2KSBnWn (last visited Aug. 7, 2018).

[28] *See* COMMISSION & MOLOO, *supra* note 15, at 187–88; app. 9A (providing information on means, medians, and detailing cases contributing to the analysis and acknowledging that ICSID may contain non-ITA cases); *see also id.* at 190, app. 9A (reflecting that for public ITA cases proceeding under UNCITRAL rules between 2010-2017, the average costs for investors' lawyers, respondents' lawyers, and arbitrators was roughly US$6 million, US$4.6 million, and US$1 million respectively). For ICSID and UNCITRAL analysis, the costs were converted to US$ on the date of the award, but there is no indication of adjustment for inflation, and figures lacked standard deviations. *Id.* at 187.

[29] *Legalised Profiteering?*, TRANSNAT'L INST. & CORP. EUROPE OBSERVATORY 2, 6 (Nov. 2011), http://bit.ly/17Zj7jS (last visited Aug. 7, 2018).

[30] Pia Eberhardt & Ceclia Olivet, *Profiting from Injustice: How Law Firms, Arbitrators and Financiers Are Fueling an Investment Arbitration Boom*, CORP. EUROPE OBSERVATORY & TRANSNAT'L INST. 13, 15, 18–19, 22 (Nov. 2012), http://bit.ly/1e30kHT (last visited Aug. 7, 2018).

costs award in *Philip Morris v. Australia*.[31] More recently, after obtaining documents under Freedom of Information requests, some suggested costs were roughly US$29 million;[32] yet even those figures contain multiple ambiguities. To prevent undue anchoring, it is critical to recall that the Australian government explained the US$29 million figure "may not solely relate to the Philip Morris Asia dispute," and fees from other tobacco-related litigation "have not been disaggregated,"[33] meaning the amount attributable to ITA is likely less, thereby creating an irrelevant anchor that improperly pulls perception of actual cost. Moreover, that dispute is not necessarily representative and, while acknowledging the impact of that case is critical, using an outlier as a rallying cry or condemnation of an entire process or a basis for systemic reform, is problematic.

While startling numbers may make attention-grabbing headlines, it is neither good science nor appropriate to draw strong inferences from assertions that are unsupported by data gathered in accordance with quality ex ante research protocols.[34] Emotive rather than data-driven narratives invoke intuitive reasoning, and, whether by design or by accident, facilitate reliance on cognitive illusions that lead to predictably irrational decision-making. Yet the claims provide a valuable hypothesis for examination to confirm, disprove, or contextualize conventional wisdom and test theories against data.

C. COSTS IMPACT STAKEHOLDER EXPECTATIONS

It is one thing to spend millions of dollars in legal fees to pursue or defend a claim. It is quite another to pay an award, pay for one's own lawyers, pay for the entirety of tribunal costs, and then pay for the opposing lawyers—particularly when one had no control over opposing counsel's billing. Moreover, when tribunals fail to articulate their approach to cost allocation in advance, it is problematic for parties to learn at the end about the fiscal reality of cost-shifting.

Previous research identified that tribunals poorly articulated the legal basis and rationale for their cost assessments.[35] Yet, managing costs and derivative expectations can affect stakeholder satisfaction with ITA and aid evaluation of the net costs and benefits of treaties. Offering greater guidance about possible costs and cost outcomes prepares stakeholders, permits expectation management, and aids resource conservation.[36]

---

[31] BBC News, *Philip Morris: Tobacco Giant Ordered to Compensate Australia*, BBC.COM (July 10, 2017), https://bbc.in/2u9W2M6 (last visited Aug. 7, 2018) ("The exact sum was redacted . . . but the *Sydney Morning Herald* reported it was as high as A$50m (£30m; $38m)."); Adam Gartell, *Philip Morris Ordered to Pay Australia Millions in Costs for Plain Packaging Case*, 22 SYDNEY MORNING HERALD (July 9, 2017), https://bit.ly/2uIoO43 (last visited Aug. 7, 2018) ("While the exact figure is a closely-guarded secret—and is redacted from the Permanent Court of Arbitration's new ruling—it's believed the bill could be as high as $50 million.").

[32] Gareth Hutchens & Christopher Knaus, *Revealed [AUS]$39m Cost of Defending Australia's Tobacco Plain Packaging Laws*, THE GUARDIAN (July 1, 2018), https://bit.ly/2lQsEF6 (last visited Aug. 7, 2018).

[33] *Id.*

[34] *See* Susan D. Franck, *The Promise and Peril of Empiricism and International Investment Law Disputes*, *in* CAMBRIDGE COMPENDIUM OF INTERNATIONAL COMMERCIAL AND INVESTMENT ARBITRATION (Andrea Bjorklund et al., forthcoming 2019).

[35] Franck, *supra* note 11; Riesenberg, *supra* note 23; Smith, *supra* note 23.

[36] Franck, *supra* note 11, at 787; Susan D. Franck, *Managing Expectations: Beyond Formal Adjudication*, *in* PROSPECTS IN INTERNATIONAL INVESTMENT LAW AND POLICY: WORLD TRADE FORUM 371 (Roberto Echandi & Pierre Suave eds., 2013).

Without proper planning, parties may find themselves in a worse position than anticipated. "Such uncertainty is clearly undesirable in terms of foresee ability and legal certainty and compromises the calculability of risk and potential liability for an investor who decides to bring an action under an international investment treaty."[37] While losing on the merits may be upsetting, parties consented to the risk of loss when granting substantive rights and opting to resolve disputes through ITA. By contrast, cost-shifting determinations could be unanticipated, uncontrollable, and material in fiscal exposure. Nevertheless, parties do not typically appear to agree in advance about cost allocation or offer tribunals clear cost guidelines.[38] Instead, parties place costs in a vacuum and leave the issue to the arbitrators' wide discretion. An optimism bias may mean parties have an unrealistic view about winning and improperly presume that they would benefit from cost-shifting. States that were not fully cognizant of arbitration risks when signing an investment treaty may not have appreciated the complete scope of risk regarding arbitration costs.[39] Such informational deficits may, in part, explain why many parties have not addressed cost allocation ex ante. This research, even with its limitations, provides stakeholders an opportunity to reassess that choice with data.

D. COSTS INFORM DISPUTE RESOLUTION CHOICES

Assessing arbitration costs aids stakeholders in weighing arbitration's value. Costs could be leveraged to induce party conduct before or during disputes.[40] Costs create incentives (and disincentives) for initiating and defending claims, settling claims, bringing motions, or engaging in potentially dilatory tactics.[41]

Presuming investors and states (and their counsel) are rational actors—or at least exhibit bounded rationality—and interested in ex ante analysis of dispute resolution's fiscal elements, having valid and reliable costs data is critical. Otherwise, parties and counsel must guess, engaging in speculation potentially no better than random chance or influenced by cognitive illusions. In an information vacuum, poor judgment risks error, controversial awards, and the ITA-equivalent of buyer's remorse.[42] A more data-driven approach to "bargain[ing] in the shadow of arbitration" can aid the ex ante and ex post management of investment treaty conflict, as well as assessment of procedural mechanisms in treaties or institutional rules for resolving disputes.

---

[37] Stephan W. Schill, *Arbitration Risk and Effective Compliance: Cost-Shifting in Investment Treaty Arbitration*, 7 J. World Inv. & Trade 653, 656 (2006).

[38] *Infra* notes 82, 88.

[39] Franck, *supra* note 11, at 787.

[40] Barnali Choudhury, *Recapturing Public Power: Is Investment Arbitration's Engagement of the Public Interest Contributing to the Democratic Deficit?*, 41 Vand. J. Transnat'l L. 775, 820 n.329 (2008); *see also* Jack J. Coe, Jr., *Taking Stock of NAFTA Chapter 11 in Its Tenth Year: An Interim Sketch of Selected Themes, Issues, and Methods*, 36 Vand. J. Transnat'l L. 1381, 1400–01 (2003) (discussing NAFTA settlements, entities with "adequate funding contemplate a vigorous, protracted campaign," and tribunals "exhibit[ing] a disinclination to award costs").

[41] Franck, *supra* note 11, at 787–88.

[42] Simmons, *supra* note 25.

E. COSTS INTERSECT WITH LEGITIMACY

Cost assessments implicate ITA's legitimacy, namely assessing capacity to provide clear, coherent, and determinate law; offering access to justice to both disempowered investors and states; and providing for equality of treatment. One might question if the law of cost allocation and cost-shifting in ITA is coherent, determinate, and predictable. Literature on norms for cost-shifting, as well as the practice of tribunals, is mixed. One aspect commentators—and tribunals—agree upon is that cost allocation in ITA is "arbitrary and unpredictable," and the state of the field is largely unknown and often confusing.[43] Some commentators complain arbitrators "give cursory attention to fixing arbitration costs."[44] Earlier research identified, despite small pockets of consistency, that there was minimal justification for cost decisions, and it was not possible to identify reliable links between losing and cost allocations.[45] One commentator identified that the "negative consequences of inaccurate and opaque valuations can extend to the entire arbitral system, beginning with lost confidence in awards and unreliable expectations about future cases [particularly as] unexplained large awards may strain the budget of a developing country and give rise to significant domestic political opposition."[46] With the lack of legal clarity,[47] scope of discretion, and challenge of assessing outcomes in advance, it has been difficult to predict the magnitude of costs, which parties will bear the costs, and the basis for cost allocation. A better understanding—supported by data—about costs is central to an understanding of ITA and to creating a normative framework reflecting stakeholder normative objectives.

Costs allocations can have a disparate effect on economically disadvantaged stakeholders. Smaller investors may not be able to access justice if costs of bringing claims makes it economically untenable and potential legal fees are larger than amounts claimed.[48] Likewise, countries with limited resources may end up allocating scarce public funds to shoulder arbitration costs. Professor Salacuse observed that "the costs of an investor-State arbitration . . . may prove to be a significant burden for developing

---

[43] Mondev Int'l Ltd. v. United States, ICSID Case No. ARB(AF)/99/2, Award, ¶ 159 (Oct. 11 2002), 42 I.L.M. 85 (2003); *see also* CHRISTOPH SCHREUER ET AL., THE ICSID CONVENTION: A COMMENTARY 1229 (2d ed. 2009); Franck, *supra* note 11, at 775–90 (collecting sources); Lester Nurick, *Costs in International Arbitration*, 7 ICSID REV.-FOREIGN INV. L.J. 57 (1992); *see also* Ank A. Santens, *Costs in International Arbitration: A Plea for a Debate on Early Guidance by the Arbitral Tribunal on the Principles It Will Apply when Deciding on Costs*, KLUWER ARB. BLOG (June 10, 2009), http://bit.ly/1arGrsv (last visited Aug. 7, 2018); Gotanda, *supra* note 21, at 421.

[44] Lawrence W. Newman & David Zaslowsky, *Assessing Costs in International Arbitration*, N.Y. L.J. (Jan. 29, 2010).

[45] Franck, *supra* note 11, at 777–78, 821–32.

[46] Simmons, *supra* note 25, at 198.

[47] *See infra* Section III(C).

[48] Lindsay C. Nash, Response, *Adam McBeth, Crushed by an Anvil: A Case Study on Responsibility for Human Rights in the Extractive Sector*, 11 YALE HUM. RTS. & DEV. L.J. 167, 174 (2008). Debates about third-party financing, although controversial and evolving, are relevant to this debate. *See, e.g.*, ICCA-QUEEN MARY TASK FORCE REPORT ON THIRD-PARTY FUNDING IN INTERNATIONAL ARBITRATION 162, 174–75, 177, 200, 202–06 (Apr. 2018), https://bit.ly/2J44bpz (last visited Aug 7. 2018); JONAS VON GOELER, THIRD-PARTY FUNDING IN INTERNATIONAL ARBITRATION AND ITS IMPACT ON PROCEDURE 367–423 (2016).

countries."[49] Economically disadvantaged stakeholders—be they states or investors—may need more information about what to expect and how to plan for ITA costs to promote equality of arms and access to justice.[50]

ITA's legitimacy depends on creating a system that is seen to—and actually does—provide a level playing field permitting stakeholders to understand real risks and to make economic, legal, and political choices. A process that appears arbitrary or unpredictable generates questions about its equity, sustainability, and integrity.[51] Yet, a lack of uniformity in cost decisions need not destroy legitimacy if there are respectable reasons for divergence. If investment treaties and their dispute resolution mechanisms are to foster rule-of-law or otherwise contribute to the law market,[52] there are challenges when cost allocations are made without justification.[53] If stakeholders deem costs too high or the process of allocation unfair, states may abandon ITA, mandate other forms of dispute resolution, return to international diplomacy, or reject international law altogether.[54]

II. Doctrinal and Policy Bases for ITA Costs

Various doctrinal sources affect ITA costs. Treaties are often silent on how tribunals should allocate costs, whether PLC (Parties' Legal Costs) or TCE (Tribunal-related Costs and administrative Expenses). Institutional rules vary, typically granting tribunals nearly unfettered discretion. Meanwhile, national laws vary, and international law has its own traditions. This section explores the history, policy, and doctrine of cost allocation. It first offers three normative standards for cost assessments before moving to doctrinal standards for cost-shifting.

A. NORMATIVE BASELINES FOR COST-SHIFTING

Norms in international dispute resolution come from various sources, including international conventions, national laws, institutional rules, and international practices. One observer astutely explained "[f]rom a doctrinal standpoint, it is not obvious how legal costs should be awarded" in ITA.[55] Despite the uncertainty in the legal framework for costs in international arbitration, allocation of PLC and TCE derives from norms in Roman, U.S.,

---

[49] Jeswald W. Salacuse, *Is There a Better Way? Alternative Methods of Treaty-Based, Investor-State Dispute Resolution*, 31 FORDHAM INT'L L.J. 138, 142 (2007); *see also* Hena Schommer, *Environmental Standards in U.S. Free Trade Agreements: Lessons from Chapter 11*, 8 SUSTAINABLE DEV. L. & POL'Y 36, 36 (2007); Luke Eric Peterson, *All Roads Lead Out of Rome: Divergent Paths of Dispute Settlement in Bilateral Investment Treaties*, INT'L SUSTAINABLE & ETHICAL INV. RULES PROJECT 18 (2002).

[50] Franck, *supra* note 11, at 788; Eric Gottwald, *Leveling the Playing Field: Is It Time for a Legal Assistance Center for Developing Nations in Investment Treaty Arbitration?*, 22 AM. U. INT'L L. REV. 237 (2007).

[51] John Y. Gotanda, *Awarding Costs and Attorneys' Fees in International Commercial Arbitrations*, 21 MICH. J. INT'L L. 1, 21–22 (1999); Fulvio Fracassi, *Confidentiality and NAFTA Chapter 11 Arbitrations*, 2 CHI. J. INT'L L. 213, 221 (2001); Carlos G. Garcia, *All the Other Dirty Little Secrets: Investment Treaties, Latin America, and the Necessary Evil of Investor-State Arbitration*, 16 FLA. J. INT'L L. 301, 324 (2004).

[52] *See, e.g.*, ERIN A. O'HARA & LARRY E. RIBSTEIN, THE LAW MARKET (2009).

[53] Franck, *supra* note 11, at 788–89; Rubins, *supra* note 23, at 119.

[54] Franck, *supra* note 11, at 789–90.

[55] Riesenberg, *supra* note 23, at 995.

and Swedish law. These approaches in ITA are best viewed as: complete cost-shifting ("loser-pays"),[56] no cost-shifting ("pay-your-own-way"),[57] and partial cost-shifting derived from parties' relative success or other factors ("factor dependent").[58]

The first norm comes from Roman law traditions.[59] The "loser-pays" rule—or "costs follow the event"—requires losers to compensate winners for costs.[60] Various civil law jurisdictions use the principle in adjudication.[61] The objective is to indemnify successful parties; discourage frivolous actions, defenses, or motions; and put wronged parties in the position where they would have been but for the wrong.[62]

A hybrid uses a one-way cost-shifting approach, namely only one type of party receives costs when successful.[63] One-way fee-shifting provisions occur in standardized contracts, often operating in favor of the drafting party.[64] One-way fee shifting is *not* policy neutral; rather, it encourages suits that further public policy goals or penalize egregious behavior.[65] Stephan Schill argued, in ITA, there is a one-way, pro-claimant cost-shifting rule whereby, when investors win and states lose, an investor's costs will be shifted onto the state; whereas, if investors lose and a state wins, parties will split costs.[66] Recognizing not all cost awards fall into this pattern, Schill nevertheless argued such a rule is normatively desirable.[67] Others suggest the backlash against ITA provides a reason to rethink this, as "a uniquely pro-investor

---

[56] This is sometimes referred to as the "English" rule or the "costs-follow-the-event" rule. *Id.* at 989–90; Smith, *supra* note 23, at 751.

[57] Riesenberg, *supra* note 23, at 989–90; Smith, *supra* note 23, at 751. This is sometimes referred to as the "American" rule. Franck, *supra* note 1, at 792.

[58] Some might combine categories one and three, on the theory that both reflect an element of "costs-follow-the-event" approach. *See* Int'l Thunderbird Gaming Corp. v. United Mexican States, UNCITRAL, Award, ¶ 213 (Jan. 26, 2006), 18 WORLD TRADE & ARB. MATERIALS 59 (2006); Baiju S. Vasani & Anasttasiy Ugale, *Cost Allocation in Investment Arbitration: Back Toward Diversification*, 100 COLUMBIA FDI PERSP. (July 29, 2013), https://bit.ly/2uMGptk (last visited Aug. 7, 2018).

[59] Gotanda, *supra* note 51, at 5; Werner Pfennigstorf, *The European Experience with Attorney Fee Shifting*, 47 L. & CONTEMP. PROBS. 37, 40–42 (1984).

[60] Schill, *supra* note 37, at 654. Even using "costs follow the event," there are exceptions in national law. Micha Bühler, *Awarding Costs in International Commercial Arbitration*, 22 ASA BULL. 249, 262 (2004); Gotanda, *supra* note 51, at 6–7; Manciaux, *supra* note 3, at 277.

[61] Pfennigstorf, *supra* note 59, at 44.

[62] Gotanda, *supra* note 51, at 6; Arthur L. Goodhart, *Costs*, 38 YALE L.J. 849, 851–55 (1929); Murry L. Smith, *Costs in International Commercial Arbitration*, 56 APR. DISP. RESOL. J. 30, 30 (2001).

[63] Eisenberg & Miller, *supra* note 8, at 330; Thomas D. Rowe, Jr. & David A. Anderson, *One-Way Fee Shifting Statutes and Offer of Judgment Rules: An Experiment*, 36 JURIMETRICS J. 255, 273 (1996); Robert V. Percival & Geoffrey P. Miller, *The Role of Attorney Fee Shifting in Public Interest Litigation*, 47 LAW & CONTEMP. PROBS. 233, 240–41 (1984); Thomas D. Rowe, Jr., *The Legal Theory of Attorney Fee Shifting: A Critical Overview*, 1982 DUKE L.J. 651, 662 (1982).

[64] Katz, *supra* note 1, at 66; *see also* Eisenberg & Miller, *supra* note 8, at 359, 361–63 (identifying one-way fee shifts in lending, credit commitment, pooling and services, and security agreement contracts).

[65] Avery W. Katz & Chris William Sanchirico, *Fee Shifting*, *in* PROCEDURAL LAW AND ECONOMICS 271–73 (Chris William Sanchirico ed., 2012); Douglas C. Rennie, *Rule 82 & Tort Reform: An Empirical Study of the Impact of Alaska's English Rule on Federal Civil Case Filings*, 29 ALASKA L. REV. 1, 4 (2012).

[66] Schill, *supra* note 37; *see also* Riesenberg, *supra* note 23, at 990.

[67] Schill, *supra* note 37, at 657, 674.

procedural advantage [that] disincentivizes host states from participating in the investment arbitration regime [and] the overall aim of investment protection would be better served by a more balanced approach."[68]

A second norm is the "pay-your-own-way" approach. Although other states use it, the so-called "American rule" mandates parties cover their own adjudication costs, irrespective of the outcome.[69] U.S. law generally presumes there is no cost-shifting unless expressly permitted by contract, statute, or arbitration rules.[70] The "pay-your-own-way" approach has limited exceptions to grant discretion to shift costs, primarily for extreme cases of bad faith during adjudication, for three reasons. First, where litigation is uncertain, it is unfair to penalize losers if there was a good-faith basis for bringing or defending a lawsuit. Second, there is a desire to avoid unjustly discouraging the poor or those with limited economic resources from vindicating their rights. Third, with an eye to administrative convenience, detailed proceedings about cost would create an unnecessary burden.[71]

Professor Welamson, later a Swedish Supreme Court justice, championed a third approach, where parties pay for costs given relative success and conduct. Welamson advocated "a sliding scale" proportionate for parties' claims to provide "both parties with an incentive to make the claims/offers as realistic as possible" and promote settlement on reasonable terms.[72] Using multiple variables (i.e., a "factor-dependent" approach), the objective involves incentivizing good conduct, promoting precision in claims, and avoiding pernicious dispute resolution strategies.[73]

Some suggest the loser-pays approach is universal[74] or axiomatic.[75] But as others disagree,[76] the reality is worth testing. With three theoretical norms for addressing costs, the

---

[68] Riesenberg, *supra* note 23, at 993.

[69] Kateryna Bondar, *Allocation of Costs in Investor-State and Commercial Arbitration: Towards a Harmonized Approach*, 32. ARB. INT'L 45, 46–49 (2016); Bühler, *supra* note 60 at 250; Arthur R. Miller, *The Adversary System: Dinosaur or Phoenix*, 69 MINN. L. REV. 10 (1984); Rubins, *supra* note 23, at 109–10; Gotanda, *supra* note 51, at 10.

[70] *See* THOMAS H. OEHMKE, COMMERCIAL ARBITRATION § 123:01 (1999); Bühler, *supra* note 60, at 257; Gillis Wetter & Charl Priem, *Costs and Their Allocation in International Commercial Arbitrations*, 2 AM. REV. INT'L ARB. 249, 280–82 (1991); Thomas J. Stipanowich, *Rethinking American Arbitration*, 63 IND. L.J. 425, 453 (1988).

[71] *See* John F. Vargo, *The American Rule on Attorney Fee Allocation: The Injured Person's Access to Justice*, 42 AM. U. L. REV. 1567, 1575–78, 1593–96, 1634–35 (1993); Gotanda, *supra* note 51, at 11; Jeffrey S. Brand, *The Second Front in the Fight for Civil Rights: The Supreme Court, Congress, and Statutory Fees*, 69 TEX. L. REV. 291, 297–98 n.22 (1990).

[72] Wetter & Priem, *supra* note 70, at 274; Lars Welamson, *Principer om Rattegangskostnader under Debatt, in* FESTSKRIFT TILL OLIVECRONA 684–709 (1964); Lars Welamson, *Svensk Rattspraxis: Civil-och Straffprocessratt 1980–1987*, 74 SVENSK JURISTTIDNING 497, 531 (1989).

[73] *But see* Wetter & Priem, *supra* note 70, at 275 (suggesting complex approaches may require "[c]omputer models . . . to properly master the intricacies of the system.").

[74] *See* Bühler, *supra* note 60, at 259; AMERICAN LAW INSTITUTE, PRINCIPLES OF TRANSNATIONAL CIVIL PROCEDURE 176, art. 25 (2004); JULIAN D.M. LEW ET AL., COMPARATIVE INTERNATIONAL COMMERCIAL ARBITRATION 654 (2003) (suggesting an emerging trend for tribunals to order losing parties to bear TCE and PLC).

[75] Rubins, *supra* note 23, at 109; Marc J. Goldstein, *Some Thoughts About Costs in International Arbitration*, INT'L ARB. NEWS 16, 18 (Summer 2003); Smith, *supra* note 62, at 32; FOUCHARD, GAILLARD, GOLDMAN ON INTERNATIONAL COMMERCIAL ARBITRATION 686 (Emmanuel Gaillard & John Savage eds., 1999).

[76] Christopher Koch, *Is There a Default Principle of Cost Allocation in International Arbitration?–The Importance of the Applicable Provisions and Legal Traditions*, 34 J. INT'L ARB. 485, 497 (2014); *see also* Wendy J. Miles,

concerns about inconsistency, unpredictability, and wide variation on cost determinations[77] mirrors general critiques of ITA.

B. LAW OF COST-SHIFTING

Given the theoretical variation, it is useful to explore applicable law. This section explores doctrinal foundations of ITA cost allocation, including party agreement, institutional rules, national law, practice of international courts and tribunals, and soft law.[78] Variance in applicable law can mandate different costs treatment.[79] While tribunals may "routinely award costs and attorneys' fees, usually without discussion [of] questions of applicable law,"[80] cost assessments should be based on law to encourage rule-of-law adjudication. This requires states to provide legal directives, so as to permit tribunals to follow those directives and provide legal reasoning with a nexus between reasoning and result. It remains an open question whether these aspirations reflect reality.

1. Party Agreement

Parties can agree on cost allocations, and adjudicators often enforce those agreements.[81] Express agreements provide a degree of predictability, offer a clear mandate, and capture discretion. This approach was recently championed by Neil Kaplan.[82] Party agreement may, however, need to be quite express and precise.[83]

Costs Allocation in Investor-State Arbitration, 80 ARB. 413, 416–18 (2014) (offering information on potential "presumptions" about cost-shifting and analyzing data from 2006–2013 to conclude "there is no trend in investor-state arbitral awards in favour of any particular approach to costs. The statistics demonstrate that less than half of unsuccessful parties were ordered to bear some part (but not necessarily all) of the successful party's costs and the remaining costs decisions, where one was taken, determined that each party would bear its own costs").

[77] Bühler, *supra* note 60, at 249.

[78] Franck, *supra* note 11, at 796–97; *see also* FOUCHARD ET AL., *supra* note 75, at 685–86; Peter Schlechtriem, *Attorney's Fees as Part of Recoverable Damages*, 14 PACE INT'L L. REV. 205, 207 (2002).

[79] The ICSID Convention is a self-contained, exclusive forum requiring consideration of parties' agreement and treaty rules. Convention on the Settlement of Investment Disputes Between States and Nationals of Other States art. 42 (Mar. 18, 1965), 4 I.L.M. 524, 541 (1966), *compiled in* ICSID CONVENTION, REGULATIONS, AND RULES, at 11 (2006), https://bit.ly/2sjVvVg (last visited Aug. 7, 2018) [hereinafter ICSID Convention]. ITA under other doctrinal regimes (i.e., ICSID-Additional Facility cases, ad hoc, SCC, or ICC arbitrations under the New York Convention) have a different applicable law. HEGE E. KJOS, APPLICABLE LAW IN INVESTOR-STATE ARBITRATION: THE INTERPLAY BETWEEN NATIONAL AND INTERNATIONAL LAW (2013); Yas Banifatemi, *The Law Applicable in Investment Treaty Arbitration*, *in* ARBITRATION UNDER INTERNATIONAL INVESTMENT AGREEMENTS: A GUIDE TO KEY ISSUES 191 (Katia Yannaca-Small ed., 2010).

[80] Gotanda, *supra* note 5?, at 18 (quoting GARY B. BORN, INT'L COMMERCIAL ARBITRATION IN THE UNITED STATES 626 (1994)).

[81] Marc Blessing, *Mandatory Rules of Law Versus Party Autonomy in International Arbitration*, 14 J. INT'L ARB., 23–24, 40 (Dec. 1997).

[82] Neil Kaplan, *Winter of Discontent*, 34 J. INT'L ARB. 376 (2017).

[83] *See* Crystallex Int'l Corp. v. Bolivarian Republic of Venez., ICSID ARB(AF)/11/2, Award, ¶¶ 951–960 (Apr. 4, 2016), https://bit.ly/2LQc5Uf (last visited Aug. 30, 2018) (observing both parties agreed to using a loser-pays approach but, given residual discretion under the treaty and ICSID Additional Facility Rules, opting

Theoretically, parties have multiple opportunities to agree on cost allocation. Ex ante, parties could agree on cost allocation through an express contract, reference to institutional rules with cost guidelines,[84] or obligations in a treaty's offer to arbitrate.[85] The 2012 U.S. Model BIT provides guidance about cost allocation, noting that tribunals:

> may, if warranted, award to the prevailing disputing party reasonable costs and attorney's fees incurred in submitting or opposing the objection. In determining whether such an award is warranted, the tribunal shall consider whether either the claimant's claim or the respondent's objection was frivolous, and shall provide the disputing parties a reasonable opportunity to comment.[86]

Parties could also agree on cost allocations after disputes arise. The ICSID Convention permits parties to make specific cost agreements,[87] and this could occur before the first procedural order. Despite partisanship mid-adjudication, parties have made agreements on costs—typically during settlements and discontinuances.[88] Yet, "ex ante agreements rarely provide guidance on the distribution of legal costs,"[89] and during a polarizing dispute, parties may become intractable and either unable (or unwilling) to agree on cost allocation. When parties fail to provide an express choice, tribunals then consult applicable arbitration rules to assess how those rules supplement (or supplant) otherwise applicable law.

2. Institutional Rules

Institutional rules provide guidance on cost allocation. Treaties can opt into specific rules—and cost standards—by carefully selecting arbitration rules and institutions with preferred standards. Likewise, treaties could set their own rules for optimal cost assessment. The 2012

---

to exercise that discretion to not shift costs against the losing state); *see also* Guarachi Am. Inc. v. Republic of Bolivia, UNCITRAL, PCA Case No. 1011–17, Award, ¶¶ 331–332, 618–622 (Jan. 31, 2014), https://bit.ly/2No5bKO (last visited Aug. 30, 2018) (exercising residual discretion under UNCITRAL Rules but using parties' relative success and good counsel conduct to shift neither PLC or TCE).

[84] Later sections of this chapter address textual flexibility woven into institutional rules. While Chapter 9 argues for greater specificity in treaties and institutional rules, Chapter 7 provides a content analysis of how tribunals actually used law and discretion to explain costs.

[85] Jan Paulsson, *Arbitration Without Privity*, 10 ICSID Rev.-Foreign Inv. L.J. 232, 236–41, 250–51, 255–66 (1995); *see also* Agreement Between the Kingdom of the Netherlands and the Republic of Poland on Encouragement and Reciprocal Protection of Investments, Neth.-Pol., Sept. 7, 1992, 2240 U.N.T.S. 387, 399, 400 (providing an express agreement on responsibility for costs); Won Kidane, *China and India's Different Investment Treaty Dispute Resolution Experiences and Implications for Africa*, 49 Loyola U. Chi. L. Rev. 405, 459 (2018) (identifying the new Indian model BIT has express rules on costs).

[86] 2012 U.S. Model Bilateral Investment Treaty, arts. 28(6), Apr. 20, 2012, http://1.usa.gov/UglyXP (last visited Aug. 7, 2018) [hereinafter 2012 U.S. Model BIT]. For state-to-state arbitration, the 2012 Model provides that costs "shall be paid for equally" but that "the tribunal may, in its discretion, direct that a higher proportion of the costs be paid by one of the Parties." *Id.* at art. 37(3).

[87] Schreuer et al., *supra* note 43, at 1226.

[88] *See, e.g.*, Joseph Charles Lemire v. Ukraine [I], ICSID Case No. ARB/06/18, Award (Sept. 18, 2000), 15 ICSID Rev.-Foreign Inv. L. J. 528, 537 (2000) (providing an ex ante agreement on cost allocation).

[89] Riesenberg, *supra* note 23, at 998; *see also* Bühler, *supra* note 60, at 253.

U.S. Model BIT, for example, expressly permits tribunals to award "costs and attorneys' fees in accordance with this Treaty and the applicable arbitration rules."[90] Institutional rules thereby become implied terms to guide cost assessments.[91]

Yet rules diverge. Some institutional rules do not distinguish between PLC and TCE; others do not expressly permit party autonomy, and others provide different standards for tribunals' cost decisions. Variance expands when states offer arbitration under multiple arbitration rules (with different cost-related rules), as investors then select applicable cost rules from the set of choices states offer.[92]

For ICSID Convention cases, the Convention, the ICSID Arbitration Rules, and ICSID Financial Regulations govern costs.[93] The draft ICSID Convention provided parties would cover their own PLC and bear TCE equally.[94] As enacted, however, cost rules were far from clear. There was no default cost rule, leaving tribunals with general discretion.[95] Rather than addressing costs only at the end, ICSID Arbitration Rules theoretically permit tribunals to be proactive and consult parties about costs.[96] Although tribunals can assess costs and allocate proportions[97] "at any stage of the proceeding," final awards must contain any decision regarding costs.[98] Although the current Rules are clear on *when* tribunals can address costs, they are silent as to *how* and *why* tribunals should exercise their authority.[99] ICSID's Additional Facility Rules are similarly vague.[100] ICSID's August 2018 rule reform efforts have put costs front and center—proposing new duties to act in a cost-effective manner, encouraging tribunals to make more interim decisions, and offering factors for tribunals to consider when assessing costs.[101]

---

[90] 2012 U.S. Model BIT, *supra* note 86, at art. 34.

[91] *See* Republic of Ecuador v. Chevron Corp., 638 F.3d 384, 394–95 (2d Cir. 2011); Republic of Argentina v. BG Group PLC, 665 F.3d 1363, 1371 (D.C. Cir. 2012); Bühler, *supra* note 60, at 254 ("If the parties have adopted a certain set of arbitration rules, it must be assumed that such reference includes the provisions therein relating to the determination and allocation of costs.").

[92] Franck, *supra* note 11, 798–99.

[93] ICSID Convention, *supra* note 79. The ICSID Financial Regulations refer to "direct costs of individual proceedings," which involve the fees and expenses of arbitrators. ICSID Administrative and Financial Regulations, Regulation 14, *compiled in* ICSID Convention, Regulations, and Rules, at 69 (2006), https://bit.ly/2nhow1w (last visited Aug. 7, 2018) [hereinafter ICSID Financial Regulations].

[94] Schreuer et al., *supra* note 43, at 112; *see also* Nurick, *supra* note 43, at 59–60.

[95] ICSID Convention, *supra* note 79, art. 61; ICSID Financial Regulations, *supra* note 93, reg. 14. Article 61(2) demarcates among party expenses, tribunal expenses, and ICSID charges. Schreuer et al., *supra* note 30, at 1222–23; *see also* Lucy Reed et al., Guide to ICSID Arbitration 93 (2004).

[96] ICSID Rules of Procedure for Arbitration Proceedings, Rule 20(1)(f) *compiled in* ICSID Convention Regulations, and Rules, at 111 (2006), https://bit.ly/2nhow1w (last visited Aug. 7, 2018) [hereinafter ICSID Arbitration Rules].

[97] *Id.* art. 28(1).

[98] *Id.* art. 28(2).

[99] Gotanda, *supra* note 51, at 23; Smith, *supra* note 23, at 751.

[100] The current Additional Facility Rules require tribunals to consult parties on cost allocation and provide cost decisions in the award, and do not provide standards for cost allocation. ICSID, Additional Facility Rules, 58, 67, 69 (2006), https://bit.ly/2OjNXel (last visited Aug. 7, 2018) [hereinafter ICSID/AF Rules].

[101] International Centre for Settlement of Investment Disputes, *Proposals or Amendment of the ICSID Rules—Synopsis: Volume I*, 3–4, 9, (Aug. 2, 2018), https://bit.ly/2MhlTrv (last visited Aug. 7, 2018); *see also* Chapter 9.

The UNCITRAL Arbitration Rules, typically used in ad hoc arbitration, provide specific cost rules.[102] First, regardless of the dispute's procedural posture, the 1976 Rules permitted an assessment of costs in any award.[103] Second, they demarcated between TCE (tribunal cost)[104] and PLC (party legal costs).[105] Third, the 1976 Rules gave tribunals guided discretion about allocating TCE, using a "loser-pays" approach and considering "the circumstances of the case."[106] PLC decisions, in contrast, offered tribunals more discretion to consider "the circumstances" and reasonableness.[107] The 2010 UNCITRAL Rules are similar,[108] setting a "loser pays" baseline but permitting tribunals to "tak[e] into account the circumstances of the case"[109] but without defining relevant circumstances.

The SCC rules make a clear distinction between TCE and PLC,[110] permits parties to retain autonomy about cost apportionment, and provides tribunals with limited guidance. SCC Rules direct tribunals to allocate TCE and PLC "having regard to the outcome of the case and other relevant circumstances."[111] The SCC, however, neither identifies how to exercise that discretion nor suggests which "circumstances" are relevant. Other institutions,

---

[102] UNCITRAL, UNCITRAL Arbitration Rules, G.A. Res. 31/98, art. 40(1)–(2), U.N. GAOR, 31st Sess., Supp. No. 17, U.N. Doc. A/31/17 (Dec. 15, 1976), https://bit.ly/2v8CbhD (last visited Aug. 7, 2018) [hereinafter 1976 UNCITRAL Rules].

[103] *See id.*, arts. 32, 38 (providing the tribunal authority "to make interim, interlocutory, or partial awards" and stating the tribunal "shall fix the costs of arbitration in its award"). The 2010 Rules state tribunals "shall in the final award or, if it deems appropriate, in any other award, determine any amount that a party may have to pay to another party as a result of the decision on allocation of costs." UNCITRAL, UNCITRAL Arbitration Rules (as revised in 2010), Aug. 20, 2010, art. 42(2), https://bit.ly/2tYM9Aa (last visited Aug. 7, 2018) [hereinafter 2010 UNCITRAL Rules].

[104] 1976 UNCITRAL Rules, *supra* note 102, at art. 38.

[105] *Id.* art. 38(e) ("The costs for legal representation and assistance of the successful party if such costs were claimed during the arbitral proceedings, and only to the extent that the arbitral tribunal determines that the amount of such costs is reasonable.").

[106] *Id.* art. 40(1).

[107] 1976 UNCITRAL Rules, *supra* note 102, at art. 40(2). The 2010 UNCITRAL Rules are similar, reflecting costs "shall in principle be borne by the unsuccessful party" and that the tribunal can apportion costs as it determines is "reasonable, taking into account the circumstances of the case." 2010 UNCITRAL Rules, *supra* note 103, at art. 42. They also, however, require separate accountings for arbitrators, reasonableness for arbitrator fees, and arbitrators "inform[ing] the parties as to how it proposes to determine its fees and expenses." *Id.* art. 41.

[108] 2010 UNCITRAL Rules, *supra* note 103, at arts. 40–41. The UNCITRAL Rules on Transparency for ITA do not generally address costs. UNCITRAL, UNCITRAL Rules on Transparency in Treaty-based Investor-State Arbitration, art. 3(5) July, 30, 2013, https://bit.ly/2nlgDZg (last visited Aug. 7, 2018).

[109] 2010 UNCITRAL Rules, *supra* note 103, at art 42(1). Those rules provide tribunals clear authority to assess costs at any stage. The 2012 Permanent Court of Arbitration's Arbitration Rules provide nearly identical language on costs. *See* Permanent Court of Arbitration, Arbitration Rules 2012, art. 42 (2012), https://bit.ly/2ermjA1 (last visited Aug. 7, 2018). Theoretically, although none of the cases in the dataset used these rules, future cases arising under these presumptive baselines may "nudge" tribunals to follow the loser-pays rule.

[110] Stockholm Chamber of Commerce, Arbitration Rules art. 43, (2007) https://bit.ly/2MiySod (last visited Aug. 7, 2018) [hereinafter SCC Rules] (providing that "Costs of the Arbitration" include tribunal and institutional fees and describing separate rules for party costs, which can include "any reasonable costs incurred by another party, including costs for legal representation").

[111] *Id.* arts. 43(5), 44.

such as the London Court of International Arbitration (LCIA),[112] Hong Kong International Arbitration Centre (HKIAC),[113] and International Chamber of Commerce (ICC)[114] likewise use case "circumstances" in an amorphous way; and the Singapore International Arbitration Center (SIAC) demarcates among cost types but without any textual guidance for tribunal discretion.[115]

Where parties have not agreed on costs, the failure of arbitration rules to provide predictable and clear rules on cost allocation matters. Without party guidance (particularly states drafting treaties), tribunals become free—and are arguably required—to exercise considerable discretion in allocating costs. In the legal vacuum governing costs, tribunals "faced with the opaque statements from each set of arbitration rules have reached scattershot outcomes."[116]

3. National Law

National law may implicate ITA costs,[117] but countries vary on approach.[118] Some laws are silent on costs, particularly states adopting the UNCITRAL Model Law on International Commercial Arbitration.[119] Other states give tribunals unfettered discretion. Swiss and

---

[112] LCIA Arbitration Rules, art. 28.2-28.4 (1998), http://bit.ly/14NCwz6 (last visited Aug. 7, 2018); *see also* Franck, *supra* note 11, at 801 (discussing institutional rules).

[113] The HKIAC rules are intriguing, inserting potentially two levels of discretion. First, they initially define costs to only include a series of "reasonable" costs involving PLC and TCE; and the arbitral tribunal is given discretion, namely the tribunal "may apportion all or part of the costs . . . if it determines that apportionment is reasonable, taking into account the circumstances of the case," even potentially limiting the "reasonable costs to a specified amount." HKIAC, Administered Arbitration Rules, arts. 33.1-33.3 (2013), https://bit.ly/20AOEp5 (last visited Aug. 7, 2018).

[114] ICC Rules historically granted discretion without guidance. W. Laurence Craig et al., International Chamber of Commerce Arbitration 91–96 (3d ed. 2000). The newest ICC rules provide tribunals shall "take into account such circumstances as it considers relevant, including the extent to which each party has conducted the arbitration in an expeditions and cost-effective manner." International Chamber of Commerce, Arbitration Rules, art. 38(2)(5) (Dec. 2017), https://bit.ly/2G7YSEw (last visited Aug. 7, 2018).

[115] The Singapore International Arbitration (SIAC) makes a clear break between TCE (Rules 35-36) and PLC (Rule 37), but without providing any guidance as to standards for cost allocation. SIAC Arbitration Rules, Rules 35-36, https://bit.ly/2MI6vJo (last visited Aug. 17, 2018).

[116] Smith, *supra* note 23, at 752.

[117] For non-ICSID Convention cases, national law may apply through *lex arbitri* or other substantive law.

[118] *See, e.g.*, John Y. Gotanda, *Awarding Damages Under the United Nations Convention on the International Sale of Goods: A Matter of Interpretation*, 37 Geo. J. Int'l L. 95, 132 n.168 (2005); John Y. Gotanda, *Attorney's Fees Agonistes: The Implications of Inconsistency in the Awarding of Fees and Costs in International Arbitrations*, 5–8 (Villanova Univ. School of Law Pub. Law & Legal Theory, Working Paper No. 2010-01, 2009), http://bit.ly/18KKgSK (last visited Aug. 7, 2018).

[119] The 1985 Model Law did not address costs. UNCITRAL, UNCITRAL Model Law on International Commercial Arbitration, U.N. Doc. A/40/17/Annex I (June 21, 1985), http://bit.ly/4DGwVx (last visited Aug. 7, 2018); *see also* UNCITRAL, Possible Future Work in the Area of International Commercial Arbitration, Note by the Secretariat, ¶¶ 106–114, U.N. Doc. A/CN.9/460 (Apr. 6, 1999), https://bit.ly/2LAlbpU (last visited Dec. 27, 2013) (suggesting costs were an inappropriate subject for the UNCITRAL Model Law); Peter Binder, International Commercial Arbitration and Conciliation in UNCITRAL Model Law Jurisdictions 356–57 (2d ed. 2005). The 2006 revisions also failed to address costs. UNCITRAL, UNCITRAL Model Law on International Commercial Arbitration 1985 with amendments as adopted in 2006, United Nations Publication, Sales No. E.08.V.4, art. 17G (2008), https://bit.ly/1z3UHjv (last visited Aug. 7, 2018).

French law historically failed to guide arbitrator decision-making.[120] Some states offer legal baselines, with Argentina, Germany, and England following a "loser-pays" baseline;[121] but the United States and Japan instead follow the "pay-your-own-way" model.[122]

4. Public International Law Cases

In public international law, the historical baseline has been the pay-your-own-way rule.[123] The International Court of Justice (ICJ) has a clear rule: "Unless otherwise decided by the Court, each party shall bear its own costs."[124] The ICJ applies this rule rigorously, stating that "the basic principal regarding the question of costs in contentious proceedings before international tribunals . . . [is] that each party shall bear its own in the absence of a specific decision of the tribunal awarding costs."[125] Other international adjudicative bodies, such as the World Trade Organization (WTO), likewise follow the pay-your-own-way rule.[126]

Meanwhile, the Iran-U.S. Claims Tribunal (IUSCT)—involving claims brought by investors and states—uses procedures derived from the 1976 UNCITRAL Rules.[127] Both countries agreed to pay tribunal costs, but attorney costs and limited administrative expenses are subject to cost-shifting.[128] The rules presume the unsuccessful party will bear

---

[120] Bühler, *supra* note 60, at 253–54; Swiss Public International Law, Ch. 12, Art. 379 (2012); *but see* Philipp Habegger, *The Revised Swiss Rules of International Arbitration*, 5 N.Y. Disp. Resol. L. 63, 63 (2012) (identifying the new Swiss law permits tribunals to consider "participant's behavior when allocating the costs of the arbitration."). French international arbitration law historically had no standard or authority for costs. Décret no 2011-48 du 13 jan. 2011 portant réforme de l'arbitrage [Decree 2011-48 of Jan. 13, 2011 on arbitration reform], https://bit.ly/2mGsiBz. (last visited Aug. 7, 2018).

[121] Bürgerliches Gesetzbuch [BGB] [Civil Code] (Jan. 1, 1998), Zivilprozessordnung [ZPO] b. X c. VI, § 1057(1) (Ger.) (*translated in*, Georges R. Delaume, *Germany: Act on the Reform of the Law Relating to Arbitral Proceedings*, 37 I.L.M. 790 (1998)); English Arbitration Act, 1996, c. 23, § 61(2), sch. 1 (Eng.), http://bit.ly/1aVteaK (last visited Aug. 7, 2018); Guido Santiago Tawil & Rafael Mariano Manovil, *Argentina*, *in* International Comparative Legal Guide to: International Arbitration 43 (Steven Finizio & Wendy Miles eds., 2005).

[122] Franck, *supra* note 11, at 794, 802.

[123] Statute of the International Court of Justice, art. 38(1), 59 Stat. 1055, 8 U.N.T.S. 993 (June 26, 1946) [hereinafter ICJ Statute].

[124] ICJ Statute, *supra* note 123, at art. 64.

[125] *Application for Review of Judgment No. 158*, Advisory Opinion, 1973 I.C.J. 166, 39–40 (July 12, 1973); *but see The Factory at Chorzów* (Claim for Indemnity) (The Merits) (Ger. v. Pol.), 1928 P.C.I.J. (Ser. A), No. 17, 47 (Sept. 13) ("[A]s far as possible, [reparation must] wipe out all the consequences of the illegal act and reestablish the situation which would, in all probability, have existed if the act had not been committed.").

[126] At the WTO and European Court of Human Rights, the general rule is to not shift costs. Chester Brown, A Common Law of International Adjudication 193–95, 216–20 (2007); Marc L. Busch et al., *Does Legal Capacity Matter? A Survey of WTO Members*, 8 World Trade Rev. 559, 570–71 (2009); *but see* Dinah Shelton, Remedies in International Law 368 (2d ed. 2005) (indicating that ECHR and Inter-American Court of Human Rights successful claimants and "indigent, social outcasts or marginalized" may benefit from a one-way cost shift).

[127] Alan Redfern et al., Law and Practice of International Commercial Arbitration 50–51 (2d ed. 1991); Charles N. Brower & Jason D. Brueschke, The Iran-United States Claims Tribunal 16–20, 760–62 (1998).

[128] Iran–U.S. Claims Tribunal, Tribunal Rules of Procedure, May 3, 1983, art. 38, https://bit.ly/2JQCOiH (last visited Aug. 7, 2018).

administrative costs but the tribunal will "tak[e] into account the circumstances of the case" to determine a reasonable apportionment.[129] IUSCT decisions analyzing costs have focused upon inhibiting dilatory tactics, promoting compliance with tribunal decisions, or avoiding inappropriate conduct—sometimes even making winners pay.[130]

5. Soft Law and Practice

Other sources of law include international practice, academic commentary, and other arbitral awards.[131] Soft law and perceived "tradition," however, are a moving target. This necessitates empirical consideration to ensure that cognitive illusions—such as recency, negativity, or confirmation bias—do not inadvertently (and wrongly) drive legal conclusions.

Commentary about current practice runs the gamut. The *EDF v. Romania* majority found a "growing application" of the loser-pays rule justified its decision, but the dissent questioned the value of departing from ICSID tradition.[132] Professor Scheuer, meanwhile, argued tribunals "appear to be motivated by these principles [from ICSID's *travaux preparatoires*] in most of their decisions."[133] He pinpointed factors including the loser-pays principle, party responsibility for case development, procedural (mis)conduct, and relative success as core aspects of cost liability.[134] Others, however, disagree, positing international practice is "every bit as chaotic as the costs regime that it seeks to describe."[135]

These commentators offer a starting point for consideration, despite limitations of underinclusivity, overinclusivity, temporal gaps, failure to explain methodology, and sample bias.[136] The limitations create a risk that those objecting to a "single model" of costs practice are perhaps influenced by cognitive illusions,[137] with data providing a baseline for testing assessments.

---

[129] *Id.* at art. 40.

[130] Mauro Rubino-Sammartano, International Arbitration Law & Practice 818 (2d ed. 2001); *see also* Int'l Inc. v. Islamic Rep. of Iran Air Force et al., 27 Iran–U.S. Cl. Trib. Rep. 218 (Oct. 29, 1991) Sylvania Technical Sys., Inc. v. Iran, 8 Iran–U.S. Cl. Trib. Rep. 298, 323–24, 329, 332–36 (June 25, 1985); Nurick, *supra* note 43, at 66–68.

[131] Franck, *supra* note 11, at 804–05.

[132] EDF (Servs.) Ltd. v. Republic of Rom., ICSID Case No. ARB/05/13, Award, ¶ 327, Dissent, ¶¶ 4–12 (Oct. 8, 2009), https://bit.ly/2Tk2xVW (last visited Dec. 27, 2018); *see also* Int'l Thunderbird Gaming Corp. v. United Mexican States, Separate Opinion, ¶¶ 124–129 (Dec. 1, 2005), https://bit.ly/2QYhZdE (last visited Dec. 27, 2018).

[133] Schreuer et al., *supra* note 43, at 1236.

[134] *Id.* at 1229–36.

[135] Smith, *supra* note 23, at 754.

[136] *See* Franck, *supra* note 11 (describing challenges with previous research, including her own); Franck *supra* note 34 (identifying core standards for quality research).

[137] Beyond those discussed in Chapter 2, other cognitive illusions could play a role, including: expectation bias (identifying information agreeing with expected outcomes and downgrading data in conflict with expectations), selective perception (tendency for expectations to affect perceptions), and projection bias (tendency to assume unconsciously that others share similar thoughts, beliefs, or positions). *See, e.g.*, Scott Plous, The Psychology of Judgment and Decision Making (1993); Justin Kruger & David Dunning, *Unskilled and Unaware of It: How Difficulties in Recognizing One's Own Incompetence Lead to Inflated Self-Assessments*, 77 J. of Personality & Soc. Psych. 1121 (1999); Donald C. Langevoort, *Behavioral Theories of Judgment and Decision Making in Legal Scholarship: A Literature Review*, 51 Vand. L. Rev. 1499 (1998); Ronald Chen & Jon Hanson, *Categorically Biased: The Influence of Knowledge Structures on Law and Legal Theory*, 77 S. Cal. L. Rev. 1103 (2004).

III. Setting the Stage: Cost Baselines

After identifying the unit of analysis and awards analyzed, this section offers descriptive data on PLC and TCE to assess conventional wisdom on costs. It then contextualizes the data using cognitive psychology insights.

A. SCOPE OF COST DECISIONS

The research analyzed PLC and TCE in 272 awards (from 202 cases). Despite inevitable limitations from data collection, the objective was to use data derived from rigorous coding protocols to assess hypotheses about cost amounts, allocations, and justifications.

Tribunals, unfortunately, did not consistently provide clear and complete cost articulations. Tribunals regularly provided less than complete information about PLC, TCE, and basic details about cost shifts—meaning data on fascial data was limited.[138] For example, tribunals might provide an assessment of overall "costs," but fail to demarcate between which costs are attributable to parties' lawyers or tribunal fees.[139] Other tribunals might state a party was responsible for paying a particular proportion of TCE, but fail to quantify the amounts or otherwise address PLC.[140] The failure to provide precise cost information was most pronounced in the earliest data,[141] but over time, tribunals reliably improved.[142]

---

[138] *See* Chapter 4 (failing generally to find meaningful differences between awards missing and providing costs and extensively analyzing the difference between cases including and missing PLC and TCE).

[139] *See* Wena Hotels Ltd. v. Islamic Republic of Egypt, ICSID Case No. ARB/98/4, Award, ¶ 130 (Dec. 8, 2000), 41 I.L.M. 896, 919 (2002) (making general claims about costs which, given text from an previous award, was assumed to be PLC); Ron Fuchs v. Republic of Geor., ICSID Case No. ARB/07/15, Award, ¶¶ 687, 692 (Mar. 3, 2010), https://bit.ly/2whb8hr (last visited Aug. 7, 2018), and Ioannis Kardassopolous v. Republic of Geor., ICSID Case No. ARB/05/18, Award, ¶¶ 689–691 (Mar. 3, 2010), https://bit.ly/2whb8hr (last visited Aug. 7, 2018), (lumping together lawyer fees, expert fees, and other disbursements); AIG Capital Partners, Inc. v. Republic of Kaz., ICSID Case No. ARB/01/6, Award ¶ 14 (Oct. 7, 2003), https://bit.ly/2EWahKq (last visited Dec. 27, 2018) (identifying a US$1.25 million cost shift without distinguishing between PLC and TCE); PSEG Global, Inc. v. Republic of Turk., ICSID Case No. ARB/02/5, Award, 90 (Jan. 19, 2007), 19 WORLD TRADE & ARB. MATERIALS 107, 198 (2007) (referring to around US$21 million in costs for both parties but failing to identify which costs were attributed to which parties and failing to demarcate between PLC and TCE).

[140] *See* Asian Agricultural Prods. Ltd. v. Republic of Sri Lanka (AAPL v. Sri Lanka), ICSID Case No. ARB/87/3, Award, ¶¶ 116, 627 (June 27, 1990), 30 I.L.M. 580, 619 (1991) (identifying US$165,917 in "reasonable costs" and discussing 33% of PLC but without permitting calculation); Methanex Corp. v. United States, UNCITRAL, Final Award of the Tribunal on Jurisdiction and Merits, Part V ¶¶ 1–4 (Aug. 3, 2005), 44 I.L.M. 1345, 1462–63 (2005) (indicating generally claimant's PLC was between US$11–12 million); Tembec Inc. v. United States, UNCITRAL, Joint Order on Costs, ¶ 74 (July 19, 2007), https://bit.ly/2QWTqoq (last visited Dec. 27, 2018) (identifying investor's partial PLC as US$101,052.50); *but see* William Nagel v. Czech Republic, SCC Case No. 049/2002, Award, ¶ 338 (Sept. 9, 2003), https://bit.ly/2JvwYTC (last visited Aug. 7, 2018). (requiring 80% cost shift but purporting to calculate that ratio using "reasonable" rather than actual state costs).

[141] Franck, *supra* note 11, at 814–86.

[142] For claimant PLC, G1 data had seven cases (ninety-five with missing information), G2 had fourteen cases (sixty-six missing information), and G3 had thirty-four cases (fifty-six missing). An omnibus chi-square test

This has implications for the data studied. Only 161 awards contained PLC decisions.[143] For claimant's PLC, 34% of awards contained complete information on amounts, and 37% contained complete respondent PLC data. Only 32% of awards contained PLC totals for both parties. Barely a quarter of awards recorded either the percentage of PLC shifted (26.7%) or the fiscal impact of the cost shift (25.5%). Similarly, tribunals made decisions about TCE in 160 awards.[144] For nearly all those awards (95.6%), tribunals allocated—or provided sufficient information to permit calculation of—the proportions for which parties were responsible. Yet, tribunals did not necessarily detail the fiscal implications; barely 38% of awards contained complete financial details about party TCE.

Some tribunals failed to mention costs in any respect. Previous research identified that cost assessments were only made in approximately 10% of non-final cases, but in 94% of final cases.[145] The pattern extended into the newer data. The predominant approach (96%) was to make cost assessments in final awards. For non-final awards, only 6% of awards contained a substantive costs decision, but predominantly to defer the issue. Put simply, despite their authority, it was rare for tribunals to decide costs in a non-final award—or identify planned cost-shifting methodology—at an early phase. *See* Table 6.1.

TABLE 6.1

Breakdown of Treatment of PLC Decisions in Both Non-final ($n = 113$) and Final Awards ($n = 159$) in Complete Dataset.[146]

	Percentages (n) of Treatment of Costs in All Awards			
Award Finality	*No Costs Reference*	*Cost Decision Reserved*	*Substantive Decision Made*	Total
Non-Final Award	22.1% (25)	69.9% (79)	8% (9)	100% (113)
Final Award	4.4% (7)	0.0% (0)	95.6% (152)	100% (159)
Total	*(32)*	*(80)*	*(161)*	*(272)*

revealed a meaningful group (χ^2 (2) = 28.847; $p < .01$; $r = .310$; $n = 272$). Tribunals in G2 provided more cost information than G1 tribunals, and G3 tribunals were better at providing costs than both G1 and G2 tribunals. Follow-up comparisons demonstrated tribunals gave more information about claimant PLC (comparing G1 with G2: χ^2 (1) = 4.97; $p = .03$; $r = .17$; $n = 182$; comparing G1 with G3: χ^2 (1) = 27.209; $p < .01$; $r = .28$; $n = 192$; comparing G2 with G3: χ^2 (1) = 8.594; $p < .01$; $r = .23$; $n = 170$).

143 The remaining seventy-nine awards referred to PLC but reserved PLC assessments, and thirty-two awards did not mention PLC at all, reflecting a limited number of non-final awards where tribunals made PLC determinations.

144 In eighty other awards, tribunals discussed TCE but reserved the TCE decision. In the remaining thirty-two awards, tribunals failed to reference TCE in any manner.

145 Franck, *supra* note 11, at 807–08.

146 The breakdown of TCE assessments were nearly identical to the PLC figures provided in Table 6.1. For non-final awards, there were twenty-seven awards without any reference to costs, eighty awards reserving costs, and six awards making substantive cost assessments. For final awards, five awards did not discuss costs, and the remaining 154 made a substantive assessment.

Chapter 9 advocates for normative reform deriving from this data, encouraging costs transparency—whether through party agreement, treaty text, or institutional rules—requiring tribunals to provide early costs guidance, including legal norms and conduct impacting tribunal cost allocation. By providing advance guidance about the possible payoff matrix for conduct, tribunals could create incentives for efficient and productive behavior. The existing gap between what tribunals *could* do and what they *actually* do suggests tribunals are missing a critical opportunity. Providing early guidance affects tactical choices,[147] assessment of dispute resolution options, settlement opportunities given the risk calculus, and management of parties' and counsel's expectations, and otherwise enhances ITA's legitimacy by offering clear and determinate guidance about where, when, why, and how tribunals will exercise their discretion.[148]

B. RAW ITA COSTS: TESTING CONVENTIONAL WISDOM

Commentators have made claims about fiscal exposure of costs but sometimes in an evidence-free or error-prone manner. Meanwhile, the LCIA's analysis of costs in its 2013–2016 (primarily commercial) caseload acknowledged that "it is not currently possible to provide detailed statistics" on parties' legal costs.[149] To prevent commentary being skewed via cognitive illusions or providing emotionally satisfying—but empirically weak—assessments, testing claims is key, particularly as arbitration historically was lauded for cost savings.

The earliest historical snapshot focused on the fiscal implications of shifting PLC, noting the average shift was approximately US$655,000 and average total TCE was approximately US$581,000.[150] In slight contrast, former ICSID officials indicated that parties' PLC totals were in the "millions," and average TCE fees for ICSID cases from 2005–2009 was roughly US$540,000.[151] The question is, as earlier data was not adjusted for inflation, how those findings held up over time. The next subsection offers another historical snapshot of ITA-related costs, recognizing limitations due to time and poor tribunal reporting.

1. PLC: Cost of Counsel

An earlier section noted that the majority of tribunals failed to identify the precise fiscal implications of both claimants' and respondents' counsel. This creates an inevitable risk of case selection effects; yet extensive testing[152] was generally unable—with one material exception—to identify major variances between cases with and without costs data. The core variation was that awards missing PLC data tended to be from before 2007. This suggests more recent cases were better represented, raising the possibility that older cases could be

[147] To the extent permissible by law, parties might explore the possibility of providing early cost-related guidance during interviews of potential party-appointed arbitrators.

[148] Franck, *supra* note 11, at 808.

[149] LCIA, Facts and Figures—Costs and Duration: 2013–2016 (Oct. 3, 2017), https://bit.ly/2uKjJKd (last visited Aug. 7, 2018).

[150] Franck, *supra* note 22.

[151] Manciaux, *supra* note 3, at 280 (citing Nassib G. Ziade, *Les Frais et dépens dans l'arbitrage CIRDI*, *in* CIRDI: 45 Ans Après, Bilan d'un Systèm 263, 269 (Ferhat Horchani ed., 2011)).

[152] *See* Chapter 4.

meaningfully different. The next historical snapshot should be appreciated with that limit in mind.

Adjusted for inflation to 2011 (and including outliers),[153] the average combined costs for *both* parties' legal teams (namely combined costs for investors and states) was roughly US$9.3 million.[154] In 2018 values, that value has the same buying power as roughly US$10.7 million.[155]

The most expensive case analyzed was *Libananco v. Turkey* where parties' combined PLC amounted to slightly over US$60 million.[156] Although it settled,[157] *Abaclat v. Argentina*'s jurisdictional award was the second highest total PLC, with fees of nearly US$40 million for jurisdiction alone.[158] By contrast, *Grynberg v. Grenada* had the lowest PLC total of US$243,595;[159] *Pantechniki v. Albania* had the second least expensive lawyers, with a PLC total of US$627,857.[160] PLC totals were nontrivial. The mean the PLC total was an order of magnitude similar to the mean award in all cases analyzed (US$16.6 million), meaning that, proportionately, the average PLC total was roughly 60% of the average amount awarded. In slight contrast, for the cases where investors won anything, average PLC total was roughly 20% of average amount awarded (US$45.6 million).[161]

Identifying costs on a party-by-party basis offers further context and a bit of nuance. For awards containing claimant PLC data, the inflation-adjusted average cost for investors' counsel was approximately US$5 million.[162] These figures were roughly similar to recent

---

[153] The Codebook, Appendix IV, details inflation-adjustments processes. Original and inflation-adjusted amounts (and transformations) are available in the dataset in Appendix V. Figures were generally adjusted for inflation from the date they were rendered to a common date reflecting the last year of awards (2011). *See also* Appendix I. With the passage of time, inflation-adjustments have continued to trend higher. For example, in the *Pope & Talbott v. Canada* award rendered in November 2002, investor's legal fees were US$3,780,088. Using the U.S. Bureau of Labor Statistics (BLS) inflation calculator reveals that amount, in June 2018, had the same buying power as US$5,253,947.02. *See* https://data.bls.gov/cgi-bin/cpicalc.pl.

[154] $M = 9{,}317{,}669$; $SD = 10822504$; $n = 51$. The 25th percentile was US$3,702,874, median (50th percentile) was US$5,387,784, and the 75th percentile was US$12,542,254.

[155] The amount was calculated using the BLS inflation calculator reflecting the mean cost and median costs were, respectively, US$10,661,693.35 and US$6,164,943.27 in June 2018.

[156] *Libananco v. Turkey, supra* note 21, at 182–83 (US$60,083,973.76). Using the BLS website for conversion, the combined PLC of US$60 million equates to roughly US$67 million in June 2018.

[157] Caroline Simson, *Argentina Settles Historic ICSID Row with Italian Bondholders*, LAW360 (Feb. 2, 2016), http://bit.ly/2dN803p (last visited Aug. 7, 2018).

[158] The original amount from the award was US$38,929,944. Abaclat v. Argentine Republic, ICSID Case No. ARB/07/5, Decision on Jurisdiction, 269–70 (Aug. 4, 2011), https://bit.ly/2C1a489 (last visited Aug. 7, 2018). Using the BLS website for conversion, this equates to roughly US$58 million in June 2018.

[159] The original amount was US$236,219.33. Rachel S. Grynberg v. Gren., ICSID Case No. ARB/10/6, Award, 45–46 (Dec. 10, 2010), 23 WORLD TRADE & ARB. MATERIALS 483 (2011). Using the BLS website, this equates to US$271,580.18 in June 2018.

[160] The original amount was US$598,963. Pantechniki S.A. Contractors & Engineers v. Republic of Alb., ICSID Case No. ARB/07/21, Award, 26 (July 30, 2009), https://bit.ly/2b81FkL (last visited Aug. 7, 2018). Using the BLS website for conversion, this is equivalent to US$700,861.51 in June 2018.

[161] These figures were based upon overall averages from awards, rather than case-by-case averages. While a potential way of thinking in broad arcs about ITA costs, this inevitably injects error and the possibility that general analyses were not comparing data from the same case. Providing some information is preferable to losing data or continuing in an information vacuum.

[162] $M = 4{,}972{,}601$; $SD = 5780156$; $n = 55$. For the raw inflation-adjusted data (containing outliers), the 25th percentile of investor PLC was US$1,335,066, the median (50th percentile) was US$3,144,147, and the 75th

analysis from Commission and Moloo who found (albeit using non-inflation-adjusted data) that mean costs for claimants in ITA-related cases were around the US$5–6 million mark.[163]

Of analyzed data, the most expensive investor legal team was *Abaclat* (US$27,309,605), which never reached the merits;[164] investors' counsel in *Libananco* were a close second (US$24,381,556).[165] The lowest cost for claimant lawyers were *Grynberg* (US$32,063)[166] and *Swembalt v. Latvia* (US$86,220).[167] Despite some evidence that cases involving an investor related to a FT500 entity paid reliably more for their counsel,[168] most tests could not identify a reliable pattern between investor type and cost of their counsel.[169]

Costs for respondents' PLC was somewhat similar to claimants' legal fees.[170] The average cost for state counsel (adjusted for inflation to 2011) was roughly US$4.1 million.[171] These

---

percentile was US$7,246,320. *See also supra* note 153; *see also* Figure 6.1 (visualizing quartile breakdowns in boxplot form). Using the BLS inflation-calculator, the nearly US$5 million average PLC had roughly the same buying power as US$5.7 million in June 2018.

[163] Commission and Moloo examined awards from 2011–2017. While recognizing ICSID arbitrations can contain non-ITA cases, they identified the average claimant cost was around US$6 million (US$3.6 million median) and 61% of cases involved claimant costs below US$5 million. Likewise, in analyzing UNCITRAL tribunals, they found that the average claimant costs were roughly US$6.1 million (median unavailable), and 72% of cases involved claimant costs under US$5 million. Commission & Moloo, *supra* note 15, at 187–88, 190.

[164] *Abaclat v. Argentina, supra* note 158, at 269. The original and inflation-adjusted amounts were the same. Investors' legal teams in *Abaclat* consisted of White & Case, Grimaldi e Associati and Pérez Alati, Grondona, Benites, and Arntsen & Martínez de Hoz. Using the BLS calculator, the figure equated to roughly US$30.4 million in June 2018.

[165] *Libananco v. Turkey, supra* note 21, at 182. The original and inflation-adjusted amounts were the same. The team representing the investors in *Libananco* consisted of Crowell & Moring and Lellos P. Demetriades Law Office. Using the BLS calculator, the figure equated to roughly US$27.1 million in June 2018.

[166] The original amount was US$31,093. *Grynberg v. Grenada, supra* note 159, at 45. RSM Production Company and Daniel L. Abrams represented investors in *Grynberg*.

[167] The original amount was US$66,012. Swembalt AB v. Republic of Lat., UNCITRAL, Award, 16 (Oct. 23, 2000), https://bit.ly/2vqtJsu (last visited Aug. 7, 2018).

[168] Comparing claimant PLC in cases with and without an FT500 investor (including a potential FT500-parent in the immediate corporate chain) using logged data identified a reliable mean difference (t (52) = −2.480; p = .02; r = .31; n = 54), with cases where at least one investor (or a parent) was an FT500 entity experienced reliably higher investor PLC than cases where no investor (or parent) was an FT500 entity. A test of medians likewise identified a meaningful pattern (U = 50.0; p = .01). Results failed to replicate when using a partial correlation to control for case length (r (50) = .18; p = .21).

[169] It was not possible to identify a link between investor type when comparing cases with individuals, corporations, or a combination thereof and mean investor PLC using logged data (F (2, 52) = 0.729; p = .47; r = .17; n = 55). A Kruskal-Wallis test of medians likewise failed to identify a pattern (χ^2 (2) = 3.975; p = .14; r = .26; n = 44) between investor type and claimant PLC. Likewise, a partial correlation, controlling for case length, failed to reveal a reliable relationship (r (51) = −.05; p = .70). As the sample was underpowered, caution is warranted, as the possibility of a reliable but latent effect cannot be excluded.

[170] Chapter 4 explores patterns of legal representation for investors and states, reflecting states in-house representation. Discrepancies in relative costs could be a function of variables such as: in-house counsel costing less, state procurement and competitive bidding process for legal services whereby states may be required to choose lower cost counsel, or potential price discrimination by counsel charging lower fees to states (as compared to investors).

[171] M = 4,123,366; SD = 5976146; n = 60. For states' PLC, using raw inflation-adjusted data (containing outliers), the 25th percentile was US$907,260, the median (50th percentile) was US$1,644,354, and the 75th percentile was US$4,562,928. *See also* Figure 6.1 (visualizing quartile breakdowns in boxplot form). Using the BLS inflation-calculator, this is roughly US$4.7 million in June 2018.

figures were, again, roughly similar to Commission and Moloo's analysis finding mean costs for respondents were around the US$4.5–5 million mark.[172]

Given broad deviations in PLC, the gap between investors' and respondents' costs was not necessarily meaningful. The most expensive respondent counsel was the team representing Turkey in *Libananco*, topping the tables at US$35,702,418;[173] and the next largest runner-up was *EDF v. Romania* at US$19,470,692.[174] In contrast, laying aside *Mohammad Ammar al-Bahloul v. Tajikistan*, where Tajikistan incurred no fees after failing to appear,[175] the lowest cost state counsel were in *Tembec v. United States* (US$102,743)[176] and *Link-Trading v. Moldova* (US$180,579).[177] All tests were unable to identify a reliable link between investor type and states' counsel cost.[178]

Multiple tests were unable to confirm PLC costs changed over time in a meaningful way.[179] The inability to detect an increase (or decrease) in PLC—for both investors

---

[172] The awards from 2011–2017 analyzed by Commission and Moloo, which were not adjusted for inflation, revealed that for ICSID cases (which theoretically may include non-ITA cases), the average respondent cost was around US$5.2 million (US$2.6 million median) and, for 65% of cases, respondent costs were below US$5 million. For UNCITRAL tribunals, the average respondent cost was around US$4.6 million (median unavailable) and 66% of cases involved respondent costs under US$5 million. Commission & Moloo, *supra* note 15, at 187–88, 190. Unfortunately, standard deviations and inflation-adjustments were not provided. Gaps between the data analyzed for this book, which inflation-adjusted to 2011 levels, and Commission and Moloo's data could be attributable to inflation-adjustments and broad standard deviations in party costs.

[173] The original and inflation-adjusted amounts were the same. Respondent's lawyers in *Libananco* were Freshfields and Cosar Avukatlik Burosu. *Libananco, supra* note 21, at 183. Using the BLS website, the figures equate to roughly US$39.7 million in June 2018.

[174] The original amount in the award was US$18,574,642. The team representing Romania was White & Case and Tuca Zbârcea & Asosiati. EDF v. Romania, *supra* note 132, at ¶ 321. Using the BLS website, the amounts equate to roughly US$21.7 million in June 2018.

[175] Mohammad Ammar al-Bahloul v. Republic of Taj., SCC Case No. V (064/2008), Final Award, 29 (June 8, 2010), https://bit.ly/2AOuS1Z (last visited Dec. 27, 2018).

[176] The costs of the Office of the Legal Advisor in the U.S. Department of State, which represented the U.S. in *Tembec*, were US$94,720.68. Tembec v. United States, *supra* note 140, at 2, 85.

[177] Mihail Buruiana represented Moldova in *Link-Trading*. Link-Trading Joint Stock Co. v. Republic of Mold., UNCITRAL, Award, 8, 29 (Apr. 18, 2002), https://bit.ly/2TiU3hU (last visited Dec. 27, 2018).

[178] First, tests could not identify a link between investor type (individual, corporations, or a combination thereof) and mean respondent PLC using winsorized data (F (2, 57) = 1.860; p = .17; r = .25; n = 60); a test of medians likewise failed to identify a meaningful pattern (χ^2 (2) = 2.264; p = .32; r = .21; n = 60). The non-significant results replicated using a partial correlation to control for case length (r (56) = .02; p = .89). Second, tests could not detect a reliable relationship comparing states' mean counsel cost for cases with and without an investor related to an FT500 entity (t (57) = 0.523; p = .60; r = .07; n = 59); a test of medians also failed to detect a meaningful relationship (U = 120.0; p = .33). Those non-significant results replicated when using a partial correlation to control case length (r (55) = −.15; p = .26) As the sample is underpowered and requires over 780 total awards to reliably identify potential latent effects, caution is warranted.

[179] A bivariate correlation failed to detect a linear relationship between year of award and claimant PLC (r (55) = .07; p = .64), respondent PLC (r (60) = .24; p = .06), or total PLC (r (51) = .01; p = .92). An ANOVA using logged data failed to detect a meaningful difference in total PLC over three different time periods (F (2, 48) = 0.017; p = .98; r = .03; n = 51); and follow-up tests failed to identify meaningful differences. A Kruskall-Wallis test of medians failed to find a statistically significant difference in PLC costs for claimants (χ^2 (2) = 2.170 p = .34; r = .20; n = 55), respondents (χ^2 (2) = 2.071; p = .36; r = .18; n = 60), and in for parties' combined legal costs (χ^2 (2) = 0.032; p = .98; r = .03; n = 51) over three generations of data. Finally, although

and respondents—over time even held true controlling for case length.[180] This is unsurprising as the typical combined PLC costs fluctuated over time, ranging from roughly US$8–10 million.[181]

As ever, inferences should be made carefully, as missing data from early cases means expanded data could change results. One might imagine that low PLC costs were omitted from final awards, as tribunals viewed the costs as negligible. Alternatively, a selection effect could pull in the other direction, where tribunals somewhat embarrassed about large counsel costs omitted the PLC information. Or, tribunals lacked or thought the information irrelevant, potentially making PLC randomly distributed. Firm conclusions about the impact of the missing data is, unfortunately, not possible; but the limitation must be acknowledged.

2. TCE: Tribunal and Administrative Costs

As a reminder, despite 160 awards with TCE decisions,[182] less than 40% of tribunals provided full fiscal details about their own costs and administrative expenses. Unlike PLC, cases with (and without) TCE were evenly dispersed over time.

The scale of TCE was different from PLC. Unlike PLC, average total TCE using 2011 inflation-adjusted raw data was under US$1 million—sitting comfortably around US$800,000,[183] translating into just under US$1 million in 2018 dollars.[184] These figures were similar to Commission and Moloo's analysis, finding tribunal and administration expenses in investment-related cases were regularly under US$1 million.[185] To reflect the distribution of tribunal costs and comparing its scale to other costs, Figure 6.1 offers

linear regressions exploring award year and case length was significantly linked with investors' PLC (F (2, 51) = 14.591; p < .001; R^2 = .35; n = 53) and states' PLC (F (2, 56) = 4.476; p = .02; R^2 = .14; n = 58), that was largely a function of the number of months required to complete a case. The year a tribunal rendered the award was a non-significant predictor of costs of both investors' (B = –.015; SE = .027; t = –0.562; p = .577) and states' (B = 222542; SE = 166231; t = 1.339; p = .19) PLC.

180 Partial correlations, controlling for case length, failed to detect a reliable link between award year and: (1) claimant PLC (r (51) = –.08; p = .58), (2) respondent PLC (r (56) = .18; p = .19), or (3) total PLC (r (47) = –.12; p = .43).

181 Using raw inflation-adjusted data, for G1 (through 2006), the mean total PLC was roughly US$7.6 million ($SD$ = 5392942; n = 5); for G2 (2006–2009), the mean was US$7.6 million ($SD$ = 4932990; n = 13), and for G3 (2009–2012), the mean was US$10.2 million ($SD$ = 12787383; n = 33). It should be recalled that the earliest G1 data was the most likely to be missing PLC data. *See* Chapter 4.

182 In eighty awards, the tribunal discussed TCE but reserved a TCE decision for a future phase. In the remaining thirty-two awards, tribunals failed to reference TCE in any manner.

183 M = 816,215; SD = 848742; n = 61. For total TCE using the raw inflation-adjusted data (containing outliers), the 25th percentile was US$326,566, the median (50th percentile) was US$602,208, and the 75th percentile was US$1,010,39. *See also* Figure 6.1 (reflecting quartile breakdowns in boxplot form).

184 Using the BLS website to adjust figures to June 2018, the previous mean equated to the same buying power of US$933,949.69 and the median of US$689,073.31.

185 For ICSID cases (possibly containing non-ITA cases) for the period analyzed, they identified average TCE costs of US$922,087 (US$876,816 median). For UNCITRAL tribunals, the average claimant cost was around US$6 million (US$3.6 million median), and 61% of cases involved claimant costs below US$5 million. Likewise, analyzing UNCITRAL tribunals, average TCE was under US$1 million (median unavailable). COMMISSION & MOLOO, *supra* note 15, at 188–89, 190–91.

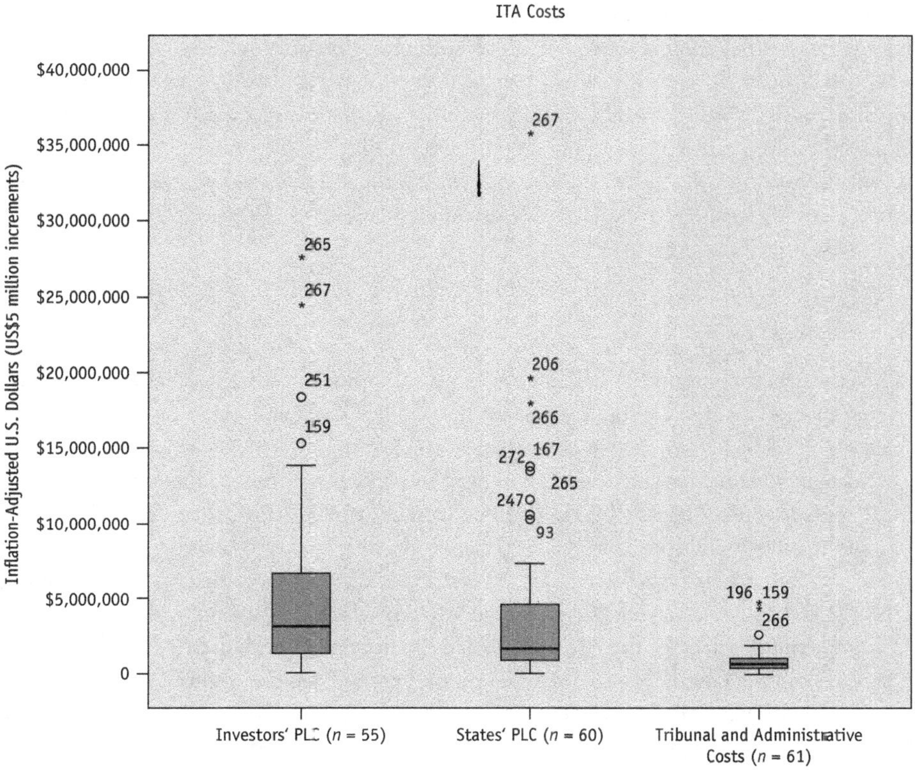

FIGURE 6.1 Side-by-Side Boxplots Reflecting Median and Quartile Distributions of Inflation-adjusted Raw ITA Costs, namely Investors' PLC ($n = 55$), States' PLC ($n = 60$), and TCE ($n = 61$).

side-by-side boxplots of investors' PLC, states' PLC, and TCE. The thick black central lines represent median costs; the shaded boxes represent the second and third quartiles; the lower black stem reflects the lowest quartile; the upper black stem reflects the upper quartile. Circles reflect statistical outliers and stars reflect the most extreme outliers.

The two lowest TCE totals were *Yury Bogdanov v. Moldova* and *Iurii Bogdanov v. Moldova*, with 2011 inflation-adjusted TCE totals of US$24,990[186] and US$35,805[187] respectively. By contrast, *Walter Bau v. Thailand* and *Victor Pey Casado v. Chile,* were the most expensive, with tribunals and institutional support totaling inflation-adjusted amounts of roughly US$4.6 million[188] and US$4.4 million[189] respectively.

[186] The original TCE was EUR18,000 (converted to US$24,232.85). Yury Bogdanov v. Republic of Mold., SCC Arb. No. V (114/2009), Award, 22 (Mar. 30, 2010), https://bit.ly/2mqlurE (last visited Aug. 7, 2018).

[187] The original TCE was EUR25,347 (converted to US$31,088). Iurii Bogdanov v. Republic of Mold., SCC Arb., Award, 20–21 (Sept. 22, 2005), https://bit.ly/2vAc5Ds (last visited Aug. 7, 2018).

[188] Walter Bau AG v. Kingdom of Tha., UNCITRAL, Award, 161–63 (July 1, 2009), 22 World Trade & Arb. Materials 681 (2010). As detailed in the Codebook (n.116), Appendix IV, *Walter Bau* was the only case requiring an single assumption to calculate costs. Although originally described in Euros, calculations suggested the original TCE was equivalent to US$4,372,270. If the tribunal was more precise about its own costs (as distinct from parties' costs) there would have been no need for any assumption or calculation.

[189] The original amount was US$4,182,524.45. *Victor Pey Casado, supra* note 11, at 234 n.658.

TCE was roughly similar to earlier research, finding average TCE totals around US$600,000.[190] Various tests failed to detect a reliable change in TCE over time.[191] The inability to detect an increase (or decrease) in TCE remained when controlling for case length.[192] Nevertheless, caution is warranted, as these tests cannot prove the absence of a relationship; rather they simply identify the inability to demonstrate a meaningful relationship over time. Definitive conclusions are improper; but as any potential latent effect was statistically small, over 781 final awards would be required to rule out the possibility of an increase in tribunal costs.

C. SYNTHESIS

While the data support aspects of some conventional wisdom, it disrupts other narratives that might generate cognitive ease but are nevertheless wrong. Like Goldilocks, some assertions were "too cold," while others are "too hot," and some were "just right."

Older claims about lawyers' fees, such as early UNCTAD commentary, about average PLC for states being approximately US$1–2 million were arguably too low; but this may be a function of the time-bound (pre-2006) data. Other claims were "too hot," including *Profiting from Injustice*'s reference to cases where PLC involved tens of millions of dollars.[193] Some recent UNCTAD data, copied by the EC (perhaps due to textual error),[194] did not withstand scrutiny.

Commentary, such as the OECD data estimating that each party spends roughly US$4 million for a total of roughly US$8 million per case, was "just right." Practitioner data was roughly similar.[195] It is noteworthy that, using different data and measurement tools but analyzing a similar temporal pool of data, OECD's findings were equivalent to these findings of parties spending roughly US$4–5 million each, for a grand total of lawyers' fees of around US$10 million.

TCE data supported conventional wisdom from earlier research and former ICSID officials. The historical baseline was roughly similar to newer analyses indicating a typical cost of an arbitral tribunal, and related institutional support was roughly US$600,000–800,000.

---

[190] *See* Franck, *supra* note 22, at 69 (but failing to adjust for inflation).

[191] A bivariate correlation failed to detect a linear relationship between award year and total TCE using logged data (r (61) = .12; p = .36). Similarly, an ANOVA using logged data failed to detect a meaningful difference in total TCE over three different time periods across the three generations of data (F (2, 58) = 1.026; p = .37; r = .19; n = 61); follow-up tests failed to identify meaningful differences among time periods. A Kruskall-Wallis test of medians also failed to find a statistically significant difference in TCE (χ^2 (2) = 1.321; p = .57; r = .15; n = 61) over the three generations of data. Finally, although a linear regression exploring case year and the number of months to complete the case was significantly linked with TCE (F (2, 57) = 16.357; $p < .001$; R^2 = .365), the year a tribunal rendered the award was a non-significant predictor of TCE (B = −.002; SE = .014; t = 0.161; p = .873).

[192] A partial correlation, controlling for case length, failed to detect a reliable link between the year of an award and total TCE (r (60) = −.02; p = .92).

[193] These claims may have reflected a micro-trend at the time, but as the caseload has evolved, it is possible that costs have increased. In any event, historical data provides context.

[194] *See supra* notes 15–16.

[195] *See supra* notes 15, 26–28 (discussing Hodgson, Commission, and Moloo's findings).

Although using data primarily from the commercial disputes (rather than ITA), the LCIA's data provides an intriguing counterpoint. Their recent analysis of their primarily commercial caseload indicated, for claims over US$100 million, average TCE was roughly US$323,000.[196]

The data disrupted conventional wisdom that legal costs were "skyrocketing" during the period analyzed. The analyses could never confirm a meaningful increase in ITA costs over time. It is possible that, rather than being accurate, the cognitive illusions facilitate the impressionistic gestalt that promulgates a narrative of increased costs. Those illusions might be facilitated by focusing on recent and negative cases. For example, recent news stories related to *Philip Morris v. Australia* have focused on legal fees that could be "up to $50 million."[197] Even use of a phrase "up to $50 million" could mean that the phrase "up to" is ignored and, instead the $50 million figure becomes an anchor that is difficult to ignore—or forget. Moreover, hearing these extreme and recent cases—particularly disputes piquing the interest of John Oliver[198] and entering the public domain in a humourous and sticky way—stakeholders might remember those extreme cases easily. This, in turn, can lead to a series of intuitive jumps, namely a presumption that ease of recall of a dispute leads to an inference that those cases occur frequently; and representativeness can then facilitate the feeling that the single case is representative of the larger whole. When combined with regular press references, an availability cascade can generate the intuitive, rather than data-driven, conclusion that large costs are typical, even if they are not.

Focusing on *Philip Morris*, without a larger context, prevents balanced consideration. One need only recall press headlines claiming plaintiffs' attorneys in the tobacco litigation from the 1990s obtained over US$8 billion in legal fees.[199] Even after some attorneys' set aside contingency fee arrangements, their fees decreased to a mere US$1.5 billion.[200] As Professor Deborah Rhode explained, "tobacco litigation is a stunning example of the inordinate health and legal costs . . . At last count, trial lawyers were set to pocket more than [US]$75 billion over the next quarter-century; some of these lawyers netted fees amounting to [US]$150,000 per hour."[201] This makes one wonder whether arguably excessive fees may be a complex matrix related to the specific dispute, the law applicable to the reasonableness of lawyers' fees, or the value in investing in thoroughly adjudicating matters involving sensitive public health issues.

Using another frame, the management of other transnational business conflicts, which are embedded with government regulation, can involve visually staggering figures. While it is not

[196] *See supra* notes 31–32.

[197] *See* LCIA, *supra* note 149, at 12–13 (noting that while average TCE costs were just under US$100,000, the amounts for claims in excess of US$100 million were around US$323,000, but failing to provide standard deviations or an indication of inflation-adjustments).

[198] John Oliver, *Tobacco: Last Week Tonight with John Oliver*, HBO (Feb. 15, 2017), https://bit.ly/1CznuMr (last visited Aug. 7, 2018) (discussing Philip Morris' ITA claims against Australia and Uruguay).

[199] Barry Meier, *Layers in Early Tobacco Suits to Get $8 Billion*, N.Y. TIMES (Dec. 12, 1998), https://nyti.ms/2uGab24 (last visited Aug. 7, 2018).

[200] Daniel J. Capra et al., *The Tobacco Litigation and Attorneys' Fees*, 67 FORDHAM L. REV. 2827, 2827 (1999).

[201] Deborah L. Rhode, *Frivolous Litigation and Civil Justice Reform: Miscasting the Problem, Recasting the Solution*, 54 DUKE L.J. 447, 470 (2004).

clear how representative the figures are, the popular press reported that fees for transnational investigations "quickly exceed $100 million—and that's before the lawsuits even begin;"[202] and Siemen's 2008 investigation of corrupt activities in Germany, China, and the United States "racked up 1.5 million billable hours" leading to legal fees costing Siemens "more than $1 billion."[203]

Framing costs against other ITA variables offers another context. PLC totals, for example, provide food for thought about costs and the value of ITA. Average costs of roughly US$11 million (roughly US$10 million for parties' combined PLC and US$1 million for total TCE) implicate the relative value of lawyers.[204] For PLC, this means when considering the average damages awarded for all cases (US$16.6m), lawyers' costs were 60% of the average award, and for the smaller subset of cases where investors obtained damages, the average PLC total was nearly 20% of the average amount awarded (US$45.6 million). In contrast, TCE was approximately 5% of overall amounts awarded (2% for those cases where investors obtained damages).[205] Although a nearly US$1 million paycheck for a tribunal is not insignificant, it is a different order of magnitude compared to lawyers' fees.

While there are ebbs and flows in adjudication—with average case length at 3.5 years—this suggests a potential rule of thumb that each party pursuing ITA spends roughly US$1.4 million per year for lawyers and US$100,000 on the tribunal. The net costs of ITA, the uncertainty of ultimate liability, and yearly expenditures, taken together, suggest untapped value in alternative dispute resolution or streamlining ITA to decrease time and costs.

There is an unattractive worst-case scenario for investors: not only will they have lost their investment, they will have lost any capacity to recoup their losses and pay for that privilege by potential costs liability around US$10 million. These negative fiscal consequences provide a deterrent to small and medium-sized enterprises and could create challenges for access to justice. Investors—particularly with the advent of third-party funding[206]—may be willing to

---

[202] Peter J. Henning, *The Mounting Costs of Internal Investigations*, N.Y. TIMES (Mar. 5, 2012), https://nyti.ms/2wH5TbA (last visited Aug. 30, 2018); *see also* Mary Shaddock Jones, *The High Costs of Non-compliance*, FCPACOMPLAINCEREPORT.COM (Nov. 13, 2012), https://bit.ly/2oA5O67 (detailing legal fees worth hundreds of millions of dollars for compliance with anticorruption laws in international business).

[203] Siri Schubert & T. Christian Miller, *At Siemens, Bribery Was Just a Line Item*, N.Y. TIMES (Dec. 20, 2008), https://nyti.ms/2CfJrN7 (last visited Aug. 30, 2018); David Gow, *Record US Fine Ends Siemens Bribery Scandal*, THE GUARDIAN (Dec. 15, 2008), https://bit.ly/2Cd8pfZ (last visited Aug. 30, 2018).

[204] Even adjusting medians to June 2018 values, the median cost for all lawyers and arbitrators was around US$6.85 million. *See supra* notes 154–155, 183–184.

[205] Using 100 nonpublic commercial arbitration awards analyzed by the ICC, Webster identified tribunal and administrative expenses in ICC commercial arbitration accounted for approximately 16–18% of arbitration-related costs. Webster, *supra* note 208, at 493–94, 513 (citing REPORT FROM THE ICC COMMISSION ON ARBITRATION, TECHNIQUES FOR CONTROLLING TIME AND COSTS IN ARBITRATION, ICC Pub. 843 (2007)). Although ITA tribunals facially cost nearly twice the amount of ICA tribunals, the lack of underlying data prevents analysis of whether the relative percentage of costs was meaningfully different; the facial distinction could reflect chance alone. There also could be variation in costs across institutions conducting ICA. *See* LCIA, *supra* note 149, at 19–21 (identifying cost variations among institutions).

[206] Only one award in the dataset—the consolidated cases of *Ron Fuchs v. Georgia* and *Ioannis Kardassopoulos v. Georgia*—mentioned third-party funding when making cost assessments and allocations. Increases in third-party funding and ICSID's proposal for disclosure of third-party funding (Chapter 9) could affect future costs.

take risks on ITA. By contrast, for states, the standard "worst-case-scenario" involves paying average damages of US$45 million plus US$10 million in legal fees. These figures may be substantial for developing states, particularly after currency conversions and relative to their gross domestic product or tax base.

As argued in Chapter 9, the fiscal reality suggests there is real value in exploring non-adjudicative methods of dispute resolution—such as negotiation and mediation—to contain costs and regain control over outcomes. Given concerns about state "policy space," regaining control through other dispute resolution processes seems sensible. Yet, if outsourcing dispute settlement to arbitrators provides states with commercial or domestic political cover,[207] the value of shifting blame onto another entity—rather than taking internal responsibility—may create value for states. In any event, stakeholders should be prepared for substantial legal costs along with the resulting uncertainty of ultimate liability for those costs.

IV. Baselines of Cost Allocation

There is wide speculation about the dominant pattern of ITA cost allocation. Some commentators suggest a "traditional" or "universal" approach to costs, without recognizing the three different normative "traditions." Some suggest that tribunals' dominant approach is to shift costs or that shifting is an "emerging trend"; others disagree and argue that costs have historically not been shifted. [208] This may, in part, be a function of the different doctrinal bases for cost-shifting decisions and reflect people intuitively believing their domestic legal standards or personal experiences are representative. While cost-shifting may be traditional in international commercial arbitration, public international law has a different tradition based upon state sovereign equality The quest for a normative baseline for costs in ITA mirrors ITA's identity crisis about whether its traditions should be dominated by either a public or private international law framework.

A growing literature considers the empirical reality of ITA cost-shifting. Earlier research identified the standard pattern in ITA is for parties to share costs, and while cost-shifting occurred, the pattern was not dominant.[209] Lucy Reed's analysis of 2004–2010 ICSID cases

---

[207] Todd L. Allee & Paul K. Huth, *Legitimizing Dispute Settlement: International Legal Rulings as Domestic Political Cover*, 100 AM. POL. SCI. REV. 219 (2006).

[208] AMERICAN LAW INSTITUTE, ALI/UNIDROIT PRINCIPLES OF TRANSNATIONAL CIVIL PROCEDURE 176 (2004); Franck, *supra* note 11, at 809–11; *supra* notes 74–76; *compare* Thomas H. Webster, *Efficiency in Investment Arbitration: Recent Decisions on Preliminary and Costs Issues*, 25 ARB. INT'L 469, 471, 473 (2009) (analyzing "59 ICSID and UNCITRAL awards rendered in the period between 2005 and 2009" and finding "in more than half the cases, tribunals have adopted the 'costs follow the event' principle . . . [and] that trend appears to be becoming dominant") *with* Lucy Reed, *Allocation of Costs in International Arbitration*, 26 ICSID REV. 76, 79 (2011) (reviewing "all available decisions on costs rendered by ICSID tribunals between January 2004 and January 2010" and concluding "in 43 out of 67 cases, or almost two-thirds of cases" tribunals used the pay-your-own-way approach).

[209] Franck, *supra* note 11.

identified that most cases did *not* use a loser-pays approach,[210] and Wendy Miles reached a similar conclusion.[211]

Others disagree.[212] Using data from 2008–2009,[213] Smith found that the pay-your-own-way baseline was becoming dominant. For the two years analyzed, Smith found that 41.9% of awards involved some degree of either a PLC or TCE shift[214] and posited there was an increasing preference for shifting costs.[215] Recognizing the narrowness of his dataset and need for replication, Smith cautiously noted the "shift is relatively small and may not be indicative of a longer-term trend, the percentage of awards which include some cost-shifting appears to have risen slightly—at least over the short term."[216]

Using the variant of cost-shifting, Schill argued, in ITA, there is a one-way cost-shifting operating *only* in favor of successful investors.[217] Two students writing articles set out to test Schill's theory. Using two years of data, Smith identified "victorious claims may have an easier time winning costs than victorious respondents."[218] In contrast, Riesenberg suggested a one-way fee-shifting approach in favor of investors was not dominant but argued any such approach was normatively unjustifiable given the ITA backlash.[219]

Presuming ITA is path-dependent—and existing baselines facilitate future behavior—it is critical to identify *what* that standard baseline has been for cost-shifting and identifying whether patterns were reliable (or reflected chance alone). This section considers cost assessment patterns, first offering information about how tribunals addressed PLC and TCE. Second, it provides descriptive information about cost allocation patterns to test conventional wisdom. Third, it considers the relative allocation of cost-shifting.

A. TO SHIFT OR NOT TO SHIFT: ASSESSING PLC AND TCE CHOICES

PLC and TCE are doctrinally and practically distinct. ITA tribunals need not—and often do not—address PLC and TCE decisions identically. Nevertheless, the question remains as to what divergences or congruity there may be for the two costs. The data revealed that, generally,

---

[210] Reed, *supra* note 208 (noting two-thirds all ICSID cases—including decisions, awards, and annulments—between 2004–2010 did not exhibit cost-shifting).

[211] Miles, *supra* note 76; *see also* Bondar, *supra* note 69 (reviewing "available studies" to come to similar conclusions about ITA regarding the lack of a consistent approach; failing to statistically test the claims, but suggesting there is variation in how ICSID and UNCITRAL tribunals address cost-shifting).

[212] *See* Vasani & Ugale, *supra* note 58, at 1 (suggesting some tribunals are "paving a trend" for cost-shifting but arguing such a "single harmonized approach" is inappropriate).

[213] Smith transparently explains he focused on two years, did not include non-final awards, and did not differentiate between PLC and TCE. Smith, *supra* note 23, at 753–54, appx. A.

[214] *Id.* at 753, 768.

[215] *See also* Manciaux, *supra* note 3, at 278, 280–84 (identifying 2011 data indicating tribunals increasingly used a loser-pays approach); Webster, *supra* note 208 (suggesting loser-pays has become dominant); Riesenberg, *supra* note 56 (intimating the loser-pays approach is dominant).

[216] Smith, *supra* note 23, at 753; *but see* Webster, *supra* note 208, at 472–73, 493–94.

[217] Schill, *supra* note 37; *see supra* notes 63–68 (describing potential unilateral variation of the loser-pays rule).

[218] Smith, *supra* note 23, at 756, 763–64.

[219] Riesenberg, *supra* note 23, at 989–95.

tribunals tended not to shift either PLC or TCE. While tribunals were somewhat more likely to shift smaller TCE-related sums, that slight preference was not statistically meaningful.[220]

1. PLC Assessments

Data failed to demonstrate that tribunals predominantly shifted PLC. Like earlier research, tribunals generally followed the pay-your-own-way paradigm, making parties responsible for their own legal fees and expenses. For those awards making PLC assessments, irrespective of award, 67.6% of tribunals (n = 109) made parties responsible for their own PLC and did not shift costs. For the remaining awards (32.3%), tribunals shifted costs; and there was an equal divide in which party was responsible for contributing. In 16.15% of awards (n = 26), respondents contributed to investors' PLC, and for the remaining 16.15% (n = 26), claimants paid some element of states' PLC. Figure 6.2 offers a frequency distribution, breaking out PLC determinations for both final and non-final awards.

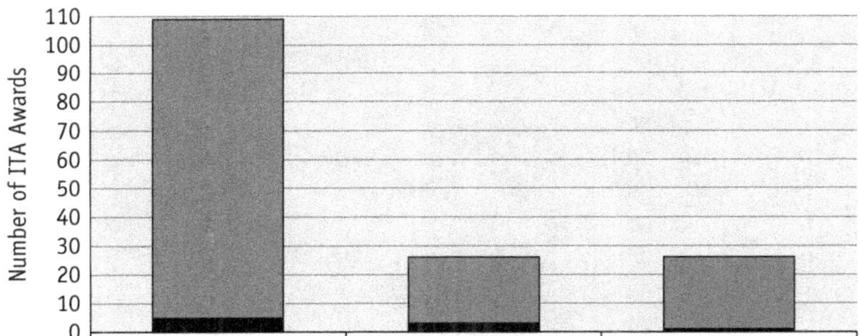

	No PLC Shift (*n* = 109)	Respondent must pay Claimant PLC (*n* = 26)	Claimant must pay Respondent PLC (*n* = 26)
Final Awards	104	23	25
Non-Final Awards	5	3	1

FIGURE 6.2 Frequency Distribution of PLC Allocations in All Awards (n = 161), including Non-final and Final Awards.

These figures contradict claims that cost-shifting was the dominant practice of PLC assessments. Award finality did not play a role, as both non-final and final awards were roughly in parity for PLC assessments.[221] The results provide initial evidence casting doubt on claims of "one-way" cost-shifting, as shifts were split equally between investors and states. Yet that facial pattern does not trace the variance linked to outcomes, which is discussed later

[220] When comparing PLC awards failing to shift (n = 109), and those that did shift costs (n = 52), and TCE awards with a 50/50 cost allocation (n = 98) and those that did shift costs (n = 58), it was not possible to detect any meaningful pattern (χ^2 (1) = 0.833 p = .36; r = .05; n = 317). Given non-significant results and less than statistically small effect size, there may be no latent difference between the patterns; but with low statistical power, ex ante power analysis suggests replication would require more than 781 cases.

[221] For the nine non-final awards, five awards did not shift costs, three shifted costs to the state, and one shifted costs to the investor. For the 152 final awards, 104 awards did not shift costs, twenty-three shifted costs to the state, and twenty-five shifted costs to the investor.

and provides considerable food for thought. Rather, the initial data support commentary (including by Reed and Miles) about the lack of cost-shifting as the more typical practice.

2. TCE Assessments

The data also failed to support the claim that most tribunals shifted TCE. Rather, tribunals predominantly followed the pay-your-own-way approach and parties shared equally in tribunal costs and administrative expenses.

For those awards allocating TCE obligations, parties shared TCE on an equal basis in 61.3% of awards (n = 98). In the remaining awards, tribunals shifted costs and did so on a roughly equivalent basis. In 18.1% of the awards (n = 29), states experienced a cost shift and paid some element of the investors' TCE. For the remaining 20.6% (n = 33), investors were required to contribute to the state's TCE. *See* Figure 6.3 offers a frequency distribution, breaking out TCE determinations for both final and non-final awards.

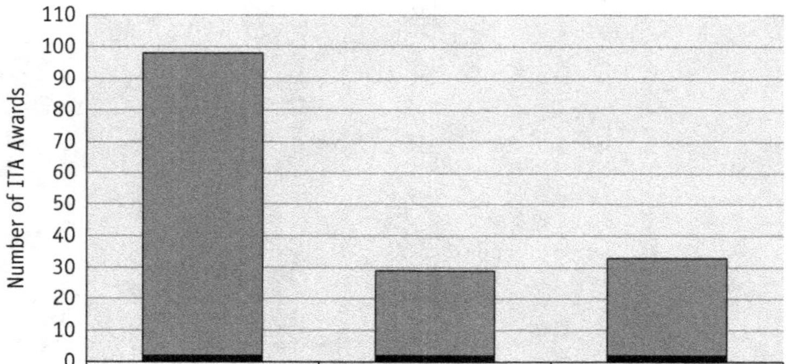

	No TCE Shift (n = 98)	TCE Shifted to Respondent (n = 29)	TCE Shifted to Claimant (n = 33)
Final Awards	96	27	31
Non-Final Awards	2	2	2

FIGURE 6.3 Frequency Distribution of TCE Allocations in All Awards (n = 160), including Non-final and Final Awards.

Although tribunals appeared slightly more likely to shift TCE amounts than PLC, there was no indication that these small variations were statistically meaningful or different from chance alone. The data nevertheless contradicted claims that cost-shifting was the dominant method of TCE assessment, and award finality did not impact the assessments.[222] The facial data also suggested that "one-way" cost-shifting was not a dominant method, as TCE shifts occurred in roughly equivalent patterns for investors and states.

[222] For six non-final awards, two awards did not shift TCE, two made the state pay more than 50% of TCE, and two made the investor pay more than 50% of TCE. For the 159 final awards, ninety-six awards did not shift TCE, twenty-seven awards made the state pay more than 50% of TCE, and thirty-one awards made the investor pay more than 50% of TCE.

B. NET COST ALLOCATIONS AND OUTCOMES

Rather than focusing on PLC and TCE allocations generally, to provide another frame, it is useful to consider the case as a whole. Overall, nearly 60% of ITA awards followed the "pay-your-own-way" approach and required equal fee allocation (57.4%; $n = 93$). For the remainder, tribunals shifted costs to investors (20.4%; $n = 33$) and states (22.2%; $n = 36$) in roughly equivalent proportions.[223]

The way tribunals used cost tools, however, exhibited broad variation. Tribunals used multiple methods for cost allocation, creating unusual combinations to generate a diffuse set of approaches. Theoretically, there were eight different ways for tribunals to shift costs; and seven were used, albeit in different proportions. For tribunals shifting costs, the most common allocations involved either a shift of *both* PLC and TCE to either the investor or the state. These assessments—shifting multiple costs simultaneously—happened in roughly equivalent levels. *See* Table 6.2.

TABLE 6.2

Awards Making Cost Determinations on PLC and TCE as a Function of Case Status ($n = 161$).

Cost Decisions	*Number (%) of Awards*	Case Status[224]
No PLC Shift and TCE Shared Equally	93 (57.8%)	Claimant Wins = 25 Respondent Wins = 55 Settled / Discontinued = 10[225] Non-final awards = 3[226]

(Continued)

[223] These figures contained 162 observations, as the *Eastern Sugar* case generated two cost-shifting awards only months apart, shifting PLC against the state and TCE against the claimant. Eastern Sugar B.V. v. Czech Republic, SCC Case No. 088/2004, Partial Award, 71 (Mar. 27, 2007), https://bit.ly/2Rs7aQA (last visited Dec. 27, 2018); Final Award, 2–3 (Apr. 12, 2007), https://bit.ly/2LFLsDl (last visited Dec. 27, 2018).

[224] This subsection defines investor "wins" as in Chapter 5 (i.e., an award or other agreement to pay damages over US$0).

[225] This includes: Terminal Forest Prods. Ltd. v. United States, UNCITRAL, Joint Order on Costs and Termination (July 19, 2007), https://bit.ly/2QWTqcq (last visited Dec. 27, 2018) (termination); Canfor Corp. v. United States, UNCITRAL, Joint Order on Costs and Termination (July 19, 2007), https://bit.ly/2QWTqoq (last visited Dec. 27, 2018) (termination); Trans-Global Petroleum, Inc., v. Hashemite Kingdom of Jordan, ICSID Case No. ARB/07/25, Consent Award (Apr. 8, 2009), https://bit.ly/2GNLH04 (last visited Dec. 27, 2018) (consent award); TCW Group, Inc. v. Dominican Rep., UNCITRAL, Consent Award (July 16, 2009), https://bit.ly/2GIQn7u (last visited Dec. 27, 2017) (consent award); EVN AG v. Republic of Maced., ICSID Case No, ARB/09/10, Award (Sept. 2, 2011), 24 World Trade & Arb. Materials 139 (2012) (settlement); Joseph Lemire v. Ukraine [I], ICSID Case No. ARB/06/18, Award (Sept. 18, 2000), 15 ICSID Rev.- Foreign Inv. L.J. 528 (2000) (settlement); Vattenfall AB v. Federal Republic of Germ., ICSID Case No. ARB/09/6, Award (Mar. 11, 2011), https://bit.ly/2EVjHG7 (last visited Dec. 27, 2017) (settlement); Goetz v. Burundi [I], ICSID Case No. ARB/95/3, Award (Feb. 10, 1999), https://bit.ly/2uOtLYt (last visited Dec. 27, 2018) (settlement); Rail World LLC v. Republic of Est., ICSID Case No. ARB/06/6, Order of the Tribunal (Feb. 5, 2007), https://bit.ly/2rWownc (last visited Dec. 27, 2018) (discontinuance); Impreglio S.p.A. v. Islamic Republic of Pak., ICSID Case No. ARB/03/3, Order of Discontinuance of the Proceeding (Sept. 25, 2005), https://bit.ly/2QSoYBL (last visited Dec. 27, 2018) (discontinuance where tribunal indicated TCE was equally shared but failing to mention PLC).

[226] This includes non-final awards: Abaclat v. Argentina, *supra* note 158, (jurisdiction); Sergei Paushok v. Government of Mong., UNCITRAL, Award on Jurisdiction and Liability (Apr. 8, 2011), https://bit.ly/2GVHJCy (last visited Dec. 27, 2018) (jurisdiction and merits); United Parcel Serv. v. Government of Can.,

TABLE 6.2

(Continued)

Cost Decisions	*Number (%) of Awards*	Case Status[224]
Claimant Pays PLC Shift and more than 50% of TCE	25 (15.5%)	Respondent wins = 20[227] Settlement/Discontinuance = 4[228] Non-final awards = 1[229]
Respondent Pays PLC Shift and more than 50% of TCE	20 (12.4%)	Claimant wins = 18[230] Non-final awards = 2[231]
No PLC Shift, but Claimant pays more than 50% of TCE	6 (3.7%)[232]	Respondent wins = 6

UNCITRAL, Award on Jurisdiction (Nov. 22, 2002), https://bit.ly/2CDQZXU (last visited Dec. 27, 2018) (jurisdiction).

[227] This includes *Nova Scotia Power*. Nova Scotia Power, Inc. v. Bolivarian Republic of Venez., UNCITRAL, Award on Costs (Aug. 30, 2010), https://bit.ly/2SqSwGh (last visited Dec. 27, 2018). The *Nova Scotia* merits award was rendered four months earlier; it involved a respondent win (US$0 awarded), and reserved all PLC and TCE for future consideration. It was omitted from Table 6.2.

[228] This includes: (1) Quadrant Pacific Growth Fund L.P. v. Republic of Costa Rica, ICSID Case No. ARB(AF)/08/1, Order of the Tribunal and Allocation of Costs (Oct. 27, 2010), https://bit.ly/2QXooHh (last visited Dec. 27, 2018) (discontinuance); (2) Piero Foresti v. Republic of S. Afr., ICSID Case No. ARB(AF)/07/01, Award, (Aug. 4, 2010), https://bit.ly/2EWJOMi (last visited Dec. 27, 2018) (discontinuance and award); (3) Melvin J. Howard v. Governemnt of Can., UNCITRAL, PCA Case No. 2009-21, Correction of Order for the Termination of Proceedings and Award on Costs (Aug. 9, 2010) (termination order), https://bit.ly/2EYAkQi (last visited Dec. 27, 2018); and (4) Tembec Inc. v. United States, UNCITRAL, Joint Order on Costs and Termination (July 19, 2007), https://bit.ly/2QWTq0q (last visited Dec. 27, 2018) (costs). Tembec v. United States, UNCITRAL, Order for Termination with Respect to Tembec (Jan. 10, 2006), https://bit.ly/2EWNrm3 (last visited Dec. 27, 2018) (termination order reserving PLC and TCE for future consideration), was omitted from Table 6.2.

[229] This includes *Ethyl*. Ethyl Corp. v. Government of Can., UNCITRAL, Award on Jurisdiction (June 24, 1998), https://bit.ly/2VbfAKW (last visited Dec. 27, 2018).

[230] *Wena Hotels v. Egypt* was coded as only involving a PLC decision in an award with a claimant win, but is referred to here as a case involving both PLC and TCE decisions for the sake of convenience. *Walter Bau v. Thailand* was placed in this category despite the tribunal's bizarre approach to costs; for PLC, the tribunal required each party to contribute to the others' legal costs, but the net result left Thailand contributing to the investor; the tribunal also ordered Thailand to contribute fractionally more to TCE. *Walter Bau, supra* note 188, at 162–63. This also includes *S.D. Myers*. S.D. Myers, Inc. v. Government of Can., UNCITRAL, Final Award, 19 (Dec. 30, 2002), https://bit.ly/2LErZTk (last visited Dec. 27, 2018) (decided on the merits and involving an investor win of US$3,844,443). The award reserved PLC and TCE for future consideration and was omitted from Table 6.2.

[231] This included the August 2005 partial award in *Eureko v. Poland*, which held the respondent breached the treaty but was non-final given the failure to specify the scope of loss, and the 2001 partial award in *CME v. Czech Republic*, which addressed jurisdiction and merits. The final award in *CME* addressed costs but failed to shift either PLC or TCE and is included in Table 6.2. CME Czech Republic B.V. v. Czech Republic, UNCITRAL, Final Award, 161 (Mar. 14, 2003), 42 I.L.M. 919, 971 (2003).

[232] *HICEE v. Slovak Republic* had two awards addressing costs. As one award omitted a PLC analysis, but the TCE analyses consistently shifted in the same manner, the net cost-shifting result codes only the first award.

TABLE 6.2

(Continued)

Cost Decisions	*Number (%) of Awards*	Case Status[224]
No PLC Shift, but Respondent pays more than 50% of TCE	10 (6.2%)	Claimant wins = 9[233] Respondent wins = 1
Claimant Pays PLC Shift and TCE shared Equally	1 (0.6%)	Respondent wins = 1
Respondent Pays PLC Shift and TCE shared Equally	5 (3.1%)	Claimant wins = 4 Respondent wins = 1
Respondent experiences PLC shift and Claimant experiences TCE Shift	1 (0.6%)	Claimant wins = 1[234]
Claimant experiences PLC Shift and Respondent experiences TCE Shift	0 (0.0%)	Not Applicable

While contradicting conventional wisdom, the results offer insights for costs and outcomes. First, the loser-pays paradigm was not the dominant model in ITA.[235] Second, the data contradict the narrative of an "emerging trend" toward a reliable implementation of a loser-pays model. Earlier research identifying that roughly 63.5% of awards failed to shift costs[236] was not much different from data here reflecting 58% of tribunals did not shift costs. The 5–6% variation was small, and not statistically meaningful, and could reflect chance alone.[237] The failure to identify a reliable effect likely reflects that, despite a near tripling of the awards analyzed, the proportion of awards *not* shifting costs was relatively stable over

[233] This included the *Pope & Talbot v. Canada* costs award. The *Pope & Talbot* merits award was rendered six months earlier, involved an investor win (US$407,646 awarded), and reserved PLC and TCE for future consideration; it was omitted from Table 2. Pope & Talbot, Inc. v. Government of Can., UNCITRAL, Award in Respect of Damages, 41 (May 31, 2002), 41 I.L.M. 1347, 1362 (2002).

[234] In *Eastern Sugar*, two separate awards addressed costs fully. *See supra* note 223. For net-cost shifting, the two awards were analyzed together.

[235] The ITA experience may not reflect practice in international commercial arbitration. *See* Webster, *supra* note 206, at 493–94; *see also* Bondar, *supra* note 69, at 50, 53; Philippe Cavalieros, *In-House Counsel Costs and Other Internal Party Costs in International Commercial Arbitration*, 30 ARB. INT'L 145 (2014).

[236] Franck, *supra* note 11, at 810 (noting thirty-three of fifty-two awards shared PLC and TCE equally).

[237] When comparing the oldest (G1) with the combined newest (G2–G3) data, it was not possible to detect a meaningful change over time for proportions of tribunals following the pay-your-own-way or loser-pays norms (χ^2 (1) = 1.021; p = .31; r = .08; n = 161). Likewise, a regression was unable to reliably predict either the year of the request for arbitration (F (2, 136) = 0.552; p = .58; R^2 = .01) or the award year (F (2, 136) = 2.920; p = .06; R^2 = .04) using two dummy variables to explore variance in whether: (1) an investor or state won the dispute and (2) there was any shift of some ITA cost (whether PLC or TCE) or no cost-shifting or all. Given miniscule effect sizes, analyses were technically underpowered requiring replication.

time. And while time has marched on since the historical snapshot offered, it nevertheless creates a baseline for consideration, particularly as the promulgation of a "loser pays" approach is part of the debate about ITA reform at ICSID and the European Union.[238]

The results demonstrated, when tribunals shifted costs, they did so for the benefit of both investors and states. While this might initially suggest worries that one-way cost-shifting benefitting investors are overstated, that assessment is premature. There is more to the story.

Second, a statistical test identified a reliable relationship between outcomes and overall cost assessments that—*for the first time*—did reflect a one-way loser-pays rule that reliably operated to investors' benefit—rather than to the benefit of states or operating in a neutral way.[239] Table 6.3 provides outcomes and cost assessments reflecting the significant pattern, which exhibited a small to medium-sized effect.

TABLE 6.3

Cost Decisions for PLC and TCE as a Function of Case Outcome (either a claimant or respondent win).

Case Outcome	*No Shift of PLC or TCE*	*Cost Shifted for Either PLC or TCE*	*Total*
Claimant Wins	43.86% (n = 25)	56.14% (n = 32)	100% (n = 57)
Respondent Wins	65.48% (n = 55)	34.52% (n = 29)	100% (n = 84)
Total	*80*	*61*	*141*

Unlike earlier analysis finding insufficient data to support the one-way cost-shifting theory,[240] the detectable and significant pattern was that tribunals did not treat parties' success equally. Tribunals demonstrated a propensity to shift costs for winning *investors*; the same was *not* true for *winning states*. Rather, when states won, tribunals tended to follow the pay-your-own-way approach. The pattern was: for each case an investor won, tribunals were roughly as inclined to use either the loser-pays or pay-your-own-way approach to assess costs. In contrast, for state wins, tribunals were twice as likely to use the pay-your-own-way approach. Including settlements and discontinuances did not change matters.[241] In other words, the link between outcomes and cost-shifting—with a preference for shifting costs for winning investors—was robust.

Although the door of de jure cost-shifting theoretically swings both ways, the door swung de facto more comfortably toward winning investors. Having identified data confirmed

[238] *See generally* Kate Brown de Vejar & Chloe Baldwin, *The Economics of Access: Systemic Imbalances in ISDS, in* ICCA Congress Proceedings (forthcoming) (arguing for implementing the loser-pays approach); Jones, *supra* note 5 (suggesting ICSID revise its rules by "keeping costs in the discretion of the tribunal but with extra criteria that should be considered including the outcome of the proceeding and conduct of the parties"); *see also* European Parliament, *supra* note 15, at 20 (discussing a possible multilateral investment court and noting three recent European treaties "establish the 'loser pays all' principle"); Chapter 9.

[239] χ^2 (1) = 6.464; p = .01; r = .23; n = 141.

[240] Franck, *supra* note 11, at 826–27, 831–32.

[241] When comparing cost-shifting in cases where investors won against cases involving state wins or settlements with no cost shifts (n = 65), and state wins or settlements involving any cost shifts (n = 33), the pattern

Schill and Smith's theory about a one-way cost-shifting baseline—and identifying initial assessments from earlier research were no longer supported—the question becomes whether the result is normatively desirable. This issue is poignant as, in two cases, states were not found liable but tribunals required those winning states to pay costs. While those cases—*Al-Bahoul v. Tajikistan* and *Encana v. Ecuador*[242]—may be outliers confined to their peculiar facts, there is a reasonable basis to ask whether the propensity to shift fiscal responsibility to states is appropriate. As Chapter 9 argues in greater detail, with states having a monopoly on drafting treaty provisions, they could become more proactive in addressing costs given the statistical evidence. For example, states may wish to choose fixed cost-shifting in advance, expressly forbid one-way cost-shifting in favor of investors,[243] or even require one-way cost-shifting in favor of the state.

Finally, most awards (85%) treated PLC and TCE similarly. Yet, PLC and TCE are doctrinally and fiscally distinct, and the costs could be allocated differently depending on states' policy objectives when negotiating treaties and tribunals' approach to delegated discretion. In a vacuum where states have not provided a clear treaty mandate, tribunals could allocate TCE equally to follow a pay-as-you-go model to prevent imbalance in adjudicator costs but promote a factor-dependent approach to PLC if they wanted to strongly incentivize behaviors—including proper conduct during proceedings or encouraging party settlement. Given the doctrinal distinction and the utility of signaling different payoff matrices, it is surprising that tribunals have not generally made more distinctions between cost elements. Nevertheless, tribunals using a broad brush to address PLC and TCE replicates the extreme co-linearity between PLC and TCE in earlier research.[244] The lesson is: although separating costs is theoretically useful, as a practical matter, it is underutilized.

Ultimately, data suggest three critical takeaways. First, the pay-your-own way remained dominant in ITA, and where tribunals diverged from that baseline to shift costs, there was

---

remained significant (χ^2 (1) = 7.47; p = .01; r = .22; n = 155). When comparing cost-shifting experiences in cases where states won against the group of combined cases involving investor wins or settlements with no cost shifts (n = 35), and investor wins or settlements involving cost shifts (n = 36), the pattern was again significant (χ^2 (1) = 4.137; p = .04; r = .16; n = 155).

[242] In *Al-Bahloul*, despite repeated tribunal requests to be involved, Tajikistan never appeared and incurred no PLC. *Al-Bahloul*, *supra* note 175, at 31–32. By contrast, the investor was successful at jurisdiction and incurred moderate PLC amounts. Mohammad Ammar Al-Bahloul v. Republic of Taj., SCC Case No. V (064/2008), Partial Award on Jurisdiction and Liability, 96–97 (Sept. 2, 2009), https://bit.ly/2s2kKM5 (last visited Dec. 27, 2018). *EnCana* rejected jurisdiction but expressed concern about the nature of Ecuador's conduct and the merits of the underlying claim. EnCana Corp. v. Republic of Ecuador, LCIA Case No. UN3481, Partial Award on Jurisdiction, 18 (Feb. 27, 2004), https://bit.ly/2Q85Qxj (last visited Dec. 27, 2018).

[243] One-way cost-shifting in favor of investors could be normatively appropriate for customary international law. Case Concerning the Factory at Chorzów (Ger. v. Pol.), 1927 P.C.I.J. (ser. A) No. 9 (July 26); Int'l Law. Comm'n, *Draft Articles on Responsibility of States for Internationally Wrongful Acts*, art. 31(1), U.N. Doc. A/56/10 (Nov. 2001), https://bit.ly/1MIyM9V (last visited Aug. 7, 2018); Gotanda, *supra* note 21, at 434; *see also* Guaracachi America Inc. v. Plurinational State of Bolivia, UNCITRAL PCA Case No. 2011-17, Dissent of Co-Arbitrator Manuel Conthe, ¶ 16 (Jan 31, 2014), https://bit.ly/2wHdoj3 (last visited Aug. 7, 2018). Although it generates fragmentation in international law, states vary custom through the *lex specialis* of treaties. Krista N. Schefer, International Investment Law 191 (2013); M. Sornarajah, The International Law on Foreign Investment 175–77 (2010); Stephan W. Schill, International Investment Law and Comparative Public Law 362–63 (2010).

[244] Franck, *supra* note 11, at 832–34.

variance in how tribunals approached cost-shifting. Cognitive illusions, including recency bias, may affect the conversation. Simply because there was one case that occurred in a temporally proximate time frame does not mean the recent case is a representative example; rather it may simply be recent, and other examples may be more typical of systemic tendencies. Moreover, when commentators focus upon a new "trend" in an effort to be newsworthy, different, or in an honest belief that limited examples may reflect something new, this can facilitate an availability cascade. Persistent conversation or media reporting about new "trends" may not reflect reality any better than statistical noise. Yet, to the extent the information is available, cognitive illusions can trick stakeholders into easily recalling the information, presuming it is true, failing to fact-check the assessment, and making errors about what reality is. Confirmation bias could compound those influences and generate cognitive ease whereby stakeholders seek out data confirming existing assessments. In that vein, to the extent there is a time lag between today and data analyzed, one might acknowledge the possibility that data has evolved; but to avoid the risk of error of cognitive illusions, stakeholders should absorb the statistical base rate information to redress potential error.

Second, tribunals could have made clear demarcations between PLC and TCE to send distinct signals. They failed to do so, however. The "in for a penny, in for a pound" approach meant tribunals missed an opportunity to incentivize behavior and make subtle cost decisions.

Third, there was a reliable pattern between outcomes and costs, but states and investors were not equal de facto beneficiaries of the same de jure dispute settlement process. Rather, when cost-shifting occurred, successful investors were more likely than successful states to benefit. While not every case exhibited such a "one-way" cost shift, the results bear watching and justify some remedial action. States, particularly those interested in redressing perceived "pro-investor bias," should give serious consideration to establishing baselines as to cost allocations, such as requiring a "pay-as-you-go" approach so that neither claimants nor respondents are advantaged, creating more guided tribunal discretion with mandates on cost allocation, or perhaps even instituting a one-way cost-shifting rule in favor of states.

C. COST-SHIFTING: PROPORTIONS, FISCAL VALUES, AND OUTCOMES

Despite the fiscal impact, little empirical literature focuses on cost-shifting. This section initially explores the percentage allocation of ITA costs (for PLC and TCE) and changes over time. It then considers the fiscal value of shifts and potential temporal shifts.

1. Percentage of Allocation: PLC and TCE

Some commentators historically suggested that, when tribunals shifted costs, they shifted approximately one-third of PLC.[245] Earlier research could not confirm that baseline, instead identifying a broad range of PLC shifts. For TCE, the dominant approach was a 50/50 allocation. It was rare for a tribunal to make a 100% cost shift. Where there was a 100% TCE shift, those awards were split equally in favor of cases won by investors and respondents.[246] The question is whether the pervious baseline persisted.

---

[245] Wetter & Priem, *supra* note 70, at 292–93.

[246] Franck, *supra* note 11, at 813–16.

While percentages of PLC and TCE shifts continued to vary, there were some patterns. For cases with PLC available to analyze, when tribunals shifted PLC, they shifted an average of 63.5%.[247] There was a cluster of awards shifting roughly one-third to one-half of a party's PLC, but the most frequent allocation was a 100% shift. Those findings mirrored research indicating that tribunals tended to shift an average of 60% of a party's costs but roughly one-third of cases provided a 100% PLC shift.[248] Given the stability, it is unsurprising that tests were unable to determine that PLC proportional shifts changed over time.[249]

For TCE, most awards provided a 50/50 cost-sharing, consistent with the pay-your-own-way approach. Both means and medians of average TCE responsibility for investors hovered at 50%.[250] There were, however, two variations. One cluster contained a 0/100 shift in favor of the investor, and another group clustered in a cost shift of 100/0 shift in favor of the state. In other words, there was a degree of balance in responsibility for tribunal cost. *See* Table 6.4.

TABLE 6.4

Percentages of Cost-shifting for PLC and TCE for all Awards ($n = 272$).

Cost Issue	*Frequency of Awards*	*Valid Percent of Awards with Available Data*
Percentage of PLC Shift ($n = 43$)[251]		
2.0%	1	2.3%
4.0%	1	2.3%
11.1%	1	2.3%
13.4%	1	2.3%
13.5%	1	2.3%
14.0%	1	2.3%
15.4%	1	2.3%
23.9%	1	2.3%
25.0%	1	2.3%
32.0%	2	4.7%

(*Continued*)

[247] $SD = 34.70$; $n = 43$. Similarly, the median shift was 60%.

[248] Franck, *supra* note 11, at 813–14.

[249] An ANOVA analyzed mean differences in PLC percentage over three generations of data. The mean PLC shift in G1 data was 55.3%, 57.6% in G2 data, and 70% in G3 data. Despite a facial increase in G3, the difference was non-significant ($F(2, 40) = 0.811$; $p = .45$; $r = .20$; $n = 43$). HSD follow-up tests failed to find latent meaningful group differences. Similarly, it was not possible to identify a linear relationship between PLC shifts and the year the investors filed the case ($r(43) = -.03$; $p = .85$) or award year ($r(43) = .19$; $p = .21$). Given that the sample was small, future research with expanded data could detect a latent shift, and firm conclusions are unwarranted.

[250] $M = 53.12$; $SD = 24.82$; $n = 153$. The median cost responsibility for investors was 50%.

[251] Data was unavailable in 229 awards because: tribunals did not shift PLC in 109 awards, tribunals made no substantive assessment of PLC in 111 awards, and nine awards failed to provide sufficient information to calculate PLC shift percentages.

TABLE 6.4

(Continued)

Cost Issue	*Frequency of Awards*	*Valid Percent of Awards with Available Data*
40.0%	2	4.7%
42.0%	1	2.3%
50.0%	4	9.3%
52.0%	1	2.3%
54.0%	1	2.3%
56.6%	1	2.3%
60.0%	1	2.3%
70.0%	1	2.3%
75.0%	2	4.7%
83.0%	1	2.3%
98.0%	1	2.3%
99.0%	1	2.3%
100%	15	34.9%
Percentage of Claimant Responsibility for TCE (n = 153)[252]		
0%	12	7.8%
25%	3	1.9%
27%	1	0.7%
30%	2	1.3%
33%	2	1.3%
35%	1	0.7%
40%	1	0.7%
42%	1	0.7%
45%	1	0.7%
49%	1	0.7%
50%	98	64.1%
60%	2	1.3%
67%	2	1.3%
70%	1	0.7%
75%	1	0.7%
90%	1	0.7%
100%	23	15.0%

[252] The data reflects the claimant percentage of responsibility; the respondent percentage is the reverse (100% – Claimant%). Data was unavailable in 119 awards because: tribunals made no substantive assessment of TCE in 112 awards, and it was not possible to calculate TCE proportions in seven awards.

TCE allocations were also relatively stable. Earlier research indicated that 68% of cases did not involve TCE shifts, and only 8% of parties obtained a complete TCE shift. Although the dataset nearly tripled in size, the small shift (only 4%) away from the pay-your-own-way approach was minor. The more noteworthy aspect was that the proportion of cases where the *claimant* was 100% responsible for TCE doubled. Given the stability of TCE allocations, it was not possible to identify a meaningful change in TCE allocation over time.[253] *See* Table 6.5.

TABLE 6.5

Mean Percentage of TCE Allocations in Cases over Time across Generations of Data.

	Claimant's TCE	*Respondent's TCE*	*Total*
Generation 1 (until June 1, 2006)	50.38%	47.64%	50
Generation 2 (June 1, 2006–June 1, 2009)	51.96%	48.04	46
Generation 3 (June 1, 2009–January 1, 2012)	56.47%	43.53	57
Total	53.12	46.23	153

The data exhibited some variation. The primary pattern was roughly equivalent "splitting" of ITA, with one party obtaining a roughly 60% PLC shift and sharing TCE equally. The minority pattern reflected an "all or nothing" model. Despite claims that the arguably micro-trend is "growing" or "dominant," tests could not confirm a reliable new trend. This creates the possibility that perceived ebbs and flows in the treatment of cost shifts could reflect chance alone, and commentators' desire to impose a rational order upon randomness could simply reflect cognitive predispositions to see patterns confirming one's existing theories, or otherwise reflect a recent case, easily retrievable information, or a paradigm providing cognitive ease. While data may continue to evolve, cognitive illusions may be affecting assessments of perceived "new" trends in PLC shifts or TCE allocation. Rather than relying on statistical base rate information about a historical norm, cognitive illusions—including availability, recency, negativity, and representativeness—can influence perceived reality. Confirmation bias could also facilitate a self-referential process through which the *belief* in the truth of an

[253] The mean percentage of TCE shifts to claimants in G1 was 50.38%, 51.96% in G2 data, and 56.47% in G3 data. Despite slight facial shifts, an ANOVA was unable to identify that the shifts in TCE over time were statistically meaningful (F (2, 150) = 0.874; p = .42; r = .10; n = 153); and follow-up tests failed to find any reliable latent differences. Similarly, it was not possible to identify a linear relationship between TCE and either the year investors filed the arbitration (r (153) = .12; p = .14) or award year (r (153) = .11; p = .19). Given the sample size, future research involving a larger sample could detect a latent shift, and firm conclusions are unwarranted. Replication requires a sample of 1,172 awards before making a definitive assessment.

assertion leads to enquiries reflecting that desire. As data revealed the updated baseline was not reliably different, extreme positions about ITA cost allocations are unwarranted. As the caseload grows, however, being vigilant about potential variations in cost patterns is prudent.

2. Fiscal Shifts of PLC and TCE

Proportions are one way to appreciate cost shifts. Yet, they hide the fiscal magnitude. As PLC and TCE are nontrivial, this section explores costs using dollar values and assesses changes over time.

a. PLC Shifts Generally

The available data offer a sense of the larger picture of typical PLC shifts as a whole. The average PLC shift was roughly US\$2.5 million.[254] The smallest PLC shifts—all under US\$30,0000—were in *Howard v. Canada* (case discontinued),[255] *Link-Trading v. Moldova* (Moldova prevailed),[256] and *Swembalt v. Latvia* (investor won).[257] In contrast, the three largest PLC shifts were over US\$8 million and occurred in *Spyridon Roussalis v. Romania* (Romania prevailed),[258] *ADC v. Hungary* (investor won),[259] and *Libananco v. Turkey* (Turkey prevailed).[260]

Generally, the average PLC shift was visually distinct from the under US\$700,000 shift reported in earlier research.[261] Controlling for case length, multiple tests identified a reliable mean difference in PLC amounts shifted over time.[262] Table 6.6 summarizes mean PLC shifts over time.

[254] $M = 2{,}540{,}754$; $SD = 3099867$; $n = 41$. The median shift was US\$1,446,787. Converting the figures using the BLS website to June 2018 buying power, the mean PLC shift equates to US\$2,907,244.29, and the median equates to US\$1,644,479.35.

[255] Melvin J. Howard v. Government of Can., UNCITRAL, PCA Case No. 2009-21, Order for the Termination of Proceedings & Award on Costs, ¶ 24 (Aug. 2, 2010), https://bit.ly/2M6whW9 (last visited Aug. 7, 2018) (US\$4,673).

[256] *Link-Trading v. Moldova, supra* note 177, at 8, 31 (US\$27,758).

[257] *Swembalt v. Latvia, supra* note 167, at ¶ 16 (US\$86,932).

[258] Spyridon Roussalis v. Republic of Rom., ICSID Case No. ARB/06/1, Award, 143-44 (Dec. 7, 2011), 24 World Trade & Arb. Materials 343 (2012) (US\$8,102,230).

[259] *ADC v. Hungary, supra* note 11, at ¶ 103 (US\$8,116,366).

[260] *Libananco v. Turkey, supra* note 21 (US\$15,000,000).

[261] Franck, *supra* note 22, at 69 (identifying an average shift of US\$655,407).

[262] An ANOVA using logged data ($F(2, 38) = 3.494$; $p = .04$; $r = .39$; $n = 41$) identified a reliable mean difference in the PLC shifted across the different generations of data. A Kruskall-Wallis test identified a statistically meaningful change in median PLC amounts shifted ($\chi^2(2) = 8.981$; $p = .01$; $r = .47$; $n = 41$) over time. A correlation found a reliable, positive linear relationship between the year tribunals rendered awards and PLC amount shifted using logged data ($r(41) = .42$; $p = .01$). The direction of the effect was, in more recent awards, PLC shifts were larger. A partial correlation, controlling for case length, replicated the results using logged data ($r(37) = .33$; $p = .04$). Likewise, a linear regression reliably predicted PLC shifts ($F(2, 39) = 10.256$; $p < .001$; $R^2 = .357$), as a function of the number of months to resolve the dispute and year of the award, and both variables were significant predictors of PLC shifts.

TABLE 6.6

Mean PLC Shifts in Cases over Time across Generations of Data using Inflation-adjusted Raw U.S. Dollars for All Awards with Data Available ($n = 41$).

	Mean PLC Shifted	*Standard Deviation*	*Total*
Generation 1 (until June 1, 2006)	786,581	1008510	11
Generation 2 (June 1, 2006–June 1, 2009)	2,510,852	3011287	11
Generation 3 (June 1, 2009–January 1, 2012)	3,573,639	3569853	19
Total	2,540,754	3099867	41

Follow-up comparisons[263] revealed the reliable effect was driven by comparisons between the earliest data (G1), when the ITA was in its infancy, and the most recent data (G3). By contrast, it was not possible to detect meaningful differences in PLC shifts for other direct comparisons. Given the small number of awards with PLC and potential selection effects, these results must be viewed cautiously. Yet, they suggest that—as a function of dollar values shifted—there was a pocket of increased PLC shifts, with the most recent cases involving the largest shifts compared to the oldest cases.

The results are at odds with other PLC findings, where analyses were unable to find tribunals changed their approach to PLC allocation. One explanation might be, as legal teams expanded, and cases became more complex, counsel fees increased—and it would be unsurprising that the amount of PLC tribunals shifted increased commensurately. Yet that narrative is limited, as other tests were unable to revealed that parties' total PLC expenses increased over time.[264] While the results create a small mystery, they also raise an interesting possibility. Commentators making assertions about "new" trends in cost-shifting may have intuitively identified a real change—but mis-attributed the change to the wrong variable. Rather than a general change to tribunal's PLC cost-shifting practice, there was instead only a change to actual dollar values shifted. Coupled with the non-meaningful micro-trend of more "all or nothing" cases, intuitive cognition may have facilitated an instinctive

[263] As a reminder, Appendix I contains detailed information about data coded and analyzed, transformations made, statistical tests (including follow-up tests), and effect sizes (r-values).

[264] An ANOVA analyzing mean differences in parties' combined PLC across generations of data using logged data failed to reveal a reliable difference ($F(2, 48) = 0.197$; $p = .82$; $r = .09$; $n = 51$). A test of medians on total PLC failed to reveal a shift over time across generations of data ($\chi^2(2) = 0.882$; $p = .25$; $r = .13$; $n = 51$). Similarly, bivariate correlations using logged data were unable to identify a reliable link between parties' total PLC and either the year the case was initiated ($r(51) = .12$; $p = .41$) or the year the award was rendered ($r(51) = -.02$; $p = .62$). A partial correlation, that controlled for case length, also failed to find a reliable relationship between total PLC expenses and either year of case filing ($r(47) = .03$; $p = .83$) or award year ($r(47) = -.21$;

mis-attribution and prevented identification of genuine change. As the data reveals, the real story was more complex.

b. PLC: Party-Specific Shifts

Previous discussions of cost shifts combined the experiences of investors and states. As about half of PLC shifts were in investors' favor and half were in states', the question is whether the experiences of investors and states differed from the overall pattern. Or put another way, was there a variance in how investors and states experienced PLC cost shifts?

In 2011 inflation-adjusted dollars, the average contribution that states made to investors' PLC was around US$2 million,[265] whereas the mean contribution investors made to states' PLC was nearly US$3 million.[266] Adjusting the averages to 2018 levels reveals those average amounts were roughly US$2.2 million and US$3.4 million respectively.[267]

Although the averages that investors as a group paid roughly US$1 million more in PLC, that conclusion is erroneous and deceptive. First, it fails to consider that, due to high variation in costs, median PLC contributions by *both* investors and states was roughly US$1.5 million each. Second, statistical tests failed to confirm that investors' obligation to pay states' PLC was meaningfully larger (or smaller) than states' PLC obligations to investors.[268]

Average PLC shifts for respondents and investors appeared facially distinct from earlier research identifying the average state obligation to pay for investor PLC was under US$500,00, whereas the average investor obligation to pay a state was around US$900,000.[269] Given wide standard deviations, most tests were unable to identify a meaningful difference over time in PLC shifts for either investors[270] or states.[271]

Only one test identified a reliable increase in fiscal amounts *states* were required to contribute to investors' PLC. The effect was confined to the comparisons between the oldest

---

p =.14). It is possible that the tests were underpowered, as the effect sizes were around small (r = .10) or lower, meaning replication may be required.

[265] M = 2,023,049; SD = 2296317; n = 19. The median was US$1,446,788.

[266] M = 2,987,863; SD = 3651232; n = 22. The median was US$1,470,507.

[267] Using the BLS website to convert averages for inflation to reflect June 2018 buying power, the mean state contribution to investors of US$2,314,863.09 and a mean investor contribution to states of US$3,418,846.39.

[268] An ANOVA analyzing mean PLC contributions by claimants and respondents failed to find a reliable difference using winsorized (F (1, 39) = 0.665; p = .42; r = .13; n = 41) or logged (F (1, 39) = 0.001; p = .98; r = .01; n = 41) data. A Mann-Whitney two-sample U-test failed to reveal a significant difference in median PLC contributions for investors and states (U = 190.5; p = .63) Given small effect sizes and missing data, the tests were theoretically underpowered and would benefit from replication.

[269] Franck, *supra* note 22, at 69–70.

[270] An ANOVA analyzing investors contributions to states' PLC over time failed to identify a reliable difference using logged data (F (2, 19) = 1.002; p = .39; r = .31; n = 22) across generations; follow-up comparisons failed to identify any meaningful (but latent) differences. A test of medians likewise failed to find a reliable difference in investors' fiscal contributions to state PLC over time ((χ^2 (2) = 3.696; p = .16; r = .39; n = 22).

[271] For cases where states contributed to investors' PLC, tests were unable to identify a reliable mean difference in PLC contributions over time using winsorized data (F (2, 16) = 2.054; p = .16; r = .42; n = 19), with no latent difference in follow-up tests.

cases against the most recent cases.[272] Because of data gaps in the oldest cases and lack of robust findings across tests, some caution is required. Nevertheless, the statistically large effect size in the one significant test suggests that states' increased obligations to pay investors' PLC could evolve to identify a robust effect. The overall interesting historic remnant was the rough parity in typical fiscal PLC shifts for both investors and states.

c. TCE Shifts

The available data offers one glimpse into typical cost-shifting for tribunal expenses. There was a facial similarity in the fiscal responsibility of TCE for investors and states. Using 2011 inflation-adjusted data, the mean TCE investors paid was roughly US$430,000.[273] Similarly, the mean TCE for states was just shy of US$390,000.[274] Adjusting averages to 2018 levels, those amounts were roughly US$492,000 and US$441,000 respectively.[275]

Earlier research, which had not adjusted for inflation, found investors and states each paid roughly US$300,000 for TCE.[276] The updated, inflation-adjusted data suggests tribunal costs were relatively steady. Tests generally confirmed that TCE fiscal obligations were somewhat stable over time for both investors[277] and states.[278] But there was a small twist. Namely, tests suggested that states' fiscal TCE obligations to pay for tribunals reliably *decreased* over time.[279] Table 6.7 provides parties' TCE obligations.

---

[272] An ANOVA using logged data identified general reliable relationship between the generation of the data and fiscal amounts states contributed to investors' PLC ($F(2, 16) = 3.937; p = .04; r = .57; n = 19$). The effect, however, was confined to comparisons between the earliest (G1) and most recent (G3) PLC shifts; all other post hoc comparisons were non-significant. A test of medians likewise identified a reliable change in median PLC shifts over generations of data ($\chi^2(2) = 6.374; p = .04; r = .58; n = 19$).

[273] $M = 430{,}023; SD = 420{,}229; n = 61$. The median was US$334,756.

[274] $M = 385{,}511; SD = 568875; n = 61$. The median was US$180,573.

[275] Using the BLS website for conversion to June 2018 buying power, the mean investor TCE was roughly US$492,051.54 million and the mean state TCE was roughly US$441,118.92.

[276] Franck, *supra* note 22, at 69.

[277] An ANOVA was unable to identify a meaningful difference in investors' mean TCE obligations across generations of winsorized data ($F(2, 58) = 0.840; p = .44; r = .17; n = 61$); no follow-up tests revealed latent differences. A test of medians failed to reveal a meaningful difference in investors' TCE obligations over time ($\chi^2(2) = 2.805; p = .25; r = .21; n = 61$). A bivariate correlation using winsorized data was on the cusp of significance when analyzing award year and investors' TCE payment ($r(61) = .25; p = .05$); however, when using a partial correlation to control case length, the non-significant results replicated and were no longer on the cusp ($r(57) = .15; p = .27$).

[278] An ANOVA could not identify a meaningful difference in respondents' mean TCE allocations across generations of logged data ($F(2, 58) = 2.009; p = .14; r = .26; n = 61$); follow-up tests failed to reveal latent differences. A test of medians failed to reveal a meaningful difference in states' TCE obligations ($\chi^2(2) = 1.458; p = .48; r = .16; n = 61$).

[279] A bivariate correlation found a negative and reliable link between the year a tribunal rendered award and states' TCE cost using logged data ($r(61) = -.25; p = .049$). The result persisted controlling for case length through a partial correlation ($r(57) = -.27; p = .04$).

TABLE 6.7

Mean TCE Allocations over Time across Generations of Data using Inflation-adjusted Raw U.S. Dollars ($n = 61$).

	Mean TCE Obligation	*Standard Deviation*	*Total*
Generation 1 (until June 1, 2006)			
Claimants	350,384	432088	17
Respondents	358,218	374688	17
Generation 2 (June 1, 2006–June 1, 2009)			
Claimants	426,940	287725	18
Respondents	490,676	766084	18
Generation 3 (June 1, 2009–January 1, 2012)			
Claimants	484,228	490575	26
Respondents	330,550	525492	26

For investors, average TCE responsibility increased roughly US$50,000 during each three-year period, but that trend was non-significant and could reflect chance alone. In slight contrast, for states, while there was wider variation in TCE responsibility, with one time period reflecting a small spike in respondent TCE obligation but with an ending pattern of states paying less TCE. The other intriguing visual element was, in the most recent data, investors appeared to pay somewhat more TCE than states. Replication should continue to explore parties' TCE exposure over time to evaluate stability or continued evolution.

d. Discussion

Overall, the percentage of and ultimate fiscal liability for cost shifts exhibited several patterns. First and foremost, as a whole, tribunals generally engaged in relatively balanced treatment in cost-shifting for both investors and states, both for costs as a function of percentage shift or real fiscal values.

Second, for percentage shifts, for PLC and TCE, proportions were relatively stable over time. There was limited evidence supporting the conventional wisdom of an "increasing" number of cases exhibiting extreme cost-shifting. For PLC, tribunals exhibited great variation in the percentage of fees shifted, and average PLC shifts were approximately 60% of a party's legal fees and expenses. Also, only roughly one-third of the cases generated an extreme PLC shift 100% in favor of investors or states. For TCE, most allocations were still roughly 50/50, with parties splitting tribunal fees equally. While there were pockets where investors paid no TCE, the relative percentage of that allocation (8%) was identical to earlier research. In slight contrast, the proportion of cases where states were not responsible for paying TCE increased to 15%, but the change was not meaningful.

Third, there were a few wrinkles. Generally, cost-related parameters were stable over time. But for PLC, dollar values of PLC shifted increased over time—but only when comparing awards rendered after 2009 with awards rendered before 2006. One test reflected that the increase was particularly pronounced for states making an increased contribution to investors' legal fees. By contrast, for TCE, there was generally no change, except for the set of tests demonstrating states experienced a slight decrease in the fees paid to tribunals.

Ultimately, inferences must be done cautiously given tribunals' failure to regularly particularize PLC and TCE. Tribunals' failure to itemize costs undermines the legitimacy of tribunals' cost assessments, especially as the available data suggested the PLC amounts were nontrivial, involving millions of dollars. Tribunals' fiscal confidentiality seems inappropriate given the sheer scope of funds. Chapter 9 argues for enhanced standards of costs transparency information, particularly as arbitrators are privy to the remuneration paid for their own professional services.

7 The Evolution of Cost Rationalization—Explaining Cost Assessments

ITA INVOLVES STATES, public resources, large fiscal risk, and adjudicative processes. As such, ITA should demonstrate the rule-of-law, rather than a rule of irrationality. A fundamental normative aspiration is that adjudicators should explain decisions involving international law obligations with real fiscal implications. As Chapter 6 revealed, ITA costs involve material fiscal exposure; and providing well-reasoned decisions offers benefits to parties, counsel, arbitrators, states, and other stakeholders making strategic decisions about ITA. Jurisprudential care and clear reasoning stand to promote clearer, more predictable jurisprudence and to facilitate settlement.[1] Yet, some perceive that "tribunals award costs and fees without discussion."[2]

There are divergent narratives about whether and how tribunals rationalize ITA costs.[3] One group argues ITA cost awards are neither justified nor rationalized, suggesting arbitrators "rarely discuss in detail the reasons for their decisions on costs"[4] or that

[1] Joshua B. Simmons, *Valuation in Investor-State Arbitration: Towards a More Exact Science*, 30 BERKELEY J. INT'L L. 196, 213–14 (2012).

[2] John Y. Gotanda, *Consistently Inconsistent: The Need for Predictability in Awarding Costs and Fees in Investment Treaty Arbitration*, 28 ICSID REV. 420, 435 (2013).

[3] *See, e.g.,* Susan D. Franck, *Rationalizing Costs in Investment Treaty Arbitration*, 88 WASH U. L. REV. 769, 816–20.

[4] Lester Nurick, *Costs in International Arbitration*, 7 ICSID REV.-FOREIGN INV. L.J. 57 (1992).

Arbitration Costs. Susan D. Franck.

arbitrators pay "short shrift" to costs, making it the "Achilles' heel" of ITA.[5] Schill argued, "reasons for adopting a certain cost decision are rarely given," as awards do not make "reference to specific policy considerations."[6] Smith likewise suggested that the "landscape of costs in investment arbitration lacks fundamental consistency," and "virtually anything can become a factor in a costs decision because the relevant textual provisions are so vague."[7] Perhaps this is not surprising, as leading investment arbitration scholars find little consistency in cost-shifting explanations, with Schreuer identifying ICSID tribunal practices as being "neither clear nor uniform" and Gotanda calling cost awards "often arbitrary and inconsistent."[8]

Yet others suggest ITA cost awards *do* provide reasoning, but subgroups disagree on the dominant rationale. These subgroups mirror theoretical paradigms for cost assessments described in Chapter 6. A first group advocates reasoned awards reflecting a "pay-your-own-way" approach, arguing tribunals follow the "traditional rule" about equal allocation of costs where parties pay their own PLC and tribunals equally split TCE.[9] A second group promotes the loser-pays approach, suggesting that tribunals follow variations on a costs-follow-the-event rule.[10] A third group, suggesting reasoning depends on various factors, explains tribunals use multiple matrixes to assess costs. Reflecting a "borderless balancing standard," some tribunals use a plethora of factors such as "identity of the victorious party," "fraudulent claims, delays, and unnecessary expense caused by one party or the other; excessive filings; frivolous arguments; the relative skill and professionalism of the parties' counsel; the difficulty and novelty of legal issues involved; and occasionally the relative wealth of the parties."[11] Each group presumes that the dominant rationale tribunals tend to provide

---

[5] Kenneth Riesenfeld & Joshua Robbins, *The Achilles' Heel of Investor-State Arbitration* Awards, LAW360.COM (Dec. 6, 2016), https://bit.ly/2vo8DQQ (last visited Aug. 7, 2018); *see also* Klaus Reichert & James Hope, *Costs–The Sting in the Tail*, GLOBAL ARB. REV. (Apr. 1, 2006), https://bit.ly/2QWeWCz (last visited Dec. 27, 2018).

[6] Stephan W. Schill, *Arbitration Risk and Effective Compliance: Cost-Shifting in Investment Treaty Arbitration*, 7 J. WORLD INV. & TRADE 653, 659 (2006); J. Gillis Wetter & Charl Priem, *Costs and Their Allocation in International Commercial Arbitrations*, 2 AM. REV. INT'L ARB. 249, 261 (1991).

[7] David Smith, *Shifting Sands: Cost-and-Fee Allocation in International Investment Arbitration*, 51 VA. J. INT'L L. 749, 756, 775 (2011).

[8] CHRISTOPH SCHREUER ET AL., THE ICSID CONVENTION: A COMMENTARY 1229 (2d ed. 2009); Gotanda, *supra* note 2.

[9] *See* LUCY REED ET AL., GUIDE TO ICSID ARBITRATION 91–93 (2004); Noah D. Rubins, *The Allocation of Costs and Attorney's Fees in Investor-State Arbitration*, 18 ICSID REV.-FOREIGN INV. L.J. 109, 126 (2003); Steven Smith et al., *International Commercial Dispute Resolution*, 42 INT'L LAW. 363, 393–94 (2008).

[10] *See* SCHREUER ET AL., *supra* note 8, at 1231–32; Smith et al., *supra* note 9, at 393; U.N. Conference on Trade and Dev., *Latest Developments in Investor-State Dispute Settlement: IIA Monitor No. 1*, UNCTAD/WEB/DIAE/IA/2009/6/Rev1 3–4 (2009), http://bit.ly/1Dgaa (last visited Aug. 7, 2018); *compare* Schill, *Cost-Shifting*, *supra* note 6, at 660, 672, 657 (suggesting one-way cost-shifting operates to investors' benefit) *with* David P. Riesenberg, *Fee Shifting in Investor-State Arbitration: Doctrine and Policy Justifying Application of the English Rule*, 60 DUKE L.J. 977 (2011) (advocating a pure loser-pays approach).

[11] Smith, *supra* note 7, at 756.

mirrors its own normative approach to (or experience with) cost-shifting, possibly reflecting confirmation and blind spot illusions.

The issue of how tribunals explain their costs is not a small matter, particularly given ongoing reform efforts. ICSID's August 2018 consultation process suggested clarifying the bases for awards on costs and possibly adopting a presumption in favor of awarding costs with a view toward parties' relative success. Meanwhile, UNCITRAL's procedural reform efforts and the European Union's investment court proposal have put costs—and cost assessments—front and center.[12]

Empirical analysis offers a baseline for assessing descriptive accuracy of paradigmatic approaches. Earlier research identified that, although tribunals rarely cited legal authority and provided only minimal rationalization of their decisions, much like the factor-dependent model, tribunals' approaches varied. Some rationales—such as relative success, equity considerations, encouraging appropriate behavior, underlying tribunal discretion, and concerns about the underlying substantive dispute—predominated.[13] The question is whether those findings persisted

To facilitate an evidence-based dialogue, this chapter explores tribunals' rationalization of cost decisions. It first assesses how many awards contained any rationalization for either PLC or TCE and identifies gaps between non-final and final awards. Second, it provides content analysis of rationalization offered by tribunals for PLC and TCE. Third, it explores whether—both for PLC and TCE—tribunals' ability to explain their cost decisions changed over time, and then synthesizes main themes from the data.

I. Introduction and the Gap between Final and Non-final Awards

There were stark findings about tribunals' rationalization of costs. One glaring point involved the large constituency of tribunals failing to ground cost determinations in established legal doctrine or offer an analytical justification for cost-related activity. Using a negative frame, for PLC, 63% of tribunals failed to rely upon any legal authority, and roughly 30% of tribunals failed to provide a legal rationale. Using a positive frame, PLC tribunals explained their cost assessments by relying on legal authority in approximately 37% of the total awards and offered at least one legal reason justifying their decision in nearly 70% of awards. *See* Figure 7.1. Tribunals could have provided both these elements in 100% of the awards. Tribunals' approach to TCE was similar to the gap in PLC justifications, in that they failed to uniformly offer a legal basis or ratio for cost assessments.[14]

---

[12] *See* Kate Brown de Vejar & Chloe Baldwin, *The Economics of Access: Systemic Imbalances in ISDS*, *in* ICCA Congress Proceedings (forthcoming) (discussing cost-related reform efforts).

[13] Franck, *supra* note 3, at 824–32.

[14] For all TCE awards, 61.4% ($n = 167$) of tribunals failed to rely on legal authority, and 28.8% ($n = 78$) failed to justify the decision with a legal rationale. *See infra* Table 7.2.

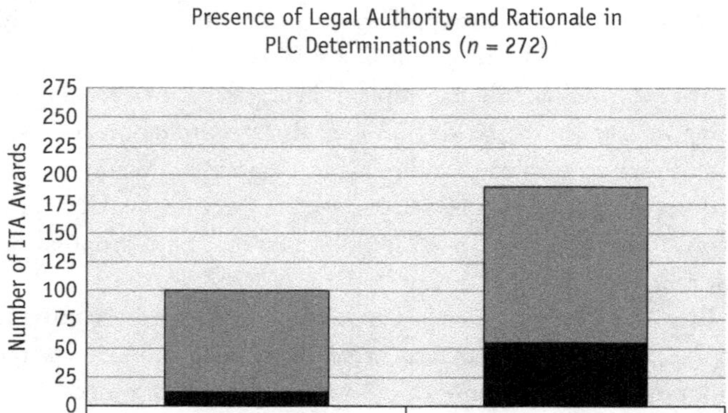

	Award Relies on Legal Authority	Award Relies on Legal Rationale
Final Awards (n = 159)	88	135
Non-Final Awards (n = 113)	12	55

FIGURE 7.1 Frequency of Tribunal Use of Legal Authority and Rationale to Explain PLC Decisions (n = 272) in Non-final and Final Awards.

One explanation for the failure to offer justification may be distinctions between non-final and final awards. Tribunals often failed to mention cost assessments in non-final awards. Figure 7.1 reflects, for PLC, that tribunals in final awards appeared to be comparatively better in relying upon underlying doctrine and legal justifications to make cost assessments. A test confirmed the facial pattern was statistically meaningful, with tribunals more reliably using both legal authority[15] and reasoning[16] to explain their cost assessments in final awards. *See* Table 7.1.

Irrespective of tribunal's better comparative performance in final awards, *only 55% of final awards relied upon any form of legal authority for PLC determinations.* This is normatively unacceptable, given how easy it is for tribunals to explain their assessments by virtue of readily available rules, treaties, and existing awards. For the PLC rationale, tribunals were better; approximately 85% of final awards provided some form of reasoning. While some failure of the gap could be attributed to settlement or discontinuances, only three awards fell into that category.[17]

Instead, most cases failing to offer a costs rationale were typical ITA disputes. For example, in *Alpha Projektholding v. Ukraine*, the tribunal simply concluded that "Each party shall bear

[15] A chi-square test analyzed the use (or absence) of legal authority in final and non-final awards, finding tribunals were reliably better at using legal authority in final awards (χ^2 (1) = 56.84; p < .001; r = .46; n = 272).

[16] When comparing non-final and final awards, tribunals in final awards were more likely to offer more rationale in final awards (χ^2 (1) = 41.18; p < .001; r = .39; n = 272).

[17] S&T Oil Equip. & Mach. Ltd. v. Republic of Rom., ICSID Case No. ARB/07/13, Order of Discontinuance (July 16, 2010), https://bit.ly/2ESW4x8 (last visited Dec. 27, 2018); Impreglio S.p.A. v. Islamic Republic of Pak., ICSID Case No. ARB/03/3, Order of Discontinuance (Sept. 25, 2005), https://bit.ly/2QSoYBL (last visited Dec. 27, 2018); Canfor Corp. v. United States, UNCITRAL, Joint Order on Costs and for Termination (July 19, 2007), https://bit.ly/2QWTqoq (last visited Dec. 27, 2018).

TABLE 7.1

Reliance on Legal Authority and Rationale for PLC Decisions as a Function of Award Finality.

PLC Justification	Tribunal References		Total
	Not Present	*Reliance Present*	
Treaty Claim Not Final			
Reliance on Legal Authority	101	12	113
Rationale Explained	58	55	113
Treaty Claim Final			
Reliance on Legal Authority	71	88	159
Rationale Explained	24	135	159

its own legal fees and expenses" with no further enumeration, and other tribunals have been similarly amorphous in their failure to provide any explanation for their cost assessment.[18] Likewise, in *CMS Gas Transmission v. Argentina*, despite being one of the largest awards studied (presumably with matching legal fees), the tribunal failed to particularize PLC and just concluded, "Each party shall bear the expenses incurred by it in connection with the present arbitration."[19]

---

[18] Alpha Projektholding GMBH v. Ukraine, ICSID Case No. ARB/07/16, Award, ¶ 515 (Nov. 8, 2010), https://bit.ly/2yjVlCt (last visited Dec. 27, 2018).

[19] CMS Gas Transmission Co. v. Argentine Republic, ICSID Case No. ARB/018, Order, ¶ 472 (Aug. 31, 2009), https://bit.ly/2LBOh88 (last visited Dec. 27, 2017); *see also* American Mfg. & Trading, Inc. v. Republic of Zaire, ICSID Case No. ARB/93/1, Award, 42 (Feb. 21, 1997), 36 I.L.M. 1534, 1555 (1997) (stating "each of the Parties shall bear . . . the entirety of its own expenses and fees for its own counsel" without further explanation); ATA Constr., Indus. & Trading Co. v. Hashemite Kingdom of Jordan, ICSID Case No. ARB/08/2, Award, ¶ 133(6) (May 18, 2010), 22 World Trade & Arb. Materials 945, 995 (2010) (ordering, without explanation, that the parties "shall each bear their own legal costs"); Empresa Eléctrica del Ecador, Inc. v. Republic of Ecuador, ICSID Case No. ARB/05/9, Award, ¶ 137 (June 2, 2009), https://bit.ly/2Vcm1om (last visited Dec. 27, 2018) (stating "each Party shall assume its own costs and expenses of representation" without indicating what particular circumstances warranted that conclusion); Empresas Lucchetti, S.A. v. Republic of Peru, ICSID Case No. ARB/03/4, Award, 25 (Feb. 7, 2005), 17 World Trade & Arb. Materials 163, 188 (2005) (concluding without further discussion that "The Tribunal decides that each Party shall . . . bear its own legal costs"); EnCana Corp. v. Republic of Ecuador, LCIA Case No. UN3481, Award, ¶¶ 202, 204 (Feb. 3, 2006), https://bit.ly/2VeGWQi (last visited Dec. 27, 2018) (deciding to shift TCE to the winning state given its discretion, but failing to indicate why it failed to shift either parties' PLC); Joy Mining Mach. Ltd. v. Islamic Republic of Egypt, ICSID Case No. ARB/03/11, Award on Jurisdiction, 25 (Aug. 6, 2004), https://bit.ly/2SrK8pV (last visited Dec. 27, 2018) (stating, without further analysis, that "Each Party shall bear its own legal costs."); Occidental Exploration & Prod. Co. v. Republic of Ecuador, LCIA Case No. UN3467, Final Award, ¶ 216 (July 1, 2004), https://bit.ly/2ERoQhz (last visited Dec. 27, 2018) (providing an explanation for TCE assessment, but then stating that "Each party shall bear its own legal expenses" without explaining why); Mihaly Int'l Corp. v. Democratic Socialist Republic of Sri Lanka, ICSID Case No. ARB/00/2, Award, ¶ 63(b) (Mar. 15, 2002), 14 World Trade & Arb. Materials 21, 41 (2002) (stating only "Each Party shall bear its own costs and expenses in respect of legal fees for counsels"); TSA Spectrum de Argentina S.A. v. Argentine Republic, ICSID Case No. ARB/05/5, Award, ¶ 180 (Dec. 19, 2008), https://bit.ly/2AlIhw2 (last visited Dec. 27, 2018) (stating that "the Tribunal finds the circumstances to be such that each party shall bear its

Tribunals' TCE assessments were akin to their treatment of PLC. Tribunals typically provided better reasoning in final TCE decisions, as compared to non-final awards. While barely half of final awards (58.5%) used legal authority to justify their cost assessments, the vast majority of tribunals (88.7%) provided some legal reasoning to explain their decisions. *See* Table 7.2. Like PLC, more recent awards reflected that tribunals more reliably used legal authority[20] and reasoning[21] in final awards.

TABLE 7.2

Presence of Legal Authority and Rationale for TCE decisions as a Function of Award Finality.

	Tribunal References		
TCE Justification	*Not Present*	*Reliance Present*	Total
Treaty Claim Not Final			
Reliance on Legal Authority	101	12	113
Rationale Explained	60	53	113
Treaty Claim Final			
Reliance on Legal Authority	66	93	159
Rationale Explained	18	141	159

Unfortunately, legal authority and rationalization of TCE was decidedly lacking in non-final awards, with a whopping 89% of tribunals failing to use any legal authority and 53% failing to provide any rationale. To the extent that an early explanation and discussion of costs generates benefits—including notice to parties, aiding streamlined dispute settlement, and enhancing tribunal legitimacy—one would hope that tribunals would seize the opportunity to improve the coherence, predictability, determinacy, and integrity of ITA.

Given the significant difference (and statistically large effect) in how tribunals treated costs in non-final and final awards, the remainder of this chapter focuses on final awards. Rather than focusing on a large component where tribunals failed to explain their

own expenses" while failing to identify any specific circumstances that justified that decision); Tokios Tokelés v. Ukraine, ICSID Case No. ARB/02/18, Award, ¶ 146 (July 26, 2007), https://bit.ly/2Tk5qpP (last visited Dec. 27, 2018) (stating that the tribunal "reviewed the entire conduct of the parties" and then, without providing any further guidance, concluded: "each side must bear its own legal costs and expenses"); United Parcel Serv. v. Government of Can., UNCITRAL, Award on the Merits, ¶ 188 (May 24, 2007), 18 WORLD TRADE & ARB. MATERIALS 107, 185 (2007) (stating that "given the substance and overall course of the proceedings the Tribunal rules that the parties . . . bear their own costs" but failing to identify what factors in the proceedings warranted that conclusion).

[20] To test for reliable differences in use of legal authority, a chi-square compared tribunals' use in final and non-final TCE assessments, finding tribunals more reliably used legal authority in final awards (χ^2 (1) = 63.87; $p < .001$; $r = .49$; $n = 272$).

[21] Comparing non-final and final awards, tribunals in final awards were more likely to offer at least one rationale for TCE decisions (χ^2 (1) = 56.37; $p < .001$; $r = .46$; $n = 272$).

decision-making on a fundamental fiscal element, the objective is to explore key doctrinal and analytical justifications for ITA cost decisions where they were actually present.

II. Rationalizing PLC: Justifying Attorneys' Costs and Expenses

Tribunals could have done better in explaining their choices about allocating PLC. This subsection explores tribunals' use of legal authority (where tribunals were particularly poor) and analytical justification using legal reasoning (where they were better).

A. LEGAL AUTHORITY

Recalling only 55% of final awards offered legal authority for PLC, the average tribunal barely used one authority to justify the PLC determination.[22] Given tribunals' lack of regular reliance on authority, it is useful to consider what that authority was and what was doctrinally available.

In theory, tribunals could have relied upon multiple doctrinal sources. The research explored reliance on the ICSID Convention, investment treaties, arbitration rules, previous ITA awards, jurisprudence from other international tribunals, or toher authority from national legislatures or courts. The most heavily doctrinal source for PLC assessments in final awards was the ICSID Convention, followed closely by UNCITRAL arbitration rules. *See* Table 7.3.

Although institutional rules were readily available, many tribunals did a poor job of using them. For ICSID Convention cases, only 44% referred to either the ICSID Convention or ICSID Arbitration Rules. For ICSID Additional Facility cases, 45.5% referred to the Additional Facility Rules. For SCC cases, 40% relied upon underlying SCC rules for making PLC decisions. By contrast, for ad hoc arbitrations using UNCITRAL Rules, tribunals' dominant approach (85%) involved using UNCITRAL Rules to justify PLC decisions.

The cases analyzed *never* revealed tribunals used national law to ground PLC assessments. A notable portion of tribunals referred to "other authority," typically expert commentary. Four awards referred to Professor Schreuer's ICSID commentary (one using a discussion to the ICSID *traveaux*), two cited to Professor Gotanda's costs article, one cited to Redfern and Hunter's treatise on commercial arbitration, one cited to Wetter and Priem's costs article, and a final tribunal cited Professor David Caron's commentary on the UNCITRAL rules. Although unlikely to constitute "the teachings of the most highly qualified publicists" within

[22] $M = 0.97$; $SD = 1.105$; $n = 159$. The median was 1; but the mode was 0. For the 159 final awards, nearly half of tribunals used *no* authority (44.7%; $n = 71$), roughly a quarter of tribunals cited to one authority (25.4%; $n = 42$), and less than 9% ($n = 14$) of tribunals cited to three or more legal authorities. For non-final awards, the failure to provide authority was more marked, with the mean number of authorities being close to zero ($M = 0.12$; $SD = .38$; $n = 113$); barely 10% ($n = 12$) used one or more authorities to justify their PLC decision.

TABLE 7.3

Legal Authority Relied upon by Tribunals for PLC Decisions in Final Awards (n = 159) (more than one authority possible for each award).

	Tribunal References		
PLC Justification	*Not Present*	*Reliance Present*	Total
ICSID Convention[23]	120	39	159
ICSID Arbitration Rules[24]	140	19	159
ICSID Additional Facility Rules[25]	149	10	159
SCC Rules[26]	155	4	159
UNCITRAL Rules[27]	130	29	159
Investment Treaty	144	15	159
Investment Treaty Awards	137	22	159
International Tribunals	153	6	159
National Law	159	0	159
Other	149	10	159

the meaning of Article 38(1) of the ICJ statute, *ADC v. Hungary* relied upon an article from *Global Arbitration Review*.[28]

It is unfortunate that tribunals were not proactive in providing legal authority to legally ground their decisions. The finding is striking, as research on other issues has demonstrated tribunals increasingly rely on other arbitral decisions.[29] The gap in legal authority for costs is troubling given the scale of costs, namely the possibility of absorbing two sets of lawyers' fees from domestic and multinational law firms over several years. The phenomenon of arguably lazy, perhaps cognitively depleted, arbitral reasoning has material consequences. Other

[23] There were ninety-three final awards arising under the ICSID Convention; all thirty-nine awards citing the ICSID Convention were ICSID Convention awards.

[24] All nineteen awards citing the ICSID Arbitration Rules were ICSID Convention cases; all but two of those awards also cited to the Convention.

[25] There were twenty-two final awards arising under the ICSID Additional Facility Rules; all ten awards citing those rules were Additional Facility cases.

[26] There were ten final awards arising under the SCC Rules; all four awards citing the SCC rules were SCC cases.

[27] There were thirty-three final awards arising under the UNCITRAL Arbitration Rules; twenty-eight of the awards referring to UNCITRAL rules were organized pursuant to those rules, whereas one, *Cargill v. Mexico*, *infra* note 63, was an ICSID-Additional Facility case.

[28] ADC Affiliate Ltd. v. Republic of Hun., ICSID Case No. ARB/03/16, Award, ¶¶ 532-533 (Oct. 2, 2006), https://bit.ly/2Tgmc8W (last visited Dec. 27, 2018). In addition, *Tza Yap Shum v. Peru* used the ICJ Statute, and *Mohammad Ammar al-Bahloul v. Tajikistan* referred to parties' *lack* of agreement. No other authorities were offered. Mohammad Ammar al-Bahloul v. Republic of Taj., SCC Case No. V (064/2008), Final Award (June 8, 2010), https://bit.ly/2AOuS1Z (last visited Dec. 27, 2018); Tza Yap Shum v. Republic of Peru, ICSID Case No. ARB/07/6, Award (July 7, 2011), https://bit.ly/2zWATcP (last visited Aug. 7, 2018).

[29] Jeffrey P. Commission, *Precedent in Investment Treaty Arbitration*, 24 J. Int'l Arb. 129 (2007); Ole K. Fauchald, *The Legal Reasoning of ICSID Tribunals—An Empirical Analysis*, 19 Eur. J. Int'l L. 301 (2008);

stakeholders—including other tribunals, professors synthesizing commentary, lawyers advising clients, or governments adjusting normative baselines—are using inchoate reasoning to draw conclusions from cases that may not be thoroughly grounded in the law. The only arguable bright spot, given historical concerns about tribunals' poor performance on costs justification,[30] was there was some evidence that tribunals, over time, became somewhat better at offering a doctrinal basis explaining PLC decisions.[31]

B. LEGAL RATIONALE

By contrast to authority, most PLC decisions offered some sort of reasoning to explain tribunal PLC decisions. For the final awards, tribunals offered an average of at least two rationales to justify PLC choices. Put another way, tribunals were twice as likely to explain their reasoning as they were to ground the decision in a legal framework.[32]

Given the prevalence of reasoning, it is useful to examine those factors. A content analysis explored the rationales influencing decision-making[33] using a classification system from previous research focusing on four clusters of factors.[34] The first cluster mirrored factors related to party success and failure. Recognizing the possibility of framing effects, the research used three variables. It initially analyzed negative framing, focusing on punishing the loser or imposing a penalty;[35] it then identified possible positive framing, focusing on rewarding the winner or creating a gain.[36] Last, a variable considered the effect of parties' relative success or failure.[37] The second cluster, again recognizing framing effects, explored party behavior during arbitration in three ways. The negative frame assessed whether tribunals identified parties had "acted frivolously, in bad faith or otherwise irresponsibly"[38] and used costs to

---

but see Gabrielle Kaufmann-Kohler, *Arbitral Precedent: Dream, Necessity or Excuse*, 23 ARB. INT'L 357 (2007).

[30] Franck, *supra* note 3, at 821–24.

[31] *See infra* Section IV.

[32] For final awards, the mean was 2.28, the median was 2, and the mode was 1 ($SD = 1.835$; $n = 159$). Tribunals most typically cited to one ($n = 43$) or two ($n = 32$) rationales. Sixty tribunals offered three or more bases; of that group, eleven tribunals offered six or more justifications. For non-final awards, tribunals provided less rationalization: on average, less than one per award ($M = .64$; $SD = .887$; $n = 113$). The median and mode were 0.

[33] Mentioning a factor was not defined as "influencing" the decision. Factors were only coded where there was a textual basis for asserting the factor affected a PLC and/or TCE decision.

[34] *See* Franck, *supra* note 3, at 824–25 (defining categories of rationales provided by tribunals); *infra* notes 37, 43, 47, 51 (operationalizing variables).

[35] The "loser-pays" rationale involved expressing "a desire to have the loser pay for making losing arguments." *See* Codebook, Appendix IV.

[36] The Codebook operationalized rewarding the winner for "making winning arguments and/or compensat[ing] the winner and making them whole for either: (1) needing to expend legal fees to fully compensate their losses or, (2) to put the party in the position they would have been but for the need to bring the claim." *Id.*

[37] "Welamson" reflected parties' relative success (i.e., parties could win some arguments but lose others) where tribunals determined "costs should be allocated *inter partes* on a sliding scale proportionate to the assessment by the [tribunal] of the claims made by the parties." *Id.*

[38] Schill, *supra* note 6, at 673; Thomas D. Rowe, Jr., *The Legal Theory of Attorney Fee Shifting: A Critical Overview*, 1982 DUKE L.J. 651, 653, 653, 660–61 (1982); Rubins, *supra* note 9, at 126; Wetter & Preim, *supra* note 6, at 327. Reed explores this factor in greater detail, indicating that it involves "the reprehensible conduct of the unsuccessful party" in four categories related to patently unmeritorious or legally untenable claims; abuse of process by attempting to create an investment for no bona fide reason, or otherwise bringing a fraudulent claim;

penalize and to deter inappropriate behavior.[39] A positive frame considered tribunals' assessments of parties' cooperativeness and efficiency[40] and used costs to reward and to encourage appropriate behavior.[41] The last aspect examined whether parties' attempted settlement negotiations[42] and tribunals' reaction to party settlement efforts,[43] particularly as several national legal systems use parties' unreasonable refusal to attempt negotiation or mediation as a factor in cost-shifting.[44]

A third cluster involved the dispute itself. One focus was to assess the novelty or challenge of establishing claims, defenses, or other legal issues.[45] Another element assessed substantive concerns regarding parties' behavior related to the claim or derivative party conduct.[46] A last element explored public interest considerations.[47] The final cluster involved concerns about administrative justice and procedural integrity. One element focused on situational equities and examined tribunals' focus upon considerations of equity and reasonableness.[48] Another aspect considered how tribunals focused upon the scope of their own discretion when assessing costs.[49] While one variable explored tribunals' desire to make informed

---

presenting poor quality or inefficient pleadings; or engaging in egregiously wrongful underlying conduct. Lucy Reed, *Allocation of Costs in International Arbitration*, 26 ICSID Rev. 76, 84 (2011).

[39] Deterring inappropriate behavior was: "[P]revent[ing] or sanction[ing] inappropriate behavior including: (1) bad faith conduct in adjudicating the proceedings, (2) poor pleadings or proof, (3) delays in making arguments, (4) inefficient administration of the arbitration, (5) repetitive or unfounded conduct, (6) unwillingness to produce documents, (7) reliance on annulled cases, or (8) lack of cooperation with the tribunal." *See* Codebook, Appendix IV.

[40] Franck, *supra* note 3, at 818; Fouchard Gaillard Goldman on International Commercial Arbitration 686 (Emmanuel Gaillard & John Savage eds., 1999).

[41] Encouraging appropriate behavior as expressing a desire to praise or reward appropriate behavior, including professionalism of parties and/or their attorneys; constructive nature of parties' pleadings or proof; efficiency in making arguments; efficiency in the administration of the arbitration; and the absence of inappropriate behavior. *See* Codebook, Appendix IV.

[42] Franck, *supra* note 3, at 819; Jeswald W. Salacuse, *Is There a Better Way? Alternative Methods of Treaty-Based, Investor-State Dispute Resolution*, 31 Fordham Int'l L.J. 138, 142 (2007).

[43] The Codebook operationalized settlement efforts influencing cost decisions as references that parties have made settlement efforts whether through mediation, negotiation, or some other facilitative process; or the parties' recorded settlement agreement. *See* Codebook, Appendix IV.

[44] Jackeline Nolan-Haley, *Mediation Exceptionality*, 78 Fordham L. Rev. 1247, 1248–49, 1256–63 (2009); Jackeline Nolan-Haley, *Is Europe Headed Down the Primrose Path with Mandatory Mediation?*, 37 N.C. J. Int'l L. & Com. Reg. 981, 1004–06 (2012).

[45] "Novelty" rationale was present when the "claim or argument made is novel and/or is challenging to establish." Codebook, Appendix IV.

[46] The Codebook defined "substantive" as tribunal concern with party conduct related to the underlying substantive dispute, including concerns parties won/lost based upon procedural issues (i.e., burdens of proof or evidentiary rules) or there was an issue regarding inappropriate nature of a party's substantive conduct. *Id.*

[47] Public interest implicated concerns that "the public, issues of policy, or matters of public importance are implicated by the claim and/or the issues raised in the arbitration." *Id.*

[48] The Codebook operationalized "equity" as expressing a desire to be based upon principles of fairness, justice, equity, appropriateness, or reasonableness. For PLC, "reasonableness" also related to the PLC amount charged. *Id.* at 110, 119 nn.124, 147.

[49] The Codebook defined a decision based upon "discretion" as "more than a mere reference to a rule that references the possibility of a tribunal exercising discretion; rather the award must demonstrate that the tribunal was exercising that discretion." *Id.* at 110, 119 nn.130, 148.

decisions,[50] another variable also assessed tribunals' interest in comporting with norms from existing cases.[51] Last, but by no means least, coding identified whether tribunals expressed a concern about party equality of arms.[52]

With this framework, content analysis examined the sources tribunals used to explain their PLC decisions. A critical finding was the broad number of different types of justifications tribunals used to substantiate decisions about the proper allocation of parties' costs. The lack of uniformity becomes clear when one considers that no single justification was present in more than 40% of awards. Rather, rationale was dispersed widely. There were, however, clusters of rationale regularly used.

The most heavily cited basis, present in 38.4% of final awards, was parties' relative success or failure. Equity and reasonableness considerations were also popular, used in 38.4% of final awards. Tribunal discretion was also in the top tier of most utilized justifications and was present in 32.7% of final awards. The importance of outcome-related rationales was underscored by the "loser-pays" (15%) and "rewarding-winner" (12%) rationales being in the secondary tier of prominent justifications. In other words, considerations about outcome and justice were the most prominent factors to explain tribunal PLC decisions in final awards. *See* Table 7.4

Another set of rationales were regularly cited but of secondary importance. These "mid-tier" justifications tended to focus on party behavior and the content of the case itself. Specifically, tribunals referred to rewarding appropriate conduct in 23.9% of cases and punishing inappropriate activity in 18.9% of cases. Although rewarding positive conduct and punishing poor behavior may appear to function as two sides of the same coin, the prevalence of the focus on positive party behavior is intriguing. Aspects of the claim, particularly issues of claim novelty (15.7%) or underlying state conduct (12.6%) were secondary considerations.

Several aspects barely registered on tribunals' PLC assessments. Like earlier research,[53] no tribunal used informed decision-making in final awards, and only a few tribunals articulated the value of settlement efforts (6.9%), public interest (3.8%), equality of arms (3.8%), or stare decisis (3.1%). Only two cases—*Kardassopoulos v. Georgia* and *Fuchs v. Georgia*—contained express references identifying third-party funding, which the tribunal declared irrelevant to cost decisions.[54]

---

[50] An "Informed Decision" reflected a tribunal's "desire to make a full and informed decision on costs or asks for information about costs". *Id.* at 110, 119.

[51] Like *jurisprudence constante*, "Stare Decisis" was defined as an effort "to adhere to previous cases" and, beyond mere citation to other materials, involved "an interest in adhering to established precedent and principles of *stare decisis* (i.e. treating like cases alike), or analyzes the application of or distinctions from previous investment treaty awards." *Id.* at 109, 118 nn.126, 144.

[52] The Codebook operationalized equality of arms as reflecting "inequalities between the parties, whether based upon power, size or finances." *Id.* at 110, 119.

[53] Franck, *supra* note 3, at 824–27.

[54] Leaving aside debates about whether third-party funding (TPF) can or must be disclosed, it is noteworthy that, when the dataset closed, TPF availability was only beginning to gather steam. This likely means that ICSID's proposed disclosure of funding-related obligations, or similar obligations required by national or other applicable law, require ongoing consideration of this historical baseline.

TABLE 7.4

Type of Rationale Tribunals Relied upon for PLC Determination in Final Awards ($n = 159$) (more than one rationale possible for each award).

	Tribunal References		
PLC Justification	*Not Present*	*Reliance Present*	Total
Outcome Related			
Loser Pays	133	26	159
Rewarding Winner	140	19	159
Relative Success or Failure	98	61	159
Party Behavior			
Deter Inappropriate Behavior	129	30	159
Encourage Appropriate Behavior	121	38	159
Party Settlement Efforts	148	11	159
Nature of Claim			
Novelty of Claim or Defense	134	25	159
Substantive Reasons	139	20	159
Public Interest Considerations	153	6	159
Justice			
Equity Considerations	99	60	159
Discretion of Tribunal	107	52	159
Making Informed Decisions[55]	159	0	159
Stare Decisis	154	5	159
Party Equality of Arms	153	6	159
Other	155	4	159

In contrast to commentary suggesting that a loser-pays approach or punishing negative behavior were dominant justifications for cost decisions,[56] tribunals used other rationales more frequently. Tribunals often used sophisticated approaches. Rather than a blunt loser-pays rule, they more typically considered the range of party successes and failures. Moreover, when focused on whether to use a carrot or a stick, tribunals tended to frame cost decisions using *positive* conduct—including professionalism and efficiency—rather than dwelling on negative framing.

Overall, rather than an extreme "outcome" or "costs-follow-the-event" focus, tribunals used multiple factors to justify PLC assessments. Tribunals heavily emphasized relative success, discretion, and equity. This suggests that, as a descriptive matter, ITA tribunals used a factor-dependent approach to cost-shifting.

---

55 While not used in final awards, forty-five of the 113 non-final awards used this for cost decisions, typically reserving costs for the future.

56 *See* Franck, *supra* note 3, at 817–19, 826 (gathering sources).

Tribunals arguably overweighted unimportant factors and underweighted valuable factors. One wonders—when there is an opportunity to address substantive concerns about the underlying dispute in the merits and damages phase—why substantive considerations regularly affected costs decisions. Meanwhile, the lack of focus on equality of arms, public interest, stare decisis norms, and other core rule-of-law values is disappointing. Given the focus on public interest, the desire to encourage settlements or to enhance party autonomy and sovereignty in controlling outcomes, and the value in promoting efficient dispute resolution, it is unfortunate that tribunals did not focus upon these aspects. Normatively, the gap and lack of focus on these aspects during arbitration may impact parties' strategic adjudication choices and potentially inhibit consideration of other forms of dispute resolution, such as mediation or negotiation. Stakeholders—including those engaged in reform—should therefore consider what ex ante standards or guidance treaties and institutional rules should provide to capture or guide tribunal discretion to promote efficient dispute resolution processes while regulating PLC, which demonstrably outweighted other costs.

III. TCE Rationalization

Tribunal and other administrative costs are doctrinally and economically distinct from parties' legal fees. Although the scale of TCE pales by comparison to parties' legal fees, tribunal expenses are a critical component of ITA costs. This section explores how tribunals justify TCE and whether tribunals rationalize decisions for their own fees differently than counsel costs.

A. LEGAL AUTHORITY

As previously indicated, a surprising proportion of awards failed to provide legal authority justifying TCE choices. Even for final awards where tribunals tended to offer more authorities, 41.5% of awards failed to rely upon any legal source, translating into the average tribunal barely citing to one basis on average to justify TCE allocations.[57]

For cases providing authority, like PLC, content analyses explored tribunals' use of doctrinal authorities for explaining TCE, namely: the ICSID Convention, investment treaties, arbitration rules, previous ITA awards, jurisprudence from other international tribunals, or reference to some other proceedings, including national courts. The most heavily used source was the ICSID Convention, followed closely by UNCITRAL arbitration rules. *See* Table 7.5.

[57] $M = 0.97$; $SD = 1.105$; $n = 159$. The median was 1, but the mode was 0. For the 159 final awards, 41.5% of tribunals used *no* authority ($n = 55$), 30.2% of tribunals cited one authority ($n = 48$), 20.8% tribunals used two forms of authority ($n = 33$), and 7.5% tribunals used three or more bases ($n = 12$) to justify their final TCE decision.

TABLE 7.5

Type of Legal Authority Relied Upon by Tribunals for TCE Determination in Final Awards ($n = 159$) (more than one authority possible for each award).

	Tribunal References		
TCE Justification	*Not Present*	*Reliance Present*	Total
ICSID Convention[58]	120	39	159
ICSID Arbitration Rules[59]	139	20	159
ICSID Additional Facility Rules[60]	149	10	159
SCC Rules[61]	151	8	159
UNCITRAL Rules[62]	129	30	159
Investment Treaty	145	14	159
Investment Treaty Awards	138	21	159
International Tribunals	155	4	159
National Law	159	0	159
Other	150	9	159

Although rules and treaties were readily available, ICSID tribunals did a poor job invoking these authorities. For cases under the ICSID Convention, only 44% referred to either the Convention or ICSID's Arbitration Rules. For Additional Facility cases, less than half (45.5%) cited Additional Facility Rules. Awards from other institutions, by contrast, regularly proffered rules to explain TCE assessments. SCC tribunals used SCC rules in 80% of SCC cases, and for arbitrations organized under the UNCITRAL Rules, tribunals relied upon the UNCITRAL rules in 88% of final awards. Oddly, one ICSID-Additional Facility case used UNCITRAL Rules to justify the TCE decision.[63]

Tribunals likewise did not normally use national law for TCE decisions. One lone tribunal—*CME v. Czech Republic*—used the Czech civil code when allocating TCE.[64] For the remaining tribunals, three referred to Professor Schreuer's ICSID commentary and two

[58] There were ninety-three awards arising under the ICSID Convention; all thirty-nine awards citing to the ICSID Convention were ICSID Convention awards.

[59] All twenty awards citing the ICSID Arbitration Rules were ICSID Convention cases, and all but two of those awards also cited to the Convention.

[60] Twenty-two awards arose under the ICSID Additional Facility Rules; all ten awards citing those rules were Additional Facility cases.

[61] There were ten awards under SCC Arbitration Rules; all eight awards citing SCC rules were SCC cases.

[62] Thirty-three awards arose under the UNCITRAL Arbitration Rules.

[63] Cargill, Inc. v. United Mexican States, ICSID Case No. ARB(AF)/05/2, Award, 158 (Sept. 18, 2009), https://bit.ly/2OS7rbe (last visited Aug. 7, 2018).

[64] CME Czech Republic B.V. v. Czech Republic, UNCITRAL, Final Award (Mar. 14, 2003), https://bit.ly/2tzYriK (last visited Dec. 27, 2018). In a more recent case, *Enkev Beheer v. Poland*, the tribunal used German law (the *lex arbitri*) to direct costs analysis to the treaty text. Enkev Beheer B.V. v. Republic of Pol., UNCITRAL, PCA Case No. 2013-01, Award on Costs, ¶ 56 (June 13, 2014), https://bit.ly/2VdmOy4 (last visited Dec. 27, 2018).

cited Professor Gotanda's costs article about commercial arbitration. One tribunal also relied on an article from *Global Arbitration Review*.[65]

It is unfortunate that tribunals did not proactively use legal authority to justify their decisions. In one case, *Eureko v. Poland*, the failure to use authority had serious ramifications, as the failure to use the applicable law meant that its presumption of unfettered discretion ran counter to treaty text. Even though the treaty forbade cost-shifting, *Eureko* shifted both PLC and TCE,[66] and did so in an eighty-one-page award, on the basis of two sentences: "Claimant has prevailed. Consequently, its costs and those of the Tribunal shall be borne by the Respondent."[67] To place this in a cognitive psychology context, "quick" intuitive thinking—rendering a decision in under twenty words that lazily avoided the rationality required by slower thinking—facilitated the creation of legal error. Whereas slower deliberation or reliance on legal authority can aid accurate resolution, as the tribunal in *Enkev Beheer v. Poland* learned from the past, and, in a case involving the same treaty, both cited to the treaty and used treaty standards as the rule of decision.[68]

Like PLC, the failure to offer authority for TCE decisions was striking when compared to scholarship identifying tribunals' increased reliance on other ITA decisions. One wonders, given the scope of new cases, why only 10% of final awards provided any kind of reference to existing jurisprudence to guide the arbitrators' thinking and manage party expectations. Thankfully, some evidence suggested, over time, tribunals improved and reliably increased their reliance on legal authority.[69]

B. LEGAL RATIONALE

As contrasted with their capacity to cite to legal authority, tribunals were better at providing *some* form of explanation for TCE decisions. Tribunals offered legal reasoning for TCE assessments in 88.7% of final awards.[70] The average tribunal offered at least two reasons to justify TCE choices—nearly twice the number of legal authorities offered.[71] Content analysis

---

[65] *ADC v. Hungary, supra* note 28. *Tza Yap Shum v. Peru, supra* note 28, used the ICJ Statute, and *Mohammad Ammar al-Bahloul v.* Tajikistan, *supra* note 28, referred to parties' lack of agreement. There were no other authorities offered.

[66] *See* Agreement Between the Kingdom of the Netherlands and the Republic of Poland on Encouragement and Reciprocal Protection of Investments, Neth.-Pol., Sept. 24, 1996, arts. 8(2), 12(3-9) (establishing the pay-your-own-way rule for ITA). Poland later issued a press release indicating the tribunal issued a supplementary award retracting its cost decision. Franck, *supra* note 3, at 830 n.307.

[67] Eureko B.V. v. Republic of Pol., UNCITRAL, Partial Award, ¶ 161 (Aug. 19, 2005), https://bit.ly/2ETImc8 (last visited Dec. 27, 2018).

[68] Enkev Beheer v. Poland, *supra* note 64, at ¶¶ 57–58.

[69] *See infra* Section IV.

[70] Tribunals provided minimal explanation of TCE choices in non-final awards, however, where the average number of rationales provided was less than one ($M = 0.61$; $SD = 0.86$; $n = 113$), the median and mode were 0. Although 53.1% of tribunals provided no rationale ($n = 60$), 40.7% of tribunals provided a single rationale ($n = 46$), and 6.3% of awards offered two or more explanations ($n = 7$).

[71] The mean was 2.16, the median was 2, and the mode was 1 ($SD = 1.591$; $n = 159$). Tribunals most typically cited to either one ($n = 49$) or two ($n = 37$) rationales. Fifty-five tribunals offered three or more authorities to justify their decision; of that group, six tribunals offered six or more.

explored the extent and type of reasoning using four categories: outcomes, party conduct, underlying claim, and underlying judicial mandate.

Tribunals used a variety of bases to explain and rationalize TCE choices. Like the broad variance for PLC decisions, no single justification was present in more than 40% of awards. There were, however, clusters of rationale for tribunals decisions' allocating their own costs and administrative expenses.

Once again, relative party success, equity, and reasonableness were the most prominent considerations affecting TCE assessments. Relative success remained the most prevalent basis for TCE, with tribunals using it in 39.6% of final awards. Although not as prominent as parties' relative success, the importance of case outcome was reflected in tribunals' reliance on factors such as having losers pay (17.6%) or rewarding winners (10.7%). Other fundamental drivers included equity and discretion, respectively used in 37.7% and 31.4% of final awards. *See* Table 7.6.

TABLE 7.6

Type of Rationale Tribunals Relied upon for TCE Determination in Final Awards ($n = 159$) (more than one rationale possible for each award).

TCE Justification	Tribunal References		
	Not Present	*Reliance Present*	Total
Outcome Related			
Loser Pays	131	28	159
Rewarding Winner	142	17	159
Relative Success or Failure	96	63	159
Party Behavior			
Deter Inappropriate Behavior	129	30	159
Encourage Appropriate Behavior	127	32	159
Party Settlement Efforts	145	14	159
Nature of Claim			
Novelty of Claim or Defense	137	22	159
Substantive Reasons	140	19	159
Public Interest Considerations	154	5	159
Justice			
Equity Considerations	109	50	159
Discretion of Tribunal	108	51	159
Making Informed Decisions	159	0	159
Stare Decisis	155	4	159
Party Equality of Arms	154	5	159
Other	155	4	159

The second tier of prominent rationales for TCE implicated party conduct. The core focus tended to be rewarding and encouraging appropriate conduct, with 20.1% of tribunals using these justifications. Although only slightly edged out by the positive frame, 18.9% of final awards referred to deterring and punishing inappropriate behavior. Other standard justifications for TCE involved the case itself. Tribunals used claim novelty to justify 13.8% of final decisions. States' substantive conduct also formed a basis for TCE assessments, being used in 11.9% of final awards.

Much like PLC, when rendering TCE decisions in final awards, some factors barely registered on tribunals' radar. Tribunals seemed particularly uninterested in party settlement efforts, as this was only referenced in 8.8% of final awards. Public interest (3.1%), equality of arms (3.1%), and stare decisis (2.5%) likewise had a barely perceptible impact on TCE decisions. Although regularly used for non-final awards, no tribunal used the informed decision-making factor in final awards.[72] For "other" potentially relevant considerations, only *Kardassopoulos v. Georgia* and *Fuchs v. Georgia* included tribunal statements about third-party funding, identifying it was irrelevant for cost assessments.[73]

Although tribunals facially offered multiple explanations when allocating their own costs, in reality, PLC and TCE rationales offered by tribunals exhibited great similarity, with minor fluctuations. The only slight differences were: the focus on positive party conduct was somewhat more prevalent in PLC, as opposed to TCE; and fewer tribunals justifying TCE were focused upon equity. Like PLC, in contrast to commentary suggesting that a pure loser-pays approach and a desire to punish behavior form the core paradigm for cost assessments, tribunals instead relied upon other reasons. Tribunals' core motivators involved relative party success, promoting positive party behavior, equity, and exercising the tribunal's discretion. Rather than the purported "costs follow the event," the reality was that ITA tribunals used a factor-dependent approach for TCE decisions.

Like PLC, when it came to TCE, tribunals arguably overused less important factors and underemphasized valuable factors. One wonders—when those elements can be addressed during merits and damages phases—why substantive considerations about state conduct leaked into TCE determinations. Meanwhile, failure to consider factors such as equality of arms, public interest, stare decisis norms, and core aspects of procedural justice and rule-of-law was peculiar. Given the public interest involved in ITA, the enhancement of state sovereignty to directly control outcomes in settlement terms, and the value of promoting efficient dispute resolution, it is unfortunate that tribunals did not regularly focus on these aspects. Normatively, lack of focus could affect parties' approach to dispute resolution and inhibit consideration of other forms of dispute resolution. Stakeholders should therefore consider setting out ex ante standards, whether in treaties or otherwise, to capture and guide tribunal discretion to promote more efficient dispute resolution.

IV. The Growth of Rationalization

Research on pre-2006 awards found that tribunals were poor at rationalizing costs.[74] While tribunals were particularly bad at consulting legal authority, they were somewhat better in

---

[72] Nearly 41% of tribunals in non-final awards (46 of 113) used "informed decisions" to justify a cost decision, which generally involved reserving costs for the future.

[73] The only other bases of the "other" coding related to unique, non-replicable expressions of concerns peculiar to the underlying facts in *Azinian v. Mexico* and *Sedelmayer v. Russia.*

[74] *See generally* Franck, *supra* note 3.

using reasoning. The question is whether, over time, tribunals became better at explaining a major fiscal component of dispute settlement. While tests generally revealed that tribunals improved their cost assessments over time, the core differences related to comparisons between the very earliest cases and the most recent awards.

A first set of tests explored potential improvements in the presence of *any* reliance on legal authority or rationale. With one small exception, all the tests identified a reliable pattern whereby tribunals improved over time. For example, tribunals exhibited a larger propensity to provide authority in the most recent awards both for PLC[75] and TCE.[76] Follow-up tests revealed the significant pattern was driven by comparisons between the most recent and oldest awards.[77] Similarly, tribunals were reliably better at explaining their TCE determinations, but the reliable improvement was limited to comparisons between the oldest and newest awards.[78] The only minor variation was, only for PLC rationale, that it was not possible to identify that the period when an award was rendered was reliably associated with increased reasoning, although the data trended toward that pattern.[79]

A second set of models tested whether the *magnitude* of tribunals' explanations increased over time to explore whether tribunals provided more thorough and substantive explanations of their cost decision-making as the case law evolved. Every test indicated that, for the sheer number of ratios tribunals used to explain cost decisions, more recent awards were most likely to offer the fullest explanation of costs. That single sentence requires unpacking to focus on

---

[75] A Pearson's Chi-Square Test of Independence using a 3 x 2 cross-tabulation of final awards identified a reliable pattern in presence (or absence) of rationalization in different generations of data (χ^2 (2) = 8.805; p = .01; r = .23; n = 159). A t-test likewise found there a reliable relationship between the year a tribunal rendered an award and presence of PLC authority whereby, the older the award, the less likely the tribunal used any authority (t (157) = −3.082; p = .002; r = .24; n = 159).

[76] A chi-square test identified a reliable pattern in the generation of awards and PLC authority (χ^2 (2) = 6.554; p = .04; r = .20; n = 159). The t-test revealed the presence of TCE authority was reliably linked to newer awards (t (157) = −3.215; p = .003; r = .25; n = 159), with the mean award year without TCE authority reflecting older awards.

[77] For PLC authority, in G1, twenty-one of fifty-two final awards provided PLC authority; in G2, twenty-six of forty-seven final awards provided PLC authority; and in G3, forty of sixty final awards provided PLC authority. For TCE authority, in G1, twenty-four of fifty-two final awards gave TCE authority; in G2, twenty-seven of forty-seven final awards gave TCE authority; and in G3, forty-two of sixty final awards gave TCE authority. The meaningful difference came from comparing G1 and G3 data for both PLC (χ^2 (1) = 8.804; p = .01; r = .28; n = 112) and TCE (χ^2 (1) = 6.544; p = .01; r = .24; n = 112).

[78] For TCE rationale, in G1, 78.9% (41 out of 52) of final awards provided TCE rationale; in G2, 91.5% (43 out of 47) of final awards provided TCE rationale; and in G3, 95% (57 out of 60) of final awards provided TCE rationale. Using a chi-square 3 x 2 cross-tabulation to analyze the final awards in three different generations of data revealed a meaningful pattern between the presence (or lack) of TCE rationale. χ^2 (2) = 7.766; p = .02; r = .22; n = 159. The meaningful difference came from the distinction between the oldest and most recent awards (χ^2 (1) = 6.646; p = .01; r = .24; n = 112). A t-test similarly found a reliable link between the year the tribunal rendered an award and any explanation for the TCE decision (t (157) = −2.612; p = .01; r = .20; n = 159).

[79] A chi-square test was unable to detect a pattern between the generation of the data and presence of PLC rationale (χ^2 (2) = 3.99; p = .14; r = .16; n = 159). For PLC rationale, in G1, 23.1% (12 out of 52) of final awards provided PLC rationale; in G2, 87.2% (41 out of 47) of final awards provided PLC rationale; and in G3, 90.0% (54 out of 60) of final awards provided PLC rationale. Follow-up tests comparing G1 and G3 awards failed to identify a meaningful pattern, although it was close to significant (χ^2 (1) = 3.106; p = .08; r = .17; n = 109). A t-test analyzing final awards with and without PLC rationale was unable to detect a mean difference in the year of the award (t (159) = −1.620; p = .11; r = .13; n = 159).

doctrinal authority for justifying PLC and TCE; and legal reasoning to rationalize PLC and TCE assessments.

First, various tests identified that, over time, there was a meaningful change in the number of authorities that tribunals used to justify PLC[80] and TCE[81] determinations in final awards. The general direction was: recent awards provided more cost justification, whereas the oldest awards were least likely to provide authority. Follow-up tests revealed the meaningful effect existed only when comparing between the oldest and most recent awards.[82] Table 7.7 provides an illustrative example of the effect in TCE. In the earliest data, the average tribunal provided *less than one* PLC authority to justify a decision in a final award, whereas the most recent data demonstrated tribunals used one or more legal sources to justify the decision. *See* Table 7.7.

TABLE 7.7

Mean Number of Authorities Relied upon to Justify TCE Decisions in Final Awards ($n = 159$).

	Mean TCE Authorities	*Standard Deviation*	*Total*
Generation 1 (until June 1, 2006)	0.67	0.923	52
Generation 2 (June 1, 2006–June 1, 2009)	0.94	0.987	47
Generation 3 (June 1, 2009–January 1, 2012)	1.27	1.133	60
Total	0.97	1.049	159

Second, even though legal rationales started out with a high proportion of cases offering explanations for cost decisions, tribunals increased the number of justifications offered over time for both PLC[83] and TCE[84] decisions. Once again, the general direction was that more

[80] A between-subjects factorial analysis of variance (ANOVA) identified a reliable difference between the mean number of authorities offered for PLC and the different generations of data ($F(2,156) = 5.178; p = .01; r = .27; n = 159$). In G1, the mean number of PLC authorities offered was .65 ($SD = .99; n = 52$); in G2, the mean was .89 ($SD = .98; n = 47$); and in G3, the mean was 1.30 ($SD = 1.21; n = 60$). A correlation coefficient also identified a reliable positive relationship between the total number of PLC authorities provided and the year of the award ($r(159) = .26; p = .001$). The direction was: the more recent the award, the higher the number authorities cited.

[81] An ANOVA found a reliable relationship between TCE authorities offered and different generations of data ($F(2, 156) = 4.716; p = .01; r = .24; n = 159$). A correlation coefficient also identified a positive relationship between number of TCE authorities provided and year the award was rendered ($r(159) = .27; p = .001$).

[82] For PLC authority, HSD follow-ups indicated the reliable effect was confined to comparisons between G1 to G3 awards. TCE authority follow-ups revealed the same pattern driving the overall significant effect.

[83] An ANOVA found a reliable relationship between PLC justification and different generations of data ($F(2, 156) = 4.675; p = .01; r = .24; n = 159$). In G1, the mean number of reasons was 2.12 ($SD = 1.99; n = 52$); in G2, the mean dropped slightly to 1.79 ($SD = 1.37; n = 47$); and in G3, the mean was 2.82 ($SD = 1.90; n = 60$). A correlation coefficient identified a positive relationship between number of PLC rationales used and award year ($r(159) = .16; p = .04$).

[84] An ANOVA found a reliable relationship between TCE explanations provided and different generations of data $F(2, 156) = 4.384; p = .01; r = .24; n = 159$). A correlation coefficient also identified a positive relationship between number of TCE rationales offered and year the award was rendered ($r(159) = .22; p = .01$).

recent awards explained assessments using more legal reasoning. Follow-up tests revealed, however, the meaningful effect existed only when focusing upon the newest awards.[85] Table 7.8 provides the average number of explanations offered over time.

TABLE 7.8

Mean Number of Rationales Relied upon to Justify TCE Decisions in Final Awards ($n = 159$).

	Mean TCE Authorities	*Standard Deviation*	*Total*
Generation 1 (until June 1, 2006)	1.88	1.700	52
Generation 2 (June 1, 2006–June 1, 2009)	1.87	1.296	47
Generation 3 (June 1, 2009–January 1, 2012)	2.63	1.615	60
Total	2.16	1.591	159

As other research identified a similar growth of tribunal reasoning occurring in substantive decisions,[86] increased use of authority and rationale for costs is perhaps unsurprising and even warranted. While tribunals could have done better at the outset, the data nevertheless sends the message that tribunals have begun taking cost assessments more seriously, improving their explanations, and providing greater clarity in decision-making. They should continue to do so in the future, particularly given the scope of direct fiscal costs.

V. Discussion

The analyses revealed four core findings that implicate debates about ITA costs. First, tribunals exhibited mixed success in offering clear and full explanations of cost decisions. Given the ease with which tribunals could provide explanation of cost assessments—particularly when the average costs of parties' lawyers and tribunals were roughly US$11 million—it would behoove tribunals to exhibit more care. Parties pay for the privilege of arbitral reasoning and judgment, and those explanations—while not necessarily requiring a hundred or even twenty pages of justification—are worthy of careful, explicit, and honest consideration. Others observe that, where millions of dollars of costs are involved but costs are a "study in brevity," this is a problematic misalignment.[87]

[85] For PLC rationale, HSD follow-ups indicated the effect was confined to comparisons between G2 to G3 awards; but a more liberal LSD follow-up identified the effect persisted when comparing G1 to G3 and G2 to G3, with awards rendered latest in time always having the largest mean number of reasons offered. For TCE rationale, HSD and LSD follow-ups demonstrated that the effect existed when comparing: (1) G1 with G3 awards, and (2) G2 with G3 awards, with later-in-time final awards offering reliably more rationale.

[86] *See* Commission, *supra* note 29; Fauchald, *supra* note 29.

[87] Riesenfeld & Robbins, *supra* note 5 (describing tribunals giving short shrift to costs, describing *Philip Morris v. Uruguay* as a "study in brevity" as it reflected "eight paragraphs out of an award that exceeded 76 pages (not including the 45-page dissent)" when "Morris's costs were about $17 million, Uruguay's slightly over

Second, tribunals' justifications were visually weaker in providing authority but stronger providing analytical justification of decisions. For either PLC or TCE, tribunals could easily refer to various treaties, arbitration rules, previous awards, and scholarship to explain the basis of cost assessments.[88] Tribunals could consider baselines from national law, particularly when parties come from states sharing a doctrinal approach to costs. Yet only one tribunal analyzed, *CME v. Czech Republic*, ever considered domestic legal authority related to tribunal costs. It is troubling that—when sources are easy to locate (and probably readily known)—tribunals failed to provide authority for cost decisions. Because referring to existing law is straightforward and easy—demonstrating ITA decision-making is bounded by agreed legal principles and preventing legal errors—one would hope that future tribunals would increasingly refer to legal authority. If law professors require students to cite to legal authority on examinations in order to do well, one would hope arbitrators paid hundreds of thousands of dollars for professional expertise would render decisions with a higher degree of precision. The general failure to incorporate authority is more troubling if ITA purports to demonstrate rule-of-law values. Investment treaties should provide incentives for rule-based decisions, so that parties can make grounded arguments and arbitrators can engage in decision-making that promotes legitimacy and procedural justice.[89]

Yet, lack of coherence is somewhat unsurprising.[90] Treaties and arbitration rules forming the bulk of governing law are often silent or fail to address costs. Key institutions either have not addressed cost guidelines or only vaguely reference factors such as "outcome of the case" or "other relevant circumstances."[91] Meanwhile, counsel at the end of a case suffering from cognitive depletion may give cost arguments short shrift in their briefing, particularly if tribunals do not request briefing on costs. It is then little wonder that tribunals pick reasons at their leisure to justify decisions. One might suggest that arbitrators simply give parties the result they requested, and the vacuum of guidelines left by lack of party agreement requires arbitrators to make difficult choices.[92] If stakeholders create an ITA system failing to address costs clearly, they should hardly be surprised when the system does not provide clear results.

$10 million, and the arbitration and administrative fees totaled $1.5 million."); *see also* Brown de Vejar & Baldwin, *supra* note 12.

[88] *See supra* Section II.

[89] *See* Rebecca Hollander-Blumoff & Tom R. Tyler, *Procedural Justice in Negotiation: Procedural Fairness, Outcome Acceptance, and Integrative Potential*, 33 L. & Soc. Inq. 473 (2008); Tom R. Tyler, *Governing and Diversity: The Effect of Fair Decisionmaking Procedures on the Legitimacy of Government*, 28 Law & Soc'y Rev. 809, 827 (1994) (finding "use of fair decisionmaking procedures" enhances legitimacy of national governmental authorities).

[90] *See* Schill, *supra* note 6, at 659 ("The discretion conferred upon arbitral tribunals accounts for a considerable amount of uncertainty in the allocation of costs in investment treaty arbitration.").

[91] *See* Stephen W. Schill, *Enabling Private Ordering: Function, Scope and Effect of Umbrella Clauses in International Investment Treaties*, 18 Minn. J. Int'l L. 1 (2009).

[92] If, however, parties have expressly agreed on standards to follow, whether through treaty terms or later agreement, tribunal failure to abide by parties' agreement could be problematic. *See, e.g.*, Crystallex Int'l Corp v. Bolivarian Republic of Venezuela, ICSID ARB(AF)/11/2, Award ¶¶ 951-960 (Apr. 4, 2016), https://bit.ly/2LQc5Uf (last visited Aug. 30, 2018) (noting both parties agreed the loser-pays rule should apply but deciding, given retained residual discretion under the treaty and ICSID Additional Facility Rules, to exercise discretion to not shift costs against the losing state).

Yet this also means, should stakeholders wish to enhance legitimacy, provide clarity, and contain tribunal discretion, costs are the opportunity for meaningful reform. Meanwhile, with ICSID and other entities considering investment dispute settlement costs and reform opportunities, it would be appropriate to guide arbitrator discretion to aid bounded rationality and avoid the potential nefarious aspects of intuitive decision-making.[93]

Third, the most recent tribunals generally provided better rationalization of cost decisions, as compared to the earliest tribunals. This difference suggests that, although arbitrators may not have done particularly well at the outset, ITA tribunals are slowly improving. Although commentators may have initially been correct that justifications of cost were rare or limited, the evidence suggests that the jurisprudence of ITA costs has evolved. Nevertheless, tribunals should continue to develop their cost explanations. As fiscal amounts involved were non-trivial and tribunals can at least explain their own fees, arbitrators' transparency, care, and precision on costs can demonstrate a commitment to practices comporting with rule-of-law and legitimacy.

Finally, the analyses disrupted claims that tribunals follow either a pure "loser-pays" or a "pay-your-own-way approach." Instead, tribunals followed a factor-dependent approach and used various factors to make cost determinations. Although Smith was on the right track to suggest there are multiple options that tribunals can—and do—use to explain costs,[94] it is not clear that tribunals' practice was completely unclear, arbitrary, and inconsistent. Lack of predictability is, in and of itself, a form of certainty in uncertainty. Nevertheless, the data indicated the predominant bases justifying costs involved parties' relative success, tribunal perceptions about equity and reasonableness, and tribunal discretion. Ultimately, concerns about factors affecting outcome and conceptions of justice were the primary divination rods for costs. Meanwhile, party conduct during the proceedings was secondary.

Whether that baseline is normatively desirable, however, is another matter. It is troubling that other considerations related to justice—including public interest, stare decisis norms, and party equality of arms—were rarely used, often in less than 3% of final awards. Similarly, references to settlement efforts occurred in less than 10% of final awards. If stakeholders wish to create a dispute resolution system with cost implications that promote fairness and efficiency, this latter finding requires both attention and redress.[95] To the extent states want additional cohesion on cost determinations, which is justified given the fiscal costs, states should actively consider their options. These options include whether to revise their investment treaties to provide clear guidance on cost-shifting, the factors that tribunals must consider, how to prioritize competing considerations, and how equity should guide tribunals or otherwise impact the exercise of tribunal discretion.

---

[93] *See* Brown de Vejar & Baldwin, *supra* note 12 (arguing for more precision in standards applicable to cost-shifting and "where costs are shifted because of the tribunal's concerns regarding the abusive behavior of a party, such as an investor's ulterior motive for bringing a claim, these reasons should be articulated so that they may act as an effective deterrent to such tactics going forward"); Chapter 9 (discussing ICSID's proposed rule changes).

[94] Smith, *supra* note 7.

[95] *See* Wetter & Preim, *supra* note 6, at 333 ("[A] much increased awareness of the impact and proper allocation . . . (including the proper methods of their assessment) is desirable . . . much greater care and time must be devoted in arbitral proceedings to the presentation of cost claims and to their determination.").

8 The Potential Drivers—Predicting ITA Costs

MANY VARIABLES COULD, in theory, be linked to ITA costs. This chapter explores various possibilities with an eye toward explaining ITA costs for possible future prediction. While modeling ITA costs involves a trade-off, namely an under-specification of non-identifiable costs that are challenging to measure reliably, it focuses on direct, tangible fiscal elements to aid risk management for parties, counsel, and other stakeholders. As there has never before been any explanatory modeling of ITA costs, the chapter offers a novel perspective. The chapter first sets the stage by identifying the tight, perhaps expected, link between costs of parties' counsel and the tribunal. Second, it explores cost linkages to the starting and end points of ITA, namely amounts claimed and outcomes. It then focuses on core demographics from earlier chapters to identify non-significant and significant cost predictors. Finally, it offers a descriptive model that partially explains the variance of ITA costs.

I. The Cost Nexus

Minimal research has explored links between core ITA costs, namely parties' combined legal expenses and tribunal costs. In theory, the variables should be linked, as the scope of care and attention counsel uses to arbitrate disputes are likely reflected in higher costs, and tribunals will have more work to do sifting through materials and carefully making decisions. Another theory, however, is that ITA costs should not be interlinked, as tribunals' work should be independent of counsel's efforts and simply reflect the independent effort required to complete adjudication. The question is: Which theory does the data support?

Analyses repeatedly revealed a strong relationship between parties' and tribunals' costs. A basic test revealed a statistically large, robust, and reliable relationship between parties'

Arbitration Costs. Susan D. Franck.

total legal expenses and total tribunal and administrative costs.[1] Controlling for case length, the strong, reliable relationship persisted.[2] The tests revealed that, as both parties' legal costs increased, tribunals' costs also reliably increased; and when parties' legal fees decreased, so did tribunal costs. Figure 8.1 demonstrates the effect. The strong positive nature of the relationship supported the first hypothesis: that where counsel expended more time, effort, and money to arbitrate a dispute, tribunals expended commensurate levels of energy and fiscal resources.

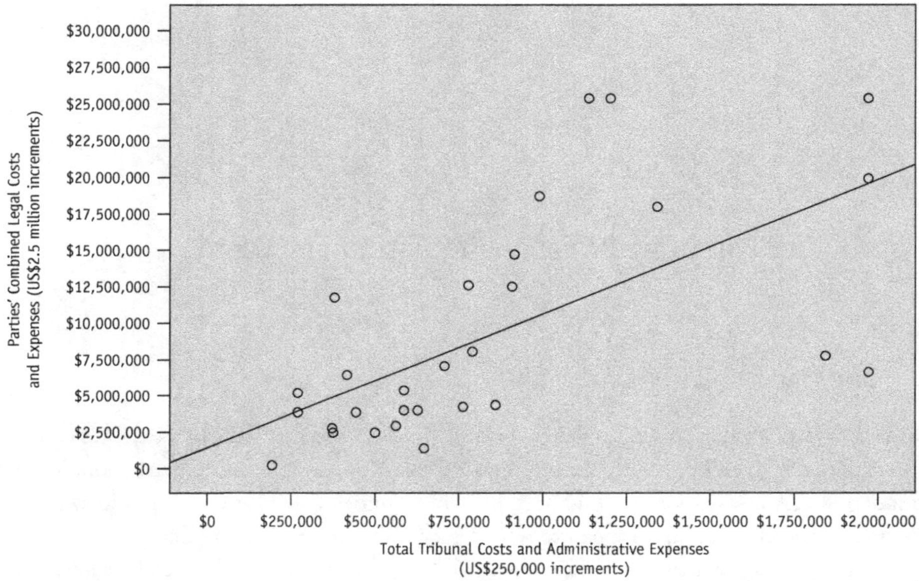

FIGURE 8.1 Final Awards using Inflation-adjusted Winsorized Data on Investors' and Respondents' Combined PLC (Total PLC), using US$2.5 Million Increments, and Total TCE, using US$250,000 Million Increments,[3] including a Line-of-Best-Fit to Demonstrate the Significant Relationship.

Correlation, however, is not causation. The test does not prove that higher counsel costs inevitably lead to higher tribunal costs. It is possible, for example, that counsel costs were a proxy for other aspects, such as seriousness, the scope of underlying documentation, or the difficulty of resolving the dispute. It is, nevertheless, a relationship to appreciate, as it undercuts the hypothesis of

[1] A bivariate correlation analyzed Total PLC and Total TCE to assess a potential linear using logged data, observing a large and reliable relationship between the two variables (r (29) = .62; p < .001). *See also* Appendix I (providing an explanation for data selection and statistical tests).

[2] Using logged data, a partial correlation controlled for case length and identified that the large and reliable link between total PLC and total TCE persisted (r (25) = .40; p = .04).

[3] Using winsorized data for total PLC that Appendix I reflects exhibited slightly high skewing, tests remained significant (r (29) = .63; p < .001), even controlling for case length (r (25) = .43; p = .03). Winsorized data is displayed, as it is easier to understand the scale of dollar-values (rather than logs).

cost independence. Yet, despite finding a strong and reliable relationship, caution is warranted given missing data.[4]

When it comes to ITA costs, given the intertwined nature, conservation of party costs are only one tool. Party costs may have been the larger fiscal thumb on the scale, yet tribunals should also push for increased efficiency to promote cost savings and efficient dispute resolution. While issues involving international law and state sovereignty are no doubt important and worthy of focused time and funds to permit thorough consideration of the issues, neither lawyers nor tribunals should tolerate conduct that generates unnecessary costs.

II. Costs and Amounts Claimed

Minimal research has explored links between amounts claimed and ITA costs. There are theoretical reasons to believe a connection could exist. For PLC, lawyers' fees could be higher when higher amounts are claimed, to ensure that the value of a claim or a defense warrants the expenditure of party resources. For tribunal expenses, where greater amounts are at risk, tribunals might take claims as an indicator of seriousness and expend more resources to consider parties' arguments and ensure the arbitration process is thorough, arguably increasing tribunal costs. Yet, one might also theorize that tribunals should take the time necessary to resolve the dispute according to case complexity, thereby making tribunal costs roughly equivalent regardless of claimed amounts. Using this paradigm, as all ITA disputes involve the sensitive consideration of international law and potential state liability, and because factual and legal questions can be complex irrespective of claimed damages, the value of an investor's claim should not dictate (or should be irrelevant to) tribunal cost.

The only known research on this topic identified that, as the size of investors' claims increased, so did *tribunal* costs.[5] The lingering question is whether, with the developing caseload, those initial findings evolved or expanded regarding parties' costs.

Multiple tests were unable to find a reliable relationship between parties' legal costs and amounts claimed, but the reliable link between amounts claimed and tribunal costs persisted.[6] That simple sentence requires unpacking a variety of implicit, embedded assessments.

First, it was not possible to identify any correlation between investors' claims and investors' legal costs,[7] even controlling for case length.[8] Second, it was also not possible to

---

[4] *But see supra* Chapter 4 (analyzing data and not generally finding fundamental group differences between awards with and without costs data).

[5] Susan D. Franck, *Rationalizing Costs in Investment Treaty Arbitration*, 88 WASH U. L. REV. 769, 835–36; *see also* Kate Brown de Vejar & Chloe Baldwin, *The Economics of Access: Systemic Imbalances in ISDS*, *in* ICCA CONGRESS PROCEEDINGS (forthcoming) (draft on file with author) (discussing links between investor claims and ITA).

[6] Readers are again reminded that Appendix I provides background on data and statistical tests used, explaining that inferential tests used inflation-adjusted data with the lowest skewness to most closely approximate assumptions underlying statistical tests.

[7] Evaluating logged amounts claimed and logged claimant PLC failed to identify a reliable linear relationship (r (38) = .21; p = .21).

[8] A partial correlation, controlling for case length, failed to reveal a reliable relationship (r (34) = .20; p = .26). Similarly, controlling for the presence (or lack) of energy disputes, failed to reveal a reliable relationship with amounts claimed (r (35) = .09; p = .60).

identify a reliable link between amounts an investor claimed and states' legal costs,[9] even controlling for case length.[10] In sharp contrast—but replicating earlier research—there was a strong, positive, and reliable relationship between tribunal costs and amounts claimed.[11] The relationship remained reliable, even after controlling for case length.[12] In other words, as amounts investors claimed increased, so did TCE; and as amounts claimed decreased, so did TCE. *See* Figure 8.2.

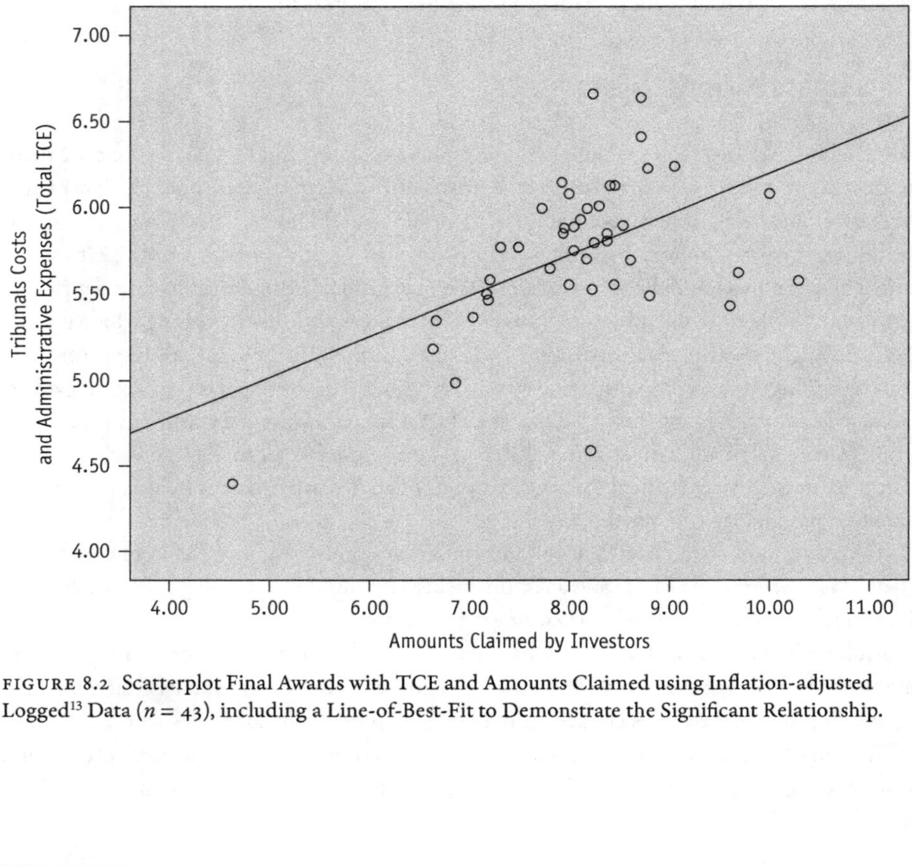

FIGURE 8.2 Scatterplot Final Awards with TCE and Amounts Claimed using Inflation-adjusted Logged[13] Data ($n = 43$), including a Line-of-Best-Fit to Demonstrate the Significant Relationship.

---

[9] A bivariate correlation using logged amounts claimed and winsorized respondent PLC failed to identify a reliable relationship (r (43) = .17; p = .27).

[10] A partial correlation, that controlled for case length, exploring respondents' legal costs and amounts claimed remained non-significant (r (39) = .18; p = .28). A partial correlation controlling for presence of energy disputes likewise was unable to detect a reliable link (r (40) = .12; p = .47).

[11] Logged amounts claimed and logged total TCE were reliably linked (r (43) = .51; p < .001).

[12] A partial correlation, that controlled case length, again identified a reliable relationship between tribunal costs and investors' claims (r (39) = .38; p = .01). Even controlling for the presence of an energy dispute, where claims were reliably higher, the link between claims and TCE using logged data remained significant (r (41) =.41; p = .01).

[13] While logged data is more challenging to understand as is on a different scale from U.S. dollar-values, the scatterplot best captured the significant relationship.

Despite replicating a strong, reliable, and positive relationship between investors' claims and tribunal costs, it is not yet proper to conclude that amounts claimed—even though it precedes a tribunal incurring costs—cause tribunal costs. It is, however, part of the effect and should be explored in any multivariate model attempting to explain or otherwise predict ITA costs.

III. PLC and TCE: Links to Outcomes

To the extent that lawyers' legal fees—for prosecution or defense—are nontrivial and represent a serious proportion of a case's net outcome, it begs the question: Are lawyers in ITA worth what clients pay? One would hope that, if one is spending more on lawyers, those increased fees generate more positive outcomes. Likewise, with tribunals being paid by parties, one wonders whether their costs are linked to outcomes. Unfortunately, literature has not explored ITA costs and outcomes.[14]

This section analyzes ITA costs using three different ways of understanding outcomes using Chapter 5's outcome variables. First, it investigates ITA costs using a dichotomous "win" or "loss" variable. Second, it explores cost links with amounts awarded (including settlements). Finally, it considers ITA costs as a function of investors' relative success.

A. ITA COSTS: LINKS WITH WINNING AND LOSING

There was a reliable link between ITA costs and binary outcomes of which party won—but the effect was strictly limited to the cost of investors' counsel. Overall the relationship was, where investors won, they were more likely to pay more for legal representation. By contrast, it was not possible to identify any link between which party won and the costs of states' counsel or tribunal cost.

Multiple tests identified a robust effect whereby the cost of counsel (PLC) for investors was reliably more expensive when investors won, and where states won, investor PLC cost reliably less.[15] With a statistically medium-sized effect, the practical significance was, for cases where investors won and using a dollar-based scale, claimants' counsel expended nearly twice as much; whereas for the cases where respondents won, investors' counsel spent roughly half the amount states' counsel spent. *See* Table 8.1.

---

[14] Earlier research failed to identify a link between one outcome variable and tribunal costs. Franck, *supra* note 5, at 837–38.

[15] A t-test using logged data identified a reliable mean difference in claimants' PLC for cases where either investors or states won ($t\,(46) = 2.496; p = .02; r = .35; n = 48$). A Mann-Whitney U-Test identified a reliable median difference in the cost of claimants' counsel ($U = 159.0; p = .01$). Controlling for the presence of an energy dispute, the reliable link persisted using logged data ($r\,(45) = -.36; p = .01$); but when controlling for case length, the link dissipated ($r\,(45) = -.18; p = .23$), suggesting some caution in drawing overly strong inferences from the otherwise significant results.

TABLE 8.1

Claimant PLC using Winsorized Inflation-adjusted Data and Winning or Losing ITA (n = 48).[16]

	Mean (US$) Claimant PLC	*Standard Deviation*	*Total*
Claimant Win— *Investor Awarded US$1 or more*	6,011,951	4473000	20
Respondent Win— *Investor Awarded US$0*	3,154,113	4758092	28
Total	4,344,879	4808450	48

A degree of caution is required, however, given the effect of outliers even in the winsorized data. Nevertheless, using logged data, with acceptable skewing, the results reflected a similar pattern for outcomes and investors' PLC, but on a different scale than reflected by Table 8.1. For cases respondents won, the logged mean for investors' PLC was 6.17 (SD = .597; n = 28), whereas the logged mean investor PLC for an investor "win" was 6.59 (SD = .530; n = 20).

By contrast, none of the tests analyzing respondents' legal costs identified a link with the party winning or losing.[17] Using inflation-adjusted winsorized data with the lowest skewing, the mean cost of respondent counsel in cases where states won was US$3.4 million.[18] In slight contrast, the average cost when the state lost was roughly US$3 million.[19] Irrespective of outcome, states' average PLC was around US$3.2 million.[20] Despite a facial suggestion that state counsel cost somewhat more when states won, it was not possible to identify a reliable link. Put another way, rather than letting a deceptive average "anchor" the debate

---

[16] With winsorized data exhibiting higher skewing, results remained significant (t (46) = 2.103; p = .04; r = .30; n = 48). The one other case involving claimant PLC involving a settlement or discontinuance were investors' legal fees in *Foresti v. South Africa*, which using inflation-adjusted data were US$5,960,598. Winsorized data is displayed, as it is easier to understand the scale of dollar-values and still sought to minimize the effects of statistical outliers. *See also* Appendix I.

[17] A t-test using winsorized data failed to identify a reliable relationship between outcome and states' legal fees (t (51) = −0.469; p = .64; r = .07; n = 53). Partial correlations, that controlled for case length (r (49) = −.01; p =.99) or presence of an energy dispute (r (50) = −.09; p = .52), were still unable to identify a link with state PLC and raw outcomes. A Mann-Whitney U-Test failed to find a meaningful difference in median state PLC (U = 319.0; p = .84). While the less than small statistical effects do not suggest a power problem, the risk of insufficient power should be acknowledged; a sample of over 700 cases with data would be required to exclude the possibility of a reliable latent effect.

[18] M = 3,380,975; SD = 3494464; n = 33.

[19] M = 2,962,633; SD = 2457052; n = 20.

[20] The mean cost of state counsel in the two cases, involving settlements and discontinuances, hovered over US$3.5 million. M = 3,749,946; SD = 3975326; n = 2.

on costs,[21] the better course is to recognize the tests suggested a possibility that the facial disparity in average costs could reflect chance alone, rather than a reliable effect that should form the basis for planning and decision-making.

Like states' legal costs, the data provided evidence that tribunal costs could function independently from outcome. None of the models analyzed detected a meaningful link between tribunal costs and which party won.[22] Using inflation-adjusted winsorized data to mitigate statistical outliers, the mean tribunal cost when investors won was around US$800,000;[23] but, when states won, the mean cost was around US$650,000.[24] The null effect (i.e., the inability to find a reliable relationship) means facial variation is an improper basis to make a meaningful inference. Moreover, irrespective of outcome, the typical tribunal cost was under US$1 million.[25]

Ultimately, only one ITA cost was reliably linked to who won or lost: namely, investors' legal costs. This provides some support for the theory that, for successful investors, the increased cost may be worth the positive outcome—and unsuccessful investors may either be happy to not have paid more for a poor outcome or may perhaps wish they invested more in prosecuting their claim. Yet, reliable links need not reflect cause. Simply spending more money on counsel does not guarantee favorable outcomes. The result may derive from other variables, including claimants with stronger cases (e.g., resulting from different treaty terms, facts, experts, or arbitrators), or the claimants being willing to invest more resources into arbitrating claims. Yet, other research suggests that expertise of claimants' counsel affected winning or losing.[26] This generates the possibility that, rather than costs driving outcome, it is the legal expertise of sophisticated, repeat counsel—which may also cost more—that drives the link with outcomes.

By contrast, neither respondents' counsel nor tribunal costs were reliably associated with who won. For respondents, the inability to demonstrate a reliable association means that counsel costs cannot cause outcomes. Yet, the null effect raises a question: For those cases where states lost, why would a state want to pay more than an average amount? To reframe the null results and minimize the suggestive pull of cognitive illusions, the data also meant that it was not possible to conclude that states paid reliably more when they lost.

---

[21] *But see* Chapter 2 (discussing cognitive illusions but noting that the concept of anchoring applies to fiscal numbers, not concepts).

[22] Using logged data, a t-test was unable to find a reliable mean difference in total TCE in cases where claimants and states won ($t\ (47) = 0.781$; $p = .78$; $r = .11$; $n = 49$). Partial correlations, controlling for case length ($r\ (45) = .04$; $p = .80$) or presence of energy disputes ($r\ (46) = -.04$; $p = .78$), were likewise unable to identify reliable relationships between TCE and which party won or lost. Similarly, a Mann-Whitney U-test found no reliable difference in tribunals' median cost ($U = 274.0$; $p = .75$).

[23] $M = 835{,}485$; $SD = 695432$; $n = 20$.

[24] $M = 649{,}351$; $SD = 333956$; $n = 29$.

[25] In slight contrast, average tribunal fees for disputes resulting in settlement or discontinuance was under US$300,000. $M = 268{,}371$; $SD = 154593$; $n = 4$. *See also* Chapter 6.

[26] Susan D. Franck & Lindsey Wylie, *Predicting Outcomes in Investment Treaty Arbitration*, 65 DUKE L.J. 459 (2015).

The lack of a relationship with tribunal costs was noteworthy, as it provides one piece of data about the potential integrity of the arbitration process. As winning or losing could not be reliably linked with tribunal costs, this provides limited evidence that tribunals as a group were not necessarily self-dealing, and outcomes could operate independently of tribunal cost. Nevertheless, caution is warranted. Like all the null analyses in this book, limited data injects the possibility of case selection effects or other alternative explanations, and for analyses failing to detect reliable differences, replication is required before concluding no effect exists.[27] In the interim, these results provide initial evidence of a reliable relationship between outcome and claimants' legal fees but also the potential lack of links to other ITA costs.

B. ITA COSTS: LINKS WITH AMOUNTS AWARDED

A second way to measure outcome involves amounts awarded. Historically, there was no analysis of relationships between amounts awarded and parties' legal costs. The only analysis of tribunal costs failed to find a relationship between those costs and amounts awarded.[28]

The analyses for amounts awarded tended to mirror findings from binary outcomes, namely increases in investors' counsel fees were associated with larger amounts awarded. Neither respondents' fees nor tribunal fees demonstrated the same pattern. Yet there is some nuance.

First, for investors' PLC, multiple tests[29] identified a link between higher amounts awarded and higher counsel cost. This was true both for the set all cases[30] and for the subset of cases where investors won.[31] The effect was, as claimants' PLC increased, so too did amounts awarded. Figure 8.3 illustrates that relationship. It also reflects that, for cases where investors failed to obtain damages, their legal costs varied; but for cases where investors' obtained damages, there was a clustering with higher legal fees and larger damage awards.

---

[27] Post-hoc power analysis indicated, to identify the smallest potentially latent relationship, to have sufficient power complete cost and outcome data would be required from over 780 cases.

[28] Franck, *supra* note 5, at 837–38.

[29] Since PLC, TCE, and amounts awarded are continuous variables using the same scale, bivariate correlations evaluated linear relationships. Given data types and skewness, the analyses presented used inflation-adjusted models with the lowest skewing to most closely approximate the assumptions underlying the test. *See* Appendix I.

[30] For all cases, there was a reliable, positive relationship ($r(48) = .35; p = .02$) between logged amounts awarded and logged claimant PLC. A partial correlation, controlling for presence of an energy dispute, also revealed a reliable relationship between logged amounts awarded and claimant fees ($r(45) = .36; p = .01$). Controlling for case length, however, rendered the link non-significant ($r(44) = .17; p = .26$), suggesting case length was the driver.

[31] $r(20) = .45; p = .046$. Using logged data and controlling case length ($r(17) = .51; p = .03$) replicated the reliable link; when controlling for presence of an energy dispute, the relationship was on the cusp of significance ($r(17) = .45; p = .05$) and the latent effect was statistically large.

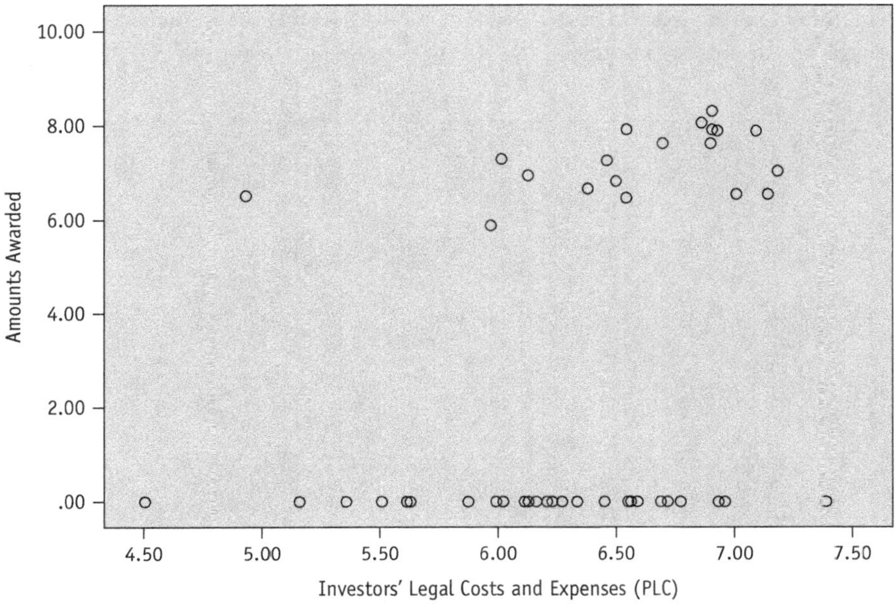

FIGURE 8.3 Scatterplot of Final ITA Awards reflecting Investor PLC and Amounts Awarded using Inflation-adjusted Logged Data ($n = 48$).[32]

It was not possible, however, to identify a reliable relationship between states' PLC and amounts awarded to investors. This held true both for tests exploring all awards[33] and the smaller subset of awards (including settlements) where investors obtained some fiscal award.[34] The superficial, but non-significant, trend was for a small negative relationship, whereby the higher states' legal fees the lower amount awarded; and the lower the respondents' PLC, the higher the amount awarded.

For tribunal costs and administrative expenses (TCE), the overall inability to detect a reliable pattern was present but with a twist. Initially, for all cases—including cases where tribunals awarded no damages—there was no identifiable link between amounts awarded and TCE.[35] Figure 8.4 illustrates the non-significant general results and the wrinkle. Namely, for the subset of cases with a damages award, there was a strong, positive, and reliable

[32] The logged data scatterplot best captured the relationship, demonstrating the variation in investor PLC for: (1) those cases claimants lost (US$0 award); and (2) those cases were claimants obtained some damage award from a tribunal or through settlement.

[33] It was not possible to identify a reliable relationship between logged amounts awarded and winsorized respondent PLC ($r(54) = -.05$; $p = .70$). The non-significant results replicated using a partial correlation to control for case length ($r(53) = -.18$; $p = .20$), and presence of energy disputes ($r(54) = -.08$; $p = .58$).

[34] $r(20) = .06$; $p = .80$. Even controlling for case length $r(20) = -.03$; $p = .89$) and energy disputes ($r(20) = .10$; $p = .70$), partial correlations replicated the non-significant results.

[35] The non-significant correlation analyzed logged amounts awarded and logged TCE ($r(52) = .16$; $p = .26$). The non-significant results between amounts awarded and TCE replicated when using a partial correlation to control for case length ($r(51) = .16$; $p = .26$) and presence of energy disputes ($r(53) = .16$; $p = .27$).

relationship between tribunal costs and damages,[36] with increased costs linked to increased damages and decreased damages associated with decreased tribunal costs.

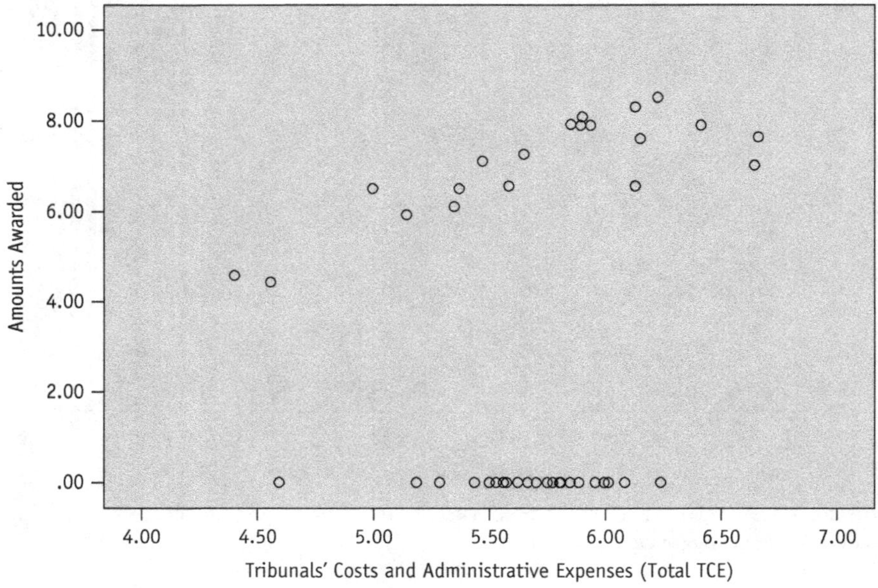

FIGURE 8.4 Scatterplot of Final ITA Awards reflecting Total TCE and Amounts Awarded ($n = 52$) using Inflation-adjusted Logged Data.[37]

Yet, strong inferences should be made cautiously. As described earlier, amounts claimed were associated with higher tribunal costs. After controlling for amounts claimed, the reliable relationship between TCE and amounts awarded became non-significant.[38] The disappearance of the link between damages and TCE, once investors' claims were held constant, begs the question whether the real variable of interest is amount claimed—perhaps as a proxy for a claim's perceived seriousness or time required to adjudicate detailed damage assessments. Awarding damages can be time-consuming for non-economists. It may require arbitrators to spend considerable time digging into underlying data, assumptions, and models. Particularly at institutions (such as ICSID) where arbitrators are paid on an hourly basis and because most cases analyzed occurred at ICSID, increased time to consider complex damage submissions easily translates into increased tribunal costs. Moreover, should tribunals appoint their own expert to aid damage calculations, the additional support

---

[36] $r(20) = .81; p < .001$. A partial correlation using the same data replicated the results when controlling for either case length ($r(17) = .79; p < .001$) or presence of an energy dispute ($r(17) = .81; p < .001$).

[37] While logged data is challenging to understand, the scatterplot most properly captured the relationship with TCE, demonstrating the variation in total TCE for: (1) cases where claimants lost (US$0 award), where TCE was somewhat normally distributed, possibly reflecting random variance, and (2) cases where investors obtained damages, where there was a strong and reliable link to cases with higher damages having higher TCE.

[38] $r(15) = -.27; p = .29$.

adds another layer of TCE expense. If data were disaggregated—to identify in which phases tribunals expended the most time resolving disputes—it could be possible to test whether the time commitment for tribunals evaluating damages generates increased tribunal costs. This is something institutions, in particular, are in a unique position to monitor. In the interim, the link between amounts awarded and TCE requires consideration in any descriptive model attempting to predict ITA costs.

C. ITA COSTS: LINKS TO RELATIVE INVESTOR SUCCESS

A final way to assess relationships with costs and outcomes involves relative investor success, namely identifying what tribunals awarded relative to claims. There has, however, been no literature exploring relative success and core ITA costs. Relative success could also potentially be a helpful, but incomplete, proxy for the relative strength of the dispute's merits.[39]

Using one simplistic theory, if lawyers provide commensurate value, their clients' relative success should be associated with the cost of their services. For investors, this translates into higher counsel fees for higher levels of investor success; and for states, driving down investors' success (i.e., states faring relatively better) should be reflected in relatively higher state legal fees. An alternative theory is that all parties vigorously pursue their rights and spend "what it takes" to pursue the dispute, and counsel cost has little to do with relative success. Under this paradigm, counsel fees reflect a party's confidence in success, the dispute's larger strategic value, idiosyncratic factors about the effort required to prosecute or defend a claim, or other factors. For tribunals' costs, one theory is that there should be no reliable link between tribunal costs and investors' relative success, as tribunal costs should function independently; but if there were to be a relationship, the direction of that relationship requires further scrutiny.

Multiple tests evaluated how investors' relative success, as the core outcome variable, impacted costs. Despite the theory that relative success would be *positively* correlated with investors' PLC and *negatively* correlated with respondents' PLC, none of the tests could isolate any meaningful relationship between investors' relative success and either party's PLC. It was also not possible to identify a reliable link between investors' relative success and TCE. Yet those statements include implicit, embedded information that are worthy of systemic consideration.

First, analyses failed to detect any relationship between investors' relative success and cost of investors' counsel.[40] The results were robust when controlling for key variables.[41]

The non-significant result may reflect, for cases where investors obtained damages, investors' experience a broad range of PLC but with a few clusters. In one cluster, investors did

---

[39] Franck & Wylie, *supra* note 26, at 486–87; *see also* Catherine A. Rogers, *The Politics of International Investment Arbitrators*, 12 SANTA CLARA J. INT'L L. 223, 234 (2013) (arguing "the relative strength of a particular party's case" serves as a control for correct outcomes).

[40] Using logged data, it was not possible to identify a reliable relationship between investors' PLC and relative success when analyzing all cases ($r(37) = .12; p = .50$) or the subset of investor wins ($r(20) = -.02.; p = .93$).

[41] A partial correlation controlling case length failed to identify a link between relative success and investors' PLC using logged data for final awards ($r(33) = .13; p = .46$) or the subset of investor wins ($r(20) = .12; p = .62$). Controlling for presence of energy disputes failed to identify a link between investors' relative success and investors' PLC in final awards ($r(34) = .13; p = .45$) or the subset of investor wins ($r(20) = -.01; p = .97$).

relatively well while expending little on fees. In *Swembalt v. Latvia*, investors received 45% of their claim and had lawyer fees that were the equivalent to under US$100,000;[42] investors in *Cargill v. Mexico* had a 62% success rate and paid under US$3.5 million in legal fees,[43] and the investors in *ADC v. Hungary*[44] and *BG Group v. Argentina*[45] had success rates ranging from 76 to 78% and fees that, using inflation-adjusted data, were in the order of US$4.5 million and US$8 million respectively. But likewise, a group of investors fared relatively poorly and paid a great deal. In *Chevron v. Ecuador*, investors obtained only 9% of claimed damages and had legal fees of roughly US$12 million,[46] and in *RosInvestCo v. Russia*, investors obtained 1% of their claim while incurring fees of around US$14 million.[47] In a more extreme case, in *Libananco v. Turkey*, investors had 0% success on a US$10 billion claim—yet expended nearly US$25 million in legal fees.[48]

Ultimately, the broad variance made it impossible to detect links between investors' relative success and higher (or lower) legal investor PLC. While providing a piece of evidence that investors' counsel fees operate independently of investors' relative success, it is possible that differently skilled lawyers have chosen to represent investors. For example, one group of counsel could provide cost-efficient services, but a second group of lawyers could arguably provide less efficient service by expending greater fees in pursuit of lower success levels, rather than settling weak claims. The challenge, for clients, is to demarcate between groups when making decisions about which counsel to retain.

For state counsel, the relationship between relative investor success and cost was somewhat more random. Multiple tests failed to detect a relationship between investors' relative success and states' counsel costs.[49] The non-significant results remained after controlling for key variables.[50] There were greater pockets of variance for states' legal fees. When investors

---

42 SwemBalt AB v. Republic of Lat., UNCITRAL, Decision by the Court of Arbitration, ¶¶ 10, 49 Section VII (Oct. 23, 2000), https://bit.ly/2KAiYZj (last visited Aug. 7, 2018); *see also* Codebook, Appendix IV (detailing coding procedures for converting non-U.S. dollar currencies).

43 Cargill, Inc. v. United Mexican States, ICSID Case No. ARB(FA) 05/2, Award, ¶¶ 158, 160 (Sept. 18, 2009), https://bit.ly/2OS7rbe (last visited Aug. 7, 2018).

44 ADC Affiliate Ltd. v. Republic of Hung., ICSID Case No. ARB/03/16, Award, ¶ 100 (Oct. 2, 2006), https://bit.ly/2M4H4kM (last visited Aug. 7, 2018).

45 BG Group Plc v. Argentine Republic, UNCITRAL, Final Award, ¶¶ 86(d), 415, 444, 458–65 (Dec. 24, 2007), https://bit.ly/2vrbvab (last visited Aug. 7, 2018).

46 Chevron Corp. & Texaco Petroleum Co. v. Republic of Ecuador, UNCITRAL Rules, Permanent Court of Arbitration Case No. 34877, ¶¶ 338, 355, Dispositif 3 (Aug. 31, 2011), https://bit.ly/2vH1BRc (last visited Aug. 7, 2018).

47 RosInvestCo UK Ltd. v. Russian Fed'n, SCC Case No. V079/2005, Final Award, ¶¶ 46–47, 692, 694 (Sept. 12, 2010), https://bit.ly/2gCH6BC (last visited Aug. 7, 2018).

48 Libananco Holdings Co. Ltd. v. Republic of Turk., ICSID Case No. ARB/06/8, Award, ¶¶ 182, 462, 559 (Sept. 2, 2011), https://bit.ly/2niSVfZ (last visited Aug. 7, 2018).

49 Using winsorized data for states' PLC, it was not possible to detect a reliable relationship when analyzing the set of all cases ($r\ (43) = -.01, p = .96$) or the subset of investor wins ($r\ (20) = .18; p = .48$).

50 Using a partial correlation to control for case length failed to reveal a link between investors' success and states' PLC using winsorized data for final awards ($r\ (39) = .004; p = .98$) or the subset of investor wins ($r\ (20) = .19; p = .44$). Controlling for the presence of an energy dispute also failed to identify a link between

lost, there was wide variation in states' PLC (costs ranging from around zero to US$10 million). For cases where investors experienced some success, there were multiple clusters. For cases with an investor success rate of less than 40%, there was a larger cluster of state PLC around US$2 million and a slightly lighter cluster around US$4 million. There were also a few cases, like *ADC v. Hungary* and *Kardassopoulos v. Georgia* where investor success rates were over 50%, and as the success rate increased, so too did states' PLC; but this is contrasted with *Chevron v. Ecaudor*, where there was less than 20% investor success but over US$17 million in state PLC. The variations could reflect, as discussed in Chapter 4, differences in states' experiences with counsel, including variations in in-house expertise, the role of external lawyers, political motification in defending potentially sensitive cases or cases with third-party funding, price discrimination potentially operating to states' benefit, or the results of procurement processes that some states use to retain lawyers. While the possibility of other explanatory variables remains, relative success and state counsel fees could also be random. While states may therefore reasonably focus less on the intersection of counsel experience, counsel cost, and relative investor success, they may nevertheless wish to actively consider the link between respondent counsel expertise and decreased levels of investor success.[51]

Finally, it was not possible to identify a reliable link between investors' relative success and tribunal costs. Multiple tests failed to detect any relationship between investors' relative success and TCE,[52] even controlling for key variables.[53] The non-significant direction of a potential latent effect was generally: the higher tribunal cost, the lower investors' relative success. Ultimately, the data could not prove that relative success was linked with higher (or lower) TCE, which provides initial evidence that investors' relative success operated independently of tribunal costs.

When thinking about relative success, parties may wish to think in a particularly careful manner about fees. For PLC and TCE, it was not possible to say that spending more obtained relatively better outcomes for either party. Nor did spending more money appear to generate reliably worse relative outcomes.

D. DISCUSSION AND SYNTHESIS

ITA costs were both linked to each other and sometimes, but not always, linked with the starting points and ending points of arbitration. First, total PLC and total TCE were reliably linked to each other. PLC was generally of a higher order of magnitude than TCE, and mean

investors' relative success and state PLC in final awards (r (40) = −.07; p = .66) or the subset of investor wins (r (20) = .10; p = .67).

[51] Franck & Wylie, *supra* note 26.

[52] Using logged TCE data, it was not possible to detect a reliable relationship when analyzing the set of all cases (r (42) = −.12; p = .44) or the subset of investor wins (r (18) = −.46; p = .06).

[53] Using a partial correlation to control for case length failed to identify a link between TCE and investor success using logged data for both final awards (r (41) = −.04; p = .79) and the subset of investor wins (r (11) = −.40; p = .77). Controlling for the presence of an energy dispute likewise failed to identify a significant link between investors' relative success and TCE in final awards (r (18) = −.43; p = .09) or the subset of investor wins (r (15) = .43; p = .08).

TCE costs were around 10% of PLC.[54] Parties can and should consider monitoring their own PLC as a possible indictor of their counterparts' costs—and certainly for gauging tribunal costs. Such consideration may also aid assessment of net value of settlement opportunities.

Second, both investors' and respondents' PLC were unrelated to amounts claimed, suggesting that claims operated independently of how much parties were willing to spend on arbitration. Yet *tribunal costs were* reliably linked to investors' claimed damages. Tribunals faced with disputes involving serious fiscal implications theoretically took their responsibilities seriously by spending more time on the dispute, thereby incurring more costs.[55] But likewise, as amounts claimed decreased, so too did TCE.

The link with amounts claimed suggests there is value in clarifying how tribunals allocate costs and suggests a need for safeguards to minimize harm (namely potentially increased costs and decreased settlement opportunities) from inflated claims. One procedural safeguard advocated in Chapter 9 involves requiring investors to accompany arbitration requests with a detailed preliminary expert report. As ITA has no good-faith pleading obligation, there is value in making clear ex ante that parties will be penalized for inflated claims or encouraging the more accurate assessments of initial damages, particularly as experimental research demonstrated that irrelevant anchors reliably increased tribunal damage awards.[56] Changing pleading obligations, requiring security for costs, or using cost-shifting standards strategically could incentivize behavior fostering efficiency and fairness. Using procedural tools to discipline timetables may lower arbitration costs for both parties, potentially decreasing arbitration-based buyer's remorse by focusing clients and counsel on ITA's net worth.[57] Likewise, it may facilitate negotiation within realistic zones of possible agreement,[58] and could, like early damage assessments in asbestos disputes, aid settlement.[59]

Third, outcomes were sometimes, but not always, linked with different ITA costs. For investors, spending more on their counsel was reliably associated with obtaining a "win" and amounts awarded—but not with relative success. In contrast, for states, paying their own counsel more did not mean they were more likely to win a case, but likewise, it did not mean

---

[54] Chapter 6 identified, using 2011 inflation-adjusted data, that parties' combined average PLC was around US$10 million (with a median around US$6 million), whereas average TCE was under US$1 million.

[55] Most cases studied occurred at ICSID or were ad hoc, meaning tribunal costs were primarily a function of hourly rates—rather than amount-in-controversy. As a reminder, none of the cases analyzed were at the ICC, where TCE would be a function of amounts claimed.

[56] *See* Chapter 2 (discussing *Inside the Arbitrator's Mind*).

[57] Although arguably unrepresentative, the successful CEO in *Metalclad* suggested the experience was "so dissatisfying that he wished he had merely entrusted his company's fate to informal mechanisms," including political options, given the lost time and arbitration costs. Jack J. Coe, Jr., *Toward a Complimentary Use of Conciliation in Investor-State Disputes—A Preliminary Sketch*, 12 U.C. Davis J. Int'l L. & Pol'y 8, 8–9 (2005).

[58] *See* Michael Watkins & Susan Rosengrant, Breakthrough International Negotiation: How Great Negotiators Transformed the World's Toughest Post-Cold War Conflicts 31–33 (2001); Michael L. Moffitt, *Will This Case Settle? An Exploration of Mediators' Predictions*, 16 Oh. St. J. Disp. Resol. 39 (2000).

[59] Asbestos litigation benefitted from addressing damages at an early procedural phase. *See* Drury Stevenson, *Reverse Bifurcation*, 75 U. Cin. L. Rev. 213, 217 (2008); Michelle J. White, *Asbestos Litigation: Procedural Innovations and Forum Shopping*, 35 J. Legal Stud. 365 (2006).

they were more likely to lose; and none of the tests ever identified reliable links between the cost of state counsel and either amounts awarded or relative success.

Finally, for tribunals, it was generally impossible to identify a reliable link between TCE and outcomes. More precisely, it was not possible to establish meaningful links to TCE with either party winning a dispute or relative investor success. Although one subset of data suggested tribunal costs were correlated with amounts awarded, the effect dissipated when amounts claimed were held constant. Moreover, one significant test does not mean tribunals *caused* the amounts awarded to be higher or support a "self-dealing" hypothesis, whereby arbitrators make large awards to generate a large personal payday. For the small subset of cases revealing a link, increased costs were arguably a rational reaction to a large and serious claim.

When assessing damage claims, tribunals must consume, consider, and evaluate a substantial amount of fiscal information, complex economic models, and competing expert reports with different theoretical assumptions. Tribunals are arguably more expert in law than financial accounting, and a copious number of hours may be required to adjudicate using a rule-of-law, rather than an intuitive, approach. As more than 75% of cases involved rules where tribunals were remunerated on an hourly basis, the number of hours devoted by the tribunal (and resulting costs) were higher given the value in carefully rendering an award. When state liability, and potential taxpayer payments are on the line, an investment of effort by tribunal members is warranted. But tribunals should not be perversely incentivized to pad their own bills simply because the amount in controversy is large. Future analysis should consider this potential relationship—keeping in mind claims are in investors' hands and those investors are not yet subject to a good-faith pleading obligation to prevent them from lodging claims disconnected from the facts.

Nevertheless, caution is required, given missing data[60] and temporal evolution. The null effects also cannot rule out the possibility of a latent link between ITA outcomes and costs. Although there is an risk of error with underpowered samples,[61] most of the potential latent effects were statistically small and typically far from significant. In the interim, these initial findings offer a constructive historical baseline for future consideration.

IV. ITA Costs and Case-Related Variables

Despite the historical lack of information on costs, Chapter 4 demonstrated that, time and money were inextricably intertwined. As "time is money"[62] in ITA, earlier analyses identified that, in final awards, there was a strong, significant, and positive link between time and

[60] Several cases lacked data on amounts claimed and/or costs. Missing data could theoretically impact the results, although preliminary analyses could not identify that cases with and without financial data exhibited meaningful group differences. *See supra* Chapter 4.

[61] Given the less than statistically small effect sizes, several analyses exhibited less than acceptable levels of power. To redress this, ex post power analysis suggests more than 780 cases with full costs information would be required to exclude the possibility of a latent effect. *See also* Appendix I (discussing effect sizes and power analyses).

[62] Benjamin Franklin, Advice to a Young Tradesman (1748), *reprinted in* The Oxford Dictionary of Quotations 323 (1999).

claimant's PLC, respondent's PLC, and total TCE.[63] As time to resolve disputes increased, so did cost—and that relationship was critical,[64] as the practical significance revealed a statistically medium-to-large effect. In other words, stakeholders ignore links between time and costs at their peril.

Yet, other potential predictors may prove useful. This section explores how other variables related to ITA costs in an effort to form a baseline for considering how to explain ITA costs and begin generating a predictive model for the future. These insights may aid counsel and clients when managing expectations about ITA's fiscal costs—and the comparative need for and utility of other forms of conflict management—and when to worry about cost management.

A. NON-SIGNIFICANT COST PREDICTORS

Tests were unable to detect a meaningful link with ITA costs for multiple variables, particularly when controlling for case length. For the primary purpose of this chapter, the variables included: ad hoc versus institutional cases, cases organized under different arbitration rules, varying participation of non-disputing parties (NDPs), and—only when controlling for case length—even bifurcated cases.[65]

1. Institutional Choices

There is a robust conversation about institutions and which arbitration venues in ITA are the most expensive.[66] One can easily imagine why, as getting it "right" with the institutional choice is theoretically a way to save money and add value to dispute resolution strategy. Some suggest *ad hoc* arbitration is cheaper and institutional arbitration is more expensive.[67] Others buttress this claim noting ICSID arbitration can "be considerably more expensive" than other forms of dispute settlement.[68] Yet others claim, in ITA, ad hoc arbitration is more expensive and ICSID is less expensive.[69] Stanimir Alexandrov has argued ICSID "is less

---

[63] The individual costs of claimant PLC, respondent PLC, and TCE tended to be co-linear; but after controlling for months required to resolve a case, it was not possible to identify reliable differences among these different cost elements, suggesting case length was the real driver of costs. *See* Chapter 4.

[64] *Id.*

[65] Other variables, when included in many different regressions, were also unable to predict ITA costs. Analyses in Chapter 6, for example, were unable to identify reliable links between investor identity and costs. *See also infra* notes 198–200, 202 (discussing tests of other potential non-significant predictors of ITA costs, including tribunal gender and Latin American respondents).

[66] Although the data analyzed did not include cases administered under LCIA Rules (but some cases were administered by the LCIA on an ad hoc basis), recent LCIA analysis explores costs and suggests comparatively that the LCIA is more cost-effective than its competitors. LCIA, FACTS AND FIGURES—COSTS AND DURATION: 2013–2016 19–21 (Oct. 3, 2017), https://bit.ly/2uKjJKd (last visited Aug. 7, 2018).

[67] JAMES CALVIN BAKER, FOREIGN DIRECT INVESTMENT IN LESS DEVELOPED COUNTRIES: THE ROLE OF ICSID AND MIGA 33 (1999); MARGARET L. MOSES, THE PRINCIPLES AND PRACTICE OF INTERNATIONAL COMMERCIAL ARBITRATION 9–10 (2008).

[68] Lester Nurick & Stephen J. Schnably, *The First ICSID Conciliation:* Tesoro Petroleum Corporation v. Trinidad and Tobago, 2 ICSID REP. 399, 402 (1994).

[69] Diana Marie Wick, *Counter-productivity of ICSID Denunciation and Proposals for Change*, 11 J. INT'L BUS. & L. 239, 284–85 (2012); *see also* Matthew Hodgson, *Counting the Costs of Investment Treaty Arbitration*, GLOBAL

expensive than UNCITRAL." Acknowledging his position "may be contrary to the conventional wisdom," he suggested ICSID is cheaper, as it "controls the fees of the arbitrators, because it provides certain facilities and services for free, because the charges for administrative support don't cover the actual expenses."[70] Meanwhile, Hodgson's most recent analysis suggests that "median tribunal costs are now closely aligned between ICSID and UNCITRAL Tribunals."[71]

There is, unfortunately, minimal research comparing cost variations at ITA venues with scientific rigor.[72] As ITA involves complex disputes with states, ad hoc arbitration could theoretically generate increased costs because of increased opportunities for mischief. Yet, lack of fees for administrative oversight and parties' options to select comparatively cheaper arbitrators could theoretically make ad hoc arbitrations cheaper. Meanwhile, ICSID has fees for administrative support and charges for its arbitrators on an hourly basis. SCC rates are partially a function of the amount in dispute; and ad hoc arbitration costs occur on a case-by-case basis.

To reality test the debate and underlying theory against reality, two sets of analyses explored variations in ITA costs as a function of institutional choice. The first set of tests explores the blunt distinction between ad hoc and institutional arbitration. Recalling the lack of cases proceeding as institutional arbitration at venues such as the HKIAC, ICC, ICDR, LCIA, and SIAC, the second group of analyses provide more nuanced analyses comparing cost differences in ICSID, SCC, and ad hoc arbitrations.

First, none of the tests supported the hypothesis that ad hoc arbitration costs were meaningfully lower (or higher) than institutional arbitration. Rather, it was not possible to identify meaningful cost variations, and all costs appeared roughly equivalent irrespective of whether ITA was ad hoc or institutional.

Arb. Rev. (Mar. 24, 2014), https://bit.ly/29UwfPi (last visited Aug. 7, 2018) (using non-inflation-adjusted data without standard deviations to suggest average UNCITRAL tribunal cost US$853,000, whereas the average ICSID tribunal cost US$769,000, and noting medians at ICSID and UNCITRAL were US$544,000 and US$714,000 respectively).

[70] Stanimir Alexandrov, *Is ICSID Losing Its Appeal... Again?*, 105 Am. Soc'y Int'l L. Proc. 193, 213–14 (2012).

[71] Matthew Hodgson & Alastair Campbell, *Damages and Costs in Investment Treaty Arbitration Revisited*, Global Arb. Rev. (Dec. 14, 2017), https://bit.ly/2NOTjPA (last visited Aug. 7, 2018); *see also id.* (identifying in post-2013 data, the average and median costs at ICSID were US$1,042,000 and US$910,000 but average mean and median costs of UNCITRAL cases were US$1,384,000 and US$905,000); *supra* note 68 (describing pre-2013 results).

[72] Commission and Moloo provide helpful descriptive data about costs at ICSID and in UNCITRAL proceedings and offered means and medians; but they properly did not try to draw inferences about meaningful group differences in the absence of standard deviations or statistical tests. Jeffery Commission & Rahim Moloo, Procedural Issues in International Investment Arbitration 185–91 (2018). While a thoughtful starting point, research by Hodgson, *supra* note 69 and 71, failed to report standard deviations, to identify whether costs were adjusted for inflation, or to conduct statistical analysis indicating whether temporal shifts were statistically meaningful (rather than reflecting random chance) while suggesting some inferences about differences.

For investors' legal fees, multiple tests,[73] including tests controlling case length,[74] were unable to detect any meaningful difference of the average cost in ad hoc and institutional arbitration. Using winsorized data with higher than normal skewing (but an more readily understandable scale), investors' legal costs were US$4 million (or US$5 million in 2018 dollars), irrespective of whether an arbitration was institutional[75] or ad hoc.[76] The results provide preliminary evidence that investors' PLC was roughly equivalent, irrespective of whether claims initiated at an institution or via ad hoc proceedings.

For states' PLC, tests were likewise unable to detect meaningful differences in the cost of states' legal fees at institutional or ad hoc arbitration,[77] even controlling for case length.[78] For both institutional[79] and ad hoc[80] arbitration, states' average legal fees were approximately US$3 million (roughly US$3–4 million in 2018 dollars). The tests provide preliminary evidence that states' legal costs in ITA were roughly equivalent across arbitration forums.

For tribunal fees and administrative expenses, tests again failed to reveal costs were meaningfully different in ad hoc and institutional arbitration.[81] Controlling case length generally replicated the non-significant findings.[82] Using winsorized data with slightly higher skewing, for institutional cases, average tribunal costs were around US$600,000,[83] whereas the mean costs for ad hoc cases were facially higher at roughly US$800,000;[84] given the large variation,

---

[73] Tests failed to identify a reliable mean difference in claimants' PLC in institutional or ad hoc arbitration using winsorized (t (49) = 0.173; p = .86; r = −.03; n = 51) or logged (t (49) = −0.226; p = .82; r = .03; n = 51) data. A test of medians was also non-significant (U = 206.0; p = .75).

[74] A partial correlation, controlling for case length, failed to find a link between investors' PLC and the use of ad hoc or institutional arbitration using logged data (r (47) = .09; p = .55).

[75] M = 4,399,088; SD = 495600; n = 40. Using the BLS inflation-calculator described in Chapter 6 to convert to June 2018 values, the mean cost of investors' PLC in institutional arbitration had the same buying-power as US$5,033,633.

[76] M = 4,283,475; SD = 3931413; n = 9. Converting the January 2011 inflation-adjusted figure with the BLS calculator revealed the average cost of investors' PLC ad hoc arbitration had the same buying power as US$4,901,344 in June 2018.

[77] t (55) = 0.539; p = .59; r = .07; n = 57. Tests were also unable to determine that rrespondents' median legal fees were significantly different (U = 254.0; p = .92).

[78] Using winsorized data, a partial correlation controlling for case length was unable to establish a link between state PLC and the use of either ad hoc or institutional arbitration (r (53) = −.08; p = .55).

[79] M = 3,296,557; SD = 3213768; n = 45. Converting the mean for states' PLC in institutional arbitration to June 2018 with the BLS calculator, the amount had the same buying power US$3,772,068.

[80] M = 2,747,985; SD = 2792652; n = 12. Using the BLS calculator, the amount of states' PLC in ad hoc arbigration had the same buying power US$$3,144,367 in June 2018.

[81] Tests using logged data were unable to detect a reliable mean difference.in TCE for ad hoc and institutional arbitration (t (56) = −0.977; p = .33; r = .13; n = 58). A test of median TCE was also unable to detect a significant difference (U = 350.0; p = .28).

[82] A partial correlation, that controlled case length and used logged data with the lowest skewing, failed to find a reliable relationship (r (54) = .20; p = .14). Using winsorized data (with acceptable but slightly higher skewing), however, revealed tribunal costs in ad hoc arbitrations were reliably higher than institutional arbitrations (r (54) = .31; p = .02), confirming the intuition of Stanamir Alexandrov.

[83] M = 594,739; SD = 418002; n = 30. Converting the mean TCE in institutional cases to June 2018 with the BLS calculator, TCE had the same buying power as US$680,527.

[84] M = 826,245; SD = 616312; n = 28. Using the BLS calculator, the mean TCE in ad hoc arbitrations converted to US$945,427.

however, it is not possible to confidently infer that the distinction between the two figures was statistically meaningful. Adjusting those two figures to 2018 values reflected that mean TCE was always under US$1 million for both types of venue.

The second set of tests permitted a more nuanced assessment of potential cost differences across arbitral forums by focusing on doctrinal rules.[85] Yet, they were also unable to detect reliable institutional differences in ITA costs.

For investors' PLC, tests were unable to find any meaningful relationship between their legal feels and the arbitral forum.[86] Using winsorized data with higher skewing but an understandable scale, the mean cost for investors' lawyers in ad hoc proceedings[87] and at ICSID were both around US$4.1 million (US$4.7–4.8 million in 2018 dollars).[88] At the SCC, investors' average PLC was US$6.5 million (US$7.4 million in 2018 dollars).[89] Although investors' lawyers appeared most expensive at the SCC, the facial difference was not statistically meaningful. This provides initial evidence that, despite some variation, investors' PLC in ICSID, SCC, and ad hoc cases were roughly equivalent. The key is to avoid being fooled by a pattern with superficial or intuitive appeal—as averages contain wide variation—and instead rely upon quantitative tests to check intuitive impulses.[90]

For respondents, analyses likewise failed to detect a meaningful differences in states' PLC across arbitration forums.[91] On average, ad hoc arbitrations cost states roughly US$2.8 million (roughly US$3.1 million in 2018 dollars);[92] and the average ICSID arbitration was US$3.5 million (nearly US$4 million in 2018 dollars).[93] While the average costs for respondents at the SCC was facially lower than the other venues at US$1.7 million (nearly US$2 million in 2018 dollars),[94] tests failed to identify statistically meaningful variations.

---

[85] Chapter 3 provides demographic data on institutions and variables, revealing no ICC cases within the dataset. The Codebook coded for five potential categories: ICSID, SCC, ICC, Other Institution, and Ad Hoc.

[86] As forum was a variable with multiple categories and costs were continuous, ANOVAs evaluated differences. Logged data, with appropriate skewing, was unable to detect a reliable mean difference in investors' PLC relationship at ICSID, SCC, or in ad hoc proceedings ($F(2, 48) = 0.133; p = .88; r = .07; n = 51$). A Kruskall-Wallis test of medians replicated the null effect on investors' PLC (χ^2 (2) = 0.441; $p = .80$).

[87] M = 4,120,404; SD = 3572704; n = 11. Using the BLS calculator, investors' mean PLC in ad hoc proceedings had the same buying power as US$4,714,750 in June 2018.

[88] M = 4,168,310; SD = 4830262; n = 36. Using the BLS calculator to transform the mean investor PLC in ICSID proceedings to June 2018, the average had the same buying power as US$4,769,567.

[89] M = 6,476,086; SD = 6576064; n = 4. Using the BLS calculator to transform the SCC average to June 2018, the mean had the same buying power as US$7,410,227.

[90] *See also* Chapter 6 (providing means, medians, quartile breakdowns, and Figure 6.1 to reflect dispersion of investors' PLC, states' PLC, and TCE).

[91] An ANOVA using winzorized data failed to detect any meaningful mean differences in respondent PLC at ICSID, the SCC, and ad hoc arbitration ($F(2, 54) = 0.710; p = .50; r = .16; n = 57$); and HSD follow-up comparisons could not detect any latent relationships. A Kruskall-Wallis test of medians likewise was unable to detect meaningful differences in respondent costs at different arbitration venues (χ^2 (2) = 0.933; $p = .63; r = .13; n = 57$).

[92] M = 2,747,985; SD = 2792652; n = 12. Using the BLS calculator, the mean amount for states' PLC in ad hoc arbitrations had the same buying power as US$3,144,367 in June 2018.

[93] M = 3,451,490; SD = 3293780; n = 41. Using the BLS calculator, the average for states' PLC in ICSID arbitrations had the same buying power as US$3,949,349 in June 2018.

[94] M = 1,708,491; SD = 1771435; n = 4. Using the BLS calculator, the average for states' PLC in SCC arbitrations had the same buying power as US$$1,954,932.

The facial distinction was likely influenced by the small number of SCC cases, which included *al-Bahloul v. Tajikistan*, an SCC case where the state failed to appear and incurred no verifiable PLC in connection with the proceedings.

For TCE, tests failed to reveal meaningful differences in arbitration forums.[95] *See* Table 8.2.

TABLE 8.2

Mean Tribunal Costs and Administrative Expenses using Inflation-adjusted Winsorized Data in Final Cases across Arbitral Forums (n = 58).

Arbitral Institution	*Mean TCE (US$)*	*Standard Deviation*	*Total Cases*
ICSID	648,463	410714	22
SCC	446,995	428704	8
Ad Hoc	826,245	616312	28
Total	706,500	531449	58

Tribunal expenses in SCC arbitration appeared to be the least expensive, although the visually lower cost may reflect that the SCC cases analyzed included multiple documents-only cases. While tribunal costs at ICSID were not the least expensive, they were facially less expensive than ad hoc disputes. Yet, the failure to identify a meaningful difference among forums and legal rules is something stakeholders might wish to consider when either offering arbitration or commencing arbitration.

Overall, the first set of results could not confirm that ad hoc arbitration was meaningfully cheaper (or more expensive) on any core cost metric. Subsequent analyses of specific venues—despite potentially facially appealing patterns—were likewise unable to identify that there were meaningful differences across ad hoc, ICSID, and SCC arbitration. This suggests, but cannot conclusively prove, that facial distinctions may reflect chance alone. It is initial evidence that ITA costs may be roughly equivalent across institutions.

The comparisons have several implications. First, when comparing core ITA costs, the failure to identify any comparative jurisdictional advantage, suggests, as a pragmatic measure, that no venue was superior to another. Likewise, using an alternative frame, no venue was inferior to another. In other words, for states thinking about which arbitration form to include in their offers to arbitrate, variations in ITA costs need not be dispositive. Likewise, for investors considering which type of arbitration to accept, costs need not be a critical

[95] Logged data, with lowest skewing, that explored possible mean differences failed to identify a reliable difference in TCE across arbitration forums ($F(2, 55) = 1.849$; $p = .17$; $r = .25$; $n = 58$). Winsorized data with slightly higher (but acceptable) skewing, which forms the basis of Table 3, was unable to find a reliable mean difference ($F(2, 55) = 2.490$; $p = .09$; $r = .29$; $n = 58$). A test of medians likewise was unable to identify meaningful variation in TCE across arbitral fora ($\chi^2(2) = 2.824$; $p = .24$; $r = .22$; $n = 58$). Given the medium effect size, the analysis had only 50% power, meaning a minimum sample of 287 cases would be required to detect latent effects.

variable for making decisions about adjudication venue. Parties could therefore focus their risk assessments on other aspects, including enforcement-related concerns or other material variations, such as whether baselines about transparency of process, treatment of third-party funding, and how the institution regulates (or otherwise incentivizes) arbitrator or counsel conduct.

Second, the results disrupt claims that ad hoc arbitration has cost efficiencies; but it also challenges claims that ad hoc proceedings exhibited reliable inefficiencies. Third, there may be value in continuing to explore whether there are potentially latent cost variations in SCC arbitrations. Should the SCC caseload become more contentious, with a lower proportion of documents-only cases or more cases where states fully defend their actions, the costs could increase commensurately as the caseload evolves; alternatively, there may be a value proposition that would justify directing cases toward the SCC. Fourth, facial differences that ICSID arbitration may be less costly than ad hoc arbitration may likewise justify ongoing consideration of the relative value of ICSID arbitration. While replication is necessary, these preliminary findings should guide stakeholders drafting treaties or making strategic choices about where to initiate ITA.

The results and inferences nevertheless warrant caution. As several tribunals failed to particularize costs, the sample was small and potentially exhibits case effects. For parties' legal costs, cases with missing costs data were similar across the vast majority of variables to cases *with* costs—including whether cases were institutional or ad hoc—and it is not clear that cases missing data were meaningfully different.[96] The small sample available likewise means non-significant analyses were technically underpowered.[97] Although effect sizes were generally small, suggesting any latent effect was minor, more than 700 additional cases are required to ascertain possible links between costs and institutional choice.

2. Non-Disputing Parties

Although Chapter 3 explored core demographics related to Non-Disputing Parties (NDPs), their role in ITA remains an evolving conversation, particularly given concerns about potential costs and net participation benefits. The theoretical value of NDP participation involves increased transparency, derivative benefits from public scrutiny, improved award quality, and protection of the public interest. On the cost side, there are concerns NDP participation is

[96] Cases with PLC data tended to take longer to resolve, and cases without PLC were statistically shorter and took less time to resolve, suggesting that cases with missing data could lower average costs. For TCE, although cases were similar on many dimensions, including the time to render an award, they were different as regards both ad hoc and institutional arbitration; institutional cases were more likely to omit TCE data. *See generally* Chapter 4 (discussing case selection challenges for cases with and without data). For cases missing TCE data, ICSID had the highest degree of omissions within its caseload (86.8%; $n = 92$). The difference was significant ($\chi^2(2) = 36.420; p < .001$) as compared to SCC and ad hoc arbitration. Other missing data derived from SCC (1.9%; $n = 2$) and ad hoc (11.3%; $n = 12$) arbitration. Cases with TCE data came from ICSID (41.5%; $n = 22$), SCC (15.1%; $n = 8$), and ad hoc (43.4%; $n = 23$) arbitration.

[97] Many tests had effect sizes around the .10 range, suggesting roughly .20 power and an 80% risk of a Type II error. For analyses of a tribunal's legal costs, effect sizes were larger, power was higher (between .30 and .40), but the risk of a Type II error was still high.

contrary to traditions of party consent and creates duplicative submissions.[98] More tangibly, there are concerns NDP activity may increase arbitration costs and generate delays from increased costs of reviewing and responding to NDP submissions and augmented tribunal workload.[99]

Keeping in mind that most NDPs were states, multiple tests failed to identify a meaningful difference in the average number of months to adjudicate a case when there was (or was not) an NDP[100] (or even an NGO)[101] present. Unsurprisingly, given the lack of reliably longer cases when NDPs were present, it was also not possible to identify increased costs associated with NDP participation. Even controlling for case length, the null-results remained for investors' PLC,[102] states' PLC,[103] and TCE.[104] The lack of a reliable link with cost for cases involving NGOs (a small subcategory of NDPs) was remarkably similar. None of the tests

---

[98] Katia F. Gomez, *Rethinking the Role of Amicus Curiae in International Investment Arbitration: How to Draw the Line Favorably for the Public Interest*, 35 FORD. INT'L L.J. 510, 523 (2012).

[99] *See* Alessandra Asteriti & Christian J. Tams, *Transparency and Representation of the Public Interest in Investment Treaty Arbitration*, *in* INTERNATIONAL INVESTMENT LAW & COMPARATIVE PUBLIC LAW (Stephan W. Schill ed., 2011); Andrea K. Bjorklund, *The Emerging Civilization of Investment Arbitration*, 113 PENN. ST. L. REV. 1269, 1292–93 (2009); Jack J. Coe, Jr., *Transparency in the Resolution of Investor-State Disputes–Adoption, Adaptation, and NAFTA Leadership*, 54 U. KAN. L. REV. 1339, 1363 (2006); Eugenia Levine, *Amicus Curiae in International Investment Arbitration: The Implications of an Increase in Third-Party Participation*, 29 BERKELEY J. INT'L L. 200, 217–18, 221 (2011).

[100] A t-test exploring differences in average case length (i.e. months between filing an arbitration and a final award) was unable to detect a reliable difference in length for arbitrations with and without an NDP ($t(154) = -1.274$; $p = .20$; $r = .10$; $n = 156$). For cases with an NDP, the mean case length was 47.5 months ($SD = 16.64$; $n = 23$); whereas, for cases without an NDP, the mean case length was 42.0 months ($SD = 19.09$; $n = 133$). Although the facial trend was for cases with NDPs to take longer, the 3–4 month difference was non-significant, statistically small, and could reflect chance alone. A Mann-Whitney U-Test likewise failed to reveal a difference in the median number of months to resolve disputes with (or without) NDPs ($U = 1225.5$; $p = .13$; $n = 156$).

[101] A t-test failed to reveal a reliable mean difference in case length and the presence (or absence) of an NGO ($t(154) = -1.932$; $p = .06$; $r = .15$; $n = 156$). Recognizing that there were broad standard deviations involved, cases without NGO participation took on average forty-two months ($SD = 18.59$; $n = 150$) to complete; whereas cases with NGO participation took on average fifty-seven months ($SD = 19.8$; $n = 6$). It was also not possible to find a reliable median difference in case length for disputes with and without NGOs ($U = 244.0$; $p = .06$; $n = 156$). Although the results were close to significant and there is a risk that the test was underpowered, the potential latent effect was statistically small and the number of cases with NGO participation was relatively small as compared to the caseload.

[102] A t-test failed to reveal any statistically meaningful link between the mean cost of investors' lawyers and NDP presence (or absence) using logged data ($t(49) = 0.173$; $p = .86$; $r = -.03$; $n = 51$). A Mann-Whitney test could not detect a reliable difference in median cost of investors' lawyers when NDPs were present or absent ($U = 149.0$; $p = .94$). A partial correlation, that controlled for case length, also failed to identify a reliable relationship ($r(50) = -.02$; $p = .92$).

[103] A t-test failed to reveal a reliable difference in states' average legal costs depending upon the presence of an NDP using winsorized data ($t(55) = -.345$; $p = .73$; $r = .05$; $n = 57$). A Mann-Whitney test could not detect a difference in median costs for state' counsel when NDPs were involved ($U = 159.0$; $p = .40$). A partial correlation, that controlled for case length, failed to find a link between NDP presence and the cost of respondent counsel ($r(56) = -.08$; $p = .58$).

[104] A t-test failed to reveal a meaningful difference in mean tribunal cost in cases with and without an NDP, using logged data ($t(56) = -1.612$; $p = .11$; $r = .21$; $n = 58$). Although one test did reveal a meaningful difference in median tribunal cost, whereby tribunals without NDPs were reliably cheaper ($U = 93.0$; $p = .04$), a partial

identified a reliable pattern between NGO presence and increased (or decreased) arbitration costs.[105]

Table 8.3 offers the average ITA costs for cases with (and without) NDPs. The core costs of counsel, both for investors and states, were roughly equivalent when NDPs were involved; and the slight facial trend toward investors paying less on average when NDPs were involved was not statistically meaningful. Although there was a facial trend suggesting tribunals cost reliably more when NDPs were involved, the potential practical significance and effect sizes were relatively small. All tribunals still cost, on average, under US$1 million, with PLC dwarfing tribunal costs.

TABLE 8.3

Mean ITA Costs using Inflation-adjusted Winsorized Data[106] (Adjusted for Inflation to 2011) for Cases With and Without an NDP.

	Mean Cost (US$)	*Standard Deviation*	*Total*
Investors' PLC			
With an NDP	3,604,474	3105992	7
Without an NDP	4,455,833	4897932	44
Respondent's PLC			
With an NDP	3,536,077	2463251	8
Without an NDP	3,123,107	3225672	49
TCE			
With an NDP	970,887	371017	7
Without an NDP	670,213	542523	51

correlation, that controlled for case length, minimized the effect and was unable to detect a reliable relationship between presence (or absence) of an NDP and TCE (r (54) = .09; p = .50).

105 For investors' PLC, using logged data, it was not possible to detect a mean difference in cases with and without an NGO (t (53) = –.630; p = .53; r = .09; n = 55), and controlling case length replicated null results (r (51) = .12; p = .41); likewise, tests could not identify a reliable median difference (U = 14.00; p = .41). For states' PLC, using winsorized data, there was no detectable mean difference (t (55) = –1.005; p = .32; r = .12; n = 57), and controlling case length failed to reveal a relationship (r (56) = .02; p = .91); a test of medians failed to reveal a difference (U = 26.00; p = .22). For TCE, tests using logged data, were unable to identify a mean difference (t (59) = –1.441; p = .16; r = .18; n = 61), and controlling case length failed to identify a relationship (r (57) = –.03; p = .80). Tests were also unable to find a reliable median difference (U = 31.00; p = .06) in TCE for cases with and without an NGO. Recognizing effect sizes ranged from small to medium, the analyses are underpowered, and strong inferences cannot be drawn. To detect the smallest possible effect, 781 cases with complete information would be required.

106 For respondent PLC, winsorized data exhibited the most appropriate skewing and was used for testing. While on the same scale as respondent PLC and easier to understand, winsorized investor PLC had high skewness. For TCE, winsorized data is on the same scale of respondent PLC, is easier to understand, and had acceptable skewness to permit testing. *See* Appendix I. Tests using winsorized TCE data replicated results from logged data.

These analyses provide preliminary evidence that there was no critical difference in core ITA costs as a function of the presence or absence of NDPs. Those results cast doubt on claims that ITA costs were meaningfully larger when NDPs are involved. This, in turn, suggests that normative reforms excluding NDP or NGO participation for costs reasons are not evidence-based reforms and would arguably create an overly broad remedy for containing costs. Nevertheless, the absence of a reliable relationship cannot prove there is no latent relationship. Given the variance, small number of cases (particularly for the subset of NGOs), and the limited costs information, a larger sample could identify a meaningful effect. As one test assessing case length and NGO presence was close to significance—but not significant at the .05 level and, in any event, NGO presence was never reliably linked with higher costs—the area is ripe for replication and a degree of both prudence and nuance when crafting ITA cost reforms.

3. Bifurcation

Bifurcation is theoretically an opportunity to save costs. Yet bifurcation could be inefficient and simply increase costs. Some tests—related only to investors' legal fees and tribunal costs—suggested initially that bifurcation was reliably associated with *higher* (not lower) arbitration costs; but subsequent analyses suggested that the real factor driving costs was case length generally—not bifurcation in particular. After controlling for case length, it was never possible to identify a reliable link between bifurcation and the core ITA costs of investors' legal fees, respondents' legal fees, and tribunal costs. Unpacking the underlying analyses provides a useful context.

For claimants' PLC, initial tests suggested fees were reliably higher in bifurcated cases. Using winsorized data with higher skewing but on an understandable scale, investors' PLC in non-bifurcated cases was US$3.6 million (US$4.1 million in 2018 dollars),[107] whereas cases involving bifurcation (or in rare cases trifurcation) the fees were roughly US$5.6 million (US$6.4 million in 2018 dollars).[108] Although initial analyses suggested the difference was meaningful,[109] after controlling for case length, it was not possible to identify a reliable difference in claimants' legal costs in bifurcated and non-bifurcated cases.[110]

---

[107] $M = 3{,}605{,}264$; $SD = 4805736$; $n = 32$. Adjusting investors' mean PLC for non-bifurcated cases to June 2018 with the BLS calculator, the amount had the same buying power as US$4,125,304.

[108] $M = 5{,}574{,}711$; $SD = 4292308$; $n = 19$. Adjusting invesotrs' mean PLC for bifurcated cases to June 2018 with the BLS calculator, the amount had the same buying power as US$6,378,834.

[109] Inflation-adjusted logged data, with acceptable skewing, revealed a significant mean difference in investors' PLC for bifurcated and non-bifurcated cases ($t(49) = -2.562; p = .02; r = .34; n = 51$). A test of medians found a reliable distinction between the cost of investors' counsel in bifurcated and non-bifurcated cases ($U = 185$; $p = .02$).

[110] A linear regression using logged data reliably predicted investors' PLC ($F(2, 49) = 13.447; p < .001; R^2 = .364$) in a model using the number of months in a case and a dummy variable for bifurcation (0 = no bifurcation; 1 = bifurcated or trifurcated case). Yet, bifurcation was a non-significant predictor ($B = .128$; $SE = .155$; $t = .823$; $p = .42$). A partial correlation, controlling case length, likewise failed to identify a reliable link between claimant PLC using logged data ($r(47) = .12; p = .42$).

For respondents' legal fees, however, none of the tests were able to identify a meaningful distinction between costs in bifurcated and non-bifurcated cases.[111] In both bifurcated[112] cases and cases with one award,[113] the average cost for states' lawyers was roughly US\$3 million (US\$3.4–3.7 million in 2018 dollars). Even controlling for case length, there was no reliable relationship between bifurcation and respondents' legal costs.[114] The data thus failed to confirm that states' legal fees were either reliably higher (or lower) in bifurcated cases, and any latent effect was statistically small.

For tribunal and administrative costs, as with investors' PLC, initial tests suggested that bifurcation was associated with higher TCE.[115] While the average tribunal in bifurcated cases cost slightly less than US\$1 million,[116] non-bifurcated tribunals were nearly 50% cheaper.[117] Yet, as ICSID arbitrators are paid on an hourly basis (and most cases occurred there), it is reasonable that bifurcated cases would cost more, as tribunals take additional time to resolve cases. After controlling for case length, it was not possible to identify reliable links between TCE and bifurcation.[118] Perhaps it should not be surprising that increased case length—but not necessarily increased costs—was associated with bifurcation, particularly for tribunals. Chapter 4 identified the average gap between final hearings and rendering an award was roughly 10–12 months, meaning the time to draft two awards inevitably takes extra deliberation and writing time.

The non-significant results for costs but the significant impact of time,[119] are double-edged. Although bifurcated cases were reliably longer, they were not necessarily more (or less) expensive. One interpretation suggests that bifurcation was unnecessary, as it did not generate

---

[111] Winsorized data failed to reveal any meaningful mean difference in states' PLC in bifurcated and non-bifurcated cases (t (55) = 0.398; p = .69; r = .05; n = 57). A test of medians likewise failed to reveal a meaningful difference in median state PLC as a function of bifurcation (U = 372; p = .84).

[112] M = 2,972,658; SD = 2824388; n = 22. Adjusting states' mean PLC for bifurcated cases to June 2018 with the BLS calculator, the amount had the same buying power as US\$3,401,448.

[113] M = 3,247,698; SD = 3229877; n = 35. Adjusting states' mean PLC in non-bifurcated cases to June 2018 with the BLS calculator, the amount had the same buying power as US\$3,716,161.

[114] A linear regression, using winsorized data, reliably predicted states' PLC (F (2, 53) = 5.022.; p = .01; R^2 = .159) in a model analyzing months in a case and a dummy variable for bifurcation (0 = no bifurcation; 1 = bifurcated or trifurcated case). Yet, bifurcation was a non-significant predictor of states' legal fees (B = −1252511; SE = 857066; t = −1.461; p = .15). A partial correlation, controlling for case length, likewise failed to find a relationship between bifurcation and states' PLC (r (53) = −.20; p = .14).

[115] A t-test using logged data identified a reliable mean difference in tribunal cost for bifurcated and non-bifurcated cases (t (56) = −2.150; p = .04; r = .28; n = 58). Likewise, a Mann-Whitney U-test of medians found a reliable difference in TCE for bifurcated and non-bifurcated cases (U = 259.0; p = .02).

[116] M = 950,554; SD = 621073; n = 23. Adjusting the mean TCE in bifurcated cases to June 2018 with the BLS calculator, the amount had the same buying power as US\$\$1,087,666.

[117] M = 552,693; SD = 403109; n = 35. Adjusting the mean TCE in non-bifurcated cases with the BLS calculator, the amount had the same buying power as US\$632,416 in June 2018.

[118] A linear regression using logged data reliably predicted TCE (F (2, 54) = 18.524; p < .001; R^2 = .407) in a model using the number of months in a case and a dummy variable for bifurcation (where 0 = no bifurcation and 1 = bifurcated or trifurcated case). Bifurcation, however, was a non-significant predictor of TCE (B = .084; SE = .102; t = .825; p = .413). A partial correlation, that controlled case length, likewise failed to identify a reliable relationship between TCE and bifurcation using logged data (r (54) = .11; p = .41).

[119] *See* Chapter 4.

clear cost savings, and the impact of delayed justice outweighs cost concerns. Another interpretation is that the lack of either higher or lower costs demonstrates that an intended efficiency of bifurcation materialized. The absence of increased costs suggests that tribunals properly distinguished between cases requiring bifurcation, and, without the bifurcation, costs would have been higher. Given the risk of hindsight bias, a third approach is that both interpretations remain plausible, but without experimental control to explore how bifurcation affects time and costs, it is not yet proper to reject either claim. This suggests, when it comes to normative reform involving bifurcation, a degree of nuance and sensitivity is prudent.

Bifurcation may be useful in the right circumstances, but bifurcation must be used carefully and with a dose of reality, as cost savings may be illusory unless time is also controlled. Parties—particularly states, with the capacity to draft treaties—should welcome strict timetables to control costs, lest timetables expand along with costs. To avoid conflating the concerns about bifurcation's impact upon time and costs, reform should focus on controlling timelines and creating incentives for parties and arbitrators to proceed expeditiously. As Chapter 6 revealed one-way cost-shifting operated reliably more often to investors' benefit, states should appreciate that—economically—avoiding bifurcation and its temporal expansion may decrease the costs potentially shifted against them, should they lose. Avoiding bifurcation may not, however, be politically palatable for states that need to launch an intensive defense to avoid state liability or states are best served by delay given the need to avoid a finalized award or flexibility adapting to evolving domestic politics. Meanwhile, investors (and third-party funders) should be concerned what bifurcation means for their dispute-resolution risk. There should be an incentive to avoid bifurcation to decrease unnecessary costs and save time.

There are inevitably limitations to these analyses. First, some cost data was unavailable. While there were not meaningful differences for tribunals and parties' counsel, cases with cost data tended to be rendered later in the caseload and were shorter, whereas cases without cost data were rendered earlier and were longer; but cases missing PLC were neither more nor less likely to be bifurcated,[120] limiting risk of a case selection effect. Second, the group analyzed was relatively small with limited power. Several analyses had less than small effect sizes, suggesting power was not the core issue. The presence of some small to medium-sized effects[121] warrants caution in drawing firm conclusions about the lack of a relationship between costs and bifurcation. This means that replication is required.[122]

In the interim, by recognizing these limitations, parties, their counsel, and arbitrators should weight potential increased case length against the lack of certainty in cost savings when making strategic decisions about bifurcation. Likewise, stakeholders—including treaty negotiators and institutional rule drafters—should focus on time (rather than cost) when considering reforms targeted to real, rather than intuitive, problems.

---

[120] *See id.*

[121] For claimant and respondent PLC, there was less than .20 power, reflecting 80% risk of a Type II error; for tribunal fees, there is a .30 power, reflecting 70% risk of a Type II error; replication is therefore required.

[122] For instance, with newer ITA disputes occurring at the ICC (where TCE is based on claimed amounts), the data could change; and it may become increasingly important to control for institutional rules.

B. SIGNIFICANT COST PREDICTORS

Some case-related elements did, however, exhibit reliable relationships with ITA costs. Some variables involved process points, whereas some variables implicated more substantive elements. Other than case length identified in Chapter 4, no other single variable ever reliably predicted all three arbitration costs (namely investors' PLC, states' PLC, or TCE). Rather, the story about the influence on costs was more nuanced.

1. Energy Disputes

The presence of an energy sector dispute is a classic example of the reliable effect on *some* ITA cost element, but never all three core costs. Specifically, disputes involving the energy sector were reliably associated with higher costs for states' legal counsel—but not higher costs for investors' counsel or tribunals. Yet, investment in the energy sector can be high-value and long-term,[123] and multiple tests confirmed that energy disputes evolved to produce larger claims than disputes in other sectors.[124] For example, using winsorized data to mediate outliers, the mean claim in an energy dispute was roughly US$60 million (US$68.7 million in 2018 dollars),[125] whereas non-energy disputes were roughly half that at US$34 million (US$39 million in 2018 dollars).[126]

With higher amounts at stake, when exploring cost differences between energy and non-energy disputes, tests only identified reliably *higher* costs for *state* legal fees in cases involving energy disputes.[127] Winsorized data, with the most appropriate skewing, revealed the mean cost of states' counsel in energy disputes was roughly US$4.7 million (US$5.4 million in 2018 dollars);[128] in contrast, the mean cost in non-energy cases was US$2.2 million (US$3 million in 2018 dollars).[129] The medium-sized statistical effect suggested the practical effect was that the cost of states' counsel was nearly doubled in energy disputes. The reliably

---

[123] *See, e.g.*, PETER CAMERON, INTERNATIONAL ENERGY INVESTMENT LAW: THE PURSUIT OF STABILITY (2009); *see also* David Elward, *ICSID Releases New Caseload Stats*, GLOBAL ARB. REV. (Sept. 6, 2010), https://bit.ly/2BPc7ca (last visited Dec. 28, 2018) *International Energy Investment Law: The Pursuit of Stability*, ICSID BLOG (Apr. 14, 2010, 10:17 PM), https://bit.ly/2vutn40 (last visited Aug. 7, 2018); Allen & Overy, *Energy Disputes*, ALLENOVERY.COM, https://bit.ly/2ARICsU (last visited Aug. 7, 2018).

[124] A t-test comparing mean claims in energy and non-energy disputes using winsorized ($t(115) = -3.612; p < .001; r = .32; n = 117$) and logged ($t(99) = -2.484; p = .003; r = .32; n = 117$) data found energy claims contained reliably higher claims. Similarly, a test of median amounts claimed identified a significant group difference in energy and non-energy cases ($U = 799.0; p = .002; n = 117$).

[125] $M = 60{,}016{,}350; SD = 59957318; n = 18$. Adjusting the mean claim in an energy-related dispute to June 2018 with the BLS calculator, the value was US$$68,673,390.

[126] $M = 34{,}066{,}779; SD = 54529100; n = 58$. Adjusting the mean claim for non-energy disputes with the BLS calculator, the June 2018 inflation-adjusted value was US$38,980,732.

[127] A t-test comparing mean state PLC in energy and non-energy disputes identified that respondent PLC was meaningfully higher in energy cases ($t(55) = -2.404; p = .02; r = .31; n = 57$). A test of the medians was on the cusp of significance ($U = 228.0; p = .076$).

[128] $M = 4{,}704{,}580; SD = 3623749; n = 16$. Adjusting the mean state PLC in energy disputes to June 2018 with the BLS calculator, the value was US$5,383,191.

[129] $M = 2{,}586{,}527; SD = 2656493; n = 41$. Adjusting state's mean PLC to June 2018 for non-energy cases, the value was equivalent to US$2,959,620 in June 2018.

higher legal costs persisted, even when controlling for case length and amount claimed.[130] Given the reliably larger risk and exposure to liability in a politically sensitive area, states were wise to defend high-risk claims actively. The higher fiscal exposure can partially explain the responsible state decision to expend more fiscal resources; yet what drives the increased cost goes beyond pure amount claimed.

For other ITA costs, however, it was not possible to identify reliably higher (or lower) costs in energy disputes. Despite investors' higher claims, tests were unable to determine that investors' counsel was reliably more expensive in cases involving an energy dispute;[131] this null effect remained after controlling for amounts claimed and case length.[132] Raw inflation-adjusted data, which includes outliers, might give the intuitive impression that investors' counsel in energy cases were twice as expensive in energy cases—with average costs of US$6.6 million (US$7.6 million in 2018 dollars)[133] for energy disputes but US$3.4 million (US$3.9 million in 2018 dollars)[134] in non-energy disputes. Yet, the superficial pattern is misleading, as there was material variance and skewing in the cost of investors' counsel, and averages could reflect random chance. *See* Table, Appendix I. Yet, as the caseload and legal fees evolve, the impact of energy disputes warrants watching, since expanded data could decrease variance or otherwise reveal a meaningful pattern.

Tribunal costs were more straightforward. Tests failed to reveal a meaningful relationship in total tribunal costs and presence of energy disputes.[135] Results were generally replicated controlling for core variables.[136] This is perhaps unsurprising, as winsorized data suggested

---

130 A partial correlation, controlling for case length, revealed a meaningful distinction in respondents' costs in energy and non-energy disputes (r (53) = .37; p = .01). Similarly, a partial correlation that controlled for amounts claimed replicated the reliable difference between states' PLC and energy and non-energy cases (r (40) = .31; p = .047).

131 A t-test using logged data, the only data with acceptable skewing for inferential tests, failed to reveal a meaningful mean difference in final ITA cases for the cost of claimant PLC in energy and non-energy disputes (t (49) = −0.912; p = .37; r = .13; n = 51). A test evaluating the median cost of investors' counsel likewise was unable to detect a reliable group difference in investors' PLC for energy and non-energy disputes (U = 203.0; p = .17; n = 51).

132 Using logged data and a partial correlation to control for amounts claimed failed to reveal a link between energy disputes and investor PLC (r (35) = .26; p = .12). Controlling for case length also failed to identify a link between investor PLC and energy disputes (r (47) = .19; p = .20).

133 M = 6,613,540; SD = 6737290; n = 15. Adjusting investors' mean PLC in energy cases to June 2018 with the BLS calculator revealed a value of US$7,567,508.

134 M = 3,391,246; SD = 3155063; n = 36. Adjusting investors' mean PLC in non-energy cases with the BLS calculator revealed a value of US$3,880,415 in June 2018.

135 Inflation-adjusted winsorized and logged data had roughly equivalent and acceptable skewing for total TCE, although logged data was somewhat better. Appendix I. Irrespective of whether winsorized (t (56) = −0.761; p = .45; r = .10; n = 58) or logged (t (56) = 1.157; p = .25; r = .15; n = 58) data was used, tests could not detect a reliable mean difference in TCE for energy and non-energy cases. A Mann-Whitney U-test replicated the non-significant results when exploring median TCE differences (U = 308.0; p = .30; n = 58).

136 Using a partial correlation to control case length, inflation-adjusted winsorized data for total TCE could not identify a relationship between TCE and energy (or non-energy) disputes (r (54) = .20; p = .14). Logged data, however, revealed a reliable link whereby tribunal costs were higher in energy disputes and lower in non-energy disputes (r (54) = .28; p = .04). Controlling for amounts claimed, however, failed to reveal a reliable link between TCE and energy (or non-energy) disputes using either winzorized (r (40) = .05; p = .77) or logged (r (40) = .03; p = .83) data.

that the average cost for energy[137] and non-energy[138] disputes hovered around US$700,000–800,000 (under US$1 million in 2018 dollars).

2. Separate Opinions

Separate opinions, whether dissenting or concurring, are a core procedural element of ITA. Chapter 4 identified how, for final awards, it was not possible to identify either increased case length or increased deliberative delay for cases with a separate opinion.[139] Yet, when it came to costs, the presence of a separate opinion *did* have a reliable influence. Much like energy disputes, the presence of a separate opinion was *only* a reliable predictor for respondent costs.

There has historically been no literature exploring how separate opinions affect ITA costs. Theoretically, separate opinions should not generate higher lawyer fees for either investors or states. Attorneys do not decide cases or render awards, and while counsel may exert time and effort in arguing their position to all arbitrators, it is not clear why the costs of investors' or states' counsel should be meaningfully different. As arbitrators draft awards, internal deliberations and the process of drafting multiple opinions increase the time spent; and where arbitrators are paid on an hourly basis, it is reasonable to hypothesize that tribunal costs increase in cases with separate opinions. Testing these assumptions against data, however, generated unusual results. These distinct theories, however, were only supported in one respect, namely: for investors' legal costs, it was not possible to reliably distinguish between the cost of counsel for cases with and without a separate opinion.

Multiple tests, even controlling for case length, failed to identify reliable relationships between investor PLC for cases with (or without) separate opinions.[140] For investors' legal costs, using winsorized data which had high skewing but offers an understandable scale, in cases with separate opinions, the mean PLC was roughly US$4.6 million (US$5.25 in 2018 dollars),[141] and investors' mean PLC in cases without a separate opinion was US$4.3 million (US$5 million in 2018 dollars).[142]

---

[137] $M = 782{,}825$; $SD = 496689$; $n = 19$. Using the BLS calculator to adjust the mean TCE in energy disputes to June 2018, the figure was US$895,7[illegible]3.

[138] $M = 669{,}316$; $SD = 5459691$; $n = 39$. Adjusting for inflation to June 2018 with the BLS calculator, the mean TCE in non-energy disputes was US$765,861.

[139] The one small exception was: there was reliably longer deliberative delay for non-final awards containing separate opinions.

[140] A *t*-test using logged data, with the most appropriate skewing, was unable to identify a reliable mean difference in investors' PLC for cases with and without a separate opinion ($t\,(49) = 0.890$; $p = .38$; $r = .1$[illegible]; $n = 5$[illegible]). A test of medians was likewise unable to detect a meaningful difference in investors' PLC in cases with and without a separate opinion ($U = 125.0$; $p = .43$). A partial correlation, controlling for case length, was also non-significant using logged data ($r\,(47) = -.12$; $p = .41$).

[141] $M = 4{,}589{,}499$; $SD = 3197078$; $n = 7$. Adjusting investors' mean PLC in cases with separate opinions using the BLS calculator revealed a value of US$5,251,510 in June 2018.

[142] $M = 4{,}299{,}124$; $SD = 4398937$; $n = 44$. Adjusting investors' mean PLC in cases without separate opinions to June 2018 using the BLS calculator revealed a value of US$4,919,249.

In contrast to what was theorized, for cases with separate opinions, respondents' average legal costs were meaningfully *higher*,[143] even controlling for case length.[144] For cases with a separate opinion, states' mean PLC was US$6.7 million (US$7.7 million in 2018 dollars)[145] whereas cases without a separate opinion cost states' an average of US$2.7 million (US$3 million in 2018 dollars).[146] Put differently, respondents experienced materially lower legal costs with a unified tribunal.

Three different theories explain the effect. An initial theory may be that higher counsel fees could be attributable to Romania, which generally paid higher-than-average legal fees for its defense. Core cases contributing to the effect—namely *EDF v. Romania*[147] and *Spyridon Roussalis v. Romania*[148]—involved some of the highest state legal fees. Yet, Romania also paid more than average fees in *Noble Ventures v. Romania*[149] for a unified tribunal. A second theory is that respondents devoted large fiscal resources to secure favorable outcomes. For five of the seven awards with separate opinions, four cases involved investor losses or settlements, namely *EDF, Spyridon Roussalis, Thunderbird v. Mexico*,[150] and *Piero Foresti v. South Africa*.[151] There were only two cases where respondents lost, namely *Lemire*

[143] Using winsorized data with the best skewing, a t-test identified a significant mean difference in respondent PLC in cases with and without a separate opinion ($t\,(55) = 3.535; p = .001; r = .43; n = 57$). Likewise, there was a significant difference in median respondent PLC in cases with and without a separate opinion ($U = 56.0; p = .004$).

[144] A partial correlation between respondent PLC and presence of a separate opinion, that controlled case length, remained significant using winsorized data ($r\,(53) = -.42; p = .001$).

[145] $M = 6{,}731{,}004; SD = 3454527; n = 7$. Adjusting states' mean PLC in cases with a separate opinion to June 2018 with the BLS calculator revealed a value of US$7,701,916.

[146] $M = 2{,}684{,}077; SD = 2751317; n = 50$. Adjusting states' mean PLC in cases without a separate opinion using the BLS calculator revealed a value of US$3,071,240 in June 2018.

[147] EDF Servs. Ltd. v. Republic of Rom., ICSID Case No. ARB/05/13, Award, 106 (Oct. 8, 2009), 21 World Trade & Arb. Materials 1401 (2009) (original, non-inflation adjusted respondent PLC fees of around US$18.6 million); EDF Servs. Ltd. v. Republic of Rom., ICSID Case No. ARB/05/13, Dissent Regarding Costs by Arthur W. Rovine (Oct. 2, 2009), https://bit.ly/2LKAXyA (last visited Dec. 27, 2018).

[148] Spyridon Roussalis v. Republic of Rom., ICSID Case No. ARB/06/1, Award, 133-34 (Dec. 7, 2011), 24 World Trade & Arb. Materials 343 (2012) (original, non-inflation adjusted state PLC fees of over EUR10 million, translating into roughly US$13.5 million); Spyridon Roussalis v. Republic of Rom., ICSID Case No. ARB/06/1, Declaration of W. Michael Reisman (Nov. 28, 2011), https://bit.ly/2RvjteZ (last visited Dec. 27, 2018).

[149] Noble Ventures, Inc. v. Republic of Rom., ICSID Case No. ARB/01/11, Award, 145 (Oct. 12, 2005), https://bit.ly/2CS2EzC (last visited Dec. 27, 2018) (original, non-inflation adjusted respondent PLC fees of over US$8.9 million). The other final case involving Romania was *S&T Oil*, which lacked respondent cost information. S&T Oil Equipment & Machinery Ltd. V. Republic of Rom., ICSID Case No. ARB/07/13, Order of Discontinuance (July 16, 2010), https://bit.ly/2ESW4x8 (last visited Dec. 27, 2018). In a case that was included in the dataset, but where the final award was rendered after the dataset closed, *Iona Micula* also spawned a separate opinion and Romanian legal fees of EUR11.5 (roughly US$15.6 million at the date of the award). Iona Micula v. Republic of Rom., ICSID ARB/05/20, Final Award, ¶ 1325 (Dec. 11, 2013), http://bit.ly/1vbdnOV (last visited Aug. 7, 2018); Iona Micula v. Republic of Rom., ICSID ARB/05/20, Separate Opinion of Georges Abi-Saab (Dec. 5, 2013), http://bit.ly/1lpVOaN (last visited Aug. 7, 2018).

[150] Int'l Thunderbird Gaming Corp. v. United Mexican States, UNCITRAL, Award (Jan. 26, 2006), 18 World Trade & Arb. Materials 59 (2006); Int'l Thunderbird Gaming Corp. v. United Mexican States, UNCITRAL, Separate Opinion of Thomas Wälde (English), (Dec. 2005), https://bit.ly/2QYhZdE (last visited Dec. 27, 2018).

[151] Piero Foresti v. Republic of S. Afr., ICSID Case No. ARB(AF)/07/01, Award (Aug. 4, 2010), https://bit.ly/2EWJOMi (last visited Dec. 27, 2018); Piero Foresti v. Republic of S. Afr., ICSID Case No. ARB(AF)/07/

v. Ukraine [II][152] and *Siag & Vecchi v. Egypt,*[153] and in both cases, respondents' counsel cost was roughly average.[154] A final explanation is that states are risk-averse and expend higher fees when warranted by the merits. High legal fees could reflect the important nature of the case and states' political investment. A novel element could also require significant attention from counsel. For a state interested in defending its legitimate government conduct, investing in strong counsel (and paying them accordingly) to secure a favorable result, even with a separate opinion, warrants expenditure of fees.

Finally, rather than separate opinions generating higher TCE as theorized, it was *not* possible to distinguish between the costs of unified tribunals and those rendering separate opinions.[155] Average tribunal costs for cases with a separate opinion was roughly US$750,000[156] whereas

---

01, Concurring Statement of Arbitrator Matthews (Aug. 3, 2010), https://bit.ly/2EV7r7H (last visited Dec. 27, 2018).

[152] Charles Joseph Lemire v. Ukraine [II], ICSID Case No. ARB/06/18, Award (Mar. 28, 2011), 23 World Trade & Arb. Materials 947 (2011); Charles Joseph Lemire v. Ukraine [II], ICSID Case No. ARB/06/18, Dissenting Opinion of Arbitrator Dr. Jürgen Voss, https://bit.ly/2LHBTU6 (last visited Dec. 27, 2018).

[153] Siag & Vecchi v. Arab Republic of Egypt, ICSID Case No. ARB/05/15, Award (June 1, 2009), 21 World Trade & Arb. Materials 1171 (2009); Siag & Vecchi v. Arab Republic of Egypt, ICSID Case No. ARB/05/15, Dissenting Opinion of Professor Francisco Orrego Vicuña, https://bit.ly/2R1MYWl (last visited Dec. 27, 2018).

[154] After expanding the analysis to evaluate both final and non-final cases, a t-test revealed a meaningful link between respondents' cost and separate opinions ($t\ (58) = 2.979; p < .01; r = .36; n = 60$). Cases contributing to the effect reflected that states typically won. *See EDF v. Romania, supra* note 147; *Sypridon Roussalis v. Romania, supra* note 148; Nations Energy Inc. v. of Republic Pan., ICSID Case No. ARB/06/19, Award and Explanation of Dissenting Vote (Nov. 24, 2010), https://bit.ly/2CGWZz9 (last visited Dec. 27, 2018); *Thunderbird v. Mexico, supra* note 150; Total S.A. v. Argentine Republic, ICSID Case No. ARB/04/01, Decision on Liability (Dec. 27, 2010), https://bit.ly/2uFlWGO (last visited Dec. 27, 2017); Total S.A. v. Argentine Republic, ICSID Case No. ARB/04/01, Individual Opinion of Henri Alvarez (Dec. 21, 2010), https://bit.ly/2St8AHB (last visited Dec. 27, 2018); Total S.A. v. Argentine Republic, ICSID Case No. ARB/04/01, Concurring Opinion of Luis Herrera Marcano (Dec. 12, 2010), https://bit.ly/2BOrykZ (last visited Dec. 27, 2018). One case involved a settlement where the state did not provide fiscal compensation. *Foresti v. South Africa, supra* note 151. Only three cases involved investor wins. *Lemire v. Ukraine [II], supra* note 152; *Siag & Vecchi v. Egypt, supra* note 153; Eastern Sugar B.V. v. Czech Republic, SCC Case No. 088/2004, Partial Award, 71 (Mar. 27, 2007), https://bit.ly/2Rs7aQA (last visited Dec. 27, 2018); Eastern Sugar B.V. v. Czech Republic, SCC Case No. 088/2004, Partial Dissenting Opinion of Robert Volterra (undated), https://bit.ly/2CEWsOm (last visited Dec. 27, 2018); Eastern Sugar B.V. v. Czech Republic, SCC Case No. 088/2004, Final Award (Apr. 12, 2007), https://bit.ly/2LFLsDl (last visited Dec. 27, 2018). By slight contrast, *Abaclat* was a non-final award with a separate opinion with US$11.6 million in respondent fees. Abaclat v. Argentine Republic, ICSID Case No. ARB/07/5, Decision on Jurisdiction (Aug. 4, 2011), https://bit.ly/2KUz7oI (last visited Aug. 7, 2018); Abaclat v. Argentine Republic, ICSID Case No. ARB/07/5, Dissenting Opinion of Georges Abi-Saab (undated), https://bit.ly/2RnqVZb (last visited Dec. 27, 2018).

[155] Analyses were unable to identify a significant mean difference in TCE for cases with and without a separate opinion using logged data ($t\ (56) = 0.666; p = .51; r = .09; n = 58$). A test of medians failed to identify a reliable difference in TCE ($U = 217.0; p = .64$). A partial correlation controlling case length replicated the non-significant results using logged data ($r\ (54) = .02; p = .89$).

[156] $M = 751{,}745$; $SD = 465317$; $n = 10$. Adjusting the mean TCE for cases with a separate opinion to June 2018 with the BLS calculator revealed a value of US$860,180.

the average cost for a unified tribunal was US$700,000.[157] In other words, multiple tests failed to find that providing a separate opinion increased costs or undermined tribunals' fiscal efficiency.

Caution is warranted before making overly strong inferences. Where tribunals failed to provide cost information, there is a risk that cases with missing data were meaningfully different, but preliminary analysis suggested that this was potentially a low risk.[158] For analyses failing to identify a relationship, there is a potential lack of statistical power, meaning that it is not possible to definitively conclude the lack of a relationship.[159] Yet effect sizes were typically small; a sample of over 780 awards would be needed to assess whether separate opinions are linked to reliable effects on time or costs. In the interim, these tests offer initial evidence about the lack of a link between separate opinions and core cost variables.

For investors' counsel and tribunals, analyses failed to reveal that separate opinions were reliably associated with increased costs. Without a reliable relationship, it is logically improper to suggest that separate opinions cause increased costs. Rather, separate opinions have doctrinal benefits, including clarifying reasoning, generating better awards, bolstering party confidence in the process, and aiding the evolution of doctrine and public discourse. The added value of separate opinions in terms of procedural and substantive justice enhances the legitimacy of ITA with minimal risk. Separate opinions thereby offer a tangible doctrinal benefit for little additional fiscal cost or for extra cost that yields a benefit, thereby generating net value for ITA.

Yet the one exception, namely the reliably higher costs for states, bares considering. Despite the increased costs, the data suggested that states potentially benefitted from expending additional fiscal resources on lawyers. More often than not, separate opinions occurred in cases where states obtained favorable results; and, in cases where states lost, states' legal fees were roughly average. While states paid more for cases with separate opinions, they obtained decent returns for favorable results. In some sense, perhaps, states wisely invested in paying more for counsel, presumably for better judgment, advocacy, tactical choices, and arbitrator selection. Put simply, while states might have paid more, their counsel succeeded in convincing two tribunal members of the state's position.

3. Repeat Player Counsel

Previous research (using the dataset from this book) explored how counsel experience—namely whether counsel were repeat players (RPs)—affected ITA outcomes.[160] Supporting Mark Galanter's classic scholarship that RPs have strategic advantages in

---

[157] $M = 697{,}074$; $SD = 548218$; $n = 48$. Adjusting the mean TCE for cases with a unified tribunal to June 2018 with the BLS calculator revealed a value of US$797,623.

[158] *See* Chapter 4.

[159] As most effect sizes were around .10, the power of the analysis was limited. The effect sizes for the link between separate opinions and respondent costs for non-significant tests were around .22, suggesting a 70% risk of a Type II error. Both results necessitate replication before drawing strong inferences.

[160] *See, e.g.*, Franck & Wylie, *supra* note 26.

dispute resolution[161] and suggestions that RP counsel's influence may be pronounced in international arbitration,[162] there were reliable differences in how RPs contributed to ITA outcomes, albeit in complicated ways.

Repeat counsel for investors were reliably associated with representing winning investors (i.e., cases where an investor obtained some damage award) and amount awarded—but not relative success. In contrast, although the presence of RPs on states' legal teams was neither linked with an investor "win" nor amounts awarded, there *was* a strong and reliable relationship whereby strongly experienced teams representing states were associated with lower levels of relative investor success—and less experienced state counsel were associated with higher investor success.[163] Yet the question remains how that expertise was linked with ITA costs and what it means for the value proposition of hiring experienced counsel.

A market-based theory might suggest that more legal experience in a complex and sensitive area should create a price premium, where experienced lawyers with insight, insider knowledge, and appreciation of nuance could justify higher costs and a more expensive legal team; whereas newer or less experienced counsel might offer discounted prices to gain access to the ITA market or reflect that less experienced firms without the subject matter expertise could not justify cost premiums. An alternate, efficiency-based theory might be that experienced counsel were particularly effective in case management, cost-containment, and pooling resources, and this could generate reliably lower legal fees, particularly for stakeholders interested in cost-efficient dispute management. Whereas new market entrants may be more inefficient, require larger sunk costs to engage in competent representation, or otherwise pass up strategic efficiencies.

Prior to this research, there was no variable for analyzing RP counsel in ITA. Drawing upon research from Mark Galanter, a classic way to classify RPs is with a binary dichotomous variable to distinguish between firms that are RPs and one-shot (OS) players. As described in Chapter 3, which offers demographics on RPs, to robustly test differences in the influence of counsel on ITA costs, the research used two core approaches. A "binary" measure only differentiated between the counsel who had (or who had not) worked on an ITA dispute in the past, and a composite version of the variable identified the total number RPs on each party's legal team. The second "weighted" approach explored counsel's relative experience within ITA and then compiled a composite score for each party's relative legal experience.[164]

In theory, RPs with additional expertise would extract additional rents to reflect their higher level of expertise and outcomes that would provide investors with increased opportunities for more investor-favorable outcomes. In practice, the hypothesis was only partially supported, only holding true for investors' counsel (but not for state counsel).

All analyses exploring counsel's expertise revealed a significant relationship between the expertise of claimants' legal teams and claimants' legal costs and expenses. First, for the binary metric, multiple tests identified a reliable link whereby the larger the number of RPs

---

[161] Marc Galanter, *Why the "Haves" Come Out Ahead: Speculations on the Limits of Legal Change*, 9 LAW & SOC'Y REV. 95 (1974).

[162] Carrie Menkel-Meadow, *Do the "Haves" Come Out Ahead in Alternative Judicial Systems?: Repeat Players in ADR*, 15 OHIO ST. J. DISP. RESOL. 19 (1999); Catherine Rogers, *The Arrival of the "Have-Nots" in International Arbitration*, 8 NEV. L.J. 341 (2007).

[163] Franck & Wylie, *supra* note 26, at 501–17. Those results held true for two ways of looking at counsel expertise, namely as either a weighted or a binary variable.

[164] *See* Chapter 3; Codebook, Appendix IV.

on investors' legal teams, the higher the PLC[165]—and the practical significance was critical, as the effect was statistically large and persisted even controlling for other variables.[166] Table 8.4 demonstrates that the average cost for investors' counsel in cases involving RPs was over 200% larger than cases where investors were represented by OS players. Second, multiple tests using the weighted variable, assessing the relative strength of an investor's combined legal team, revealed that more experienced teams tended to cost investors more; and less experienced teams tended to cost reliably less.[167] That strong and linear relationship persisted controlling for case length[168] and presence of an energy dispute.[169]

The cost of states' counsel, however, failed to reflect the same pattern. In theory, as states were often (but not always) represented by external counsel,[170] RPs representing states with greater expertise might charge more to reflect their higher expertise; likewise, states might pay a premium to have large, sophisticated internal teams supporting their defense. The data could not support the hypothesis that, as a group, states reliably paid more (or less) when their legal teams included experienced counsel.

Using the binary variable to assess experience, multiple tests were unable to detect a link between the presence of RP counsel on states' legal teams and increased state PLC,[171] even controlling for core variables.[172] Table 8.4 demonstrates that costs ranged between US$2 and US$3 million for states (US$2.5–3.8 million in 2018 dollars), irrespective of the team's expertise, and there was broad variance in the cost of state counsel.

---

[165] A t-test using logged data, with acceptable skewing, identified a reliable mean difference between the cost of investors' counsel for those teams with and without RPs ($t\,(47) = -4.016; p < .001; r = .51; n = 49$). A Mann-Whitney test replicated the results, finding a reliable difference in median investor PLC ($U = 113.0; p = .001$). Tests using the composite variable, counting number of total RPs on the investors' legal team, revealed a reliable relationship. An ANOVA identified a reliable mean difference in investors' PLC whereby, for every RP added to the team, the cost of investors' PLC increased ($F\,(4, 44) = 4.049; p = .01; r = .52; n = 49$); a Kruskall-Wallis test revealed reliable median differences in investor PLC ($\chi^2\,(4) = 11.438; p = .02; r = .48; n = 49$).

[166] Partial correlations, that controlled case length, revealed a reliable relationship between: (1) investor PLC and the presence of any RP ($r\,(45) = .40; p = .01$) or (2) investor PLC and the combined number of RPs ($r\,(45) = .36; p = .01; n = 48$) on an investor's legal team. When controlling for the presence of an energy dispute, partial correlations identified a link between: (1) investors' PLC and the presence of any RP ($r\,(46) = .57; p < .001$), or (2) investors' PLC and the combined total RPs ($r\,(46) = .50; p < .001$).

[167] A bivariate correlation analyzing the relative weight of RPs and investors' PLC identified a reliable relationship ($r\,(51) = .48; p < .001$).

[168] $r\,(45) = .39; p = .006$.

[169] $r\,(45) = .51; p < .001$.

[170] *See* Chapter 3.

[171] A t-test using winsorized data could find no reliable mean difference between cost of state counsel for teams with and without RPs ($t\,(53) = -0.702; p = .49; r = .10; n = 55$). A Mann-Whitney test replicated the null effect testing states' median PLC ($U = 76.0; p = .40$). Tests using the composite variable, counting total RPs on states' legal teams, could not find a reliable mean relationship ($F\,(4, 50) = 0.676; p = .61; r = .23; n = 55$); a Kruskall-Wallis test of medians could not detect meaningful difference in states' PLC ($\chi^2\,(4) = 3.215; p = .52; r = .24; n = 55$).

[172] A partial correlation controlling for case length found no link between: (1) states' PLC and presence of any RP ($r\,(51) = .02; p = .89$) or (2) states' PLC and the combined number of RPs ($r\,(51) = .06; p = .65$) on a state's legal team. Another partial correlation controlling for the presence of an energy dispute likewise failed to identify

TABLE 8.4

Mean Counsel Costs of Investors and States using Inflation-adjusted Winsorized Data for Cases With and Without Repeat Player Counsel.

	Mean Cost (US$)	*Standard Deviation*	*Total*
Investors' PLC**			
With an RP	5,466,055	5076316	33
No RP—Only OS Player	2,255,968	3051040	16
Respondent's PLC			
With an RP	3,324,952	3210729	51
No RP—Only OS Player	2,174,476	2033087	4

There was also evidence that an opposing sides' relative expertise was unrelated to either party's PLC or to tribunals' PLC shifts. Irrespective of whether RPs were evaluated using a binary or weighted measure, it was not possible to identify a link between the expertise of investors' legal teams and either: (1) states' PLC,[173] or (2) tribunals' PLC shifts.[174] Likewise, irrespective of whether the expertise was evaluated using a binary or weighted approach, it was also not possible to link states' counsel experience to either: (1) investors' PLC,[175] or

a link between: (1) state PLC and the presence (or absence) of any RP (r (52) = .04; p = .78), or (2) state PLC and the combined total RPs (r (52) = .04; p = .77) on states' legal teams.

173 For the binary variable, tests did not reveal a reliable mean difference (t (54) = −0.074; p = .94; r = .01; n = 56) or a reliable median difference (U = 288.0; p = .18) in having any RP on the claimant's team and a state's PLC. The non-significant results replicated when controlling for either case length (r (52) = −.13; p = .34) or the presence of an energy dispute (r (53) = .06; p = .64). An ANOVA exploring mean differences in total RPs on investors' legal teams and state PLC failed to identify a meaningful relationship (F (4, 51) = 0.190; p = .94; r = .12; n = 56); and partial correlations controlling for case length (r (52) = −.092; p = .51) and energy cases (r = −.08; p = .58) likewise failed to identify links between RPs on investors' legal teams and state PLC. Null results replicated using the weighted measure to evaluate investors' counsel expertise and respondent PLC (r (56) = −.01; p = .94), and after controlling for case length (r (52) = −.11; p = .42) or presence of an energy dispute (r (53) = .03; p = .82).

174 For the binary expertise variable, using logged data, it was not possible to detect a link between the presence of an RP on investors' legal teams and tribunals' mean PLC shifts (t (36) = −0.607; p = .55; r = .10; n = 38) or a linear relationship (r (40) = .15; p = .35) involving tribunals' mean PLC shifts. A test of the medians likewise failed to reveal a meaningful group difference in binary expertise and tribunals' PLC shifts (U = 166.5; p = .86). The null results replicated using a correlation to test the weighted variable (r (40) = .19; p = .23).

175 For the binary measure, it was not possible to detect a reliable mean difference (t (54) = −0.112; p = .91; r = .02; n = 56) or a reliable median difference (U = 288.0; p = .18) between the presence of any experienced counsel on states' legal team and investor PLC, using logged data. An ANOVA exploring mean differences in investors' PLC as a function of total RPs on states' legal teams likewise failed to reveal a significant result (F (4, 43) = 0.512; p = .73; r = .21; n = 47). Null results replicated using the weighted measure to evaluate states' counsel experience and investor PLC (r (48) = .13; p = .13), even controlling for case length (r (44) = .04; p = .81; n = 47) or presence of energy disputes (r (45) = .10; p = .49; n = 48).

(2) tribunals' PLC shifts.[176] Because there was no reliable link, it is improper to infer that the experience of one side caused the other side to "lawyer up" and pay more for their own counsel—or for tribunals to consider counsel experience when making PLC shifts. While caution is required for null effects, the lack of a link bears consideration as the caseload evolves.

As a policy matter, there may be value in paying relatively higher prices for lawyers when there is a better outcome. For investors, if one is paying a premium to retain experienced counsel, one would hope that success would be commensurate with that higher price tag. The data supported the notion that, overall, there was value in paying a premium for experienced counsel, as they also generally exhibited greater success levels. While investors might wish they could pay less to win more, presumably the findings are preferable to either paying more to receive an adverse outcome or paying less to win less. For respondents, the narrative was not overwhelmingly negative. With previous research finding that states could reliably drive down investors' relative success with experienced counsel,[177] there may be some comfort in knowing that states were not necessarily paying a relatively higher price for driving down relative investor success. If RPs generated less state success in outcomes but states paid more PLC, that result would be a more concerning result.

In contrast to parties' legal fees, potential links between counsel expertise and tribunal costs could, in theory, operate in multiple ways. First, an efficiency theory would suggest a negative relationship between counsel experience and TCE, whereby more sophisticated and experienced counsel are more efficient and make streamlined but effective arguments to tribunals. As many tribunals (particularly ICSID cases) base fees on an hourly rate, an efficiency theory means experienced counsel should facilitate lower TCE, whereas less experienced counsel may require tribunals to make additional effort to adjudicate the claim, thereby increasing costs. Alternatively, a complexity theory would suggest the opposite and reflect a positive correlation between TCE and parties' legal expertise. Under this theory, RPs familiar with the subtleties of the law, the importance of fact investigation, arbitrator appointment and challenge subtleties, and the nature of tribunal dynamics could pursue more arguments in a more complex and nuanced manner, thereby generating more materials for tribunals to consider and thereby raising tribunal costs. Yet, under a complexity theory, the relationship might be reflexive—whereby parties with challenging cases appoint an RP to address case complexity, and the inherent intricacy of the dispute could require larger quantities of tribunal time, thereby increasing TCE. Alternatively, TCE could be random or otherwise be unassociated with counsel experience.

---

176 For the binary expertise variable, using logged data, it was not possible to detect a link between presence of an RP on states' legal teams and tribunals' mean PLC shifts ($t\,(35) = -1.003$; $p = .32$; $r = .17$; $n = 37$); and a Mann-Whitney U-test likewise failed to reveal a reliable relationship between the presence of any RP on states' legal team and median investor PLC ($U = 40.0$; $p = .58$). The null results replicated using a bivariate correlation testing the weighted variable ($r\,(40) = .19$; $p = .23$).

177 Franck & Wylie, *supra* note 26.

The data supported the "complexity theory," as tests regularly revealed that increased tribunal costs were associated with the presence of expert counsel. A series of linear regressions explored expertise of investors' and states' counsel on tribunal costs. For both the binary approach[178] and weighted measures of teams' relative experience,[179] regression models reliably predicted TCE; and in those regressions, presence of RPs for both investors[180] and states[181] were generally linked with increased TCE. Bivariate tests continued to reflect that increased counsel experience for investors[182] was reliably associated with higher TCE, whereas the effect was intermittently present for experienced state counsel.[183] Table 8.5 reflects mean tribunal costs and expenses, demonstrating the average cost for tribunals nearly doubled when investors' legal team included RPs and TCE increased roughly 150% when RPs represented states.

---

[178] Using logged TCE data to analyze final cases, a regression reliably predicted TCE as a function of lawyers' expertise, namely whether investors' legal teams had at least one RP and whether states' legal teams had at least one RP (F (2, 52) = 5.361; p =.01; R^2 = .18; n = 56). Analyzing total number of RPs investors' and states' respective legal teams also reliably predicted TCE (F (2, 50) = 3.945; p = .03; R^2 = .14; n = 52).

[179] Using logged data, a regression model predicted TCE as a function of weighted expertise of counsel on both investors' and states' legal teams (F (2, 20) = 7.822; p = .001; R^2 = .24; n = 52).

[180] For the presence or absence of any RP on investors' teams, RPs were a reliable predictor of TCE (B = .307; SE = .118; t = 2.595; p = .01). The total number of RPs on investors' teams, however, was on the cusp of significance of predicting TCE (B = .122; SE = .069; t = 1.779; p = .81). The weighted variable of total relative expertise on investors' legal teams reliably predicted TCE (B = .072; SE = .026; t = 2.775; p = .01).

[181] For the presence or absence of any RP on states' legal teams, RPs were a reliable predictor of TCE (B = 314; SE = .139; t = 2.4263; p = .03). The total number of RPs on states' legal teams was likewise significant (B = .130; SE = .062; t = 2.094; p = .04). For the weighted variable, relative experience on states' legal teams reliably predicted TCE (B = .058; SE = .022; t = 2.593; p = .01).

[182] A test analyzing mean differences in TCE for cases with and without any RP on investors' teams was on the cusp of significance using logged data (t (53) = −1.795; p = .08; r = .24; n = 55); and winsorized data with higher but acceptable skewing was significant (t (53) = −2.636; p = .01; r = .34; n = 55). A test of medians identified a reliable difference in TCE for cases where investors had at least one RP on their legal team (U = 199.0; p = .02). For the weighted variable examining TCE and the total weight of investors' legal teams, the relationship was significant (r (55) = .36; p = .01); and the significant link remained after controlling for case length (r (51) =.37; p = .01) or presence of an energy dispute (r (52) = .38; p = .01). The only wrinkle was: it was not possible to identify a reliable link with TCE when analyzing the total number of RPs on investors' legal teams when considering mean (F (4, 50) = 0.810; p = .53; r = .25; n = 55) or median (χ^2 (4) = 5.425; p = .25; r = .30; n = 55) cost, but this may reflect the large number of categories within the variable.

[183] A test of mean TCE differences in cases where states had at least one RP, using logged data with the least skewing, was marginally significant (t (51) = −1.893; p = .06; r = .26; n = 53). Likewise, a test of median differences in TCE based upon whether states had at least one RP on their legal team was on the cusp of significance (U = 140; p = .09). For the weighted variable examining the total weight of states' legal teams and TCE, the relationship was significant (r (53) = .35; p = .01). While the results replicated after controlling for presence of energy disputes (r (50) = .34; p = .01), the result dissipated when controlling for case length (r (49) = .23; p = .11). Like investors' experience, the variable analyzing total number of RPs on states' legal teams was unable to identify reliable differences in means using logged data (F (4, 48) = 1.348; p = .27; r = .32; n = 53) or medians (χ^2 (4) = 5.191; p = .27; r = .30; n = 53), which may reflect the variance from having a variable with five categories.

TABLE 8.5

Mean Tribunal Expenses and Administrative Costs using Inflation-adjusted Winsorized Data in Final Awards, for Cases With and Without Repeat Player Counsel.

	Mean TCE (US$)	*Standard Deviation*	*Total*
Investors' Legal Team			
With an RP	812,445	563732	38
No RP—Only OS Players	435,144	249477	17
Respondent's Legal Team			
With an RP	760,375	533163	43
No RP—Only OS Players	489,088	400369	10

Considering the data in a more granular way using the weighted variable is also helpful, as averages have the capacity to hide a degree of variance. When considering the relative weight of investors' legal teams and TCE, there were clusters of costs. First, the most important break point was: where investors were exclusively represented by one-shot players and lacked RPs on their team, tribunal costs bunched around US$500,000 or lower. In contrast, for cases with RPs, there was a greater variance, ranging between US$500,000 and US$1.5 million.[184]

Likewise, when considering the relative weight of states' legal teams and TCE, there were pockets of cases, but the most critical distinction was whether states were represented exclusively by one-shot players. Where states were not represented by RPs, all TCE was less than US$1 million and TCE tended to cluster *under* US$500,000. In contrast, when states were represented by RPs, TCE exhibited broader variation. While there were clusters around US$800,000, some lower weighted teams had higher TCE, and some higher weighted teams had lower TCE.[185]

To the extent that lower tribunal costs were associated with less time expended by arbitrators, this could be a function of attorney representation. One-shot players may, for example, have made fewer arguments, not raised procedural issues, underdeveloped the facts or document requests, and/or used less sophisticated legal arguments; the net result was to minimize tribunal time in resolving a case and decreasing costs. An alternative explanation

[184] Only three cases involved tribunals costing *over* US$2 million. The largest TCE was in *Walter Bau v. Thailand* before Ian Barker, Marc Lalonde, and Jayavadh Bunnag, where investors were represented by Lovells and Professor James Crawford. The next highest TCE was *Victor Pey Casado v. Chile*, before Pierre Lalive, Mohammed Chemloul, and Emmanuel Gaillard where investors were represented by Garcés y Prada, Abogados and Gide Loyrette & Nouel. The third highest TCE was in *Chevron v. Ecuador* before Karl-Heinz Böckstiegel, Charles Brower, and Albert Jan van den Berg, where investors were represented by King & Spalding and Quevedo & Ponce.

[185] For the three outlier cases with TCE over US$2 million, White & Case represented Thailand in *Walter Bau*; Ministerio de Economía, Fomento y Reconstrucción de Chile, Carey & Cía. Ltda. and Arnold & Porter represented Chile in *Victor Pey Casado*; and Procuraduría General del Estado de Ecuador, Winston Strawn and Foley Hoag represented Ecuador in *Chevron*.

might be that one-shot players were less selective in accepting clients and, as such, case selection effects could mean that they represented clients with less meritorious cases that were more efficiently decided, which in turn generated lower TCE. Another explanation could be that those aspects interacted, namely if the dispute was sufficiently serious, complex, or meritorious, investors appointed sophisticated legal teams, tribunals then allocated more time than they might have otherwise given to adjudication.

V. An Initial Model of ITA Costs

Ultimately, there were some—but very few—variables reliably associated with ITA costs, which could have any potential causal influence on costs. Despite hopes that multiple variables might affect all types of arbitration costs, only one variable reliably affected investors' PLC, respondents' PLC, and TCE—namely, time. In other words, Benjamin Franklin's intuitive hypothesis that "time is money" was true in ITA.

While other variables were traceable to one cost or another, it was the exception (rather than the rule) that variables reliably predicted any ITA cost. Instead, for better or worse, it was not normally possible to detect whether most variables were reliably related to costs; and even where variables were linked, the influence was typically limited to a single type of ITA cost. In other words, for variables other than time, that data was unable to proscribe a universal narrative for ITA costs and reality required an appreciation of nuance.

To begin building a model for future prediction, this section synthesizes potential drivers to begin exploring a descriptive model to explain ITA costs in the hopes of creating a baseline for future predictive models. Recognizing the models suffer from challenges involving missing data and inevitable under-specification,[186] the longer-term objective is to provide a baseline to aid future research in identifying how arbitration costs evolve over time.

For investors' PLC, previous analyses reflected that few variables were related to cost increases (or decreases). As with all costs, time was a predictor. Otherwise, outcome—but only for choosing a winning dispute and amounts awarded—and the presence of investors' RP counsel were the only variables reliably contributing to investors' legal costs and expenses. A linear regression analysis, using inflation-adjusted logged data, identified those variables reliably predicted investors' PLC.[187] While the model predicted investor's costs, once interacting with other variables, the outcome variable ceased to have a predictive

[186] Under-specification could derive from the need to have more precision with existing variables or to add more variables to explain the variance of ITA costs.

[187] $F(3, 43) = 13.07$[illegible]; $p < .001$; $R^2 = .477$; $n = 47$. *See also* Table 8.6. Rerunning the model with the binary measure of claimant attorney experience replicated the significant results ($F(3, 43) = 13.451$; $p < .001$; $R^2 = .484$). When the experience of state counsel as RPs was added to either the binary ($F(4, 41) = 9.941$; $p < .001$; $R^2 = .492$) or weighted ($F(4, 41) = 9.913$; $p < .001$; $R^2 = .492$) model, the models remained significant; but respondents' experience was a non-significant predictor of investors' legal costs for both the bivariate ($B = .090$; $SE = .271$; $t = .332$; $p = .74$) and weighted ($B = .027$; $SE = .029$; $t = .931$; $p = .36$) models. This replicated earlier bivariate analyses suggesting the lack of a relationship.

effect.[188] Table 8.6 provides information on the beta-weights, standard errors, *t*-values, and *p*-values, denoting with a * reflecting where individual predictors were significant, namely case length and the total weight of the investors' legal team.

TABLE 8.6

Regression Model and Coefficients used for Predicting Investors' PLC using Inflation-adjusted Logged Data ($n = 47$).

Variable	B	SE	t	p
Intercept	5.578	.157	35.482	< .001
Case Length (in months)	0.012	.003	3.787	< .001*
Case Outcome (0 = Respondent Win; 1 = Claimant Win–investor awarded US$ or equivalent remedy)	0.136	.157	0.870	.389
Claimant Attorney Experience (Weighted Variable)	0.074	.033	2.279	.028*

For states, only a handful of variables were reliably associated with states' legal fees. The length of a case, presence of an energy dispute, and the presence of a separate opinion were the only robust cost predictors.[189] A linear regression analysis, using inflation-adjusted winsorized data with the lowest skewing, reliably predicted states' PLC.[190] Table 8.7 provides information on the beta-weights, standard errors, *t*-values, and *p*-values, using a * to identify the three individual predictive variables, namely case length, the presence of an energy case, and the presence of a separate opinion.

---

[188] When the model substituted inflation-adjusted logged amounts awarded in cases where investors won for the previous binary outcome variable, both the binary (F (3, 43) = 12.302; p <.001; R^2 = .462) and weighted (F (3, 43) = 11.809; p < .001; R^2 = .452) models of investors' RP expertise remained significant predictors—and amounts awarded remained non-predictive for both the binary (B = .029; SE = .020; t = 1.472; p = .15) and weighted (B = .018; SE = .021; t = .849; p = .40) models.

[189] Amounts claimed, although significant predictors of respondent PLC only in the subset of claims where investors won, was not included for multiple reasons. First, links to amounts awarded dissipated when controlling for amounts claimed. Second, it was not significant in the set of all outcomes. Third, an investor makes a claim at a moment that temporally precedes an award and is therefore a path constraint on amounts awarded.

[190] F (3, 55) = 8.567; p < .001; R^2 = .32; n = 59. *See also* Table 8.7. Replicating tests to include RP experience of state counsel, the model remained significant using either the binary (F (4, 52) = 6.477; p < .001; R^2 = .33) or weighted (F (4, 52) = 6.355; p < .001; R^2 = .33) variables; but respondents' experience was a non-significant predictor of states' legal costs for both the bivariate (B = −817048; SE = 1476489; t = −0.587; p = .56) and weighted (B = 20814; SE = 163323; t = .127; p = .90) variables, which replicated previous bivariate analyses that were unable to detect a relationship.

TABLE 8.7

Regression Model and Coefficients used for Predicting States' PLC using Inflation-adjusted Winsorized Data ($n = 59$).

Variable	B	SE	t	p
Intercept	4240836	1457206	2.910	.005
Case Length (in months)	37,835	16387	2.309	.025*
Energy Dispute (0 = Dispute in sector other than energy; 1 = case involves energy dispute)	2,074,581	779185	2.663	.010*
Separate Opinion in Award (0 = no separate opinion; 1 = separate opinion present)	−799,888	239419	−3.341	.002*

As winsorized data exhibited the lowest skewing and was in a scale (U.S. dollars) with practical significance, the beta-weights (B) offer a unique opportunity to understand the model's implications for states' legal costs.[191] Namely, beta-weights reflect that, accordingly to the model, states' PLC increased roughly US$38,000 every month; cases involving an energy dispute cost roughly US$2 million more than non-energy cases, and cases without a separate opinion cost nearly US$800,000 less than cases with a separate opinion.

Tribunal costs and administrative expenses were likewise challenging to predict. In addition to time, the most robust predictors were amounts claimed and the presence of RPs on either the investors' or states' legal teams.[192] A linear regression analysis on inflation-adjusted logged data continued to reliably predict TCE.[193] While the influence of experienced counsel for *investors* continued to be a significant predictor of TCE, when combined with other factors, the experience of states' legal team failed to predict tribunal cost. Table 8.8 provides information on the beta-weights, standard errors, t-values, and p-values, denoting with a * reflecting where individual variables were significant predictors, namely case length, amount claimed, and the total weight of the investors' legal team.

---

191 Due to high skewing, a similar analysis was not performed using winsorized data for investors' PLC, as the logged data most properly comported with the assumptions underlying the statistical modelling. *See* Appendix I.

192 Previous analysis identified a reliable link with amounts awarded, which evaporated after controlling for amounts claimed. As claims precede awards, any variance attributable to awards has its origin in claims. For this reason, and because the link was only present in the subset where investors won, the model focused on claims.

193 $F(4, 35) = 13.065$; $p < .001$; $R^2 = .599$; $n = 40$. *See also* Table 8.8. Replacing counsel experience with the binary measures for the presence of any RP on investors' or states' legal teams replicated the significant model ($F(4, 35) = 12.5436$; $p < .001$; $R^2 = .589$); case length, amount claimed, and RPs on investors' legal teams remained significant predictors, the presence of an RP on states' legal teams remained non-predictive ($B = .079$; $SE = .135$; $t = .585$; $p = .56$).

TABLE 8.8

Regeression Model and Coefficients used for Predicting TCE using Inflation-adjusted Logged Data ($n = 40$).

Variable	B	SE	t	p
Intercept	3.960	.411	9.625	< .001
Case Length (in months)	.009	.002	3.919	< .001*
Amount Claimed (inflation-adjusted logged data)	.149	.053	2.800	.008*
Claimant Attorney Experience (Weighted Variable)	.078	.023	3.425	.002*
Respondent Attorney Experience (Weighted Variable)	.009	.020	.448	.657

While logged TCE data exhibited the lowest skewing, most people do not intuitatively understand values provided in logs. Winsorized data—which is measured in an understandable scale of U.S. dollars but also had statistically acceptable skewing—permits consideration of the practical implications of the model. Focusing on beta-weights (B) of winsorized U.S. dollars permit an understanding of the costs involved using an more readily understandable scale.[194] Using the two significant predictors from the winsorized data,[195] the model reflected that tribunal costs and expenses increased roughly US$10,000[196] a month; and, when investors' legal team contained at least one RP, TCE was around US$500,000[197] more than in cases where investors' lawyers consisted exclusively of one-shot players.

It is important to understand these models in context, appreciating that, for ITA, costs may not arise on an average, monthly basis and with a healthy appreciation for the limitations of the tests. Regressions are but one window into understanding ITA costs over a dispute's lifecycle. As with all analyses in this book, inferences require caution. Like in any empirical research, there are concerns about data's temporal nature, case selection effects from missing data, measures used, and the inevitable limitations of null effects. Beyond those concerns, there are others. First, there may be limitations to the strength of the inferences, as they may not reflect population parameters. Inferences should be made cautiously given

[194] *See* Appendix I (reflecting the acdeptable skewing level of winsorized and logged TCE). The binary ($F\,(4, 39) = 9.875; p < .001; R^2 = .53$) and weighted ($F\,(4, 39) = 8.254; p < .001; R^2 = .485$) models of counsel experience, using the same variables on winsorized data, significantly predicted TCE.

[195] Using either the binary or weighted models of RP experience to predict TCE, logged amounts claimed were no longer significant predictors of TCE. Winsorized amounts claimed, which would have been on the same scale as the winsorized TCE data, were not used as skewing was slightly higher than normally accepted levels levels. *See* Appendix I.

[196] $B = 10{,}227.5; SE = 2{,}998.5; t = 3.441; p = .002.$

[197] $B = 528{,}256; SE = 148{,}153; t = 3.566; p = .001.$

the representativeness of subsets. Replication is necessary to avoid establishing parameters that could reflect random chance. Second, it is always possible that there was an insufficient sample size to predict non-significant costs. A broader pool of data, likely requiring over 700-cases based on an a priori power analysis, could confirm, contradict, or supplement these findings. Third, related to case selection effects, there may be issues related to external validity since the results come from data in publicly available awards. Publicly available awards may not be representative of the broader pool of both public and private awards. Particularly given the concerns about the missing or incomplete costs data in many awards, it is possible that the data is under-representative of ITA costs even given the public data. Accordingly, preparing for and conducting the analyses in this book, which were a mammoth undertaking, represent a historical snapshot rather than a holistic conclusion etched in stone.

Fourth, inferential tests and descriptive models predicting ITA costs could be underspecified. Omitted variables—such as the presence of third-party funding, the type of government activity at issue, the nature of the underlying dispute, or other factors—could contribute meaningfully to predicting ITA costs. None of the models have focused extensively upon party characteristics (including whether a case involved an FT500 entity in an investors' corporate chain, the presence of investors involving human beings,[198] the region or development status of respondents),[199] characteristics of NDPs, or tribunal characteristics (including the tribunals' development status, whether a chair was a repeat player, or the presence of women on tribunals).[200] The choice to omit these variables was largely because

---

[198] *But see* note 65 and accompanying text (noting Chapter 6 contained some analyses that were generally unable to identify a reliable impact of investor identity, using multiple definitions, and arbitration costs, particularly after controlling for case length); *see also infra* notes 199–202.

[199] For example, to assess the extent of the Argentine wrinkle identified in *infra note* 200, multiple analyses explored the presence (or absence) of a Latin American respondent on ITA costs. None of the tests found a reliable relationship between ITA costs and the presence (or absence) of a Latin American state. The *t*-tests were unable to detect reliable mean differences in cases with (or without) Latin American respondents for: (1) investor PLC (t (53) = −1.204; p = .23 ; r = .16; n = 55); (2) state PLC (t (58) = −0.59; p = .95; r = .08; n = 60); or (3) TCE (t (59) = −1.453; p = .15; r = .19; n = 61). Partial correlations, that controlled for case length, replicated the inability to detect reliable relationships between the presence of a Latin American state and: (1) investors' PLC (r (51) = −.14; p = .30), (2) states' PLC, (r (56) = −.13; p = .32), or (3) TCE (r (57) = .13; p = .31). Testing medians likewise failed to find group differences in cases with (or without) Latin American respondents for investors' PLC (U = 240.0; p = .18), states' PLC (U = 315.0; p = .70), and TCE (U = 269.0; p = .20).

[200] Using variables from previous work that had found some (but not all) variables predicted ITA outcomes, *see* Franck & Wylie, *supra* note 26, many regression analyses were generally unable to detect reliable differences in ITA costs, including: (1) presence of a human being (instead of a corporation) as an investor, (2) presence of an FT500 investor (or parent) in a case, (3) an Argentine respondent, (4) the presence of women on tribunals, and (5) presence of a chair who had repeat arbitration appointments. By way of example, for investors PLC, adding four variables (namely, FT500_Parent, Argentina, Gender, ChairBI) to the predictors from Table 8.6 meant the model still predicted investors' PLC (F (7, 39) = 6.302; p < .001; R^2 = .368; n = 47). Yet, the presence of an investor who was an FT500 entity (or an FT parent) was nonpredictive (B = .331; SE = .278; t = 1.191; p = .24); Argentina's presence as respondent was nonpredictive (B = −.266; SE = .305; t = −0.873; p = .39); the presence of a woman on tribunal was nonpredictive (B = .028; SE =.196; t = 0.140; p = .89); and the presence of a repeat player chair was non-predictive (B = −.381; SE = .210; t = −1.816; p = .08) of investors' PLC. The results came close to full replication for states' PLC. Adding the same four variables to the other predictors of state PLC in Table 8.7 still meant the model predicted state PLC (F (7, 50) = 5.739; R^2 = .368;

bivariate and multivariate regressions studied were unable to detect reliable relationships with ITA costs.[201] For example, since neither analysis of investor identity nor the extensive consideration of the presence of an NDP were reliably linked to any ITA costs, adding a non-significant variable to a predictive model does not necessarily add value. Nevertheless, it is possible that, as cases evolve and measurements improve, better predictors of ITA costs could be ascertained.[202]

Given these considerations, more research is needed to provide sufficient power, stability, statistical control, and enhanced validity for making more definitive conclusions. It will likely take years—if not decades—before there is a sufficient data pool. While this creates challenges, it does not diminish the baseline offered by this research. Rather, it requires respecting limitations of statistical inference and doing our best with available information in an area of controversy and at a moment in history when data—rather than emotions, ideology, and political expediency—should aid decision-making involving long-term international law consequences.

$p < .001$; = ; $n = 58$). The presence of the FT500-related entity ($B = 357572$; $SE = 1311825$; $t = 0.189$; $p = .85$), a woman on the tribunal ($B = 185004$; $SE = 1006307$; $t = 0.184$; $p = .86$), or a RP chair ($B = -385$; $SE = 970938$; $t = 0.000$; $p = .99$) all failed to be individual predictors of states' PLC. Argentina's presence, however, was a significant predictor of states' costs in cases involving Argentina ($B = -5251152$; $SE = 1703294$; $t = -3.083$; $p = .003$). Given the findings of *supra* note 199, the effect may be limited to Argentina. For TCE, adding the same four variables to the TCE predictors in Table 8.8 meant the model still reliably predicted total TCE ($F(8, 31) = 7.974$; $p < .001$; $R^2 = .589$; $n = 40$). Yet, the presence of a FT500-related entity ($B = .027$; $SE = .141$; $t = 0.193$; $p = .85$), an Argentine respondent ($B = -.078$; $SE = .247$; $t = -0.318$; $p = .75$), a woman on the tribunal ($B = -.296$; $SE = .188$; $t = -1.577$; $p = .13$), or a RP chair ($B = -.185$; $SE = .111$; $t = 01.668$; $p = .11$), were all non-predictive of TCE.

201 Space restrictions also inevitably came into play. Explaining tests slowly to ensure that the cognitive processing of System 2 occurs properly takes both time and space. *See, e.g., supra* note 199 (analyzing a single variable). While our human intuition may desire to find cases failing to conform with a larger pattern, as Chapter 2 identified, individual cases still form part of a larger whole; and the objective should be to focus on baselines when making general normative choices. Likewise, one might wish the dataset contained a different version of a variable or this book tested different hypotheses. Readers are invited to invest in exploring those questions through their own research, building upon the information that this book (and its online appendices) are putting into the public domain.

202 Multiple bivariate correlations or regression models tested whether having a woman on a tribunal was associated with increased (or decreased) TCE. For example, using the model in Table 8.7 but adding a dummy variable for tribunals with (and without) women, the model remained statistically significant ($F(4, 35) = 12.103$; $p < .001$; $R^2 = .64$; $n = 39$). All other significant and non-significant predictors persisted; but having a woman on a tribunal was not a significant predictor of TCE ($B = -.353$; $SE = .178$; $t = -1.977$; $p = .06$), although it was on the cusp, suggesting further attention is warranted. *See also supra* note 199. The null results, however, do not mean that women on arbitration tribunals were paid equivalently to men. As TCE is a composite variable—including costs of all arbitrators and administration—future analyses might seek to disaggregate individual arbitrators' costs, thereby aiding assessment of whether female arbitrators received different compensation than did male colleagues. *See* Chapter 9 (supporting ICSID's proposals to disaggregate tribunal costs and identify the fees of each arbitrator in an award).

9 The Way Forward

IRRESPECTIVE OF ITS age and evolutionary state, the foment and discontent surrounding investment treaty arbitration (ITA) must be acknowledged.[1] One cannot help but recall the folk tale from India, passed down in oral tradition, of "The Blind Men and the Elephant."[2] In the parable, a group of blind men who have never encountered an elephant before try to conceptualize what one is simply by interacting with the elephant. Each person has a specific personal experience, touching a distinct part, whether the trunk, the tusk, the body, the foot, or the tail. Having had unique interactions, each person creates a different hypothesis about the precise nature of the whole elephant. Recognizing they are in complete disagreement about the elephant's nature, some versions have the men suspecting others are dishonest and even coming to blows. The greater lesson is that humans easily presume their experiences are representative and reflect the whole truth, rather than accepting that each unique perspective can be valid but yet remains a narrow element of a broader whole. Framed differently: one's personal experiences and beliefs can be partially right and legitimate yet still only reflect partial information.

In addition to observers' disparate contemporaneous perspectives, historical observations can frame our understanding of present-day observations. Alexis de Tocqueville began his classic, *Democracy in America*, by encouraging observers of social experiments to keep assessments in perspective, recalling both the genesis of a transformation and appreciating

[1] *See, e.g.,* Chapters 1, 4.

[2] JOHN GODFREY SAXE, THE BLIND MEN & THE ELEPHANT (2016); WAS RAHMAN & PIRYA KURIEN, BLIND MEN AND THE ELEPHANT vii–viii (2007); U.S. Peace Corps, *The Blind Men and the Elephant*, https://bit.ly/2MoKePr (last visited Aug. 8, 2018).

Arbitration Costs. Susan D. Franck.

future potential. As de Tocqueville explained, "[t]he entire man [or woman] is, so to speak, to be seen in the eyes of the child. The growth of nations presents something analogous to this; they all bear some marks of their origin."[3] As another innovation involving the laws of nations, assessing ITA warrants a similar perspective. Keeping in mind Everett Rogers's classic insights about diffusion of innovations,[4] stakeholders should appreciate both where ITA started and where it may evolve, hopefully without rushing to undue praise or condemnation. The better course is to have data inform a considered conversation about the future of what is, still, a relatively new phenomenon in international law.

The lessons from these wise thinkers mean it is vital to be appreciative of and respectful toward those whose experiences have created an antagonistic, critical, sympathetic, laudatory, or even agnostic view of ITA, as all those experiences aid understanding of the larger whole and historical context. Throughout this book, there have been instances where some parts, but likely not all, resonate strongly. Each reader will likely have a different perspective, namely one reader will find an evidence-based finding surprising, whereas another will find it commonplace; one reader may find the insights helpful and supportive of existing perception, whereas another reader may find it disconcerting and failing to support previously held views and personal experience. Like the tale of the elephant, it is possible that the different reactions are reasonable, as each reader came to the "elephant" of ITA with different preexisting experiences and origin stories.

The challenges with data-driven approaches to analyzing complicated legal phenomena are threefold. First, disrupting conventional wisdom that is personally (and potentially deeply) held can be a shock to identity and perception, making it difficult to take in contradictory information or appreciate how disruptive information could be beneficial. Given the subtleties revealed by the data about ITA, it takes time and cognitive capacity to engage in nuanced analysis. Offering information that *feels* unsettling does *not* mean previous experiences are invalid; rather, the trick is to place the old information within a new context, appreciating both the prior experience and new variation. Second, the story about ITA—and its relative costs and benefits—is not easily reducible to a single, sleek, tweetable, tagline with a trendy #hashtag. This means understanding the full variance, and providing tailored reforms, requires appreciation of detail. Stakeholders (whether states, lawyers, arbitrators, institutions, international organizations, nongovernmental organizations, journalists, or law professors) may not have time to pay detailed attention and may intuitively cherry-pick elements to focus upon, rather than keeping a holistic perspective. This inevitably means core elements of the picture will be absent. Third, and perhaps more important, the ITA universe is in motion, meaning the data may be changing, generating an evolution where new analyses could reveal different results.

The author is aware that, in practical political terms, her approach is provocative. By neither being allied with "pro-ISDS" nor the "anti-ISDS" factions, there is minimal political cover when stakeholders affiliated with either intellectual tribe take issue with the results and seek to nitpick when information creates psychological discomfort.[5] The effort, however, is

---

[3] Alexis de Tocqueville, Democracy in America 39 (Richard D. Heffner ed., 1984) (1835).

[4] *See* Chapter 4.

[5] *See, e.g.*, Steven Pinker, Enlightenment Now: The Case for Reason, Science, Humanism, and Progress 355–72, 383 (2018) (discussing tribalism) *see also* Amy Chua, Political Tribes: Group Instinct and the Fate of Nations 2–13, 204 (2018) (same).

designed to align with data—data gathered and analyzed in accordance with scientific principles[6] in a genuine effort to understand "what is the elephant" with which we are dealing, as the system evolves. Reframing matters more positively, this book contains "something for everyone," namely something to both complain about and benefit from regarding the fiscal implications and practices of cost allocation in investment treaty dispute resolution.

This final chapter, then, has a rather unenviable task. Namely, given the data and analyses—with their inevitable limitations—what are the insights for creating dispute settlement norms in international investment law? Increasing scrutiny by UNCITRAL's Working Group on costs, enquiries from the European Union into alternative forms of dispute settlement, and ICSID's proposals putting costs front and center,[7] create considerable food for thought.

To synthesize preceding chapters and point the way forward with data, this chapter proceeds in five parts. It first identifies the need for enhanced transparency on costs and rationalization, particularly in early stages of disputes to manage expectations and create process efficiencies. Second, placing costs in context, it identifies relative costs and benefits of ITA, arguing an increased focus on non-adjudicative dispute resolution is warranted while acknowledging those mechanisms only work effectively when some form of legitimate adjudication permits parties to negotiate "in the shadow of the law." Third, given the data and models associated with costs, the chapter explores ICSID's recent proposals to foster a dialogue about costs. Fourth, it advocates changing the normative framework for cost-shifting to a factor-dependent model to provide a more realistic, authentic, and functional approach. Recalling potential limitations, the chapter concludes that in order for international investment dispute resolution to foster rule-of-law adjudication that is efficient, fair, reliable, and rationalized, stakeholders should implement structural safeguards to focus on *appropriate* dispute resolution to promote cost containment, predictability, and sustainable dispute resolution in an era of re-emerging nationalization and a backlash against international law.

I. The Costs Baseline

Chapter 6 demonstrated ITA costs were nontrivial and relatively high (particularly counsel cost), creating access to justice and equality of treatment challenges. The combined average cost of all parties' lawyers, arbitrators, and related expenses was slightly over US$10 million on average (with a median net cost of around US$6 million).[8] Compared to outcomes in Chapter 5, costs were proportionately large. Yet, despite the scale of fiscal risk in disputes

---

[6] Methodological enquiries to explore adherence to quality social science research are appropriate. Susan D. Franck, *The Promise and Peril of Empiricism and International Investment Law Disputes*, *in* CAMBRIDGE COMPENDIUM OF INTERNATIONAL COMMERCIAL AND INVESTMENT ARBITRATION (Andrea Bjorklund et al., forthcoming 2019).

[7] *See* Am. Soc'y Int'l L., *Unfolding the Working Paper on ICSID Rules Amendment: Interview with Meg Kinnear*, ASIL.ORG (Sept. 6, 2018) at 3:00-3:50; 35:57-41:30, https://bit.ly/2xvPMPk (last visited Sept. 22, 2018); *see also infra* notes 35, 152, 180, 185 (discussing EU and UNCITRAL efforts).

[8] The figures from the dataset directly suggested that the combined means of the 2011-inflation total PLC and TCE were around US$10 million (with a median total of roughly US$6 million). Using a calculator to adjust those values to 2018, the combined mean was close to US$11.6 million (with a median total of close to US$6.9). *See* Chapter 6; Figure 6.1.

affecting state sovereignty, and in contrast with damage explanations, tribunals regularly failed to particularize basic ITA costs. Fully appreciating ITA's costs requires evolutionary assessments, as the gaps mean that drawing conclusive inferences is improper.

The large relative values warrant increased attention by tribunals, parties, and other stakeholders to ensure all parties (both investors and states) are treated fairly and not unduly burdened. For smaller parties with fewer resources, the sheer scope of costs creates barriers in accessing justice and fully pursuing their claims or defenses should parties be unable to pay lawyers, arbitrators, or institutions. Small and economically disadvantaged investors, with few economic resources and minimal political capital, may be unable to generate incentives facilitating a negotiated resolution before initiating arbitration; lack of resources may translate into abandoning potential claims or accepting the consequences of illegal state behavior. Likewise, states with limited economic resources may have real challenges accessing and paying for quality counsel (particularly where local currencies have material exchange rate fluctuations)—or otherwise having to make a "Sophie's Choice" between financing social projects or paying defense lawyers, especially when pitted against well-financed and politically well-positioned investors. Meanwhile, there may be situations where amounts at stake are sufficiently small that, despite the seriousness of an investor's claim or a state's need for a clear ruling their conduct comports with international law, sheer economics means disputes capable of repetition, yet evading review, may never reach adjudication.[9] ITA costs are, in this respect, the dull knife that cuts both ways.

ICSID's 2018 proposals are a step in the right direction, as they create obligations making clear that parties and arbitrators have responsibilities to control costs. ICSID explains that its proposed "new rule establishes general duties for the parties and Tribunal, including equality of treatment of the parties, acting in an expeditious and cost-effective manner."[10] Specifically, tribunals must "treat the parties equally and provide each party with a reasonable opportunity to present its case," and both parties and arbitrators must "conduct the proceeding in an expeditious and cost-effective manner."[11] Yet, ICSID's guidance is that

[9] This is where third-party funding (TPF) might play a constructive role. *See, e.g.,* Clara Brillembourg, *Remarks*, 109 Am. Soc'y Int'l L. Proc. 229, 233 (2015) (discussing Bloomberg and Gates' Foundation Anti-Tobacco Trade Litigation Fund for defending developing states); Maya Steinitz, *Whose Claim Is This Anyway? Third-Party Litigation Funding*, 95 Minn. L. Rev. 1268, 1272–73 (2011) (exploring how financing adjudication can alter dynamics to permit "traditionally disempowered parties" to use adjudication and "serve as a redistributive tool by society's have-nots").

[10] ICSID Secretariat, Proposals for Amendment of the ICSID Rules—Synopsis, Vol. 1, 4 (Aug. 2, 2018), https://bit.ly/2MhlTrv (last visited Aug. 17, 2018) [hereinafter ICSID, Synopsis]. In October 2018, NAFTA parties toyed with a similar duty but only used hortatory language. United States-Mexico-Canada Agreement (Oct. 1, 2018), Ch. 14, Annex 14-D, art. 7.10, https://bit.ly/2O5Pbi1 (last visited Oct. 3, 2018) ("The tribunal and the disputing parties shall endeavor to conduct the arbitration in an expeditious and cost-effective manner.").

[11] ICSID Secretariat, Proposals for Amendment of the ICSID Rules—Consolidated Draft Rules Vol. 2, Proposed Arb. Rule 11(1),(3), Proposed AF Arb. Rule 20(1),(3) (Aug. 2, 2018), https://bit.ly/2vFo419 (last visited Aug. 17, 2018) [hereinafter ICSID, Proposed Rules]; *see also* ICSID Secretariat, Proposals for Amendment of the ICSID Rules—Working Paper, Vol. 3, 108–09 (Aug. 2, 2018), https://bit.ly/2whvXdh (last visited Aug. 17, 2018) [hereinafter ICSID, Working Paper] (indicating equality of treatment is similar to obligations in UNCITRAL Arbitration Rules but noting the cost-effectiveness duty is new).

tribunals and parties "should discuss any appropriate means to expedite a case early in the process."[12]

The devil, however, will be in the details. It remains to be seen precisely what this new duty requires, and how violations of the duty will be managed. While the proposal suggests arbitrators should consider party violations when assessing costs,[13] it is an open question as to how violations of *arbitrator* duties will be assessed and addressed. ICSID should offer details about this general standard, define the duty's scope, establish a working group to explore best practices for meeting the duty,[14] and identify how arbitrator transgressions will be addressed—including fee disgorgement[15] or commensurate sanctions, whether by a separate body or the ICSID Secretary-General.[16] Another way to address economic imbalance could involve creating a standing small claims facility for low-value disputes to resolve conflicts in a cost-efficient, streamlined manner.[17]

Given Chapter 3's findings about the number of human beings involved in ITA and the large number of developing country respondents, it may be worthwhile to establish a standing body to provide access to justice, whether by adjudication or other means such as mediation, for all parties.[18] One might also imagine such a facility could go hand in hand

---

[12] ICSID, WORKING PAPER, *supra* note 11, at 108. ICSID's proposals reflect efforts to improve efficiency throughout, including shorter timelines (i.e., streamlining arbitrator challenges), hurdles to receiving time extensions, and aspects described later in this chapter. *See, e.g.*, ICSID, SYNOPSIS, *supra* note 10, at 2; ICSID, WORKING PAPER, *supra* note 11, at 101–05.

[13] ICSID, PROPOSED RULES, *supra* note 11, Proposed Arb. Rule 19(4)(b); *id.* at Proposed AF Arb. Rule 29(4)(b).

[14] A "best practices" working group could be broader, potentially addressing similar aspects to those considered when exploring cost-containment in ICA. College of Commercial Arbitrators, *Protocols for Expeditious, Cost-Effective Commercial Arbitration: Key Action Steps for Business Users, Counsel, Arbitrators, and Arbitration Provider Institutions* (2010), https://bit.ly/2PiBnog (last visited Aug. 17, 2018); ICC Comm'n on Arb. and ADR, *Controlling Time and Costs in Arbitration* (Mar. 2018), https://bit.ly/2P3mIpk (last visited Aug 17, 2018).

[15] *See* Susan D. Franck, *The Liability of International Arbitrators: A Comparative Analysis and Proposal for Qualified Immunity*, 20 N.Y. L. SCH. J. INT'L & COMP. L. 1, 14–15, 31–32, 38, 42–44, 55–56 (2000) (identifying national laws where arbitrators breaching duties lose fees or are sanctioned); *see also* Int'l Chamber of Comm., *ICC Court Announces New Policies to Foster Transparency and Ensure Greater Efficiency* (May 1, 2016), https://bit.ly/2wkAf4H (last visited Aug 17, 2018) (providing a reduction in fees for draft awards received in an untimely manner); *see also infra* note 128 (discussing fee reduction options).

[16] For Additional Facility cases, ICSID proposed that the ICSID Secretary-General make decisions on arbitrator disqualification, suggesting a similar process could occur for fees. ICSID, PROPOSED RULES, *supra* note 11, Proposed AF Arb. Rules 39-40.

[17] Rather than a small claims facility, ICSID proposed Expedited Arbitration Rules, which may not be suitable for all cases and still require fiscal investments to constitute tribunals, albeit with streamlined proceedings. *See, e.g.*, ICSID, SYNOPSIS, *supra* note 10, at 10–11; ICSID, WORKING PAPER, *supra* note 11, at 292–95, 976–80. States could mandate expedited rules apply in treaties for small claims. Yet an ex ante choice might bind states to tight timetables and reduced submissions in disputes that, *ex post*, may be worthy of time-consuming, expensive proceedings.

[18] Susan D. Franck & Lindsey E. Wylie, *Predicting Outcomes in Investment Treaty Arbitration*, 65 DUKE L.J. 459, 525–26 (2016); Kirsten Boon, *Public Input into the ICSID Rules Revision: Rules and Regulations Reform—Expedited Procedures for Small Claims*, ICSIDWORLDBANK.ORG, https://bit.ly/2Ptxntn (last accessed Aug. 17, 2018).

with legal assistance centers to provide support for economically disadvantaged investors and states. While creating a legal assistance center has been discussed since the inception of debates about ITA,[19] nothing has happened. As a practical matter, the inertia may mean such a facility is politically infeasible. Yet given party demographics, potential power disparities, the value of rule-of-law adjudication, and the utility of creative problem-solving, keeping the possibility of creating a legal assistance center on the table is a vital policy option. If nothing else, providing a standing body and legal assistance supports a valuable hortatory norm, namely: investment treaty dispute settlement should be, functionally, an anti-bullying measure, to address (rather than facilitate) abusive conduct by bullying investors, bullying states, or bullying counsel.

Inevitably, ITA costs, while large, must be kept in context. Any form of transnational adjudication involving complex disputes likely also involves multiple jurisdictions, multiple sets of lawyers, and multiple languages, translating into high costs. Yet, little legal scholarship has explored the costs of transnational commercial or international economic adjudication (let alone with empirical rigor), making direct comparisons difficult.[20] Chapter 6 explored the billions of dollars in lawyer fees involved in the U.S. domestic tobacco litigation and transnational corruption investigations.[21] The data vacuum, however, has not stopped observations that: "ICJ [International Court of Justice] proceedings tend to last longer and cost more than ICSID or WTO panel proceedings."[22] Keeping potential comparative costs in mind is vital to understanding the value of alternatives, including a small claims facility or standing investment court. Nevertheless, even when average ITA costs are compared with other internal ITA fiscal values, the scale of costs is noteworthy, reflecting nearly 60% of the average damage award for all cases (including cases investors lost) or roughly 20% of average damages for the subset of cases where investors won.

---

[19] Eric Gottwald, *Leveling the Playing Field: Is It Time for a Legal Assistance Center for Developing Nations in Investment Treaty Arbitration?*, 22 AM. U. INT'L L. REV. 237 (2007).

[20] One effort estimated costs of WTO disputes (using "back-of-the-envelope" calculations) ranged from US$320,000 to US$882,000, suggesting those costs "create a threshold effect that effectively discriminates against small claims and countries that have them, even though such small claims are relatively large in relation to those countries' small economies." Hakan Nordstrom & Gregory Shaffer, *The Case for a Small Claims Procedure: A Preliminary Analysis*, Int'l Cen. for Trade and Sustainable Dev., ICTSD Dispute Settlement and Legal Aspects of International Trade Issue Paper No. 2, 10–11 (June 2007), https://bit.ly/2Mz7pqr (last visited Aug. 17, 2018); *see also* Jeffrey L. Dunnoff, *Less than Zero: The Effects of Giving Domestic Effect to WTO Law*, 6 LOY. U. CHI. INT'L L. REV. 279, 302–303 (2008); *but see* Diane A. Desierto, *Chad P. Bown's Self-Enforcing Trade: Developing Countries and WTO Dispute Settlement (2009)*, YALE J. INT'L L. 533, 539–41 (2010) (book review).

[21] Chapter 6; *see also* J.M. Rieger, *The Price Tag on the Russia Investigation Is Lower than Trump Claimed It Was, but He's Still Attacking It*, WASH. POST (June 1, 2018), https://wapo.st/2x8vkEh (last visited Sept. 8, 2018) (identifying, in contexts involving sensitive domestic public policy issues that "Justice Department documents . . . show the [Mueller] investigation has cost $16.7 million through the first 10½ months of the investigation, considerably less than the $47.4 million spent investigating the Iran-contra affair or the $69 million spent on the independent counsel investigation of President Bill Clinton from 1994 to 2002.").

[22] Ernst-Ulrich Petersmann, *Justice as Conflict Resolution: Proliferation, Fragmentation, and Decentralization of Dispute Settlement in International Trade*, 27 U. PA. J. INT'L ECON. L. 273, 304 (2006).

II. Enhancing Costs Transparency

Despite their materiality, ITA costs receive short shrift. Having demonstrated the substantial amounts and proportions involved, Chapter 6 observed over 95% of tribunals failed to address costs in a meaningful way before final awards and identified regular gaps in the basic cost information tribunals provide. Meanwhile, Chapter 7 revealed, despite a small but reliable improvement since ITA's inception, tribunals still failed to provide full rationalization—namely legal authority and rationale—for cost allocations. Given informational gaps, the fundamental point is: understanding ITA costs fully and accurately necessitates more data, requiring transparency from parties, institutions, and arbitrators. Since the book focuses on data from public awards, this section primarily puts arbitrators under the spotlight and focuses on transparency gaps requiring redress.

First, tribunals predominantly made cost decisions in final awards and hardly ever offered advance guidance about their anticipated approach to costs and cost-shifting. This failure is a material missed opportunity. As they can render cost decisions before the end, tribunals failed to capitalize on opportunities to generate incentives and "nudge" constructive behavior.[23] Early assessments, particularly interim orders, could provide immediate costs guidance and incentivize behavior,[24] enabling parties to understand how tribunals anticipate using their cost-related discretion. Advance articulation is a neutral, process-driven guidepost requiring application with equal measure with the goal of saving time and costs for everyone; as such, it should neither be a basis of party complaint nor arbitrator challenge.

Lucy Reed has argued that tribunals should explain their objectives for cost allocations to encourage efficiency and "apply them at the beginning of the [ITA] process as a management tool."[25] Recently, ICSID had the foresight to propose a behavioral nudge, namely expressly stating that tribunals "may at any time make interim decisions on the costs of any part of a proceeding."[26] Combined with the new duty for parties and tribunals to "conduct the proceedings in an expeditious and cost-effective manner,"[27] ICSID's proposal generates a strong incentive for early costs consideration. To avoid breaching their duty, parties have an incentive to request tribunals address cost issues early; arbitrators have clear power to act early on cost containment in support of their own obligations. By placing emphasis on early costs guidance—rather than relegating it to the mental background—ICSID beneficially uses the availability heuristic to situate early assessment at the mental foreground for direct application.

---

[23] *See, e.g.*, Richard Thaler & Cass Sunstein, Nudge: Improving Decisions About Health, Wealth, and Happiness (2008); Susan D. Franck, *Rationalizing Costs in Investment Treaty Arbitration*, 88 Wash U. L. Rev. 769, 841–42 (2011).

[24] David Smith, *Shifting Sands: Cost-and-Fee Allocation in International Investment Arbitration*, 51 Va. J. Int'l L. 749, 776 (2011). Smith identified a potential deleterious effect on smaller investors, possibly causing parties to settle from "sticker shock," rather than merits. *Id.*

[25] Lucy Reed, *Allocation of Costs in International Arbitration*, 26 ICSID Rev. 76, 85 (2011).

[26] ICSID, Proposed Rules *supra* note 11, at Proposed Arb. Rule 19(5); *id.* at Proposed AF Arb. Rule 29(5).

[27] *Id.* at Proposed Arb. Rule 11(3); *id.* at Proposed AF Arb. Rule 20(3).

Yet, the ICSID rule amendments have not yet become binding; and not all arbitration rules offer de jure incentives for early costs consideration. The Canada-European Union trade agreement (CETA),[28] 2018 draft Dutch model investment treaty,[29] and United States-Mexico-Canada-Agreement (USMCA)[30] fail to encourage early consideration, referencing costs only in connection with final awards. In the void of clear party direction (via treaty or party agreement), this leaves arbitrators with considerable latitude. There are no institutional rules that *prohibit* arbitrators from providing early and clear guidance about anticipated approaches to costs. Tribunals should actively use non-final awards or interim procedural orders strategically to offer parties clear and transparent guidance about principles upon which tribunals will exercise their mandate to address ITA costs.

At a minimum, tribunals could easily "announce early in the proceedings which theory of cost allocation they will use in the matter or, at a minimum, what factors they will consider most important."[31] This transparency permits parties to appreciate the costs and benefits of their dispute resolution strategy and prevent the loss of valuable settlement opportunities.[32] With early guidance, parties can understand the relative value of alternative methods of resolving disputes,[33] rather than compounding existing challenges related to the uncertainty of general ITA outcomes. Although some arbitrators may worry taking a firm stand on costs may subject them to challenges in an era of guerilla tactics,[34] such an approach is unwarranted when all stakeholders benefit from cost efficiencies and enhanced predictability. Reform at institutions, such as

[28] Comprehensive Economic and Trade Agreement between Canada and the European Union, Article 8.39(5), Sept. 14, 2016 (entered into force provisionally Sept. 21, 2017), https://bit.ly/1ScSoGS (last visited Sept. 8, 2018) [hereinafter CETA].

[29] Dutch Ministry of Foreign Affairs, *Nieuwe Modeltekst Investeringsakkoorden* [New draft model investment treaty], art. 22.5 (May 16, 2018), https://bit.ly/2slNa4e (last visited Aug 17, 2018) [hereinafter Dutch Model BIT].

[30] USMCA, *supra* note 10, at Annex 14-D, art. 13.4 (identifying items for inclusion in awards, noting tribunals can award costs but generally providing no direction other than institutional rules); *but see id.* at art. 7.6 (permitting tribunals to consider "frivolous" claims or defenses but only for issues of jurisdiction and claims "manifestly without legal merit").

[31] Smith, *supra* note 24, at 776; *see also* Klaus Reichert & James Hope, *Costs–The Sting in the Tail*, GLOBAL ARB. REV. (Apr. 1, 2006), https://bit.ly/2QWeWCz (last visited Dec. 27, 2018).

[32] *See* John Y. Gotanda, *Awarding Costs and Attorneys' Fees in International Commercial Arbitrations*, 21 MICH. J. INT'L L. 1, 38 (1999) (observing ICA's inability "to predict with any degree of certainty the outcome of a claim for costs . . . impairs the ability of parties to fully evaluate the case and consequently settle the dispute"); Michael Bühler, *Costs in ICC Arbitration: A Practitioner's View*, 3 AM. REV. 116, 117–19 (1992) ("[I]t must be a prerequisite to any international arbitration that the parties know well in advance what to budget for costs, and that the cost system of the administering institution is fully transparent from the outset").

[33] *See* Jeswald W. Salacuse, *Is There a Better Way? Alternative Methods of Treaty-Based, Investor-State Dispute Resolution*, 31 FORDHAM INT'L L.J. 138, 153 (2007) ("rational investor[s] will not lightly resort to [arbitration] and will examine other options for redress of its grievance before doing so. The final and perhaps most important reason for increased recourse to investor-State arbitration may be that aggrieved investors, having undertaken the search for other options, have concluded that they have no more cost-effective, reliable remedy for the settlement of disputes than investor-State arbitration").

[34] *See, e.g.*, GUERRILLA TACTICS IN INTERNATIONAL ARBITRATION (Günther J. Horvath & Stephan Wilske eds., 2013).

UNCITRAL, warrants careful focus on costs.[35] Early tribunal guidance has the potential benefit of protecting arbitrators from subsequent criticism, as parties should not be allowed to "have their cake and eat it, too" on cost containment. Namely, parties (and counsel) have less firm ground to complain about problematic costs when their own conduct (or inaction) drives costs. By placing parties on notice, offering parties space to agree upon cost rules, using discretion to provide guidance in the absence of agreement or applicable law, and following that guidance, tribunals can ensure they fulfill their duties and exercise their mandate with care.

Second, where tribunals provided fiscal information about costs and cost-shifting, overall, they were relatively sloppy. The data, particularly as discussed in Chapters 6 and 7, indicated that where tribunals specifically referenced costs—whether amounts, proportions, or rationalization—they offered minimal (or no) clarity on individual cost elements. Yet, Party Legal Costs (PLC) and Tribunal Costs and administrative Expenses (TCE) are doctrinally distinct and of decidedly different magnitudes.[36] The SCC,[37] LCIA,[38] SIAC,[39] and 1976 UNCITRAL Arbitration Rules,[40] make clear demarcations between those costs and how to use them individually. The Kingdom of Spain, commenting on ICSID reforms, has likewise articulated the value in making clear demarcations between PLC and TCE.[41] In contrast, the initial draft of ICSID reform

---

[35] U.N. Comm'n Int'l Trade Law [UNCITRAL], *Report of Working Group III (Investor-State Dispute Settlement Reform) on the Work of its Thirty-fourth Session (Vienna, 27 November–1 December 2017)*, 5–11 (Dec. 19, 2017), https://bit.ly/2LbD5Sc (last visited Aug. 7, 2018); *see also* Anthea Roberts & Zeineb Bouroui, *UNCITRAL and ISDS Reforms: Concerns about Costs, Transparency, Third Party Funding and Counterclaims*, EJIL:Talk! (June 6, 2018), https://bit.ly/2PiFsSo (last visited Aug. 17, 2018).

[36] Figure 6.1 provides a stark visualization of different scales for PLC and TCE.

[37] SCC Arb. Rules, arts. 43–44 (2007), https://bit.ly/2MiySod (last visited Aug. 17, 2018); *see also* SCC Arb. Rules, arts. 49–50 (2017), https://bit.ly/2M9kaI5 (last visited Oct. 3, 2018).

[38] LCIA Arb. Rules, art. 28 (1998), http://bit.ly/14NCwz6 (last visited Aug. 17, 2018); *see also* LCIA Arb. Rules, art. 28 (Dec. 11, 2017), https://bit.ly/2PgGoIh (last visited Aug. 17, 2018).

[39] SIAC rules make a clear break between TCE (Rules 35–36) and PLC (Rule 37), but without providing guidance on cost allocation standards. SIAC Arbitration Rules, https://bit.ly/2MI6vJo (last visited Aug. 17, 2018).

[40] UNCITRAL, UNCITRAL Arbitration Rules, G.A. Res. 31/98, arts. 38–40, U.N. GAOR, 31st Sess., Supp. No. 17, U.N. Doc. A/31/17 (Dec. 15, 1976) [hereinafter 1976 UNCITRAL Rules]. Article 38 of the 1976 UNCITRAL Rules is very specific on costs providing specific subelements of TCE (the tribunal's own fees and travel expenses, expert advice for the tribunal and approved travel, and the fees of appointing authorities); the article also identifies PLC as pertaining to the reasonable legal fees of the successful party. Article 40(1) suggests all costs use a loser-pays baseline, subject to "circumstances of the case"; but Article 40(2) provides a carveout for attorney's costs, giving greater freedom to determine "reasonable" apportionment given "circumstances of the case." The 2010 UNCITRAL Rules have a few twists. Article 40 is similar to the 1976 version in its specification of cost subelements, but 40(e) expands PLC to potentially apply to both parties (subject to a reasonableness limitation). Article 42, however, then generally provides a loser-pays baseline but subject to tribunal disction to determine what is "reasonable" given the "circumstances of the case." UNCITRAL Arbitration Rules (as revised in 2010) (Aug. 20, 2010), arts. 40, 42, https://bit.ly/2tYM9Aa (last visited Aug. 17, 2018).

[41] Ministerio de Industria, Comercio y Tourismo [Kingdom of Spain, Ministry of Industry, Trade, and Tourism], *Comentarios de España a la Propuesta de Modificación de las Reglas de los Procedimientos Regidos por el Mecanismo Complementario en la Reforma del CIADI* [Commentary of Spain on the Proposed Modification of the Rules and Procedures of the Additional Facility in the Reform of ICSID], page 6-7 (Dec. 21, 2018), https://bit.ly/2SAFWEw (last visited Dec. 28, 2018) ("[T]ambién puede ser útil distinguir entre las diferentes categorías de costes, tales como los costes de abogados, por una parte, y los costes del tribunal y administrativos,

appears to be taking the route of ICC,[42] lumping costs together.[43] In doing so, ICSID is missing a critical opportunity, namely to offer different incentivization for different arbitration costs, which are of a decidedly different scale. As parties' costs were the heavy thumb on the scale, if ICSID wishes to send a "strong" signal, then targeting PLC is appropriate; whereas if a lighter touch is desired, incentivizing through TCE is preferable. While, in theory, ICSID's proposals do not prohibit tribunals from taking this approach, the blunt treatment—without an express practice direction or explanation of best practices—risks cognitively depleted arbitrators ignoring the potential value of the demarcation. The better course, such as front-loading interim costs orders and making the idea cognitively available, is to expressly identify the distinction ex ante. Such precision creates opportunities for tribunals to redress past gaps and promotes the clarity and transparency of cost-related decision-making.[44]

Third, tribunals provided little information on fiscal costs and proportions, making precise identification of PLC and TCE challenging. To redress the gap and ensure information is available (thereby promoting procedural justice through transparency), creating precise default obligations about what tribunals should include in cost determinations is fundamental. In this respect, ICSID made a core stride forward with two proposals, first mandating that tribunals "shall request that each party file a statement of costs before allocating the costs of the proceedings"[45] and then requiring that "all decisions on costs are reasoned" in the award.[46] One would have thought these elements would be best practices,[47] but data discussed in Chapters 4, 6, and 7 reflect that tribunal practice has not matched aspirations,

---

por otra." [Also it can be useful to distinguish between the different categories of costs, such as lawyer costs, on the one hand, and court and administrative costs, on the other.]).

[42] ICC Arb. Rules, art. 38 (Mar. 2017), https://bit.ly/2G7YSEw (last visited Aug. 17, 2018); *see also* 2010 UNCITRAL Rules, *supra* note 41, at art. 42(1); *see also* HKIAC, Administered Arbitration Rules, art. 33.1-33.3 (2013), https://bit.ly/2oAOEp5 (last visited Aug. 7, 2018).

[43] ICSID, Proposed Rules, *supra* note 11, at Proposed Arb. Rule 19(2),(4); *id.* at Proposed AF Arb. Rule 29(2),(4). ICSID observes that costs are partially constrained by the ICSID Convention. *See* ICSID, Working Paper, *supra* note 11, at 124. Yet, the Convention uses separate clauses to address PLC and TCE. *See* ICSID Convention, Regulations, and Rules, art. 61(2) (2006), https://bit.ly/2nhow1w (last visited Aug. 17, 2018) ("the Tribunal shall, except as the parties otherwise agree, assess the expenses incurred by the parties in connection with the proceedings, and shall decide how and by whom those expenses, and the expenses of the members of the tribunal and the charges for the use of the facilities shall be paid").

[44] ICSID's proposed rule requiring tribunals articulate reasons for cost assessments in final awards may help. *See* ICSID, Working Paper, *supra* note 11, at 259, 262 (discussing Rule 60(1)(j)); *infra* note 46. Without a textual nudge, exhausted and cognitively depleted tribunals may fail to appreciate the opportunity. Providing post hoc explanations does not provide ex ante guidance that tribunals can treat different costs differently.

[45] ICSID, Proposed Rules, *supra* note 11, at Proposed Arb. Rule 19(3); *id.* at Proposed AF Arb. Rule 29(3); *see also* John Y. Gotanda, *Consistently Inconsistent: The Need for Predictability in Awarding Costs and Fees in Investment Treaty Arbitration*, 28 ICSID Rev. 420, 437 (2013) (recommending "separately brief[ing] issues relating to the award of costs and fees"). With ICSID proposing required publication of "documents generated in the proceedings," cost submissions could become publicly available. ICSID, Proposed Rules, *supra* note 11, at Proposed Fin. Reg. 22.

[46] ICSID, Proposed Rules, *supra* note 11, at Proposed Arb. Rules 19(6), 60(1)(j); *id.* at Proposed AF Arb. Rules 29(6), 70(1)(j); *see also supra* note 44.

[47] While not empirically demonstrated given information gaps, it could be standard practice for both parties to provide detailed cost submissions. Providing readily available, preexisting materials should be straightforward.

suggesting a legal nudge is warranted. Using hard law—whether through treaties, arbitration rules, or party agreement—to mandate inclusion of precise costs information promotes transparency, clarity, predictability, and rule-of-law. Obtaining complete cost information also means others can use derivative data that becomes available for more complete empirical analyses and better assessments of potential cost implications.

Other stakeholders may wish to require tribunals to provide full cost details in awards to redress the activity of some (but not all) tribunals and to establish best practices. Neither the Mauritius Convention[48] nor UNCITRAL Transparency Rules[49] address cost-related transparency. Building from Atul Gawande's *Checklist Manifesto*,[50] which advocates creating checklists for professionals in stressful occupations subject to cognitive depletion, one might imagine creating checklists about what tribunals should provide, requiring transparency about ITA costs. This need not require tribunals providing 200 pages of details on cost assessments; rather, it could identify streamlined, detailed, efficient, and normatively desirable costs information.[51] Although CETA and the Dutch model treaty failed to do so,[52] states could mandate what costs data is required in investment treaties. Likewise, parties could come to agreements about what tribunals must provide in their cost assessments after a dispute has arisen, and institutions could detail what must be included in awards, including articulating each arbitrator's individual hours and costs, similar to ICSID's recent proposal.[53] This aspect has the value of aiding assessment of individual arbitrators' efficiency. If arbitrators know their fees will be subject to scrutiny, this creates an incentive to be careful and precise with billing. Moreover, individualized information aids data disaggregation. Rather than lump sums that hide variance, separating costs of each arbitrator aids nuanced assessments.[54]

---

[48] G.A. Res. 69/116, United Nations Convention on Transparency in Treaty-based Investor-State Arbitration, Dec. 10, 2014; *see also* UNCITRAL, *Status: United Nations Convention on Transparency in Treaty-based Investor-State Arbitration* (New York, 2014), UNCITRAL.ORG, https://bit.ly/1R11NMK (last visited Aug. 17, 2018) (entering into force during 2017 but noting only in Canada, Cameroon, Mauritius, and Switzerland).

[49] The only mention of costs indicates those granted access to documents bare the administrative costs, rather than requiring disclosure of fiscal costs. UNCITRAL Rules on Transparency in Treaty-based Investor-State Arbitration, G.A. Res. 68/109, art. 3(5) (Dec. 16, 2013), https://bit.ly/1rHXZVU (last visited Aug. 17, 2018).

[50] ATUL GAWANDE, THE CHECKLIST MANIFESTO: HOW TO GET THINGS RIGHT (2009).

[51] Using the Codebook as a baseline, for PLC, one could imagine requiring tribunals to: request parties make cost submissions, identify raw fiscal costs attributable to investors' counsel (and what proportion is deemed reasonable), provide states' raw fiscal costs for counsel (and what proportion is reasonable), indicate the raw amounts of cost shifts and the proportion shifted, clarify which party is responsible for any cost shift, and provide doctrinal justification and legal reasoning explaining the decision. TCE could have a similar checklist.

[52] CETA, *supra* note 28, at art. 8.39; Dutch Model BIT, *supra* note 29, at art. 22; *see also* European Union, *EU-Chile Free Trade Agreement EU Textual Proposal*, art. 2.46, https://bit.ly/2yaeCF9 (last visited Oct. 3, 2018) (identifying elements for inclusion in awards and discussing costs but failing to detail required costs information).

[53] ICSID usefully recommended that tribunals state reasons for cost decisions and final awards and must identify each arbitrator's individual costs. ICSID, PROPOSED RULES, *supra* note 11, at Proposed Arb. Rule 60(1)(j) (requiring "a statement of the costs of the proceeding, including the fees and expenses of each member of the Tribunal"); *id* at Proposed AF Arb. Rule 70(1)(j); (same); *see also* ICSID, WORKING PAPER, *supra* note 11, at 124–25, 262 (identifying individualized cost statements in final awards but not other cost-related decisions).

[54] Disaggregation aids assessments of other questions, including whether female arbitrators or arbitrators from the developing world are paid differently. Similarly, it permits assessment of tribunal efficiency by looking at

As a final point, given incomplete information from arbitrators, as guardians of their holistic information, institutions administering ITA can and should take a lead in providing information on ITA costs. In commercial arbitration, the LCIA and others have begun this process.[55] One hopes that ICSID thoughtful suggested transparency reforms involving providing underlying documentation, along with its renewed commitment to publishing data,[56] will lead to publishing average, median, or (perhaps more ambitiously) quartile breakdowns of party, tribunal, and administrative costs.[57] As Hans Rosling's *Factfulness* admonishes, most of the world's variance is found between gaps; and having a sense of variance in holistic data (and how variance changes) is fundamental to having an accurate and constructive view of reality.[58]

More complete information can prevent cognitive illusions from facilitating improper inferences about ITA costs and aid strategic dispute settlement decisions. As cognitive illusions could generate an overly optimistic assessment of the merits of claims and defenses—causing clients to avoid considering settlement—data must reality test perception. Likewise, focusing on cases recently in the news or popular press (i.e., a recency illusion), focusing on poignant cases that spring readily to mind (i.e., the availability heuristic), or believing a case feels intuitively similarly to other winning cases but without references to base rates (i.e., representativeness),[59] can lead parties to make suboptimal decisions about pursuing or defending ITA disputes. With full information on costs, cost-shifting, and claim success rates,[60] stakeholders can disrupt cognitive illusions that promote inefficient dispute resolution. Instead, if transparency permits them to be armed with data, parties can focus on strategic opportunities for settlement or streamlined adjudication, rather than being driven by sunk costs or intuitive "feel" about the value of investing in arbitration. Moreover, data can aid policymakers in understanding ITA's values and drawbacks.

"wing" arbitrator (i.e., party-appointed) costs, as compared to each other or to chairs. Although disaggregation may be less meaningful in institutions such as the ICC or SCC where amount in dispute plays a role in tribunal costs, for ICSID, the LCIA and ad hoc proceedings involving hourly fees, results could prove constructive, particularly as ICSID's recent proposals still permit arbitrator rate variances.

[55] LCIA, Facts and Figures—Costs and Duration: 2013–2016 (Oct. 3, 2017), https://bit.ly/2uKjJKd (last visited Aug. 17, 2018); *see also* CMS Holborn Asia, *Costs and Duration: A Comparison of the HKIAC, LCIA, SCC and SIAC Studies*, (Mar. 19, 2018), https://bit.ly/2vRM69N, (last visited Aug. 17, 2018) (attempting to compare data across arbitration institutions using data from institutional reports).

[56] *See, e.g., ICSID, The ICSID Caseload—Statistics*, ICSD.Worldbank.org, https://bit.ly/2MvUQME (last visited Aug. 17, 2018).

[57] ICSID has unique international law confidentiality obligations. ICSID, *Confidentiality and Transparency—ICSID Convention Arbitration*, ICSD.Worldbank.org, https://bit.ly/2PjvBf8 (last visited Aug. 17, 2018). ICSID proposed changing transparency-related regulations that could affect costs information, namely, "[w]ith a view to furthering the development of international law" ICSID "*shall* publish [] information about the operation of the Centre". ICSID, Proposed Rules, *supra* note 11, Proposed Reg. 22(a). Costs data has not been published despite rules containing discretion permitting publication of data to "further the development of international law." ICSID Administrative and Financial Regulations, Reg. 22 *compiled in* ICSID Convention, Regulations, and Rules 66 (2006), https://bit.ly/2nhow1w (last visited Aug. 17, 2018). This should change in the future to aid research and cost assessments.

[58] Hans Rosling, Factfulness: Ten Reasons We're Wrong About the World—and Why Things Are Better than You Think 21–46 (2018).

[59] Chapter 2.

[60] Chapters 5–6; Franck & Wylie, *supra* note 18.

Ultimately, requiring tribunals to provide textured and particularized costs facilitates a data-driven dialogue on costs, provides key opportunities to debias discourse, and promotes informed decision-making about ITA's normative utility. ITA is best served by requiring greater costs transparency, providing parties with early costs guidance, being precise about cost distinctions, and offering full cost enumeration. There is minimal downside to offering "truth in arbitration costs" through data rather than obfuscation, particularly given what is at stake in both raw fiscal exposure and the integrity of dispute resolution.

III. Arbitration Costs and Appropriate Dispute Resolution

Abraham Maslow, the celebrated psychologist, famously observed, "I suppose it is tempting, if the only tool you have is a hammer, to treat everything as if it were a nail."[61] As the only realistic adjudicative and viable dispute resolution method in treaties,[62] it is unsurprising that investors and counsel focus on arbitration as the primary conflict management method. There are, however, a suite of options, including ombuds, negotiation, early neutral evaluation, fact-finding, mediation,[63] or the small claims facility discussed earlier.

Costs data suggests that alternatives to arbitration are warranted to provide more flexibility and expanded options. To the extent that investors, states, and counsel are economically rational actors (while recognizing people are predictably irrational[64] and domestic politics can impact states' rational decision-making), stakeholders require data to aid appraisals of ITA's net value. Net value permits stakeholders to assess adjudicative options, such as arbitration, to explore the viability of alternative processes for managing conflict, and to identify *appropriate* dispute resolution (ADR) strategies. The objective should be to avoid disputes where possible, manage conflict when it arises, and engage in systematic consideration of dispute

---

[61] Abraham H. Maslow, The Psychology of Science: A Reconnaissance 15–16 (1966).

[62] While many treaties refer to "amicable resolution," without the legal infrastructure (i.e., communication pathways within states for dispute notices, party capacity to use negotiation or diplomacy effectively, and treating pre-arbitration obligations as a condition precedent to arbitration), such obligations are functionally toothless. *See generally* Susan D. Franck, *Integrating Investment Treaty Conflict and Dispute Systems Design*, 92 Minn. L. Rev. 161, 195–201 (2007); *but see* Mark Kantor, *Negotiated Settlement of Public Infrastructure Disputes, in* New Directions in International Economic Law: In Memoriam Thomas Wälde (Todd Weiler & Freya Baetens eds., 2011) (suggesting negotiation normally occurs before initiating arbitration). The innovative Dutch Model fails to sketch out mediation, briefly referencing amicable settlement (including mediation), and suggesting such settlement can occur at any time, only restating the reality that parties already had the capacity to settle; another article identifies "consultations" as processes involving formal dispute notices, but fails to provide guidelines, parameters, timetables, and mediation standards. *See* Dutch Model BIT, *supra* note 29, at arts. 17–18.

[63] *See, e.g.*, U.N. Conference on Trade and Dev., Investor-State Disputes: Prevention and Alternatives to Arbitration II: Proceedings of Symposium held on 29 March 2010, UNCTAD/WEB/DIAE/IA/2010/8 (Susan D. Franck & Anna Joubin-Bret eds., 2011), http://bit.ly/1nCFcwC (last visited Aug. 17, 2018); Mariana Hernandez Crespo, *A New Chapter in Natural Resource-Seeking Investment: Using Shared Decisions System Design ("SDSD") to Strengthen Investor-State and Community Relationships*, 18 Cardozo J. Conflict Resolution 551, 567–74 (2017); Matthew W. Swinehart, *Institutionalism and Fact-Finding in International Disputes*, https://bit.ly/2T3mW1L (last visited Jan. 19, 2019); Chapter 1.

[64] Dan Ariely, Predictably Irrational (2008); Chapter 2.

resolution options to "fit the forum to fuss."[65] Part of making strategic choices involves understanding outcome probabilities given the variables involved and likely costs of pursuing different methodologies.

A. THE DISPUTE RESOLUTION CALCULUS AND COGNITIVE ILLUSIONS

When focusing on fiscal elements, a dispute resolution calculus requires assessment of: relative success, likely amounts awarded, cost of counsel, cost of tribunals, and likelihood of cost-shifting to determine whether the costs of pursuing the dispute over multiple years is worth the theoretical benefit.[66] Or, in Spanish: ¿Vale la pena?

Chapters 5–6 offer baserates, placing ITA's relative value in context. For all final cases (including cases where investors lost), the average award was around US$16.6 million, meaning average total PLC and TCE costs were roughly 60% of average awards. Reframed to focus on the subset of claims where investors obtained a damage award, the average amount awarded of US$45.6 million, meaning average total PLC and TCE was around 22% of average awards.[67] Meanwhile, Chapters 6–7 demonstrated that the baseline for when and how tribunals shifted costs remained relatively uncertain, with a reliable (but not guaranteed) pattern that winning investors reliably obtained the benefit of a beneficial cost shift more often than winning states. The only certain fiscal risk was: parties paid upfront costs of their lawyers and advances to arbitrators and institutions.[68] Chapter 6 estimated, for every year of ITA, each party spent roughly US$1.5 million (using aggregated averages), and one might legitimately question whether those fees could be put to a better use and whether negotiated settlements could facilitate more cost-efficient results while placing control of outcomes squarely in parties' hands.

Where ultimate substantive outcomes and cost-shifting assessments are generally uncertain ex ante,[69] costs data and possibility of a win (or risk of loss) offer baselines for decision-making. Investors may find it useful to incorporate the data, use it to judge risk, and have those assessments inform dispute resolution choices,[70] including the most likely alternatives

---

[65] Frank E.A. Sander & Stephen B. Golberg, *Fitting the Forum to the Fuss: A User-Friendly Guide to Selecting an ADR Procedure*, 10 NEGOT. J. 49 (1994); Deborah M. Kolb & Susan S. Sibley, *Enhancing the Capacity of Organizations to Deal with Disputes*, *in* NEGOTIATION THEORY AND PRACTICE 315 (J. William Breslin & Jeffrey Z. Rubin eds., 1991).

[66] Both pre-award and post-award interest are fiscal risks. Although the dataset (Appendix V) coded and contains information about interest, given major problems with missing data and tribunals' failure to particularize interest, statistical analysis was imprudent. Available data suggest interest generated meaningful fiscal exposure. Future analyses should consider interest-related variables; as with costs, tribunals could benefit from increased precision and transparency on interest-related issues.

[67] Averages reflect aggregate, rather than case-specific, data. Given missing data involving claims, relative success, PLC, and TCE, direct case-by-case comparison was not possible.

[68] For those receiving TPF, these fiscal risks may be distributed differently.

[69] The most robust predictors of case outcomes involved the presence of human beings in a dispute and the role of RP counsel, both for investors and states. *See* Franck & Wylie, *supra* note 18, at 515–17.

[70] For negotiation to work effectively, it is vital for parties to have a free hand in dispute settlement without artificial baselines. If, for example, either party was required to settle either below or above a particular amount—whether due to contract obligation or national legislation—this could inhibit constructive negotiation.

to negotiated settlements. Cognitive illusions could facilitate investors' incentives to settle. As Chapter 2 explains, when claimants are faced with the low probability of a gain, cognitive illusions of positive framing and loss aversion facilitate investors inclination to actively pursue adjudication; whereas, if there is a medium-to-high probability risk—which Chapter 5 suggests is likely given large claims—investors' predictable incentive should be to settle and take a lower, but certain, outcome.[71]

The ultimate focus should be on crafting appropriate dispute resolution. Mediation, negotiation, or working with an ombuds office (or lead government agency), particularly when combined with Dispute Systems Design[72] to identify methodologies for channeling conflict, provide core infrastructure supporting alternatives for extracting value from dispute resolution, decreasing direct costs, avoiding indirect costs (such as diverting key personnel from productive activities), and maintaining relationships, particularly when investors continue to do business within the state or region. Approaching conflict management with a broad perspective and eye toward effective use of adjudication alternatives has resolved disputes about government conduct, regulatory conflicts, and public policy issues,[73] including environmental disputes.[74] A broader perspective on conflict management, searching for appropriate tools, opens doors to dispute prevention and fostering relationships that constructively promote investment retention and expansion in collaboration with local communities.[75]

There is a possibility, however, that once armed with data, rational states may be more willing to roll the dice with ITA. Where states derive domestic political cover from blaming third-party adjudication for adverse outcomes or identify value from fighting claims to vindicate domestic policy choices, settlement may be unattractive. States may also determine that pursuing ITA is appealing, as states won in a reliably greater proportion than investors

---

[71] TPF could change the probabilities and normal application of prospect theory, as funders need not have the same incentives, potentially becoming risk-seeking when investors become risk-averse (i.e., preferring settlement).

[72] Franck, *supra* note 62; *see also* LISA BLOMGREN AMSLER, ET AL., DISPUTE SYSTEM DESIGN (forthcoming 2020); CATHY COSTANTINO & CHRISTINA SICKLES MERCHANT, DESIGNING CONFLICT MANAGEMENT SYSTEMS: A GUIDE TO CREATING PRODUCTIVE AND HEALTHY ORGANIZATIONS (1996); WILLIAM L. URY ET AL., GETTING DISPUTES RESOLVED: DESIGNING SYSTEMS TO CUT THE COSTS OF CONFLICT 41–64 (1988); Khalil Z. Shariff *Designing Institutions to Manage Conflict: Principles for the Problem Solving Organization*, 8 HARV. NEGOT. L. REV. 133 (2003).

[73] DAVID A. SCHULTZ, ENCYCLOPEDIA OF PUBLIC ADMINISTRATION AND PUBLIC POLICY 267–68 (2004); LAWRENCE SUSSKIND & JEFFREY CRUIKSHANK, BREAKING THE IMPASSE: CONSENSUAL APPROACHES TO RESOLVING PUBLIC DISPUTES (1987); Giuseppe De Palo & Mary Trevor, *Making the European Commission's Mediation Directive More Effective*, 30 ALT. HIGH COST LIT. 137 (2012); Carrie Menkel-Meadow, *Correspondences and Contradictions in International and Domestic Conflict Resolution: Lessons from General Theory and Varied Contexts*, 2003 J. DISP. RESOL. 319, 337; Howard S. Bellman & Susan L. Podziba, *Public Policy Mediation*, 18 DISP. RESOL. MAG. 14, Winter 2012; Molly M. Melin, *When States Mediate*, 2 PENN. ST. J.L. & INT'L AFF. 78 (2013); Lawrence Susskind, *Multi-party Public Policy Mediation: A Separate Breed*, DISP. RESOL. MAG. 4, Fall 1997.

[74] Stephen Higgs, *The Potential for Mediation to Resolve Environmental and Natural Resources Disputes*, 1 AM. J. MED. 101 (2007); Neil G. Sipe & Bruce Stiftel, *Mediating Environmental Enforcement Disputes*, 15 ENVIRON. IMP. ASSESS. REV. 139 (1996).

[75] Hernandez Crespo, *supra* note 63, at 551–57, 576, 619–20; Zhenwei Christine Qiang et al., *Maximizing the Potential Benefits of Foreign Direct Investment for Competitiveness and Development* (World Bank Group, Working Paper No. 114863, May 9, 2017), https://bit.ly/2zTGj62 (last visited Oct. 3, 2018).

and investors' levels of success were proportionately low.[76] Cognitive illusions may also contribute to states pursuing ITA. As Chapter 2 explains, for states experiencing a negative frame and risk aversion, a medium-to-high probability loss contributes to risk-seeking behavior (i.e., not settling). Should states focus unduly on large initial amounts claimed courtesy of cognitive illusions such as recency, negativity, and availability—rather than lower amounts awarded or relative investor success—states theoretically are more likely to gamble and avoid settlement.

Yet, data revealed that states wishing to avoid a potential loss face unpalatable economic risks, including: paying legal fees over the life cycle of an ITA, absorbing sunk costs as states did not reliably receive the benefits of cost-shifting, and exposure to the risk (should an investor win) means that states may be more prone (than a losing investor) to pay *both* their own and a prevailing investor's costs. These risks, particularly combined with social and political costs of a dispute lasting 3–4 years, provide a data-driven reason for states to explore the relative value of outcomes under alternative conflict management paradigms. Alternatives, including direct negotiation or mediation, could be pursued before initiating a case *or* during adjudication to address specific issues or narrow the scope of the dispute, to decrease the uncertainty of substantive outcomes, and to increase certainty about costs (to say nothing of minimizing fiscal exposure to accumulating interest). Using non-adjudicative methodologies has the added benefit of returning control and autonomy to resolve conflicts in accordance with sovereign preferences.

B. THE RISING VALUE OF NON-ADJUDICATIVE DISPUTE RESOLUTION

The functional value of non-adjudicative alternatives is increasing, as innovations create the legal infrastructure to support non-adjudicative methods by decreasing transaction costs and facilitating easier adoption. In 2018, there were major innovations regarding the use of alternative methods, such as mediation. The draft UNCITRAL Convention on the Enforcement of Mediation Settlements (the Singapore Convention) was finalized;[77] and once open for signature in August 2019,[78] it will likely serve as the "New York Convention" for mediated settlements with streamlined enforcement. UNCITRAL relatedly promulgated a Model Law on international mediation and settlements.[79]

---

[76] *See* Franck & Wylie, *supra* note 18; Chapter 5.

[77] UNCITRAL, *Note by the Secretariat on International Commercial Mediation: Draft Convention on International Settlement Agreements Resulting from Mediation*, UNCITRAL 51st Sess. (June 25–July 13, 2018), A/CN.9/943 (Mar. 2, 2018), https://bit.ly/2PjKOwy (last visited Aug. 17, 2018); *see also* Shahla F. Ali & Odysseas G. Repousis, *Investor-State Mediation and the Rise of Transparency in International Investment Law: Opportunity or Threat?*, 45 DENV. J. INT'L L. & POL'Y 255 (2017); S.I. Strong, *Realizing Rationality: An Empirical Assessment of International Commercial Mediation*, 73 WASH. & LEE L. REV. 1973 (2016).

[78] Erin Gleason Alvarez, *Mediation Update: UNCITRAL Finalizes Convention and Model Law Drafts on International Settlement Agreements Resulting from Mediation*, BLOG.CPR.ORG (July 3, 2018), https://bit.ly/2u96BoV (last visited Sept. 8, 2018).

[79] UNCITRAL, *Note by the Secretariat on International Commercial Mediation: Draft Model Law on International Commercial Mediation and International Settlement Agreements Resulting from Mediation*, UNCITRAL 51st Sess. (June 25-July 13, 2018), A/CN.9/943 (Mar. 2, 2018), https://bit.ly/2ONRFx3 (last visited Aug. 17, 2018).

While formal in nature (and potentially standing to benefit from providing more options for process-related protocols), ICSID's proposed Mediation Rules[80] and CETA's mediation references[81] are a nudge in the right direction. The EU's draft negotiating text with Chile is even more direct about mediation procedures and ethical standards for mediators.[82] The IBA has guidelines that offer a preliminary framework for investment treaty-related mediation,[83] and the Energy Charter Conference adopted a Guide on Investment Mediation.[84] Meanwhile, the International Mediation Institute promulgated mediator competency standards for investment treaty disputes;[85] and ICSID encourages dispute prevention and conflict management as part of best practices,[86] even offering mediator training.[87]

Scholars also focus on non-adjudicative methodologies for investment treaty disputes.[88] Perhaps it is little wonder, if mediated settlements mean disputes can be resolved within

---

[80] ICSID, Proposed Rules, *supra* note 11, at Proposed AF Mediation Rules; ICSID, *Backgrounder on Proposals for Amendment of the ICSID Rules*, ICSID.Worldbank.Org, (Aug. 3, 2018) https://bit.ly/2Mopl72 (last visited Aug. 17, 2018). Rules for submitting mediation requests are formal in nature and reminiscent of arbitration. Obligations to set out the issues during the First Session reflect adjudication norms, with a focus upon legally disputed issues rather than exploring parties' interests, concerns, and objectives. ICSID, Proposed Rules, *supra* note 11, at Proposed AF Mediation Rules 3–5, 7–10, 13–15. While rules could be developed, offering structure aids expectation management for parties (and counsel) with minimal mediation experience.

[81] Rather than providing a mediation framework—including mediation process management, issue identification, common interests, and zones of potential agreement—CETA identifies what was already implicit, namely that parties have recourse to mediation without impacting arbitration rights, identifying mediator appointment options, and suggesting mediations finish within sixty days; it retains the possibility of adding more nuanced mediation rules from the Committee on Services and Investment. CETA, *supra* note 28, at art. 8.20; *see also id.* at art. 8.19 (providing for consultation).

[82] *EU Textual Proposal*, *supra* note 52, at arts. 2.20–2.21, annexes I–II; *but see* USMCA, *supra* note 10, at annex 14-D (using the word "mediation" once but failing to discuss it further).

[83] Int'l Bar Ass'n Mediation Comm., IBA Rules for Investor-State Mediation (Oct. 2, 2012) https://bit.ly/2MwDIgr (last visited Aug. 17, 2018); *see also* Susan D. Franck & Anna Joubin-Bret, *Investor-State Mediation*, 29 ICSID Rev. 90 (2014) (demonstrating how IBA Rules apply to a simulation).

[84] Energy Charter Secretariat, *Decision of the Energy Charter Conference: Adoption by Correspondence of the Guide on Investment Mediation*, CCDEC 2016 12INV (July 19, 2016), https://bit.ly/2vXQGU7 (last visited Aug. 17, 2018).

[85] International Mediation Institute, *IMI Competency Criteria for Investor-State Mediators* (Sept. 19, 2016), https://bit.ly/2PqWDRM (last visited Aug. 17, 2018).

[86] ICSID, *Practice Notes for Respondents in ICSID Arbitration*, ICSID.Worldbank.Org (2015), https://bit.ly/2wglILR (last visited Aug. 17, 2018).

[87] ICSID, *Investor-State Mediation*, ICSID.Worldbank.Org, https://bit.ly/2BkZAjL (last visited Aug. 17, 2018).

[88] *See, e.g.*, Prospects in International Investment Law and Policy 1–10, 265–305, 371–88 (Roberto Echandi & Pierre Sauvé eds., 2013); Franck & Joubin-Bret, *supra* note 63; Ali & Repousis, *supra* note 77; Roberto Echandi & Mariana Hernadez Crespo Gonstead, *Investor-State Conflict Management*, *in* Encyclopedia of International Economic Law 335–38 (Thomas Cottier & Krista Nadakavukaren Schefer eds., 2017); Susan D. Franck, *Using Investor-State Mediation Rules to Promote Conflict Management*, 29 ICSID Rev. 66 (2014); Franck, *supra* note 62; Note, *Mediation of Investor-State Conflicts*, 127 Harv. L. Rev. 2543 (2014); Mariana Hernandez Crespo, *From Noise to Music: The Potential of the Multi-door Courthouse (Casas de Justicia) Model to Advance Systemic Inclusion and Participation as a Foundation for Sustainable Rule of Law in Latin America*, 2012 J. Disp. Resol. 335 (2012); Anna Spain Bradley, *Integration Matters: Rethinking the Architecture of International Dispute Resolution*, 32 U. Penn. J. Int'l L. 1 (2010); Nancy A. Welsh & Andrea

weeks (or months) rather than years and on creative terms acceptable to both parties. One wonders, as Everett Rogers suggested, if new innovations begin when older innovations saturate a market,[89] whether mediation will become the new wave and, over time, commonplace.[90]

C. THE REMAINING VALUE OF ADJUDICATION

For non-adjudicative methodologies to gain traction, they must have an adjudicative backstop, permitting parties to "bargain in the shadow of the law."[91] Eradicating international adjudication for resolving treaty-based disputes will fundamentally impair the efficacy of other dispute resolution options. While non-adjudicative alternatives have value given ITA's direct costs and uncertain outcomes, they cannot function in a vacuum.

Simply abandoning arbitration or rejecting the idea of a standing international adjudicative body because of direct fiscal costs is shortsighted. Both the possibility of retaining arbitration[92] and/or creating a standing international tribunal[93] have material

---

Kupfer Schneider, *The Thoughtful Integration of Mediation into Bilateral Investment Treaty Arbitration*, 18 HARV. NEGOT. L. REV. 71 (2013).

[89] *See, e.g.*, EVERETT M. ROGERS, DIFFUSION OF INNOVATION (5th ed. 2003); Chapter 4; *see also* James Ming Chen, *Leaps, Metes, and Bounds: Innovation Law and Its Logistics*, 2015 MICH. ST. L. REV. 845, 860–61 (2015) (discussing models of technology saturation and innovation) (citing J.C. Fisher & R.H. Pry, *A Simple Substitution Model of Technological Change*, 3 TECHNOLOGICAL FORECASTING & SOC. CHANGE 74, 75 (1971)).

[90] *Compare* Jean E. Kalicki, *Mediation of Investor-State Disputes: Revisiting the Prospects*, KLUWER ARB. BLOG (June 14, 2013), https://bit.ly/2OSdT13 (last visited Aug. 17, 2018) (observing the rising interest and skepticism about mediation but observing investor-state disputes historically faced similar skepticism) *with* Jacqueline Nolan-Haley, *Mediation: The Best and Worst of Times*, 16 CARDOZO J. CONFLICT RESOL. 731 (2015) (identifying challenges for over-reliance on mediation, when mediation itself becomes a saturated innovation).

[91] Robert Cooter et al., *Bargaining in the Shadow of the Law: A Testable Model of Strategic Behavior*, 11 J. LEGAL STUD. 225 (1982).

[92] Retaining arbitration has potential advantages over a standing court. The ad hoc nature permits tailor-made rules, flexibility about where parties and tribunals will have hearings to adjudicate the dispute, and party control over arbitrators to promote procedural justice. Additionally, international conventions provide for relatively straightforward enforcement to incentivize compliance. *See* Susan D. Franck, *The Legitimacy Crisis in Investment Treaty Arbitration: Privatizing Public International Law Through Inconsistent Decisions*, 73, FORD. L. REV. 1520, 1598, 1486–87 (2005) (identifying problems and potential benefits from ITA); Charles N. Brower & Jawad Ahmad, *From the Two-Headed Nightingale to the Fifteen-Headed Hydra: The Many Follies of the Proposed International Investment Court*, 41 FORD. INT'L L.J. 791 (2018). Aside from its temporary nature that aids easier dismantling and adjustment, arbitration avoids the politicization of courts. *See* Jack M. Balkin, *Constitutional Rot Reaches the Supreme Court*, BALKANIZATION (Oct. 6, 2018), https://bit.ly/2zViueo (last visited Oct. 6, 2018) ("In times of severe constitutional rot, coupled with high party polarization, courts are not the solution. They are part of the problem.").

[93] Creating an international court has potential advantages over arbitration including: generating binding precedent to aid ex ante assessment of legal correctness, an appellate body to redress legal errors and promote consistency, formalizing procedures supporting transparency (as most states have not adopted the Mauritius Convention), and opportunities to promote diversity and inclusiveness in adjudicators. Franck, *supra* note 92, at 1600–01, 1606-24; David M. Howard, *Creating Consistency Through a World Investment Court*, 41 FORD. INT'L L.J. 1 (2017); *see also* Michael Reisman, *Control Mechanisms in International Dispute Resolution*, 2 U.S.-MEX. L.J. 129 (1994) (identifying the value of a permanent standing international tribunal for resolving

merit,[94] primarily because they retain a transnational adjudication mechanism facilitating the efficient use of an array of dispute resolution options. Every methodology of managing conflict—including the choice to provide no dispute resolution or provide it in an unpalatable way—has inherent costs.

Offering no adjudicative forum for resolving international investment conflict[95] has consequences. One need only imagine a long-standing relationship where pent-up frustration from an inability to vent simmering discontent leads to a disastrous explosion.[96] Aside from raising the temperature of international relations and placing commercial activity on the geopolitical chessboard (along with gunboat diplomacy), failing to provide neutral adjudication could affect development projects. Leaving aside the viability of securing political risk insurance in the absence of investment treaties, concerns about investment risk—where mitigation opportunities are limited without international legal standards or availability of reliable, rule-of-law based adjudication for protecting property rights—means that investors with the best practices (and those most likely to build longer-term value) have the perverse incentive to avoid investment. In contrast, "cowboy" investors with less internal discipline or adherence to corporate-social-responsibility norms could become the primary investors willing to risk investment, given risk-seeking predispositions. Alternatively, investors willing to take the plunge will extract such high and prohibitive rents that investment could be ex ante unsustainable, unlikely to promote states' development objectives, and poised to cause social and economic disruption.

Requiring international law disputes to be resolved before the national courts of the state sued, in an era of rising nationalism,[97] has material challenges. First, not all national courts have the privilege of judicial independence. Even if judges are neutral, putting domestic courts "on the front lines"[98] imbibes dispute resolution with the unique variance of municipal courts, which may be byzantine, unpredictable, or perceived as biased in favor of the local sovereign party. Scholarship has identified, in cases of actual or perceived national court corruption and bias, it is "rational (though not moral) to act corruptly when litigating in the

investment disputes). There may also be theoretical cost-savings, including savings from parties' inability to make time-consuming arguments that are contrary to de jure precedent, and decreasing case length by having full-time judges dedicated to adjudication (rather than arbitrators balancing other professional obligations).

[94] A full analysis of the relative merits and costs of international arbitration rather than an international court is beyond the scope of this book, which focuses on existing empirical information about adjudication costs rather than theoretical costs of an institution that does not yet exist. The core focus should be on ensuring that there is a legitimate, neutral tribunal available to render final, binding, efficient, and accurate decisions that create incentives for parties, counsel, and adjudicators to conduct the proceedings in a manner reflecting rule-of-law values.

[95] International investment treaty conflict, which involves the exercise of government authority and arguable variance with a state's international law obligations, is distinguishable from commercial or domestic administrative law conflicts, which involve national law and may more appropriately be resolved before national courts.

[96] *See* Jeswald W. Salacuse, *BIT by BIT: The Growth of Bilateral Investment Treaties and Their Impact on Foreign Investment in Developing Countries*, 24 INT'L LAW. 655, 659 (1990) (noting the U.N. historically identified 875 acts of government takings in sixty-two countries over a fourteen-year period for which there was no remedy).

[97] Editorial, *Trump's World: The New Nationalism*, THE ECONOMIST (Nov. 19, 2016), https://econ.st/2UauhwJ (last visited Jan. 21, 2019).

[98] William S. Dodge, Loewen v. United States: *Trials and Errors under NAFTA Chapter 11*, 52 DEPAUL L. REV. 563, 577 (2002).

courts of many nations."[99] If, however, states believe that national courts are preferable because *some* (but not all) countries have sufficient rule-of-law traditions, states will quickly be in the uncomfortable position of having to "name and shame" national judiciaries deemed substandard, creating diplomatic and international relations tensions that states may sensibly wish to avoid. Second, national courts may not have the requisite appreciation of international law or may disregard international law norms in favor of isolationist interpretations that prioritize national rules, norms, or objecttives. Third, not all national courts have broad transparency, meaning core information could be lost in some (but not all) jurisdictions. Perhaps most important, as the Hague Choice of Courts Convention is of limited applicability,[100] enforcement of national judgments will be neither streamlined nor efficient, creating structural incentives for losing parties (whether a state or investor subject to an adverse costs order) to ignore national court judgments.

In a perfect world, arbitration—or any form of adjudication—could theoretically be unnecessary, as everyone could identify the value in resolving conflicts efficiently and fairly. Given limitations of human cognition, this is unlikely to occur in all disputes, and the need for final and binding adjudication remains. Put differently, economically rational and savvy parties may redress conflict before it ever crystalizes or generates a formal dispute notice.[101] With imperfect humans and a range of needs involved, having multiple viable dispute resolution options—working independently or in tandem—is sensible, enabling stakeholders to match "horses for courses."[102]

Ultimately, the data reflected high fiscal costs of ITA, suggesting parties should actively consider alternatives to address crystalized disputes and manage latent conflict.[103] Focusing on appropriate dispute resolution, stakeholders should systematically consider strategies for

---

[99] Maya Steinitz & Paul Gowder, *Transnational Litigation as a Prisoner's Dilemma*, 594 N.C. L. REV. 751, 751, 753, 812 (2016).

[100] The Convention—limited to litigation deriving from a choice-of-court clause—is only in force among Denmark, European Union members (who already have an internal enforcement regime), Mexico, Montenegro, and Singapore. Hague Convention on Choice of Court Agreements (June 30, 2005), 44 I.L.M. 1294, http://bit.ly/18x6Gbv (last visited Oct. 6, 2018). Subject to qualifications involving Brexit, the United Kingdom agreed to be bound by the Convention starting April 1, 2019. Ministry of Foreign Affairs of the Kingdom of the Neth., Convention on Choice of Court Agreeemnts (The Hague, 30 June 2005), Notification pursuant to Article 34 of the Convention, United Kingdom Accession (Dec. 28, 2018), https://bit.ly/2Ml6KGq (last visited Jan. 21, 2019).

[101] Echandi & Gonstead, *supra* note 88; Qiang et al., *supra* note 75.

[102] Capacity building of mediators, counsel, and parties will be fundamental. Mediators may have procedural sophistication in managing complex disputes and disparate interests but may lack the public international law expertise to understand the "shadow of the law" under which the parties are negotiating. Likewise, public international law experts may lack mediation skills, including an understanding of what "mediation" means and the breadth, scope, and types of mediation practice and how to effectively use state-of-the-art mediation tactics and procedural opportunities. Counsel advising clients may have an incorrect understanding of mediation (thereby being disinclined to recommend it), may not fully appreciate the potential value, or may have institutional incentives to avoid mediation. *See, e.g.*, FRANCK & JOUBIN-BRET, *supra* note 63; Franck, *supra* 62, at 208–11, 216–18; *see also* ROGER FISHER & WILLIAM URY, GETTING TO YES (1991); Michael Moffitt, *Three Things to Be Against ("Settlement" Not Included)*, 78 FORD. L. REV. 1203 (2009).

[103] *See* Wolf Von Kumberg, *International Commercial Arbitration from a User's Perspective: Are the Benefits More Theoretical than Real?*, 66 DISP. RESOL. J. 76, 78–80 (2012) (suggesting "horses for[race] courses" involves identifying adjudication's value as compared to other processes, keeping in mind a variety of factors involved to achieve that acceptable resolutions occur in the least time for the least money).

untapped value and cost savings. Formal and neutral adjudication, with procedural rules and substantive finality, serves a critical function; but given the uncertainties and exposure in ITA costs and cost-shifting, alternative ways of preventing, managing, and resolving investment-treaty related conflict may increase stakeholder satisfaction, increase access to justice, and decrease costs.

IV. Opportunities for Decreased Costs

Presuming alternative methodologies—including negotiation, ombuds, mediation, absorbing the loss, or walking away from conflict—are inapplicable, the fundamental question is how to decrease costs of the existing adjudication system provided by thousands of treaties to foster efficiency, to provide a balanced playing field, and to demonstrate rule-of-law norms. As Chapters 4 and 8 revealed, cost and time walked hand in hand. While time was the only variable reliably predicting investors' costs, states' costs, and tribunals' costs, other variables were uniquely linked with cost elements. This section explores different normative opportunities that may control (but may not always curtail) costs and provide enhanced cost predictability. Given ICSID's ongoing prevalence as an ITA forum—and because it addressed multiple issues that offer a springboard for others considering innovations to treaties or institutional rules—ICSID's reform efforts are worthy of particular focus. This section first explores ICSID's proposed revisions before addressing other opportunities for cost containment.

A. Procedural Innovations: Exploring Reform through the Lens of ICSID Rule Revision

Earlier, this chapter addressed ICSID's proposed creation of an affirmative duty for arbitrators to conduct proceedings in an expeditious and cost-effective manner. While the express obligations are a step in the right direction, there are other procedural innovations that could decrease time, theoretically facilitating decreases in ITA costs. Some proposed changes—including timing and procedures for tribunal constitution, challenges, and appointment[104]—aid reduction in overall case length.[105] While this book did not analyze arbitrator appointment, regressions in Chapter 8 suggest any rule change capable of decreasing

---

[104] ICSID, Working Paper, *supra* note 11, at 126–28, 139–66.

[105] The Working Paper does not specifically address financial resources devoted to appointment-related issues. The time (and financial resources) devoted to investigating, appointing, and challenging arbitrators are theoretically avoidable costs should there be a standing tribunal or court. The "cost" of identifying the selection criteria and making appointments to a standing adjudicative body, however, also exist, and many only transfer the same problem to a new context. While not immediately quantifiable like ITA costs, current debates about the potential membership of an investment court system—which may last years and could even continue after establishment—generate political, diplomatic, and social costs. One need only consider ongoing debates about WTO appellate body membership. Simon Lester, *Trump's Dangerous Approach to the "Supreme Court" of Global Trade*, Reuters (June 19, 2018), https://reut.rs/2OVDC8H (last visited Aug. 17, 2018); *see also* Charles Bjork, *ASIL 2018 Recap: 2018 Annual Grotius Lecture*, https://bit.ly/2nWPiNl (Apr. 9, 2018) (last visited Aug. 17, 2018) (discussing Justice Donoghue's observations about ICJ election and appointment challenges).

the time of a case's life cycle could, in theory, save states legal fees of around US$38,000 and tribunal costs of roughly US$10,000 per month.[106]

1. Expedited Rules, Case Management Conferences, and Timetable Compliance

Core procedural innovations could achieve cost savings by decreasing dispute resolution time. ICISD's proposed new set of Expedited Arbitration Rules is one of the most innovative and constructive elements. Parties could opt into these rules, streamlining timetables and imposing page limitations on submissions.[107] While a material shift for ICSID, the recommendations accord with other institutions implementing expedited procedures.[108] In theory, these procedures can be used for both high- and small-value disputes to decrease costs; and with evidence submissions potentially running into thousands of exhibits and terabytes of data, such streamlining may save counsel and tribunals considerable time and costs by requiring a more exacting focus.

A second innovation involves working within ICSID's existing framework. While the mandatory First Session is still held within sixty days of tribunal constitution, to move matters along, ICSID proposed requiring tribunals to issue a procedural order within fifteen days of the First Session.[109] The proposed rules expressly permit case management conferences (CMCs) to narrow the issues and contested facts.[110] CMCs are not, however, mandatory under ICSID's proposed rules,[111] with CMCs only indirectly referenced in discussion items for the First Session.[112] The situation is somewhat ironic, as ICSID's Working Paper encourages parties to be proactive in case management, briefly referring to issuing a guidance note with case management techniques.[113] While a step toward injecting procedural efficiency, further procedural opportunities to narrow the dispute's focus are warranted to prevent the facilitation of a free-for-all that muddies core issues by flooding the record,

[106] *See* Chapter 8 (discussing beta-weights from regressions but failing to provide beta-weights for investors' legal fees as non-logged data contained high skewing); Appendix I (discussing skewing and kurtosis of costs data). Beta-weights for monthly costs were a function of the unit of analysis and may not realisticly reflect the ITA lifecycle, as procedural timetables likely cluster costs around critical events (i.e. dates for memorials and hearings) rather having a standard monthly cost. Nevertheless, the beta-weights offer a base rate for consideration.

[107] ICSID, Proposed Rules, *supra* note 11, at Proposed AF Arb. Rules 73–81; *see also* ICSID, Synopsis, *supra* note 10, at 10–11; ICSID, Working Paper, *supra* note 11, at 292–95, 976–80.

[108] Meng Chen, *Emerging Internal Control in Institutional Arbitration*, 18 Cardozo J. Conflict Resol. 295, 300–07 (2017); *see also* ICSID, Working Paper, *supra* note 11, at 990–91 (comparing rules for expedited processes).

[109] ICSID, Proposed Rules, *supra* note 11, at Proposed Arb. Rule 34(5); *id.* at Proposed AF Arb. Rule 44(5).

[110] *Id.* at Proposed Arb. Rule 14; *id.* at Proposed AF Arb. Rule 23.

[111] *Compare* ICC Rules, *supra* note 42, at art. 24, app. IV (requiring CMCs and related case management techniques); 2017 SCC Rules, *supra* note 37, at art. 28 (requiring only an initial CMC); ICDR, Arbitration Rule art. 4, https://bit.ly/2q8KNzP (July 2016) (last visited Aug. 17, 2018) (permitting an "administrative conference" with administrative staff before the tribunal "to facilitate party discussion and agreement on issues such as arbitrator selection, mediating the dispute, process efficiencies, and any other administrative matters").

[112] *Supra* note 110; ICSID, Proposed Rules, *supra* note 11, at Proposed Arb. Rule 34(4)(j); *id.* at Proposed AF Arb. Rule 44(4)(j).

[113] ICSID, Working Paper, *supra* note 11, at 108, 114.

thereby requiring the tribunal to invest more time and costs. This suggests that at least one, if not more, CMCs should be mandatory. If parties wish to sacrifice time and fiscal efficiency, they can certainly agree to do so during a CMC; but they then stand on less solid footing to complain subsequently about the time and costs of proceedings. Parties, be they investors or states, must be willing to accept the consequences of their choices, action, and inaction.

A somewhat "softer" approach to procedural timetables involves putting pressure on parties. ICSID proposed that parties have a duty to comply with tribunal orders, and the draft rules provide that, where parties act *after* the expiration of a time limit, those activities "shall be disregarded" unless there are "special circumstances justifying the delay."[114] Yet it is unclear what justifies "special circumstances," meaning the rule remains flexible, and creative counsel can generate arguments as to what makes each instance unique.[115] To prevent potential mischief, ICSID or a delegated working group should explore guidelines for distinguishing between normal and abnormal situations. Additionally, parties can agree to extend time periods fixed by the ICSID Secretary-General or the Rules,[116] and prior to time limits expiring, a party can unilaterally—but with valid reasons—request an extension beyond tribunal-imposed time limits.[117]

Another of ICSID's proposed changes involves focusing on tribunal compliance with timelines, presumably holding arbitrators' feet to the fire to ensure that the tribunal or administration is not the core source of delay (or undue cost). The proposals obligate tribunals to fix time limits for completing procedural steps where there are gaps.[118] A core, and appropriate, innovation requires tribunals to decrease the gap in rendering an award, as the proposals state tribunals "shall deliberate . . . immediately after the last written or oral submission."[119] Likewise, there are timing obligations, including requiring arbitrators to render decisions within: 60 days after the last submissions for petitions that a dispute manifestly lacks legal merit,[120] 180 days after the last submissions for preliminary objections to jurisdiction,[121] and 240 days (or eight months) for all other matters.[122] These figures provide a cognitive anchor that, hopefully, can shift tribunal behavior in a constructive direction.

Yet, anchoring can be pernicious. As data suggested average gaps between hearings and awards of ten months, it is unfortunate that arbitrators could receive *eight months* for rendering decisions. While it is a more realistic formulation than innovations from the draft

---

[114] ICSID, Proposed Rules, *supra* note 11, at Proposed Arb. Rules 8(2), 9(3); *id.* at Proposed AF Arb. Rules 16(2), 17(3).

[115] The only guidance is, when considering a reasoned request for extension, arbitrators should recall the duty to act expeditiously. ICSID, Working Paper, *supra* note 11, at 104–05.

[116] ICSID, Proposed Rules, *supra* note 11, at Proposed Arb. Rule 8(1); *id.* at Proposed AF Arb. Rule 16(1).

[117] *Id.* at Proposed Arb Rule 9(2); *id.* at Proposed AF Arb. Rule 17(2); *see also* ICSID, Working Paper, *supra* note 11, at 494 (providing a chart about extending time limits).

[118] ICSID, Proposed Rules, *supra* note 11, at Proposed Arb. Rule 9(1); *id.* at Proposed AF Arb. Rule 17(1).

[119] *Id.* at Proposed Arb Rule 16(4); *id.* at Proposed AF Arb. Rule 26(4).

[120] ICSID, Working Paper, *supra* note 11, at 103; ICSID, Proposed Rules, *supra* note 11, at Proposed Arb. Rules 35(2)(d), 59(1)(a); *id.* at Proposed AF Arb. Rules 45(2)(d), 69(1)(a).

[121] ICSID, Proposed Rules, *supra* note 11, at Proposed Arb. Rules 36(6–7), 59(1)(b); *id.* at Proposed AF Arb. Rules 46(7), 69(1)(b); ICSID, Working Paper, *supra* note 11, at 257–58.

[122] ICSID, Proposed Rules, *supra* note 11, at Proposed Arb. Rule 59(1)(c); *id.* at Proposed AF Arb. Rule 69(1)(c); ICSID, Working Paper, *supra* note 11, at 257–58.

Dutch model treaty,[123] ICSID's proposal does little to move the needle or incentivize more efficient arbitral decisions. If anything, it entrenches the status quo, rather than shortening periods. It also creates a potentially perverse situation where, by identifying a lengthy period, tribunals may be intuitively drawn to ensuring their awards "fill the space" and are rendered after eight months.[124] While the Working Paper thoughtfully notes that fixed and overly harsh timetables could endanger the underlying award and fail to address unique complexities, the proposal still falls flat. One would hope that, even with a voluminous record (theoretically addressing merits, damages, and costs) tribunals could write up decisions in at least six (preferably three to four) months. Moreover, even the eight-month period has built-in temporal expansion, as tribunals have an obligation to use "best efforts to meet [] time limits" imposed by the ICSID Rules,[125] and the proposal fails to provide texture as to what "best efforts" means.[126] When "special circumstances" prevent tribunals from complying with their required deadlines, they simply advise parties of the delay, rather than suffering a penalty for procedural deviations.[127] One might hope that ICSID could consider, for example, imposing a shorter time period, rewarding early completion, or considering fee reductions for delay, particularly for arbitrators receiving exceptions to ICSID's standard fee of US$375 per hour.[128] Other options might involve providing data on timetable compliance and costs for individual arbitrators, thereby aiding parties in identifying arbitrators with preferred efficiency and case-management skills.[129]

---

[123] For example, the Dutch model attempts to nudge the rendering of final awards by stating tribunals "shall endeavor to issue its final award within 24 months of the date the claim." *See* Dutch Model BIT, *supra* note 29, at art. 22(1). While a laudable goal to render awards within two years, as current data suggest the average case length is 3.5–4 years, this likely sets an unreachable objective, inevitably setting stakeholders up for disappointment or possibly even an award that is null and void. Much like losing weight, slow and steady decreases over time are likely to be sustainable and preferable to radical weight loss from imposing severe restrictions.

[124] Anchoring research, for example, has found that mandatory minimums (i.e., a floor) and mandatory maximums (i.e., a ceiling) on damages can serve as anchors, with decisions pulled in the direction of the legally generated baseline, which has nothing to do with actual damages. *See, e.g.*, Jeffrey J. Rachlinski, Andrew J. Wistrichv & Chris Guthrie, *Can Judges Make Reliable Numeric Judgments? Distorted Damages and Skewed Sentences*, 90 Ind. L.J. 695, 720 (2015) ("damage caps are exactly the kind of anchor apt to have a large effect on judgment"). As anchoring has influenced international arbitrators, a long and express time period must be considered carefully. *See also* Susan D. Franck et al., *Inside the Arbitrator's Mind*, 66 Emory L.J. 1117 (2017); Chapter 2.

[125] *Id.* at Proposed Arb. Rule 8(3); *id.* at Proposed AF Arb. Rule 16(3).

[126] ICSID, Working Paper, *supra* note 11, at 103.

[127] *Id.* at Proposed Arb. Rule 8(3); *id.* at Proposed AF Arb. Rule 16(3).

[128] *See supra* notes 15–16. One might imagine requiring tribunals (or individual arbitrators) to articulate written reasons for the delay, and rules granting the ICSID Secretary-General the right to accept or reject those considerations and make reasonable fee adjustments accordingly.

[129] Professor Rogers' Arbitrator Intelligence platform offers some access to related information. *See, e.g.,* http://www.arbitratorintelligence.org (last visited Aug. 17, 2018); *see also supra* notes 53–54. Embedded information in existing awards is aggregated for three-member tribunals, creating challenges in identifying individual variance.

2. Bifurcation Norms

ICSID also proposed a new rule on bifurcation. Imposing some reform on bifurcation, to nudge more prudent use of time and potentially decrease costs, is prudent given the data. ICSID's own analysis of bifurcated cases in 2015–2017 suggested bifurcation is not necessarily the best option for all cases, as many (but not all) bifurcated cases were considerably longer.[130] Chapter 4 likewise demonstrated that case length was reliably longer in bifurcated cases, while Chapter 8 revealed investors' legal costs and tribunal costs could be meaningfully higher in bifurcated cases.[131] The data suggest bifurcation is ripe for consideration as an area of reform.

ICSID has proposed time periods for parties making bifurcation requests, requiring tribunal responses within thirty days, with tribunals retaining power to bifurcate proceedings *sua sponte*.[132] When making bifurcation decisions, tribunals "shall consider all relevant circumstances, including whether bifurcation would materially reduce the time and cost of the proceeding."[133] ICSID's Working Paper suggests automatic bifurcation was not warranted, as each case is unique and "ICSID case law has uniformly held that there is no presumption in favor of bifurcation."[134] If the goal is to eliminate unnecessary time (thereby controlling costs), the data in this book lends supports the conclusion that automatic bifurcation is unwarranted; but likewise, an inability to bifurcate could be problematic. The challenge, however, is to identify the relevant factors supporting efficient (rather than long and costly) bifurcation. ICSID thoughtfully identified other factors for consideration—including whether jurisdiction is closely intertwined with the merits, capable of resolving the dispute, or frivolous.[135] The commentary has the benefit of highlighting potentially negative effects of bifurcation, enabling parties to manage their own expectations through a reframing process.

One would hope the reality of data may temper irrational exuberance and potential optimism bias of states seeking a quick victory, but who may end up disappointed when, in reality, their case ultimately took longer than if they had opted for a unified proceeding. Bifurcation research should be an area for ongoing scrutiny about relevant factors to identify cases most likely to benefit from bifurcation, so as to develop working practices for tribunals and to guide party's making strategic decisions, which risk back-firing and generating longer proceedings rather than streamlined ones.

3. Non-Disputing Parties

ICSID has proposed rules about participation and costs of non-disputing parties (NDPs). ICSID's proposal ensures that there is a broad opportunity for observation of hearings and NDP participation.[136] This choice was sensible, particularly as Chapter 4 revealed the

---

[130] ICSID, Working Paper, *supra* note 11, at 976–80.

[131] Readers are encouraged to remember both that ICSID data included non-ITA cases, and Chapter 8 revealed that, after controlling for case length, the significant relationships between: (1) bifurcation and investor PLC, and (2) bifurcation and TCE dissipated.

[132] ICSID, Proposed Rules, *supra* note 11, Proposed Arb. Rule 37(1–3); *id.* at Proposed AF Arb. Rule 47(1–3).

[133] *Id.* at Proposed Arb. Rule 37(4); *id.* at Proposed AF Arb. Rule 47(4).

[134] ICSID, Working Paper, *supra* note 11, at 188.

[135] *Id.* at 187–89.

[136] ICSID, Proposed Rules, *supra* note 11, at Proposed Arb. Rules 47-48; *id.* at Proposed AF Arb. Rules 56–57.

dominance of states as NDPs and as Chapter 8 was unable to detect reliable increases in ITA costs or time when NDPs (or NGOs) were present.

Given the potential assistance to adjudication quality, the normative value of transparency, and the importance of mirroring rule-of-law values in ITA—where the data fails to reveal a reliable derivative cost increase—such interventions seem sensible and warranted. ICSID also proposed safeguards to ensure NDPs are not incentivized to unduly burden the process and that they add real value. Specifically, tribunals should "ensure that [a] non-disputing party does not disrupt the proceeding or unduly burden or unfairly prejudice either party." ICSID identifies conditions tribunals can impose, including: the filing date; the format, scope, and length of submission; and "the payment of funds to defray the increased costs" attributable to NDP participation.[137] This should, in theory, ensure the value of enhanced NDP participation need not disproportionately encumber the process, particularly the proposal to require fiscal contributions from NDPs.[138] It would be useful to have greater guidance about factors promoting effective and quality participation, as the Working Paper has thus far suggested only that where an "NDP might have a commercial purpose or financial capacity to contribute," tribunals might consider financial contributions appropriate.[139]

4. Security for Costs

While costs can be fiscally serious, it is vital that complying with tribunal cost determinations be a real requirement, rather than a theoretical obligation. To help make costs and payment for cost-shifting a tangible risk, it is vital to provide clear rules and cost enforcement opportunities. To this end, another critical innovation by ICSID was to create an express rule in support of costs-enforcement, so all parties treat costs seriously.[140] The EU and its

---

[137] *Id.* at Proposed Arb. Rule 48(4); *id.* at Proposed AF Arb. Rules 57(4). This is similar to CETA, which permits NDP participation, indicates documents that are generally available to NDPs, and indicates where (primarily for production of non-public evidence) that NDPs may be responsible for some costs. CETA, *supra* note 28, at art. 8.38; *compare* Dutch Model BIT, *supra* note 29, at art. 20.11 (providing for NDP activity but failing to address cost issues).

[138] Another method of managing NDP submissions involves not limiting amicus curiae submissions in any manner. In theory, NDPs could submit briefing materials and parties need not invest in responses, permitting the quality of the NDP arguments to stand on their own merits, and giving tribunals discretion to use, reject, or ignore the submissions. In the U.S. Supreme Court, there has been a surge in amicus activity; and while many submissions have little effect on Court reasoning or outcomes, empirical analysis reveals the activity reliably favors respondents. Joseph D. Kearney & Thomas W. Merrill, *The Influence of Amicus Curiae Briefs on the Supreme Court*, 148 U. PA. L. REV. 743 (2000); *see also* Lucia Manzi & Matthew E.K. Hall, *Friends You Can Trust: A Signaling Theory of Interest Group Litigation Before the U.S. Supreme Court*, 51 LAW & SOC'Y REV. 704 (2017). Other empirical evidence identifies some concerns deriving from the unfettered amicus participation involving balance, and fairness, and injecting potentially inaccurate and untested facts that improperly contaminate decision-making. *See* Allison Orr Larsen, *The Trouble with Amicus Facts*, 100 VA. L. REV. 1757, 1818 (2014); Michael Rustad & Thomas Koenig, *The Supreme Court and Junk Social Science: Selective Distortion in Amicus Briefs*, 72 N.C. L. REV. 91, 94–95 (1993); Linda Sandstrom Simard, *An Empirical Study of Amici Curiae in Federal Court: A Fine Balance of Access, Efficiency, and Adversarialism*, 27 REV. LITIG. 669, 705–06 (2008).

[139] ICSID, WORKING PAPER, *supra* note 11, at 216–17.

[140] ICSID, PROPOSED RULES, *supra* note 11, at Proposed Arb. Rule 51; *id.* at Proposed AF Arb. Rule 60; *see also* ICSID, WORKING PAPER, *supra* note 11, at 229–36.

counter-parties have taken a similar perspective, explicitly incorporating security for costs into its treaties.[141] Such an approach is sensible and provides an opportunity for case-specific assessment of the value of the interim relief, rather than mandating security in every case or leaving a legal void suggesting that security for costs may be inappropriate.

As a unique form of preliminary relief, ICSID's proposal helpfully regularizes security for costs, identifies that the remedy can be warranted, provides guidance for making requests, and offers decision timetables. Yet, it does little by way of guiding adjudicative authority, simply suggesting that tribunals consider a "party's ability to comply with any adverse decision on costs" and "any other relevant circumstances." On one hand, it notably fails to include availability of third-party funding[142] as part of required consideration for possible compliance (and whether funding covers adverse cost awards); but on the other hand, it does not require the party requesting the security to demonstrate irreparable harm, urgency, or the necessity of the security, which are high thresholds possibly preventing the imposition of preliminary relief.[143]

While ICSID's Working Paper observes that lack of assets alone will not justify granting security, it identified scope for procedural flexibility, noting "there must be other circumstances present, such as a history of noncompliance with legal orders or bad-faith." Intriguingly, those other factors are framed to focus upon investor conduct—not states.[144] This focus, rather than looking at the merits, decreases the risk that dissatisfied parties will perceive arbitrators as biased and use it as a basis for challenge. Like the SCC, ICSID's proposal also has a "stick" to ensure cost orders are taken seriously, as proceedings may be suspended or discontinued for compliance failures.[145] As it provides clarity on enforcement and reflects costs are serious—combined with the ongoing duty to treat parties equally and consider cost-efficiency—the proposed rule provides a key opportunity to put economic incentives at the foreground of strategic decision-making.

It would, however, be constructive to form a working group that explores the factors that are most fundamental in creating a fair and workable decision that work for all parties. These may be a function, for example, of economic resources and/or previous compliance (or non-compliance) with core legal obligations. One might imagine that the capitalization or the scope of indebtedness may be factors for consideration. Likewise, compliance with domestic regulatory investigations or decisions of international adjudicative bodies, availability of reserve funds and/or legal authority to pay security if necessary, or an established record of ethical violations by a party's in-house or external counsel, might also be indicators of potential compliance risk. Nevertheless, given that there is a great deal of variation in the identity

[141] EU-Vietnam Trade and Investment Agreements (Agreed Text as of August 2017), Viet.-Eur. (Sept. 24, 2018), arts. 3.37(3), 3.48, 3.54(6), https://bit.ly/2BXmYT6 (last visited Oct. 3, 2018); *EU Textual Proposal, supra* note 52, at arts. 2.39, 2.47(6); *but see* USMCA, *supra* note 10, at Annex 14-D (failing to discuss security for costs).

[142] ICSID's draft rules, however, require disclosure of the existence of TPF. ICSID, Proposed Rules, *supra* note 11, at Proposed Arb. Rule 21; *id.* at Proposed AF Arb. Rule 32.

[143] *See* Kate Brown de Vejar & Chloe Baldwin, *The Economics of Access: Systemic Imbalances in ISDS, in* ICCA Congress Proceedings (forthcoming) (overviewing jurisprudence on security for costs, and challenges in recovering costs, and suggesting security for costs are the "unicorns of investment arbitration. Everyone has heard of them, and apparently they are beautiful creatures, but no one has actually seen one").

[144] ICSID, Working Paper, *supra* note 11, at 235.

[145] ICSID, Proposed Rules, *supra* note 11, at Proposed Arb. Rule 51(4); *id.* at Proposed AF Arb. Rule 60(4).

of claimants, the nature of respondents, and the disputes involved, such variation requires some flexibility and an appreciation of the nuance of individual situations. The better course is, having established a clear rule permitting security for costs, ICSID should task a working group with exploring factors that contribute to effective (and ineffective) determinations in order to aid ongoing reform and best practice protocols.

B. ADDITIONAL OPPORTUNITIES FOR REFORM: ADVISORY COMMITTEE ON RULES REFORM, PLEADING OBLIGATIONS, ATTORNEY REGULATION, AND ENERGY DISPUTES

There were areas, however, where ICSID has *not* proposed rules but where data suggest value in potential reform to save time and costs. Should ICSID be unable to explore these matters during its revision process, states and other institutions could explore these when negotiating treaties or considering the future of investment dispute resolution. Perhaps more realistically, somewhat like the U.S. Advisory Committee on the Federal Rules of Civil Procedure that offers guidance, ICSID could form a transnational working group to provide insights supporting potential revisions or the establishment of guidelines or best practices, particularly for time efficiency and cost containment.

First, procedural reform should both impose good-faith pleading obligations and require early expert witness evidence in support of damage calculations. Chapter 5 revealed large amounts claimed but relatively small proportions of claims awarded. Should parties "weaponize" findings in this book and previous research to benefit from the cognitive illusion of anchoring, which affects international arbitrators' damage awards,[146] one can imagine some investors artificially inflating claims by 300% to address the gap. Such a result serves no rule-of-law value. Rather, such puffery creates an artificial, irrelevant, and manipulative anchor, which risks tainting by association the careful and considered damage claims from investors who meticulously identify real economic harm.

Chapter 8 also revealed a reliable link between investors' amounts claimed and tribunal costs (but not either party's legal costs). As an investor's claim temporally precede a tribunal incurring costs, the reliable link creates a risk that, not only will a subcategory of investors be incentivized to make unduly inflated claims, those same larger claims will facilitate larger tribunal costs. For this reason, beyond articulating cost-shifting standards at the beginning to provide constructive incentives, it would be worthwhile for ICSID to require parties to substantiate their damage claims at the outset, with expert reports and/or appropriate documentation. For example, a preliminary expert request could accompany the Request for Arbitration identifying the amount claimed, the economic basis, and the modeling behind the estimate. Claimants should be in a position to know the scope and extent of their own damages, particularly when they are making

[146] *See* Franck et al., *supra* note 124; Chapter 2. The Kingdom of Spain has also identified concerns about overly inflated claims. *Comentarios de España, supra* note 40, at 6 ("Es habitual que las partes demandantes sobrevaloren las compensaciones solicitadas. En ocasiones, esta sobrevaloración alcanza umbrales irracionales. Este comportamiento provoca una gran alarma en la opinión pública, generando información confusa pero con un gran impacto mediático. Además, tiene como objetivo influenciar al Tribunal en la valoración de daños.") [It is common that clamants overestimate their requested damages. On occasion, this overevaluation reaches irrational threshholds. This behavior provokes a large alarm in public opinion, generating confusing information but with a large media impact. In addition, it has has the object of influencing the tribunal in its damage valuation.].

the decision to pursue adjudication,[147] meaning they should be able to efficiently provide the information; and states bringing counterclaims should likewise be able to substantiate their claimed damages. This recommendation mirrors reforms successfully implemented in response to high-value asbestos litigation, where early focus on damages streamlined adjudication.[148]

Even in the absence of ICSID reform, states drafting treaties would be well-served by providing default rules that require parties to plead damages with specificity and in good-faith to create incentives for reasonable, evidence-based damage assessments. Such an approach should maximize the value of relevant anchors, decrease the risk of irrelevant anchors exerting improper influence, and decrease tribunal costs. Providing realistic claims also increases the potential zone of possible agreement between parties, rather than having outsized and unwarranted claims eliminate the potentially effective use of negotiation and mediation. Requiring good-faith pleading and incentivizing claim accuracy demonstrates that adjudication follows rule-of-law norms, in the hopes of rendering more accurate and reasoned awards.

Second, there is value in focusing on how to regulate attorneys during ICSID arbitration or identifying requirements for attorneys competent to arbitrate before ICSID. The data suggests the potential value in shifting a focus to counsel, as previous research identified reliable links between repeat player (RP) counsel and ITA outcomes,[149] and Chapter 8's insights that RP counsel were linked with higher ITA costs, particularly for investors' counsel and tribunal costs.

While direct regulation of counsel practicing before ICSID or other bodies would be novel, the data suggest it is a promising area as, to the extent that counsel receive fees and the RPs can cost reliably more, it may be worthwhile ensuring that they have the proper capacity to practice before international tribunals, including avoiding dilatory tactics. There are, in fact, already soft-law instruments to guide counsel conduct. The IBA Guidelines on Party Representation in International Arbitration provide a baseline with specific provisions suggesting lawyer misconduct should be a basis for shifting costs.[150] There is nothing to prevent institutions, states, and investors from adopting these guidelines. Yet, while ICSID,[151] the European Union,[152] and others[153] recognize the IBA Guidelines for Conflicts of Interest

[147] Should data on investors' damages be destroyed or no longer in their possesseion or control due to the particularies of a case, investors should nevertheless be able to identify the gap and where supporting damates documentation is located. There is also a possibility that prudent potential third-party funders have already requested preliminary damage assessments, meaning core information could already exist; and should the case proceed beyond the merits, claimants would be required to expend the effort to collect and analyze such documentation.

[148] Drury Stevenson, *Reverse Bifurcation*, 75 U. Cin. L. Rev. 213, 218 (2008); Franck, *supra* note 23, at 851.

[149] *See* Franck & Wylie, *supra* note 18, at 505–08, 512–13, 516–18, 522–23 (observing, for *investors' legal teams*, the absence of RPs was reliably associated with investor losses, RPs on investors' teams were associated with higher amounts awarded, but failing to identify any effect on relative investor success); *id.* (noting, for *states' legal teams*, it was not possible to identify a link between RPs and winning/losing or amounts awarded, but noting RP counsel was reliably associated with decreased investor success).

[150] Int'l Bar Ass'n, Guidelines on Party Representation in International Arbitration, art. 26(c) (May 25, 2013); *see also* Tom Cummins, *The IBA Guidelines on Party Representation in International Arbitration—Levelling the Playing Field?*, 30 Arb. Int'l 429 (2015).

[151] ICSID, Working Paper, *supra* note 11, at 132.

[152] European Parliament Directorate-General for External Policies, In Pursuit of an International Investment Court: Recently Negotiated Investment Chapters in EU Comprehensive FTA in Comparative Perspective, 16–17, 106–17, EP/EXPO/INTA/2017/02 (July 2017), https://bit.ly/2v2WWZx (last visited Aug. 24, 2018).

[153] *See* Dutch Model BIT, *supra* note 29, at art. 20(6) ("Arbitrators shall comply with the International Bar Association Guidelines on Conflicts of Interest in International Arbitration and any supplemental rules agreed

for Arbitrators, there has not been the same focus on regulating attorneys' ethical conduct in ITA. Should we wish lawyers to engage in high standards of professionalism to model rule-of-law conduct—rather than engaging in guerilla warfare, exploitation of regulatory arbitrage, and bullying tactics—the time is ripe for conversations about regulating lawyers or changing their incentives to reward the appropriate behavior of many counsel while addressing variance arising from misconduct. With the patchwork of counsel's comparative professional obligations, and anticipating rules ex ante applicable to transnational attorney conduct is challenging, means there is value in exploring direct regulation to create direct results.[154]

Third, as data suggested energy disputes have unique characteristics, it may be worthwhile creating specific cost-containment protocols for energy disputes. Chapter 5 identified that claims in energy disputes were reliably higher than non-energy disputes; and while energy disputes were not necessarily reliably associated with outcomes,[155] Chapter 8 revealed that energy disputes *did* reliably predict one fundamental ITA cost, namely states' legal fees. Like the Energy Charter Treaty's[156] rules or the AAA's support of energy-specific ADR,[157] ICSID and others could implement specific rules or conflict management protocols for energy disputes. As some states make carveouts from investment protection for sensitive industries,[158] states could explore measures to limit their arbitration risks—whether by narrowing substantive rights or managing procedural rights—or provide greater certainty on arbitration costs to reduce fiscal exposure.[159] While the ultimate choice of treaty rights is a prerogative of sovereign states, the data suggest a degree of value in focusing upon energy disputes to identify the relative strengths and weaknesses of dispute resolution options.

C. SEPARATE OPINIONS: BALANCING COSTS AND OUTCOMES

As a final matter, it is worthwhile identifying that ICSID failed to create rules in one area related to costs in a manner that is arguably appropriate, namely separate opinions. Although Chapter 4 was unable to identify that separate opinions were reliably associated with increased

---

upon by the Contracting Parties."); *see also* Republic of Italy, *Comments by the Italian Republic on Proposed Changes of ICSID Rules and Regulations*, https://bit.ly/2s2Dxqw (last visited Dec. 30, 2018) (promoting the Italian Chamber of Commerce Code of Ethics of Arbitrators as a recommendation for Arbitrators "Code of Conduct" but failing to offer any thoughts on attorney regulation).

154 Catherine Rogers has written the seminal work exploring ethics, for attorneys and arbitrators, in international arbitration and addressing the challenges of working in a transnational legal environment. CATHERINE ROGERS, ETHICS IN INTERNATIONAL ARBITRATION (2014); *see also* Catherine A. Rogers, *Lawyers Without Borders*, 30 U. PA. J. INT'L L. 1035 (2009).

155 *But see* Franck & Wylie, *supra* note 18, at 499, 519–20 (failing to find energy disputes robustly predicated ITA outcomes).

156 Energy Charter Treaty, 34 I.L.M. 360 (Dec. 17, 1994); *see also supra* note 84.

157 *See, e.g.*, American Arbitration Association, *Energy ADR Services*, https://bit.ly/2Lpr8nY (last visited Aug. 24, 2018); International Centre for Dispute Resolution, *ICDR Energy Dispute Resolution Services*, https://bit.ly/2PpP4KR (last visited Aug. 24, 2018).

158 *See, e.g.*, Vera Korzun, *The Right to Regulate in Investor-State Arbitration: Slicing and Dicing Regulatory Carve-Outs*, 50 VAND. J. TRANSNAT'L L. 355 (2017); Sergio Puig & Gregory Shaffer, *A Breakthrough with the TPP: The Tobacco Carve-Out*, 16 YALE J. HEALTH POL'Y L. & ETHICS 327 (2016).

159 The USMCA, however, went in the opposite direction, granting expanded rights for oil, gas, and power-generation disputes involving government contracts. USMCA, *supra* note 10, at Annex 14-E.

(or decreased) case length or deliberative delay in rendering awards, Chapter 8 demonstrated that separate opinions *were* reliably associated with increased state legal fees. At first blush, states might be tempted to eliminate separate opinions in a bid to decrease their costs.

Yet doing so arguably destroys potential value for three reasons. First, other tests were unable to identify that other ITA costs were reliably higher when separate opinions were present, particularly investors' costs (which theoretically could be shifted to states) or the comparatively small tribunal cost. Second, separate opinions creating room for considered conversation about what is appropriate (or inappropriate) in the development of international investment law. Third, and perhaps more self-interestedly, when arbitrators rendered separate opinions, the majority opinion tended to benefit states, as states tended to win those disputes where a separate opinion was present. Given the lack of reliable effect investors' and tribunals' costs, keeping the status quo of permitting separate opinions provides substantive value without impeding procedural justice.

V. Changing Standards for Cost Assessments: Towards a Factor-Based Approach

In a legal vacuum with minimal hard law restraining or guiding tribunals, cost assessments are one of the last bastions of nearly unlimited, unfettered, and unpredictable tribunal discretion. As discussed earlier, tribunals rarely signaled in advance how they would use their discretion. Chapter 7 demonstrated how tribunals' costs rationalization, although improving slightly over time, remained relatively weak, and primarily relied upon untextured notions of equity and discretion to justify assessments while ignoring justice-based concepts such as precedential concerns, equality of arms, settlement efforts, and public interest. While tribunals' cost allocations were uncertain, a statistically reliable pattern demonstrated some imbalance in ITA costs, namely that investors proportionally benefitted more than states from cost-shifting when they were successful in winning the case.

Given those patterns, stakeholders face a stark choice, namely whether or not they are content with the status quo. If historic practice is appealing, it is possible (but not guaranteed) that the baseline will continue with multiple implications. First, should states continue to predominantly win cases, the overall pay-your-own-way baseline will likely continue. Yet substantive outcomes are by no means certain ex ante, which generates two sets of material risks—namely the scope of substantive recovery and scope of costs for which a party will be responsible. Second, where investors win or should investors begin winning in larger proportions after unmeritorious claims are weeded out (either by counsel, third-party funders, or legal barriers to arbitration), states could start experiencing more adverse consequences from cost assessments, particularly given the reliable pattern of investors more regularly benefitting from cost-shifting. As evidence suggested PLC shifts reliably increased over time, changing substantive outcomes could compound states' fiscal exposure. While investors and third-party funders may find those prospects appealing, states holding the pen in treaty negotiations may be less enthralled.[160]

[160] For states that anticipate roughly equivalent claims by their investors and as respondents, the loser-pays rule could generate a degree of balance over time. *See* Appendix III (suggesting there is a degree of rough parity in claims for Canada, for example). For primarily capital-importing states, however, the long-term equities may be less attractive.

The general approach to cost assessments revealed by the data is normatively undesirable and does not serve the long-term interests of international arbitration or of stakeholders paying for access to transnational justice. While discretion offers tribunals some flexibility—and may permit tribunals to engage in negotiation about other aspects of the dispute, which can happen in elite national tribunals[161]—adjudication of a fiscal risk involving millions of dollars should involve the regular and predictable application of legal standards rather than ad hoc horse-trading or implicit negotiation. Should parties wish to resolve their disputes via negotiated outcomes, there are procedures for that, whereas tribunals with adjudicative mandates should fulfill their rule-of-law obligations. If parties wish to provide tribunals with unfettered discretion to decide million-dollar cost issues at their whimsy, they are entitled to do so; but then parties should then have no expectation of predictability and must appreciate the consequences. If, however, parties want greater self-determination, they are free to generate cost assessment baselines in advance for arbitrators to follow.

This raises the question of whether parties, particularly states drafting treaties that offer dispute resolution options, wish to capture tribunal discretion and provide guidance to direct tribunals' assessments. Should there be a desire to minimize risk and structure discretion, the question then becomes which normative baseline is preferable for cost allocation. Given how tribunals have exercised their discretion, to maximize the policy objectives of cost-shifting, a factor-dependent approach is most suitable. It permits states to enumerate factors given state-directed levels of importance,[162] and it reflects the practical reality that tribunals have rejected a uniform method of cost assessments. Rather than having an adjudicative "hide-the-ball" rule, a factor-based approach encourages transparency, facilitates advocacy, and promotes predictability in a manner deriving from sovereign priorities.

ICSID has waded squarely into the debate. Acknowledging the ICSID Convention provides a costs baseline in ICSID Convention cases[163] and the need to balance concerns of investors and states, ICSID has proposed a preliminary model that encourages enhanced cost rationalization and predictability. First, ICSID proposed an affirmative obligation for tribunals to include cost decisions in final awards and "ensure that all decisions on costs are reasoned."[164] While this is relatively low-hanging fruit, stating this value expressly nudges costs decision-making in the right direction, offering textual authority to direct tribunals toward greater rationalization. Second, ICSID recommended a factor-dependent approach requiring consideration of outcomes (in whole or in part), party conduct during the arbitration (including expeditious and cost-effective behavior), issue complexity, and cost reasonableness.[165]

---

[161] *See, e.g.,* Lee Epstein & Tonja Jacobi, *The Strategic Analysis of Judicial Decisions*, 6 ANN. REV. L. & SOC. SCI. 341 (2010); Paul J. Wahlbeck, James F. Spriggs II & Forrest Maltzman, *Marshalling the Court: Bargaining and Accommodation in the United States Supreme Court*, 42 AM. J. POL. SCI. 294 (1998).

[162] This includes using PLC and TCE elements strategically, shifting PLC to create strong incentives and TCE to create weaker incentives, given differential risks. While it would require tribunals to exercise care, particularize distinct costs, refer to legal authority, and offer careful analysis, this nuanced approach would honor party agreement, provide guided discretion, and create legal standards for assessing fiscally critical elements. *See also supra* notes 36–41.

[163] ICSID Convention, *supra* note 43, at art. 61(2); ICSID, WORKING PAPER, *supra* note 11, at 124.

[164] ICSID, PROPOSED RULES, *supra* note 11, at Proposed Arb. Rule 19(6); *id.* at Proposed AF Arb. Rule 19(6).

[165] *Id.* at Proposed Arb. Rule 19(4); *id.* at Proposed AF Arb. Rule 29(4); *see also* ICSID, WORKING PAPER, *supra* note 11, at 124–26.

An implicit question, however, is whether normative clarity is desirable. While commercial arbitration is arguably different, ITA involves state responsibility and treaty interpretation, and systematic legitimacy demands ITA provide a rule-of-law function. This means that there is tangible value in offering pockets of predictability and clarity. Costs are tangible, with risks arguably affecting investors and states in equal measure. Costs implicate the utility of arbitration over other processes; and understanding ITA costs could aid dispute resolution efficiency. Cost issues should be relatively politically neutral, particularly compared to hotly contested issues related to jurisdiction, merits, and damages; and costs are an area for clear rules—or at least improved guidance—about how tribunals can and should exercise discretion.[166] To this end, ICSID's proposed reform sets a solid initial tone, directing more precision and identifying factors for consideration, although stakeholders may wish to expand the list to reflect strategic objectives.

Recalling that legal scholars and economists have spilled a considerable amount of ink analyzing incentives and efficiencies of different fee regimes, none of that research has "resulted in agreement as to the relative social utility of [fee-shifting] rules."[167] Chapter 6 explored the three paradigms for cost assessments, namely a loser-pays approach, a pay-your-own-way approach, and a factor-dependent approach. Each normative baseline has its own relative value.

The pay-your-own-way approach, which fails to ever shift costs, has certain benefits. First, normatively, requiring parties to be responsible for their respective fees and half of tribunal fees offers equality of treatment and mimics ITA's public international law roots.[168] Second, it generates predictability that parties can use to orient their decisions.[169] Knowing they will bear their own costs, parties should theoretically pursue the most efficient arguments and know likely tribunal costs. A loser-pays rule can involve greater stakes and decreased marginal costs and may generate more adjudication costs,[170] as some experimental literature found that implementing a "loser-pays" model increased average adjudication costs and the predicted efficiencies from reducing frivolous litigation (or strategic attorney behavior) were not realized.[171] Third, self-liability for costs can facilitate settlement, with parties making informed choices about the net value of pursuing arbitration, whereas parties affected by

---

[166] Franck, *supra* note 2?.

[167] Theodore Eisenberg & Geoffrey P. Miller, *The English Versus the American Rule on Attorney Fees: An Empirical Study of Public Company Contracts*, 98 CORNELL L. REV. 327, 334–35 (2013); *see also* Avery W. Katz & Chris William Sanchirico, *Fee Shifting in* PROCEDURAL LAW AND ECONOMICS 271–73 (Chris William Sanchirico ed., 2012); Chapter 6.

[168] John Y. Gotanda, *Attorney's Fees Agonistes: The Implications of Inconsistency in the Awarding of Fees and Costs in International Arbitrations*, 5–8 (Villanova Univ. School of Law Pub. Law & Legal Theory, Working Paper No. 2010-01, 2009), http://bit.ly/18KKgSK (last visited Aug. 17, 2018).

[169] *See* Gotanda, *supra* note 45, at 323 ("the major advantage of the pay-your-own-way principle is that it provides a clear and predictable rule").

[170] Eisenberg & Miller, *supra* note 167, at 336–37; John J. Donohue III, *The Effects of Fee Shifting on the Settlement Rate: Theoretical Observations on Costs, Conflicts, and Contingency Fees*, 54 LAW & CONTEMP. PROBS. 195, 202 (1991).

[171] *See* Eisenberg & Miller, *supra* note 167, at 339–41 (gathering sources). One study found that one-way pro-plaintiff fee-shifting rules did not increase the number of lawsuits filed, suggesting cost-shifting standards need not create an unreasonable burden on the courts, but the new rule increased the number of cases proceeding to trial and the degree of plaintiff success. *Id.* at 340; Susanne Di Pietro et al., *Alaska Judicial Council, Alaska's English Rule: Attorney's Fee Shifting in Civil Cases*, 79–90, 106–18, 138–42 (1995), http://bit.ly/13wvYXr (last

cognitive illusions such as optimism bias, confirmation bias, and loss aversion may view cost-shifting as an inducement to continue adjudication.[172] Fourth, arbitrating costs adds an additional layer of argumentation, with parties compiling costs and briefing costs in an additional round of adjudication. Eliminating such briefing eliminates the costs of arbitrating costs. Finally, avoiding cost-shifting may prevent over-deterrence, which could detrimentally influence sovereign regulatory choices or deter investors from productive investment decisions.[173]

There are, however, drawbacks of the pay-your-own-way approach and potential benefits from a loser-pays rule. With worries about guerilla tactics in ITA and abusive behavior by parties and counsel, removing tribunal discretion can increase incentives for parties to engage in deleterious behavior during arbitration (knowing there will be no fiscal sanction) and fails to reward parties for success in reasonably pursuing or defending claims. While the loser-pays approach stands as the theoretical opportunity to deter unmeritorious litigation,[174] there are challenges with identifying legal correctness (particularly without an appellate body), which likely permit the theoretical value from materializing. Meanwhile, cognitive illusions could affect judgments about likely success ex ante, making it difficult to distinguish among unmeritorious and reasonable claims. Optimism bias could skew parties' assessments of the merits of their positions, and representativeness, recency, and availability can skew counsel's assessment of relative success by focusing on cases that come readily to mind or because the dispute seems to mimic (or represent) a recent case—even though it may be unrepresentative in other material respects. Should stakeholders, however, focus on statistical base rates and variables linked with outcomes,[175] the incentives of a loser-pays rule may function more effectively.[176] Whether parties, counsel, and others can set aside their cognitive illusions, however, is another matter; and experimental research demonstrated that cognitive illusions have influenced decisions by international arbitration experts.[177]

---

visited Aug. 17, 2018); Douglas C. Rennie, *Rule 82 & Tort Reform: An Empirical Study of the Impact of Alaska's English Rule on Federal Civil Case Filings*, 29 ALASKA L. REV. 1, 6 (2012).

[172] Steven M. Shavell, *Suit, Settlement, and Trial: A Theoretical Analysis Under Alternative Methods for the Allocation of Legal Costs*, 11 J. LEGAL STUD. 55, 65–66 (1982). Settlements may be suboptimal as they may deprive the legal system of precedent or reflect inaccurate estimates of underlying liability given asymmetric information or perceived differences in risk. Eisenberg & Miller, *supra* note 167, at 337–39; *see also* Owen Fiss, *Against Settlement*, 93 YALE L.J. 1073 (1984); John P. Gould, *The Economics of Legal Conflicts*, 2 J. LEGAL STUD. 279, 296 (1973).

[173] *See, e.g.,* Harold J. Krent, *Explaining One-Way Fee Shifting*, 79 VA. L. REV. 2039, 2042, 2046, 2076–82 (1993).

[174] Scholars explore how loser-pays rules can reduce net costs (minimizing parties' incentives to increase costs) and promote settlement. Albert W. Alschuler, *Mediation with a Mugger: The Shortage of Adjudicative Services and the Need for a Two-Tier Trial System in Civil Cases*, 99 HARV. L. REV. 1808, 1830–31 (1986); Eisenberg & Miller, *supra* note 167, at 336; John J. Donohue III, *Effects of Fee Shifting on the Settlement Rate: Theoretical Observations on Costs, Conflicts, and Contingency Fees*, 54 LAW & CONTEMP. PROBS. 195, 202–08 (1991); Chapter 6.

[175] *See* Franck & Wylie, *supra* note 18.

[176] Eisenberg & Miller, *supra* note 167, at 334–36; Avery Katz, *The Effect of Frivolous Lawsuits on the Settlement of Litigation*, 10 INT'L REV. L. & ECON. 3, 4, 17–19 (1990); A. Mitchell Polinsky & Daniel L. Rubinfeld, *Does the English Rule Discourage Low-Probability-of-Prevailing Plaintiffs?*, 27 J. LEGAL STUD. 141 (1998); David Rosenberg & Stephen M. Shavell, *A Model in Which Suits Are Brought for Their Nuisance Value*, 5 INT'L REV. L. & ECON. 3 (1985).

[177] Franck et al., *supra* note 124.

The European Union has focused on adopting the loser-pays rule for investment disputes, albeit in a nuanced way. CETA states: tribunals "shall order that the costs of the proceedings be borne by the unsuccessful disputing party," and other "reasonable" costs of legal representation "shall be borne by the unsuccessful disputing party."[178] Other EU proposals are similar.[179] Yet, the EU concept paper for an international investment court primarily focuses upon one set of outcomes, stating: "[w]e are making investors who bring a case and lose, pay for all the costs of the legal proceedings . . . [to] not only discourage frivolous or unfounded claims but [to make an investor pay for] the litigation costs of the state he has challenged . . . [and g]iven the financial risk, an investor will think twice before bringing any [ITA] claim."[180] While perhaps driven by political messaging objectives, the statement suggests how cognitive illusions possibly affect preferences. The commentary reflects a framing effect (perhaps combined with optimism bias) about court-derived outcomes, or more bluntly, a framing fallacy. By focusing on losing investors paying winning states, the implicit suggestion is: states will win. As the "loser-pays" is theoretically reciprocal, failing to provide an alternate frame underemphasizes the risk of losing states paying the costs of winning investors. Yet, considered from another perspective, it may be possible that EU policymakers fully appreciate the net balance of the potential trade off, are willing to pay the potential price, and see strategic value in the framing. Yet the EU may wish to tailor the narrative to ensure that its member states appreciate both the downsides *and* upsides of the proposal so as to prevent buyer's remorse, lest there be a potential backlash from mismanaged expectations.

One core benefit of the EU's approach is precisely the theoretical uniformity of the loser-pays rule, namely it operates to the benefit of winners—irrespective of who wins. Yet some have suggested, as the broad aim of damages under international law is to wipe out consequences of unlawful acts,[181] that a loser-pays rules should apply to successful investors. Chapter 6 demonstrated, despite facial neutrality, the loser-pays rule operated more reliably in favor of winning investors. Such a one-way fee-shifting for a facially neutral standard is

---

[178] CETA, *supra* note 28, at art. 8.39(5); *see also infra* note 189.

[179] European Union, *Comments to the proposed amendments to the ICSID Rules submitted on behalf of the European Union and its Member States*, ¶¶ 30-31 (undated), https://bit.ly/2Tgmc8W (last visited Dec. 28, 2018); *see also* European Commission, *Internal Draft: Transatlantic Trade and Investment Partnership: Trade in Services, Investment and E-Commerce, Chapter II—Investment*, art. 28(4), https://bit.ly/1UUwWnc (last visited Aug. 17, 2018) ("The Tribunal shall order that reasonable costs incurred by the successful disputing party shall be borne by the unsuccessful disputing party, unless the Tribunal determines that such apportionment is unreasonable in the circumstances of the case. Such a determination may also take into account whether the successful disputing party has acted improperly, for example by raising manifestly frivolous objections . . . Where only some parts of the claims have been successful the costs shall be adjusted, proportionately, to the number or extent of the successful parts of the claims."); *see also* Matthew Hodgson & Alastair Campbell, *The Allocation of Costs in Investment Treaty Arbitration, in* CONTEMPORARY AND EMERGING ISSUES ON THE LAW OF DAMAGES AND VALUATION IN INTERNATIONAL INVESTMENT ARBITRATION 398, 422–24 (Christina L. Beharry ed., 2018) (describing default approaches to cost-shifting in various investment treaties).

[180] European Union, *Concept Paper: Investment in TTIP and Beyond—The Path for Reform* (May 5, 2015), at 3, https://bit.ly/1buplLQ (last visited Aug. 17, 2018); *but see supra* note 160.

[181] Case Concerning the Factory at Chorzów (Germany v. Poland), 1927 P.C.I.J. (ser. A) No. 9 (July 26); *see also Draft Articles on Responsibility of States for Internationally Wrongful Acts*, International Law Commission, art. 31(1), https://bit.ly/1MIyM9V (last visited Aug. 17, 2018) (explaining states must make full reparation for injuries caused by an internationally wrongful act).

imbalanced and unwarranted.[182] Leaving aside data indicating the analyzed ITA caseload was *not* dominated by deep-pocket FT500 investors,[183] pro-claimant cost shifts may only be appropriate when claimants are economically disadvantaged;[184] otherwise, alternative structures may more appropriately address economic inequality while promoting access to justice, equality of arms, and rule-of-law.[185]

A potential revolutionary alternative to the one-way loser-pays rule that more reliably benefits winning investors involves flipping the entire frame, namely implementing a one-way fee-shifting rule that operates in favor of successful states. As masters of treaty language, states could strategically disrupt the statistical pattern of a reliable pro-investor shift and re-orient the scales by providing a one-way cost-shifting rule that operates purely their benefit. The objective would be to generate disincentives for investors to bring claims, redress perceived inequalities in ITA by favoring states, promote enhanced state "policy space," and create a *lex specialis* tribunals must follow.

There are, however, challenges in implementing this thought experiment. Unlike a one-way fee-shift favoring investors to compensate for unlawful acts, treaties do not currently generate affirmative international law liability for investors; it could therefore be viewed as curious to compensate states for a successful defense but without having made an affirmative claim.[186] Moreover, if international investment law values rule-of-law balance, one would hope for an equal procedural playing field where cost rules "cut both ways," rather than operating to the exclusive benefit of only one type of party. A one-way shifting rule operating only in states' favor may overcorrect for the pro-investor results from statistical tests; and states may wish to avoid unfavorable optics where, in an era of rising nationalism, states create rules designed to let them "have their cake and eat it too."[187]

---

[182] *See* David P. Riesenberg, *Fee Shifting in Investor-State Arbitration: Doctrine and Policy Justifying Application of the English Rule*, 60 DUKE L.J. 977, 1009 (2011) ("[where investors] can mobilize the Magic Circle [law firms] to retrieve millions of dollars from a tiny island republic, [it] can hardly be characterized as structurally imbalanced in favor of the respondent").

[183] *See* Chapter 3.

[184] Riesenberg, *supra* note 182, at 1009–10.

[185] There is merit in exploring the CETA model, with specific rules for claims involving natural persons or small and medium-sized enterprises. CETA, *supra* note 28, at art. 8.39(6); *see also* European Commission, *Fact Sheet: A Future Multilateral Investment Court*, MEMO/16/4350 (Dec. 13, 2016), https://bit.ly/2iaLUcG (last visited Aug. 17, 2018) (acknowledging "a multilateral context raise[s] a number of specific issues such as . . . cost allocation"); European Commission, *Fact Sheet on Investment*, 2–3, https://bit.ly/2obHUoA (last visited Aug. 17, 2018) (suggesting the need to make it easier for small investors to access adjudication, including a cap on procedural costs); European Commission, *Why the New EU Proposal for an Investment Court System in TPP Is Beneficial to Both States and Investors* (Nov. 12, 2015), https://bit.ly/1PFkA2E (last visited Aug. 17, 2018) (same). The American Bar Association echoed these concerns, noting a loser-pays rule raises challenges involving access to justice for small and medium-sized entities as well as nonprofit actors. Investment Treaty Working Group, Am. Bar Ass'n on Int'l Law, *Initial Task Force Discussion Paper: Executive Summary & Conclusions and Recommendations*, 15 (Oct. 14, 2016), https://bit.ly/2iqhyUh (last visited Aug. 17, 2018). Chapter 4 revealed the limited proportion of FT500 entities (or an FT500 entity in the corporate chain) and similar proportions of cases involving human beings.

[186] As treaties embed a one-way liability rule on the merits benefitting investors, in theory, a one-way rule on costs benefiting states offers a degree of equilibrium.

[187] *See also* Jeffrey L. Dunoff & Mark A. Pollack, *The Judicial Trilemma*, 111 AM. J. INT'L L. 225 (2017) (exploring challenges in international adjudication involving states).

The third approach involves creating a normative framework for cost-shifting while guiding tribunal discretion using pre-articulated factors. This could include using various standards to justify cost-shifting,[188] which is the approach ICSID now advocates. CETA dabbled with this approach for tribunal costs, starting with the loser-pays baseline but providing discretion in "exceptional circumstances" to apportion costs that are "appropriate in the circumstances of the claim."[189] Sadly, there is no iteration in CETA of what circumstances may be exceptional, functionally leaving the loser-pays rule intact. For parties' legal costs, CETA grants tribunals discretion to consider cost-shifting for only "reasonable" expenses, granting tribunals authority to demarcate between reasonable and unreasonable lawyers' fees and then preventing cost-shifting only when apportionment is "unreasonable in the circumstances of the claim."[190] Retaining massive discretion, CETA's only guidance on reasonableness is that PLC should be adjusted proportionately to "the number or extent of the successful parts of the *claims*."[191] Textually, it includes no opportunity to proportionately adjust for successful *defenses*. The Comprehensive and Progressive Agreement for Trans-Pacific Partnership (CPTPP),[192] a re-styled Trans-Pacific Partnership (TPP),[193] and USMCA are not markedly better. Rather than being more precise with costs and cost-shifting, the general approach was to punt, leaving cost allocations to broad discretion from applicable arbitration rules.[194] While tribunals were expressly permitted to shift costs for "frivolous" claims or defenses,[195] there was no definition or explanation of the contours of what constitutes "frivolous" claims or defenses. Given arbitration's inability to offer an appellate mechanism to assess ex ante which claims or defenses were legally correct, frivolity assessments could become the new proxy for unfettered discretion.

From the standpoint of predictability, the pay-your-own-way norm provides certainty, giving parties both advance warning for budgeting and incentives to be "good stewards" and manage their expenses, knowing they will be unable to recoup fees at the end. This provides foresight for predictive judgment and decision-making. The core weakness is the rule's unbreakable position, which leaves no other mechanism to penalize poor conduct or encourage efficiency. The pay-your-own-way approach also potentially inhibits parties' access to justice and fails to indemnify parties who have, perhaps wrongly, been required to come to the dispute resolution table and expend costs. From a cognitive psychology perspective, the "pay-your-own-way" approach has one other latent difficulty. To the extent that parties spend

[188] *See* Smith, *supra* note 24, 778–79 (exploring factors including rewarding a victorious party; bad-faith claims related to unmeritorious actions, motions, or filings; pro-rata assessment of relative success, consideration of counsel skill, and professionalism; party-derived procedural delays, compliance, evidential misconduct, or professionalism; legal novelty and claim difficulty; and factors such as parties' relative wealth and expenditures); Gotanda, *supra* note 45, at 434–35 (identifying cost-shifting factors including bad faith, misconduct, or undue hardship).

[189] CETA, *supra* note 28, at art. 8.39(5).

[190] *Id.; see also supra* notes 37, 41 (identifying arbitration rules demarcating costs for reasonable PLC).

[191] CETA, *supra* note 28, at art. 8.39(5) (emphasis added); *see also* EU-Vietnam BIT, *supra* note 141, at art. 3.53(4–5).

[192] Comprehensive and Progressive Agreement for Trans-Pacific Partnership (Mar. 8, 2018), https://bit.ly/2MBjiga (last visited Aug. 17, 2018) [hereinafter CPTPP].

[193] Trans-Pacific Partnership (Feb. 4, 2016), https://bit.ly/2Lq86O1 (last visited Aug. 17, 2018) [hereinafter TPP].

[194] CPTPP, *supra* note 192, at Ch.9 art. 9.29(3); TPP, *supra* note 191, at Ch. 9 art. 9.29(3); *supra* note 30.

[195] CPTPP, *supra* note 192, at art. 9 29(4) ("If the tribunal determines such claims to be frivolous, the tribunal may award to the respondent reasonable costs and attorney's fees.") *id.* at art 9.23(6) ("In determining whether such an award is warranted, the tribunal shall consider whether either the claimant's claim or the respondent's

money on claims or defenses, those sunk costs likely facilitate an endowment effect. When we "own" items, endowment effects mean we value the possession more than would otherwise be appropriate. Paying for one's own dispute essentially means that investors "buy" a claim and states "buy" a defense. With both parties investing time, money, and emotional energy in the dispute, they may value their positions more by "owning" them through the fiscal investment, creating entrenchment, an inability to resile from a position, or a failure to actively consider alternative forms of dispute resolution. Should stakeholders have treaty language or institutional rules following the pay-your-own-way approach, they should be prepared for the trade-off between predictability and the loss of other benefits, including potential settlement.

The second option—a pure "loser-pays" option—is also suboptimal. Given the inconsistency and breadth of the case law, it may be difficult to know in advance which party will "win" and which party will "lose," making the baseline susceptible to uncertainty and doubling-down on ITA risk. Rather than engaging in a high-stakes poker game involving adverse awards *and* costs, it is preferable to enhance determinacy and coherence by promulgating clearer guidelines for cost assessments. Strategically using costs, and perhaps one-way cost-shifting, to redress perceived imbalances within ITA is a topic worthy of discussion given the reliable variance in how tribunals applied a facially neutral rule.

The third option—a factor-based approach—is the most normatively useful but also potentially most challenging, as it requires a sea change in states' approach to costs. A factor-based approach permits stakeholders to prioritize behaviors that they wish to encourage and "nudge" to maximize desirable conduct.[196] If states wish to caveat arbitrator discretion—providing more guidance to tribunals and increasing certainty—they can and should do so in treaties[197] they negotiate and renegotiate. States must expressly make a normative choice about the factors they identify as the most appropriate and compelling. Chapter 7 suggests the most "naturally" occurring factors were relative success, situational equities, and concern about party conduct during proceedings. These are, fundamentally, the three core factors ICSID has proposed using.[198] Should states, however, wish to reinforce these factors, they can articulate these standards in treaties. If, however, states wish to incentivize other aspects—such as access to justice or other fairness considerations—this means expressly incorporating additional factors such as public policy considerations or equality of arms. Likewise, if states wish to increase settlement opportunities, they could require tribunals to consider the cost implications of meritorious arguments or the social utility of claims or defenses during the proceedings,[199] particularly should ICSID decline to include these standards in its recalibration of cost-shifting criteria.

---

objection was frivolous, and shall provide the disputing parties a reasonable opportunity to comment."); *see also* TPP, *supra* note 193, at arts. 9.23(6), 9.29(4) (same).

[196] *See, e.g.*, Stephan W. Schill, *Arbitration Risk and Effective Compliance: Cost-Shifting in Investment Treaty Arbitration*, 7 J. World Inv. & Trade 653, 666, 669 (2006) (suggesting cost-shifting can "channel the behavior" to preserve arbitral efficiency); Frances Kahn Zemans, *Fee Shifting and the Implementation of Public Policy*, 47 Law & Contemp. Prob. 187 (1984).

[197] Andrea K. Bjorklund, *Investment Treaty Arbitration Decisions as* Jurisprudence Constante, *in* International Economic Law: The State and Future of the Discipline 265 (Colin Picker et al. eds., 2008).

[198] ICSID, Working Paper, *supra* note 11, at 121–26.

[199] *See, e.g.*, Chapter 7; Jackeline Nolan-Haley, *Mediation Exceptionality*, 78 Ford. L. Rev. 1247, 1248–49, 1256–63 (2009) (exploring how national cost-shifting law incentivize settlements).

One might imagine treaty text incorporating specific costs provisions, defining PLC and TCE, and identifying parties' capacity to agree on costs, but providing a normative default. That default, like ICSID's proposed revisions, would require tribunals to identify factors affecting cost assessments at an early stage, permitting tribunals to assess costs at any stage, requiring all costs decisions to include references to legal authority and reasoning, and requiring transparency on cost details, particularly in final awards.[200] States could then choose the standards tribunals must use in allocating costs, including parties' relative success, whether cost-shifting would be equitable given parties' behavior during the arbitration, parties' settlement efforts, and policy factors states identify as central to their sovereign objectives.[201]

Although nudging conduct cannot guarantee behavior or eliminate all discretion, it can encourage stakeholders to consider key variables—and recognize what discretion they have implicitly delegated to arbitrators.[202] By establishing normatively desirable standards that reflect empirical knowledge about actual behavior, stakeholders can move beyond unbridled discretion to encourage useful behavior. Putting parties on notice about the utility of their behavior and the potential merits of claims and defenses provides opportunities to consider other forms of conflict management. Tribunals are also afforded guidance about states' original wishes and are bound by express mandates. While arbitrator discretion would remain, it would be directed toward streamlined variables that parties could use to order their conduct while promoting greater certainty and enhanced predictability.

If stakeholders—particularly states—fail to take control of the pen to address decision-making about ITA costs, there is an implicit delegation to adjudicators to make choices. And those choices could occur in the absence of clear or predictable legal standards and without a recognition of sovereigns' policy preferences. Yet, states' failure to act or the decision to provide minimal guidance is arguably understandable. States may choose to prioritize other policy issues over cost choices, including focusing on the substantive rights in investment treaties or securing the net benefits of trade agreements. Stakeholders may view changing the status quo to identify and rank factors for tribunal consideration in cost-shifting to be burdensome or politically complex. There is also value in leaving decisions to tribunals to deal with the peculiarities of unique disputes. States draft treaties that punt cost decisions to adjudicators, which means parties can: (1) blame arbitrators ex post, as a form of domestic political cover should there be dissatisfaction with the results, rather than taking responsibility ex ante, or (2) ensure arbitrators have as much discretion as possible to carry out their broader mandate given unusual facts, perhaps using costs for negotiated log-rolling[203] to secure agreement on other matters such as liability and damage. These elements by themselves, or in combination, suggest that there can be value in both the status quo and the wild west poker tournament of ITA costs.

---

[200] These could, for example, include "checklist" factors identified earlier. *Supra* note 51.

[201] Rather than direct choice, there could be implied choice by limiting arbitration to institutions with preferred cost-shifting rules. *See* Gotanda, *supra* note 45 (arguing for institutional rules providing a baseline).

[202] *See* Ariely, *supra* note 64 (discussing nudges); Thaler & Sunstein, *supra* note 23 (same).

[203] Log-rolling is a standard practice in negotiation (or mediation) where people exchange support, assistance, and favors for other desired support, assistance, and outcomes. *See, e.g.,* Carrie J. Menkel-Meadow & Andrea Kupfer Schneider, Negotiation: Processes for Problem Solving 127 (2006); Donald G. Gifford, *The Synthesis of Legal Counseling and Negotiation Models: Preserving Client-Centered Advocacy in the Negotiation Context*, 34 UCLA L. Rev. 811 (1987).

Nevertheless, the stakes are high for ITA costs, given the sheer fiscal amounts involved. One would hope, as would Aristotle,[204] that adjudication involving international law would serve a rule-of-law function, rather than a rule of intuition. Yet, making the strategic decision to delegate costs to adjudicators without clear, determinate, or predictable bases for exercising authority means—after the fact—stakeholders cannot and should not be surprised. When parties outsource nearly unfettered discretion (and provide no structural safeguards or otherwise guide interpretation), they should face the reality that costs divergence and subsequent party dissatisfaction with cost allocation is likely. To pretend otherwise is disingenuous and imposes an unrealistic burden on dispute resolution. Stakeholders cannot have it both ways. It is improper to demand precision and predictability without providing a basis for making precise choices. The better choice is to recognize the divergence in normative options, appreciate the risk of doing nothing, and then prioritize elements of greatest value.

Normatively, there is value in states, institutions, and parties building structural safeguards to control the time required to resolve disputes and provide greater clarity for cost allocation. In theory, beyond those already mentioned, various structural safeguards could constructively affect costs. The most straightforward way of enhancing the predictability of cost allocation is to be more precise and careful when addressing normative standards for cost shifting. But there are other opportunities. Creating an appellate body could provide clearer guidance about legally correct outcomes ex ante,[205] so parties can make better assessments about a case's relative value and choose the most appropriate dispute resolution method. Similarly, joint state interpretive commissions or crafting more precise treaty language could offer greater clarity about the meaning and application of investment law, increasing the certainty and reliability of the application of substantive legal principles. Likewise, as discussed in connection with ICSID's proposed reforms, so could creating a working group on best practices for cost-containment and procedural integrity.

There is much work to do in terms of implementing evidence-based normative reforms for the management of international investment conflict. The good news is that, with the enhanced public focus, there is an unusual opportunity to implement constructive change that promotes rule-of-law and anti-bullying values, provided we avoid the pernicious influence of cognitive illusions and focus upon the broad variance of stakeholder experience.

VI. Conclusion

Costs will likely continue to be the "sting in the tail" at the end of a complicated case, and law should strive to manage expectations, decrease unnecessary negative effects, increase certainty, and promote procedural justice rather than sewing confusion for material fiscal exposure, that affects businesses and sovereign choices. While the preliminary descriptive models identified some variables working together to impact costs, there are undoubtedly

---

[204] *See* Aristotle, The Politics of Aristotle, book III, ch. xi § 19, at 127 (Ernest Barker trans., Oxford 1946) ("Rightly constituted laws should be the final sovereign; and personal rule, whether it be exercised by a single person or a body of persons, should be sovereign only in those matters on which law is unable, owing to the difficulty of framing general rules for all contingencies, to make an exact pronouncement.").

[205] *See* Franck, *supra* note 92.

others—and those variables may evolve as stakeholders make decisions to change the normative boundaries of both the adjudication process and costs.

Understanding the utility of ITA and making appropriate choices about the future of international investment law requires a more dynamic and nuanced understanding of the operation and impact of ITA costs; but, at least now, there is a baseline from which to start. More detailed data and analyses could aid the assessment of structural solutions that could involve major sunk costs, such as the creation of an investment court, constructing a standing small-claims facility, or promulgating a legal assistance center for small investors or developing states. Without data, it is easy to make normative choices in an information vacuum—and perhaps generate choices reflecting intuition or ideology. It would be unfortunate if ITA costs reform permitted the "tail to wag the dog," relying on unrepresentative, recent, or emotionally memorable events that fail to represent the broad variance of ITA experiences. Given the large fiscal amounts and state sovereignty at stake, we should move beyond intuitive decisions and toward evidence-based reform in an area with critical implications for the international political economy.

With targeted reforms that promote greater costs transparency, increase support for non-adjudicative dispute settlement that work hand in hand with adjudication, use and identify cost assessment norms earlier, and adopt factor-dependent approaches to cost-shifting that incentivize constructive and cost-efficient conduct, ITA reforms stand a chance of promoting cost-containment and predictability, while offering higher quality options. The core objective should be to foster rule-of-law adjudication that is efficient, fair, reliable, and rationalized, enabling stakeholders to implement structural safeguards focusing on appropriate dispute resolution to promote cost containment, predictability, and sustainable conflict management.

Throughout this book—in analyses, footnotes, syntheses, and appendices—there have been acknowledgments of the potential limitations of data, analyses, and the inferential value for normative choices. There is also a recognition that others, coming later and asking different research questions, may explore more variables with alternative definitions and use other tests to advance knowledge. Yet this book's core objective has been to use data-driven insights to correct the potential negative effects of cognitive illusions, while recognizing that human nature inevitably injects error. At the close of this book and particularly for normative reforms, reiterating the need for prudence is proper. The recommendations were not typically tested experimentally,[206] meaning a disconnect among data, inferences, and recommended reforms remains possible.[207]

We are then left with choices about how best to value available, imperfect information. While no empirical research is perfect—just as no form of knowledge is perfect—provided it is methodologically sound ex ante and limitations are identified, empiricism is preferable to no research at all. As a form of knowledge acquisition, data is in many senses superior to the substitution of political power, chance, instinct, personal opinion, intentional manipulation,

---

[206] *But see* Franck et al., *supra* note 124.

[207] Identifying cause through experimentation in international law is challenging. Requiring states to engage in behavior due to random assignment to an experimental condition (rather than permitting free exercise of sovereignty) means, as a practical matter, it may not be possible to test normative reform with academic rigor.

or unrepresentative but emotionally "sticky" examples. Yet, one must recognize the challenges of using data from public arbitration awards (rather than broader investment conflict or confidential awards), data that is timebound, missing data deriving from omissions by tribunals (and potentially parties or counsel), limited variables, omitted variables, null-results that could reflect power problems, and under-specified models. To address these challenges with humility and honesty, the book has strived to frame the data against other data, explore variables using multiple definitions, conduct multiple tests, identify sample size required (typically more than 700 cases) to identify potentially latent effects, and urge caution even for reliable effects. Ultimately, the research is part of an evolutionary landscape, and the research must continue, as costs are serious and should not be swept under the rug.

Science, while helpful, is imperfect. Although it can help minimize intuitive blinders, we must nevertheless be cognizant of science's potential limitations, lest there be assertions that science overpromises and under-delivers, and we end up with normative solutions that are worse than the problems we hope to solve. If nothing else, the hope is that this book has aided assessment of conventional wisdom, estimation of error, and the practical operation of dispute settlement, with an eye toward unblinding risk management and opening new opportunities.

At a bare minimum, the objective has been to encourage readers to be more "fox" than "hedgehog."[208] Recognizing the difficulty in deviating from political ideology or intellectual tribalism,[209] the book is a call to entertain the possibility that data offers nuance to contextualize experience. Like the "Blind Men and the Elephant" who experienced different aspects of the same reality, being appreciative of the perspective data brings (and its limitations) facilitates increased accuracy, authentic conversations (rather than debates along established lines), and exploration of new ideas for adding value to the investment treaty dispute settlement choice matrix. We owe it to future generations to implement evidence-based reforms that demonstrate care, precision, foresight, and a concerted effort to provide sustainable, efficient, and rule-of-law international norms. While arguably a Sisyphean challenge[210] as we enter an age of creeping nationalism and social fragmentation, the journey toward fostering constructive dialogue in a contested area of international economic law is one well worth taking.

---

[208] Chapter 2 discussed Philip Tetlock's classic research on expert political judgment, which found that expert judgments generally were not better than random chance. Yet one subcategory of experts *were* more accurate than chance (and other experts). Namely, "foxes" tended to be broader thinkers amenable to receiving new data, including data potentially disrupting what they thought they believed, adjusting their assessments, and making better predictions. In contrast, "hedgehogs" were rigid thinkers, clinging to one core ideological precept; and while hedgehogs may receive more press and public attention, they have made reliably worse predictions. Philip Tetlock, Expert Political Judgment (2005); Philip Tetlock & David Gardner, Superforcasting: The Art and Science of Prediction (2016).

[209] Pinker, *supra* note 5, at 367–84.

[210] Albert Camus, The Myth of Sisyphus and Other Essays 123 (Justin O'Brien trans., Alfred A. Knopf, Inc. 1955) ("The struggle itself toward the heights is enough to fill a [woman or a] man's heart. One must imagine Sisyphus happy.").

APPENDIX I

Supporting Information on Methodology and Data Introduction

This Appendix provides background information on research methodology. In keeping with best social science protocols,[1] the objective is to promote informed assessments of the analyses, models, and value of derivative inferences. It first explores the unit of analysis and acknowledges the data's limitations. Second, it explains the process of gathering and coding data. Third, it describes transformations necessary to adjust for inflation and to conduct statistical analyses comporting with assumptions underlying those tests. Fourth, it identifies standard research hypotheses and the statistical analyses typically used for exploring various hypotheses. Fifth, it provides basic information about effect sizes and statistical power. Finally, it identifies how readers can access the underlying online materials, namey the Codebook in Appendix IV and the dataset in Appendix V.

I. Unit of Analysis

The unit of analysis was publicly available ITA awards as of January 1, 2012. This included all public awards irrespective of the language rendered, which necessarily included awards rendered in English, Spanish, and French. The method for gathering awards was the same methodology

[1] *See, e.g.,* Susan D. Franck, *The Promise and Peril of Empiricism and International Investment Law Disputes, in* CAMBRIDGE COMPENDIUM OF INTERNATIONAL COMMERCIAL AND INVESTMENT ARBITRATION (Andrea Bjorklund et al., eds., forthcoming 2019) (describing how to identify hallmarks of quality social science research and derivative best practices).

Arbitration Costs. Susan D. Franck.

used in previous research.[2] As there was no single agreed repository for ITA awards, Professor Newcombe's website, *ITAlaw.com*, was the primary source. This source was supplemented and cross-checked using resources such as the UNCTAD website, the ICSID website, the *ICSID Review*, and other sources.[3]

International arbitration, depending partially on applicable law, varies in the doctrinal definition of "award" and distinguishes among types of tribunal activity. For example, awards—namely elements of cases that resolve dispositive key legal issues—under the ICSID Convention[4] or under the UNCITRAL Model Law[5] have specific, but slightly different, meanings.

As this research cuts across all ITA cases, irrespective of doctrinal regime or venue, it adopted a definition of "award" to permit comparison of ITA cases irrespective of whether the case derived from the ICSID Convention or New York Convention. Namely, an "award" was a tribunal's written document[6] making a binding decision on one of four substantive phases of an arbitration or otherwise finally disposed of the dispute, namely awards on: (1) jurisdiction, (2) merits, (3) damages, (4) allocation of costs, or (5) settlement agreements or other orders indicating a case

---

[2] Susan D. Franck, *Empirically Evaluating Claims About Investment Treaty Arbitration*, 86 N.C. L. Rev. 1, 16–20 (2007).

[3] The U.N. Conference on Trade and Development (UNCTAD) Database of Treaty-Based Investor-State Dispute Settlement Cases was historically available at http://bit.ly/17JUSlY (last visited Aug. 11, 2014) but cases have since moved to the new Investment Policy Hub. *See* U.N. Conference on Trade and Dev., *Investment Policy Hub*, http://investmentpolicyhub.unctad.org (last visited Aug. 18, 2018).ICSID awards are searchable at http://bit.ly/13VxMvj. ICSID cases are also available in print form, including cases like AIG Capital Partners, Inc. v. Republic of Kazakhstan, ICSID Case No. ARB/01/6, Award (Oct. 7, 2003), https://bit.ly/2OcHd6N (last visited Aug. 8, 2018), which was referenced on Prof. Newcombe's website, but historically only published in the *ICSID Reports.* Likewise, cases at the Stockholm Chamber of Commerce are accessible through its website at www.sccinstituite.com or the *Stockholm International Arbitration Review.* The availability of awards was cross-checked through other sources, including websites requiring a subscription such as the APPLETON-ISR database on Westlaw, NAFTAclaims.com, the Oxford University Press website investmentclaims.com, and the Investor-State Law Guide database (after it was launched).

[4] Convention on the Settlement of Investment Disputes Between States and Nationals of Other States art. 48, *opened for signature* Mar. 18, 1965, 17 U.S.T. 1270, 575 U.N.T.S. 159 [hereinafter ICSID Convention] (defining an award); ICSID, Rules of Procedure for Arbitration Proceedings, Rules 41, 43–45 (Apr. 10, 2006), https://bit.ly/2sjVvVg (last visited Aug. 14, 2018) (providing rules related to orders for preliminary objection related to jurisdiction and other orders for discontinuance of proceeding for settlement, at the request of parties, for party inaction).

[5] U.N. Comm'n Int'l Trade L. [UNCITRAL] Model Law on International Commercial Arbitration, U.N. Doc. A/40/17/Annex I (June 21, 1985), arts. 17–17J, 30–33 (2006), http://bit.ly/1dMkdSn (last visited Aug. 14, 2018) (defining interim measures as awards capable of enforcement and defining the content of other enforceable awards).

[6] "Awards" are the actual written outcome. Usually each award only pertained to a single case. There are limited exceptions for tribunals writing a single award that embedded several separate cases (often consolidated cases). For those awards, each case was analyzed separately and treated as an individual award. Those awards were: (1) the June 6, 2006 decision for the cases *Canfor v. United States* and *Terminal Forest Prodsucts v. United States*; (2) the July 27, 2006 decision for the cases *Pan American Energy & BP Argentina Exploration v. Argentina* and *BP America v. Argentina*; (3) the August 3, 2006 combined award in *Suez, Sociedad General de Aguas de Barcelona S.A., & Vivendi Universal v. Argentina* and *AWG Group v. Argentina*; (4) the July 19, 2007 decision for the cases *Canfor v. United States, Terminal Forest Products v. United States*, and *Tembec v. United States*; and (5) the March 3, 2010 award for the cases *Kardassopolous v. Georgia* and *Fuchs v. Georgia.*

was dismissed or discontinued.[7] This definition necessarily means that other decisions that might provide sources of information or insights into the larger dispute resolution process—including interim measures, decisions on confidentiality and transparency, place of arbitration, arbitrator challenges, tribunals' interpretive decisions, ad hoc Annulment Committees and subsequent decisions by national courts—were neither a part of the unit of analysis nor coded.[8] Disputes with only a dispute notice or request for arbitration were also omitted.[9] As this research focused on adjudicative decisions from first instance tribunals, it omitted sources to provide a more nuanced picture of investment conflict and the arbitration life cycle.

There are three elements that must be kept in mind when understanding the dataset in Appendix V, unit of analysis, and derivative inferences. First, the dataset is time-bound and derives from public awards. The population continually evolves, and the research has limitations involving external validity. Awards rendered after January 2012 add additional variance. Yet, as multiple elements of the research demonstrate that core ITA elements have remained stable over time, even with the temporal limitation, and as others conducting post-2012 research have identified similar patterns, the analyses provide a core baseline for consideration; but these limitations must be kept in perspective.

Second, private awards may differ meaningfully from the public awards. The growth in the data from the first analysis to the dataset in Appendix V revealed a small number of awards that were previously private but eventually entered the public domain over time. In the interim, there did not appear to be a meaningful difference between those awards and other awards. Awards that were once private, but later became public, seemed to be reasonably similar to original cases. Even with the possible case selection bias, this may not skew the data collection process. Both investors and states have incentives to disclose awards irrespective of whether they win. Investors, for example, may wish to disclose awards because shareholders view the information of the investor-favorable result and enhanced commercial certainty positively. Likewise, states may believe that informing the public of the state's success may promote transparency, restore government confidence, or provide political utility. It is possible that where they have lost but paid an award, states will find value in demonstrating the decreased risk to other foreign investors or highlighting their compliance with rule of law. On balance, it is possible, but not certain, that case selection effects of analyzing public awards did not materially skew the data.

Finally, the chosen unit of analysis means that other investment-related conflicts were not coded. These conflicts might relate to either formalized investment treaty disputes or conflicts that never crystalized into formal disputes. First, ITA disputes with a dispute notice—such as those listed on the ICSID website—could be in the arbitration pipeline, but nonetheless constitute disputes about which there is some public discussion. It is unfortunately not possible to reliably assess information about those disputes, since a verifiable record is unavailable. Unfortunately, when ICSID publicly registers a case, it does not provide information to identify whether the

---

[7] This methodology is similar to other research analyzing ICSID awards addressing, jurisdiction, merits, settlements or other orders for discontinuances. *See* Daphna Kapeliuk, *Collegial Games: Analyzing the Effect of Panel Composition on Outcome in Investment Arbitration*, 31 REV. LITIG. 267, 302 (2012).

[8] After drafting the content of this Appendix, multiple cases have come before national courts reviewing ITA awards, such as BG Group v. Republic of Argentina, 134 S. Ct. 1198 (2014).

[9] Cases with dispute notices or arbitration requests were omitted, as the limited information prevented valid and reliable coding.

dispute involves a treaty breach or some other jurisdictional basis, such as domestic investment or commercial law. It is therefore impossible to identify the case selection effect from analyzing formalized disputes that have not generated a public award or other verifiable document. This limitation affects basic demographic information—such as that related to the identity of parties, arbitrators, lawyers, and non-disputing parties. This will likely be redressed as more awards become public, particularly if ICSID's reform efforts described in Chapter 9 permit the publication of more information about disputes.

Non-formalized investment-related problems likely arise daily; and no current dataset measures the full scope of investment conflict. There are various reasons for the difficulty in understanding latent conflict. States and investors could use alternative dispute resolution strategies—such as negotiation, mediation, or ombuds—to address conflicts before an investor submits a formal dispute notice; where this occurs, and there are no reporting obligations, the problem would never be recorded. Additionally, after client-counseling and exploring costs of dispute resolution, an investor might abandon its claim or seek alternative redress, or a state may modify a policy or engage in other activity minimizing risk of suit and/or bring its state policy into conformity with domestic and international law. The dataset therefore is only the tip of investment-treaty conflict. The full range of unreported and informal disputes is likely larger and potentially unknowable.[10] By focusing on public awards, the research necessarily omits a larger context. Nevertheless, narrowing the field of inquiry generates some basic information and offers opportunities for future research.

II. Dataset Creation

Since initial research from 2006 ("Generation 1" or "G1" research) on 102 different arbitration awards in 82 different cases, the dataset in Appendix V expanded considerably. With five additional years of data, the number of publicly available awards increased by approximately 250%, and the number of cases increased by 300%. Coding of public awards occurred over three time periods. G1 data was collected from the beginning of the first ITA case until June 1, 2006. Generation 2 ("G2") data was collected from public awards between June 1, 2006 and June 1, 2009. Generation 3 ("G3") data was collected from awards were within the public domain between June 1, 2009 and January 1, 2012. Cases that were not available before January 2012 were not coded.[11] G2 and G3

[10] *See* W. Michael Reisman, *International Investment Arbitration and ADR: Married but Best Living Apart*, 24 ICSID Rev.–Foreign Inv. L. J. 185, 186 (2009) (identifying "the number of actual disputes going to arbitration seems to be a miniscule fraction of the universe" of investment and investment conflict).

[11] These cases might include *Gallo*, where a U.S. citizen sued Canada under NAFTA in connection with an abandoned mine that was to serve as a waste disposal site, claiming CAD$105 million in damage. The tribunal dismissed the claim on jurisdictional grounds (US$0 award), required parties to pay their own costs, and required claimant to pay 100% of the tribunal's costs (US$900,000). *See* Vito G. Gallo v. Government of Can., UNCITRAL, Award (Sept. 15, 2011), http://bit.ly/1dYOApH (last visited Aug. 14, 2018). Another example is the final award in *Occidental v. Ecuador*, where U.S. companies sued Ecuador in connection with oil exploration, claiming over US$1,000,000,000. Claimants were awarded US$1,769,625,000 for expropriation and fair and equitable treatment violations, with pre-award interest compounded annually at the rate of 4.188%. The tribunal dismissed Ecuador's counterclaim (except for an element that led to a 25% reduction in investor's damage claim), required each party to bear its own costs, and split tribunal costs 50/50. *See*

data collection also looked for awards that, although once private, had become public. During every generation of coding, there was always at least one coder who had been involved in previous coding.[12] All coders received extensive four-week training, coding a core set of practice materials and using the Codebook before working with live data.

Multiple coders—two coders for G1 and G3 and three coders for G2—coded every single piece of raw data from awards. Out of the 266 raw variables coded in the three generations of data collection, there were 68,476 different raw coding decisions. Of those, there were 3,599 disagreements, which meant there was a 94.7% rate of inter-coder agreement after initial coding assessments. All divergences were then scrutinized during multiple inter-coder reliability meetings, where coders discussed every divergence and created an agreed code for the dataset. The hope was that the rigor and reference to mutually agreed standards in the Codebook would ensure coding was reliable, minimize the risk of error, and enhance the quality of derivative analyses. Of note, no funding—other than annual summer research grants provided by academic institutions where the author was employed, including American University Washington College of Law, and an small seed grant in 2005 from the University of Nebraska to fund the initial reserach—was used to finance this research. Rather, the primary source of value derived from the sweat equity of the researcher and those people who typically volunteered their time. *See* Acknowledgements.

Using 272 different awards and a Codebook (Appendix IV) with detailed coding explanations which was over 130 pages in its original Word format, the dataset (Appendix V) generated over 500 variables and over 140,000 discrete pieces of data. Not every single element of potential variance within the universe was coded, as some variables either do not exist or were not pertinent to the research questions, which was initially and primarily focused on cost elements. Making the effort to code hundreds of variables, given the limited time and finances available, was the primary objective; and retroactively creating a single variable can be a time-consuming process involving months and years of sweat equity. Should readers wish to create alternative methodologically sound variables to add nuance to the data and analyses, they are welcome to invest the time and effort to use proper social science standards to do so, using the dataset as a baseline.

As the Codebook describes, some of the initial raw data was transformed. For example, nationality was transformed to consider, at the time the tribunal rendered the award, the "development status" of investors, respondents, and arbitrators, using preexisting classifications from entities including the United Nations and World Bank. Similarly, fiscal data had originally been converted, where necessary, to a common currency of U.S. dollars using Codebook protocols; these amounts were adjusted for inflation using the Consumer Price Index. Additionally, all fiscal data (such as amounts claimed, awarded, and costs) were analyzed for skewness and transformed to reduce risk of error and ensure data conformed to underlying mathematical assumptions of statistical tests.[13]

When there is not one uniform understanding of a term, "a proxy variable must be used."[14] While no single definition is perfect, the key is to "produce definitions that are adequate to permit

---

Occidental Exploration & Prod. Co. v. Republic of Ecuador [II], ICSID Case. No. ARB/06/11, Award (Oct. 5, 2012), http://bit.ly/14wVZDd (last visited Aug. 14, 2018).

[12] Susan Franck and Melanie Neely coded G1 data. *See* Franck, *supra* note 2, at 1. Jason Ratigan, Gene Hamilton, and Brandon Hasbrouck coded G2 data. Susan Franck and Jason Ratigan coded G3 data.

[13] *See infra* Section III.

[14] Peter Kennedy, Guide to Econometrics 5 (5th ed. 2003).

a replication of all important respects by another researcher."[15] Defining "development status," for example, requires care, as there is no consistent legal definition of this concept. Even the World Trade Organization permits member states to self-define development level.[16] Without a pre-defined or exclusive measure for legal phenomenon, it is prudent to use measures deriving from "judgments made for entirely different purposes by *other researchers*."[17] Like earlier research,[18] this research used two established measures of development status but added a third.

First, development status was operationalized as a binary variable—OECD Status—that derived from a state's membership in the OECD. OECD membership is generally, but not always, associated with higher levels of development and offers a blunt proxy. States become OECD members through a complicated accession process designed to demonstrate a willingness to embrace a market economy, democratic pluralism, and respect for human rights.[19] Although OECD membership has been fairly stable,[20] the possibility of change, particularly with the 2010 expansion, was addressed by coding for OECD membership at the date of the award, which was the date for other decisions, such as currency conversions and inflation adjustments. This meant, for example, in *CSOB v. Slovak Republic* (1999), Slovakia was coded as "0" to reflect that it was not an OECD member; but in *Eureko v. Slovak Republic* (2010), Slovakia was coded as "1" to reflect its December 2000 OECD membership.

Second, development was operationalized using a more sensitive four-category variable—World Bank Status—deriving from World Bank state classification, namely as High Income, Upper-Middle Income, Lower-Middle Income and Low Income.[21] The World Bank's main criterion for classifying economies is gross national income (GNI) per capita.[22] Like OECD membership, World Bank classifications change over time, and to reflect this, World Bank Status was coded for the date of the award. This meant, in *Lauder v. Czech Republic* (2001), the Czech Republic was coded as an Upper-Middle Income state; but in *Phoenix Action v. Czech Republic* (2009), the Czech Republic was coded as High Income. Similarly, in *EnCana v. Ecuador* (2004), Ecuador

---

[15] MILDRED L. PATTEN, UNDERSTANDING RESEARCH METHODS: AN OVERVIEW OF THE ESSENTIALS 17 (7th ed. 2009) (emphasis omitted).

[16] *See* WORLD TRADE ORGANIZATION, *Who Are the Developing Countries in the WTO?*, http://bit.ly/9EBM08 (last visited Aug. 8, 2014) ("There are no WTO definitions of 'developed' and 'developing' countries. Members announce for themselves whether they are 'developed' and 'developing' countries."); Anu Bradford & Eric A. Posner, *Universal Exceptionalism in International Law*, 52 HARV. INT'L L.J. 1 n.159 (2011) ("WTO rules do not contain a definition of a 'developing country.' Instead, states self-designate themselves as developed or developing countries as part of a political calculus."); Andrew D. Mitchell & Joanne Wallis, *Pacific Pause: The Rhetoric of Special & Differential Treatment, the Reality of WTO Accession*, 27 WISC. INT'L L.J. 663, 696–97 (2010).

[17] GARY KING ET AL., DESIGNING SOCIAL INQUIRY: SCIENTIFIC INFERENCE IN QUALITATIVE RESEARCH 157 (1994) (emphasis in original).

[18] Susan D. Franck, *Development and Outcomes of Investment Treaty Arbitration*, 40 HARVARD INT'L L.J. 436 (2009).

[19] Jan Wouters & Sven Van Kerckhoven, *The OECD and the G20: An Ever Closer Relationship?*, 43 GEO. WASH. INT'L L. REV. 345 (2011).

[20] *See List of OECD Member Countries—Ratification of the Convention on the OECD*, OECD, http://bit.ly/Otiu9R (last visited Aug. 8, 2014).

[21] World Bank analytical classifications were available at http://goo.gl/LrGDO (last visited Aug. 8, 2014).

[22] *Data: How We Classify Countries*, WORLD BANK, http://bit.ly/cgOu7t (last visited Aug. 8, 2014).

was coded as a Low-Middle Income state; but in *Murphy Exploration v. Ecuador* (2010), Ecuador was coded as an Upper-Middle Income state to reflect its higher World Bank classification.

Third, development was operationalized using a continuous variable—HDI Status—that derived from the United Nations Development Programme's (UNDP) Human Development Index (HDI). Developed by Mahbub ul Haq and Amartya Sen to shift conceptions of development from economics to people-centered policies, the HDI evaluates life expectancy, education, and income. As the methodology for coding HDI changed in 2011 and applied retroactively, previously published Human Development Reports were not used to code HDI. Rather, this research used data directly provided by Dr. Milorad Kovacevic, Chief Statistician at the UNDP's Human Development Report Office. All scores Dr. Kovacevic provided used the updated 2011 methodology to re-evaluate historical and current rankings. HDI ranges from 0.0 (undeveloped) to 1.0 (completely developed). As the HDI indicators fluctuated over time, HDI was coded as of the date of the award. This meant, for example, in *Tradex Hellas v. Albania* (1996), Albania's HDI Status was 0.662; but in *Pantechniki v. Albania* (2009), Albania's HDI Status was 0.734. Likewise, in *Sedelmayer v. Russian Federation* (1998), Russia had an HDI Status of .677; but in *RosInvestCo v. Russian Federation* (2010), Russia had an HDI Status of 0.751. In *Loewen v. United States* (2001), the United States' HDI Status was 0.898, and it was similar (0.906) in *Glamis Gold v. United States* (2009).

III. Data Transformations

As described in the Codebook, all fiscal values—including claims, damage awards, investors' legal costs, states' legal costs, tribunal costs and expenses, and any cost shifts—were coded initially in the original currency as originally stated in the date of the award. Any non-U.S. dollar amounts were then converted into U.S. dollars using the date of the award as the appropriate date for currency conversions pursuant to the Codebook protocol. These variables were typically were marked with "CC" to reflect the U.S. dollar as the "Common Currency" and identified in the dataset as the "raw" amount to reflect that the amounts came directly from the award. There were only two material transformations to decrease error in making statistical analyses. The first was to promote adjustments for inflation, and the second was to clean data to ensure it was fit for its purpose in conducting statistical tests.

For the inflation transformation, as the cases spanned awards issued during 1990–2011, as described in the Codebook, each of those fiscal amounts was adjusted for inflation using a metric from the Consumer Price Index and calculated according to computators directly available from the U.S. federal government to 2011-based values. The objective was to ensure comparisons occurred according to a common scale. Variables with inflation adjustments typically used some form of "CPI" to ensure it was clear where amounts were (and were not) adjusted for inflation.

In order to use inferential statistics properly to test potential relationships, particularly for associative hypotheses exploring potential predictive relationships,[23] variables generally need appropriate levels of skewness. While debate ranges about the proper number, typically accepted levels of

[23] *See* Section IV, *infra*.

skewness are in the -1.0 through 1.0 range,[24] whereas acceptable kurtosis levels are in the -3.0 to 3.0 range. The idea is to ensure the data ranges fit the statistical parameters of the test to ensure a match between the data analyzed and tests performed. When there is a mismatch (i.e., the data analyzed is too skewed), this risks inaccurate results and undermines tests' statistical conclusion validity.[25]

Three standard methods for transformation to permit statistical analysis are trimming, winsorizing, and logging. Winsoring and log transformations, in particular, are standard practices used to reduce data skew and kurtosis to aid the validity of statistical tests.[26]

Trimming requires identifying the range of the distribution, and then isolating the upper and lower bounds to detect outliers in the hinge spread (typically using Tukey's Hinges), so as to pinpoint the acceptable maximum and minimum values. Trimming, however, receives its name because outliers are simply "trimmed" (i.e., removed) from the analysis and never measured, meaning relevant data, that is pertinent to the research hypothesis, is omitted.

Winsorizing involves identifying and then converting extreme values in the data to the upper or lower bounds of the distribution in a manner consistent with the normal curve.[27] Winsorizing data has similarities to trimming—in that it looks for upper and lower bounds using the hinge spread. But rather than eliminating outliers, on the highest end, it substitutes the actual raw value for the highest value from the hinge spread. This ensures the variance attributable to the outlier is not omitted from the analysis, but rather includes the data in a manner that does not disrupt the assumption of statistical test, which would otherwise undermine a test's inferential value.

Logging, like winsorizing, uses all original data—including outliers. It requires taking the original (but skewed) data and applying a logarithmic function to compute a new value.[28]

When inferential statistics were used—particularly comparing means, analyses of variance, correlations, partial correlations, and regressions—the data tested had the lowest skewing and kurtosis(**).[29] Variations were typically identified. For ease of reference, the following Table App. 1 identifies fiscal variables that required transformation, reporting original skewing and kurtosis as well as post-transformation skewing and kurtosis, and identifying values typically analyzed.

---

[24] Some have suggested that the range is ±0.80 while others suggest the amount is ± 2.0. In keeping with more typical protocols, this research used the standard ±1.0 as an indicator of acceptability.

[25] *See* Franck, *supra* note 1.

[26] *See* Valerie P. Hans & Theodore Eisenberg, *The Predictability of Juries*, 60 DePaul L. Rev. 375, 386 (2011) (discussing the value of data transformation to minimize skewness and other problems); Melanie Sauderland & Anna Sagana, *Assessing Nonchoosers' Eyewitness Identificacy Accuracy from Photographic Showups by Using Confidence and Response Times*, 36 L. & Humn. Beh. 394, 396 (2012) (using winsorization to address skewness); Justin Sevier, *Vicarious Windfalls*, 102 Iowa L. Rev. 651, 674–76 (2017) (using "logs" or logarithmic transformations to address skewness).

[27] *See, e.g.*, W.J. Dixon, *Simplified Estimation from Censored Normal Samples*, 31 Annals Math. Stat. 385, 385 (1960); John W. Tukey, *The Future of Data Analysis*, 33 Annals Math. Stat. 1, 18–19 (1962).

[28] Krishnan D. Broota, Experimental Design in Behavioural Research 48 (1989); *see also* Theodore Eisenberg, Geoffrey Miller & Roy Germano, *Attorneys' Fees in Class Actions: 2009–2013*, 92 N.Y.U. L. Rev. 937, 942 (2017) (discussing data logging and indicating attorneys' fees were "transformed into base 10 logarithms").

[29] ** denotes data typically analyzed for inferential tests due to acceptable skewing and kurtosis, that was used when needed to adjust for test assumptions in a way that neither lead to omission of data nor was incompatible with statistical conclusion validity. Raw data with outliers, but adjusted for inflation, was typically used for analyzing: (1) descriptive data, to aid comprehension using an intuitively understandable scale, or (2) medians, as medians are less susceptible to skewing and tests exploring medians are not normally tested using transformed data. *See also infra* note 40.

TABLE APP. I.A

Table Identifying Variables, Skewness, Skewness Standard Error, Sample Size (n), Kurtosis, and Kurtosis Standard Error for Fiscal Values and Case Length.

Variable Name	Skewness	Skewness Standard Error	n (number)	Kurtosis	Kurtosis Standard Error
CC_Claimed_CPI (Inflation-Adjusted Amount Claimed)	6.278	.224	117	43.602	.444
CCC_CPI_trim (trimmed version)	1.445	.239	102	1.614	.474
CCC_CPI_winz (winsorized version)	1.125	.224	117	−.121	.444
CCC_CPI_log ** (logged version)	.86615	−.500	117	2.283	.444
CC_Awarded_CPI (Inflation-Adjusted Amount Awarded)	3.938	.192	159	17.969	.383
CCA_CPI_All_trim (trimmed version for *all* cases)	2.58	.212	131	6.396	.420
CCA_CPI_All_Winz (winsorized version for *all* cases)	1.210	.192	159	−.343	.383
CCA_CPI_All_log** (logged version for *all* cases)	.639	.192	159	−1.526	.383
CCA_CPI_1$_trim (trimmed version *subset* of awards when investors obtained damages)	1.593	.322	55	1.633	.634
CCA_CPI_1$_winz (winsorized version *subset* of awards where investors obtained damages)	1.472	.314	58	1.008	.618
CCA_CPI_1$_log** (logged version *subset* of awards where investors obtained damages)	−.716	.314	58	.628	.618

(Continued)

TABLE APP. I.A

(Continued)

Variable Name	Skewness	Skewness Standard Error	*n* (number)	Kurtosis	Kurtosis Standard Error
Cplc_CPI (Inflation-Adjusted Claimant Legal Fees)	2.179	.322	55	5.209	.634
CC_Cplc_CPI_trim (trimmed version)	1.213	.333	51	.961	.656
CC_Cplc_CPI_winz (winsorized version)	2.179	.322	55	5.209	.643
CC_Cplc_CPI_log** (logged version)	−.882	.322	55	1.185	.643
Rplc_CPI (Inflation-Adjusted Respondent Legal Fees)	3.228	.309	60	13.204	.608
CC_Rplc_CPI_trim (trimmed version)	.981	.330	52	−.089	.650
CC_Rplc_CPI_winz** (winsorized version)	1.183	.309	60	.191	.608
CC_Rplc_CPI_log (logged version)	−4.510	.309	60	28.697	.608
PLCshift_CPI (Inflation-Adjusted amount of legal fees shifted by tribunal)	2.075	.369	41	5.423	.724
PLCshift_CPI_trim (trimmed version)	1.248	.383	38	.606	.750
PLCshift_CPI_winz (winsorized version)	1.136	.369	41	.063	.724
PLCshift_CPI_log** (logged version)	−.978	.369	41	1.181	.724
CTCE_CPI (Inflation-Adjusted amount claimant contributes to tribunal and administrative expenses)	2.101	.306	61	5.777	.604
C_TCE_CPI_trim (trimmed version)	.761	.319	56	.302	.628
C_TCE_CPI_winz** (winsorized version)	.789	.306	61	−.271	.604
C_TCE_CPI_log (logged version)	1.704	−2.520	61	4.980	.604

TABLE APP. I.A

(Continued)

Variable Name	Skewness	Skewness Standard Error	*n* (number)	Kurtosis	Kurtosis Standard Error
RTCE_CPI (Inflation-Adjusted amount respondent contributes to tribunal and administrative expenses)	3.052	.306	61	12.100	.604
R_TCE_CPI_trim (trimmed version)	1.054	.314	58	.006	.618
R_TCE_CPI_winz (winsorized version)	1.084	.306	61	.069	.604
R_TCE_CPI_log** (logged version)	−.850	.306	61	−1.220	.605
TotalPLC_CPI (Inflation-Adjusted total amount of parties combined legal fees and expenses)	2.776	.333	51	9.665	.656
TotalPLC_CPI_trim (trimmed version)	1.102	.347	47	.368	.681
TotalPLC_CPI_winz (winsorized version)	1.212	.333	51	.492	.656
TotalPLC_CPI_log** (logged version)	−.386	.333	51	.599	.656
TCEtotal_CPI (Inflation-Adjusted total amount of tribunal fees and administrative expenses)	2.883	.306	61	10.220	.604
TotalTCE_CPI_trim (trimmed version)	.794	.314	58	−.033	.618
TotalTCE_CPI_winz (winsorized version)	.897	.306	61	.026	.604
TotalTCE_CPI_log** (logged version)	−.766	.306	61	1.356	.605
CaseLength_Details**	1.075	.195	155	2.370	.378
CaseLength	1.158	.212	131	3.150	.420

IV. Hypothesis Testing and Standard Statistical Tests

Statistical tests were performed using normal social science protocols. As the dataset was built in SPSS, SPSS was used for conducting all analyses. Readers interested in learning more are encouraged to take classes in social science research methodology, read social science textbooks, and explore how to use social science data processing software. The author received postgraduate training in statistics and statistical analysis at the University of Nebraska in its Law and Psychology Program with Professor Calvin P. Garbin. Coursework from Dr. Garbin is available online: http://psych.unl.edu/psycrs/. Although the course design has shifted somewhat since the author's training, readers are encouraged to consider exploring the research design and analysis materials in both Psychology 941 and Psychology 942. To provide a primer to aid novice readers in understanding methodological choices, this section explains tests used and the basis for the choice.

There are three types of research hypotheses in empirical research, namely: descriptive, associative, and causal. Descriptive hypotheses test the world around us by defining, classifying, or measuring social phenomenon. This often requires a means of separating, discriminating, or distinguishing among similar experiences. The objective is to use statistics to identify basic information, describing the world using a common nomenclature that can be readily understood. This often involves counting data and providing basic identification and definitional information. In ITA this might include: which industries are involved in disputes, where are cases resolved, which law firms have been involved in representation, what are the outcomes, and what are the arbitration costs? Even in a descriptive hypothesis, a researcher may have to make distinctions and classify the variable using categories. For example, the development status of states—depending upon which ex ante metric one uses for operationalizing "development status"—could be a two-category binary variable (i.e., OECD or non-OECD member), a four-category variable (i.e., World Bank's Development Status), or a continuous variable (i.e., UNDP's Human Development Index on a scale of 0–1).

The Codebook, Appendix IV, offers a detailed definition and explanation of the coding and classification process of each variable. When descriptive variables were analyzed to test descriptive hypotheses—including information in Chapters 3–7—information was provided about the category of the variables involved, the number of cases (*n*), and where appropriate for the research question the means (*M*), medians, and standard deviations (*SD*). While standard error (*SE*) terms were not always reported, they are easily replicable through an SPSS analysis; and in any event, *SD* was included as a metric of potential error and variation. As descriptive analyses are not inferential tests, raw (but inflation-adjusted) data directly from awards was often used.[30]

[30] When analyzing basic descriptive statistics, it is critical to identify the proper unit of analysis, as identified in Chapter 3. Given that the dataset includes nested data (i.e., a single case could spawn multiple awards, but awards were the coded unit of analysis), filters may or may not be necessary to separate out aspects of the dataset for analysis to ensure a proper fit between the hypothesis and the statistical test. For example, where the analysis is focusing on all awards (including final and non-final awards), it is not necessary to filter the analysis. For amounts claimed, it is necessary to use a filter that analyzes the awards with the most recent amounts claimed (pursuant to Codebook protocol), so that the proper claim is analyzed and cases with multiple awards are not double-counted. Where there is a focus on cases with final outcomes or the smaller sub-set of cases involving investor wins, it is necessary to use filters that limit the cases analyzed, so that non-final or other improper awards are excluded and do not skew the analysis.

Second, testing associative hypotheses involves exploring potential patterns, reliable relationships, or group differences among variables.[31] Some might call these "predictive" hypotheses, as the objective is to identify and to predict one phenomenon on the basis of another. Yet, one must never confuse correlation and causation.[32] In a classic example, research found a high positive correlation between murder rates and ice cream sales. Yet, a confounding variable—namely heat—influenced both the increased ice cream sales and the murders.[33]

There are multiple, commonly accepted methodologies for testing potential relationships among variables. Test selection is largely a function of one's research hypothesis and variables.[34] For example, when trying to explore patterns of group differences—where there are two variables that are both categorical in nature (rather than on a continuous numerical scale)—conducting a Pearson's Chi-Square Test of Independence is appropriate.[35] The nonparametric test then evaluates whether there is a meaningful pattern in the relationship between the two variables. The chi-square statistic is frequently used in a 2 x 2 design, where each of the two variables analyzed is binary (and has only two categories each) to assess whether a pattern arose from chance alone.[36] A classic binary categorical variable ($k = 2$) might be OECD status (i.e., is the respondent state an OECD member or not an OECD member), has counsel served as an attorney in an ITA dispute before or not (i.e., is the lawyer a repeat player or not), or birth gender (i.e., was an arbitrator born as a man or a woman). With some care, as it likely requires additional 2 x 2 follow-up analyses after the main Omnibus test, a chi-square test can also analyze variables containing three or more categories.[37] An example of such a categorical variable with multiple conditions would be World Bank Development status, with four categories ($k = 4$), namely High Income, Upper-Middle Income, Lower-Middle Income, and Low Income.

Most of the research in this book, however, relates to costs. Costs, namely direct fiscal amounts, are a continuous variable (not a categorical variable). Therefore, other tests are appropriate for

[31] When analyzing inferential statistics, as it is also important to apply the proper filter. *See supra* note 30. The objective should be to select the proper unit of analysis so there is an appropriate fit between the data analyzed, the test used, and the inferences made.

[32] *See* Franck, *supra* note 1.

[33] ENCYCLOPEDIA OF EPIDEMIOLOGY 234–35 (Sarah Boslaugh ed., 2008).

[34] Tests involve Null Hypothesis Significance Testing (NHST). NHST involves testing the null hypothesis (namely, there is no relationship between variables) against the research hypothesis (namely, there is some relationship among variables), in an effort to falsify and test theory. NHST tests the null hypothesis against the research hypothesis using probabilistic approaches to ascertain whether a relationship is likely to exist to a particular level of certainty. Chris Spattz, *Statistical Techniques and Analysis*, *in* 21ST CENTURY PSYCHOLOGY: A REFERENCE HANDBOOK VOL. 1 48–53 (Stephen F. Davis & William Buckist eds., 2008). Confidence intervals are an alternate way to test, typically yielding similar results to NHST. Confidence intervals use probabilities but focus on identifying a range of values within which a relationship may (or may not) exist, focusing on identifying the range within which the true value of the unknown population parameter may exist. GEOFF CUMMING & ROBERT CALLIN-JAGEMAN, INTRODUCTION TO THE NEW STATISTICS: ESTIMATION, OPEN SCIENCE, AND BEYOND 97–159 (2017); TIMOTHY C. URDAN, STATISTICS IN PLAIN ENGLISH 60–73, 84–89 (2d ed. 2005) NHST can be augmented by including effect sizes (r-values), which are common in tests using confidence intervals, to identify the size and practical significance of reliable differences (or the potential size of any latent effect). For this reason, this book typically provides r-values during significance-testing.

[35] URDAN, *supra* note 34, at 161–63; *see also* ROBERT M. LAWLESS, JENNIFER K. ROBBENNOLT & THOMAS S. ULEN, EMPIRICAL METHODS IN LAW 248–54 (2010) (discussing the chi-square statistic).

[36] Franck, *supra* note 18, at 456–59 (discussing and conducting chi-square tests).

[37] LAWLESS, ET AL., *supra* note 35, at 254–58 (discussing the basic chi-square statistic).

exploring cost-related differences. When one is trying to identify mean differences between groups, for binary variables with two categories, an independent samples *t*-test can analyze meaningful group differences for a normally distributed continuous variable (such as amounts claimed or tribunal costs); [38] and tests may require the use of transformed data comporting with the assumption of a normal distribution.[39] Alternatively, when examining group differences in a binary variable (such as OECD status), a Mann-Whitney *U*-test can evaluate median differences, even using data where means are skewed.[40] To cross-check robustness, therefore, many analyses in this book explore both mean differences (using transformed data with minimal skewing with an inflation adjustment) and median differences (using original but skewed data with an inflation adjustment). As one example, when examining differences in tribunal costs where there is (or is not) a separate opinion, Chapter 8 explored differences in mean tribunal costs and used the test of medians as a robustness check. Likewise, when testing the binary categorical variable either institutional or ad hoc arbitration to assess differences in tribunal costs, more *t*-tests (and *U*-tests) in Chapter 8 analyzed potential differences between the two groups.

When one is interested in group differences—but there are three or more groups involved—across a continuous variable (such as costs, claims, or damages) slightly different tests are required. It is still possible to assess mean group differences when there is a continuous variable (such as tribunal costs), but the test required is somewhat different. Namely, assuming that the data is normally distributed (which requires use of transformed data to address unacceptable skewing or kurtosis), to compare three or more different groups against one independent variable, an independent between-groups factorial Analysis of Variance (ANOVA) is appropriate.[41] Where ANOVAs are conducted, it is also possible to conduct post-hoc follow-up tests to identify if there are any potentially latent differences by making specific comparisons between two groups (i.e., a simple effect). To do so, follow-up tests primarily used Tukey's HSD (Honestly Significant Difference) to demarcate between significant and non-significant simple effects.[42] Relatedly, to compare median group differences across a continuous variable that is not normally distributed, a Kruskall-Wallis test can compare the group differences for a multi-category variable.[43] In this

---

[38] URDAN, *supra* note 34, at 93–96; LAWLESS ET AL., *supra* note 35, at 264–71 (discussing *t*-tests).

[39] *See* Section III, *supra; see also* Susan D. Franck et al., *Inside the Arbitrator's Mind*, 66 EMORY L. J. 1115, 1146, 1156 (2017) (identifying when a *t*-test was appropriate).

[40] *See generally* GREGORY W. CORDER & DALE I. FOREMAN, NONPARMETRIC STATISTICS FOR NON-STATISTICIANS: A STEP-BY-STEP APPROACH (2009); *see also* URDAN, *supra* note 34, at 97, 205; *see also supra* note 29.

[41] URDAN, *supra* note 34, at 113–18; LAWLESS ET AL., *supra* note 35, at 277–82 (discussing ANOVAs); *see also* Franck, *supra* note 18, at 454, 456–57 (explaining when ANOVAs are appropriate); Susan D. Franck et al., *The Diversity Challenge: Exploring the "Invisible College" of International Arbitration*, 53 COLUM. J. TRANSNAT'L L. 429, 483, 494 (2015) (same).

[42] As it is the most conservative and least likely to reveal a false positive, HSD was primarily used for follow-up tests. URDAN, *supra* note 34, at 107. Other follow-up tests, such as an LSD (Least Significant Difference), were another potential way of conducting post-hoc follow-ups, but they were not typically used given higher degree of error. *See* CLIVE IRELAND, EXPERIMENTAL STATISTICS FOR AGRICULTURE & HORTICULTURE 110–11 (2010).

[43] A Kruskal-Wallis test analyzes non-normal continuous variables and group differences in multi-categorical variables. CORDER & FOREMAN, *supra* note 40; URDAN, *supra* note 34, at 205; *see also* Franck et al., *supra* note 41, at 487–88 nn.201–203 (discussing appropriateness of using a Kruskall-Walllis test of medians).

book, for example, Chapter 8 analyzed differences in tribunal costs across a multi-categorical variable, namely whether the tribunal was administered at ICSID, the SCC, or in an UNCITRAL-based proceeding. ANOVAs using transformed inflation-adjusted data explored mean differences in tribunal costs, and Kruskall-Wallis tests examined inflation-adjusted non-transformed median data to assess robustness. As they test slightly different things with slightly different data, more often than not, tests of both means and medians were conducted to check robustness.

Where, however, one is interested in examining the relationship between two continuous variables, yet another kind of test is required. A Pearson's Product Moment Correlation Coefficient (otherwise known as a bivariate correlation) explores potential linear relationships between two continuous variables but without establishing a causal link.[44] Relatedly, a partial bivariate correlation can control for the effect of a third variable (by holding it constant) to analyze the correlation between two continuous variables of interest. In this book, case length (namely the number of months between filing of an arbitration request and rendering the final award) is a continuous variable; and a party's legal fees and expenses is also continuous. Therefore, to assess the potential link between time and costs, it is reasonable to use a correlation. Given the collinearity of case length and various costs, it was sensible to control for case length in partial correlations, lest tests of other relationships be tainted by the effect of case length.

Thus far, all of the tests analyzing potential associative relationships tended to focus on bivariate analyses, namely relationships between two (or possibly three) variables. Where, however, one is interested in considering how three or more variables all work together to contribute toward an outcome—when that outcome variable is a continuous variable—regression analysis becomes possible and prudent. In the words of the classic empirical legal studies textbook, "regression allows for the simultaneous consideration of more than two variables" and as those authors observe, entire books and multi-semester courses are spent on that topic.[45] Like previous research using this data using regression models to identify significant predictors of ITA outcomes,[46] this book used regression models. As costs are continuous variables, having identified potential predictors previously, Chapter 8 used multiple regressions to examine how several independent variables could discretely contribute to each ITA cost.

When reporting results of inferential statistics, this book assumes that the appropriate level for testing for statistical significance[47] level is < .05,[48] and therefore probability values (p) were tested

[44] URDAN, *supra* note 34, at 165–73; *see also* LAWLESS ET AL., *supra* note 35, at 289–93, 297–300 (discussing correlations); Franck et al., *supra* note 41, at 483, 488 (discussing use of correlation coefficients).

[45] LAWLESS ET AL., *supra* note 35, at 300–01.

[46] Susan D. Franck & Lyndsey E. Wylie, *Predicting Outcomes in Investment Treaty Arbitration*, 65 DUKE L.J. 459 (2015).

[47] Readers interested in basic definitions of statistical significance are encouraged to review Earl Babbie's classic book on social science research. EARL R. BABBIE, THE PRACTICE OF SOCIAL RESEARCH 633 (5th ed. 2014); *see also id.* at 460–70.

[48] Many studies use the .05 probability level (reflecting 5% risk of error of a false positive, called a Type I Error) for determining whether a result is significant. Some areas use a .10 probability level, reflecting a 10% risk of error. Use of probabilities does not prevent error (and false positives) from creeping into analysis, but the objective is to identify the likely risk using pre-established levels. *See, e.g.,* NEIL J. SALKIND, ENCYCLOPEDIA OF MEASUREMENT & STATISTICS VOL. 1 889–91, 1019–22 (2007). As there is no scientific basis for rejecting the dominant scientific practice for international investment law, and the law is relatively new and still evolving,

against and reported using that cutoff value. The book regularly reports the test-statistic (whether a t-value, U-value, F-value, χ^2-value or otherwise), the sample size (n), and the r-value to indicate both the effect size and (particularly for the null effects) aid the calculation of the power and, for null results, permit estimation of risk of a Type II Error.

Finally, having established a reliable link between two variables, causal hypotheses explore whether one variable actually *causes* the relationship.[49] This requires a causal variable to temporally precede an effect, a statistical relationship between the two variables (the presumed cause and effect), and no alternative causes for the effect (including confounds or interactions). Typically, causal hypotheses are only appropriate to test using experimentation—or sufficiently high levels of statistical control. Given limited data and large variance in ITA, it is not yet prudent to use modeling to make causal attributions, as it may overstep the mark. Experimental control, however, seems an appropriate basis to discuss cause.

For this reason, the book discusses—but does not conduct—experimental analyses.[50] While in the immortal words of Professor Cal Garbin, "humans lust for cause" in our rush for intuitive and cognitively appealing explanations, causal hypothesis testing requires more caution, precision, and care. Until a controlled experiment properly constrains variance by random assignment to experimental conditions, and there are a sufficiently small number of conditions to permit precise attribution to the causal variable, strong causal conclusions are improper.

V. Effect Sizes and Power Analysis

Effect sizes (r-values) serve multiple purposes in empirical analyses. First, effect sizes indicate the practical significance of a statistically reliable relationship. These are useful as, it is one thing to distinguish between two experiences, but it is another matter to understand the *magnitude* of the difference.[51] To provide a sticky example, identifying statistically reliable differences may be equivalent to distinguishing between eating at fast food and a locally run restaurant, but effect sizes help identify the magnitude of the difference of eating at McDonalds or a restaurant with a Michelin 3-star rating. Luckily, methodologically minded psychologists have explored effect sizes to provide a baseline for identifying practical significance. Cohen's standard conventions suggest that tests with r-values of under .10 are trivial or less than small; whereas a "small" effect involves $r = .10$, a "medium" effect involves $r = .11\text{-}.30$,

---

caution is warranted and therefore a .05 level for statistical significance was methodologically prudent. *See* ERICH L. LEHMANN, FISHER, NEYMAN, AND THE CREATION OF CLASSICAL STATISTICS 10, 17–20 (discussing Fisher's creation and use of .05 cutoffs for statistical significance as a useful ex ante standard); *but see* James K. Skipper Jr., Anthony L. Guenther & Gilbert Nass, *The Sacredness of .05: A Note Concerning the Uses of Statistical Levels of Significance in Social Science*, *in* THE SIGNIFICANCE TEST CONTROVERSY 155, 155–57 (Donald E. Morrison & Ramon E. Henkel eds., 2006) (observing that others believe cutoff levels for statistical significance may vary by context when there are grounds for doing so).

[49] DONALD H. MCBURNEY & THERESA L. WHITE, RESEARCH METHODS 15–16 (8th ed. 2010) (explaining the importance of description, looking for reliable associations, and, eventually, cause).

[50] *See, e.g.*, Franck et al., *supra* note 39.

[51] FREDERICK J. GRAVETTER & LARRY B. WALLNAU, ESSENTIALS OF STATISTICS FOR THE BEHAVIORAL SCIENCES 198–201, 345–48 (5th ed. 2007); *see also* Franck, *supra* note 18, at 357–58.

and a "large" effect involves *r*-values over .50.[52] These conventions are applied in this book, as there are no studies suggesting deviations from that traditional baseline is warranted in ITA, and cherry-picking cutoffs without a scientific basis is unsound.

Effect sizes have a second, and critical, set of functions involving statistical power. As discussed in Section IV, they aid an assessment of the power of the analysis conducted and permit estimation of the size of future samples to reliably detect an effect.[53] Where a statistical test identifies a significant relationship, it is by definition sufficiently powered. But, where there is a null effect and analyses were unable to detect reliable relationships (like many analyses in this book), *r*-values aid calculation of potential power using established power tables.[54] For this reason, this book regularly identifies *r*-values and identifies, when appropriate, where there are power problems. With reported *r*-values of .10 or lower, for analyses with a null effect, power tables suggest that any sample with *less* than 781 cases analyzed would have insufficient power to detect latent relationships. In some cases, where variables contained multiple categories and exhibited a small effect size, more than 1,000 cases would be required to reliably detect latent effects. While efforts were made in the footnotes to acknowledge this throughout the book, it is fundamentally a generally applicable caveat for all null effects.[55] The good news is, having identified *r*-values and aided identification of underpowered samples, *post-hoc* power assessments permit identification of how many cases are required to chase down statistically small effects.

VI. Information on Underlying Sources

Two core pieces of information are vital to understanding analyses in this book, namely the Codebook used to aid coding assessments and increase inter-coder reliability and the dataset. The Codebook (Appendix IV) and the underlying dataset (Appendix V) are available online. The Codebook contains raw coding from original coding protocols as well as a variety of transformation related information. The dataset contains all the data. Given the length of the Codebook, readers seeking to understand values and coding may find it easier to review the Appendix V dataset in "Variable View", as the dataset contains embedded information including both: (1) a "Label" category with background descritiptive information about the meaning of a variable; and (2) a "Value" category providing information, where applicable, on the numerical coding and categorical classification of individual variables. Appendix II contains a detailed listing of awards in the dataset.

---

[52] Jacob Cohen, Statistical Power Analysis for the Behavioral Sciences 25, 113–16 (2d ed. 1988); Frederick J. Gravetter & Larry B. Wallnau, Essentials of Statistics for the Behavioral Sciences 198–201, 345–48 (6th ed. 2007); *see also* Franck, *supra* note 18, at 357–58.

[53] Franck, *supra* note 18, at 461.

[54] The power of analysis is determined through power tables, such as those found in Cohen, *supra* note 52, as a function of the size of the sample (n) and effect size (r). Using the table with these two values permits an estimation of the sample's power. This, in turn, permits estimation of the probability of having committed a Type II error (a false negative, or a failure to identify a reliable effect that actually exists) using the formula: Type II error rate = 1 – power. In social science literature, a result with .80 power (i.e., a 20% risk of a Type II error) is considered acceptable.

[55] The author apologizes for any inadvertent omissions, particularly as word count limitations created restrictions for how many times it was possible to reproduce the same type of power analysis.

APPENDIX II

Awards in Dataset (Listed Alphabetically)

1. *Abaclat, et al. (Case formerly known as Giovanna a Beccara and Others) v. Argentine Republic*, ICSID Case No. ARB/07/5, Decision on Jurisdiction and Admissibility (Aug. 4, 2011).
2. *ADC Affiliate Limited and ADC & ADMC Management Limited v. Republic of Hungary*, ICSID Case No. ARB/03/16, Award of the Tribunal (Oct. 2, 2006).
3. *ADF Group Inc. v. United States*, ICSID Case No. ARB(AF)/00/1, Final Award (Jan. 9, 2003), 6 ICSID REP. 470 (2004).
4. *AES Corporation v. Argentine Republic*, ICSID Case No. ARB/02/17, Decision on Jurisdiction (Apr. 26, 2005).
5. *AES Summit Generation Limited and AES-Tisza Erömü Kft v. Republic of Hungary*, ICSID Case No. ARB/07/22, Award (Sept. 23, 2010).
6. *African Holding Company of America, Inc. and Société Africaine de Construction au Congo S.A.R.L. v. Democratic Republic of the Congo*, ICSID Case No. ARB/05/21, Award on the Ouster of Jurisdiction and Admissibility (July 29, 2008).
7. *Aguas del Tunari S.A. v. Republic of Bolivia*, ICSID Case No. ARB/02/3, Decision on Respondent's Objections to Jurisdiction (Oct. 21, 2005), 10 ICSID REV. 250 (2005).
8. *AIG Capital Partners, Inc. and CJSC Tem Real Estate Company v. Republic of Kazakhstan*, ICSID Case No. ARB/01/6, Award (Oct. 20, 2005).
9. *Alasdair Ross Anderson et al. v. Republic of Costa Rica*, ICSID Case No. ARB(AF)/07/3, Award (May 19, 2010).
10. *Alpha Projektholding GMBH v. Ukraine*, ICSID Case No. ARB/07/16, Award (Nov. 8, 2010).
11. *Alps Finance and Trade AG v. Slovak Republic*, UNCITRAL Arbitration, Award (Mar. 5, 2011).

12. *American Manufacturing and Trading, Inc. v. Republic of Zaire*, ICSID Case No. ARB/93/1, Final Award (Feb. 21, 1997), 5 ICSID REP. 14 (2002).
13. *Mohammad Ammar al-Bahloul v. Republic of Tajikistan*, SCC Case No. V (064/2008), Partial Award on Jurisdiction and Liability (Sept. 2, 2009).
14. *Mohammad Ammar al-Bahloul v. Republic of Tajikistan*, SCC Case No. V (064/2008), Final Award (June 8, 2010).
15. *Archer Daniels Midland Company and Tate & Lyle Ingredients Americas, Inc. v. United Mexican States*, ICISD Case No. ARB(AF)/04/05, Award (Nov. 21, 2007).
16. *Asian Agricultural Products Ltd. v. Republic of Sri Lanka*, ICSID Case No. ARB/87/3, Final Award (June 27, 1990), 4 ICSID REP. 526 (1991).
17. *ATA Construction, Industrial and Trading Company v. Hashemite Kingdom of Jordan*, ICSID Case No. ARB/08/2, Award (May 18, 2010).
18. *Austrian Airlines v. Slovak Republic*, UNCITRAL Arbitration, Final Award (Oct. 9, 2009).
19. *AWG Group Ltd v. Argentine Republic*, UNCTRAL Arbitration, Decision on Jurisdiction (Aug. 3, 2006).
20. *AWG Group Ltd. v. Argentine Republic*, UNCITRAL Arbitration, Decision on Liability (July 30, 2010).
21. *Robert Azinian, Kenneth Davitian, & Ellen Baca v. United Mexican States*, ICSID Case No. ARB(AF)/97/2, Final Award (Nov. 1, 1999), 5 ICSID REP. 272 (2002).
22. *Azpetrol International Holdings B.V., Azpetrol Group B.V. and Azpetrol Oil Services Group B.V. v. Republic of Azerbaijan*, ICSID Case No. ARB/06/15, Award (Sept. 8, 2009).
23. *Azurix Corp. v. Argentine Republic*, ICSID Case No. ARB/01/12, Decision on Jurisdiction (Dec. 8, 2003), 43 I.L.M. 262 (2004).
24. *Azurix Corp. v. Argentine Republic*, ICSID Case No. ARB/01/12, Award (July 14, 2006).
25. *Bayindir Insaat Turizm Ticaret Ve Sanayi A.S. v. Islamic Republic of Pakistan*, ICSID Case No. ARB/03/29, Decision on Jurisdiction (Nov. 14, 2005).
26. *Bayindir Insaat Turizm Ticaret Ve Sanayi A.S. v. Islamic Republic of Pakistan*, ICSID Case No. ARB/03/29, Award (Aug. 27, 2009).
27. *Bayview Irrigation District et al. v. United Mexican States*, ICSID Case No. ARB(AF)/05/1, Award (June 19, 2007).
28. *Vladimir Berschader & Moise Berschader v. Russian Federation*, SCC Case No. V (080/2004), Award (Apr. 21, 2006).
29. *BG Group Plc v. Republic of Argentina*, UNCITRAL Arbitration, Final Award (Dec. 24, 2007).
30. *Biwater Gauff (Tanzania) Ltd. v. United Republic of Tanzania*, ICSID Case No. ARB/05/22, Award (July 24, 2008).
31. *Iurii Bogdanov, Agurdino-Invest Ltd., and Agurdino-Chimia JSC v. Republic of Moldova*, SCC Arbitration, Arbitral Award (Sept. 22, 2005).
32. *Yury Bogdanov v. Republic of Moldova*, SCC Case No. V (114/2009), Final Arbitral Award (Mar. 30, 2010).
33. *BP America Production Company, Pan American Sur SRL, Pan American Fueguina, SRL and Pan American Continental SRL v. Argentine Republic*, ICSID Case No. ARB/04/8, Decision on Preliminary Objections (July 26, 2006).

34. *Bureau Veritas Inspection Valuation Assessment and Control BIVAC B.V. v. Republic of Paraguay*, ICSID Case. No. ARB/07/9, Decision of the Tribunal on Objections to Jurisdiction (May, 29, 2009).
35. *Burlington Resources Inc. v. Republic of Ecuador*, ICSID Case No. ARB/08/5, Decision on Jurisdiction (June 2, 2010).
36. *Camuzzi International S.A. v. Argentine Republic*, ICSID Case No. ARB/03/2, Decision on Objections to Jurisdiction (May 11, 2005).
37. *Camuzzi International S.A. v. Argentine Republic*, ICSID Case No. ARB/03/7, Decision of the Arbitral Tribunal on Objections to Jurisdiction (June 10, 2005).
38. *Canadian Cattlemen for Fair Trade v. United States*, NAFTA Arbitration, Award on Jurisdiction (Jan. 28. 2008).
39. *Canfor Corporation v. United States*, NAFTA Arbitration, Decision on Preliminary Question (June 6, 2006).
40. *Canfor Corporation v. United States*, NAFTA Arbitration, Joint Order on the Costs of Arbitration and for the Termination of Certain Arbitral Proceedings (July 19, 2007).
41. *Cargill, Inc. v. United Mexican States*, ICSID Case No. ARB(AF)/05/2, Award (Sept. 18, 2009).
42. *CCL v. Kazakhstan*, SCC Case No. 122/2001, Jurisdictional Award (Jan. 1, 2003).
43. *Cementownia "Nowa Huta" S.A. v. Republic of Turkey*, ICSID Case No. ARB(AF)/06/2, Award (Sept. 17, 2009).
44. *CEMEX Caracas Investments B.V. and CEMEX Caracas II Investments B.V. v. Bolivarian Republic of Venezuela*, ICSID Case No. ARB/08/15, Decision of Jurisdiction (Dec. 30, 2010).
45. *Československá Obchodní Banka, a.s. v. Slovak Republic*, ICSID Case No. ARB/97/4, Decision on Objections to Jurisdiction (May 24, 1999), 14 ICSID REV. 251 (1999).
46. *Champion Trading Company, Ameritrade International, Inc., James T. Wahba, John B. Wahba, Timothy T. Wahba v. Arab Republic of Egypt*, ICSID Case No. ARB/02/9, Decision on Jurisdiction (Oct. 21, 2003), 19 ICSID REV. 275 (2004).
47. *Champion Trading Company & Ameritrade International v. Arab Republic of Egypt*, ICSID Case No. ARB/02/9, Award (Oct. 17, 2006).
48. *Chemtura Corporation v. Government of Canada*, UNCITRAL Arbitration, Award (Aug. 2, 2010).
49. *Chevron Corporation and Texaco Petroleum Company v. Republic of Ecuador*, PCA Case No. 34877, Interim Award (Dec. 1, 2008).
50. *Chevron Corporation and Texaco Petroleum Company v. Republic of Ecuador*, PCA Case No. 34877, Partial Award on the Merits (Mar. 30, 2010).
51. *Chevron Corporation and Texaco Petroleum Company v. Republic of Ecuador*, PCA Case No. 34877, Final Award (Aug. 31, 2011).
52. *CME Czech Republic B.V. v. Czech Republic*, UNCITRAL, Partial Award (Sept. 13, 2001).
53. *CME Czech Republic B.V. v. Czech Republic*, UNCITRAL Arbitration, Final Award (Mar. 14, 2003).
54. *CMS Gas Transmission Company v. Argentina*, ICSID Case No. ARB/01/8, Decision on Objections to Jurisdiction (July 17, 2003), 7 ICSID REP. 492 (2005).
55. *CMS Gas Transmission Company v. Republic of Argentina*, ICSID Case No. ARB/01/8, Award (May 12, 2005), 44 I.L.M. 1205 (2005).

56. *Commerce Group Corp. and San Sebastian Gold Mines, Inc. v. Republic of El Salvador*, ICSID Case No. ARB/09/17, Award (Mar. 14, 2011).
57. *Compañía de Aguas del Aconquija S.A. and Compagnie Generale des Eaux v. Argentine Republic*, ICSID Case No. ARB/97/3, Final Award (Nov. 21, 2000), 16 ICSID REV. 641 (2001).
58. *Compañía de Aguas del Aconquija S.A. and Vivendi Universal S.A. v. Argentine Republic*, ICSID Case No. ARB/97/3, Decision on Jurisdiction (Nov. 14, 2005).
59. *Compañía de Aguas del Aconquija S.A. and Vivendi Universal S.A. v. Argentine Republic*, ICSID Case No. ARB/97/3, Award (Aug. 20, 2007).
60. *Consortium Groupement L.E.S.I.- DIPENTA v. Republic of Algeria*, ICSID Case No. ARB/03/8, Final Award (Jan. 10, 2005), 19 ICSID REV. 426 (2005).
61. *Consortium R.F.C.C. v. Kingdom of Morocco*, ICSID Case No. ARB/00/4, Decision on Jurisdiction (July 16, 2001).
62. *Consortium R.F.C.C. v. Kingdom of Morocco*, ICSID Case No. ARB/00/6, Award (Dec. 22, 2003), 20 ICSID REV. 391 (2005).
63. *Continental Casualty Company v. Argentine Republic*, ICSID Case No. ARB/03/9, Decision on Jurisdiction (Feb. 22, 2006).
64. *Continental Casualty Company v. Argentine Republic*, ICSID Case No. ARB/03/9, Award (Sept. 5, 2008).
65. *Corn Products International, Inc. v. United Mexican States*, ICSID Case No. ARB(AF)/04/01, Decision on Responsibility (Jan. 15, 2008).
66. *Desert Line Projects LLC v. Republic of Yemen*, ICSID Case No. ARB/05/17, Award (Feb. 6, 2008).
67. *Duke Energy Electroquil Partners & Electroquil S.A. v. Republic of Ecuador*, ICSID Case No. ARB/04/19, Award (Aug. 18, 2008).
68. *Eastern Sugar B.V. v. Czech Republic*, SCC Case No. 088/2004, Partial Award (Mar. 27, 2007).
69. *Eastern Sugar B.V. v. Czech Republic*, SCC Case No. 088/2004, Final Award (Apr. 12, 2007).
70. *EDF (Services) Limited v. Romania*, ICSID Case No. ARB/05/13, Award (Oct. 8, 2009).
71. *El Paso Energy International Company v. Argentine Republic*, ICSID Case No. ARB/03/15, Decision on Jurisdiction (Apr. 26, 2006), 21 ICSID REV. 541 (2006).
72. *El Paso Energy International Company v. Argentine Republic*, ICSID Case No. ARB/03/15, Award (Oct. 31, 2011).
73. *Empresa Eléctrica del Ecuador Inc. v. Republic of Ecuador*, ICSID Case No. ARB/05/9, Award (June 2, 2009).
74. *Empresas Lucchetti, S.A. and Lucchetti Peru, S.A. v. Republic of Peru*, ICSID Case No. ARB/03/4, Award (Feb. 7, 2005), 19 ICSID REV. 359 (2004).
75. *EnCana Corporation v. Republic of Ecuador*, LCIA Case UN3481, Partial Award on Jurisdiction (Feb. 27, 2006).
76. *EnCana Corporation v. Republic of Ecuador*, LCIA Case UN3481, Award (Feb. 3, 2006).
77. *Enron Corporation and Ponderosa Assets, L.P. v. Argentine Republic*, ICSID Case No. ARB/01/3, Decision on Jurisdiction (Aug. 2, 2004).
78. *Enron Corporation and Ponderosa Assets, L.P. v. Argentine Republic*, ICSID Case No. ARB/01/3, Decision on Jurisdiction (Jan. 14, 2004).

79. *Enron Corporation and Ponderosa Assets, L.P. v. Argentine Republic*, ICSID Case No. ARB/01/3, Award (May 22, 3007).
80. *Ethyl Corporation v. Government of Canada*, NAFTA Arbitration, Award on Jurisdiction (June 26, 1998).
81. *Eureko B.V. v. Republic of Poland*, Ad Hoc Arbitration, Partial Award (Aug. 19, 2005).
82. *Eureko B.V. v. Slovak Republic*, PCA Case No. 2008-13, Award on Jurisdiction, Arbitrability and Suspension (Oct. 26, 2010).
83. *Europe Cement Investment & Trade S.A. v. Republic of Turkey*, ICSID Case No. ARB(AF)/07/2, Award (Aug. 13, 2009).
84. *EVN AG v. Former Yugoslav Republic of Macedonia*, ICSID Case No. ARB/09/10, Award (Sept. 2, 2011).
85. *F-W Oil Interests, Inc. v. Republic of Trinidad and Tobago*, ICSID Case No. ARB/01/14, Award (Mar. 3, 2006).
86. *Fedax N.V. v. Republic of Venezuela*, ICSID Case No. ARB/96/3, Decision on Objections to Jurisdiction (July 11, 1997), 5 ICSID REP. 186 (2002).
87. *Fedax N.V. v. Republic of Venezuela*, ICSID Case No. ARB/96/3, Final Award (Mar. 9, 1998), 5 ICSID REP. 200 (2002).
88. *Marvin Roy Feldman Karpa v. United Mexican States*, ICSID Case No. ARB(AF)/99/1, Interim Decision on Preliminary Jurisdictional Issues (Dec. 6, 2000), 7 ICSID REP. 327 (2005).
89. *Marvin Roy Feldman Karpa v. United Mexican States*, ICSID Case No. ARB(AF)/99/1, Final Award (Dec. 16, 2002), 7 ICSID REP. 341 (2005).
90. *Fireman's Fund Insurance Company v. United Mexican States*, ICSID Case No. ARB(AF)/02/1, Award on Jurisdiction (July 17, 2003).
91. *Fireman's Fund Insurance Company v. United Mexican States*, ICSID Case No. ARB(AF)/02/01, Award (July 17, 2006).
92. *Piero Foresti, Laura de Carli et al. v. Republic of South Africa*, ICSID Case No. ARB(AF)/07/1, Award (Aug. 4, 2010).
93. *Fraport AG Frankfurt Airport Services Worldwide v. Republic of the Philippines*, ICSID Case No. ARB/03/25, Award (Aug. 16, 2007).
94. *Frontier Petroleum Services Ltd. v. Czech Republic*, UNCITRAL Arbitration, Final Award (Nov. 12, 2010).
95. *Ron Fuchs v. Republic of Georgia*, ICSID Case No. ARB/07/15, Award (Mar. 3, 2010).
96. *Bernardus Henricus Funnekotter et al., v. Republic of Zimbabwe*, ICSID Case No. ARB/05/06, Award (Apr. 22, 2009).
97. *GAMI Investments Inc. v. United Mexican States*, NAFTA Arbitration, Final Award (Nov. 15, 2004).
98. *Gas Natural SDG, S.A. v. Argentine Republic*, ICSID Case No. ARB/03/10, Decision of the Tribunal on Preliminary Questions on Jurisdiction (June 17, 2005).
99. *GEA Group Aktiengesellschaft v. Ukraine*, ICSID Case No. ARB/08/16, Award (Mar. 31, 2011).
100. *Gemplus S.A., SLP S.A., Gemplus Industrial S.A. de C.V. v. United Mexican States*, ICSID Case No. ARB(AF)/04/3, Award (June 16, 2010).
101. *Generation Ukraine, Inc. v. Ukraine*, ICSID Case No. ARB/00/9, Final Award (Sept. 16, 2003), 44 I.L.M. 404 (2005).

102. *Alex Genin, Eastern Credit Limited, Inc. and A.S. Baltoil v. Republic of Estonia*, ICSID Case No. ARB/99/2, Final Award (June 25, 2001), 17 ICSID REV. 395 (2002).
103. *Glamis Gold, Ltd. v. United States*, NAFTA Arbitration, Award (June 8, 2009).
104. *Global Trading Resource Corp. and Globex International, Inc. v. Ukraine*, ICSID Case No. ARB/09/11, Award (Dec. 1 2010).
105. *Goetz et al. v. Republic of Burundi*, ICSID Case No. ARB/95/3, Award embodying the parties' settlement agreement (Feb. 10, 1999), 6 ICSID REP. 5 (2004).
106. *Grand River Enterprises Six Nations, Ltd, et al. v. United States*, NAFTA/UNCITRAL Arbitration, Decision on Objections to Jurisdiction (July 20, 2006).
107. *Grand River Enterprises Six Nations, Ltd, et al. v. United States*, UNCITRAL Arbitration, Award (Jan. 12, 2011).
108. *Philippe Gruslin v. Malaysia*, ICSID Case No. ARB/99/3, Final Award (Nov. 27, 2000), 5 ICSID REP. 484 (2002).
109. *Rachel S. Grynberg, Stephen M. Grynberg, Miriam Z. Grynberg, and RSM Production Corporation v. Grenada*, ICSID Case No. ARB/10/6, Award (Dec. 10, 2010).
110. *Gustav F W Hamester GmbH & Co KG v. Republic of Ghana*, ICSID Case No. ARB/07/24, Award (June 18, 2010).
111. *Helnan International Hotels A/S v. Arab Republic of Egypt*, ICSID Case No. ARB/05/19, Decision of the Tribunal on Objection to Jurisdiction (Oct. 17, 2006).
112. *Helnan International Hotels A/S v. Arab Republic of Egypt*, ICSID Case No. ARB/05/19, Award (July 3, 2008).
113. *HICEE B.V. v. Slovak Republic*, PCA Case No. 2009-11, Partial Award (May, 23 2011).
114. *HICEE B.V. v. Slovak Republic*, PCA Case No. 2009-11, Supplementary and Final Award (Oct. 17, 2011).
115. *Hochtief AG v. Argentine Republic*, ICSID Case No. ARB/07/31, Decision on Jurisdiction (Oct. 24, 2011).
116. *Melvin J. Howard, Centurion Health Corp. & Howard Family Trust v. Government of Canada*, PCA Case No. 2009-21, Order for the Termination of the Proceedings and Award on Costs (Aug. 2, 2010).
117. *Hulley Enterprises Limited (Cyprus) v. Russian Federation*, PCA Case No. AA 226, Interim Award on Jurisdiction and Admissibility (Nov. 30, 2009).
118. *IBM World Trade Corp. v. Republic of Ecuador*, ICSID Case No. ARB/02/10, Decision on Jurisdiction (Dec. 22, 2003).
119. *Impregilo S.p.A. v. Argentine Republic*, ICSID Case No. ARB/07/17, Award (June 21, 2011).
120. *Impregilo S.p.A. v. Islamic Republic of Pakistan*, ICSID Case No. ARB/03/3, Decision on Jurisdiction (Apr. 22, 2005).
121. *Impregilo S.p.A. v. Islamic Republic of Pakistan*, ICSID Case No. ARB/03/3, Order of Discontinuance of the Proceeding (Sept. 25, 2005).
122. *Inceysa Vallisoletana, S.L. v. Republic of El Salvador*, ICSID Case No. ARB/03/26, Award (Aug. 2, 2006).
123. *Inmaris Perestroika Sailing Maritime Services GmbH and Others v. Ukraine*, ICSID Case No. ARB/08/8, Decision on Jurisdiction (Mar. 8, 2010).
124. *International Thunderbird Gaming Corporation v. United Mexican States*, NAFTA Arbitration, Arbitral Award (Jan. 26, 2006).

125. *Itera International Energy LLC and Itera Group NV v. Georgia*, ICSID Case No. ARB/08/7, Decision on Admissibility of Ancillary Claims (Dec. 4, 2009).
126. *Jan de Nul N.V. and Dredging International N.V. v. Arab Republic of Egypt*, ICSID Case No. ARB/04/13, Decision on Jurisdiction (June 16, 2006).
127. *Jan de Nul N.V. and Dredging International N.V. v. Arab Republic of Egypt*, ICSID Case No. ARB/04/13, Award (Nov. 6, 2008).
128. *Joy Mining Machinery Limited v. Arab Republic of Egypt*, ICSID Case No. ARB/03/11, Award (Aug. 6, 2004), 19 ICSID REV. 486 (2004).
129. *Ioannis Kardassopoulos v. Republic of Georgia*, ICSID Case No. ARB/05/18, Decision on Jurisdiction (July 6, 2007).
130. *Ioannis Kardassopoulos v. Republic of Georgia*, ICSID Case No. ARB/05/18, Award (Mar. 3, 2010).
131. *L.E.S.I. S.p.A. et ASTALDI S.p.A. v. Republic of Algeria*, ICSID Case No. ARB/05/3, Decision (July 12, 2006).
132. *L.E.S.I. S.p.A. et ASTALDI S.p.A. v. Republic of Algeria*, ICSID Case No. ARB/05/3, Award (Nov. 12, 2008).
133. *Lanco International Inc. v. Argentine Republic*, ICSID Case No. ARB/97/6, Preliminary Decision on Jurisdiction (Dec. 8, 1998), 40 I.L.M. 457 (2001).
134. *Ronald S. Lauder v. Czech Republic*, UNCITRAL Arbitration, Final Award (Sept. 3, 2001).
135. *Joseph Charles Lemire v. Ukraine* [Lemire I], ICSID Case No. ARB(AF)/98/1, Award embodying the Parties' settlement agreement (Sept. 18, 2000), 6 ICSID REP. 60 (2004).
136. *Joseph Charles Lemire v. Ukraine* [Lemire II], ICSID Case No. ARB/06/18, Decision on Jurisdiction and Liability (Jan. 14, 2010).
137. *Joseph Charles Lemire v. Ukraine* [Lemire II], ICSID Case No. ARB/06/18, Award (Mar. 28, 2011).
138. *LG&E Energy Corp., LG&E Capital Corp. and LG&E Int'l Inc. v. Argentine Republic*, ICSID Case No. ARB/02/1, Decision of the Arbitral Tribunal on Objections to Jurisdiction (Apr. 30, 2004), 21 ICSID REV. 155 (2006).
139. *LG&E Energy Corp., LG&E Capital Corp. and LG&E Int'l Inc. v. Argentine Republic*, ICSID Case No. 02/1, Decision on Liability (Oct. 3, 2006), 21 ICSIC REV. 203 (2006).
140. *LG&E Energy Corp., LG&E Capital Corp. and LG&E Int'l Inc. v. Argentine Republic*, ICSID Case No. ARB/02/1, Award (July 25, 2007).
141. *Libananco Holdings Co. Limited v. Republic of Turkey*, ICSID Case No. ARB/06/8, Award (Sept. 2, 2011).
142. *Limited Liability Company Amto v. Ukraine*, SCC Case No. 080/2005, Final Award (Mar. 26, 2008).
143. *Link-Trading Joint Stock Company v. Republic of Moldova*, UNICTRAL Arbitration, Award on Jurisdiction (Feb. 16, 2001).
144. *Link-Trading Joint Stock Company v. Republic of Moldova*, UNCITRAL Arbitration, Final Award (Apr. 18, 2002).
145. *Loewen Group, Inc. and Raymond L. Loewen v. United States*, ICSID Case No. ARB(AF)/98/3, Decision on Hearing of Respondent's Objection to Competence and Jurisdiction (Jan 5, 2001), 7 ICSID REP. 421 (2005).
146. *Loewen Group, Inc. and Raymond L. Loewen v. United States*, ICSID Case No. ARB(AF)/98/3, Award (June 26, 2003), 7 ICSID REP. 442 (2005).

147. *M.C.I. Power Group L.C. and New Turbine, Inc. v. Republic of Ecuador*, ICSID Case No. ARB/03/6, Award (July 31, 2007).
148. *Emilio Agustín Maffezini v. Kingdom of Spain*, ICSID Case No. ARB/97/7, Decision on Objections to Jurisdiction (Jan. 25, 2000), 5 ICSID Rep. 396 (2002).
149. *Emilio Agustín Maffezini v. Kingdom of Spain*, ICSID Case No. ARB/97/7, Final Award (Nov. 13, 2000), 5 ICSID Rep. 419 (2002).
150. *Malaysian Historical Salvors SDN, BHD v. Government of Malaysia*, ICSID Case No. ARB/05/10, Award on Jurisdiction (May 17, 2007).
151. *Malicorp Limited v. Arab Republic of Egypt*, ICSID Case No. ARB/08/18, Award (Feb. 7, 2011).
152. *Merrill & Ring Forestry L.P. v. Canada*, NAFTA Arbitration, Award (Mar. 31, 2010).
153. *Metalclad Corp. v. United Mexican States*, ICSID Case No. ARB(AF)/97/1, Final Award (Aug. 30, 2000), 5 ICSID Rep. 212 (2002).
154. *Metalpar S.A. and Buen Aire S.A. v. Argentine Republic*, ICSID Case No. ARB/03/5, Decision on Jurisdiction (Apr. 27, 2006).
155. *Metalpar S.A. and Buen Aire S.A. v. Argentine Republic*, ICSID Case No. ARB/03/5, Award on the Merits (June 6, 2008).
156. *Methanex Corporation v. United States*, NAFTA Arbitration, Preliminary Award on Jurisdiction and Admissibility (Aug. 7, 2002).
157. *Methanex Corporation v. United States*, NAFTA Arbitration, Final Award of the Tribunal on Jurisdiction and Merits (Aug. 3, 2005).
158. *Ioan Micula, Viorel Micula, S.C. European Food S.A, S.C. Starmill S.R.L. and S.C. Multipack S.R.L. v. Romania*, ICSID Case No. ARB/05/20, Decision on Jurisdiction and Admissibility (Sept. 24, 2008).
159. *Middle East Cement Shipping and Handling Co. S.A. v. Arab Republic of Egypt*, ICSID Case No. ARB/99/6, Final Award (Apr. 12, 2002), 7 ICSID Rep. 173 (2005).
160. *Mihaly International Corporation v. Democratic Socialist Republic Sri Lanka*, ICSID Case No. ARB/00/2, Award and Concurring Opinion (Mar. 15, 2002), 6 ICSID Rep. 310 (2004).
161. *Millicom International Operations B.V. and Sentel GSM SA v. Republic of Senegal*, ICSID Case No. ARB/08/20, Decision on the Jurisdiction of the Arbitral Tribunal (July 16, 2010).
162. *Mobil Corporation, Venezuela Holdings BV, Mobile Cerro Negro Holding, Mobil Venezolana de Petroleos Holdings Inc., Mobil Cerro Negro Ltd. and Mobil Venezolana de Petroleos Inc. v. Bolivarian Republic of Venezuela*, ICSID Case No. ARB/07/27, Decision on Jurisdiction (June 10, 2010).
163. *Mondev International Ltd. v. United States*, ICSID Case No. ARB(AF)/99/2, Final Award (Oct. 11, 2002), 6 ICSID Rep. 192 (2004).
164. *MTD Equity Sdn. Bhd. & MTD Chile S.A. v. Republic of Chile*, ICSID Case No. ARB/01/7, Award (May 25, 2004).
165. *Murphy Exploration and Production Company International v. Republic of Ecuador*, ICSID Case No. ARB/08/4 Award on Jurisdiction (Dec. 15, 2010).
166. *Mytilineos Holdings SA v. State Union of Serbia & Montenegro and Republic of Serbia*, UNCITRAL Arbitration, Partial Award on Jurisdiction (Sept. 8, 2006).
167. *William Nagel v. Czech Republic*, SCC Case No. 049/2002, Final Award (Sept. 9, 2003).
168. *National Grid plc v. Argentine Republic*, UNCITRAL Arbitration, Decision on Jurisdiction (June 20, 2006).

169. *National Grid plc v. Argentine Republic*, UNCITRAL Arbitration, Award (Nov. 3, 2008).
170. *Nations Energy Inc., Electric Machinery Enterprises Inc. and Jaime Jurado v. Republic of Panama*, ICSID Case No. ARB/06/19, Award (Nov. 24, 2010).
171. *Noble Energy, Inc. and Machalapower CIA. LTDA. v. Republic of Ecuador and Consejo Nacional de Electricidad*, ICSID Case No. ARB/05/12, Decision on Jurisdiction (Mar. 5, 2008).
172. *Noble Ventures, Inc. v. Romania*, ICSID Case No. ARB/01/11, Award (Oct. 12, 2005).
173. *Nova Scotia Power Incorporated (NSPI) v. Bolivarian Republic of Venezuela*, UNCITRAL Arbitration, Decision on Jurisdiction (Apr. 22, 2010).
174. *Nova Scotia Power Incorporated (NSPI) v. Bolivarian Republic of Venezuela*, UNCITRAL Arbitration, Award on Costs (Aug. 30, 2010).
175. *Nykomb Synergetics Technology Holding AB v. Republic of Latvia*, SCC Case No. 118/2001, Arbitral Award (Dec. 16, 2003).
176. *Occidental Exploration and Production Co. v. Republic of Ecuador*, LCIA Case No. UN3467, Final Award (July 1, 2004).
177. *Occidental Petroleum Corporation and Occidental Exploration and Production Company v. Republic of Ecuador*, ICSID Case No. ARB/06/11, Decision on Jurisdiction (Sept. 9, 2008).
178. *OKO Pankki OYJ, VTB Bank AG, and Sampo Bank PLC v. Republic of Estonia*, ICSID Case No. ARB/04/6, Award (Nov. 19, 2007).
179. *Eudoro Armando Olguín v. Republic of Paraguay*, ICSID Case No. ARB/98/5, Decisions on Objections to Jurisdiction (Aug. 8, 2000), 6 ICSID REP. 156 (2004).
180. *Eudoro Armando Olguín v. Republico f Paraguay*, ICSID Case No. ARB/98/5, Final Award (July 26, 2000), 6 ICSID REP. 164 (2004).
181. *Pac Rim Cayman LLC v. Republic of El Salvador*, ICSID Case No. ARB/09/12, Decision on the Respondent's Preliminary Objections Under CAFTA Articles 10.20.4 and 10.20.5 (Aug. 2, 2010).
182. *Pan American Energy LLC and BP Argentina Exploration Company v. Argentine Republic*, ICSID Case No. ARB/03/13, Decision on Preliminary Objections (July 27, 2006).
183. *Pantechniki S.A. Contractors & Engineers v. Republic of Albania*, ICSID Case No. ARB/07/21, Award (July 30, 2009).
184. *Parkerings-Compagniet AS v. Republic of Lithuania*, ICSID Case No. ARB/05/8, Award (Sept. 11, 2007).
185. *Sergei Paushok, CJSC Golden East Company and CJSC Vostokneftegaz Company v. Government of Mongolia*, UNCITRAL Arbitration, Award on Jurisdiction and Liability (Apr. 28, 2011).
186. *Perenco Ecuador Ltd. v. Republic of Ecuador and Empresa Estatal Petróleos del Ecuador*, ICSID Case No. ARB/08/6, Decision on Jurisdiction (June 30, 2011).
187. *Petrobart Limited v. The Kyrgyz Republic*, SCC Case No. 126/2003, Award (Mar. 29, 2005).
188. *Victor Pey Casado and President Allende Foundation v. Republic of Chile*, ICSID Case No. ARB/98/2, Award (May 8, 2002).
189. *Victor Pey Casado and President Allende Foundation v. Republic of Chile*, ICSID Case No. ARB/98/2, Final Award (May 8, 2008).
190. *Phoenix Action, Ltd. v. Czech Republic*, ICSID Case No. ARB/06/5, Award (Apr. 15, 2009).

191. *Plama Consortium Limited v. Republic of Bulgaria*, ICSID Case No. ARB/03/24, Decision on Jurisdiction (Feb. 8, 2005), 20 ICSID REV. 262 (2005).
192. *Plama Consortium Limited v. Republic of Bulgaria*, ICSID Case No. ARB/03/24, Award (Aug. 27, 2008).
193. *Pope & Talbot, Inc. v. Government of Canada*, NAFTA Arbitration, Interim Award on Merits (Apr. 10, 2001).
194. *Pope & Talbot, Inc. v. Government of Canada*, NAFTA Arbitration, Interim Award on Merits (June 26, 2000).
195. *Pope & Talbot, Inc. v. Government of Canada*, NAFTA Arbitration, Interim Award on Damages (May 31, 2000).
196. *Pope & Talbot, Inc. v. Government of Canada*, NAFTA Arbitration, Final Award on Costs (Nov. 26, 2002).
197. *PSEG Global, Inc., North American Coal Corporation, and Konya Ingin Electrik Üretim ve Ticaret Limited Sirketi v. Republic of Turkey*, ICSID Case No. ARB/02/5, Decision on Jurisdiction (June 4, 2004).
198. *PSEG Global and Konya Ingin Elektrik Üretim ve Ticaret Limited Sirketi v. Republic of Turkey*, ICSID Case No. ARB/02/5, Award (Jan. 19, 2007).
199. *Quadrant Pacific Growth Fund L.P. and Canasco Holdings Inc. v. Republic of Costa Rica*, ICSID Case No. ARB(AF)/08/1, Order of the Tribunal Taking Note of the Discontinuance of the Proceeding and Allocation of Costs (Oct. 27, 2010).
200. *Rail World LLC, Railroad Development Corp and EEIF Rail BV v. Republic of Estonia*, ICSID Case No. ARB/06/6, Order of the Tribunal Taking Note of the Discontinuance of the Proceeding (Feb. 5, 2007).
201. *Railroad Development Corporation v. Republic of Guatemala*, ICSID Case No. ARB/07/23, Decision on Objection to Jurisdiction CAFTA Article 10.20.5 (Nov. 17, 2008).
202. *Railroad Development Corporation v. Republic of Guatemala*, ICSID Case No. ARB/07/23, Second Decision on Objections to Jurisdiction (May 28, 2010).
203. *Renta 4 S.V.S.A., Ahorro Corporacion Emergentes F.I., Ahorroa Corporacion Eurofondo F.I., Rovime Inversiones SICAV S.A., Quasar de Valors SICAV S.A., Orgor de Valores SICAV S.A. and GBI 9000 SICAV S.A. v. Russian Federation*, SCC Case No. V (024/2007), Award on Preliminary Objections (Mar. 20, 2009).
204. *Romak S.A. v. Republic of Uzbekistan*, PCA Case No. AA280, Award (Nov. 26, 2009).
205. *Rompetrol Group N.V. v. Romania*, ICSID Case No. ARB/06/3, Decision on Respondent's Preliminary Objections on Jurisdiction and Admissibility (Apr. 18, 2008).
206. *RosInvestCo UK Ltd. v. Russian Federation*, SCC Case No. V (079/2005), Award on Jurisdiction (Oct. 1, 2007).
207. *RosInvestCo UK Ltd. v. Russian Federation*, SCC Case No. V (079/2005), Final Award (Sept. 12, 2010).
208. *Spyridon Roussalis v. Romania*, ICSID Case No. ARB/06/1, Award (Dec. 7, 2011).
209. *Rumeli Telekom A.S. and Telsim Mobil Telekomikasyon Hizmetleri A.S. v. Republic of Kazakhstan*, ICSID Case No. ARB/05/16, Award (July 29, 2008).
210. *S & T Oil Equipment and Machinery Ltd. v. Romania*, ICSID Case No. ARB/07/13, Order of Discontinuance of the Proceeding (July 16, 2010).
211. *S.D. Myers, Inc. v. Governemnt of Canada*, NAFTA Arbitration, Partial Award on the Merits (Nov. 13, 2000).

212. *S.D. Myers, Inc. v. Government of Canada*, NAFTA Arbitration, Damages Award (Oct. 21, 2002).
213. *S.D. Myers, Inc. v. Government of Canada*, NAFTA Arbitration, Final Award on Costs (Dec. 30, 2002).
214. *Saba Fakes v. Republic of Turkey*, ICSID Case No. ARB/07/20, Award (July 14, 2010).
215. *Saipem S.p.A. v. People's Republic of Bangladesh*, ICSID Case No. ARB/05/07, Decision on Jurisdiction and Recommendation on Provisional Measures (Mar. 21, 2007), 22 ICSID REV. 100 (2007).
216. *Saipem S.p.A. v. People's Republic of Bangladesh*, ICSID Case No. ARB/05/7, Award (June 30, 2009).
217. *Salini Costruttori S.p.A. and Italstrade S.p.A. v. Hashemite Kingdom of Jordan*, ICISD Case No. ARB/02/13, Decision on Jurisdiction (Nov. 9, 2004), 20 ICSID REV. 148 (2005).
218. *Salini Costruttori S.p.A. and Italstrade S.p.A. v. Hashemite Kingdom of Jordan*, ICSID Case No. ARB/02/13, Award (Jan. 31, 2006).
219. *Salini Costruttori S.p.A. and Italstrade S.p.A. v. Kingdom of Morocco*, ICSID Case No. ARB/00/4, Decision on Jurisdiction (July 23, 2001), 6 ICSID REP. 400 (2004).
220. *Saluka Investments BV v. Czech Republic*, Decision on Jurisdiction over the Czech Republic's Counterclaim (May 7, 2004).
221. *Saluka Investments BV v. Czech Republic*, UNCITRAL Arbitration, Partial Award (Mar. 17, 2006).
222. *Sedelmayer v. Russian Federation*, SCC Case No. 93/2004, Arbitration Award (July 7, 1998).
223. *Sempra Energy v. Argentine Republic*, ICSID Case No. ARB/02/16, Decision on Objections to Jurisdiction (May 11, 2005).
224. *Sempra Energy v. Argentine Republic*, ICSID Case No. ARB/02/16, Award (Sept. 28, 2007).
225. *SGS Société Générale de Surveillance S.A. v. Islamic Republic of Pakistan*, ICSID Case No. ARB/01/13, Decision on Objections to Jurisdiction (Aug. 6, 2003), 8 ICSID REP. 406 (2005).
226. *SGS Société Générale de Surveillance S.A. v. Republic of the Philippines*, ICSID Case No. ARB/02/6, Decision of the Tribunal on Objections to Jurisdiction (Jan. 29, 2004), 8 ICSID REP. 518 (2005).
227. *Waguih Elie George Siag and Clorinda Vecchi v. Arab Republic of Egypt*, ICSID Case No. ARB/05/15, Decision on Jurisdiction (Apr. 11, 2007).
228. *Waguih Elie George Siag and Clorinda Vecchi v. Arab Republic of Egypt*, ICSID Case No. ARB/05/15, Award (June 1, 2009).
229. *Siemens A.G. v. Argentine Republic*, ICSID Case No. ARB/02/8, Decision on Jurisdiction (Aug. 3, 2004), 132 J. DU DROIT INT'L 142 (2005).
230. *Siemens v. Argentine Republic*, ICSID Case No. ARB/02/8, Award (Feb. 6, 2007).
231. *Sociedad Anónima Eduardo Vieira v. Republic of Chile*, ICSID Case No. ARB/04/7, Award (Aug. 21, 2007).
232. *Societe Generale v. Dominican Republic*, LCIA Case No. UN7927, Award on Preliminary Objections to Jurisdiction (Sept. 19, 2008).
233. *Hussein Nuaman Soufraki v. United Arab Emirates*, ICSID Case No. ARB/02/7, Award (July 7, 2004).
234. *Suez Sociedad General de Aguas de Barcelona S.A. and InterAguas Servicios Integrales del Agua S.A. v. Argentine Republic*, ICSID Case No. ARB/03/17, Decision on Jurisdiction (May 16, 2006).

235. *Suez, Sociedad General de Aguas de Barcelona S.A., and Vivendi Universal S.A. v. Argentine Republic*, ICSID Case No. ARB/03/19, Decision on Jurisdiction (Aug. 3, 2006).
236. *Suez, Sociedad General de Aguas de Barcelona S.A., and Vivendi Universal S.A. v. Argentine Republic*, ICSID Case No. ARB/03/19, Decision on Liability (July 30, 2010).
237. *Suez, Sociedad General de Aguas de Barcelona, S.A. and InterAgua Servicios Integrales del Agua S.A. v. Argentine Republic*, ICSID Case No. ARB/03/17, Decision on Liability (July 30, 2010).
238. *Swembalt AB v. Republic of Latvia*, UNCITRAL Arbitration, Decision by the Court of Arbitration, Oct. 23, 2000.
239. *Talsud S.A. v. United Mexican States*, ICSID Case No. ARB(AF)/04/4, Award (June 16, 2010).
240. *TCW Group, Inc. and Dominican Energy Holdings, L.P. v. Dominican Republic*, UNCITRAL Arbitration, Consent Award (July 16, 2009).
241. *Técnicas Medioambientales Tecmed S.A. v. United Mexican States*, ICSID Case No. ARB(AF)/00/2, Final Award (May 29, 2003), 19 ICSID REV. 158 (2004).
242. *Telefónica S.A. v. Argentine Republic*, ICSID Case No. ARB/03/20, Decision of the Tribunal on Objections to Jurisdiction (May 25, 2006).
243. *Telenor Mobile Communications A.S. v. Republic of Hungary*, ICSID Case No. ARB/04/15, Award (Sept. 13, 2006), 21 ICSID REV. 603 (2006).
244. *Tembec Inc. et al. v. United States*, NAFTA Arbitration, Order for the Termination of the Arbitral Proceedings with Respect to Tembec et al. (Jan. 10, 2006).
245. *Tembec Inc. et al. v. United States*, NAFTA Arbitration, Joint Order on the Costs of Arbitration and for the Termination of Certain Arbitral Proceedings (July 19, 2007).
246. *Terminal Forest Products Ltd. v. United States*, NAFTA Arbitration, Decision on Preliminary Question (June 6, 2006).
247. *Terminal Forest Products Ltd. v. United States*, NAFTA Arbitration, Joint Order on the Costs of Arbitration and for the Termination of Certain Arbitral Proceedings (July 19, 2007).
248. *Tokios Tokelės v. Ukraine*, ICSID Case No. ARB/02/18, Decision on Jurisdiction (Apr. 29, 2004), 20 ICSID REV. 205 (2005).
249. *Tokios Tokelės v. Ukraine*, ICSID Case No. ARB/02/18, Award (July 26, 2007).
250. *Total S.A. v. Argentine Republic*, ICSID Case No. ARB/04/1, Decision on Objections to Jurisdiction (Aug. 25, 2006).
251. *Total S.A. v. Argentine Republic*, ICSID Case No. ARB/04/1, Decision on Liability (Dec. 27, 2010).
252. *Toto Costruzioni Generali S.P.A. v. Republic of Lebanon*, ICSID Case No. ARB/07/12, Decision on Jurisdiction (Sept. 11, 2009).
253. *Tradex Hellas S.A. v. Republic of Albania*, ICSID Case No. ARB/94/2, Decision on Jurisdiction (Dec. 24, 1996), 5 ICSID REP. 47 (2002).
254. *Trans-Global Petroleum, Inc. v. Hashemite Kingdom of Jordan*, ICSID Case No. ARB/07/25, Decision on the Respondent's Objection under Rule 41(5) of the ICSID Arbitration Rules (May 12, 2008).
255. *Trans-Global Petroleum, Inc. v. Hashemite Kingdom of Jordan*, ICSID Case No. ARB/07/25, Consent Award (Apr. 8, 2009).

256. *TSA Spectrum de Argentina S.A. v. Argentine Republic*, ICSID Case No. ARB/05/5, Award (Dec. 19, 2008).
257. *Tza Yap Shum v. Republic of Peru*, ICSID Case No. ARB/07/6, Decision on Jurisdiction and Competence (June 19, 2009).
258. *Tza Yap Shum v. Republic of Peru*, ICSID Case No. ARB/07/6, Award (July 7, 2011).
259. *United Parcel Service of America, Inc. v. Government of Canada*, NAFTA Arbitration, Award on Jurisdiction (Nov. 22, 2002).
260. *United Parcel Service of America, Inc. v. Government of Canada*, NAFTA Arbitration, Award on the Merits (May 24, 2007).
261. *Vannessa Ventures Ltd. v. Bolivarian Republic of Venezuela*, ICSID Case No. ARB(AF)/04/6, Decision on Jurisdiction (Aug. 22, 2008).
262. *Vattenfall AB, Vattenfall Europe AG, Vattenfall Europe Generation AG v. Federal Republic of Germany*, ICSID Case No. ARB/09/6, Award (Mar. 11, 2011).
263. *Veteran Petroleum Limited (Cyprus) v. Russian Federation*, PCA Case No. AA 228, Interim Award on Jurisdiction and Admissibility, Nov. 30, 2009.
264. *Walter Bau AG v. Kingdom of Thailand*, UNCITRAL Arbitration, Award (July 1, 2009).
265. *Waste Management, Inc. v. United Mexican States* [Waste Management I], ICSID Case No. ABR(AF)/98/2, Award and Dissenting Opinion (June 2, 2000), 15 ICSID REV. (2000).
266. *Waste Management, Inc. v. United Mexican States* [Waste Management II], ICSID Case No. ARB(AF)/00/3, Decision on Mexico's Preliminary Objection Concerning the Previous Proceedings (June 26, 2002), 6 ICSID REP. 549 (2004).
267. *Waste Management, Inc. v. United Mexican States* [Waste Management II], ICSID Case No. ARB(AF)/00/3, Award (Apr. 30, 2004), 43 I.L.M. 967 (2004).
268. *Wena Hotels Limited v. Arab Republic of Egypt*, ICSID Case No. ARB/98/4, Decision on Jurisdiction (June 28, 1999), 6 ICSID REP. 74 (2004).
269. *Wena Hotels Limited v. Arab Republic of Egypt*, ICSID Case No. ARB/98/4, Final Award (Dec. 8, 2000), 6 ICSID REP. 89 (2004).
270. *Wintershall Aktiengesellschaft v. Argentine Republic*, ICSID Case No. ARB/04/14, Award (Dec. 8, 2008).
271. *Yaung Chi Oo Trading PTE Ltd. v. Government of the Union of Myanmar*, ASEAN I.D. Case No. ARB/01/1, Final Award (Mar. 31, 2003), 42 I.L.M. 540 (2003).
272. *Yukos Universal Limited (Isle of Man) v. Russian Federation*, PCA Case No. AA 227, Interim Award on Jurisdiction and Admissibility (Nov. 30, 2009).

APPENDIX III

Demographics on Investor Nationality, States, and Counsel Involved in the Dataset's Public Pre-2012 ITA Awards

TABLE APP III.A

Table reflecting Investors' Claimed Nationality, Number of Cases where the Claimed Nationality was Present, and Total Number of Investors Claiming that Nationality in All Cases.

Country	Number of Cases where Investors Present	Total Investors
United States	66	104
Canada	15	28
Netherlands	19	26
Italy	13	24
Germany	11	15
Spain	8	14
United Kingdom	13	13
France	6	9
Belgium	4	9
Sweden	4	8
Russia	3	7
Greece	6	6
Cyprus	5	6
Argentina	3	5

(*Continued*)

TABLE APP. III.A

(Continued)

Country	Number of Cases where Investors Present	Total Investors
Austria	4	4
Switzerland	4	4
Turkey	3	4
Chile	2	4
Luxembourg	3	3
Malaysia	2	3
Israel	2	2
Norway	2	2
Poland	2	2
Bahamas	1	2
Finland	1	2
China	1	1
Czech Republic	1	1
Denmark	1	1
Hungary	1	1
Kazakhstan	1	1
Latvia	1	1
Lithuania	1	1
Mexico	1	1
Oman	1	1
Peru	1	1
Senegal	1	1
Singapore	1	1
Total	214[1]	318[2]

[1] Although there are 202 separate cases, 12 cases had investors with multiple nationalities. This accounts for the variation in the total number of cases.

[2] These totals reflect the first five named investors and excludes eight cases involving six or more investors.

TABLE APP. III.B

Abbreviated Table Containing Number of Cases where a State's Investors Arbitrated an Investment Treaty Dispuate against another State as Compared to when the State was a Respondent (excluding cases where local investor is the same as the respondent state).

Country	Cases Brought by Investors Against Other Governments	Cases as Respondent Government
Argentina	3	28
Canada	15	7
Chile	2	3
Czech Republic	1	7
Germany	11	1
Latvia	1	2
Lithuania	1	1
Malaysia	2	2
Peru	1	2
Poland	2	1
Russia	3	7
Spain	8	1
Turkey	3	5
United States	66	10

TABLE APP. III.C

Frequency of Cases when: (1) Nationals of State Arbitrated Investment Treaty Dispute against Another State, (2) State was the Respondent in an Investment Treaty Dispute; and (3) a State's Nationals were Appointed as Arbitrators in a Case issuing at least One Award.

Country	Cases Brought by National Against Other Government	Cases as Respondent	Number of Cases where Nationals were Arbitrators
Albania	0	2	0
Algeria	0	2	3
Argentina	3	28	14
Australia	0	0	14
Austria	4	0	4
Azerbaijan	0	1	0
Bahamas	2	0	0
Bangladesh	0	1	0
Belgium	4	0	12
Bolivia	0	1	0
Brazil	0	0	6
Brunei	0	0	0

(Continued)

TABLE APP. III.C

(Continued)

Country	Cases Brought by National Against Other Government	Cases as Respondent	Number of Cases where Nationals were Arbitrators
Bulgaria	0	1	3
Burundi	0	1	0
Canada	15	7	63
Chile	2	3	19
China	1	0	0
Colombia	0	0	7
Congo (formerly Zaire)	0	2	0
Costa Rica	0	2	5
Croatia	0	0	1
Cyprus	5	0	0
Czech Republic	1	7	4
Denmark	1	0	1
Dominican Republic	0	2	0
Ecuador	0	12	6
Egypt	0	8	9
El Salvador	0	3	0
Estonia	0	3	0
Finland	1	0	1
France	6	0	51
Georgia	0	3	0
Germany	11	2	25
Ghana	0	1	1
Greece	6	0	2
Grenada	0	1	0
Guatemala	0	1	1
Hungary	1	3	0
India	0	0	5
Israel	2	0	3
Italy	13	0	16
Jordan	0	3	1
Kazakhstan	1	3	0
Kyrgyzstan	0	1	0
Latvia	1	2	0
Lebanon	0	1	4
Lithuania	1	1	0
Luxembourg	3	0	0

TABLE APP. III.C

(Continued)

Country	Cases Brought by National Against Other Government	Cases as Respondent	Number of Cases where Nationals were Arbitrators
Macedonia	0	1	0
Malaysia	2	2	0
Mexico	1	15	25
Moldova	0	3	1
Mongolia	0	1	0
Morocco	0	2	0
Myanmar	0	1	0
Netherlands	19	0	21
New Zealand	0	0	8
Norway	2	0	3
Oman	1	0	0
Pakistan	0	3	1
Panama	0	1	0
Paraguay	0	2	0
Peru	1	2	1
Philippines	0	2	3
Poland	2	1	1
Romania	0	6	0
Russia	3	7	4
Senegal	1	1	1
Serbia	0	1	1
Singapore	1	0	2
Slovakia	0	5	3
South Africa	0	1	0
Spain	8	1	30
Sri Lanka	0	2	1
Sweden	4	0	15
Switzerland	4	0	46
Tajikistan	0	1	0
Tanzania	0	1	0
Thailand	0	1	4
Trinidad and Tobago	0	1	0
Turkey	3	5	0
Ukraine	0	9	0
United Arab Emirates	0	1	0

(Continued)

TABLE APP. III.C

(Continued)

Country	Cases Brought by National Against Other Government	Cases as Respondent	Number of Cases where Nationals were Arbitrators
United Kingdom	13	0	59
United States	66	10	102
Uruguay	0	0	4
Uzbekistan	0	5	0
Venezuela	0	5	6
Yemen	0	1	0
Zimbabwe	0	1	0
Totals	214[3]	202	622[4]

TABLE APP. III.D

Top Twenty-One Legal Entities from the Dataset Representing Investors and States in ITA.

Rank	*Legal Representative*	*Cases Representing Claimant*	*Cases Representing Respondent*	*Total*
1.	Freshfields Bruckhaus Deringer	16	13	29
2.	Procuración del Tesoro de la Nación Argentina	0	27	27
3.	White & Case LLP	5	11	16
4.	Dirección General de Consultoría Jurídica de Negociaciones de la Secretaria de Economía de Mexico	0	15	15
5.	King & Spalding LLP	13	0	13
6.	Matrix Chambers	4	8	12
7.	Sidley Austin LLP	7	4	11
8.	Office of the Legal Adviser, U.S. Department of State	0	10	10
8.	Procuraduría General del Estado de Ecuador	0	10	10

---

[3] *See supra* note 1.

[4] As there were 202 cases in the dataset (five sole arbitrators and 197 cases with three arbitrators), assuming there were no substitutions, the theoretical number of total appointments was 596. With multiple awards and arbitrators changing during proceedings, in reality, there were 806 different arbitrators, including 184 duplicate arbitrators (i.e., listed twice within a case). Excluding duplicates, there were 622 valid arbitrator appointments within the cases.

TABLE APP. III.C

(Continued)

Rank	Legal Representative	Cases Representing Claimant	Cases Representing Respondent	Total
10.	Judge Stephen M. Schwebel	6	3	9
10.	Shearman & Sterling LLP	8	1	9
12.	Covington & Burling LLP	7	1	8
12.	Appleton & Associates	8	0	8
14.	Allen & Overy LLP	3	4	7
14.	Arnold & Porter LLP (currently Arnold & Porter Kaye Scholer LLP)	0	7	7
14.	Essex Court Chambers	4	3	7
14.	Squire Sanders (currently Squire Patton Boggs)	2	5	7
14.	Department of Foreign Affairs and International Trade, Department of Justice, Trade Law Bureau, Canada	0	7	7
14.	Egypt State Lawsuits Authority	0	7	7
14.	Debevoise & Plimpton LLP	7	0	7
14.	Pillsbury Winthrop Shaw Pittman	1	6	7

Based upon 272 public awards in 202 different cases where there was information about legal representatives, which generated 420 different legal entities involved with an average of 1.89 (*SD* = 2.687) cases per legal entity.

Readers are reminded to refer to Appendix V for specific coding protocols, as legal entities were classified on the basis of information in the public awards.

Index

The index does not include references to every instance of any person, institution, country, term, or concept. For a full accounting, please read both the primary text and accompanying footnotes.